THE PROUDEST DAY

India's Long Road to Independence

ANTHONY READ
and
DAVID FISHER

PIMLICO

Published by Pimlico 1998

2 4 6 8 10 9 7 5 3 1

First published by Jonathan Cape 1997
Pimlico edition 1998

Pimlico
Random House, 20 Vauxhall Bridge Road,
London SW1V 2SA

Random House Australia (Pty) Limited
20 Alfred Street, Milsons Point, Sydney,
New South Wales 2061, Australia

Random House New Zealand Limited
18 Poland Road, Glenfield,
Auckland 10, New Zealand

Random House South Africa (Pty) Limited
Endulini, 5A Jubilee Road, Parktown 2193, South Africa

Random House UK Limited Reg. No. 954009

A CIP catalogue record for this book
is available from the British Library

ISBN 0-7126-6142-5

Papers used by Random House UK Limited are natural, recyclable products made from wood grown in sustainable forests. The manufacturing processes conform to the environmental regulations of the country of origin

Printed and bound in Great Britain by
Mackays of Chatham

To Rosemary and Barbara,
with love and gratitude.

'Come what may, self-knowledge will lead to self-rule, and that would be the proudest day in British history.'

Lord Macaulay, Minute on Indian Education, 1835

Contents

List of Illustrations   xi

Glossary   xii

Maps   xv

Acknowledgements   xxiii

Prologue   I

1 'In Quiet Trade'   10

2 'The Strangest of all Empires'   27

3 'The Moaning of the Hurricane'   45

4 'The Mildest Form of Government is Despotism'   55

5 'If Fifty Men Cannot be Found ...'   69

6 'The Gravity of the Blunder'   83

7 'No Bombs, No Boons'   102

8 'A Spontaneous Loyalty'   114

9 'An Indefensible System'   132

10 'God Bless Gandhi'   142

11 'A Himalayan Miscalculation'   162

12 'The Very Brink of Chaos and Anarchy'   179

13 'A Butchery of Our Souls'   197

14 'A Year's Grace and a Polite Ultimatum'   211

15 'A Mad Risk'   226

16 'Civil Martial Law'   245

17 'The Empty Fruits of Office'   260

18 'The Congress Asked for Bread and it has Got a Stone'   277

19 'A Landmark in the Future History of India'   293

20 'A Post-dated Cheque on a Bank that is Failing'   310

21 'Leave India to God – or to Anarchy'   325

22 'The Two Great Mountains have Met – and not even a Ridiculous Mouse has Emerged'   341

23 'Patriots not Traitors'   359

24 'We are on the Threshold of a Great Tragedy'   372
25 'If India Wants Her Blood-bath she shall have it'   390
26 'Possible New Horror Job'   409
27 'Plan Balkan'   424
28 'Thirteen Months Means Mischief to India'   442
29 'A Treaty of Peace without a War'   459
30 'A Tryst with Destiny'   476
Epilogue   494

Source Notes   509

Bibliography   533

Index   540

List of Illustrations

1 The Mughal Emperor Shah Alam and Robert Clive, 1765. (Hulton-Getty Collection)
2 Lord Macaulay. (Hulton-Getty Collection)
3 Alan Octavian Hume. (Hulton-Getty Collection)
4 The first National Congress, 1885. (By permission of the British Library)
5 Gopal Krishna Gokhale. (Hulton-Getty Collection)
6 Mohandas Karamchand Gandhi and his staff. (Hulton-Getty Collection)
7 Motilal Nehru, his wife, Swarup Rani, and his son, Jawaharlal. (Hulton Getty-Collection)
8 Lord Curzon. (Popperfoto)
9 Sir Michael O'Dwyer. (The Illustrated London News Picture Library)
10 Brigadier-General Rex Dyer. (The Illustrated London News Picture Library)
11 Annie Besant. (Hulton-Getty Collection)
12 Edwin Montagu. (Hulton-Getty Collection)
13 Gandhi Day, 1922. (Hulton-Getty Collection)
14 Lord and Lady Reading, and Lord and Lady Willingdon. (By permission of the British Library)
15 Black Flag processions. (Hulton-Getty Collection)
16 Indian princes at Imperial Conference, 1930. (Popperfoto)
17 Lord Irwin. (Hulton-Getty Collection)
18 Gandhi defies Salt Tax Law, 1930. (Hulton-Getty Collection)
19 Round-table conference in London, 1931. (Popperfoto)
20 Gandhi and Subhas Chandra Bose, 1938. (Hulton-Getty Collection)
21 Lord Linlithgow and his wife. (Hulton-Getty Collection)
22 Leo Amery. (Hulton-Getty Collection)
23 Jawaharlal Nehru and Gandhi. (Popperfoto)
24 Sir Stafford Cripps and Maulana Azad, 1946. (Hulton-Getty Collection)
25 Political leaders at Viceregal Lodge, Simla. (Hulton-Getty Collection)
26 Indian leaders arrive in London, 1946. (Associated Press)
27 Calcutta killings, 1946. (Hulton-Getty Collection)
28 Lord Wavell greets Lord and Lady Mountbatten, 1947. (Poperfoto)
29 Lord and Lady Mountbatten enthroned. (Hulton-Getty Collection)
30 Jinnah with Mountbatten and Edwina. (Hulton-Getty Collection)
31 The new government of Pakistan moves in. (Associated Press)
32 Muslims awaiting transport to Pakistan. (Popperfoto)
33 Riots in the Punjab. (Hulton-Getty Collection)
34 Suhrawardy and Gandhi. (Associated Press)
35 Independence celebrations in Calcutta. (Hulton-Getty Collection)
36 Gandhi lying in state. (Hulton-Getty Collection)

Glossary

ahimsa	non-violence
amir	Muslim prince or counsellor
ashram	a place of Hindu religious retreat
azad	free, freedom
bagh	a garden
Bande Mataram	'Hail to Thee, Mother': the first Indian national anthem
bania	member of the Hindu merchant caste, originally from Gujarat: a grocer
bapu	father: affectionate term for Gandhi
begum	a Muslim noblewoman of high rank; title of a married Muslim woman, the equivalent of Mrs
bhadralok	'gentlefolk': the intellectuals of Bengal
Bhagavad Gita	'Song of the Blessed One': Krishna's lessons to Arjuna, part of the Mahabharata, the great Hindu epic
brahmacharya	chastity; the total suppression of sexual desire
Brahman	a Hindu priest; member of the first of the traditional four-fold hierarchy of caste Hinduism
burka	one-piece garment which covers an orthodox Muslim woman from the crown of her head to her feet
Caliph (or *Khalifa*)	Deputy of Allah, Commander of the Faithful, i.e. the community of orthodox Muslims
chaat	a spicy sauce used with savoury dishes in the Punjab
chaprassi	a domestic servant, waiter
charkha	simple spinning wheel: the Congress symbol
charpoy	a bed of knotted string on a wooden frame
dak	mail, postal service
Dar-ul-harb	an accursed land, in which Muslims may not dwell
dewan	revenue collector; Indian ruler's chief minister
dharma	Hindu religion, law, duty or responsibility
dharna	a peaceful protest, usually by sitting outside the door of someone who has committed an injustice to the protestor
dharshan	reflected holiness in presence of holy person, place or object
dhoti	loin cloth worn by Indian men
durbar	a princely levee
feringhee	a foreigner
ghadr	rebellion

ghats	landing place on a river bank; also the name given to the coastal mountain ranges on both sides of southern India (literally 'steps')
goonda	a gangster, hoodlum, hired thug
Gurdwara	Sikh temple and community centre (literally: 'the Guru's doorway')
guru	teacher
Haji	one who has made the Muslim pilgrimage to Mecca (the Haj)
Harijan	an Untouchable, (literally: 'child of God')
hartal	the closing of shops and businesses as a mark of protest or mourning
hijrat	Muslim religious emigration or flight
Id (or Eid)	two great Muslim festivals, one celebrating the end of Ramadan, the other the deliverance of Isaac from sacrifice by Abraham
jai	victory (*Jai Hind*: 'Victory to India')
Jain	a follower of Jainism, a religion similar to Bhuddism and Hinduism
Jat	a Rajput tribe from the Punjab, traditionally farmers
jawan	soldier
kaffir	infidel
khadi	cotton cloth spun and woven by hand
khalsa	'the pure': the Sikh army of the pure
Khan	a tribal leader in the northern frontier region, Afghanistan and central Asia
khir	a savoury dish of milk and rice
Khudai Khidmatgars	organization led by Abdul Gaffar Khan, 'the Frontier Gandhi' (literally 'servants of God')
kirpan	the Sikh sword
kisan	peasant
kisan sabha	a peasant association
kshatriya	a warrior; member of the second main class in the Hindu caste hierarchy
kurta	the long, loose, Indian shirt, worn over pyjama trousers
lathi	long cane, often tipped with metal, used as a weapon by Indian police
Maha	prefix meaning large or great
Maharaja	Great king or prince
Mahatma	'Great-souled one' – title by which Gandhi was popularly known
maidan	an open space, park or common in or near a town
majlis	meeting or assembly
masjid	mosque
maulana	honorific title granted to a Muslim scholar or learned man
mlechcha	impure, unclean
mofussil	rural hinterland
mullah	a Muslim teacher, learned in Islamic theology and law
munsif	a junior judge
Nawab	a princely title, originally a Muslim provincial governor or viceroy
Netaji	Leader (Bengali)
Nizam	title taken by rulers of Hyderabad; originally a Mughal administrator of criminal justice and military affairs
Padishah	the Mughal emperor

Parsi	a member of the Zoroastrian religious community
Peshwa	Maratha prime minister
pindaris	Pathan mercenaries turned bandit
purdah	the system of screening women from view by means of a veil or curtain, common to orthodox Muslims and some Hindu castes
Quaid-i-Azam	'Great leader': title bestowed on Jinnah by Muslim League followers
Raj	rule, government (commonly British rule in India)
Ram	the Hindu name for God
ryot	a peasant cultivator
ryotwar	the peasantry
sabha	association, society, council
sardar	leader or chief, usually of a tribe
sati	the self-immolation of a Hindu widow on her husband's funeral pyre (litterally: 'the true one')
satya	truth
satyagraha	Gandhi's method of non-violent non-co-operation (literally: 'hold fast to the truth')
sepoy	Indian foot soldier
seth	Hindu banker or moneylender
shalwar kameez	long tunic and matching trousers, worn mainly by women in northern India and by both sexes in Pakistan
Sheikh	Muslim religious or tribal leader; a person known for his piety
sherwani	Muslim long frock coat
sowar	Indian cavalry soldier
sudra	a menial: the fourth class in the Hindu caste system
swadeshi	Indian-made goods (literally: 'of our own country')
swaraj	self-rule (*purna swaraj*, complete self-rule)
Syed	(also Sayeed, Sayyid, Saiyid, etc) a direct descendant of the Holy Prophet
taluqdar	a landed baron
tehsil	a revenue-collecting sub-district
tehsildar	officer in charge of a tehsil
thugi	ritual murder by strangulation in the cause of the mother goddess
Ulama	the community of Muslim learned men
Umma	the totality of Islam
vakil	an advocate or lawyer, a court pleader
Vazir (or Vizir)	Muslim premier
Zamindar	a revenue-collecting landlord, usually Muslim

Maps

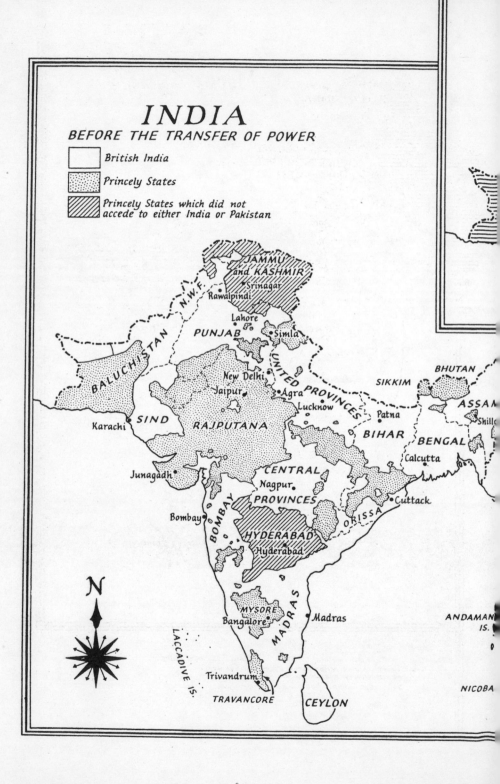

INDIA
BEFORE THE TRANSFER OF POWER

British India

Princely States

Princely States which did not
accede to either India or Pakistan

JAMMU and KASHMIR
Srinagar
N.W.F.
Rawalpindi
Lahore
PUNJAB
Simla
BALUCHISTAN
UNITED PROVINCES
New Delhi
Jaipur
Agra
BHUTAN
SIKKIM
Lucknow
ASSAM
Shillo
SIND
Karachi
RAJPUTANA
Patna
BIHAR
BENGAL
Calcutta
Junagadh
CENTRAL
Nagpur
PROVINCES
ORISSA
Cuttack
Bombay
BOMBAY
HYDERABAD
Hyderabad
N
MYSORE
Bangalore
MADRAS
Madras
ANDAMAN
IS.
LACCADIVE IS.
Trivandrum
TRAVANCORE
CEYLON
NICOBA

INDIA
ON THE DAY OF PARTITION
15 August 1947

JAMMU and KASHMIR

Rawalpindi • Srinagar •

PAKISTAN

Bilaspur • PUNJAB

Patiala • Simla • HIMACHAL PRADESH

PEPSU • Chandigarh

RAJASTHAN • UTTAR PRADESH

ASSAM

Delhi • Jaipur • Agra

Ajmer • AJMER • Gwalior • Lucknow

Shillong

W.B.

Manipur MANIPUR

KUTCH • BHARAT • VINDHYA Rewa PRADESH

BIHAR • Patna •

Bhuj • BHOPAL

W. BENGAL

Agartala

Rajkot • MADHYA • Indore • MADHYA PRADESH

W. BENGAL Calcutta •

TRIPURA

SAURASTHRA

Nagpur •

EAST PAKISTAN

BOMBAY • HYDERABAD • ORISSA • Cuttack

Bombay •

Hyderabad •

Kurnool •

ANDHRA

ANDAMAN IS.

COORG • MYSORE • Madras •

Coorg • Bangalore

MADRAS

N

NICOBAR IS.

Trivandrum •

LACCADIVE IS.

TRAVANCORE COCHIN

CEYLON

| 0 | 200 | 400 | 600 | 800 | 1000 Miles |

| 0 | 200 | 400 | 600 | 800 | 1000 Kilometers |

M. Verity

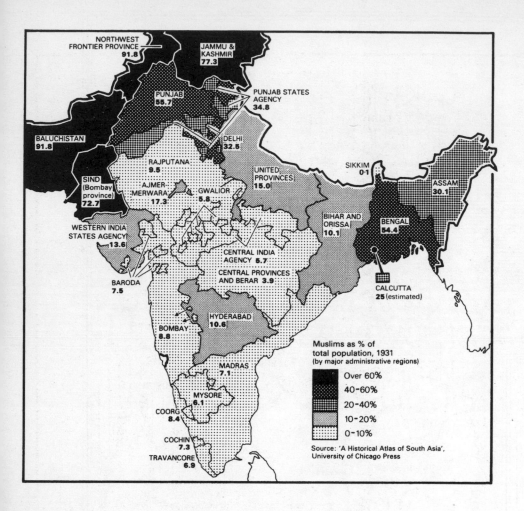

NORTHWEST
FRONTIER PROVINCE
91.8

JAMMU &
KASHMIR
77.3

PUNJAB
55.7

PUNJAB STATES
AGENCY
34.8

BALUCHISTAN
91.8

DELHI
32.5

RAJPUTANA
9.5

SIND
(Bombay
province)
72.7

AJMER-
MERWARA
17.3

GWALIOR
5.8

UNITED
PROVINCES
15.0

SIKKIM **0·1**

ASSAM
30.1

WESTERN INDIA
STATES AGENCY
13.6

BIHAR AND
ORISSA
10.1

BENGAL
54.4

CENTRAL INDIA
AGENCY **5.7**

BARODA
7.5

CENTRAL PROVINCES
AND BERAR **3.9**

CALCUTTA
25 (estimated)

BOMBAY
8.8

HYDERABAD
10.6

MADRAS
7.1

MYSORE
6.1

Muslims as % of
total population, 1931
(by major administrative regions)

COORG
8.4

COCHIN
7.3

TRAVANCORE
6.9

Over 60%

40-60%

20-40%

10-20%

0-10%

Source: 'A Historical Atlas of South Asia',
University of Chicago Press

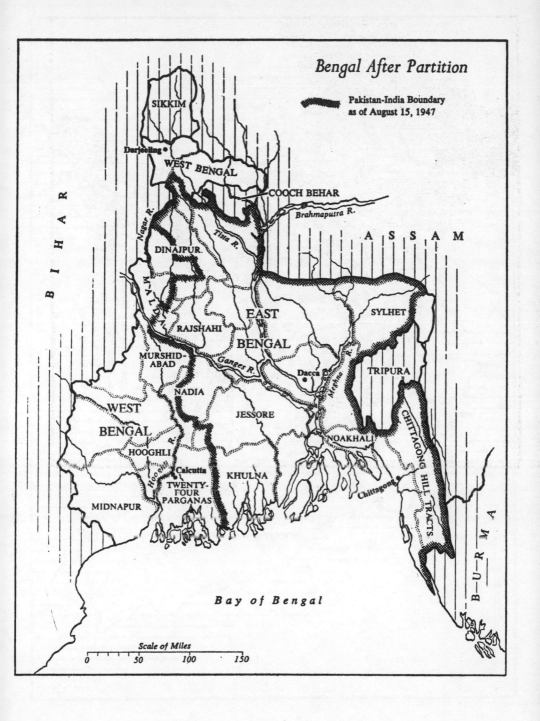

Bengal After Partition

Pakistan-India Boundary
as of August 15, 1947

SIKKIM

WEST BENGAL

Darjeeling

COOCH BEHAR

Brahmaputra R.

A S S A M

B I H A R

Nagar R.

Tista R.

DINAJPUR

EAST
BENGAL

SYLHET

RAJSHAHI

MURSHID-
ABAD

Ganges R.

Dacca

Meghna R.

TRIPURA

NADIA

WEST
BENGAL

JESSORE

NOAKHALI

CHITTAGONG HILL TRACTS

HOOGHLI

Hooghly R.

Calcutta

KHULNA

TWENTY-
FOUR
PARGANAS

Chittagong

MIDNAPUR

B–U–R–M–A

Bay of Bengal

Scale of Miles

0   50   100   150

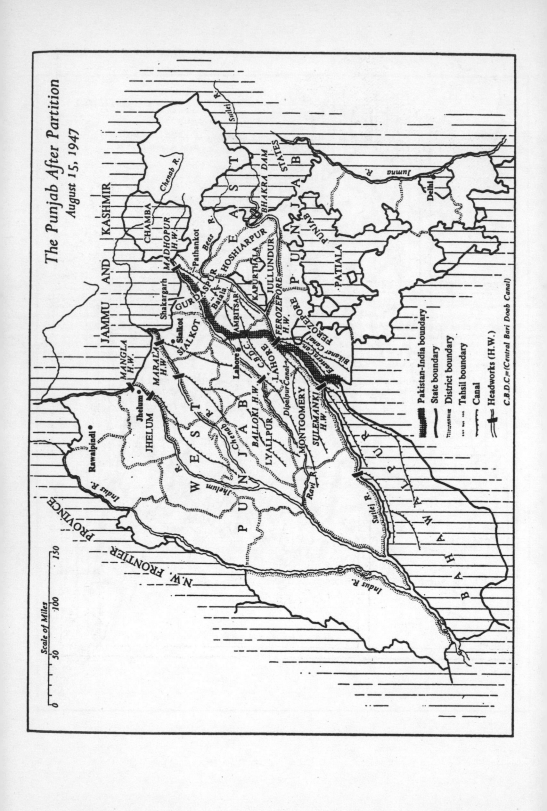

The Punjab After Partition
August 15, 1947

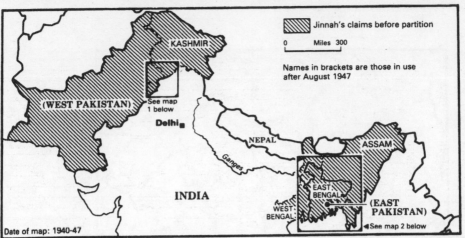

Jinnah's claims before partition

0   Miles   300

Names in brackets are those in use
after August 1947

KASHMIR

(WEST PAKISTAN)

See map
1 below

Delhi

NEPAL

Ganges

ASSAM

INDIA

EAST
BENGAL

WEST
BENGAL

(EAST
PAKISTAN)

◄See map 2 below

Date of map: 1940-47

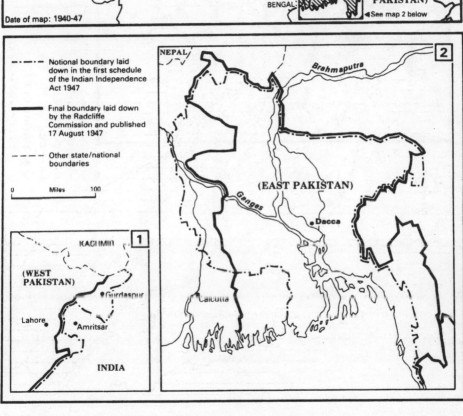

—··—··— Notional boundary laid
down in the first schedule
of the Indian Independence
Act 1947

———— Final boundary laid down
by the Radcliffe
Commission and published
17 August 1947

— — — Other state/national
boundaries

0   Miles   100

NEPAL

Brahmaputra

2

(EAST PAKISTAN)

Ganges

Dacca

Calcutta

KASHMIR

1

(WEST
PAKISTAN)

Gurdaspur

Lahore

Amritsar

INDIA

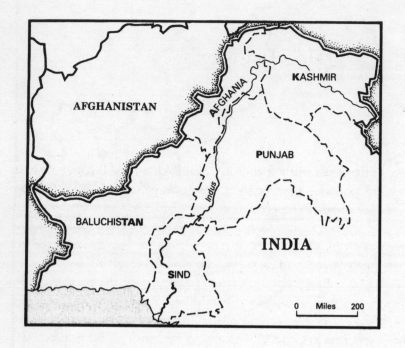

Acknowledgements

We would like to thank our many friends in India, Pakistan and Britain who have helped and advised us during the writing of this book, particularly the following: Patwant Singh, Delhi-born Delhi-phile, bon viveur and good friend, who wined and dined us and opened many doors; Meher Wilshaw; Kushwant Singh, the Doctor Johnson of Delhi, who is talented enough to be his own Boswell, and his wife, who encouraged us and told us jokes; Rear Admiral (Rtd) Krishna Nayyar, Mountbatten's token Indian, who regaled us with stories of the great man; Dr Freddie Mehta, Tata's man in Bombay, who helped us with introductions and advice, and who did his best to explain Indian economics to us; our old friend Maneck Dalal, Tata's man in London, who gave us the benefit of his guidance and immense experience from the outset of this enterprise; Syed Wajid Ali and Mian Mumtaz Muhammad Khan Daultana, both of whom remembered Jinnah not as an austere politician but as a warm and often jolly family friend; Mr Neil O'Brian, who put the case for the Anglo-Indian community most forcefully; Joya Chatterjee, who trekked across Delhi to lend us a copy of her excellent PhD thesis; Professor Ravinder Kumar, director of the Nehru Memorial Museum and Library, New Delhi; Dr S.H.M. Jafri and Dr Mohammad Ali Siddiqui, of the Pakistan Study Centre, University of Karachi, for their help and guidance; Niyatee Shinde and, as always, Vijay Nesargi, for much advice, many contacts, and for arranging a much-appreciated temporary membership of the Cricket Club of India, Bombay; Qutubuddin Aziz, passionate advocate of Pakistan and loyal defender of the late General Zia-ul-Haq; Rear Admiral (Rtd) Satyindra Singh, an unlikely Sikh sea-dog who writes English comic verse and has one of the shrewdest strategic brains we have met; Gorbachan Singh, diplomat and knowledgeable commentator on world affairs; Judge Narula, whose cold, clear eye on the people he met illuminated for us such diverse characters as Gandhi and Zulfikar Ali Bhutto; Balbir Singh Grewal, for his memories of the Mountbattens and the period of partition; Professor David Taylor of the School of Oriental and African Studies, London University; Mark Tully and Gillian Wright for their courtesy and help; Barun De and H. M. Seervhai, historians extraordinary.

For giving us their time, memories, advice and hospitality, we also thank:

Dr Jarari, Dr Anwar Shaheen, Mrs Kiani, Mrs Ishrat Aftab, Dr Hakim M. Ahsan, M.J. Akbar, S. Babar Ali, Mani Shankar Ayar, Ghulam Nabi Azad, I. Manzoor Ilhahi, Dr Hashid Ahmad Jullhandhri, John Bowman, Dr Nandakumar, Larry Fernandez, Sultan Salahuddin Owaisi, Aveek Sarkar, Mr Singhai, Saran Singh, Lieutenant-General (Rtd) Harbaksh Singh, Major-General D. 'Monty' Palit, D. Padgoakanda, Madhu Limaye, Ahmed Ali Khan, Saiyyid Hashim Raza, A. Madhavan, Farzana Khan, Justice Mahmood Ali Sayeed, Dr Durra Shalway Syed, Waseem Ahmad, Begum Faridi, Veena Lakshumalini, Ijaz Husain Batalvi, Shelagh McDonald, Mary Watson, and many others who helped to educate us about the sub-continent.

Our thanks are also due to Byram Avari, hotelier extraordinary, who opened so many doors for us in Karachi and Lahore; Mrs Bhasin of the Hotel Imperial, New Delhi, for her help and kindness; Vinati Mishra of the Taj Mansingh, New Delhi; Mr Wadia of the Taj Mahal Hotel, Bombay; the management, staff and members of the Cricket Club of India, Bombay, for their warm hospitality; the management and staff of the splendidly traditional Faletti's Hotel, Lahore.

We also thank our friends in the Indian High Commission, London, especially Talmiz Ahmad and Mrs Hemalata Bhagirath; Mohammad Abbas and his staff in the Pakistan High Commission; and Mossud Mannan of the Bangladesh High Commission.

We are particularly grateful to the staffs of the various libraries who have given us invaluable help in our researches. These include: The London Library; The India Office Library, Records and Print Department, with special thanks to Rod Hamilton; The Public Record Office; The Imperial War Museum Library; School of Oriental and African Studies Library; Nehru Memorial Library, New Delhi; India International Centre Libary, New Delhi; Indian National Archives, New Delhi; Asiatic Library, Bombay; Netaji Centre, Calcutta; University of Karachi, Pakistan Study Centre; Pakistan National Archives, Islamabad; US National Archives, Washington, DC; the public libraries of Maidenhead, Slough, Eye, Diss, Norwich and Bury St. Edmunds.

We owe a particular debt to Neil Belton for commissioning this book in the first place, to Will Sulkin for his patience, faith and encouragement over a long gestation period, and to Kirsty Dunseath for her editorial care and morale-boosting cheerfulness in the face of adversity; to Murray Pollinger for his guidance and support at the beginning, as over so many years, and to Sara Menguc for taking up the torch from him so smoothly.

And, as always, our most special thanks must be saved for our wives, Rosemary and Barbara, for their amazing forbearance and support over what has been a very long haul.

We wish to thank the following authors and publishers for permission to quote from the books listed: David Higham Associates, for *Mission with Mountbatten*, by Alan Campbell-Johnson; the Jawaharlal Nehru Trust and The Bodley Head, for Jawaharlal Nehru's *Autobiography*; William Heinemann Limited, for Lord Ismay's *Memoirs*; Hodder and Stoughton Limited, for *Two Alone, Two Together*, edited by Sonia Gandhi; Indus Publishers, an imprint of HarperCollins for *Compassion* by Saadat Hasan Manto, from *Stories About the Partition of India*, edited by Alok Bhalla; Lotus Collection, Roli Books, for *Hospitality Delayed* by Saadat Hasan Manto, from *India Partitioned: The Other Face of Freedom*, edited by Mushirul Hasan, Vol. I; also for *Who Killed India?* by Khwaja Ahmad Abbas, from *India Partitioned* Vol. 2; Orient Longman Limited, for *India Wins Freedom*, by Maulana Abul Kalam Azad, and the *Selected Works of Jawaharlal Nehru*; Oxford University Press, for *The Viceroy's Journal* by Field Marshal Lord Wavell; the Ministry of Information, Government of India, for the *Collected Works of Mahatma Gandhi*; the Pakistan National Publishing House, for *Foundations of Pakistan: All-India Muslim League Documents*, edited by S. S. Pirzada; and Her Majesty's Stationery Office, for Cabinet Papers and *The Transfer of Power*, edited by Nicholas Mansergh and E.W.R. Lumby.

Prologue

April in the north Indian province of the Punjab, the 'land of the five rivers', is a time of flowers and festivals. In 1919, the festival of Ram Naumi, when Hindus parade through the streets carrying statues of their gods anointed with ghee – clarified butter – and garlanded with flowers, fell on 9 April. It merged into the Baisakhi fair, several days of festivity culminating in Baisakhi Day itself, the start of the solar new year, on Sunday, 13 April. On Baisakhi Day, Hindus and Sikhs bathe in sacred rivers and tanks and worship at their temples or *gurdwaras*. In the Sikhs' holy of holies, the Golden Temple, around which the city of Amritsar was founded in the sixteenth century AD, water brought from all the sacred rivers of India is poured into the tank, and those who bathe in it emerge purified, their sins washed away.

For Sikhs and Hindus alike, Baisakhi is a family occasion, a time for exchanging presents, for feasting and laughter and enjoyment, for *chaat* and ice-cream and the innumerable sweetmeats Indians adore. In the Punjab, it is also a harvest festival: the rabi crop, the first of the year, has been gathered and sold, farmers have money in their pockets and are in a mood to give thanks and celebrate. They congregate in vast numbers at traditional horse and cattle fairs to meet friends and to buy and sell stock.

'They told me there were 200,000 people present at a fair I attended in the Punjab. I could believe it. They looked a million to me,' wrote Fred B. Fisher, an American who had lived and worked in India for many years.

Turbans of orange, salmon color, brilliant greens, blues and Indian red, punctuated here and there with shining black hair and shaven heads, made a flaming top to the picture. The mass of flowing robes of saffron, rose and orange, was streaked with bare bronze legs and backs and vivid rags, while the many white draperies glistened like flashes of iridescence in the dazzling sunshine.

Dust was over everything. The grass was white with it. We ate and breathed and swallowed it. Tent flies were stretched over some of the most valuable cattle; the rest stood patiently in the sun and dust while groups of

Indians gathered round to bargain and trade. Preachers of all religions distributed tracts and pictures, and, when they could get an audience, made speeches. Crouching in the dust were vendors of betel-nùt, puffed rice, coconut candy, chapatis, and ghee ... Wherever there is the smallest open space, snake charmers spread out their mats and try to cajole you into stopping to watch their tricks.[1]

Fisher was writing in 1918. By 1919, the picture in the Punjab was very different. The monsoon had failed – the rains never came – and the weather that year was among the hottest ever recorded in India. In April the temperature was regularly soaring above 115°F and tensions rose with it. For the crowds who thronged into Amritsar, the second city of the Punjab, the heat aggravated a powerful undercurrent of discontent running through the Baisakhi celebrations. The Punjab had provided almost a third of the 1,440,437 Indians who had enlisted to fight for the British in the First World War, and its men had suffered heavy casualties.[2] The survivors of the trenches in France had seen how the peoples of Europe lived. They had brought back to their towns and villages not only tales of war and fighting but expectations of a better life, and a share of the democracy for which they had been told they were fighting. Instead, they had found soaring inflation, high taxes, an uncontrolled influenza epidemic that claimed 12 million lives throughout India – 20 per cent more than the entire death toll for all sides during the war – and the threat of increased repression from the government. 'From one cause and another,' wrote Miles Irving, the newly appointed deputy commissioner in Amritsar, 'the people are restless, and discontented and ripe for revolution.'[3]

Since the 1917 revolution in Russia, and the subsequent civil war that was still raging, Bolshevism had become the bugaboo of political establishments everywhere. Revolutionary regimes had sprung up in Berlin, Munich, Hungary, Portugal and Romania; there was martial law in Spain, civil war in Mexico, and food rioting in Japan. In Britain itself, there had been widespread strikes, especially in coal mines, cotton mills and railways. In Glasgow a general strike had led to violence in January 1919, with the Riot Act being read and police making baton charges against strikers. The police themselves had been out on strike in August 1918 and were threatening to do so again – as they did in July 1919, when thousands of officers were dismissed.

Meanwhile, the Troubles in Ireland, which had flared so alarmingly with the Easter Rising of 1916, had started again in earnest. Sinn Fein members of Parliament, who had all but swept the board in the elections of December 1918, refused to go to Westminster and established their own assembly in Dublin. There, they declared all Ireland an independent republic, which the IRA set about forcing the British government to recognize. Further afield, extra troops had to be sent to quell nationalist unrest in Egypt – not officially part of the empire but 'protected' by Britain, since the Suez Canal was vital to British imperial interests. Against this background, it is not surprising that the British in India were jittery.

During the two weeks before Baisakhi Day in 1919, there had been a number of demonstrations and disturbances in various parts of northern India, but most had passed off with no serious trouble. In Amritsar, the demonstrations had all been peaceful until 10 April, though Europeans had been disquieted to see Muslims joining the Hindus in the Ram Naumi procession the day before: when the two joined together, the old India hands cautioned, it usually meant trouble. On the morning of 10 April, however, Miles Irving secretly arrested the two principal Indian leaders and had them removed from the city. Through a series of mishaps and blunders, the protest that followed turned into a full-scale riot, with a 40,000-strong mob rampaging through the city. Some 25 Indians were shot, many of them fatally, by troops or police. The mob killed five British men and seriously injured a respected woman doctor and mission school supervisor, Miss Marcia Sherwood, who was rescued by an Indian family after being left for dead.

By the evening of 10 April, all was quiet again. An eerie calm hung over the wrecked city, lit by the flames of still-burning banks, offices and godowns. One hundred and thirty terrified European women and children had taken refuge in a primitive fort, under the protection of an inadequate force of British and Indian troops, aided by 50 men of the Gurkha Rifles who had been pressed into service when the train carrying them to their depot at Peshawar fortuitously stopped at Amritsar. With all the telegraph lines cut, Miles Irving had managed to get a junior officer out on a light railway engine to fetch help, and at 11.00 p.m. 130 men of the 2/6th Battalion Royal Sussex Regiment, plus 181 men from the 124th Baluchis arrived by train from Lahore. During the night, they were joined by 107 men of the 25th (Cyclist) Battalion of the London Regiment, supported by 230 Indian soldiers, from Jullunder. This brought the total number of troops to just under 1,200, still a pitifully small number to control an agitated population swollen far beyond the city's normal 160,000.

At 9.00 p.m. on 11 April, though all was still quiet, Brigadier-General Reginald Edward Harry Dyer, commander of the Jullundur Brigade, arrived by car to take personal charge of the troops. Irving, according to Dyer, 'looked like a man broken by fatigue, anxiety and the weight of responsibilities too heavy for his shoulders'.[4] Dyer had little difficulty persuading him to sign a statement handing over his city to the military:

Handed over to G.O.C. 45th Brigade and signed by the Deputy Commissioner midnight 11–12 April 1919. The troops have orders to restore order in Amritsar and to use all force necessary. No gathering of persons or processions of any sort will be allowed. All gatherings will be fired on. Any persons leaving the city in groups of more than four will be fired on. Respectable persons should keep indoors.

As well as the troops, the military authorities in Jullundur had sent an aeroplane to Amritsar, a BE2c biplane, known to First World War pilots as 'the flying bird cage' or, more ominously, as 'Fokker fodder'. It was flown by Captain D.H.M. Carberry, MC, DFC, of 31 Squadron RAF, based at Risalpur, who had seen more than his fair share of action in the skies over France. First thing in the morning of Saturday, 12 April, Dyer sent him up to fly a reconnaissance mission over the city: he returned to report that he had seen crowds gathering at various points.

At 10.00 a.m., Dyer paraded his force of 474 British and 710 Indian and Gurkha soldiers for review. They were not impressive – few of them were front-line troops. However, he also had two armoured cars equipped with machine guns, which gave him a considerable edge against civilians armed only with sticks and knives. Deciding that a show of strength might intimidate the population, he took a third of his men plus the armoured cars, and marched them through the main streets. He encountered no resistance, except when a crowd at one of the city gates jeered, spat on the ground, and refused to disperse. Dyer said later that he contemplated firing on them, but refrained. Instead, he issued warnings that the city was now under military law, and that all meetings were banned and would be dispersed at once. For the rest of the day, Amritsar simmered in sullen silence.

Next morning, despite Dyer's warnings, crowds of Indians from the surrounding countryside began pouring into the city to celebrate Baisakhi Day. They came to worship in the temples and bathe in the Pool of Immortality, to visit the disrupted horse fair and, in some cases, to grab as much loot as they could from the wreckage – many of them had brought carts to carry it away. Furious that his orders were being flouted, Dyer decided to go back into the streets with another show of force and another proclamation.

At 10.30 a.m., with the city already sweltering in the heat, the column marched in. It was led by an Indian police inspector on a white horse, with his sub-inspector riding alongside, followed by the Indian town crier, the *naib tahsildar*, sitting in a bamboo cart with a Punjabi translator and a man beating a large drum. Behind this marched a mixed detachment of Indian and British soldiers, ahead of two cars carrying Dyer, Captain F.C. 'Tommy' Briggs (his brigade major), Miles Irving, and Amritsar's two European police officers, Superintendent J.F. Rehill and his deputy, R. Plomer. The two armoured cars brought up the rear.

For three and a half hours, the procession wound its way through the brown maze of narrow streets and crowded bazaars, halting at nineteen points. At each stop, the drum was banged to attract the crowds, the *naib tahsildar* read out the proclamation two or three times in Urdu, the translator shouted it out two or three times in Punjabi, the main local language, and printed leaflets were handed out, giving the text in Urdu. It read:

1. It is hereby proclaimed to all whom it may concern, that no person residing in the city is permitted or allowed to leave the city in his own private or hired conveyance, or on foot, without a pass from one of the following officers:

    The Deputy Commissioner
    The Superintendent of Police, Mr Rehill
    The Assistant Commissioner, Mr Beckett
    Mr Connor, Magistrate
    Mr Seymour, Magistrate
    Agher Mohammad Hussain, Magistrate
    The Police Officer in charge of the city Kotwali

This will be a special form and pass.

2. No person residing in Amritsar City is allowed to leave his house after 8.00 p.m. Any persons found in the streets after 8.00 p.m. are liable to be shot.

3. No procession of any kind is allowed to parade the streets in the city or outside of it at any time. Any such processions or gatherings of four men will be looked upon and treated as an unlawful assembly and dispersed by force of arms if necessary.

The last two words, 'if necessary', had been added by Irving, apparently his only contribution to Dyer's text.

    By 2.00 p.m., the heat in the city had become unbearable even for the iron-willed general, and he reluctantly conceded that the troops had had enough and should return to base. Although there were large areas of the city which he had not visited, especially the southern quarter beyond the Golden Temple, he reasoned that his message would have spread to them. In fact, it is open to question how many actually heard the proclamation, never mind passed it on, for the sight of the soldiers and the armoured cars was enough to send people fleeing, expecting trouble. Most of those who had heard it were contemptuous, crowding round to clap their hands – a sign of disrespect in the Punjab – and to laugh and catcall. There were cries of 'The British Raj is ended!' 'We will hold a meeting,' some of them shouted at police Sub-inspector Obaidullah. 'Let us be fired on!'

    A second, Indian, procession led by a boy banging an empty kerosene can trailed the official one, with speakers announcing defiantly that there would be a meeting that afternoon in an open space known as the Jallianwala Bagh. Dyer was told of this at 12.40 p.m., but choose to disregard it, confident that his authority would not be flouted. However when he received confirmation at 4.00 p.m. that a great crowd had gathered in the Jallianwala Bagh and the meeting was definitely about to take place, he could ignore it no longer.

Jallianwala Bagh literally means the garden of Jalli – though no one knows who Jalli was, and the place bore little resemblance to any European idea of a garden. One Englishman remembered it as 'a piece of unused ground covered ... by building material and debris, and entirely surrounded by the walls of buildings'.[5] Lying in the heart of the city barely 250 yards south-east of the Golden Temple, it was roughly rectangular, measuring about 200 yards by 100 yards, and contained three dusty peepul trees, a domed, broken-down tomb, and a well. A few buffaloes were kept there, barely managing to survive on the meagre vegetation. Estimates of the number of people crammed into the *bagh* that Sunday afternoon vary between 15,000 and 50,000 – the larger figure was the one preferred by the British authorities in the later inquiries.

It is not clear how many of the people in the Jallianwala Bagh had heard or even knew of General Dyer's proclamation – surprisingly, it was one of the places he had not visited with his column that morning. Nor was it clear if they had gathered there to listen to the illegal political speeches. Many were Hindu and Sikh peasants who had come in from the surrounding villages with their wives and children to celebrate Baisakhi, and were camping in the *bagh*, unable to afford hotels. Others had come to meet friends, gossip, play cards or dice, because that is what they usually did on Sunday afternoons. Water carriers moved through the crowd dispensing drinks and enjoying the general ribaldry. The buffaloes did their best to go on grazing amid the crush.

The densest part of the crowd was gathered around a wooden platform erected near the well, from which an assortment of politicians and poets – in those days, no Indian political occasion was complete without poets – were addressing the assembled multitude on the most recent iniquities of British rule. Durgas Dass, editor of the Lahore Urdu newspaper *Waqt*, was in full flow when the aeroplane flew over: he was the seventh speaker of the afternoon – the poet Brij Gopi Nath had just read one of his own works, inciting the crowd to murder the British.

Hindus believe that if they see some auspicious sight on Baisakhi Day, they will enjoy good fortune in the year to come. No doubt some of those in the Jallianwala Bagh saw Captain Carberry's BE2c in that light and gazed up at it in wonder – few of them had ever seen an aircraft before. Though it soon disappeared, others were alarmed, and started trying to leave, anticipating trouble. Getting out was not easy for such a crowd: there were only three narrow exits, one of which was closed. The remaining two were a side gate, the Hasaligate, only 4 feet 5 inches wide, leading from the south-eastern corner of the *bagh* into the Bazar

Burj Meva Singh, and a seven-foot-wide alleyway on the western side, leading to the main gate on Bazar Jallianwala. This was the way the soldiers came.

Dyer arrived shortly before 5.15 p.m. in an open car with his personal bodyguard, Sergeant William Anderson, and Captain Briggs, following a column of 90 men: 25 from the 1/9 Gurkhas and 25 from the 54th Sikhs Frontier Force and 59th Rifles Frontier Force, all armed with .303 Lee Enfield rifles, plus 40 Gurkhas armed only with *kukris*, their traditional curved fighting knives. Behind Dyer came the two police officers, Rehill and Plomer, in a second open car, and bringing up the rear were the two armoured cars. A further 50 riflemen had been dropped off at strategic points along the route as pickets. Dyer had ordered the men's British officers to stay behind at camp – 'If there's anything to be done,' he told them, 'I'll do it alone.' He had not even informed Deputy Commissioner Irving, who was catching up on his sleep in his bungalow.

The convoy came to a halt in Bazar Jallianwala, outside the entrance to the *bagh*. Deciding not to risk his armoured cars in the confined space of the narrow alleyway, Dyer left them outside the gate while he led his troops at the double into the field. The sight that met their eyes, according to Briggs, was of 'an immense crowd, packed into a square, listening to a man on a platform, who was speaking and gesticulating with his hands'. Dyer asked Briggs how many people he thought faced them. 'About five thousand or so,' Briggs replied – a figure that was to grow alarmingly in later estimates, its size depending on which side was seeking to exploit the situation.[6]

The point at which the passage opened out into the *bagh* was a raised terrace, under which ran the canal carrying water to the Golden Temple. Dyer deployed his troops on this high ground, the Gurkha riflemen to the left, the Sikhs and Baluchis of the 54th and 59th to the right, giving them a clear field of fire over the entire area. The remaining forty Gurkhas stood behind them with drawn *kukris* – whether to protect them from the mob or to prevent a possible mutiny is not clear.

Seeing the soldiers, some of the crowd began shouting '*Agaye! Agaye!*' (They come, they come!), and started to run as the riflemen knelt and raised their weapons to take aim. On the platform, Durgas Dass stopped in mid-sentence – he was moving a resolution criticizing the Punjab government for adopting repressive measures – and tried to calm the people, telling them not to worry, the soldiers would not fire, and even if they did they would only fire blanks.

Dyer gave the crowd no warning, no order to disperse. Even as Dass was reassuring the people, he barked the order to his men and 50 rifles rattled out the first volley. The first shots were fired high, according to Sardar Arjan Singh, a shopkeeper who was waching from the roof of one of the houses whose walls enclosed the *bagh*. 'But the sahib ordered them to fire straight and low,' he recalled.

At the second volley people began to fall. These were no blanks. Horrified, Dass dived for cover behind the platform. His audience panicked and began to run in all directions, seeking some way out of the killing ground. They jammed the one remaining gateway and tried to scramble up the walls where they were low enough to be climbed, trampling over those who had already fallen. In the crush, the steel-jacketed bullets, fired at close range, tore through flesh and bone and muscle, often passing right through one body to strike the one behind. Dyer was remorseless. He directed his men to fire at those trying to escape as well as aiming where the crowd was thickest. Even people in the surrounding houses or, like Sardar Arjan Singh, watching from rooftops, were not safe. Many people in second and third storey rooms were hit.

The shooting was as calm, deliberate and carefully aimed as target practice at the butts, with every bullet made to count. It was broken only when the troops paused to reload their magazines. 'I fired and continued to fire,' Dyer later told the government's official committee of inquiry, 'until the crowd dispersed, and I consider this is the least amount of firing which would produce the necessary moral and widespread effect ... If more troops had been at hand, the casualties would have been greater in proportion.' When he finally ordered his men to cease firing, they had used 1,650 rounds of .303 mark VI ammunition, killing an estimated 379 men, women, and children and wounding some 1,200 more. Satisfied that he had achieved his purpose, Dyer ordered the troops to withdraw. Turning on his heel, he marched away without a backward glance at the carnage he had inflicted.

Jallianwala Bagh had never looked much like a garden, but now it resembled nothing so much as a Roman arena after a particularly bloody games. Bodies lay in great heaps, the dead, the dying and the wounded piled on top of each other. There was blood everywhere – on the walls, on the trees, soaking into the ground. Even the water in the well had turned crimson, stained with the blood of those who had been shot while trying to clamber over the low wall seeking safety. Several had fallen on top of those already sheltering in the well, drowning them under the press of bodies.

Few of the wounded had any chance of receiving medical assistance: the resources were simply not available in Amritsar, and in any case, most were too scared to go to a doctor or hospital for fear of being betrayed to the British as having been at the forbidden gathering. Many of the relatives of those who were wounded or killed did not learn of the massacre until later, and with the curfew coming into operation at 8.00 p.m. they risked being shot on sight if they ventured out to search for their loved ones. The scavengers of India, the jackals, pi-dogs, vultures and kites – 'shite hawks' as they were called by the British soldiery – had no such inhibitions. They soon appeared to gorge themselves on the flesh of the dead, turning what was already a nightmare into a vision of Hades as night fell. The Baisakhi celebrations were well and truly over.

General Dyer was firmly convinced that he had saved the Indian empire. In fact, he had signed its death warrant. The shooting at Jallianwala Bagh lasted just ten minutes from beginning to end, but in those ten minutes Dyer had destroyed the trust in British justice and fair play that had been built up over one and a half centuries. He had shattered the myth of benevolent paternalism which had allowed a tiny group of barely 1,000 British civil servants, backed up by sometimes as few as 15,000 British soldiers, to govern some 400 million Indians. As a result, what had been a desultory campaign by minority groups seeking home rule for India within the British empire was transformed virtually overnight into a vigorous, determined and popular national independence movement. Britain's time in India was up. From that moment, for Indian nationalists, the only question was how soon could they get rid of their British rulers.

I

'In Quiet Trade'

The movement towards Indian independence began as soon as the British took power in the middle of the eighteenth century, and it was started not by the Indians, but by the British themselves. They had come to the sub-continent seeking trade not territory, and were, initially at least, reluctant rulers. When Parliament declared in 1783 that 'to pursue schemes of conquest and expansion of dominion in India are measures repugnant to the wish, the honour and policy of this nation'[1] most people in Britain readily agreed. For many years, the British in India had successfully avoided entanglements, because entanglements led to responsibility, and responsibility interfered with profit. The hard-headed London merchants of the East India Company wanted wealth not glory: to them, glory was an expensive luxury that counted for nothing on a balance sheet.

The Honourable East India Company had been founded on the last day of 1600 by a royal charter from Queen Elizabeth I, to capitalize on the lucrative trade in spices from the Molucca islands in what is now Indonesia. Unfortunately, the Dutch East India Company, backed by ten times the English company's £50,000 capital, was already there, having displaced the first western traders, the Portuguese. The first cargo of cloves shipped back to Holland had made a profit of some 2,500 per cent, and the Dutch had no intention of sharing such riches with anyone. When English merchants had the temerity to set up a trading post or 'factory' – junior merchants were known as factors – the Dutchmen defended their monopoly by massacring them.

In the face of such ferocious opposition, the English merchant adventurers looked around for a safer alternative. They chose India, where they had recently managed to establish a small foothold, as their second-best bet. The pickings would be nowhere near as spectacular, but neither would the risks. It proved to be a wise decision. After a decidedly shaky start, the company settled down to an average annual return of 25 per cent on capital investment, rising at times to as much as 50 per cent in cash plus 100 per cent in bonus shares for every share held; a handsome profit by almost any reckoning, apart from that of the Dutch.

For almost 150 years, the company went on trading quietly, shipping cargoes of textiles, indigo, saltpetre and sugar, plus a little pepper and other spices from India, and carrying back tin, lead, mercury, mechanical novelties, and, most importantly, silver bullion and coins. During that time, Parliament in London gave the company increasing jurisdiction over its British servants until it virtually became an autonomous state, with the right to dispense its own justice, mint its own coins and employ its own soldiers for protection – a small force that was to grow into a powerful army.

While exercising total authority over its own people, the company was content, apart from one mercifully brief aberration, to remain humble petitioners to the Mughal emperors. The aberration came in the late 1680s, when the company's autocratic chairman, Sir Josiah Child, decided the time had come 'to lay the foundation of a large, well-grounded, sure English dominion in India for all time to come'[2], and sent an expedition to Chittagong in eastern Bengal to do just that. It failed miserably, and the company almost found itself kicked out of India altogether. The lesson was well learned, and the company did nothing to challenge the Mughal empire again until the empire was already in a state of collapse.

The Mughals, nomad warriors from central Asia whose Tartar blood was a mixture of Turk and Mongol, were the latest of the Muslim invaders who for more than half a millennium had swept down through the Khyber Pass to rampage across northern India. The invasions had started at the end of the tenth century with Mahmud, 'the Sword of Islam', who led 17 bloody forays from his Afghan fortress of Ghazni, smashing Hindu temples, looting, pillaging, raping and killing in the name of Islam. Successive waves of raiders continued the process, capturing Peshawar, Lahore and Delhi and establishing a series of Turku-Afghan dynasties. The Rajputs, the indigenous Hindu warrior race of northern India, fought back bravely but adherents of India's other great religion at the time, Buddhism, were driven out, never to return in any significant numbers.

Mostly, the Muslim rulers were defeated by others of their own kind, such as Timur, otherwise known as Tamerlane, the Tartar Khan of Samarkand, who occupied Delhi in 1398, slaughtering and plundering on such a scale that he left 'towers built high' of the heads and bodies of Hindus. Timur did not stay, but rode home with his booty, taking with him tens of thousands of slaves, among them the stone-masons of Delhi whom he forced to build the fabulous great mosque of Samarkand.

The Mughals who came to stay just over 100 years later were led by

Babur, 'the Tiger'. Descended from Timur on his father's side and Ghengis Khan on his mother's, Babur justified his fearful pedigree on 21 April 1526, when his 10,000 Chagatai Turks and Afghans took just half a day to destroy the grand army of the Sultanate of Delhi, with its 100,000 men and 1,000 elephants. He then marched on without a pause to conquer the second city of Agra the following day. Over the next three years, he secured his grip over the whole of northern India with victories over Rajputs, Afghans and Bengalis. The Mughals had arrived, with Babur as their first *padishah* or great emperor.

Like most of his remarkable clan, Babur was much more than a ruthless military genius: he was also a poet and a man of fine sensitivity. One of the first things he did when he settled in Agra was to create a beautiful garden in the Persian style, an earthly vision of paradise. He died soon after the last of his battles, having called on Allah to take his life in exchange for that of his son, Hamayun, who was mortally ill. Allah obliged, but it proved to be a poor bargain for the Mughals: Hamayun was not half the man his father had been, preferring opium and astronomy to fighting battles. It was a fatal combination – he met his death by falling down the steps of his observatory and cracking his head while high on opium.

Hamayun was succeeded in January 1556 by his grandson, the 13-year-old Akbar, an illiterate youth with no time for book learning but a natural genius for conquest, conciliation and control. It was Akbar who built on his great-grandfather's foundations to consolidate the Mughal empire, defeating all attempts to unseat him for 49 years, until he was poisoned by his son Salim in 1605. Akbar won over the powerful Rajputs by marrying the daughter of Raja Bharmal of Amber and slaughtering all those who refused to join the ensuing alliance. He conquered Gujarat in the west and Bengal in the east, pacified Afghanistan, and added Orissa and Baluchistan to his dominions, to control the whole of northern and central India.

Akbar was unique in practising religious tolerance, and went a long way towards reconciling Hindu and Muslim, even banning cow slaughter throughout the empire. Sadly, Akbar's tolerance did not survive his death. But two of his other great achievements were more lasting: the foundations of a superb system of administration and revenue collection which the British, and later the Indian and Pakistani governments, would inherit, and the Mughlai culture with its Persian-influenced works of art and architectural treasures.

It was Akbar's murderous son Salim, under his imperial name Jahangir, 'World Seizer', who received the first English emissaries of the East India Company. The first to arrive was Captain William Hawkins, who sailed into the Gujarat port of Surat on 24 August 1608 carrying 25,000 pieces of gold and a personal letter to the emperor from King James I. It was not a happy beginning. Hawkins was humiliated by Mughal officials who stole his gold, and was in constant fear of the Portuguese, who tried to murder him several times and seized his ship and crew while he was ashore. He spent two fruitless and frustrating years trying to negotiate a trade treaty with Jahangir, who had no need of anything the west had to offer and therefore no interest in a treaty. In any case, the very idea of treaties was meaningless in a society where everything, including life and death, depended on the personal whim of the ruler, whose priorities could change from day to day.

Hawkins did at least survive two whole years before returning home empty-handed. The next envoy, Paul Canning, managed only a few months. It was not until 29 November 1612, when Captain Thomas Best sailed the good ship *Red Dragon* into Surat harbour and used his cannons to rout four Portuguese galleons and 'a whole fleet of frigates', that the Mughal attitude to the English changed. With no sea power of their own, the Mughals had depended on the Portuguese to escort their annual pilgrim voyages across the Arabian Sea to Mecca. After Best's impressive display, they turned to the English for protection at sea, and when the company's next ambassador, Sir Thomas Roe, presented himself in 1615, he was well received.

Roe spent three and a half years in India, and never quite approved of the place. 'They have no written law,' he complained. 'The King by his own word ruleth.' Perceiving the dangers in such a regime, he warned: 'Let this be received as a rule, that if you will profit, seek it at sea and in quiet trade.'[3] In spite of his doubts, however, he persevered, and won the emperor's consent to begin trading.

The company established itself in Agra, the seat of Jahangir's court, and its merchants sensibly dressed and lived like locals, wearing white linen coats and turbans and 'sitting on the ground at our meat or discourse'.[4] It built its first factory and headquarters at Surat, then the principal port on India's west coast. There, its merchants lived in more formal European style, with a growing network of smaller factories and settlements throughout India.

The factory at Surat, however, was always under pressure from the Portuguese, the Mughals and the rebellious Hindu Marathas, who regularly raided and looted the port. The factory itself always held out, but it was an uncomfortable situation, and in 1668 the company was happy to accept an offer from King Charles II of an island about 150 miles down the coast, which had come to him as part of the dowry of Catherine, his Portuguese queen. Always short of money, Charles was eager to off-load it in return for a substantial loan. The island was Bombay, which then had a population of 10,000, and it soon superceded Surat as the company's headquarters. Although it was entirely dependent for supplies on the mainland, which was held by the Marathas, Bombay was much more popular with the traders who flocked to it from Surat, feeling more secure on an English-held island.

Bombay, in fact, was the company's second sovereign base in India. In

1639, it had bought a strip of land six miles long by one mile wide on the Coromandel coast in the south-east of India, on which it built a new factory with a governor's house, accommodation for merchants, factors and writers, and the beginnings of a new town which became Madras. Within the strip, the company claimed full sovereignty. In 1690, it bought a fourth piece of territory from the Marathas to build a new factory, Fort St. David, opposite the town of Cuddalore further down the coast from Madras. The deal included all the land within 'ye randome shott of a piece of ordnance' – whereupon the company sent to Madras for the cannon with the longest range, and the most expert gunner to fire it. Fort St. David was always subsidiary to Madras, and never a major centre in its own right.

The 'tripod' of factories in the north-west, south, and north-east of India on which the company was to base its activities was completed in the same year, when it was given permission to build a new factory, Fort William, in Bengal. The site, 100 miles up the Hooghly river from the ocean, was in the middle of a malarial swamp, but it had the benefit of a secure, deep-water anchorage. It was centred on a village shrine to the goddess Kali, from which steps, 'ghats', led down to the water: its name, Kali-ghat, was soon Anglicized into Calcutta. By the turn of the century, it already had a European population of 1,200 and had become a honey-pot attracting people and money from all over Bengal, Bihar and Orissa, particularly rich men who could bank there with relative security. Within 50 years, Calcutta had become the chief centre of British power and influence in India, a position it was to hold for more than two centuries. Until 1773, however, the three factories, or presidencies as they came to be known, were independent of each other and answerable only to London.

When one looks at the serenity of Mughal architecture, which produced some of the most beautiful buildings ever seen on the face of the planet, and those exquisite miniature paintings of Mughal court life, one gains the impression of a world of harmony, peace and elegance. It is an illusion; nothing could be further from the truth. During the entire century of the great Mughals, there was constant unrest – coming not only from palace intrigues and attempted *coups d'état*, but also from a deep groundswell of despair and discontent among the population. The Mughals' Hindu subjects bitterly resented the foreign rule which imposed an insupportable burden of taxation on them. Someone had to pay for the elaborate bureaucracy and sublime buildings, and for military follies like the failed expeditions to reclaim the Mughals' ancestral home of Samarkand. Inevitably, the money came from the people of India: as the splendours and excesses of the Mughals increased, so did the poverty of the Hindu masses.

Resentment reached its peak in 1658 when Akbar's great-grandson Aurangzeb seized the throne after a family power struggle that was exceptionally bloody, even by Mughal standards. Aurangzeb ended the family tradition of building architectural masterpieces that had reached its apogee when his father, Shah Jahan, built the world's most beautiful tomb, the Taj Mahal. Aurangzeb did not build pleasure gardens, palaces or tombs, only mosques. Yet he still needed money. His wars of succession had drained the treasury, and he needed a bigger and better-paid army than any of his predecessors to keep him in power, which it did for 49 brutal years. To pay for the army, Aurangzeb bled his Hindu subjects dry, reintroducing the poll tax on non-Muslims which had been abolished by Akbar, and charging Hindu merchants more than double the excise duty paid by Muslims on the same goods. His revenue collectors increased taxes on the peasants to insupportable levels, both to pay for the local cavalry that kept them subjugated, and to line their own pockets. The peasants were left with too little to live on and nothing to buy seed for new crops. Millions faced starvation and famine.

Characteristically, Aurangzeb took as his imperial name Alamgir, 'World Conqueror'. His courtiers and subjects preferred to call him 'the prayer-monger'. A puritanical Muslim, he began his reign by banishing wine, song and dance from the court. He went on to impose strict Muslim laws throughout the empire, on Muslim and non-Muslim alike, appointing censors of public morals in every large city to enforce his decrees. These included bans not only on gambling and illicit sex, but also on Hindu festivals and the building and repair of temples, an interference with their religion that stoked the fires of hatred in Hindus.

All over the empire, rebellions flared, but they remained local and uncoordinated. In Maharashtra, the region of western India around and below Bombay with Poona as its capital, the warlike Marathas were a continuous source of trouble, harrassing and plundering the empire under their heroic leader Shivaji. Rajputs, too, began attacking the Moghuls in Jodphur and Mewar, and in the central Indian region of the Deccan there was constant warfare.

The revolts were put down with the utmost cruelty. Rebellious peasants were blown away by artillery. When Hindu merchants gathered outside the Red Fort in Agra to protest against ruinous new taxes, Aurangzeb sent the imperial war elephants out to trample them to death. The savagery of the Mughal repression left scars that in many cases have not healed to this day, for memories have always been long in India, and the Hindu concept of time, geared as it is to eternity, shrinks years and even centuries to insignificance.

The hostility of the Hindus was matched and even exceeded by that of the Sikhs. Aurangzeb's zealotry turned them from being a pacific, liberal sect – the word Sikh means disciple – into a militant new order of vengeful warriors. Sikhism had been created in the early sixteenth century as an attempt to bring harmony between Hindu and Muslim by synthesizing the best elements of the two faiths. It attracted recruits from both, though it was generally regarded as a protestant offshoot of Hinduism, 'purified' by the adoption of the Islamic principles of monotheism and anti-idolatry. The Sikhs' holy city, Amritsar, and the Golden Temple at its heart, were built on land given to the faith's fourth guru by Akbar, for services rendered.

The saga of oppression and wholesale slaughter of the Sikhs was started by Akbar's son Jahangir, who tortured the fifth guru to death in 1606, and culminated in the beheading of the ninth guru, Tegh Bahadur, by Aurangzeb in 1675 for his refusal to abandon the faith. His son Gobind Rai, the tenth and last guru, vowed to avenge his father's murder, and that of his own two sons who were put to death by the Muslim governor of Sirhind. On Baisakhi Day, 1699, Gobind Rai announced that he was taking the new name Singh, meaning lion. He then baptised his closest followers with the same name, and inaugurated the 'five Ks' which the *khalsa*, the 'army of the pure', would always carry or wear as the visible symbols of their faith: *kes*, the unshorn hair and beard; *kangha*, the comb to keep it tidy; *kach*, the knee-length shorts worn by soldiers of the time; *kara*, the steel bracelet worn on the right wrist; and *kirpan*, the short sword that was to be carried at all times, so that a Sikh would always be ready for battle. There were to be no more gurus: the guru would become immortal by merging with the community, to be represented in future by the will of the majority.[5]

The Mughal empire effectively died with Aurangzeb in 1707, the same year the English and Scots became the British when their two Parliaments were joined in the Act of Union. True, there was a Mughal emperor in Delhi until 1857, but he was emperor in name only, the shadow of a memory, described by Lord Macaulay as 'a mock sovereign immured in a gorgeous state prison'.[6] During the seventeenth century, the English merchants had continued to prosper, their trade secure under the protection of the Mughals. Now, the Mughals could not even protect themselves, as Aurangzeb's 17 sons and grandsons squabbled and fought over their inheritance.

Their empire split initially into two parts, with the Nizam of Hyderabad holding power in central and much of southern India, and the rest becoming fragmented. Kabul, Sind, Gujarat and Surat, Oudh and the Punjab were all lost to former Mughal governors, Hindu princes and soldiers of fortune. The Marathas regained control of Maharashtra, forming themselves into a confederacy headed by a hereditary minister known as the Peshwa, before that too disintegrated as their chiefs began fighting among themselves. Bengal still sent tribute to the emperor in Delhi, but was to all intents and purposes an independent state ruled by the nawab, the governor.

Macaulay described the situation later with his usual pungency:

Society was a chaos ... In the course of a single generation a hundred dynasties grew up, flourished, decayed, were extinguished, were forgotten.

Every adventurer who could muster a troop of horse might aspire to a throne. Every palace was, every year, the scene of conspiracies, treasons, revolutions, parricides ... A Persian invader penetrated to Delhi, and carried back in triumph the most precious treasures of the House of Tamerlane [including the Kohinoor diamond and the Peacock Throne]. The Afghan soon followed, by the same track, to glean whatever the Persian had spared. The Jauts [Jats, a Hindu community in the Punjab] established themselves on the Jumna. The Seiks [Sikhs] devastated Lahore. Every part of India, from Tanjore to the Himalayas, was laid under contribution by the Mahrattas ... All the evils of despotism, and all the evils of anarchy, pressed at once on that miserable race ... Such was the state of India when the Company began to take part in the disputes of its ephemeral sovereigns.[7]

To safeguard their trade and their bases, the British were forced to start intervening in those disputes. The main threat, however, came not from the Indians but from the French, by then the only other European power with a significant presence in India. The French East India Company (Compagnie des Indes Orientales) had been founded in 1664 and had set up its Indian headquarters 10 years later at Pondicherry, 85 miles south of Madras, with subsidiary factories at Surat and on the Hooghly. The two companies competed vigorously but peacefully until 1743, when Britain and France went to war in Europe and the conflict spread to India. The British captured several French ships. The French under the command of the president of the Pondicherry factory, Joseph Francois Dupleix, retaliated, calling their fleet from Mauritius, and taking Madras in 1746. When the Nawab of the Carnatic, the south-east coastal region around Madras and Pondicherry, running down to the southernmost tip of India, Cape Comorin, tried to make the French hand over Madras to him, Dupleix refused. The nawab sent an army of 10,000 of his best cavalry, but Dupleix, with a force of 230 Frenchmen and 700 trained sepoys (Indian foot soldiers), roundly defeated them with disciplined European-style warfare, using muskets and cannons.

When the war in Europe ended three years later, Madras was returned to Britain in exchange for Cap Breton Island in Nova Scotia, but it was now surrounded by territory under the hostile influence of the French. Dupleix's victory over the forces of the nawab had brought about a sea change in political power in India as decisive as when Babur's warriors smashed the great army of the Delhi Sultanate. Until then the Europeans, conscious of their tiny numbers, had paid court to the Indian rulers. Now, they could dictate to them.

Dupleix was a highly intelligent man with a taste for power and a talent for intrigue. By a judicious mixture of bribery, assassination, and the threat of force, he soon installed not only his own puppet Nawab of the Carnatic, but also a puppet Nizam of Hyderabad, the overall ruler of the southern part of the old Mughal empire. In order to survive in Madras, and ultimately in the whole of India, the British had to start playing Dupleix's game, promoting their own candidate as the rightful Nawab of the Carnatic.

Among those taken prisoner by the French when they captured Madras had been the 21-year-old Robert Clive, who had escaped by blacking his face and disguising himself as an Indian interpreter. Clive, described by a fellow writer as 'short, inclined to be corpulent, awkward and unmannerly, his aspect gloomy, his temper morose and untractable'[8], was the problem son of a country lawyer from Market Drayton in Shropshire. It was largely to keep him out of trouble at home that he had been sent to India as a writer, or clerk, at £10 a year. After only a few weeks, Clive had become so bored by his job in the counting house that he twice tried to blow his brains out with a pistol. Fortunately, it misfired both times. If it had not, India might well have become the jewel in the French crown rather than the British.

In 1751, the British puppet nawab, with a few British soldiers, was besieged by the French-backed nawab and his army in the rock fortress of Trichinopoly, some 175 miles south of Madras. Heavily outnumbered, the British puppet was near surrender. Once he went, it would be the end for the British in south India. It was Clive, the troublesome clerk, who perceived that in taking his army to besiege Trichinopoly, the French-backed nawab had left his capital, Arcot, virtually undefended. Clive came up with an audacious plan to seize Arcot behind the nawab's back, relieving the pressure on Trichinopoly by forcing the French nawab to pull out his troops to recapture his capital. Specially commissioned as a captain, Clive scraped together a scratch force of 200 Englishmen and 300 sepoys, with eight officers – six of whom had never seen action, four of them newly commissioned clerks. Dragging three small artillery pieces, they marched more than 100 miles in five sweltering days to take Arcot and the nawab's fortress palace without firing a shot: the 1,200 defenders fled at their approach and the citizens simply gaped in wonder as the tiny contingent marched boldly through the streets.

News of Clive's achievement spread quickly, but was soon eclipsed by what followed. Four thousand of the nawab's men were withdrawn from Trichinopoly as expected, and supported by French troops from Pondicherry, laid siege to Arcot. Outnumbered by up to 40 to one, Clive and his band of heroes held out for 50 days and nights, until they were relieved by a larger British force. By that time, the tide of the war had been turned by the arrival of a great Maratha army as allies of the British and their nawab, who was duly enthroned.

Dupleix had lost the game and was recalled to France in disgrace. The 26-year-old Clive went back to trade, making his first fortune as supplier of provisions for company troops. With £40,000 in his account, and a new wife on his arm, he sailed home to London, where he bought a house and a seat in Parliament. After only 18 months, however, he was on his way back to India to find still greater fame and fortune.

With the French and British at war again in Europe and North America, Clive, now second-in-command of the company's troops in the south, was preparing to lead an army to Hyderabad to remove the French-backed nizam. Before he could leave, however, he was ordered to sail north to Bengal, whose new nawab, Siraj-ud-daula, had seized Calcutta, ostensibly in retaliation for British insolence at fortifying their factory without permission.

It was a sorry tale: Fort William's defences were poor, with an inadequate garrison, an untrained militia, and indecisive leadership. When Siraj swooped, eager to get his hands on Calcutta's immense riches, the governor took to his boat and fled downriver with most of the able-bodied men, leaving many women and children behind. The 170 British soldiers who remained were hampered by worm-eaten ammunition and damp powder. They were overcome by noon. That night, according to their commander, J.Z. Holwell, 146 English prisoners, including one woman and 12 wounded officers, were locked up in Fort William's punishment cell, an airless dungeon measuring 18 feet by 14. It was the hottest and most oppressive night of the year – the monsoon broke next day. Again according to Holwell, 23 people emerged alive next morning. In fact, there were only 64 prisoners, and although 43 of them died, this was by accident, not design – Siraj had simply given orders that they be locked up overnight. It was Holwell's account that was heard, however, and the imperial myth of the Black Hole of Calcutta was born. It was the first in a long line of 'native atrocities' that were to strike panic into the hearts of the British in India, justifying all kinds of repressive measures up to and even beyond General Dyer's action at the Jallianwala Bagh.

Clive, with an army of 900 Europeans and 1,500 sepoys, and escorted by a fleet of five warships under the command of Admiral Watson, had no difficulty in driving Siraj out of Calcutta. He and Watson then turned on the French, removing them from Bengal by capturing their bases at Chandarnagar and on the Hooghly. When Siraj still proved troublesome, Clive formed an alliance with the fabulously rich Hindu banker, Jagat Seth, to pay Siraj's more pliable uncle, Mir Jafar, to betray his nephew and take his place.

On 23 June 1757, Clive led his troops to meet Siraj's army of 50,000 at the village of Plassey, between Calcutta and the nawab's capital of Murshidabad. The battle of Plassey has always been regarded as the decisive moment in establishing British hegemony in Bengal, paving the way for the domination of all India. And so it was, but it was hardly a battle at all, more a confused scuffle. It began with a cannonade from the nawab's artillery. Clive prudently withdrew his men behind a hill, at which point a monsoon downpour drenched the nawab's ammunition while Clive's men kept their powder dry under tarpaulins. When the rain stopped, Clive opened fire again, and after a few skirmishes, Siraj and his army turned and ran. It was not Clive's guns, however, that had truly won the day, but Mir Jafar's treachery and Jagat Seth's money: Mir Jafar, the nawab's chief general, had simply held his own men back, and Jagat Seth had laid out a small fortune to pay Siraj's soldiers not to fight. All told, the battle that settled India's future cost the British 63 men killed or wounded, and the nawab about 500.

Clive personally escorted Mir Jafar to the throne in Murshidabad, and asked the Mughal emperor in Delhi to confirm him as Nawab of Bengal, noting persuasively: 'I have 25,000 matchless sepoys.' The emperor duly recognized Mir Jafar, and with him the fact that the British had arrived as a major power in India. The company received huge compensation, including the right to collect and keep the revenues from various provinces of Bengal which brought a profit of about half a million pounds a year. Clive's personal share of the official compensation was £234,000 and a land grant worth another £30,000 a year. He returned home in 1760 with, by his own reckoning, £401,102, to buy a controlling interest in the company for £100,000, plus enough rotten borough seats in Parliament to give him and the company protection. The peerage he received two years later as Lord Clive of Plassey was an Irish barony, enabling him to continue to sit in the Commons.

Clive had made a fortune in bribes, presents and profits, but he was more scrupulous than most. Other Calcutta traders spread out across the country, plundering its people mercilessly. Their rapacity brought misery to Bengalis of all ranks, provoked attacks from the nawab and the remnants of the Mughal empire, and brought the once-wealthy region close to bankruptcy. It almost bankrupted the company, too, since the individual merchants kept the spoils for themselves and paid nothing in tax or duty.

After the most shameful five years of the entire British presence in India, the former 'poacher' Clive was forced to turn gamekeeper, returning to Calcutta to sort out the mess. The year before, a small company force under Major Hector Munro had decisively defeated the Mughal army at Buxar, on the Ganges between Benares and Patna. With the French confined to a few unfortified enclaves and the rest of northern and central India in turmoil from repeated Afghan invasions and marauding Marathas, there was nothing to prevent Clive marching on Delhi and seizing the Mughal throne. Nothing, that is, except the fact that the British still had no imperial ambitions. In a letter to his directors, Clive explained:

If ideas of conquest were to be the rule of our conduct, I foresee that we should, by necessity, be led from acquisition to acquisition, until we had the whole empire up in arms against us; and whilst we lay under the great disadvantage of fighting without a single ally (for who could wish us well?)

the natives, left without European allies, would find, in their own resources, means of carrying on war against us in a much more soldierly manner.[9]

Clive chose instead to restore the Mughal emperor, Shah Alam, to his throne, and to become the emperor's servant, if only in name. It must have been sweet revenge completing his triumph over the French in this way – Dupleix had held the strings of puppet nawabs and nizams; Clive now controlled a puppet emperor. On 12 August 1765, Shah Alam proclaimed the company his *diwan*, revenue minister, for the provinces of Bengal, Bihar and Orissa, with the right to collect their multi-million pound revenue 'from generation to generation, for ever and ever'. In return for being allowed to keep what it collected, and to trade freely and without tax throughout the region, the company was to pay the emperor £260,000 a year to support him in reduced circumstances at Allahabad. The triple province was still officially governed by the nawab, but with financial and military power in its hands, the company was ruler in all but name.

After two hectic years, during which he had more or less brought the traders to heel, forbidding private dealings and limiting presents, Clive's health failed and he returned home again. But he was not to enjoy the fruits of his success. He had made many enemies along the way, and in 1773, he was censured by Parliament for the way he had made his own Indian fortune. The following year, at the age of 49, he finally succeeded in committing suicide by cutting his throat.

In Bengal, the monsoon rains failed in 1769, and famine followed. One third of the peasantry died; many of the survivors were forced to resort to cannibalism, while merchants made fortunes from the grain they had hoarded in their warehouses. The company did nothing, claiming that administrative responsibility lay with the nawab. It was not this catastrophe, however, that roused the government in London, but the fact that the company was unable to pay its annual tax of £400,000. Despite Clive's efforts to curb corruption, the merchants were again diverting most of the profits into their own coffers, and the tax revenues alone were not enough to cover the company's costs.

To avoid bankruptcy, the company begged for a loan of £1,500,000. Lord North's government agreed to provide it, but it came with strings attached: the Regulating Act of 1773 gave the British government a direct involvement in India for the first time. The independent presidencies of Bombay and Madras were to come under the control of a governor-general in Calcutta, paid by the company but appointed by the government, which would also nominate four members of his council. The first governor-general was to be the 40-year-old governor of Bengal, Warren Hastings, a weasel of a man, small, thin-faced and balding.

Hastings, like Clive, was a company servant. But there the resemblance ended. While Clive was an intuitive hot-blooded adventurer, Hastings was all cool calculation. Without the fire of Clive, the British empire in India would never have been born; without the ice of Hastings, it would never have survived. What Clive started, Hastings consolidated, often in the face of obstruction by the government's nominees on his council, men with no knowledge of India who tried to block his every move. The antagonism between them was so strong, indeed, that one of the government directors, Philip Francis, ended up fighting – and losing – a pistol duel with Hastings. The wounded Francis returned to London, to continue his fight in the political arena, behind the governor-general's back.

Hastings, like Clive, had no wish to extend British rule. He knew that 'the dominion of all India' was possible, but declared that it was 'an event which I may not mention without adding that it is what I never wish to see'.[10] What he did wish to see was a successful company establishing the peaceful conditions needed for trade by ruling India indirectly as the power behind many thrones. He set about achieving this, starting by balancing the books. He stopped payments to the Mughal emperor, halved the amount paid to the Nawab of Bengal, and abolished the passes which allowed British merchants to trade without paying taxes or duties. Then, most importantly, he reorganized the revenue-collecting system. To make sure all the money came to the company, he replaced Indian agents with a British collector in each district, supervising Indian subordinates who gathered the taxes. This was the real beginning of the British system of administration in India.

Establishing peace outside Bengal was much more difficult. Hastings began by lending a brigade of soldiers to the Nawab-Vizier of Oudh, the state on the north-west of Bengal and Bihar which formed a valuable buffer against both the Marathas to the west and the Afghans to the north, who were then attacking it. Hastings's use of British troops in the service of an Indian ruler was heavily criticized both in London and Calcutta, but it paid off handsomely. The nawab-vizier paid a substantial sum for the military assistance, and the company gained the lasting friendship and support of Oudh, which played a vital part in the intricate mechanism of alliances constructed by Hastings.

The formerly independent presidencies of Bombay and Madras bitterly resented the appointment of Hastings as their superior – the British governor and council in Madras even suspended their agent at the nizam's court in Hyderabad for having 'betrayed the secrets of his trust to the governor-general and Council of Bengal'.[11] Both remained jealous and insubordinate, causing Hastings considerable problems at a time when he could expect little help from home, since Britain was preoccupied with the American War of Independence. The French had also reappeared on the scene, and were threatening to re-establish themselves in India.

Hastings had managed to get away with hiring out troops to an Indian ruler. However when the governors and councils of Bombay and Madras interfered in local Indian politics, they provoked wars with the Marathas in the west, united again under the Peshwa, and with the powerful ruler of Mysore in the south. To make matters even worse, they almost brought Hyderabad into a triple alliance against the company which could have proved fatal. Only Hastings's foresight and some daring military moves worthy of Clive himself saved the two presidencies. At the same time, he managed through skilful diplomacy to break up the potential triple alliance, thus freeing his own forces to see off the French fleet and the army it landed in the south-east.

In saving Bombay and Madras, Hastings brought them permanently under the control of the governor-general in Calcutta, to establish a single British government as one of the great powers in India. His reward was impeachment and disgrace. His enemies, led by Philip Francis, had been hard at work in London recruiting the redoubtable Irish parliamentarian Edmund Burke, the man who had opposed the use of force in North America, and Charles James Fox, leader of the Whigs.

After 14 years as ruler of British India, Hastings found it hard to tolerate interference from politicians back home who, in his eyes, knew nothing of India. It was a complaint that was to echo repeatedly down the years until the very end of British rule. Hastings wanted virtual independence. Burke was concerned with the supremacy of Parliament. To him, 'The East India Company did not seem to be merely a Company formed for the extension of British commerce but in reality a delegation of the whole power and sovereignty of this kingdom sent into the east.'[12] It was Parliament that delegated the power, and therefore Parliament should control it.

Obsessed with his mission to clean up the company, Burke drafted several bills giving the British government direct charge of its property and affairs, and binding it to serve the public interest. But it was his political opponent, William Pitt the Younger, who finally produced an acceptable compromise with his India Act of 1784. This forbade any further territorial expansion, and gave the home government ultimate power through a Board of Control in London consisting of six men: the chancellor of the exchequer, a secretary of state for India, and four privy councillors. For its first 18 years, the board was presided over by Henry Dundas, later Lord Melville, an astute Scottish lawyer and close associate of Pitt. The board – which meant Dundas – had a free hand, without consulting anyone either in India or Britain, on anything 'concerning the levying of war or making of peace, or negotiating with any of the native princes or states in India'.[13] It also had the power to recall the governor-general or any other company servant. This was all too much for Hastings, and he resigned before he could be fired. Back in London, Burke joined Fox and the playwright and politician, Richard Brinsley Sheridan, in leading a grand impeachment of him on charges of corruption. The trial in Westminster Hall was marked by coruscating displays of malicious vituperation. It was easily the best show in town, running for 142 days spread over seven years, until a weary and embittered Hastings proved his complete innocence.

Hastings was succeeded as governor-general by Lord Cornwallis, still smarting from his defeat at the hands of George Washington at Yorktown. Having presided over the death of Britain's empire in the west, he was now to be the midwife of its new empire in the east. Hastings had been a company man, governing Bengal on behalf of the company. Cornwallis was the first of the new line of aristocrats who would be sent out one after another until 1947 to rule India on behalf of the British government; men who already had fortunes in England and so would have no need to make more in India.

Cornwallis's first task was to continue the cleaning-up process started by Clive and Hastings. He began by separating the political functions of the company from its commercial dealings. Its merchants were still allowed to deal on their own account, but its administrators were to be a breed apart. In keeping with the Whig belief in public service for the welfare of the governed, they were expected to perform their duties selflessly, in return for security, prestige and handsome salaries that removed any need for accepting bribes. A new name was invented for them: 'civil servants' – often shortened to 'civilian', especially in the higher reaches – to distinguish them from soldiers in the company's military service and from the commercial sector. They were also to be a breed apart from the Indians. Hastings had believed in partnership with the Indians who had been running the day-to-day administration of government since the beginning of Mughal rule. Cornwallis would have none of this. Convinced of the innate superiority of the British, he declared: 'Every native of Hindustan I verily believe is corrupt.'

And so began the alienation of the Indian official classes. In Cornwallis's view, Indians were acceptable only in subservient roles. Higher civil servants, all those earning over £500 a year, were to be entirely British. So, too, were the officers of the Bengal army, of which Cornwallis was commander-in-chief. After 1790, no Indian could become a commissioned officer, a situation that would not be changed until the Second World War, and only then because Britain could not provide enough officers for all the Indian regiments fighting for the Allied cause. Those most affected by Cornwallis's measures were the Muslims. Under the Mughals, their co-religionists, they had enjoyed a privileged position: the great majority of army officers had been Muslims, as were at least 85 per cent of higher officials.[14] Now, at a stroke, they were relegated to a lower status; the old Muslim middle class was destroyed. It would take the best part of the following century before a new one began to emerge.

Two of Cornwallis's other measures were equally far-reaching. One was the introduction of the rule of law, separating the judiciary from the executive, with a system of supreme and district courts, all presided over by British judges.

His other innovation was a concept that had not previously existed in India: the private ownership of land. In the past, kings and emperors had granted favoured servants the right to administer an area and collect revenue on its crops and harvests for life. The holder of that right, known in Bengal as a zamindar and usually, though by no means always, a Muslim, shared the proceeds with the ruler. The king's share now went to the company as ruler of Bengal, but the amounts it received fluctuated wildly, depending on the harvests and the rigour of the zamindars. With the higher salaries it was now paying its civil servants, this uncertain income was a major disadvantage to the company. Cornwallis resolved it by giving the zamindars title to the land in return for regular payments fixed at the rate prevailing in 1793. The permanent settlement, as it was known, changed Indian society profoundly, though the real effects were not to be seen for some years: while the amount to be paid by the zamindar to the company, and later the government, was fixed, there was no limit on what he was allowed to extract from his tenants.

In other parts of India, particularly in the south where Mughal rule had never reached, there were no zamindars, no intermediaries between the peasant cultivator and collector, so when revenue settlements were agreed, the title went to the peasant himself, the *ryotwar*, rather than to a landlord.

Cornwallis's secondary aim, of creating a local aristocracy loyal to the company because it had a stake in the future prosperity of Bengal, soon backfired. Many zamindars got themselves hopelessly in debt to Hindu bankers in Calcutta who charged up to 150 per cent interest and then took over their deeds and became absentee landlords, displacing men who, though often Muslim, had been an integral and important part of the local community. However, there was a compensation for the British. Although the local Mughal aristocracy had lost out, they were replaced by prominent Hindu families with names like Roy, Seth and Tagore, who were to become the most fervent supporters of the British for well over a century.

Despite the fact that he was a distinguished career soldier, Cornwallis was essentially a bureaucrat, content to obey his orders not to extend the company's territory in India. But when Tipu, the Sultan of Mysore whose father had dragged Hastings into war in the Carnatic, attacked the British-protected state of Travancore on the extreme south-western tip of India in 1789, Cornwallis had to act. Tipu was defeated, and forced to cede most of the Malabar coast including the port and city of Calicut to the British, giving them their first firm foothold in the deep south.

The Malabar coast was Britain's first substantial territory outside of Bengal, Bihar and Orissa, and so it remained for five years after Cornwallis departed, handing over to his former revenue commissioner, John Shore. Shore was succeeded in 1798 by Richard Colley Wellesley, a governor-general with a very different view of Britain's role. As the eighteenth century drew to a close, the age of British imperialism was about to begin.

2

'The Strangest of all Empires'

In striking contrast to all his predecessors as governor-general, Lord Wellesley, a 37-year-old Anglo-Irish aristocrat, went out to India in 1798 as a convinced imperialist. His stated aim was 'the complete consolidation of the British Empire in India and the future tranquillity of Hindustan'. He arrived just as Napoleon Bonaparte captured Malta and invaded Egypt, clearly intent on destroying British trade. It did not take much imagination to see where the Corsican general's next step might be. Wellesley was married to a Frenchwoman, and had experienced the horrors of the revolution at first hand in Paris. As a result, he was violently opposed to the French and determined to thwart their ambitions. His first priority as governor-general, therefore, was to secure India for Britain, and to get rid of any lingering pockets of French influence among the native rulers — a policy in which he was encouraged by Henry Dundas, the autocratic president of the Board of Control in London, who was even more rabidly Francophobe than Wellesley himself.

    Wellesley had hardly unpacked his boxes in India before he found an excuse to take action against the perpetually troublesome Sultan Tipu in the south. Like his father before him, Tipu had always flirted with the French, if only to upset the British, whom he hated. Now, he made the mistake of receiving a stranded French party. It was enough to allow Wellesley to put on his general's hat and mount a well-prepared expedition to destroy Tipu and put an end to French ambitions once and for all. Tipu died fighting bravely against overwhelming odds. Wellesley annexed half of his state to the company's existing territory in the Carnatic, which now stretched from coast to coast; he gave its northern part to the Nizam of Hyderabad as a reward for deserting the French and supporting the British; and he took control of what was left of Mysore by putting on its throne a child maharaja whose family had been deposed by Tipu's father.

Both the nizam and the maharaja became client rulers, bound to the British by subsidiary treaty, a wonderful device that allowed Wellesley to extend British power throughout India at minimal expense and bloodshed. The system was beautiful in its simplicity. The British gave an Indian state and its ruler protection against neighbours and usurpers by stationing company troops in its capital, under the control of a British resident. The British took total responsibility for the state's external affairs, but avoided trouble and expense by leaving its internal affairs entirely to the ruler. The troops were, of course, very much a two-edged weapon: while they were protecting the prince, they were also keeping him in line, a privilege for which he was expected to pay.

In some cases, Hyderabad and Oudh in particular, Wellesley demanded the cession of territory to provide permanent revenue for the upkeep of the troops. In this way he obtained the cotton-rich region of Berar from the nizam, and took the larger part of the nawab-vizier's lands, including Rohilkhand, the same territory that Warren Hastings had hired out company troops to capture.

Politically, the sub-continent had slid back into the twelfth century, becoming a jungle of feuding and feudal territories, each constantly in fear of attack both by its neighbours and by gangs of marauding freebooters. In their fear, the rulers began turning to the British, as the British resident in Rajputana, one of the largest states, reported:

> They said that some power in India had always existed to which peaceable States submitted, and in return obtained its protection against the invasion of upstart chiefs and the armies of lawless banditry; that the British Government now occupied the place of their protecting power and was the natural guardian of weak States, which were constantly exposed to the cruelties and oppression of robbers and plunderers owing to the refusal of the British Government to protect them.[1]

In filling the power vacuum left by the final collapse of the Mughals, the British totally emasculated local rulers. At the same time, however, they eliminated the local wars, internal rebellions and bloody succession struggles that had bedevilled most of India for so long, draining its strength and leaving social disorder and decay in their wake. *Pax Britannica* began to spread across India. But first, there were the Marathas to be dealt with. Britain's sole remaining rivals for power in India were too divided among themselves to present any serious threat to British interests. They had, however, gone on harrassing and plundering their neighbours. 'These Maratha gentlemen,' the nizam's chief minister told Wellesley's protégé, John Malcolm, 'need a lesson and we shall have no peace till they receive it.'[2]

Wellesley sent his younger brother Arthur, the future Duke of

Wellington, to administer the lesson in the north-west, where he routed the Marathas in less than three months. Meanwhile, another British general, Lord Lake, was capturing Aligarh, Agra and Delhi. With the Mughals' imperial city under British control, the blind emperor Shah Alam, his eyes put out by an Afghan raider, became a British pensioner. He was reduced in status to king of Delhi, but even that title was purely nominal – his word was law only inside the Red Fort. The victory was almost complete when the company's directors got cold feet at the appalling realization that they were about to become the rulers of virtually the whole of India. Wellesley had always made the fullest possible use of the six months' distance between Calcutta and London to act first and report later, but this time he had gone too far. He was recalled, accused of having 'goaded the whole country into a state of revolt'.

Cornwallis was sent out again, to undo what he could of Wellesley's efforts. In the year before he died in office, Cornwallis made peace with the Marathas and withdrew from Rajputana and central India. This resulted in 13 years of brutal lawlessness surpassing anything that had gone before, as the peoples of central India were terrorized both by Maratha chiefs and by gangs of Pindaris, their Pathan mercenaries who turned bandit. No one dared travel, or even move outside his town or village, without a powerful armed escort. Everywhere, the land was laid waste and communities were destroyed.

It was not until 1818 that the then governor-general, the Marquis of Hastings (no relation to Warren Hastings, whose impeachment he had managed in London) decided the time had come to complete Wellesley's grand design and so put an end to the anarchy that was threatening the stability of British India. Notably aided by two of Wellesley's young men, John Malcolm and Mountstuart Elphinstone, he went after the Pindaris, picking them off gang by gang, before finally crushing their masters in the third and last Maratha war, and annexing huge tracts of their lands to Bombay. The Rajputs, freed from Maratha domination, hurried to sign subsidiary treaties with the British, content to live under the protection of the 'new Mughals' as they had done under the old.

The British now had undisputed hegemony over the whole of India, from the tip of Cape Comorin in the south to the river Sutlej in the north. They had fought a brief war with the Gurkhas to establish a common frontier between Oudh and Nepal, from which the two sides had emerged with a mutual respect that was to outlast the empire. Even before the peace treaty was signed, Gurkhas were rushing to sign up as soldiers for the British, and many of them fought in the armies that defeated the Marathas. Only the north-west remained for the moment outside Britain's grasp: Sind, the Sikh-ruled Punjab and the mountainous Afghan territories.

Hastings had fulfilled Wellesley's ambition of consolidating a British empire in

India, but he had done it reluctantly, with little of Wellesley's certainty about its future. Even as he completed the task, in 1818, he wrote: 'A time not very remote will arrive when England will, on sound principles of policy, wish to relinquish the dominion which she has gradually and unintentionally assumed over this country and from which she cannot at present recede.'[3]

The 'unintentional' dominion was Wellesley's main memorial in India, but it was by no means his only one. Known as 'The Glorious Little Man' to his supporters and 'Old Villainy' to his young protégés, he had seen himself as a new Mughal, and had begun to behave like one. The Mughals had built themselves grandiose palaces, and Wellesley had followed suit by constructing a new Government House in Calcutta as a symbol of power and permanence. There was nothing Mughal in its design, however, for Wellesley despised everything Indian. A classical, three-storey, stone-clad mansion with an imposing portico and four wings radiating from a central hall, the new building was a faithful copy of a great English country house – Robert Adam's Kedleston Hall in Derbyshire, home of the Curzon family. Nearly a century later, a Curzon would be one of its last occupants as governor-general, the only one of Wellesley's successors who could match his magnificent conceit.

With typical arrogance, Wellesley did not bother to inform the directors in London about the new building until he presented them with the bill for £140,000. He did not tell them, either, about the College of Fort William, which he set up to teach the young men coming out from England, most of them in their mid-teens, some, like John Malcolm, as young as 13. Almost all had had their education cut short. Wellesley's plan was that they should spend three years at the college, studying Indian history and law, oriental languages, international law, general history, and ethics. The college was to be run on the lines of an Oxford or Cambridge college, with teachers drawn not only from the growing numbers of British orientalists but also from Brahman scholars who were moving into the city as their rural estates were taken over by bankers and money-lenders.

Fort William College was already operating smoothly by the time the directors in London discovered its existence. Although they saw the value of Wellesley's aims, they objected to his high-handedness and decided it would be better to educate the young men under their own supervision, before they went out to India. So, in 1806 they opened the East India College in Hertford Castle, moving it after three years into its own buildings at Haileybury. It lasted until 1858, by coincidence the same year as the demise of the East India Company; five years after that it was reopened as an English public school. At Haileybury, as at the company's military academy at Addiscombe, generations of young Britons were imbued with the belief that they had been born to lead the Indians out of the darkness of superstition and into the light of western civilization. Their lessons in Indian history began with the Black Hole and Plassey.

With the opening of Haileybury, the college in Calcutta was reduced to a school of oriental languages for Bengal alone, but it swiftly grew into an important centre of linguistic and cultural research. In its first five years, it published more than 100 original works in oriental languages, and by 1818 its library contained the largest collection of oriental books and manuscripts in the world. The Brahmans brought in as teachers found themselves exposed to British education and western thinking, including such alien notions as the rights of man, constitutional government, and nationalism. They also gained a renewed confidence in their own culture that was to fuel a Bengali renaissance; the first, essential step on the long road to independence.

The new Charter Act of 1813 had ordered the company to provide an annual budget of not less than 100,000 rupees (£10,000) for Indian education – a full 20 years before the British government made its first grant of £20,000 for state schools at home. The trouble was, no one could agree on whether the schools should provide western education in English, or the study of Indian civilization in Sanskrit, Persian and Arabic. But while the orientalists in the company agonized over the dangers of offending the Brahmans, one Brahman at least had no doubts. Raja Rammohan Roy was horrified when the company finally decided – after prevaricating for 10 years – to found a new college for Sanskrit studies. If the government wanted to 'keep this country in darkness', he told the governor-general, the best way of doing it was with a school that could 'only be expected to load the minds of youth with grammatical niceties and metaphysical distinctions of little or no practical use to the possessors or to society'. What the young men of Bengal wanted, he said, was 'mathematics, natural philosophy, chemistry, anatomy, and other useful sciences, which the natives of Europe have carried to a degree of perfection that has raised them above the inhabitants of other parts of the world'.[4]

Roy knew what he was talking about. In 1816 he and a group of friends, both Indian and British, had founded the Hindu College in Calcutta, to offer a full western education. It was followed by a growing number of similar schools and colleges for Hindus – the newly emerging Hindu middle classes were ravenous for the new knowledge, and in particular for the English language, which they rightly saw as the essential passport to advancement. In marked contrast, the Muslims remained aloof, refusing to co-operate with the people who had supplanted them as rulers, clinging instead to their traditional ways and isolating themselves as far as was possible from western influences.

Rammohan Roy, the son of an impoverished Brahman zamindar, is now hailed by many Bengalis as the father of modern India. Though that claim may be stretching things a little, what is certain is that he was the father of the Hindu renaissance and leader of the first modernizers, convinced that India needed to assimilate western ideas as well as reforming its own. Roy was the first of a long line of Indians who embraced western culture and ideas, becoming outwardly Anglicized yet remaining completely Indian within. He welcomed British rule, he said, because 'though a foreign yoke, [it] would lead most speedily and surely to the amelioration of the native inhabitants'.[5]

After a traditional Brahman education in Sanskrit, followed by Persian and Arabic, Roy joined the company's revenue department, rising to the position of native assistant to the collector of Rangpur, the highest office an Indian could then hold. He had become fluent in English and had also mastered Latin and Greek before retiring at the age of about 42, to devote the rest of his life to promoting social and religious reform. He founded the first Indian newspapers, fought for press freedom against the new censorship measures which were introduced in 1823, corresponded on judicial reform with Jeremy Bentham, whose utilitarian ideas dominated British political thought for much of the nineteenth century, and started an association in which Calcutta intellectuals met to discuss philosophy and religion.

Roy also founded the Brahmo Samaj, or Sacred Society, a group devoted to purifying Hinduism by stripping it of centuries of superstition. He attacked such practices as *sati* – the burning of widows on their husbands' funeral pyres – idolatry, and the abuse of caste. His purpose was partly philosophical: he had emerged with a fresh understanding of Hinduism's basic tenets after studying the ancient Hindu scriptures so that he could refute the arguments of Christian missionary friends who tried to convert him. It was also political: he was convinced that while Hindus continued to think of themselves in terms of class or caste, they could not think of themselves as Indian. In 1828, he wrote:

> I regret to say that the present system of religion adhered to by the Hindus is not well calculated to promote their political interest. The distinctions of caste introducing innumerable divisions and sub-divisions among them has entirely deprived them of patriotic feeling, and the multitude of religious rites and ceremonies and the laws of purification have totally disqualified them from undertaking any difficult enterprise. It is, I think, necessary that some change should take place in their religion at least for the sake of their political advantage and social comfort.[6]

Roy's radical view of Hinduism meant that, uniquely for a Brahman at that time, he was not afraid to go abroad. For an orthodox Hindu, crossing the 'black water' of the ocean meant automatic pollution and loss of caste, a deadly serious matter, since it barred him from all contact with his fellows and broke the cycle of rebirth and regeneration, condemning him in effect to eternal damnation. Roy went to England as the first and only 'raja' ambassador of the Mughals to the

Court of St James. Sadly, although he enjoyed the social and intellectual climate of Britain, he could not cope with its natural climate. He fell ill and died in Bristol, in 1833.

The Brahmo Samaj was not a mass movement – there were never more than a few hundred members – but it was the forerunner of a number of other reform movements in various parts of India. It also influenced generations of young Indians, and paved the way for later reformers, including Mahatma Gandhi and the poet Rabindranath Tagore. Tagore's father and grandfather, Debendranath and Dwarkanath, were both among Roy's immediate followers and associates: in fact, Debendranath took over the leadership of the Brahmos after Roy's death. Grandfather Dwarkanath, like Roy a zamindar who began as assistant to a collector, played his own part in the Bengali renaissance by pioneering Hindu involvement in commerce and industry, cultivating and processing jute, indigo, silk and sugar, and sinking India's first colliery. He became the first Indian bank director in 1828, founded the Calcutta Union Bank a year later, and formed the first Anglo-Indian managing agency, Carr, Tagore and Company, in 1834. By a sad coincidence, Dwarkanath Tagore, as unafraid of pollution as Roy, also died in England, while visiting London.

By the time Hastings took over as governor-general, the company had changed out of all recognition. Trade had given way to land revenue as its main source of income, and administration had replaced commerce as its main interest. The company seemed to have forgotten that the British were only in India for trade. The government in London, however, had not. With the industrial revolution in full flood, Britain's factories were producing far more than the home market could possibly absorb. New outlets were desperately needed, and where better than India, with its vast population? 'A trade might suddenly grow up beyond the Cape of Good Hope,' declared one enthusiast, 'to take off all the surplus manufactures that Britain can produce.'[7]

The ruling free market doctrines of Adam Smith and Jeremy Bentham regarded monopoly as a sin. So it is hardly surprising that when the company's charter came up for its 20-year renewal in 1813, the new Act brought more than the vague instruction to provide a budget for Indian education. It also ended the company's trading monopoly in everything other than China tea and the opium it shipped out of India to pay for it.

The new trade brought many things that were of benefit to India, if only in helping the burgeoning middle classes to live like Englishmen. But it also brought disaster. For literally thousands of years, Indian cottons had not only clothed the people of the sub-continent, but had also been exported all over the civilized world. In the days of the Pharaohs, ancient Egyptians had worn cottons and muslins from India. Handloomed Indian fabrics had been one of the staples of the East India Company's own early trade. But now, there were hundreds of mills in Lancashire churning out textiles by the mile at costs no hand weaver could hope to match. And just to make sure they couldn't, in 1813 the Lancashire mill-owners persuaded the British government to impose a prohibitive duty of 78 per cent on imported Indian muslins – the English idea of free trade was always a one-way street.

The Indian cotton trade had already been brought to its knees by the anarchy in non-British areas between 1805 and 1818. While it was at this low ebb, protected imports from Lancashire began pouring in to deliver the death blow. In the 20 years between the charter renewals of 1813 and 1833, Bengal's vast, 4,000-year-old cottage industry collapsed, throwing millions of men and women into destitution. 'The misery hardly finds a parallel in the history of commerce,' Lord William Bentinck wrote in his governor-general's report for 1834–5. 'The bones of the cotton weaver are bleaching the plains of India.'[8] While in Europe agricultural workers were being sucked from the land into the industrial towns and cities, in India craftsmen were being forced to try and scratch a living in an already overburdened rural economy. By 1840, the population of Dacca, for example, had fallen from 150,000 to 30,000, and Sir Charles Trevelyan, Macaulay's brother-in-law, reported that 'the jungle and malaria are fast encroaching upon the town'.[9]

The ruin of the weavers was soon followed by that of other craftsmen such as potters and metal workers, who could not compete with the industrial products of the English midlands. Meanwhile, the industrial revolution was only allowed to invade India through its products. It wasn't only India that was affected by Britain's determination to protect its position as the workshop of the world. Until 1825, skilled artisans and craftsmen were not allowed to emigrate from Britain, and the export of textile machinery was prohibited by law until 1843, though the East India Company continued to ban all imports of machinery until the very end of its existence. Nevertheless as both source of raw materials and captive market for finished goods, India suffered more than most.

Bengal had changed abruptly from a relatively prosperous, self-sufficient economy to a state of foreign dependence. The change may have been inevitable, part of the grand economic cycle in which a revived Indian textile industry would destroy its Lancashire counterpart little more than a century later. But at the time it was a cruel blow, and it is remarkable that the Bengalis accepted their fate with so little rancour. Even at the height of the disaster, Rammohan Roy could write:

Thanks to the Supreme Disposer of events of this universe for having unexpectedly delivered this country from the long-continued tyranny of its former rulers and placed it under the government of the English – a nation who are not only blessed with the enjoyment of civil and national liberty,

but also interest themselves in promoting liberty and social happiness ...
among those nations to which their influence extends.[10]

   But Roy was a wealthy intellectual, grateful for the opportunities offered
by the new learning. He and his like were not poor peasants driven into starvation
in rural slums.

   The third major provision of the 1813 Charter Act sprang from the
evangelical religious revival in England. It provided for the establishment of the
Church of England in India, and allowed Christian missionaries unrestricted
access to the country, though without government support. Experienced civilians,
even those who were themselves devout Christians, were strongly opposed to
missionary activity, an opposition that remained to the very end of British rule.
They thought it was bound to cause trouble – and they were right.

   The advent of the missionaries was only one sign of the changing attitude
of the British government to India, which was a reflection of the changes in British
political life itself. It was Britain's turn in the sun, and nothing seemed impossible.
The industrial revolution had made Britain the greatest economic power in the
world, as well as being the greatest sea power and the leading imperial power. Such
success bred an unshakeable superiority complex, and with it a belief in a divinely
ordained mission to bestow the benefits of British civilization on less fortunate
peoples. When Bentinck was sent out as governor-general in 1828, the president
of the Board of Control, Lord Ellenborough solemnly told him: 'We have a great
moral duty to perform in India.' Bentinck, a liberal humanist with a strong
evangelical streak, needed no second bidding.

Bentinck began performing his moral duty by outlawing *sati*. The word *sati* means
devotion, and a widow showed her devotion to her dead husband by voluntarily
throwing herself on to his funeral pyre. For many widows this was undoubtedly
true, and some continued to sacrifice themselves of their own free will until well
into the twentieth century. But others went unwillingly, strapped helpless and
terrified to the pyre by desperate or greedy relatives – desperate because a Hindu
widow was not allowed to remarry, and so became another mouth to feed; greedy
because there was often property to be grabbed. Bentinck made no distinction. His
law defined assisting *sati* as murder. Many of the reformers like Rammohan Roy
were as appalled by the practice as Bentinck, but disapproved of banning it by law.

   Bentinck took care to emphasize that his action was purely for the benefit
of Hindus, and did not imply any wish to convert anyone to Christianity. He trod
warily, because he had had personal experience of Hindu reaction to interference
with religious customs. In 1803, at the age of 29, he had been appointed governor
of Madras under Wellesley. Three years later, the company's Indian troops at
Vellore, 75 miles inland from Madras, had mutinied when their British

commanding officer tried to smarten them up by ordering them to trim or shave their beards, remove caste marks from their faces, and wear leather stocks and hats with leather cockades instead of turbans. These were serious matters – the beard was a mark of his religion to a Muslim, as were caste marks for Hindus, for whom leather was taboo. As for hats, they were normally only worn by untouchables converted to Christianity. One hundred and fourteen British officers and men were murdered; 19 mutineers were executed and the rest dismissed. Bentinck was recalled in disgrace.

It had taken Bentinck 20 years to get back to India, and in the meantime there had been a second mutiny. In 1824, the 47th Bengal Native Infantry, composed of high-caste Hindus, refused to cross the black water to fight the troublesome Burmese, in the war that added the provinces of Assam, Arakan and Tenasserim to British India. Trouble came to a head with an official refusal to provide special transport for the individual sets of cooking pots needed by each man under caste usage. The army had responded by opening fire on the mutineers with British-manned artillery. Eleven of the surviving ringleaders were hanged, and hundreds of men were condemned to 14 years' hard labour. The threat of further mutinies, however, did not deter Bentinck in 1829. Even though he acknowledged that abolishing *sati* would 'inspire extensive dissatisfaction', he was inspired by 'the moral goodness of the act and our power to enforce it'.[11] In the end, it was all accepted peacefully.

Bentinck next turned his attention to *thugi*, the ritual murder of travellers as human sacrifices to the mother goddess Kali, by gangs of men known as thugs. The thugs would befriend groups of travellers, suggesting they join forces for safety on the road. For some days they would journey and camp together, until one night when sitting round the fire, joking and talking happily, the thug leader would suddenly clap his hands and shout 'Bring the tobacco!' At this signal, the thugs would leap into action, strangling their victims with special handkerchiefs, with a coin dedicated to the goddess bound into one corner to give extra grip for the left hand. It would all be over in minutes. The bodies would be stripped and bundled into waiting graves, which were then covered over, and the thugs would be on their way, taking their victims' possessions as their earthly reward from Kali.

Thugi had been going on for centuries in central and northern India, but it had grown rapidly during the years of unrest. By Bentinck's time there were probably about 10,000 thugs in 40 or 50 great gangs, probably claiming 20–30,000 victims a year – no one can be sure because *thugi* was surrounded with secrecy, and there were no survivors to tell the tale. It first came to British attention when sepoys going home on leave, or returning to their regiments, began disappearing en route. This time, Bentinck had no qualms about interfering in ancient customs. He gave the job of rooting out and destroying *thugi* to the young Captain William Sleeman who, aided by 12 assistants, took a mere six years to get over 3,000 thugs convicted in the courts and sentenced either to hanging or transportation to a penal colony for life. One of them admitted to personally killing 719 people, and only regretted that he had not killed more. The cult of *thugi* was eradicated, the craft forgotten, and no one but the thugs themselves mourned its passing.

Bentinck's 'positive interference' in Indian customs ended there. Once those two great social evils had been dealt with, he was happy to leave other traditions, which did not offend his western sense of morality, well alone. He was far from idle, however. He made a grand tour of northern India and created a revised system of land revenue collection that was to remain basically unchanged during the rest of British rule. Turning his attention to the company's armies – the three presidencies each supported a separate army – he abolished flogging a full 50 years before the British army did so. He started ambitious programmes of road building and land reclamation, based on experience with his own estates in the fen country of East Anglia. The star project in this was the beginning of the Grand Trunk Road linking Calcutta, Delhi and eventually Peshawar, that great highway so familiar from Kipling's *Kim*.

Bentinck went out of his way to make personal friends not only with leading Hindu thinkers but also with Eurasians, people normally shunned by both sides of the racial divide. His attitude to race clearly influenced the report of the Parliamentary committee on the company's affairs in 1833. 'It is recognised as an indisputable principle,' it stated, 'that the interests of the Native Subjects are to be consulted in preference to those of Europeans, whenever the two come in competition; and that therefore the Laws ought to be adapted rather to the feelings and habits of the Natives than to those of Europeans.'

Concern for Indians' rights was also evident in the new charter itself – the Liberal Charter, as it was instantly dubbed. Article 87 stated: 'No Native of the said Territories, nor any natural-born Subject of His Majesty resident therein, shall, by reason only of his religion, place of birth, descent, colour, or any of them be disabled from holding any Place, Office, or Employment under the said Company.' Cancelling Cornwallis's ban on Indians attaining higher positions, this was a landmark declaration. The directors carefully neglected to implement it. Although all civil service recruits were now to be chosen from four candidates for every position, the selection would be made in London, and only from Haileybury graduates.

It is easy to dismiss the noble sentiments expressed in the 1833 report and charter as nineteenth-century hypocrisy, fine words never intended to be acted upon. But most of the men behind them were not hypocrites, even though they were politicians. One such man was Thomas Babington Macaulay, the 33-year-old son of a Scottish anti-slavery campaigner. In a great speech in the House of Commons on 10 July 1833, Lord Macaulay, who was then secretary to the board of control, made a vigorous and sustained attack on imperialism for its own sake. 'We are free, we are civilised, to little purpose,' he declared, 'if we grudge to any portion of the human race an equal measure of freedom and civilisation.'[12] Although he agreed that for the moment it was 'utterly out of the question' to introduce western-style representative government to India, the future was a different matter:

It may be that the public mind of India may expand under our system till it has outgrown that system; that by good government we may educate our subjects into a capacity for better government; that, having become instructed in European knowledge, they may, in some future age, demand European institutions. Whether such a day will ever come I know not. But never will I attempt to avert or retard it. Whenever it comes, it will be the proudest day in English history. To have found a people sunk in the lowest depths of slavery and superstition, to have so ruled them as to have made them desirous and capable of all the privileges of citizens, would indeed be a title to glory all our own.[13]

Turning to more immediate matters, Macaulay said the government had seriously considered taking over the governing of India. 'The Company,' he said, 'is an anomaly; but it is part of a system where everything is an anomaly. It is the strangest of all governments; but it is designed for the strangest of all Empires.'[14] If the government got rid of the company, it would have to create something to take its place – and there was no guarantee that the new arrangement would be any better. What was more, the problems of compensation were virtually insurmountable. It would be impossible to separate the company's commercial and territorial assets – it regarded the whole of Calcutta, for example, as its private estate. Nevertheless, the company's dual role of governor and trader was no longer acceptable. Something had to give, and that something was its commercial activities, which could be quantified much more easily. And so, the company was ordered 'to close their commercial business, and make sale of all their merchandise, stores and effects'. From then on, the company would be solely the agent of the British government in India. In return, it would receive £630,000 a year from the revenues of the country.

With India now wide open, shoals of private traders soon began landing in Bombay, Calcutta and Madras, creating a new caste in the British social order, the 'box wallahs'. Civilians of any rank were always the Brahmans of British society, followed by army officers, the equivalent of the Hindus' second twice-born class, the warrior Kshatrias. The box wallahs came some distance behind, like the Hindu merchant class, the Vaishyas, and were always considered inferior. Even 90 years later, the future Lord Ismay, having failed to qualify for the civil service, joined the Indian army as his only alternative, because 'in those days commerce was not considered suitable employment for a gentleman'.[15]

As the non-official British population in India began to grow, so did racial prejudice. It was all right for the civilians, secure in their position at the top of the tree, to have easy relations with Indians, but the lower orders, as in any caste-ridden society, needed to feel there was someone beneath them. The box wallahs were themselves divided into two sub-castes, commerce and trade, one considered more or less respectable, the other quite beyond the pale – the difference between them was essentially whether a man bought and sold by the ton or by the pound, from behind a desk or a counter.

Without the basic understanding of Indian history, languages and culture instilled by Haileybury or Fort William College, most box wallahs of either sort saw only a primitive society riddled with ignorance and superstition. It was easy, therefore, for them to regard all Indians as inferior, no matter what the charter said. The increasing numbers of British women coming out to join or marry their husbands reinforced that attitude. None of the memsahibs, not even the wives of senior civilians and army officers, enjoyed the benefits of a company education, and so found themselves afloat in an alien and often frightening environment. They dealt with their fears by establishing a new social structure with rules as rigid, as complex and as exclusive as any Hindu caste laws. Initially, this was no great problem, but as the years passed this exclusion of even the most cultured and highly-educated Indians from British society inevitably created division and resentment.

A year after steering the new charter through Parliament, Macaulay found himself sailing east to become the law member of Bentinck's supreme council, a position specially created for him. 'I believe that no country ever stood so much in need of a code of laws as India,' he had told Parliament. India after the fall of the Mughals, he said, was like Europe after the fall of the Roman empire, with a hopeless jumble of laws introduced by different conquerors, rulers and religions. But he had no wish to impose British laws willy-nilly throughout India. 'I know', he said, 'that respect must be paid to feelings generated by differences of religion, of nation, and of caste. Much, I am persuaded, may be done to assimilate the different systems of law without wounding those feelings.' His aim was simple: 'uniformity where you can have it; diversity where you must have it; but in all cases certainty.'[16]

For all his high principles, Macaulay made no secret of the fact that he had taken the job for the money, hoping it would set him up for life – as it more or less did. But that did not stop him throwing himself into his immense task with all his heart and soul. His codification of Anglo-Indian law was a magnificent achievement which, when it was finally ratified in 1860, unified the disparate regions and provinces of the empire. The essence of his work survives in India to this day. So, too, do the results of an unforeseen side effect: by introducing English-style courts he created the environment that would breed generations of Indian lawyers who would lead the movement for independence.

There was another element that was equally important in equipping those lawyers for the fight, and Macaulay was responsible for that too. It was the use of English as a common language. With at least 14 major languages and literally hundreds of distinct dialects in India, men from different regions could not communicate without a lingua franca. The use of English, a foreign tongue, avoided jealousies by not favouring one Indian nationality against another, as the use of Bengali, or Hindi, or the northern Muslim Urdu, would have done. And, of course, English was the essential key to western knowledge.

Although he was in India to deal with the law, Macaulay's literary reputation was such that Bentinck also asked him to deal with the knotty subject of education. It was typical of the man's incredible energy that he was able not only to take on this extra work, but also to write a long essay on Francis Bacon and almost complete *The Lays of Ancient Rome* in his spare time! The arguments between the orientalists and the westernizers were still unresolved, but Macaulay settled them quickly. There were good practical reasons for choosing English as the medium of education. For a start, the company needed Indians as clerks and assistants in its various branches, and they had to be able to speak and write English – it would be much cheaper to teach the Indians English than to try to teach the English all the Indian languages. Then there was the question of books – all the textbooks were in English, and it would cost a fortune to translate and reprint them.

Macaulay, however, had more than economy in mind. In spite of the fact that he saw himself as 'the guardian of the people of India against the European settlers', he was curiously blind to the qualities of Indian culture. In his 'Minute on Indian Education', he stated with sublime confidence:

All the historical information which has been collected from all the books written in the Sanskrit language, is less valuable than what may be found in the most paltry abridgements used at preparatory schools in England ... The question now before us is simply whether, when it is in our power to teach the [English] language, we shall teach languages in which ... there are no books on any subject which deserve to be compared to our own ... whether, when we can patronize sound philosophy and true history, we shall countenance at the public expense medical doctrines which would disgrace an English farrier, astronomy which would move laughter in girls at an English boarding school, history abounding with kings thirty feet high and reigns 30,000 years long, and geography made up of seas of treacle and rivers of butter?[17]

Macaulay was convinced that exposure to western ideas and ethics through education would lead Hindus to embrace Christianity: in 30 years' time, he prophesied to his father, there would not be a single idolater among the respectable classes of Bengal. On a less dubious note, he was also convinced that western education would lead the Indian people to independence. Echoing his House of Commons speech, he wrote in his Minute: 'Come what may, self-knowledge will lead to self-rule, and that would be the proudest day in British history.'

On 7 March 1835, Bentinck announced his decision. 'His Lordship is of the opinion,' the resolution began, 'that the great object of the British Government ought to be the promotion of European literature and science among the natives of India, and that all the funds appropriated for the purpose of education would be best employed on English education alone.' Within three years, there were 40 schools of English in Bengal alone, open to boys of all castes, and the Calcutta School Book Society had sold well over 30,000 English texts. The final fillip to learning English came when it replaced Persian as the official state language. Now, Mughal rule was just a memory. Only the King of Delhi was left, and his days were numbered: when he succeeded his father in 1837, the same year that Victoria became queen in London, Bahadur Shah II was informed that his titles would expire with his death.

In the 20 years after Bentinck and Macaulay, western education brought growing Indianization of the judiciary and the lower and middle ranks of the administration. Indians also became increasingly involved with modern science and engineering through great public works – roads, canals and, after 1853, railways. The Calcutta Medical College began training Indian doctors in western medicine, another development seized on eagerly by educated Hindus.

During this time, the British completed their occupation of the sub-continent, but only after a rare military disaster. With the threat of Napoleon removed from Europe, the Russians had replaced the French as Britain's bogey-man. For most of the nineteenth century, British policy in India was governed by fear of Russian invasion from the north.

There were two possible routes the Russians could take. The easy one was via low-lying Baluchistan and Sind, but this would require co-operation from Persia. The British had treaties with the amirs of Sind to keep out all 'Europeans and Americans', themselves included, but these would be of little use in the event of a Russian attack. The other, more direct but more difficult route, was through Afghanistan and over the Khyber Pass. By 1838, the British were convinced the

Afghan ruler Dost Mohammed was about to strike a deal with the Russians which would allow the Cossacks to pour into India through the Hindu Kush, like their Tartar predecessors.

The company prepared a massive army to march on Kabul, to depose Dost Mohammed and install a British puppet ruler in his place. Barred by the Sikh ruler Ranjit Singh from the direct route across the Punjab, the British broke their treaty with Sind and sailed the army up the Indus, then marched north. All told, the expedition took seven months to reach Kabul, taking it by storm after savage fighting. But as other would-be conquerors have discovered, getting into Afhganistan is one thing, staying there is another. After enduring two extremely uncomfortable years of guerrilla warfare, assassinations, local uprisings and general resistance, the army was forced to pull out. Sixteen thousand five hundred people in all left Kabul early in 1842; 700 Britons, 3,800 Indian sepoys, and their camp followers. Ten days later, a half-dead horse carried one man, Surgeon William Brydon of the Army Medical Corps, into the British fort at Jalalabad, where he announced that he was the army of the Indus. The Afghans had slaughtered every one else along the way.

The dented image of British invincibility was partly restored the following year, when they conquered Sind, the mainly low-lying, fertile country around the Indus river, and its subsidiary territory, the harsh desert of Baluchistan. The Sindis were not a warlike people. They were mostly passive tenant farmers, ruled chaotically and oppressively by Muslim amirs. They were overcome in a short, sharp campaign commanded by General Sir Charles Napier, a sadistic and cynical zealot with a thirst for glory, who believed himself to be divinity incarnate. He described the annexation of Sind as 'a very advantageous, useful, humane piece of rascality'[18], and was promptly appointed its first British governor.

Mountstuart Elphinstone, Wellesley's protégé who had played a major part in putting down the Pindaris and defeating the Marathas almost a quarter of a century earlier, was horrified by Napier's action. Elphinstone, who had served as ambassador in Kabul before completing his time in India as governor of Bombay, said the conquest of Sind was made in the spirit of 'a bully who has been kicked in the streets and goes home to beat his wife in revenge'.[19] There were many Britons who agreed with him, but times had changed. Imperialism had become respectable, cloaked by the excuse of bringing 'the blessings of civilization' to the benighted inhabitants of supposedly primitive lands.

There were other excuses for seizing Sind. The need for permanent and safe navigation along the Indus for British commercial and strategic interests was one. The other was the need for security against attack from the north – by Afghans as well as Russians now. The same excuse served to justify Britain's next move, to seize the Punjab. The Punjab was always a turbulent and ill-defined region, inhabited by a volatile cocktail of nationalities, tribes and religions, some indigenous, others left behind over the centuries by invasions and settlements. Although there were many similarities between the various peoples, there was no single Punjabi nation and even religious identity was broken down into separate groupings: Hindus thought of themselves as Rajputs or Jats, for example, and Muslims as Gujars or Pathans. Everywhere, the population was mixed, though there were more Muslims in the north-west and in Kashmir, which was then part of the Punjab, and more Hindus in the south-east. And, of course, it was the homeland of the Sikhs.

In the time of Aurangzeb, the Sikhs had been driven to take refuge in the mountains, but once Mughal power collapsed they had emerged in a number of well-disciplined bands, whose leaders set up their own little states. Since 1820, these and all the other different elements in the Punjab had been welded together into a single state by the charismatic Sikh leader, Ranjit Singh, a one-eyed military and political genius with a well-trained army that included powerful artillery and was partly officered by Europeans. However, when Ranjit died in 1839, the unity he had imposed on both the Sikhs and the Punjab began to fall apart. Ranjit's army held the ring, but there was no clear champion among the various contenders for overall power.

After six years of in-fighting and assassination, one of the contenders tried to reunite the Sikhs by leading them to war against the only power worth fighting (apart from the Afghans, that is, but no one would be foolish enough to take them on). The British were waiting – indeed, they had been heavily involved in the internecine intrigues from the start. Ever since Ranjit's death, they had been building up their forces on the other side of the Sutlej river. From 2,500 men guarding the frontier in 1839, their number had grown to 14,000 by 1843, mostly sepoys of the Bengal army. A year later, when Governor-General Lord Ellenborough described Anglo-Sikh relations as being in a state of 'armed truce', there were 32,000 troops and 68 field guns, with 100,000 men in reserve only 250 miles away at Meerut, just north of Delhi.[20]

After three months and three exceptionally bloody battles in which 20,000 Sikhs and sepoys were killed, the British conquered Lahore. To the amazement of the Sikhs, they then offered a remarkably generous settlement. Instead of annexing the whole of the Punjab, they were content to take relatively small pieces, leaving the rest of the Sikh kingdom intact as a useful buffer against the Afghans. They did, however, demand an indemnity of a million pounds. The Sikhs had nothing left in the treasury, but a subsidiary chief, who had adroitly changed sides at the opportune moment, came to the rescue. The raja of Jammu, Gulab Singh – despite his name not a Sikh, but a Dogra Hindu Rajput – offered to pay the money, in return for Kashmir. The Sikhs accepted his offer, and so it was that the overwhelmingly Muslim state came to be ruled by a Hindu. No one could have imagined how much future trouble the raja's million pounds had bought. After the Sikh army rebelled two years later, prompting a second Anglo-Sikh war, the victorious British took control of the whole of the Punjab, 100,000 square miles including some of India's most fertile land. But Kashmir, with Jammu, remained outside as a princely state under British protection.

The last piece of the jigsaw was in place. Ranjit Singh, when he was shown a map of India with British territory marked in red, had commented sagely: 'All will one day become red.' His prophecy had come true. Even the princely states were coloured pink, which is only a slightly paler shade of red. After precisely 50 years of expansion, Britain controlled the entire sub-continent.

'The Moaning of the Hurricane'

Ever since the British had taken over in Bengal, there had been a continuous string of minor rebellions, mostly reactions against the changes imposed by the new regime. As British rule spread, so did the rebellions – between 1763 and 1856, there were no fewer than 40 armed revolts in various parts of British India.[1] But the troubles had always been localized, often led by deposed rulers and their descendants, or dispossessed zamindars and landlords with personal grievances. They had been supported by peasants who were suffering from the rapid changes introduced by the British. In the first 30 years of British rule, land revenue collection in Bengal was nearly doubled, and the same pattern was repeated in other provinces. To cover the cost of this and still show a profit, the bankers and money-lenders who had replaced many traditional landlords pushed up rents to ruinous levels, evicting those who couldn't pay. One result was that there were 12 major and a number of minor famines between 1770 and 1857, fuelling a growing discontent.

     The general uneasiness might well have passed as the changes became the norm and revenue levels were sorted out. But there were other factors at work. In the eighteenth century, Britons had treated Indians and their customs with respect if not understanding. Once the excesses of the early years in Bengal had been rooted out, most civilians had seen themselves as trustees guarding an ancient culture on a temporary basis. By the 1840s, the more enlightened civilians still believed this: even a tough, no-nonsense character like Henry Lawrence, who with his brother had been sent to take charge of the Punjab in 1849, could write:

> We cannot expect to hold India for ever. Let us so conduct ourselves . . . as, when the connexion ceases, it may do so not with convulsions but with mutual esteem and affection, and that England may then have in India a

noble ally, enlightened and brought into the scale of nations under her guidance and fostering care.[2]

But by then, the Lawrences were in a minority, and the 'mutual esteem' they preached was being replaced by an arrogant insensitivity. As more and more British arrived in India, their relationship with Indians deteriorated rapidly.

Nowhere was this more evident than in the army, where older sepoys mourned the passing of the days when their British officers had lived in close contact with them, sharing their pleasures and solving their problems. As one retired soldier wrote in his memoirs:

When I was a sepoy, the captain of my company would have some of the men at his house all day long and he talked with them ... I know that many officers nowadays only talk to their men when obliged to do so, and they show that the business is irksome and try to get rid of the sepoys as quickly as possible. One sahib told us that he never knew what to say to us. The sahibs always knew what to say, and how to say it, when I was a young soldier.[3]

One of the causes of this disaffection was the arrival of the memsahibs, who disapproved of such intimacy with natives – they expected their husbands to live with them and not with their men. The problem was exacerbated by the drastic shortage of trained civilians caused by the rapid expansion of the company's rule. Officers already in the company's service were a ready source of men to fill the new posts. Many were only too eager to switch, since the civil service was more comfortable, better paid and offered better prospects of promotion than the military. Consequently, few stayed long enough with Indian regiments to get to know their men, or were even interested in doing so. Inevitably, the civil service wanted the best officers, with the result that the company's armies were drained of good leaders. Thirty years earlier, officers would have been aware of the dangerous undercurrents flowing among their men, and would have been able to allay their fears. Now, those who were aware were not listened to, either by their men or by their own superiors.

Unlike the British common soldier, who usually joined the army only because he was incapable of doing anything else, the Indian soldier was following a respected and honourable tradition. Some were Muslims, hereditary soldiers whose roots were in the great Mughal armies, but most were high-caste Hindus – Brahmans or Rajput Kshatrias – who had followed their fathers into the army, and whose sons would follow them. They were also landowners, with their own plots back in their ancestral villages, and they brought their own servants to carry their bundles and follow them on campaigns. They were proud men, whose quarters within a military cantonment were like complete Indian villages; simple accommodation but far superior to the squalid barracks of British other ranks. In taking the sahib's salt they had pledged their lives to his service. Their loyalty to their regiment was total; the only thing they placed above it was their religion.

The great mass of Indians were deeply conservative, deeply suspicious of change. Since their religions governed every aspect of their lives, any change posed a threat to their religion. The early British rulers had known this, and walked with care. Even Macaulay, anxious as he was to 'engraft on despotism those blessings which are the natural fruits of liberty,' had warned 'it behoves us to be cautious, even to the verge of timidity'.[4]

Unfortunately, the Marquess of Dalhousie, governor-general from 1848 until 1856, was not a cautious man. Utterly convinced of the superiority of western ideas, he was determined to turn India into an Asian Britain. Dalhousie was probably the most able of all the nineteenth-century governors-general. He was also incurably energetic. Having been involved as president of the Board of Trade in overseeing the railway boom in Britain, he set about providing India with what he called the 'three great engines of social improvement, which the sagacity and science of recent times had previously given to the Western nations – I mean Railways, uniform Postage, and the Electric Telegraph'.[5] Together with the new educational system, Dalhousie's three great engines were to revolutionize communications throughout India, playing a vital part in its unification and making a national independence movement possible in little more than 30 years.

Creating the right conditions for independence was not, of course, Dalhousie's intention. He saw the telegraph carrying instant warnings of trouble from the furthest corner of India, which could be put down swiftly by troops transported from their depots by rail. And, of course, there were commercial considerations too. The new postal and telegraph network would aid business, while the railways would open up the interior of India to imported British goods and transport raw materials like cotton, jute and coal for the factories and mills of Lancashire, Dundee and, later, Calcutta. Hindu businessmen in Bengal and Bombay enthusiastically seized the opportunities these developments offered. But the rural masses regarded them as yet more threats to their traditional way of life. In some places, this was aggravated by the pulling down of temples which stood in the way of the railways. Also, many peasants believed the engines were driven by the force of demons trying to escape from the iron box in which the foreigners had imprisoned them, demons which were soon to rule the world in the accursed age forecast in ancient prophesies.[6]

Dalhousie's energetic efforts to spread the benefits of British civilization as widely as possible brought resentment in other areas. The method he devised for acquiring further territory – and substantially increasing revenue – with minimal expense and no bloodshed was an ingenious extension of Wellesley's subsidiary treaties. Those treaties provided for continuity through a ruler's 'heirs and successors', which according to ancient Indian custom included adopted sons. Hinduism requires prayers and sacrifices to be made by a man's sons to save him from punishment in the next life, so a man with no sons will adopt one or more, whose prayers are considered equally efficacious. Traditionally, adopted sons have all the rights and privileges of natural sons. Dalhousie, however, decided that 'heirs and successors' should be interpreted as meaning only natural-born sons. This meant that whenever the ruler of a princely state died without a natural male heir, the subsidiary treaty could be torn up and his territory annexed.

Dalhousie's 'doctrine of lapse', as it was called, was first put into effect in 1848, against the raja of Patiala, a direct descendant of the Maratha chief Sivaji. Over the next six years, Dalhousie used it ruthlessly to appropriate six more central Indian states, culminating in 1854 with Nagpur, a huge state bordering Hyderabad, with more than 4 million Maratha inhabitants. He also applied the doctrine to the titles and pensions paid to the former rulers of territories previously seized by the British, thus preventing adopted heirs from inheriting either. The company's finances were considerably improved, but Dalhousie's successors would reap the whirlwind.

In February 1856, as his final act before departing, exhausted, from India, Dalhousie annexed the kingdom of Oudh, the heartland of the Gangetic plain and one of the richest regions of India. This time, the excuse was not lapse but misrule by the corrupt and debauched ruler, Wajid Ali. The temptation of the potential revenues, which, even where they were collected at all, were wasted on 'slothful, lazy, and stupid' courtiers, was simply too much for Dalhousie. Wajid Ali surrendered to a military expedition without a shot being fired. But when first the governor-general in Calcutta and then the British government in London remained deaf to his pleas, he returned to India to begin conspiring with his taluqdars, the landed barons of Oudh, who had lost all their power and privileges. Twenty-one thousand of them had had their estates confiscated. Deprived of their only source of income, they found themselves 'unable to work, ashamed to beg, condemned to penury'.[7]

There were 75,000 sepoys from Oudh in the Bengal army, all of whom had families who were affected by the changes. Fourteen thousand sepoys sent petitions protesting against the hardships caused by the new British revenue system. A senior officer had warned Dalhousie about the effects his policies would have on the army: 'Your army is derived from the peasantry of the country ... they are part of the population, and in every infringement you make upon the rights of the individuals, you infringe upon the rights of men who are either themselves in the army or upon their sons, their fathers, or their relations.'[8] The governor-general chose to ignore the advice.

During his first year of office in 1856, Dalhousie's successor, Lord

Canning, stoked the fires of discontent by bringing in his General Service Enlistment Act. This required all Indian soldiers to go wherever they were sent, which meant high-caste Hindus could no longer refuse service overseas on religious grounds, as the 47th Bengal Native Infantry had tried to do in 1824, and the 38th as recently as 1852 during a second Burmese war. With trust already at a low ebb, the sepoys and sowars (cavalry soldiers) were ready to believe that this was a deliberate conspiracy, fostered by Christian missionaries, to send all Brahmans and Kshatrias overseas, thus destroying their caste and making them ripe for conversion. This was a very real fear – sepoys who had fought in the disastrous Afghan campaign had been outcasted on their return because they had been forced to eat and drink whatever they could lay their hands on in order to stay alive. What was more, in gaols convicts of different castes were being forced to eat together in messes, rather than individually, which was a violation of caste rules.

Still reeling from Dalhousie's edicts on adoption and a new law allowing converts to Christianity to inherit property, Hindu orthodoxy was dealt yet another blow when Canning introduced an act allowing Hindu widows to remarry. Coming on top of the outlawing of *sati*, and the abolition of slavery, female infanticide, human sacrifices to river gods, the burying alive of lepers and 'euthanasia' of the old and sick at centres of pilgrimage, the threat to the old order seemed very real indeed. Even the ending of *thugi*, welcome as it was, could be seen as an interference in religious practices. And all the time, the Christian missionaries were increasingly active. Many colonels allowed them to preach to their regiments; some officers openly tried to convert their own men.

By early 1857, there was a great groundswell of unrest throughout the Bengal army, aggravated by discontent over pay and conditions. Feelings were further inflamed by agents of Wajid Ali and his crony Nana Sahib, the adopted and therefore dispossessed son of the deposed Peshwa of Bithur. Both were bitter men, eager for revenge and the restoration of the old order. Their agents moved among the troops, encouraging grievances, reminding them that the British had been trounced by the Afghans and so were not invincible. They said there were only 100,000 people in Britain, and therefore they could easily be swept aside. What was more, they had just been defeated by the Russians in the Crimea, who had now annexed Britain. By this time, the company itself had few white troops, but units of the regular British army, known as Queen's regiments, were sent out on five-year tours to supplement the native regiments. The ratio was usually one British soldier to every three Indian, but so many British regiments had been sent to fight in the Crimean war and had not yet been replaced, that the figure was now less than one to seven. There were now only 34,000 British soldiers in the whole of India, as against 257,000 Indian sepoys and sowars. Hopelessly outnumbered, the British would have little chance if India ever rose in a co-ordinated rebellion.

On the morning of Sunday, 29 March 1857, Mangal Pande, a sepoy of the 34th Native Infantry at Barrackpore, a few miles north of Calcutta, went berserk. High on bhang and opium, he wounded two Britons, the adjutant and the sergeant-major, before trying to shoot himself. He was eventually disarmed, court-martialled and hanged, which most Indians and many Europeans thought was unduly harsh – on the day after his outburst, he couldn't even remember what had happened. It would have been an insignificant incident, soon forgotten, in normal times. But times were not normal, and the Mangal Pande incident was the first tremor of an earthquake that would shake the very foundations of British India.

Pande had been trying to incite his fellow sepoys to rebel, because he believed the British were intent on defiling every Hindu and Muslim in the army. The devilish device they had invented for this purpose was a cartridge for use in a new Enfield rifle. By combining bullet and powder for the first time, the cartridge gave an increase of at least 50 per cent in the rate of fire. The rifle, however, was still a muzzle-loader, and the paper cartridge needed to be heavily greased to ease it down the barrel. Before loading, the end of the paper had to be nipped off to expose the powder, and the quickest and simplest way of doing this was by biting it off with the teeth.

Unfortunately, the paper cartridges were lubricated with tallow, and tallow is made from various animal fats, including beef and pork. The new system had been developed in England, for the British army, and the ordnance department had not considered its impact on the sepoys of the company's Indian army. That impact was devastating: to put cow's fat into his mouth is more than disgusting to a Hindu; it is an abomination that will damn him for eternity. For a Muslim, pig's fat is almost as bad. When they heard about the new cartridges, both Hindu and Muslim sepoys determined never to use them.

In fact, the danger was spotted almost as soon as the new rifles and ammunition arrived at the musketry depots. Within three days – the cartridges had arrived on a Friday – orders went out that the greased cartridges were to be kept strictly for British troops. Indian troops were to grease their own with beeswax and vegetable oil; the loading drill was to be changed so that the ends were not to be bitten but torn off with the fingers. But by then it was too late. Word was out, and in the prevailing climate of mistrust and resentment, the sepoys refused to believe their officers' protestations that the cartridges were safe.

Captain E.M. Martineau, commander of the musketry depot at Ambala, wrote an urgent report to the army staff at Simla, the hill station where the governor-general and his aides stayed during the hot weather each year, and where the commander-in-chief had his permanent headquarters:

I know that at the present moment an unusual agitation is pervading the ranks of the entire native army, but what it will exactly result in, I am afraid to say. I can detect the near approach of the storm, I can hear the moaning of the hurricane, but I can't say how, when or where it will break forth ... I don't think they know themselves what they will do, or that they have any plan of action except of resistance to invasion of their religion, and their faith.

But, good God! Here are all the elements of combustion at hand; 100,000 men, sullen, distrustful, fierce, with all their deepest and inmost sympathies, as well as worst passions, roused, and we thinking to cajole them into good humour by patting them on the back, saying what a fool you are for making such a fuss about nothing. They no longer believe us, they have passed out of restraint and will be off at a gallop before long. If a flare-up from any cause takes place at one station, it will spread and become universal.[9]

The staff refused to heed Martineau's warning. They insisted that firing practice with the new cartridges should continue. And so it did – but the night after the first practice, the officers' bungalows and the huts of the sepoys who had used the cartridges were burned down. A Sikh reported that the men had sworn to put the entire station to the torch.[10]

In the following weeks, regiment after regiment refused to load the new cartridges, and regiment after regiment was disbanded under the guns of British-manned artillery. Sepoys were stripped of their insignia, dismissed with ignominy, and sent walking back to their villages without pay, pension or the pride they had always felt for their uniform. The bitterness increased, and with it the rumours: the new rifles had been smeared with cow and pig fat; wells had been polluted with dead pigs; cow bones had been ground down and added to sugar and flour. Nothing was beyond the devious and faithless British.

The storm that Captain Martineau had predicted finally broke on the morning of Sunday, 9 May 1857, at Meerut, one of the largest and most important military stations in India, about 40 miles from Delhi. The day before, all the troops at Meerut had been paraded to witness sentence being carried out on 85 sowars of the 3rd Light Cavalry who had been court-martialled for refusing to load their rifles, even though the cartridges they had been given were not the offensive new type. The 1,700 British troops were armed, guns and rifles at the ready. The sepoys and sowars were not. As they watched, their comrades were disgraced by being stripped of their uniforms, then shackled and made to shuffle away in irons to serve 10 years' hard labour. Many of them did not go quietly, swearing both at their British officers and at their fellow Indian soldiers for doing nothing to help them. At about 6.00 p.m. the next day, Monday, 10 May, as the British officers and their families prepared for evensong, the Indian soldiers rose in revolt. They broke open the gaol and freed the prisoners, killed as many British officers and their wives and children as they could, then set out for Delhi.

There were no British troops in Delhi, apart from the officers commanding Indian detachments, most of whose men went over to the mutineers almost immediately. And for some inexplicable reason, British troops in Meerut, of whom there were almost as many as there were Indians, were never ordered to pursue the rebels. In spite of valiant efforts by the officers and European residents, Delhi soon fell to the mutineers, who 'restored' a very reluctant Bahadur Shah II to the Mughal throne. The 82-year-old emperor was a quiet soul, more interested in Sufi poetry and miniature paintings than in power. He was dismayed to find himself the symbol of the rebels' hopes for a restoration of the old regime, and at first tried to persuade them to go away. But by then, they had killed all the Britons they could find in Delhi, and there was no turning back.

The upheaval of 1857–8 was more than the 'Great Mutiny', as the British have always called it, but less than the 'Great War of Independence' that many modern Indian historians claim. It was, in truth, a great revolt, and it spread like a forest fire in a drought across a great swath of north-eastern India from Patna to Delhi, encompassing Bihar, Oudh and what was then known as the North-Western Provinces (later the United Provinces, today's Uttar Pradesh). But the country as a whole was never behind the rebels. Except in Oudh, the peasants were not particularly interested. Like peasants everywhere, they were used to being ruled from afar and did not much care by whom, as long as they were left alone. The merchants, educated Hindus, and most rulers, on the other hand, actively supported the British – they even organized meetings in Bombay and Calcutta to pray for their success.

The revolt affected only a relatively small part of India. The rest remained mostly calm. In the south, the west and most of the centre, life went on quietly, very much as usual. The Punjab stood firmly behind the British – if only because of the Sikhs' hatred of the Muslims and fear of any possible revival of Mughal rule. In Bengal proper, as in Bombay, what little unrest there was was swiftly and easily brought under control. In Calcutta, the annual ball was held on the queen's birthday with no extra security precautions. Canning even refused the offer of a white volunteer company to stand by in case of trouble, insisting on the house and guests being protected by the normal guard of Indian soldiers. And at the height of the revolt, new, western-style universities were founded in Calcutta, Bombay and Madras.

The Bombay and Madras armies were virtually unaffected by the mutiny. Only the Bengal army, with its atmosphere of tense unrest, was involved, and less than half its sepoys joined in: the larger part fought loyally with the British against their own countrymen. The force that eventually recaptured Delhi after fierce fighting consisted of 3,200 Indians and only 1,700 British. The most vital operation in the attack, the blowing up of the Kashmir gate, was carried out by a squad of 6 British officers and NCOs and 24 Indians, 10 of whom were Punjabis, with 14 from Agra and Oudh.

The centre of the revolt was always Oudh, which had been seething with discontent ever since its annexation. The take-over and the reforms that followed had been handled by arrogant and often inept British officials. Sir Henry Lawrence, late of the Punjab, had been sent in by Canning to put things right, but he had only arrived on 20 March and had had no time to make much of an effect before the storm broke. Wajid Ali remained in Calcutta, where he was put under arrest. But the courtiers in his capital, Lucknow, and dispossessed taluqdars and landlords throughout Oudh, saw the revolt as a golden opportunity to reclaim their own possessions and positions. They were supported by peasants still smarting under the new revenue demands. Most of them were related to mutinying sepoys; some were themselves sepoys who had been ignominiously discharged. So, in Oudh, there were civil and agrarian risings alongside the military mutiny. The old order had been corrupt, inefficient and often cruel, but it was what people had always known, and they wanted it back.

Apart from Delhi, the only important centres of the revolt were Lucknow, the capital of Oudh, and the former Maratha stronghold of Cawnpore (Kanpur), some 45 miles to its south-east. Both were to take their places in the mythology of British India. Lucknow, like Arcot, would always be remembered for an incredible tale of heroic defence against impossible odds: nearly 3,000 men, women and children, including 1,400 loyal Indians, barricaded themselves inside the British residency and its compound at the end of June and held out against almost continuous attack until 23 November, when the last survivors were evacuated.

Cawnpore, on the other hand, would rank with the Black Hole of Calcutta on the roll of infamy. Nana Sahib, who had proclaimed himself the new Peshwa of the Marathas, first massacred the men of the British garrison as they boarded boats, after giving them a promise of safe passage down the Ganges to Allahabad. Then, having saved 200 British women and their children from the slaughter, he had them quite literally butchered when a relief column appeared – his soldiers refused to shoot them, so he sent in butchers from the bazaar to do the job with their knives.

At the start of the revolt, there had been only one British battalion between Calcutta and Agra, so the rebels had had little difficulty in seizing power in the region. The British faced a long, hard struggle to regain it, but regain it they inevitably did. In the end, however, neither side emerged with much credit. The knowledge of the massacres at Cawnpore and various smaller stations, at some of which sepoys had sworn loyalty one day and murdered British officers and their families that same night, released a thirst for vengeance that bordered on the psychotic. Conventional punishments for captured mutineers were no longer thought to be sufficient; even a normally sane and decent man like the Irish-born Brigadier John Nicholson proposed 'flaying alive' any Indian who had killed a British woman. Mutineers were tied to the muzzles of canons and blown to pieces on parade grounds, after having first been smeared with the blood of those they had killed. Whole villages were razed, with men, women and children put to the sword. In recaptured Delhi, where every rebel soldier was slain without mercy, Lieutenant William Hodson completed the grotesque revenge by murdering the sons of Bahadur Shah in cold blood, to ensure 'the total extinction of a dynasty, the most magnificent the world has ever seen'.[11] Bahadur Shah himself was sent into exile in Rangoon, where he died on 7 November 1862.

The great revolt was a last, desperate effort to reject change, and as such it was doomed from the start. It had involved a military mutiny, a rural rebellion, and an attempt by various deposed native rulers to regain their former positions, but nothing had been organized or co-ordinated, either geographically or politically. All those involved had been fighting for their own ends, united only by a common fear of the future. When the dust began to settle, in the middle of 1858, it could be seen that three great institutions had finally died: the Mughals, Maratha power in central India, and the Honourable East India Company. The way was now open for a new era in the long history of India.

4

'The Mildest Form of Government is Despotism'

On 1 November 1858, Lord Canning, wearing court dress and riding a large black horse, emerged from the fort at Allahabad, leading a procession of civil and military officers in full dress uniforms. An honour guard of scarlet-clad Indians, each carrying a silver wand of office, escorted him to a raised platform shaded by a crimson cloth, where a gilded throne under a canopy of crimson and gold embroidered with the royal arms, awaited him. Field guns thundered a salute as he mounted the platform to read a long proclamation from Queen Victoria. When he had finished, the proclamation was read out again, this time in Urdu, for the benefit of the few Indians present. After another salute, Canning and his staff rode back into the fort, to prepare for a dinner and fireworks later that evening. That same day, the proclamation was read out in every British station in India.

The proclamation was the first official act of the new British Raj – the word *raj* means simply 'rule' in Hindi, but it was to take on a special connotation, coming to mean the entire British presence in India. The days of company rule were over. The company itself was no more, wound up by the Government of India Act, passed in London on 2 August 1858. India was now ruled by the British crown, through Parliament. The governor-general was given the additional title of viceroy: as the queen's deputy he took precedence over everyone except the sovereign, including other members of the royal family and the prime minister. He was still answerable to London, but the board of control and the company's court of directors were replaced by a secretary of state and his India council – India was and would remain the only colony with its own minister of the crown.

Queen Victoria's proclamation had, of course, been drawn up by the government in London, with the advice of many people, including Lord Canning and his senior civil servants. But the queen, then 38 years old and still happily married to and guided by the progressive Prince Albert, had taken a close personal interest in it. She had rejected the first draft out of hand, telling Lord Derby to rewrite it, 'bearing in mind that it is a female sovereign who speaks to more than a hundred millions of Eastern people'. 'Such a document,' she insisted, 'should breathe feelings of generosity, benevolence, and religious toleration.'[1] And so it did, when it was revised to her satisfaction.

The queen's hand is clearly visible in many of the statements made in her name in the proclamation:

> It is Our earnest desire to stimulate the peaceful industry of India, to promote works of public utility and improvement, and to administer the government for the benefit of all Our subjects resident therein. In their prosperity will be Our strength, in their contentment Our security, and in their gratitude Our best reward ...
>
> We declare it to be Our royal will and pleasure that none be in anywise favoured, none molested or disquieted, by reason of their religious faith or observances, but that all shall alike enjoy the equal and impartial protection of the law; and We do strictly charge and enjoin all those who may be in authority under Us that they abstain from all interference with the religious belief or worship of any of Our subjects on pain of Our highest displeasure ... in so far as may be, Our subjects, of whatever race or creed, be freely and impartially admitted to office in Our service, the duties of which they may be qualified by their education, ability, and integrity duly to discharge.[2]

It was perhaps the most remarkable statement of policy by any imperial power in history. Over the following 90 years, the reality rarely matched the fine sentiments, but the principles remained unchanged. The British in India may have regarded the proclamation with some cynicism, not to mention hypocrisy: British officials always carefully ignored those provisions which they found unpalatable. Educated Indians, however, accepted it readily. In the early years at least, there seemed to be no resentment at its heavy paternalism – or perhaps maternalism in Queen Victoria's case.

Throughout her reign, India and the Indians always held a special place in the queen's affections. Since she never visited the country and met few of its people, the truth was that she had fallen in love with a romantic idea of India – she was not the first and by no means the last to do that. At the very height of the revolt, she had sent a message of support to Canning, whose wife, Charlotte, a former lady-in-waiting, remained one of her closest personal friends: 'The Indian people should know that there is no hatred to a brown skin, none; but the greatest wish on their Queen's part to see them happy, contented and flourishing.'[3]

The Indian people reciprocated, holding their queen in an esteem unmatched by any ruler since Akbar, somehow managing to dissociate her from the less admirable actions of her representatives. It was an important factor in the loyalty expressed even by some of the most unlikely Indians, which helped to maintain British rule during the rest of the nineteenth century. Forty years later, Mohandas Gandhi could still rely on her proclamation in his claims for equal treatment for Indians in South Africa.

It was not until 8 July 1859 that the viceroy was able to declare: 'War is at an end; Rebellion is put down ... Order is re-established; and peaceful pursuits have everywhere been resumed.' Pockets of resistance had continued long after the main struggle was over, led by a few native chieftains, most notably the Rani of Jhansi, the Joan of Arc or Boadicea of India, whose central Indian state had been snatched from her by the doctrine of lapse, and Nana Sahib's artillery expert, Tantia Topi. But they did not last long. Nana Sahib himself faked suicide and escaped to Nepal, where he died of a fever. Tantia Topi was captured and hanged. The Rani died in the saddle, her sword in her hand.

In some ways, the great revolt had lanced a boil that had been swelling for almost 20 years, providing an enormous opportunity for a fresh start. But it had left a great deal of bitterness on both sides, tempered only by the determination of Canning and a small group of his advisers not to allow the thirst for revenge to take control. The viceroy's calm and reasoned approach earned him the nickname among the British of 'Clemency Canning'. It was meant as a term of abuse; it became a badge of pride as he set about tackling the enormous problems of reconstruction and reconciliation.

For all Canning's efforts, the distrust and fear remained. Britons began building new suburbs for themselves on the edges of towns and cities, 'civil lines' consisting of spacious bungalows set back from broad, tree-lined roads which could be defended more easily in the event of trouble. At their centre was the club, strictly for Europeans only, a secure haven where the only native faces belonged to servants. The larger clubs were housed in extremely grand classical mansions, echoes of Pall Mall designed to impress the local population, particularly the 'upstarts' of the Indian middle class who could be kept firmly in their place, outside the wrought-iron gates.

The racial divisions were deepening and hardening, and as they did so, a marked change was taking place in British thinking. The concept of introducing western ideas and education in order to prepare India for early self-government was replaced by a belief that the British were there to stay, collectively if not individually, for very few had any thought of retiring there: 'home' always meant Britain. Now, they began to see India as Britain's property, a vast estate whose people were to be looked after and dealt with as a great landlord would his tenants, or perhaps more aptly as a feudal lord his serfs and vassals.

British society has always been based on property. For centuries, the right to vote depended on the ownership of property, and the penalties for theft were as severe as those for violence to the person and even murder. English aristocrats had consolidated their power by adding common land to their estates through enclosure – a process that was still continuing through the first 30 years of Victoria's rule. Once they had acquired the land, the aristocrats guarded it jealously as a mark not only of wealth but also of status. They now brought the same attitudes to India. Their great public works became symbols of permanence, designed to serve an enduring Raj rather than its people.

There were, however, many Britons both in India and in Britain who remained committed to the ideal of handing India back to the Indians as soon as they had been prepared for responsible government in the western pattern. By now, the old Whigs had metamorphosed into the Liberal Party, whose members were already beginning to inscribe social justice alongside free trade on the banner of their creed. Disapproving of colonies and empires on principle, they saw British rule in India as an unfortunate necessity, a temporary responsibility. The concept of trusteeship was not dead, therefore, though many thought it would unfortunately need to extend far beyond the foreseeable future.

As long as the British were in India, the dichotomy between the liberals and the imperialists, the givers and the takers, remained. It was never quite that simple, of course. Some imperialists saw brutal repression as the only way of holding on to what was theirs by right. Others saw themselves as benevolent father figures. The Victorian paterfamilias, however, could be forbiddingly stern, always mindful that to spare the rod was to spoil the child, a dictum that many Britons were all too ready to apply to their Indian 'children'. The Liberals, though equally paternalistic, insisted that India belonged to the Indians, claiming an infuriating moral superiority over their opponents, who included almost everyone with a vested interest in continuing British rule. These opponents ranged from businessmen who depended on India for profit to bureaucrats who depended on it for position, power and a comfortable living with a handsome pension to be enjoyed in the civilized surroundings of Cheltenham or Tunbridge Wells.

The first priority after the revolt was security, which meant reorganizing the army. The few remaining white units were absorbed into the British army; native regiments became the Indian army. To ensure loyalty, Indian troops were to be recruited only from so-called 'martial races', a spurious British invention that excluded men from Bengal, Oudh and the Maratha states, who had been the most active mutineers. Men from the north, mainly Sikhs and Gurkhas, plus selected Jats and Rajputs from the Punjab and some Pathans from the frontier regions, were now the most favoured recruits. The proportion of native troops to queen's regiments was set at two to one except in Bengal, where it was set at parity to begin with, only coming into line with the rest of India a few years later. Each British regiment was to be brigaded with two Indian regiments, which were to come from distant parts of the country, preferably speaking different languages, both from each other and from the local population. Where possible, each Indian regiment was further divided into Hindu, Muslim and Sikh companies. Artillery and other 'scientific branches' were strictly reserved for British units. British officers of the Indian army were expected to live closer to their men once more, to regain their trust and be more aware of their concerns. They soon became a caste apart from the rest of British India, identifying fiercely with the men they commanded, but becoming far more reactionary than any other Britons in their attitudes to other Indians.

By stating unequivocally that there was to be no interference with Indian religions and no official backing for religious conversion, the queen's proclamation had dealt with one of the major causes of the revolt. The other main cause was addressed in even clearer terms: 'We desire no extension of our territorial possessions.' As a reward to the vast majority of princes who had supported the British during the revolt, either actively or passively, there were to be no more annexations. The doctrine of lapse was repudiated; heirs by adoption were once again recognized. Thus, 601 Indian states,[4] some as big as France, others covering only a few square miles and with populations of less than 30,000, were clearly defined for the next 90 years. All were nominally self-governing, but all acknowledged Britain as the paramount power in India.

The princely states even in 1858 were an anomaly, but in the eyes of the British government they would serve as bulwarks against future revolt, obligated to the power that guaranteed their future. It was a shrewd move, and it worked. The zamindars of Bengal, who had been turned into landowners by Cornwallis's permanent settlement, had remained staunchly loyal throughout the revolt; now, to ensure similar loyalty, the taluqdars of Oudh were given back their confiscated lands to hold in perpetuity. And both taluqdars and zamindars, together with the landed gentry in other provinces, were appointed local magistrates. At a stroke, they became members of British India's establishment, with a personal stake in its future.

In choosing to put its money on the aristocracy, the British government had turned its back on another section of Indian society that had supported it faithfully and well throughout the revolt: the *bhadralok* or gentlefolk, the rising middle class of lawyers, teachers, journalists and businessmen. It was a snobbish, short-sighted decision, typical of its time, which was to cost Britain dear in the years to come. The educated middle classes were better equipped to act as mediators between the rulers and the masses, certainly in the towns and cities, and as agents of modernization they were incomparably better than the rural barons, whose roots remained firmly in the past. They were, however, ambitious as well as clever, and so were seen as dangerous. When three Indians were appointed as members of the viceroy's Legislative Council in 1861, all were princes, and all were Hindus: two were rajas and one a maharaja. The professional men were ignored, though they went on eagerly embracing British ways and British knowledge. It was a situation that was to remain virtually unchanged for the next 30 years.

Having dealt with two of the main causes of the great revolt, the British turned on those they believed were really to blame for the whole thing: the Muslims. 'After the Mutiny,' Sir William Hunter, a British civil servant, wrote in 1870,' the British turned upon the Mussulmans as their real enemies so that failure of the revolt was much more disastrous to them than the Hindus.'[5] Despite the fact that the greased cartridges had been rejected and feared by more Hindus than Muslims, and that the Marathas had been at the centre of the fighting and responsible for many of the atrocities, including the massacre at Cawnpore, the British were convinced that the Muslims were the prime instigators. Their aim had been to restore the Mughal dynasty, as a proclamation from Delhi in the name of Bahadur Shah II had made clear:

It is well known that in these days all the English have entertained these evil designs – first, to destroy the religion of the whole Hindustan army, and then to make the people by compulsion Christians. Therefore we, solely on account of our religion, have combined with the people, and have not spared alive one infidel, and have re-established the Delhi dynasty on those terms.

Could there be any clearer proof of guilt? It seemed not. 'The Hindus were not the contrivers,' wrote Henry Harrington in a pamphlet in 1858, 'the primary movers of the rebellion, the Mohammadans, planned and organised the rebellion for their own aggrandisement alone and the Hindu sepoys of the Bengal army were their dupes and instruments.'[6] Whether this was a true assessment or not, the Muslims were made to suffer for it.

Traditionally, upper-class Indian Muslims had made their living as landlords, administrators or soldiers but, one by one, these three pillars had been knocked out from under them. Most Muslim landlords had lost their estates earlier in the century, either through confiscation or to Hindu money-lenders – the Muslim gentry had been notoriously extravagant and irresponsible. This had serious repercussions throughout the Muslim community, as one British civil servant wrote: 'Hundreds of ancient families were ruined, and the educational system of the Mussulmans, which was almost entirely maintained by rent-free grants, received its death blow.'[7] Muslims lost their places in the administration when English replaced Persian as the language of government and the law. Until 1851, there had been more Muslim lawyers on the roll of the Calcutta court than Hindus and Christians put together; during the following 15 years, only one Muslim lawyer was enrolled. Now, they were largely barred from the army, too.

Everywhere, doors were being closed to them. For the next quarter of a century, they would be forced to live apart.

By 1861 the changes that needed to be made to the government of India under crown rule were agreed. The Indian Councils Act split the old governor-general's advisory council into two separate bodies. The Executive Council was an inner cabinet consisting of five officials, each responsible for a government department – home, revenue, finance, military and law – with the viceroy himself handling foreign affairs, and the commander-in-chief of the army as an extraordinary member. These people formed the core of the larger Legislative Council, where they were joined by between six and 12 hand-picked nominees, either British or Indian, at least half of whom had to be non-officials.

The Legislative Council, meeting on average for 25 days each year, was purely consultative: it was not even allowed to discuss the actions of the administration, or the budget, or any important bill, without the previous approval of the government. Its European non-official members generally represented British business, whose interests they defended ruthlessly. Its Indian members were not there to represent their people, but supposedly to keep the viceroy in touch with Indian opinion, so that any disquiet in the future could be nipped in the bud. Although they were 'token' Indians, their inclusion marked the first, tiny step towards Indian participation in government. The Legislative Council on which they sat was never intended to have any powers – those were reserved entirely for the government. As the secretary of state, Charles Wood, declared while moving the bill in Parliament: 'All experience teaches us that where a dominant race rules another, the mildest form of government is despotism.'[8]

Among the other changes introduced in 1861, two were particularly important. Both were concerned with the law and both were intended to tighten Britain's grip on India: Macaulay's codification of Indian law finally came into effect, and the Indian Police Act introduced a uniform police service throughout India. Each district was now to have a British superintendent of police, supported by deputy superintendents and inspectors, who could be Indian.

For administrative purposes, the country had been divided into provinces, the three presidency provinces ruled by governors, the others by lieutenant-governors. The provinces were split into divisions under a commissioner, and then into sub-divisions and districts, the basic administrative unit. There were 400 districts in British India, under the control of district officers, who enjoyed a great deal of delegated authority. All were members of what had now become the Indian Civil Service, that most élite body of administrators known among caste-conscious Indians as 'the heaven-born', placing them higher even than merely twice-born Brahmans.

There were never more than 1,200 members of the ICS at any time, and generally rather less than 1,000, to administer a country whose population was about 200 million at the start of the Raj, and 400 million by its end. After Haileybury was closed down all candidates spent at least two years at either Oxford or Cambridge – Balliol was their favourite college – before taking their final examinations, which besides academic subjects included the ability to jump a five-barred gate on horseback with arms folded and stirrups crossed.

As the ICS developed, it divided into separate departments: the executive, which administered the districts, and collected the revenue; the judicial, providing judges for district courts and the high courts in each provincial capital; the political, which was in effect the viceroy's diplomatic corps, providing envoys to foreign countries, and residents and agents in the princely states; and the secretariat, the Whitehall of India, providing senior officials for both provincial and central governments. Added to these were various minor branches such as salt, opium, and customs and excise. Below them came the uncovenanted civil servants including the police and later the Indian medical service, the forestry service, agriculturalists and engineers, adding perhaps a further 2,000 to the total.

ICS men learned their business the hard way: immediately after their probationary period they were sent out to run districts with an average size of 4,430 square miles – more than half the size of Wales – dispensing justice, settling disputes and gathering revenue in their twin roles as magistrate and collector. It was not unusual for a man still in his twenties to have authority over a million people, albeit with the help of a number of Indian subordinates and clerks, and possibly a younger British assistant.

Over the years, a great deal of romance has been spun around the role of the district officer. At its best, particularly in the early years, it was an immensely satisfying life, but it could also be hard and lonely – a man could expect to be in the saddle and under canvas for a regulation 90 days a year in a small district and 120 days in a larger one. Such isolation could breed eccentrics and obsessives, though happily their obsessions were often with scholarly pursuits such as anthropology or ornithology, or valuable public works like canals and irrigation. Some ICS men were undoubtedly brilliant, some were insufferable, others were inutterably dull, despite their good brains. Close contact with the people of his district led a man to identify with them, particularly with the peasants who treated him as a father figure. ICS men who had learned in their early years to love the simple rural folk as their children found it extremely difficult to deal with highly-educated urban Indians who demanded to be treated as equals. Many ICS officers carried such attitudes with them as they moved on up the ladder, and as the number of educated Indians grew, so did the tensions.

The ICS is rightly remembered as probably the finest civil service ever. Its members were famously incorruptible – they accepted no gifts other than flowers or fruit – and they were indefatigable in attending to the interests of the people they were responsible for. They took pride in seeing themselves as the modern equivalent of Plato's Guardians, men bred, selected and trained to govern, selflessly and devotedly. In many respects the comparison was fair: like the Guardians of Plato's ideal republic, they were forbidden to own land or take part in trade; but, also like the Guardians, they were servants of an authoritarian state. Their greatest drawback was that, like bureaucrats everywhere, they were generally intent on maintaining the status quo. They were highly skilled at resisting change – and the change they resisted most of all was the advancement of Indians into the higher reaches of the service.

The final charter renewal in 1853 had decreed that entrance to the civil service was to be through open competition, no longer confined to Haileybury men. Since the queen's proclamation, the ICS was in theory open to Indians as well as Britons, but it was another 10 years before the first Indian, Satyendranath Tagore – it was almost inevitable that he should have been a member of that famous family – went to London to take and pass the entrance examination. That same year, 1868, four more Hindus braved the sea-crossing to study and prepare for the examination in 1869. One, S.B. Thakur, was from Bombay; the others were all members of the Calcutta *bhadralok*: Romesh Chandra Dutt, Behari Lal Gupta and Surendranath Banerjea. All were successful – an achievement that was celebrated with a civic reception in their honour when they returned to Calcutta. Thakur and Gupta went on to solid but unremarkable careers in the ICS, and have since been forgotten. Dutt and Banerjea, however, were to leave their marks in no uncertain manner.

Paving the way for generations of Indian lawyers, Dutt had also been called to the bar before sailing home to take up his place in the ICS. Beginning as assistant magistrate at Alipur, he went on to become the first Indian to take charge of a district, and the only one in the nineteenth century to become a commissioner, first of Burdwan and then of Orissa, a division that was shortly to become a full province under a lieutenant-governor. He was also an official member of the Bengal Legislative Council, and was appointed a Companion of the Indian Empire before retiring after 27 years' distinguished service.

Dutt was a notable scholar, translating several works from Sanskrit into Bengali and English, and he became a lecturer in Indian history at University College, London. But although he served the empire well, he was by no means uncritical of its failings. His *Economic History of India*, written at the end of the century, had as its major theme the 'drain' of Indian substance by the British:

Taxation raised by a king, says the Indian poet, is like the moisture sucked up by the sun, to be returned to the earth as fertilizing rain; but the moisture raised from the Indian soil now descends as fertilizing rain largely on other lands, not on India . . . So great an Economic Drain out of the resources of a land would impoverish the most prosperous countries on earth; it has reduced India to a land of famines more frequent, more widespread, and more fatal, than any known before in the history of India, or of the world.[9]

The 'drain' theory, first propounded in 1867 by Dadabhai Naoroji, a prominent Parsi businessman from Bombay, became the economic battle cry of the nationalists against British rule. Naoroji and his followers argued that one half of all government revenues, equal to more than the entire land revenue and one third of India's total savings, was being drained from India into Britain each year. It went in salaries and pensions paid to British officials and military officers, the interest on loans taken out by the Indian government, the profits of British firms in India, and the expenses of the Indian government in London and elsewhere. This 'sad bleeding', Naoroji declared, 'the thoughtless and pitiless action of British policy', was the basic cause of India's poverty, and was destroying India.[10]

Like so many of his fellow campaigners, however, Naoroji, who was to become known as the Grand Old Man of Indian nationalism, was a convinced Anglophile. For many years, he divided his time between India and England, where he set up the first Indian business in London and Liverpool in 1855. Later, in 1892, he was even elected to the House of Commons as Liberal MP for the London constituency of Central Finsbury.

Unlike Naoroji, R.C. Dutt could not become actively involved in politics until he retired in 1897. Surendranath Banerjea, on the other hand was able to start much earlier after suffering a disgraceful example of racial discrimination. He had obtained a first-class degree in English literature at Calcutta University, and had then passed the ICS examinations near the top of the list in London. However, he and one of his fellows were disqualified when it was discovered that according to the ages they had given at school examinations four years earlier, they were past the ICS age limit of 21. The apparent discrepancy was easily explained: Indians traditionally counted their age from conception rather than birth. But the Civil Service Commission refused to accept this and accused them of lying. Banerjea sued the secretary of state in the Queen's Bench, and won. It was a pyrrhic victory: after being allowed to keep his hard-earned position for three years, he was dismissed for 'a palpable misuse of his judicial powers' and being 'guilty of a falsehood'. In fact, he had simply failed to correct a clerical error made by a subordinate, a mistake for which any ordinary civilian would merely have had his knuckles rapped. But Banerjea was no ordinary civilian: he was a marked man. This time, his appeal in London was unsuccessful. His dismissal stood, branding him for life.

'I had suffered because I was an Indian,' Banerjea wrote later. 'The personal wrong done to me was an illustration of the helpless impotency of our people.' He could hardly be blamed for feeling frustrated and bitter, but he reserved his bitterness entirely for 'the system', retaining an abiding affection for Britain and counting many individual Britons as personal friends. Returning to Calcutta, he set to work as a teacher and journalist, dedicated to 'redressing our wrongs and protecting our rights, personal and collective'.[11] In those aims, he was to be more successful than almost any other Indian in the nineteenth century, playing a major role in the development of Indian nationalism.

There had been pseudo-political organizations in various parts of the country for some years, but they were all local, and most were little more than rich men's clubs devoted to protecting the interests of landlords. The most anti-western of them, which had as its snappy title The Society for the Promotion of National Feeling among the Educated Natives of Bengal, was formed in 1861 to invite Bengalis to abandon the use of English language and customs and revert to purely indigenous culture, including traditional Hindu medicine.

There were also various groups dedicated to religious reform and revival. Some, like the liberal Prarthana Samaj (Prayer Society), a Bombay version of the Brahmo Samaj, believed that India could learn a great deal from the British, but needed to put its own house in order before it could begin thinking about western-style self-government. Others, like the aggressively fundamentalist Arya Samaj (Society of Noble Men), aimed to rid Hinduism and India not only of the superstitious accretions of centuries but also of all western influences.

None of these organizations was a suitable outlet for the growing nationalist feelings of young educated Hindus like Banerjea and his friends, who were more interested in joining the British rather than evicting them. If the *bhadralok* was to make itself heard, it would need to create its own platform.

For once, the first positive move came not from Bengal but from the old Maratha stronghold in the west of India, where the PSS, the Poona Sarvajanik Sabha (All People's Association), was formed in 1870 by Mahadev Govind Ranade, who was also the founder of the Prarthana Samaj. After graduating with first-class honours from Bombay University, Ranade took a law degree in 1866, and was appointed a subordinate judge in his native Poona in 1871. In spite of his undoubted gifts, he had to wait 25 years before he was raised to a judgeship in the high court, no doubt partly because he was a member of the former Peshwa's Brahman community, and partly because of his championing of Indian causes. In 1873–4, he led the PSS to a notable political victory in persuading the government to revise its land revenue settlement in Maharashtra, after a well-organized campaign among the peasants. Like Banerjea, Ranade somehow managed to remain an Anglophile, always presenting his case with sweet reason backed by an impressive knowledge of the law.

For all its success, Ranade's PSS was still a local association, pursuing a Maratha rather than an all-Indian nationalism. By 1876, there was a need for something wider. As Banerjea himself put it: 'The conception of a united India, derived from the inspiration of Mazzini [the Italian patriot, founder of the Young Italy movement] or, at any rate, of bringing all India upon the same common political platform, had taken firm possession of the minds of the Indian leaders in Bengal.'[12] And so, he created Bengal's first nationalist political organization, the Indian Association.

The new association started by aligning itself with popular causes which apparently had little political significance – its first, successful, campaign was for lavatories in third-class railway coaches. Nevertheless its first public meeting in 1877 was a protest against something close to Banerjea's heart: the discrimination against Indian candidates for the ICS. The age limit for the entrance examinations had been lowered from 21 to 19, making it much more difficult for young Indians to compete with native English speakers in London. The Indian Association proposed that examinations should be held simultaneously in London and Calcutta to make things fairer. It would be over 40 years before this was conceded, but there was one immediate outcome of that first meeting: Banerjea was deputed to tour India, to raise awareness of the need for national unity. At packed public meetings in towns and cities, he preached:

the great doctrine of peace and good will between Hindus and Musulmans, Christians and Parsees, aye between all sections of the great Indian community. Let us raise aloft the banner of our country's progress. Let the word 'Unity' be inscribed there in characters of glittering gold ... There may be religious differences between us. But there is a common platform where we may all meet, the platform of our country's welfare.[13]

It was a message that was to be heard repeatedly from Indian leaders over the following 70 years and it struck a chord in many of India's 'new men'. When Disraeli succeeded in drawing Queen Victoria out of her 15-year seclusion by proclaiming her Empress of India in 1877, they joined in the celebrations wholeheartedly. But their declarations of loyalty did not stop them demanding greater participation in the process of government, nor protesting vigorously the following year against another lunatic excursion into Afghanistan.

The viceroy at that time, Lord Lytton, had been sent out to India with the specific brief of bringing the Afghans to heel – both he and his political masters in London had clearly forgotten the lessons of the earlier catastrophe. The second Afghan war was a result of exactly the same blind fear of Russia, and exactly the same arrogant over-confidence, that had led to the first; it followed precisely the same pattern as all previous invasions of Afghanistan; and it produced the same disastrous results before the nightmare ended in 1880.

During the two futile and bloody years of the war, educated Indians were almost unanimous in condemning it and in protesting against India's having to pay for it. They made their voices heard through their own newspapers, which had become increasingly important from about 1870 onwards. From the very beginning, Indians embraced the press with great gusto. Indian newspapers have always been livelier, noisier and less respectful than those of any other country. In those early years, before the days of mass meetings, they were virtually the only means the nationalists had for spreading their ideas. With no representative assembly to debate government measures, the papers had to play the part of the opposition. They wielded an influence far in excess of normal circulation figures, because each copy would be read aloud by one of the few literate members of a community to an audience of many others, who would then discuss and debate what they had heard. And newspapers were not confined to the large towns and cities, but reached the most remote villages, often giving the inhabitants their very first knowledge of the greater world outside.

The British authorities were naturally well aware of the power of the native press, and regularly took steps to control it. Rammohan Roy had protested in vain against the heavy hand of censorship as early as 1824. From 1870, editors laboured under a new clause in the penal code which laid down penalties of transportation for life, or imprisonment for up to three years, for 'whoever attempts to excite feelings of disaffection to the Government established by law in British India'. In 1878, while still smarting from criticisms of his government's handling of a serious famine in the preceding two years, Lytton decided to silence opposition in the Indian papers to his Afghan war with a new law, drawn up in great secrecy and passed at a single sitting of the Imperial Legislative Council.

The Vernacular Press Act, which was directed only at newspapers in Indian languages, provided for the confiscation of the printing press, paper and other materials of any newspaper which the government believed was publishing seditious material. The Act was not a great success – most Indian papers got around it very neatly by reprinting critical articles from British and Irish papers, including *The Times*, which were outside the jurisdiction of the government of India. The main target of the new act was the Calcutta *Amrita Bazar Patrika*, the sharpest thorn in the side of the administration, published by the Gosh brothers, Sisir Kumar and Motilal, who were friends and close associates of Surendranath Banerjea. The paper was published half in English and half in Bengali, but the morning after the act was passed, officials moving in to close it down discovered to their dismay that it had been converted overnight into a purely English language paper, and could not be touched.

Ironically it soon became clear that the new act had seriously backfired, unifying and strengthening the opposition of the nationalists, who staged a protest meeting against it in Calcutta town hall. It was India's first great public demonstration on a political issue. The second, some five years later, was also over press freedom, when Banerjea was charged with contempt of court after writing an angry editorial in his own newspaper, the *Bengalee*, condemning a British judge for an insulting verdict in a dispute over a family idol. Comparing Justice Norris with the notorious Judge Jeffreys, Banerjea had said he was unworthy of his high office, and went on to suggest that 'some steps should be taken to put a quietus on the wild eccentricities of this young and raw Dispenser of Justice'.[14]

A bench of five judges in the Calcutta High Court found Banerjea guilty by a majority of four to one — the lone dissenter was the only Indian, the others were all British — and sentenced him to two months in gaol. The verdict provoked a huge popular reaction, with angry demonstrations all over Calcutta, in other parts of Bengal, and even in far-away Lahore; an indication of the spread of nationalist feeling, and of Banerjea's position as a national figure. What was also significant was that events in Calcutta centred around a *hartal*, a particularly Hindu form of protest in which all businesses close down, bringing life in a town or city to a standstill. Traditionally, the *hartal* is a form of mourning, and those taking part spend their time in prayer, fasting and rites of purification. It is essentially peaceful and non-violent, though inevitably passions often boil over: in Calcutta, students from the university smashed windows in the High Court and stoned the police. It was the first time the *hartal* had been used against the British government. It would not be the last.

'If Fifty Men Cannot be Found ...'

From the Indian point of view, the only good thing to come out of the second Afghan war was that it brought down Disraeli's Tory government in the spring of 1880, and opened the door to Gladstone and the Liberals. Gladstone sent out Lord Ripon as Viceroy, with instructions 'to give India the benefits and blessings of free institutions'. Ripon approached his task with evangelical fervour, putting a stop to Lytton's Afghan adventure, repealing the Vernacular Press Act, and boosting the spread of education. Then he set about introducing a measure of local self-government in districts, sub-divisions and municipalities, with elected representatives rather than nominated stooges on their governing boards.

In practice the new boards were controlled and bullied into submission by the British ICS officers who chaired them, but at least it was a start. At last, what Ripon himself described as 'the rapidly growing ... intelligent class of public spirited men who it is not only bad policy, but sheer waste of power, to fail to utilise'[1] could begin gaining vital experience of government. In fact, that was Ripon's intention, as he clearly stated: 'It is not primarily with a view to improvement in administration ... it is chiefly desirable as a measure of political and popular education.'[2] How Macaulay would have applauded – his 'proudest day' was back on the political agenda.

Although the 100,000 Britons in India – the Anglo-Indians as they now described themselves – disliked Ripon's local government changes, they grudgingly accepted them, knowing the ICS would always have the last word. But when he tried to put an end to racial discrimination in the courts by allowing Indian judges to try cases involving Europeans, it was a very different matter.

Ripon had seen this as an innocuous bit of tidying up, suggested by the law member of his Executive Council, Sir Courtney Ilbert. For some time, Indian justices had had the right to try Europeans in towns and cities, but not in country districts: the Ilbert Bill merely sought to remove this anomaly. It did not affect the normal legal safeguards, including the right of appeal against any sentence. Nevertheless, the British reaction was one of fury and outrage. The howls of protest were led by planters, always the most reactionary section of Anglo-Indian society, who habitually treated their Indian labourers like slaves: Indian magistrates, they cried, might try to stop them 'beating their own niggers'. White magistrates could be relied on to take a more understanding attitude – a planter who murdered his Indian coachman at about that time was fined the equivalent of £2.

Yet the planters were not alone. Businessmen, lawyers, and officialdom at all levels – including the lieutenant-governor of Bengal, the chief justice and 10 judges of the Calcutta court – joined in the *brouhaha*. Anglo-Indian newspapers, led by *The Englishman*, ranted and raved and carried advertisements attacking Ripon and all Indians in the most virulent language. The hysteria reached such a pitch that there was even a plot to kidnap the viceroy, bundle him on board a ship and remove him from India. A circulated letter, signed 'Britannicus', shrieked: 'The only people who have any right to India are the British. The SO-CALLED Indians have no right whatever.'[3] A Canning or a Dalhousie would probably have carried on regardless, but Ripon caved in under the pressure. The bill was redrafted and passed in a thoroughly watered-down version. The following year Ripon departed, unlamented by most Britons but given a send-off by the Indians that would not be equalled until the very last viceroy left the country in 1948.

The bigoted clamour against the Ilbert Bill was a far cry from the spirit of Queen Victoria's proclamation, but it had shown Indians what could be achieved by concerted agitation. Their own campaign in support of the bill had failed, partly because it had been uncoordinated. So, too, had various other campaigns since 1875 – the Indians' solitary success had been in persuading the British government to pay some of the cost of the Afghan war. Their demands for greater Indianization of government services had gone largely unheeded, and a continuous four-year battle to keep import duties on British textiles had been a total failure. India's first modern mills, in Bombay and Ahmedabad, were still struggling to establish themselves in 1879, and needed all the help they could get, particularly as the surrounding region was suffering a serious famine. Lytton had ignored their pleas and overruled his entire council to remove all duty from imported Lancashire cottons, while keeping excise duties on home-produced Indian textiles.

Clearly, educated Indians needed a national organization to co-ordinate and present their views. The Calcutta newspaper the *Indian Mirror* began running a continuous campaign calling for one, but in a country so vast, so fragmented by language and religion, how was it to be achieved? Surendranath Banerjea's Indian Association held its first all-India conference in Calcutta that December, timed to coincide with an industrial exhibition in the city. But it remained largely a local affair with three-quarters of the delegates coming from Bengal, and it failed to ignite. At the same time, however, a retired English official, Allan Octavian Hume, sent a letter to all the living graduates of Calcutta University, and this did strike the necessary spark:

> There are aliens, like myself, who love India and her children ... but the real work must be done by the people of the country themselves ... If fifty men cannot be found with sufficient power of self-sacrifice, sufficient love for and pride in their country, sufficient genuine and unselfish patriotism to take the initiative and if needs be to devote the rest of their lives to the Cause — then there is no hope for India. Her sons must and will remain mere humble and helpless instruments of foreign rulers.[4]

Hume found not 50 men but 72 — including 39 lawyers, 14 journalists and one doctor — who met in Bombay on 28 December 1885, for the first session of the Indian National Congress.

It was a small beginning, but one Briton at least recognized its significance: Florence Nightingale sent a goodwill message from England, saying: 'We are watching the birth of a new nationality in the oldest civilization in the world.'[5] The delegates had planned to meet in Poona, at the invitation of Justice Ranade, who no doubt considered the home of Maratha nationalism more suitable than Calcutta. But at the last minute, Poona had been struck by a cholera epidemic. Perhaps it was just as well. Only six years earlier, another Poona Brahman, Vasudeo Balwant Phadke, had tried to raise an army to drive out the British and restore Maratha power. It had taken four years to flush him and his followers out of the hills, and the memory was still fresh on both sides.

From the beginning, it was decided that the Congress should meet annually around the end of December, each year in a different province to ensure its national character. Each year's president was to come from a province other than that in which the Congress was being held. That first year, the honour went to a Calcutta barrister, Womesh C. Bonnerjee. The two most obvious candidates were not available: Ranade was a serving judge, and in any case was a local man; Banerjea was occupied in Calcutta at the second conference of his own association, though he was soon to abandon this and become an energetic Congress member. Hume was appointed secretary, a position he was to occupy with great distinction for the next 23 years.

Allan Octavian Hume was another of those remarkable Englishmen who fell in love with India. He joined the company's civil service in 1849 and spent his early years as an outstanding district officer in Etawah, between Delhi and Cawnpore, where he found himself in the thick of the revolt in 1857. He was decorated for his bravery after leading irregular forces to victory in several pitched battles, but his conduct afterwards raised doubts in the minds of Anglo-Indians. While other Britons were blowing rebels from guns and slaughtering whole villages in mindless vengeance, Hume insisted on holding scrupulously fair trials. Moreover, he showed a marked reluctance to impose the death penalty: he hanged only seven mutineers, and even then designed a new form of gallows to make their end as quick and painless as possible.

In spite of the shadow of 'unreliability' that hung over him, Hume went on to become commissioner of customs for the North-West Province, then secretary of the newly created department of revenue, commerce and agriculture in the government of India, a post he held for the unusually long time of nine years. But his proposed elevation to the viceroy's Executive Council was blocked because of his 'obvious faults'.[6] It was entirely in character that when he retired in 1882, he should decide not to go home, but to stay on in Simla and devote himself to Indian advancement.

Hume had always been a man of great enthusiasms. He was deeply interested in eastern religions, spiritualism and the supernatural. In 1879, he came under the spell of the Theosophist Madame Blavatsky. For a while, Madame Blavatsky used his splendid Simla home, Rothney Castle, to hold her seances, at which messages from her mystic 'mahatmas' floated down from the ceiling inscribed on palm leaves, and she 'found' lost jewellery and teacups buried in the garden. Hume declared he was never completely taken in – he described Blavatsky as the most marvellous liar he had ever met – but he excused her shameless charlatanry as a means of attracting converts to 'a higher faith'.

Although Hume soon turned his back on Theosophy, he continued to follow the mystic path. He told Lord Ripon, with whom he was on close terms, that he had been in touch with his own ethereal gurus since 1848, and that they had used their occult powers to save Europe in that revolutionary year and the British empire in 1857. They were now acting through him and other devotees, he said, to help Ripon introduce reforms and so avoid 'the possibility of such a cataclysm recurring'.[7] Ripon may not have taken all this too seriously, but he was obviously prepared to overlook this little foible in a man who could offer so much valuable knowledge and experience, and who was undoubtedly excellent company.

Lord Dufferin, Ripon's mediocre successor, was not prepared to make allowances, describing Hume as 'cleverish, a little cracked, excessively vain, and absolutely indifferent to truth'.[8] Hume was well aware of such opinions, complaining that 'most Europeans look upon me either as a lunatic or a liar'.[9] Therefore when he talked to Dufferin about his advisers and informants, he omitted to mention that they only existed on an astral plane, or at best in some secret Tibetan Shangri-La. And when he spoke of having seen 30,000 reports contained in seven large volumes, warning of an impending revolt throughout

India, he did not tell the viceroy that the reason he was unable to show them to him was because they had no *physical* reality.

The story of Hume's seven volumes has been enlarged, embroidered and used by politicians and writers over the years. Unaware that the volumes never actually existed, they have treated them as evidence that Dufferin instructed Hume to set up the Indian National Congress as a safety valve for politically minded Indians who were likely to cause trouble. In fact, Dufferin had no part in the creation of the Congress, and in common with most of his senior officials regarded it with suspicion. In May 1885, he told Lord Reay, the governor of Bombay: 'At his last interview he [Hume] told me that he and his friends were going to assemble a political convention of delegates, as far as I understand, on the lines adopted by O'Connell previous to Catholic emancipation.'[10]

Dufferin's biggest fear, as he told the then secretary of state, Lord Randolph Churchill, was that the 'Bengali Baboos and Mahratta Brahmins' planned to start revolutionary agitation along the lines of the 'Fenian outrages' of the Irish Republican Brotherhood in London and Manchester.[11] By the time of its third annual session, he was writing to his finance member, Sir Aukland Colvin, wondering 'in what way the happy despatch may best be applied to the Congress, [for] we cannot allow the Congress to continue to exist'.[12]

It is hard now to see why Dufferin was so worried. The first thing Bonnerjee did at the opening session was to affirm Congress's unswerving loyalty to the crown. And to make quite sure they could not be labelled seditious, the delegates passed a resolution declaring 'the continual affiliation of India to Great Britain, at any rate for a period far exceeding the range of any practical political forecast, to be absolutely essential to the interests of our own National Development'. This may have seemed a strange beginning for a nationalist organization, but these men were still feeling their way. What they wanted, for the moment, was not independence but, as Bonnerjee put it, 'that the Government should be widened and that the people should have their proper and legitimate share in it'.

It is all too easy, more than a century later, to see the Congressmen's protestations of loyalty as cynical flattery intended to keep the authorities happy and avoid arrest — a man could still be gaoled without trial under Regulation III of 1818 if he was 'known to be hostile to the Government'. But although many of those early leaders enjoyed using a little irony in their speeches and writings, their loyalty was genuine. They were well aware of the benefits of the Raj, as well as its disadvantages, and they were proud to share in the glory of the British empire, convinced that they would eventually progress to a more equal share, alongside Canada, Australia and South Africa. It would be another 20 years before disillusion set in. Until then, their main priorities were getting to know each other and building Congress into an organization that could create a sense of Indian nationality among peoples with as little in common as Icelanders and Turks.

Of course, Congress criticized the Indian government, but it did so in the spirit of Her Majesty's Loyal Opposition. Delegates griped about bureaucratic inefficiency, about their own limited opportunities in government service, and about what we would now call human rights issues. But, above all, they complained about India's finances, a subject that the Legislative Council was not allowed to discuss.

In 1885, they condemned the war earlier that year to grab the remainder of Burma before the French could add it to their expanding Indochinese empire. Their reason for condemning it, however, was not that it was imperialistic, but that India had had to pay for it, using up all the revenue that should have gone to fund Ripon's local government reforms. They also called for the abolition of the secretary of state's council in London, partly because it obstructed progress, but mainly because its costs were charged to India. Led by Dadabhai Naoroji, who presided over the second Congress, they complained regularly about the drain of India's resources to Britain. Year after year, they called for the reduction of military expenditure which was swallowing 40 and sometimes even 50 per cent of the country's total revenue. And, year after year, successive viceroys listened politely to Congress resolutions and then ignored them, convinced that the government was more concerned with the fate of India's masses than what Dufferin described as 'this self-appointed microscopic minority'.

In many ways, the viceroys were right. At the time Congress was founded the *bhadralok* throughout the whole of India numbered no more than 300,000 and though this was three times bigger than the entire Anglo-Indian population, almost all its members were westernized urban professionals who had little contact with the rural millions. The main concerns of Congress delegates, as seen through the resolutions they debated in strictly parliamentary fashion, were overwhelmingly matters that affected their own opportunities for advancement.

Despite Bonnerjee's reminder that one of its main objectives was 'the eradication, by direct friendly personal intercourse, of all possible race, creed, or provincial prejudices amongst all lovers of our country', Congress was overwhelmingly Hindu in character from the start[13] – the first session in Bombay met in a Brahman institution, the Goculdas Tejpal Sanscrit College. There were several Jains present, and a strong representation of Parsis, the established leaders of Bombay's business and legal communities: alongside Naoroji, who was elected president three times, was India's first Parsi barrister, Pherozeshah Mehta, who had formed the Bombay Presidency Association earlier that year. Known as 'the uncrowned king of Bombay', Mehta was to serve as a member of the city's municipal council for 46 years, holding its chair no fewer than four times. Both

Naoroji and Mehta, president in 1900, were to be among the most prominent leaders of Congress until their deaths during the First World War.

There were also several Englishmen besides Hume, notably Sir William Wedderburn and Sir Henry Cotton, both of whom were to be elected president twice. But among the 72 delegates to the first Congress there were only two Muslims, R.N. Sayani and A.N. Dharamsi, both from the Bombay presidency. The following year, in Calcutta, there were 33 Muslims out of 431 delegates, a marked improvement, but still nowhere near the one in five that would have matched the proportions in the general population. Ten years later, there were still only 54 out of 784, and 10 years after that, in 1906, only 45 out of 1,663. Only the sessions of 1888 in Allahabad and 1899 in Lucknow bucked the trend, with 222 out of 1,248 and 313 out of 789 respectively, but these were cities with large Muslim populations.[14]

One of the reasons for the Muslims' poor showing was that they were still at least 50 years behind the Hindus in western education. By the start of the 1880s, there were 36,686 Hindus studying in English high schools, but only 363 Muslims, and while 3,155 Hindus held university degrees, there were only 57 Muslim graduates in the whole of India.[15] One prominent Muslim was trying to drag his people into the modern age, but ironically he was the other main reason why so few of them were becoming involved with the Congress: Syed Ahmed Khan, the great advocate of western education for Muslims, was publicly urging them to stay away. Indeed, in 1888, he went even further, and founded the United Indian Patriotic Association, specifically to counter Congress. Its aim was 'to strengthen the British Rule, and to remove those bad feelings from the hearts of the Indian people which the supporters of Congress are stirring up throughout the country, and by which great dissatisfaction is being raised among the people against the British Government'.

Sir Syed Ahmed Khan – he was knighted in 1870 – was born in 1817 into the Muslim nobility in Delhi, where his grandfather had the impossible task of managing the finances of the penultimate Mughal emperor, Akbar Shah II. The young Syed Ahmed was raised traditionally in the closed world of the *haveli*, the family mansion, carefully isolated from the impurity of the streets. He was educated at home in Urdu, Persian and Arabic, mathematics and oriental medicine. But his privileged existence came to a sudden end when his father, grandfather and elder brother died in quick succession, leaving him to support the rest of the family.

Before taking up his position in the emperor's court, Syed Ahmed's grandfather had worked for the company in Calcutta, Burma and Iran. Syed Ahmed followed suit, finding employment as a reader in the law courts and later becoming a *munsif*, or junior judge. During 1857, he was serving in Bijnor, only 40 miles from the great revolt's epicentre at Meerut. He refused to join the rebels, and even managed to save the British collector, a man called Shakespeare, and the rest of the small British community from being massacred. When the local nawab offered him a prime position in his administration, he declined angrily. 'By God, Nawab Sahib,' he declared, 'I say that British sovereignty cannot be eliminated from India.'[16]

Not even finding his house in Delhi looted and his mother dying of starvation could end Syed Ahmed's love affair with the British, though the shock turned his hair and full, flowing beard white. Already a respected author of two books on Mughal history written in superb Urdu prose, he now turned his literary talents to wooing the rulers away from their distrust of the Muslims. He started in 1858 with *Essay on the Causes of the Indian Revolt*, a clear-sighted analysis which Allan Hume claimed inspired him to found the Indian National Congress. Two years later, he followed up with *The Loyal Muhammadans of India*, a book that contained such toe-curling blandishments as: 'Without flattering the English, I can truly say that the natives of India, high and low, merchants and petty shopkeepers, educated and illiterate, when contrasted with the English in education, manners and uprightness, are as unlike them as a dirty animal is to an able and handsome man.'[17] It is hardly surprising that he was one of the very few Muslim judges to keep his job after the revolt. Or that he should decide to devote his life to creating a *rapprochement* between Muslims and the British: he was convinced that only the British could protect the Muslims against total domination by the Hindus, and therefore the British had to stay.

Getting the Muslims to co-operate with the British was just as difficult as getting the British to trust the Muslims. First, Syed Ahmed had to persuade Muslims to stop looking back resentfully to past glories. 'The rule of the former emperors and rajas,' he reminded them, 'was based on nothing but tyranny and oppression; the law of might was that of right; the voice of the people was not listened to.'[18] If they were ever to catch up with the Hindus, he told them, Muslims had to swallow their pride and learn English, embrace western thinking, and stay out of politics.

Before he could persuade Muslims to stop skulking in their self-imposed isolation and join the modern world, Syed Ahmed first had to wrest power from the *ulama*, the clerics who had taken control of the community when the old Mughal aristocracy had abdicated their leadership in the early years of the century. It was the *ulama* who were holding the Muslims back, resisting any incursions of western culture. Syed Ahmed was never completely successful – religious extremists would always exert a powerful influence over the faithful – but he never gave up the struggle. In a continuous stream of speeches, articles and pamphlets, and through the schools and scientific societies which he set up, he preached that the word of Allah, as revealed in the Qur'an, was at one with the work of Allah, as revealed in the laws of physical science and nature. In an almost exact parallel with Rammohan Roy's efforts to reform Hinduism 50 years before, Syed Ahmed was determined to strip Islam of superstition. And by emphasizing the basic similarities between Islam and Christianity, with their shared Judaic heritage, he hoped to bring Muslims and British closer together.

In 1875, five years after travelling to England, Sir Syed founded the Muhammadan Anglo-Oriental College at Aligarh, some 60 miles south-east of Delhi. The viceroy himself laid the foundation stone. Modelling it on the colleges of Cambridge, Sir Syed dreamed of its becoming a western-style university for Muslims, a status it finally achieved in 1920, 22 years after his death. Aligarh was the cradle of the Muslim revival, its influence spreading into every aspect of Muslim life. Other schools and colleges were set up in its image, turning out educated young Muslims to compete with their Hindu counterparts. It was Sir Syed's greatest achievement, giving hope and self-confidence to a community that had lost both.

At first sight, it seems strange that Sir Syed should want to keep Muslims out of the Indian National Congress, which was set up to promote the advancement of all Indians. One reason was the fear that they would become involved in political agitation and revive British mistrust, which he had worked so hard to dispel: 25 years after the revolt, the British were at last beginning to realize that they had been wrong in blaming the Muslims for everything. The British also needed a counterbalance to the growing strength of the Hindus: 'divide and rule' was never officially acknowledged policy, but as a strategy it was too valuable to ignore. Sir Syed's other, more significant, reason was that Congress was committed to representative democracy, and representative democracy meant rule by the majority, which meant the Hindus. English-style elections, he said, 'would be like a game of dice, in which one man had four dice and the other only one'.[19]

Congress went to great lengths to prove that it was a purely secular organization, and to attract Muslims and other minorities. After the Hindu Bonnerjee, and the Parsi Naoroji, the third president, at the Madras Congress, was Justice Badruddin Tyabji, India's first Muslim high court judge. In his presidential address Tyabji, a liberal secular modernist, spoke out for integration: 'I, for one, am utterly at a loss to understand why Mussulmans should not work shoulder to shoulder with their fellow-countrymen, of other races and creeds, for the common benefit of all ... this is the principle on which we, in the Bombay Presidency, have always acted.'[20] But Tyabji was a member of the minority Shiite Khoja sect, and the Khojas, unlike most Indian Muslims, were always an outgoing, mercantile group. For all Tyabji's pleading, most Muslims listened to Sir Syed, and stayed away.

Sir Syed was never anti-Hindu as such. He had a large circle of Hindu friends and worked closely with Hindu social workers; Aligarh had Hindus on its faculty and as students, and received financial support from rich Hindus. One of his most famous sayings was that India was like a beautiful bride whose two eyes were Hindu and Muslim – but he went on to add that her beauty depended on the two eyes shining with equal lustre. Even before Congress came into being, Sir Syed was speaking in the viceroy's Imperial Legislative Council, to which he was appointed in 1878, against 'the introduction of the principles of election, pure and simple, in a country like India, where caste distinctions still flourish, where there is no fusion of the various races, where religious distinctions are still violent'.[21] He believed, he said later, that 'the Hindus and Muslims were two different nations even though they drank from the same well and breathed the air from the same city'.[22] It was a prophetic statement, the first public airing of the two nations idea that was to bedevil the final years of the Raj.

As Muslim self-confidence grew during the last 15 years of the nineteenth century, so also did the tensions between the two main communities. Hindus were increasingly suspicious of Muslim resurgence, while Muslims became increasingly resentful of the Hindus' dominant position. By the mid-1890s, communal riots were endemic in most major cities. Many nationalists blamed the British for fomenting trouble between the two communities, claiming that, before they came, Hindus and Muslims had always intermingled happily in cities, towns and villages throughout India. This is pure myth. The British may have utilized the division between Hindus and Muslims, but they certainly did not invent it: there had been communal friction since at least the time of Aurangzeb – the time, incidentally, when Sikhs became sworn enemies of Muslims.

Hindus and Muslims lived in different villages and separate, clearly defined quarters in towns and cities, coming into contact only when they had to. Hindus regarded all Muslims, like lower castes and untouchables, as *Mlechcha*, unclean; even if he were dying of thirst, no Hindu would drink a glass of water offered by a Muslim, or allow a Muslim to drink from one of his cups. Generally speaking, personal friendships were possible only among the upper classes, and even then were hedged in by rules of caste and Qur'anic taboos. The masses on either side, wearing different clothes, eating different foods, often speaking different languages and writing in different scripts, merely tolerated each other's presence and quietly got on with their lives.

Trouble could always flare up, especially during religious festivals, when heightened passions often led to deliberate acts of provocation on both sides. Hindu processions were always noisy affairs, and they would often make a point of stopping outside mosques, where their bands would play at full volume. Since music in mosques was forbidden by Islam, infuriated worshippers whose silent prayers had been so rudely interrupted would be goaded into a fury, pouring out into the street for a fight.

Muslims had their processions, too, and enraged their Hindu neighbours in various ways. They might, for instance, try to cut down branches that had grown on a pipal tree since the previous year and which interfered with the passage of the high paper towers representing the tombs of Hasan and Hussein, the martyred grandsons of the Prophet. Any deviation, however minor, from the procession's traditional route was, of course, unthinkable. Since the pipal tree was sacred to Hindus, they would be ready to defend it with whatever force was needed – another sure recipe for a riot.

The Muslim practice of slaughtering cows during the religious festival of Id-ul-Adha was another regular source of conflict. For Hindus, killing a cow could be considered a greater sin than killing a man – even a Brahman – and invited retribution. For Muslims, sacrificing a cow rather than a sheep or goat was a matter of prestige and economics: a cow was worth seven sheep, and it would feed many more people. It was also a guaranteed way of provoking their Hindu neighbours, particularly when the cows to be slaughtered were paraded through Hindu districts. Many Muslim leaders, including Sir Syed, tried to persuade their people to abandon cow slaughter, but old customs die hard, particularly when pride is involved, and it continued to be an irritant for many years, causing serious communal riots throughout the 1880s. Hindus all over India formed cow protection societies, a thinly veiled excuse for anti-Muslim activity. The British, of course, also killed and ate cows, but somehow the Hindus, though strongly disapproving, usually managed to look the other way.

The difference in Muslim and Hindu thinking at that time was epitomized by two books, published in 1879 and 1882 respectively: *Musaddas* (*The Ebb and Flow of Islam*), by Altaf Husain Hali, and *Anandamath* (*The Abbey of Bliss*), by Bankim Chandra Chatterjee. Hali appealed to Indian Muslims to throw off their ignorance, indolence and self-centredness and seek progress as a disciplined and industrious single nation. Chatterjee, one of the first two graduates of Calcutta University, was a member of the ICS, though he never advanced beyond his original appointment as a deputy magistrate. His novel, set in the time of the decline of Muslim power in Bengal, describes Hindus taking up arms against the degenerate and oppressive Muslim rule, with the British shown as liberators who had come to India to free them from Muslim tyranny. A community of children of Kali rampage through the countryside burning and plundering Muslim villages and slaughtering Muslims wholesale. When they have finally succeeded, the holy man guiding the movement appears and instructs the children to stop fighting and co-operate with the British, who will purify the country in God's good time then hand it over to the Hindus.[23] Although it was set in the past, the message of *Anandamath* was unequivocal. It became an enormous best-seller, creating much resentment among educated Muslims and fuelling the Hindu nationalism which the Congress was at such pains to disavow.

Not all Congressmen turned their backs on Hindu nationalism. One prominent member who pursued it relentlessly was Bal Gangadhar Tilak, a brilliant journalist who used his native Marathi language to carry his message of Hindu patriotism to the lower middle classes in Deccan towns and villages through his newspaper, *Kesari* (*The Lion*). Born to a prosperous Chitpavan Brahman family one year before the revolt of 1857, Tilak received a western education at the Deccan College in Poona. He developed a personal philosophy that reflected both his background and his education – a heady mix that combined the polemics of Hegel, Kant, Mill, Bentham, Voltaire and Rousseau, with the ancient Hindi classics, particularly the *Bhagavad Gita*. He went on to found a number of schools where western science was restated in traditional Hindu terms. In many ways Tilak's schools were a counterpart to the educational work of Syed Ahmed Khan among the Muslims, but unlike Sir Syed, Tilak was concerned with undermining British rule, not reinforcing it.

Tilak achieved national prominence in 1891, when he bitterly opposed the Age of Consent Act, introduced after the death of a child bride from sexual injuries. The Act raised the age at which a marriage could be consummated from 10 to 12 – in Britain, it had been raised from 12 to 16 in 1885. This was the first significant social reform instituted by the British since the great revolt, and Congress supported it wholeheartedly. Tilak, however, raised the battle cry of interference with religion, and soon became recognized as Hinduism's champion, in opposition to the liberal, progressive attitudes of most Congressmen.

Tilak created or revived two major Hindu festivals in Maharashtra, one commemorating the birth of Shiva's elephant-headed son, Ganesh, the other honouring the local hero Shivaji, founding father of the Maratha nation, who had fought the Mughals in the seventeenth century. Both were noisy, chauvinistic affairs, calculated to alienate Muslims: the Shivaji festival was even timed to coincide with the Muslim Muhurram. Tilak was given the title 'Lokamanya' (Revered by the Nation) – but the nation concerned was a strictly Hindu one.

In 1897, bubonic plague spread from Bombay to Poona, interfering with that year's Shivaji festival. British plague officers, led by a Mr Rand, the assistant collector of Poona, took immediate and brutal measures to control the outbreak, including isolating people from infected areas in special camps and destroying property believed to be contaminated. Inevitably, mistakes were made – people who were not infected were carted away, 'clean' houses were pulled down, soldiers searching for victims or carriers damaged shrines and helped themselves to property. Rand and his fellow plague officers did not trouble to explain their actions, which the inhabitants of the city soon came to fear more than the plague itself. It was a monumental example of arrogance and insensitivity.

Tilak described Rand and his men as 'this vast engine of oppression', and warned of trouble. 'What people on earth, however docile,' he wrote in *Kesari*, 'will continue to submit to this sort of mad terror?'[24] On 15 June, he published a poem praising Shivaji, for stabbing a Mughal official in the back while they were signing a peace treaty. He followed this up with inflammatory speeches at the Shivaji festival and articles preaching Krishna's message from the *Bhagavad Gita* that no blame could be attached to anyone who killed an oppressor without thought of reward. On 27 June, Rand and his assistant were shot dead. Tilak was arrested for sedition, and charged with incitement to murder British officials. After the most cursory of trials he was sentenced to 18 months imprisonment. It was another mistake: Tilak was now a Hindu martyr as well as a national hero. When he emerged from prison, he adopted a new slogan: '*Swaraj* is my birthright, and I will have it!' *Swaraj*, a demand made by Shivaji two centuries earlier, means self-rule. Shivaji wanted it from the Mughals for Maharashtra; Tilak now demanded it from the British for India as a whole, and he was prepared to fight for it.

In marked contrast to Tilak's fiery extremism, another Chitpavan Brahman from Poona emerged in the 1890s as a national leader with a gentler, less militant style. Born into a poor family in 1866, 10 years after Tilak, Gopal Krishna Gokhale was a protégé of Justice Ranade, shared most of his mentor's ideas and started his political life as secretary of Ranade's PSS, the Poona All People's Association. He was no firebrand but an outstanding intellectual with a particularly fine grasp of economics, who relied not on oratory but on sweet reason and detailed, logical argument. When he later became a member of the Imperial Legislative Council, his courteous, precise and devastating speeches deconstructing each year's budget became an annual event eagerly anticipated by Indians and dreaded by the government.

Like Tilak, Gokhale edited a newspaper, *Sudharak*, but unlike Tilak he was never in danger of arrest. And unlike Tilak, who looked back nostalgically to a golden past of Maratha glory, Gokhale looked forward to progress, admired the British and embraced western ideas. Tilak demanded rights; Gokhale politely requested concessions. Tilak wanted *swaraj* now, and saw no need for social reforms to make it work. Gokhale believed India would not be ready for independence until it had made the social and religious reforms that would allow all its peoples to live together in harmony – and he was prepared to work patiently towards this goal, even if it did not come in his own lifetime.

Although he was a Brahman, Gokhale sought a secular government, based on Hindu-Muslim unity. While Tilak created Hindu festivals and the militant cult of Shivaji, Gokhale founded the Servants of India Society, a select, quasi-monastic band of workers dedicated to selfless service to the motherland and its people, regardless of caste or creed. 'Its members', he wrote, 'frankly accept the British connection, as ordained, in the inscrutable dispensation of Providence, for India's good. Self-government on the lines of English colonies is their goal. This goal, they recognize, cannot be attained without years of earnest and patient work and sacrifices worthy of the cause.'[25] Gokhale's saintly work with the SIS earned him the title of Mahatma, great soul, some 15 years before Gandhi achieved the same honour.

By the end of the nineteenth century, though most of the older leaders like Ranade, Dadabhai Naoroji, Surendranath Banerjea and Pherozeshah Mehta were still around, Gokhale and Tilak had become the acknowledged leaders of the two wings of Congress, known simply as the Moderates and the Extremists. For the moment, the Moderates were still in control, for Congress was overwhelmingly middle class and conservative; its members were mostly professional men, industrialists or property owners, whose interests would be damaged by violence.

For all its caution, Congress had achieved some small successes by that time. It was largely due to Congress pressure that the Indian Councils Act of 1892 extended the legislative councils of the viceroy and the governors of Bombay and Madras to include 'elected' members for the first time. It was hardly a revolutionary step – municipalities, chambers of commerce, landowners' associations and universities submitted lists of elected representatives, from which the viceroy and governors would then select members of their actual councils. The official members were still in the majority and always voted in a solid block, faithfully supported by the princes and other placemen. It was far less than Congress had wanted, but at least a council seat offered a platform, and an opportunity to examine and criticize government policies and decisions without fear. Even Tilak accepted the chance to sit on Bombay's council from 1895 to 1897. Gokhale succeeded him, before being elected in 1901 to represent Bombay on the Imperial Legislative Council in Calcutta, in place of Pherozeshah Mehta, who resigned because of ill health.

The 1892 Act was a small but significant step on the long road to self-government. But it did little to improve the position of Congress in the eyes of the British, who still regarded it at best with suspicion and at worst with derision. When internal divisions between Extremists and Moderates widened as the new century approached, Lord Curzon, who arrived as viceroy in 1899, declared: 'The Congress is tottering to its fall, and one of my greatest ambitions while in India is to assist it to a peaceful demise.' In fact, it was Curzon who would be responsible for turning the Congress from near moribund respectability into a militant political force.

'The Gravity of the Blunder'

The British Raj reached its apogee in 1903, with a grand *durbar* in Delhi, a ceremonial gathering to which all the princes and leaders of India were summoned to celebrate the accession of the new king-emperor, Edward VII, and to swear their fealty. Spread over two weeks, it was the most splendid display of wealth and power ever seen in the sub-continent, far outweighing the magnificence of the Mughals. And it was the brainchild of Lord Curzon, the most splendid of all the governors-general. Curzon, who had been appointed viceroy in 1898 at the tender age of 39, had been branded for life by a rhyme written by two fellow undergraduates at Balliol College, Oxford:

> My name is George Nathaniel Curzon,
> I am a most superior person.
> My cheeks are pink, my hair is sleek,
> I dine at Blenheim twice a week.

The doggerel may have been mocking, but it was accurate. Curzon was always a decidedly superior person, especially in his own eyes. Curzon had many qualities, but he also had two overriding faults: like so many clever people, he was utterly insensitive to the feelings of others, particularly those less fortunate than himself; and he was politically obtuse. Indeed, he seemed to despise politics, as though its intrigues were beneath him.

No one could have been better qualified for the position of viceroy than George Curzon. He had spent most of his life preparing himself for it, having decided as a boy that there were only two worthwhile goals in life: to be viceroy of India and prime minister of Great Britain. He saw no reason why he should not achieve both, using one as a stepping-stone to the other. As part of his preparation for the viceroyship, he had travelled widely in the Far East, in Persia, Afghanistan and central Asia, as well as in India itself. He had also served terms as a junior minister in both the India Office and the Foreign Office. As though to confirm his suitability, Government House in Calcutta was an almost perfect copy of his own country seat at Kedleston – almost perfect, because the Calcutta mansion was missing the row of urns that adorned the roofline of Kedleston Hall. Curzon, of course, added them.

　　Curzon was a mass of contradictions. He was probably the most able of all the governors-general, but he was also the most disastrous. He was an out-and-out imperialist, whose stated aim was 'to rivet the British rule more firmly on to India and to postpone the longed-for day of emancipation'; but he also hoped to help India towards 'the position which is bound one day to be hers – namely that of the greatest partner in the Empire'.[1] He was intellectually brilliant, tirelessly energetic, and an impatient perfectionist obsessed with the pursuit of efficiency. But although he was contemptuous of the institutionalized pettifoggery of his bureaucrats, he was incapable of delegating responsibility, attempting to oversee every detail of the administration, no matter how insignificant. 'It is no good trusting a human being to do a thing for you,' he wrote. 'Do everything yourself.'[2] He came to India with a firm resolve to reduce paperwork, but insisted on reading every document rather than rely on summaries made for him by his officials. It was nothing for him to be presented with a hundredweight or more of papers each night, many of which he proceeded to rewrite in the interests of good English and clear thinking.

　　Although he was the grandest of grandees, Curzon had a deep love for India's peoples and their culture, and was appalled at the arrogance of most Anglo-Indians. He was distressed to discover that although 84 Indians had been killed by Europeans during the last 20 years alone, only two Europeans had been hanged for murder since 1857. 'You can hardly credit the sympathy with wrong-doing there is here – even among the highest,' he wrote, 'provided that the malefactor is an Englishman.'[3] Shortly after his arrival in India, infantrymen of the West Kent Regiment raped an old woman near Rangoon. As usual, the military closed ranks to protect the offenders. Curzon reacted by having the regiment posted to Aden, always regarded as a punishment station because of its isolation and unbearable heat.

　　In 1902, when drunken troopers of the 9th Lancers beat an Indian to death outside the gates of their barracks, Curzon was again convinced that the officers were covering up. The 9th Lancers was one of the smartest regiments in the British army. Its officers came from the highest families in Britain, with powerful connections. But Curzon remained oblivious to all threats and pressures, even from the king-emperor himself. 'The argument seems to be that a native's life does not count; and that any crime ought to be concealed and almost even condoned sooner than bring discredit to the army,' he wrote to the commander-in-chief, Field Marshal Lord Roberts. 'I have set my face like flint against such iniquity.'[4] He ordered that since they refused to produce the individuals responsible, the whole regiment must be punished. A severe reprimand was issued, all leave was cancelled for nine months – officers were even recalled from England – and as the ultimate disgrace, sentries from a more plebeian regiment were posted outside each barrack block. There was a huge outcry from Anglo-Indians, their newspapers ranted and raved, but Curzon was unmoved – unlike Ripon during the Ilbert Bill controversy, he did not give a fig what people thought about him.

When the British government asked Curzon to provide 20,000 Indians as indentured labourers for railway construction in South Africa, he refused, siding instead with an Indian lawyer in Durban, a certain M.K. Gandhi, who was campaigning for the rights of Indians in South Africa. Many Indians, Curzon said, found the concept of the British empire disreputable, because 'in practice it means to India a full share of the battles and burdens of Empire, but uncommon little of the privileges and rights'.[5] Gandhi could hardly have put it better himself.

Curzon's achievements on behalf of India were considerable. He improved the economy by encouraging inward investment from Britain and creating a Department of Commerce and Industry, with its own member of the Executive Council. He created a separate Department of Agriculture with a modern research station, and pushed through vast irrigation projects in the arid semi-desert regions, which increased irrigated land by 6.5 million acres. In fact, most of the major works of the twentieth century were originated in his time. He freed the railways from the Public Works Department and enabled them to add another 6,000 miles of track to the existing network. His proposals for reforms of the police and the administration, which only came into effect after his departure, paved the way to provincial self-government. He drove through educational reforms increasing primary and secondary schooling, personally drafting all 150 resolutions at the conference of educationalists which he called. And, perhaps most memorably for the future, he resurrected some of India's past by revitalizing the archaeological department: as well as discovering lost treasures, it rescued many known monuments that were in terminal decay, including the Taj Mahal, Fatehpur Sikri, the Pearl Mosque in Lahore, the palace at Mandalay, and the temples at Khajuraho.

By any standards, Curzon's successes were impressive. His blunders, however, were equally monumental, particularly in Calcutta, where he made no secret of his deep distrust of its educated élite. He introduced a postgraduate faculty and a residential system in Calcutta University, but made enemies of the bhadralok by interfering in their control of higher education, which they regarded as a deliberate attack on the new nationalism. The university's administration, he declared with his usual lack of tact, had 'fallen into the hands of a coterie of obscure native lawyers who regard educational questions from a political point of view'. He then added insult to injury by telling students at the university: 'I hope I am making no false or arrogant claim when I say that the highest ideal of truth is to a large extent a western conception.' And as final proof of his disdain, he effectively abolished the representative government which the city had enjoyed since 1876, by reducing the number of elected members on Calcutta's 75-man municipal council from 50 to 25, thereby ensuring a permanent majority for the official members with their chairman's deciding vote.

Curzon pacified the Pathan and Afghan frontiers, and created a new province to administer the region. But in doing so, he caused deep and lasting resentments in the Punjab, from whose territory the North-West Frontier Province was carved. Pathologically suspicious of Russia, he sent a military expedition under the command of a personal friend, Major Francis Younghusband, on what was, in effect, an invasion of defenceless Tibet, which was disavowed by the home government. The same Russophobia led him to inflame the Afghans again with incursions into their territory and interference in their affairs: further trouble was only averted by Curzon's acting replacement when he returned to London on leave at the end of his first term as viceroy.

Curzon's lack of political nous finally caught up with him early in his second term of office. His new commander-in-chief, whom he had personally recommended, was Lord Kitchener, the only man in India – maybe the only man in the whole British empire – whose ego was a match for Curzon's. It was inevitable that they should quarrel, and so they did – over control of the Indian army, and over Kitchener's chagrin at being merely an ex-officio member of the viceroy's Executive Council, while a subordinate officer sat on it as military member. It had always been thus, but Kitchener took it as a personal affront. In the increasingly bitter row that developed, he enlisted the support of the prime minister, the king, and the ambitious but undistinguished secretary of state, St John Brodrick. Brodrick had been at school and at Oxford with Curzon, and had resented living constantly in his shadow. No doubt he had experienced many of the slights which Curzon habitually inflicted on lesser mortals. In October 1903, however, when he was appointed secretary of state, he had become Curzon's immediate superior. With great relish, he sided with Kitchener. Curzon took umbrage, and resigned.

The fight with Kitchener and Brodrick may have seemed too piffling an affair to have brought down such a glittering star. But by then Curzon was in deep trouble over something far more serious: the partition of Bengal.

The Bengal presidency was a huge, unwieldy province of 189,900 square miles and 78.5 million souls, more than a quarter of the entire population of the country. Besides historic Bengal, it included Bihar, Orissa and Chota Nagpur, and was undoubtedly too big for one governor to rule. For 20 years, the civil servants had been talking about dividing up this cumbersome beast to make it more easily manageable. Curzon, typically, decided it was time to stop talking and act. In April 1902, he wrote to the secretary of state about possible boundary changes, pointing out among other things that the eastern districts of Bengal had long been neglected and that the province of Assam was, in contrast to its giant neighbour, too small for efficient administration.

A few days after Curzon had written his letter, a file arrived on his desk crammed with papers from departmental discussions that had been going on without his knowledge. Curzon was furious. But, being Curzon, he did not rant. Instead, he penned one of his most famous caustic comments:

> For fourteen months it never occurred to a single human being in the Departments to mention the matter or to suggest that it should be mentioned. Round and round like the diurnal revolution of the earth went the file, stately, solemn, sure and slow; and now in due season it has completed its orbit and I am invited to register the concluding stage. How can I bring home to those who are responsible the gravity of the blunder ... ?[6]

In Curzon's eyes, the 'blunder' was the delay in involving him in the discussions. For the Raj, the blunder was dividing Bengal. The plan looked simple on paper: to create two new provinces, Bengal and East Bengal, by a line drawn down the centre of the old one just east of Calcutta and the Hughli river — almost exactly the boundary of present-day Bangladesh. Assam would be added to the eastern half, which would then have a population of about 31 million. Western Bengal, with a population of 54 million, would include Bihar, Chota Nagpur and Orissa. Curzon saw no need to consult or consider Indian opinion. The division seemed a logical solution to a long-standing administrative problem, admirably satisfying his passion for efficiency.

Logic and efficiency, however, were the last things on the minds of the Hindus of Bengal, who were convinced that the partition was a deliberate and dastardly plot to destroy their power base. They would be reduced to a minority in East Bengal, which would have 18 million Muslims and only 12 million Hindus. And while the new Bengal would have a clear Hindu majority, its 17 million Bengali speakers would be vastly outnumbered in their own land by 37 million speaking Hindi or Oriya.

It is hard to believe that Curzon was unaware of the political implications of the partition, but it is a mark of his political naivity that he chose to disregard them. He later dismissed contemptuously the suggestion that he was pursuing the policy of divide and rule: 'It is a calumny so preposterous that it scarcely seems worthy of notice.'[7] Curzon believed that the damage partition would do to the Congress was merely a convenient side effect. His principal civil servants, however, realized it was a very significant factor. H.H. Risley, the home secretary in the government of India, said: 'Bengal united is power. Bengal divided, will pull several different ways. That is what the Congress leaders feel: their apprehensions are perfectly correct and they form one of the great merits of the scheme ... one of our main objects is to split up and thereby weaken a solid body of opponents to our rule.'[8]

The proposal was made public on 3 December 1903, and immediately provoked a tidal wave of dissent. Within the first two months, more than 500 protest meetings were held in East Bengal alone, mostly in Dacca, and nearly 50,000 pamphlets were distributed all over Bengal. More meetings packed the town hall and every open space in Calcutta. Hundreds of petitions, some of them signed by as many as 70,000 people, were presented. The campaign, using all the lessons learned from the Anglo-Indians' battle against the Ilbert Bill, was led by Surendranath Banerjea and his newspaper, the *Bengalee*, earning him the nickname 'Surrender-not Bengal'.

Curzon seemed astonished by the outcry, but remained convinced that it would die away. Bengalis, he observed loftily, 'howl until a thing is settled and then they accept it'. This time, however, they would not accept it, and the howls did not die away after the partition was put into effect on 16 October 1905. Even so, Curzon tried to ignore them. 'If we are weak enough to yield to their clamour now,' he counselled Brodrick in London, 'we shall not be able to dismember or reduce Bengal again; and you will be cementing and solidifying a force already formidable and certain to be of increasing trouble in the future.'[9]

Partition came like a political gift from heaven for Congress, which had been fading fast under an ineffectual moderate leadership. Gokhale, elected president in 1905, seized the opportunity to rally his members in his opening address at that year's session in Benares. 'A cruel wrong has been inflicted on our Bengalee brethren, and the whole country has been stirred to its deepest depths in sorrow and resentment,' he told them. And there was not a man present who did not share his indignation.

Gokhale's speech may have been stirring, but it was far from the truth. The whole country was not in the depths of sorrow and resentment: the 18 million Muslims of East Bengal were delighted. While the Hindus were mourning the day of partition with a *hartal* in Calcutta, Muslims in Dacca were celebrating with prayers of thanksgiving. Ninety per cent of Bengali Muslims were poor peasants who had converted *en masse* from the lowest orders of Hinduism in earlier centuries, and they were still despised by caste Hindus. They looked forward with relief to escaping from the political and economic domination of Calcutta and Hindu landlords, lawyers and money-lenders, declaring that they 'would be spared many oppressions which they had hitherto had to endure from Hindus'.[10]

In a visit to Dacca before partition, Curzon had promised Muslims 'the preponderating voice in the province', giving them 'a unity which they have not enjoyed since the days of the old Mussulman Viceroys and Kings'. Dacca would be transformed from a sleepy town in the *mofussil*, the rural backwaters, into their own thriving provincial capital. Chittagong would emerge from the giant shadow of Calcutta to become an important port in its own right, serving the new province's trade. It sounded good, and the Muslims grabbed it gratefully. Over the next 12 months, meetings all over the province adopted memorials to the new secretary of state, Lord Morley, thanking him for declaring, in the face of growing Hindu agitation, that the partition was 'a settled fact'.[11]

Most Hindus, however, refused to accept that the partition was permanent. The Congress was still, of course, overwhelmingly Hindu – only 20 out of the 756 delegates at Benares were Muslims. It had always been a predominantly Brahman club, but now Hindus of all castes began looking to it to lead the agitation for the reversal of the partition. With an immediate, popular issue to fight for, its image was transformed almost overnight from an élite talking shop into a national political movement. As one East Bengali provincial Congress leader, Abdul Rasul – one of its few Muslims – put it the following April: 'What we could not have accomplished in 50 or 100 years, the great disaster, the partition of Bengal, has done for us in six months. Its fruits have been the great national movement known as the *swadeshi* movement.'[12]

Swadeshi, which literally means 'of our own country', was a new and powerful weapon fashioned by Tilak and the Extremists. The polite constitutional methods of Gokhale and the Moderates – speeches, press campaigns, petitions – which Tilak scathingly described as 'mendicancy', had clearly failed. It was time for something stronger – a boycott of foreign goods.

The *swadeshi* movement began with a boycott resolution passed at a public meeting in Calcutta Town Hall on 7 August 1905. Gokhale tried to restrict it to Bengal, but Tilak took it to Bombay and Poona, and Lala Lajpat Rai, leader of the Hindu revivalist organization Arya Samaj, took it to his native Punjab. Even moderates like Surendranath Banerjea toured the country urging people to boycott Lancashire cloth and Liverpool salt. Throughout India, people made bonfires of their British material and clothing, while Indian-owned cotton mills in Bombay, Ahmedabad and Nagpur worked flat out trying to meet the unprecedented demand for *swadeshi* cloth. There was even a revival of the old cottage industry of hand-spinning and weaving.

Swadeshi was a movement the Indian middle classes could support wholeheartedly, since it called for passive resistance, with no riots, no violence and no damage to property. None supported it more wholeheartedly than the mill owners and industrialists, who stood to make fortunes from the sudden boom. As prices of home-produced goods rose, so too did complaints of profiteering. But these were soon forgotten as wearing home-produced cottons, even though they were of poorer quality than imported fabrics, became a badge of pride. *Swadeshi* was not limited to cottons, of course: other imports from Britain such as sugar, soap, chemicals, glassware, shoes, matches and metal hardware, were replaced by home-produced goods. If there were immense profits, at least they were being made by Indians, and not by British companies, and the money was staying in India.

Swadeshi caught the imagination of the Hindu population as nothing had before. Sections of the community who had never taken any interest in politics joined in, workers and the lower middle classes in towns and cities, students – even women came out of their homes for the first time to join in processions and picketing. Women refused to wear foreign bangles. Washermen refused to launder clothes made from British cloth. Cobblers refused to mend British-made shoes. Students and schoolchildren refused to write on British paper. Priests refused to accept temple offerings made from British sugar. The new spirit of nationalism was spurred on by the news that an Asian nation, Japan, had inflicted a crushing defeat on a European power, Russia, killing 200,000 Russian soldiers in a great land battle at Mukden, Inner Mongolia, on 10 March, and wiping out the Imperial Russian Navy in the straits of Tsushima on 28 May. 'The Russo-Japanese War had created a wave of enthusiasm among the Asiatic nations,' G.D. Birla, founder of the Birla commercial and industrial empire, recalled later, 'and India did not escape this surge. As a child my sympathies were definitely with Japan, and the ambition of seeing India free began to excite me.'[13]

While Birla was dreaming the dreams of youth, India's other great industrial dynasty, the Tata family, was practising *swadeshi* on the grand scale by building India's first iron and steel works on a rural site in west Bengal. They named the town that grew up around it Jamshedpur, after the founder of the dynasty, Jamshed N. Tata, another of Bombay's remarkable Parsi community, who had already made a great fortune from cotton mills in Bombay and Nagpur, and who had died in 1904. His sons received no government help or encouragement in building the new works. For technical advice and equipment, they turned to America – a small irony, since the idea of *swadeshi* had been inspired by the Chinese boycott of American goods started earlier that year in protest at US domination of the Chinese economy and mistreatment of Chinese immigrants in America. From this point on, the Tata family became Congress's main financial supporters, to be joined later by the Birlas.

As the *swadeshi* movement gathered pace, it came more and more under the control of Tilak and the Extremists, and more and more Hindu in character. The Bengali festival of Durga Puja, always one of the highlights of the Hindu year, was celebrated in 1905 with greater intensity than ever. Fifty thousand devotees gathered at the temple of Kali, at Kalighat in south Calcutta – the malevolent Kali and the demoness Durga are both forms of the mother goddess, consort of the great god Shiva, the creator and destroyer of life. There, in the heart of a sudden, violent storm, they solemnly vowed to Durga never to buy British goods, never to use British shops, and never to employ Britons. As the priests dismissed each batch of worshippers, they enjoined them: 'Swear to serve your Motherland! Offer your lives to her service! Worship the Motherland before all deities!'[14]

The idea of the motherland as a deity to be worshipped was anathema to Muslims, bound by the Qur'an to worship only the one true god, Allah. Nevertheless, it became a central tenet of Congress thinking, emphasized by the choice of the poem *Bande Mataram* (*Hail to thee, Mother*), set to music by Rabindranath Tagore, as the Congress anthem:

> Hail to thee, Mother!
> Rich with thy hurrying streams,
> Bright with thy orchard gleams,
> Cool with thy winds of delight,
> Dark fields waving, Mother of might,
> Mother free, Glory of moonlight dreams,
> Over thy branches and lordly streams –
> Clad in thy blossoming trees,
> Mother, giver of ease,
> Laughing low and sweet!
> Mother I kiss thy feet,
> Speaker sweet and low,
> Mother to thee I bow!

Bande Mataram came from Bankim Chaterjee's anti-Muslim novel, *Anandamath*, a fact that served to alienate Muslims still further. Before long, there was a steep increase in communal rioting. Muslims refused to support what they saw as a Hindu boycott and insisted on continuing to buy and sell British goods. Hindu agitators tried to stop them, and to force Muslim shopkeepers to close their businesses and declare a *hartal*. Muslim meetings were broken up, Muslim leaders were insulted, and Muslim workers assaulted. Passions spilled over, and violence and bloodshed followed.

It was against this background that in October 1906, a delegation of 35 Muslim princes and nobles from various parts of India, led by the young Aga Khan, travelled to the summer capital of Simla to meet the viceroy, Lord Minto. A Tory landowner, Minto had been appointed in the dying gasp of Arthur Balfour's Conservative government, just two weeks before it was swept away by the electoral landslide that carried the Liberals back into power under Sir Henry Campbell-Bannerman. Because of the unrest in Bengal, Campbell-Bannerman felt it would be unwise to replace the viceroy so soon. It proved to be a disastrous decision, for Minto, always seeking the quiet life, was happy to leave the governing of India to Kitchener and the ICS machine, both of whom believed that the only way of dealing with political turbulence was savage repression.

Lord Minto, whose great-grandfather had been governor-general from 1807 to 1813, was no Curzon, but one of the most pragmatic, as well as the oldest, at 60, of all the viceroys. He was best described by Sir Harcourt Butler, twice governor of the United Provinces and once of Burma, as 'not a great man ... but a very straight one who saw things simply and clearly and saw them whole'.[15] Minto had recently been governor-general of Canada, but was best known as a horseman rejoicing in the nickname 'Mr Rolly' – his main claim to fame being that he had ridden in a steeplechase at Sandown only a few months after breaking his neck riding in the Grand National. His boss as secretary of state in London was the 70-year-old Lord Morley, a Liberal intellectual who, his opponents claimed, had spent his life writing books about books.

Politically, John Morley was a good choice for India. He knew and loved the country, and in his first parliamentary speech as secretary of state, he announced his determination to bring about meaningful reforms which would allow Indians to play a greater part in government. In 1906, he invited Congress president Gokhale to London for lengthy discussions, along with a former president, R.C. Dutt, who was then lecturer in Indian history at University College, London. It all seemed too good to be true – a secretary of state actually listening to what Indians had to say. And so it was. For all his good intentions, Morley was in London while Minto and the machine were in India, where they found no difficulty in sabotaging most of his efforts at liberalization.

The Muslim delegation to Simla on 1 October 1906 was a response to Gokhale's visit to London, as well as to events in Bengal. The leaders wanted to put their point of view to Minto, to counterbalance any pro-Congress bias from London. Fearful of Morley's plans to introduce liberal parliamentary reforms, they pleaded with the viceroy to safeguard the interests of India's Muslims. 'We Muhammadans', they told him, 'are a distinct community with additional interests of our own which are not shared by other communities, and these have hitherto suffered from the fact that they have not been adequately represented.'[16] Echoing Sir Syed Ahmed Khan's warnings of majority rule, they demanded – with exquisite courtesy in an address inscribed on vellum – reserved positions for Muslims in the services, courts and administration, and reserved seats in any elected councils. Furthermore, they wanted separate electorates, with only registered Muslims voting for Muslim candidates.

Minto welcomed the delegation and its proposals. He praised Aligarh and its achievements, thanked the Muslims of East Bengal and Assam 'for the moderation and self-restraint they have shown', and assured them that they could rely on 'British justice and fair play'. 'The Muhammadan community,' he declared, 'may rest assured that their political rights and interests as a community will be safeguarded by any administrative reorganization with which I am concerned.'[17] At the tea-party that afternoon in the grounds of Viceregal Lodge members of the delegation told Lady Minto: 'Now we feel the viceroy is our friend.' Later that evening, a British official told her that the result of the meeting was 'nothing less than the pulling back of 62 million of people from joining the ranks of the seditious opposition'.[18]

Flushed with their success in Simla, the Muslim leaders decided it was time they had a political organization of their own, as a counterweight to Congress. That year, Aligarh's Muhammadan Educational Conference was holding its annual meeting in Dacca, and the city's leading landowner, Nawab Salimullah Khan, suggested that a 'Muslim All-India Conference' should be convened at the same time. Fifty-eight delegates from every corner of the sub-continent met in Dacca's Shah Bagh (Royal Garden) on 30 December 1986, where they founded the All-India Muslim League.

The League's main objects were declared to be:

(a) To promote among the Musalmans of India feelings of loyalty to the British Government and to remove any misconceptions that may arise as to the intentions of Government with regard to any of its measures
(b) To protect and advance the political rights and interests of the Musalmans of India and respectfully represent their needs and aspirations to Government
(c) To prevent the rise among Musalmans of India of any feelings of hostility towards other communities without prejudice to other objects of the League.[19]

These modest ambitions reflected the League's character as an élite upper-class club, restricted to a membership of 400 conservative aristocrats and wealthy landowners, with just a few lawyers, journalists and academics. The Aga Khan was rewarded for his financial support with the honorary position of permanent president.

For most ordinary Muslims, the League held little interest, and so it remained until the eve of the First World War. But some were actively opposed to its aims. One man in particular, the Aga Khan complained later, 'came out in bitter hostility toward all that I and my friends had done and were trying to do. He was the only well-known Muslim to take this attitude ... He said that our principle of separate electorates was dividing the nation against itself.'[20] The man the Aga Khan described as 'our doughtiest opponent in 1906', was a rising new

star of Congress. His name was M.A. Jinnah, the man who would one day make
the Muslim League his own.

At the time of the founding of the Muslim League, Mohammad Ali Jinnah had,
by his own reckoning, just celebrated his thirtieth birthday. His own reckoning
because there was always some doubt about his exact age: the municipality of
Karachi did not issue birth certificates until 1879, and while Hindus note every
detail of a child's birth so that an accurate horoscope can be cast, Indian Muslims,
scornful of such superstition, were always careless of birth dates. When the need
arose, Jinnah settled for 25 December 1876. His choice of Christmas Day may
have reflected the brief time he spent as a pupil at the exclusive Christian Mission
High School on Lawrence Road, Karachi – the register at his first school, the Sind
Madressa-tul-Islam, gives his date of birth as 20 October 1875.

      Whatever the true date, Jinnah was born Mohammad Ali Jinnahbhai, the
first child of Jinnahbhai Poonja and his wife Mithibai, in Karachi. The family
were members of the Shiite Khoja sub-sect, disciples of the Ismaili Aga Khan, so
Jinnah started life as a member of a minority sect of the minority branch of India's
minority religion, which may well explain why he was never afraid of standing
alone.

      The Ismailis came originally from Persia between the tenth and sixteenth
centuries, some fleeing from persecution, others travelling to India as missionaries,
for they were always a proselityzing sect. They converted large numbers of Hindus
in Gujarat and the Punjab, but their greatest successes were among the Afghan
tribe of Lohanas, who formed the basis of the Khoja community. Jinnah claimed,
however, that his male ancestors were Rajputs from the Punjab, one of whom
migrated to the Kathiawar peninsula, a region of small princely states between
Bombay and Karachi. He married a Khoja bride and settled in her village of
Paneli, in the small state of Gondal. By coincidence, this was barely 30 miles south
of Rajkot, the home of Mohandas Gandhi.

      The Khojas were a mercantile community, far more outgoing and
adaptable than most Indian Muslims. With a sharp eye for business and generally
keen intelligence, many of them built up considerable fortunes through trade.
Jinnah's father was one who did so, when he and his new bride moved in the mid-
1870s from Paneli to the port city of Karachi. Although it still had a population
of under 50,000, Karachi was just starting to boom following the opening of the
Suez Canal. Jinnahbhai took a second-floor apartment in the three-storey Wazir
Mansion on Newnham Road, centre of the cotton market, where he quickly
developed a thriving import-export business handling a wide range of produce –
raw cotton, wool, hides, oil-seed, grain and so on going out, and cotton piece-
goods from Lancashire, metalware from Birmingham, refined sugar from

Liverpool and London, coming in. Before long, his profits were so high that he was making a second fortune as a banker providing finance for his customers.

By the time his eldest son, affectionately known in the family as Mamad, was six, Jinnahbhai could afford to hire a private tutor to teach him reading, writing and mathematics. But although he was highly intelligent, Mamad was never a willing scholar. He was 'indifferent' to most subjects, 'positively loathed' arithmetic, and was always eager to leave his books to play marbles or *guli danda* (tip-cat) in the street with his friends. At the age of nine, he was sent to school, but his attitude did not improve and he fell behind, regularly failing his examinations.

In 1887, Jinnahbhai's only sister, Manbai, a sparkling and witty woman known to her adoring nephew as Auntie Poofi, came on a visit from her home in Bombay. Manbai was married to an even more successful Khoja merchant than Jinnahbhai, and lived in some style in the bustling, cosmopolitan city. Mamad was entranced by Auntie Poofi's stories of Bombay, and she, in turn, doted on her bright, handsome young nephew. No one knows whose idea it was that he should go to live with her – no doubt aunt and nephew colluded enthusiastically – but Jinnahbhai clearly felt that it would at least remove his son from the bad influence of his playmates. It seems to have worked, at least in part – Mamad managed to pass his fourth grade Gujarati exams at his Bombay school, qualifying him to move on to first standard English. But his mathematics remained woefully poor.

Bombay was a revelation to the young Jinnah. With its white crescent beaches, fringed with royal palm trees and elegant buildings, its sparkling bays dotted with islands, it was India's most beautiful port, as well as its most cosmopolitan city. Its Gothic monuments, its court houses and government buildings all exuded confidence in the future. Its central railway station, the brand new Victoria Terminus, was an exuberant celebration of modern technology teeming with multi-national crowds on their way to and from the furthest reaches of the empire. The boy from Karachi fell in love with the sheer energy of the place. After six months, he was called back home, as his mother could bear the separation from her 'darling son' no longer. But by then the damage had been done – he was to remain hopelessly smitten with Bombay for the rest of his life.

Back in Karachi, Mamad found school more boring than ever. An excellent rider, he regularly cut classes to gallop off across the desert sands of Sind with his friend Karim Kassim, on the Arab horses his father had bought, along with several carriages, to show off his success. Eventually, Mamad's name was withdrawn from the school register, because of his 'long absences'. He had still not matriculated, and was struggling to pass fourth standard English.

Jinnahbhai began to despair of his wayward son. He discussed the problem with an English friend, Sir Frederick Leigh Croft, a 32-year-old baronet who was general manager of Douglas Graham and Company, Karachi's leading

British managing agency, with which Jinnahbhai's own firm had close connections. Sir Frederick, who liked the sparky boy and considered he had potential despite his poor academic record, came up with a radical suggestion. He could arrange a three-year commercial apprenticeship for Mamad with Graham's head office in London. At the end of that time, he would return to India, well qualified to join his father's business.

London sounded even more exciting than Bombay, but Mamad's poor mother was heartbroken at the prospect of losing him for three whole years. She wept and pleaded for weeks, but it was hopeless – even at the age of 15 it was almost impossible to persuade Jinnah to change his mind once he had made it up. Eventually she gave up, on condition that he married a good Khoja girl before he sailed. As Jinnah's sister Fatima recalled later: 'England was a dangerous country to send an unmarried and handsome young man like her son. Some English girl might lure him into marriage and that would be a tragedy for the Jinnah Poonja family.'[21] Jinnah hesitated, but then 'behaved like an obedient son' out of regard for his mother's feelings, and consented to a traditional arranged marriage. Mithibai found a good Khoja girl, 14-year-old Emibai, from Paneli, and the wedding took place there. The celebrations lasted several days, and would have gone on even longer, but Jinnahbhai was anxious to return to his business, and Mamad, with an authority that surprised the girl's parents in one who was still only 15, overruled their objections and left with his father, taking his new wife with him. Only days later, he sailed from Bombay on a P&O liner, never to see either his wife or mother again.

The first few months in London, shrouded in the fogs and frosts of winter, were not particularly happy for the teenage Mamad. 'I was young and lonely. Far from home,' he wrote later. 'Except for some employees at Grahams, I did not know a soul, and the immensity of London as a city weighed heavily on my solitary life ... But I soon got settled to life in London, and I began to like it before long.'[22] He quickly became Anglicized, shortening his name from Jinnahbhai to Jinnah, and discarding his long yellow Sindhi coat for the first of his many Savile Row suits, stiff-collared shirts and silk neckties. For the rest of his life, he was always the very model of sartorial elegance – in his later years he had as many as 200 immaculately tailored suits in his wardrobe and prided himself on never wearing the same tie twice. He even took to wearing a monocle. After living in a succession of hotels and rooming houses, he became a lodger with a widow, Mrs F.E. Page-Drake, and her daughter at 35 Russell Road, backing on to the District Railway immediately behind the recently opened exhibition halls of Olympia.

There is some confusion about the exact timing of Jinnah's arrival in London, as there is about all his early life. But he is believed to have arrived in 1892, in time to hear the heated debates in Parliament over the Indian Councils

Act, and to witness the general election that year which swept the Liberals to power and put Gladstone in Downing Street for the fourth time. Jinnah is said to have helped as a volunteer in the election campaign of Dadabhai Naoroji, who scraped home in Central Finsbury by three votes, earning the nickname 'Mr Narrow-Majority'. Whether Jinnah actually worked for Naoroji at that time or not, he certainly sat in the public gallery of the House of Commons and 'thrilled' to hear his maiden speech.

Naoroji became Jinnah's hero. When the defeated Tory premier Lord Salisbury sneered at Naoroji – a fair-skinned Parsi – as a 'black man', Jinnah reacted furiously. 'If Dadabhai was black, I was darker,' he told his sister later. 'And if this was the mentality of the British politicians, then we would never get a fair deal from them. From that day I have been an uncompromising enemy of all forms of colour bar and racial prejudice.'[23]

During his four years in London, Jinnah became an ardent disciple of Naoroji, imbibing his philosophy of secular liberal nationalism. But Naoroji was not his only guide. His other great hero was the future secretary of state for India, 'Honest John' Morley, Gladstone's most trusted lieutenant and a disciple of John Stuart Mill. Morley was at that time leading the fight in Parliament for Irish Home Rule, an issue which caught Jinnah's imagination, but it was Morley's book, *On Compromise*, which 'like a flame' burned into his mind Morley's belief that truth is the most important of all principles.

Jinnah had been bitten by the political bug, and began to sit in the gallery of the House of Commons whenever he could – fortunately, many of the best debates took place in the evenings. At weekends, he joined the throng at Speakers' Corner in Hyde Park, where orators on their soapboxes enjoyed the traditional freedom to say what they liked, how they liked. It was all heady stuff. By comparison, his work in the counting house of Graham's, which consisted mainly of sitting on a high stool copying columns of figures from one ledger to another, was soulless drudgery. It was worse than being back at school. Inevitably, he rebelled after only a few months, but this time he did not seek escape by riding off into the desert. Instead, he turned to the law, which was clearly the passport to success in politics, both in Britain and in India. He applied for admission to the Inns of Court, passed the examination on 25 May 1893, and enrolled at Lincoln's Inn, the Alma Mater of John Morley, who was elected a bencher that year.

Back in Karachi, Jinnahbhai Poonja was furious that Jinnah had decided to abandon his business apprenticeship. But there was little he could do about it. Before his son had left India, he had opened a bank account for him in London, and deposited enough money in it to cover his living costs for three years. 'He thought business success is as capricious as a wind; it can change its direction without notice,' Fatima Jinnah recalled. 'As it turned out, the prudence of a businessman, who had come up the hard way, proved to be highly beneficial, and without it my brother's career in London might have terminated abruptly.'[24]

Jinnahbhai was ruined by the world collapse in the value of silver between 1892 and 1894, following the discovery of vast new deposits in America. While sterling, which was on the gold standard, was strengthened, the Indian silver rupee dropped in value by more than a half, halting investment and triggering a deep depression that was aggravated by widespread famine and plague.

As headstrong as ever, Jinnah ignored his father's letters ordering him to return home to help save the failing business. To make sure he would not weaken, he paid all his fees for admission to the bar in advance, with one cheque for £138 19s. Then he settled down to three years of study, following his pupil master in chambers and in court, and taking an active part in discussions with benchers, barristers and fellow students in the great hall of Lincoln's Inn. Like many another political figure, he made good use of the circular reading room of the British Museum, where he devoured political biographies and the works of men such as Burke, John Stuart Mill and the radical John Bright, the Quaker champion of electoral reform and free trade. During almost 40 years in Parliament, Bright had fought for 'an end to social, political and religious inequalities between individuals and between peoples'. This was a cause to which the young Jinnah could subscribe with all his heart, and Bright became another of his lasting heroes.

Jinnah was called to the bar on 11 May 1896. But his future was immediately put in doubt by another of his impulsive changes of direction. If his decision to abandon business in favour of the law had upset his father, his new choice of career almost caused a permanent rift: he wanted to go on the stage. A story that he played the lead in an amateur production of *Romeo and Juliet* is unsubstantiated, but he admitted years later that his secret ambition had been 'to play the role of Romeo at the Old Vic'.[25] After hearing him read, a theatrical manager offered him a job on the spot – Jinnah was extremely handsome and his great presence must have been as obvious on stage as it was in a courtroom or a political council.

Having signed a contract, Jinnah wrote to his father asking for his blessing, assuring him that he would be able to support himself as an actor and arguing that 'the law was a lingering profession where success was uncertain'. Jinnahbhai was horrified, and wrote a long letter pleading with his son to change his mind. The same letter, it seems, included the shattering news that Jinnah's mother and wife had both died. According to Jinnah himself, one phrase in his father's letter – 'Do not be a traitor to the family' – achieved what had always been impossible.[26] For once, he backed down, persuaded the manager to release him from his contract, and packed his bags. He had somehow managed to save £71 1s 10d from the sum his father had deposited in his name three years before – a testimony to the habitual thrift which he practised even after he had become hugely rich. With that and his bar certificate he sailed home on 16 July 1896, heading not for Karachi but for Bombay.

Jinnah was enrolled as a barrister in the high court of Bombay on 24 August 1896, either 10 months after or four months before his twentieth birthday. Either way, he was still very young. He rented a room in the Apollo Railway Hotel on Charni Road, within an easy walk of the high court, and waited for his first brief. It proved to be a long wait. For the first three years, he did little more than deal with litigation against his father following the liquidation of his business. Gradually, however, Jinnah began to build a reputation, and in 1900, an influential friend introduced him to John Molesworth MacPherson, the acting advocate-general, who gave him a job in his office.

From being a struggling young unknown, Jinnah was suddenly transported to the heart of the Bombay legal scene. Only a few months later, he heard that a position as one of the city's four magistrates was about to become vacant. Seeing an empty Victoria cab passing the window, he dashed out, grabbed it, and drove straight to the office of Sir Charles Ollivant, the judicial member of the governor's council, who was so impressed by his energy and ambition that he gave him the post on a six-month trial basis. It was a testing but invaluable experience for the young lawyer, sitting on the bench day after day dealing with a wide variety of cases. Jinnah acquitted himself well. At the end of his six months, Ollivant offered him a permanent place, at the respectable salary of 1,500 rupees a month. But Jinnah did not want respectability, he wanted fame and fortune. He turned down the offer, with thanks, telling Ollivant: 'I will soon be able to earn that much in a single day.'[27]

Now Jinnah began to thrive as a barrister, impressing everyone with the sharpness of his legal mind and dazzling courtroom performances making full use of his talents as an actor manqué. Soon, he was making enough money to support his father in retirement and pay for his sister Fatima's education, first as a boarder at Bombay's Bandra Convent School and then as a dental student at Calcutta University. Through his Auntie Poofi and her husband, he was able to move easily in Bombay society, making valuable contacts and friends not only among Muslims but also among Hindus, Parsis and Christians. Many of them were influential members of Congress, such as Justice Tyabji, who had been its third president back in 1887. Tyabji, now aged 57 and still very active, was a secular liberal modernist, and a Khoja, like Jinnah himself. It may have been to please him that Jinnah changed his religious allegiance, leaving the Aga Khan's Ismaili sect and joining the more orthodox Shiite Isna Asharis, of which Tyabji was a member. In any case, Tyabji was happy to take him under his wing.[28] He acquired an even more powerful patron by working for a time in the chambers of the legendary Pherozeshah Mehta, who had also been a protégé of Dadabhai Naoroji while studying for the bar in London in the 1860s.

With friends like Tyabji, Mehta and Naoroji, who had returned to
Bombay in 1896, Jinnah was building a solid base of support for his political
career. By 1904, when Congress met in Bombay, he was ready to make a start.
Although that year's president was an Englishman, Sir Henry Cotton, no one had
any doubt that Mehta was running the show. Anticipating that the next general
election in Britain would bring a Liberal government back to power, Mehta
proposed that Congress should send two delegates to London the following year,
to lobby the Liberal leadership. The two men he suggested were Gokhale and
Jinnah. Gokhale was already a Congress star, of course, but to most delegates
Jinnah was a nobody, and they refused to provide funds for his passage. It didn't
really matter – Mehta had made sure that everyone now knew who Jinnah was. He
had been launched with a suitable splash, clearly marked as a man to watch.

During the following two years, Jinnah worked to establish himself in
Congress, declaring that his aim was to become 'the Muslim Gokhale'. He had
met Gokhale for the first time at the 1904 session, and the two men had become
firm friends. They shared the same approach to the independence struggle: both
wanted India to advance along a strictly constitutional path to secular self-
government. Both believed in Indian rather than Hindu or Muslim nationalism.
Both agreed wholeheartedly with the elder statesman who had befriended them
both, Pherozeshah Mehta, who as Congress president in 1890 had dismissed
Hindu-Muslim conflict as nothing more than 'a convenient decoy to distract
attention and to defer the day of reform'. 'Can anyone doubt,' he had asked, 'that
Sir Syed Ahmed Khan was greater and nobler when he was devoting the great
energies and talents with which he is endowed ... for the benefit of all Indians in
general, than when, as of late, he was preaching a gospel of selfishness and
isolation?'[29]

Jinnah had said nothing in public about the partition of Bengal in 1905.
If he opposed it, it would have been not only because he disapproved of the
communal element involved, but also because he agreed with Gokhale's complaint
that it had been

> concocted in the dark and carried out in the face of the fiercest opposition
> that any Government measure has encountered during the last half-century,
> [and] will always stand as a complete illustration of the worst features of the
> present system of bureaucratic rule – its utter contempt for public opinion,
> its arrogant pretensions to superior wisdom, its reckless disregard of the
> most cherished feelings of the people, the mockery of an appeal to its sense
> of justice, its cool preference of Service interests to those of the governed.[30]

Jinnah had not spoken out against it, but at the 1906 Congress session in

Calcutta, he did so through no less a figure than the grand old man of Indian nationalism, Dadabhai Naoroji himself.

By 1906, the strain between the Moderates and the Extremists was fast approaching breaking point. Gokhale, Mehta and the Moderates had vetoed the election of Tilak as that year's president, and a split had only been avoided by drafting in the 81-year-old Naoroji, to whom not even Tilak dared object. The old man was too weak to make his presidential speech himself, so it was read for him by Gokhale – but it had been largely written by his 'political secretary', Jinnah, who celebrated his thirtieth birthday on the platform.

The speech called the partition 'a bad blunder for England' but one that 'may yet be rectified through agitation'. It went on to call for 'a thorough political union among all the Indian people of all creeds and classes ... They must sink or swim together. Without this union, all efforts will be in vain.' The efforts, the speech announced, were to be directed towards a new goal: no longer merely a share in running the country but 'self-government or *swaraj* like that of the United Kingdom or the Colonies'.[31] In his own maiden speech to the Congress, Jinnah threatened that Bombay would be another Boston, but this time it would not be chests of tea that were thrown into the sea but 'cartloads of live Britishers'.

'No Bombs, No Boons'

By the spring of 1907, Minto and his officials had completed their report on Morley's reform proposals, which were to form the basis of a new Indian Councils Act. As always, the proposals fell far short of Indian demands, but Morley had insisted on taking them further than Minto and the machine wanted. As a mark of his liberal intentions, while the new Act was still being drafted and debated, he appointed two Indian members to his council in Whitehall: a Hindu, K.G. Gupta, who had been an official on Calcutta's Board of Revenue, and a Muslim, S.H. Bilgrami, who had served the Nizam of Hyderabad and was a member of the Muslim League. Gokhale and the Congress moderates applauded the gesture, though not the choice of two such undistinguished individuals – Morley himself admitted that 'their colour is more important than their brains'.[1]

The Moderates were grateful for the proposed reforms. Gokhale, indeed, had helped to draft them during his discussions at the India Office in London, and he knew what could and could not be achieved. He trusted and admired Morley, 'the one friend fighting night and day in our interests'. 'If only our countrymen will have a little more patience, for, say, six months more,' he wrote, 'they will have no cause to regret their confidence in the present Secretary of State.'[2] He believed the new Act would be a significant advance towards eventual self-rule, as indeed it proved to be. The Extremists, on the other hand, dismissed the proposals contemptuously, and the division between the two wings of Congress began to widen alarmingly.

Tilak's Extremist wing had been growing in strength since 1905, and had formed itself into a separate body within Congress, calling itself the New Party. It was led by 'Lal, Bal and Pal' as the militant students liked to chant – Lala Lajpat Rai, the Arya Samaj leader from the Punjab, Bal Gangadhar Tilak himself, and Bipin Chandra Pal, a militant Bengali youth leader, founder and editor of the emotively named journal *Bande Mataram*. They and their followers now regarded the rescinding of Bengal's partition as 'the pettiest and narrowest of all political objectives.'[3] No longer content with *swadeshi* alone, they wanted a revolutionary struggle to achieve *swaraj* at once.

The revolutionary struggle was to start with a full-scale non-co-operation movement, extending the boycott on British-made goods to all British institutions, including government schools and colleges, law courts, council chambers and all forms of government service, and the return of honours and titles. The aim was to

> make the administration under present conditions impossible by an organized refusal to do anything which shall help either the British Commerce in the exploitation of the country or British officialdom in the administration of it ... If the *chowkidar* [watchman], the constable, the deputy and the *munsif* [junior judge] and the clerk, not to speak of the sepoy, all resign their respective functions, *feringhee* [foreign] rule in the country will come to an end in a moment. No powder and shot will be needed, no sepoys will need to be trained.'[4]

The New Party's intentions were admirably peaceful, but unfortunately most of its followers were hot-headed young men, and their impatience soon spilled over into violence. At the beginning of May, there were riots in Rawalpindi, East Bengal and the Punjab, where Sir Denzil Ibbetson, a close friend of Curzon, had just been appointed lieutenant-governor. Ibbetson believed 'strong medicine' was the only cure for public disorder, and wired Minto for 'emergency' authority to arrest and deport Lala Lajpat Rai and his Sikh associate, Ajit Singh. The two men were whisked away to prison in Mandalay on 6 May, just three days before the fiftieth anniversary of the great revolt of 1857. Morley hated such measures, but Minto insisted that 'the strong hand carries more respect in India than even the recognition of British justice'.[5]

To forestall any violent reaction, Minto then invoked the repressive Police Act of 1861. When Morley heard of this, he stormed around his office in Whitehall shouting to his private secretary: 'No, I can't stand that; *I will not have that.*' But he did nothing, impotent in the face of the machine, which ground inexorably into action. Troops were ordered into Lahore to clamp down on any unrest. The streets were cleared, and agitators were imprisoned without trial, for unspecified 'reasons of state'. District officers were given emergency powers to suspend all public meetings without warning or reason. The editor and proprietor of Lahore's most popular Indian newspaper, the *Punjabee*, were arrested for sedition and sentenced to two years and six months of 'rigorous imprisonment'. An uneasy peace was maintained, but the price was high.

Throughout the rest of 1907, the threat of trouble loomed constantly. It was inflamed by the first chairman of the British Parliamentary Labour Party,

James Keir Hardie, who visited India in September and October, and publicly accused Britain of running India 'like the Czar runs Russia'. It was the Labour Party's first official statement on India, and it set the tone for its policy during the next 40 years. The Anglo-Indians blamed Keir Hardie for the riots that raged through Calcutta for two days, after clashes between students and police. A week later, Minto imposed a nationwide ban on all public meetings.

By December 1907, as the annual meeting of Congress approached, Lala Lajpat Rai was back in circulation again. His exile and imprisonment had made him a national hero, and it was only natural that the New Party should propose him as that year's president. Mehta, Gokhale and the Moderates were no more prepared to accept him than they had Tilak the year before, but this time they had no grand old man to put up in his place. Instead, they proposed a distinguished but unexciting Bengali educator, Dr Rash Behari Ghose, and provoked the crisis that finally tore Congress apart.

The Congress that year was held in the Gujarati seaport of Surat, a stronghold of the Moderates, where Sir Pherozeshah Mehta – he had been knighted by Curzon in 1905 – felt confident he could keep control. He was proved wrong even before the first session got under way. For three days before the opening, the Extremists whipped up feelings against the Moderates at a series of mass meetings. By the time the 1,600 delegates took their seats in the official tent on 26 December, the atmosphere was charged with angry emotion.

As Dr Ghose mounted the rostrum to make his presidential address – which was to be a call for unity and a closing of the ranks – Tilak rose to his feet with a cry of 'Point of order!' He marched on to the platform, intending to announce Lajpat Rai's candidature for the presidency. Several young guards tried to stop him, but Gokhale leapt to his defence, putting his arms about him to protect him. By this time, there was uproar in the tent. Most of the delegates were on their feet, shouting and gesticulating. Someone threw a shoe, which hit first Surendranath Banerjea and then Mehta. From then on it was a free-for-all. Turbans and hats were trampled into the ground. Chairs and fists flew. The police had to be called to clear the tent, and the Surat session of Congress was abandoned. The long-threatened split had become a gaping wound that would not be healed for nine long years. Minto gleefully cabled Morley with the news. 'The Congress collapse,' he said, 'was a great triumph for us.'[6]

Tilak, just as much as Gokhale, regarded the split as a catastrophe for the nationalist movement. He did his best to end it by accepting Dr Ghose as president and promising to work for unity. But it was too late: Mehta and the older moderates were glad of an excuse to be rid of the troublemakers. 'The union of these men with the Congress,' wrote H.A. Wadya, one of Mehta's closest associates, 'is the union of a diseased limb to a healthy body, and the only remedy is surgical severance, if the Congress is to be saved from death by blood poisoning.'[7]

The youth of Bengal had looked to the New Party for leadership. Deprived of its guidance when the party was thrown into complete disarray, they turned to revolutionary terrorism, embracing the politics of the bomb. The heroes of Bankim Chatterjee's novels, Irish nationalists and Russian anarchists became their role models. They formed secret societies based on the worship of Kali and Durga, echoing the long-gone days of *thugi*. The new assassins, however, were far less successful than the thugs. An attempt on the life of the lieutenant-governor of Bengal in 1907 failed miserably. Next, on 30 April 1908 in Muzzafarpur, two young Bengalis, Prafulla Chaki and Kudiram Bose, threw a bomb at a carriage which they believed was carrying a district judge, Douglas Kingsford. Unfortunately, they chose the wrong carriage – it was occupied not by Kingsford, a notorious flogger of dissenting Indians, but by two innocent Englishwomen, who died in the blast. Mortified by their mistake, Chaki shot himself dead. Bose was caught, tried and hanged. Both, of course, became popular national heroes.

British newspapers screamed for vengeance, demanding the arrest and execution of all terrorists; demands that grew even more insistent when a police raid uncovered a cache of arms in Calcutta on 2 May. But in *Kesari*, Tilak leapt to the defence of the assassins, pointing out that the bomb had not been thrown 'because of hatred of any individual, or simply owing to the whim of an irresponsible madman. Even Kudiram, the bomb thrower, himself feels sorry that the innocent women of Mr Kennedy's family fell victims instead of Mr Kingsford.' The young revolutionaries of Bengal, he said, had adopted the tactics of the Russian anarchists 'not for the sake of self-interest but owing to the exasperation produced by the autocratic exercise of power by the unrestrained and powerful white official class'. The Raj, he concluded, had brought destruction upon itself. The only solution was the granting of immediate *swaraj*.[8]

Even in its state of vengeful hysteria, the Raj at first turned a blind eye to Tilak's statements. But when he began describing the bomb as 'magic', 'a sacred formula' and an 'amulet', it was too much. He was arrested for 'seditious writings'. Held without bail, he retained Jinnah to plead for his release – a remarkable choice of advocate for the leader of the Hindu Extremists, but one which testified to the growing stature of the Muslim Moderate lawyer and his open-mindedness in agreeing to represent a political opponent. Not even Jinnah's skilful arguments could move the authorities, however, and Tilak remained in custody until his trial before Mr Justice D.D. Davar at the Third Criminal Sessions of the high court in Bombay on 13 July 1908.

Tilak chose to defend himself in court. It was perhaps just as well: he could hardly have expected Jinnah to pursue his chosen line of defence, which turned on Hindu religious belief. Tilak chose to justify his actions using the concept of *dharma*, the duty laid upon people by their occupation. It was the *dharma* of a king, for example, to rule wisely and well, and that of a warrior to fight bravely. A newspaper editor's *dharma*, Tilak argued, required him to speak freely on public events, without fear or favour. He also pointed out that it was the *dharma* of a jury to defend the freedom of the press. The jury, consisting of seven Europeans and two Parsis, disagreed. They and the judge decided Tilak's *dharma* was to serve six years' imprisonment in Mandalay, where there were few Hindus to be excited by his presence.

With Tilak out of the way, the iron hand of the British authorities clamped ever tighter on the dissidents. New laws suspended trial by jury, increased the penalties for sedition, gave magistrates further powers to close down newspapers and seize their presses, and restricted meetings still further. Literally hundreds of suspected terrorists were rounded up in Bengal, and nine of their leaders were deported. Bipin Chandra Pal and Lala Lajpat Rai escaped to London, though Lajpat Rai moved on to New York, where he scraped a meagre living for several years as a writer.

Several other leading figures retired from the political scene. Some chose the religious life, others left the country, either voluntarily or forcibly – the leader of the movement in Madras, Chidambaram Pillay, was sentenced to transportation for life for making seditious speeches. When the judge at his trial declared that 'there was no lawful occasion, so far as he could see, for any man in the country to make a political speech,' the Anglo-Indians applauded. But Morley, in London, sadly commented: 'This explains Bombs.'[9] For once, he and Tilak were in complete agreement.

The bombs continued, sporadically and with little success. A policeman was shot dead in Calcutta, but four attempts on the life of the viceroy failed. The terrorists' only notable success was in London, where Morley's political aide, Lieutenant-Colonel Sir William Curzon-Wyllie, was shot on 1 July 1909. Minto's comment after the first attempt on his own life seems a masterpiece of British sang-froid: 'I hope that public opinion won't take the unreasonable view that the deeds of a few anarchists are proof of the disloyalty of all India.'[10]

In fact, what Minto said was true. The terrorists represented a minuscule minority of the population of India, which had just been recorded at about 300 million, and their activities were still confined to two centres, Bengal and Maharashtra. As always, the great mass of Indians went quietly about the business of making a living. The tedium of their everyday life was relieved by the occasional Hindu-Muslim riot, but those were essentially domestic affairs, a local form of blood sport, and nothing to do with government.

✽

In the mean time, Morley pressed on with his plans for reform, ably supported by his Parliamentary under-secretary, Edwin Montagu, who shared his master's passionate concern for India. In 1908, while the Indian Councils Act was still being drafted, Morley managed to get an Indian appointed as law member of the viceroy's holy of holies, the Executive Council. This in itself was a significant advance: only seven years earlier, Curzon had dismissed the idea with his usual hauteur: 'It is often said why not make some prominent native a member of the Executive Council? The answer is that in the whole continent there is not an Indian fit for the post.'[11]

The man Morley and Minto chose for this ground-breaking role was a Moderate Congressman and highly successful barrister, Satyendra P. Sinha (later Lord Sinha, under-secretary of state for India), who was then the advocate-general of Bengal. Minto's reason for choosing Sinha over the other candidate, P.M. Mukherjea, a leading zamindar, was revealing: 'Sinha is comparatively white, whilst Mookerjee is as black as my hat!'[12] To Minto's chagrin, Sinha at first refused the honour, calculating that it would cost him some £10,000 a year in lost fees from his legal practice. The Congress leadership dispatched Gokhale and Jinnah to Calcutta to persuade him to change his mind. It took several visits, but Jinnah eventually managed it, pointing out that Gokhale voluntarily limited his own income to a beggarly 75 rupees a year from the Servants of India, while Jinnah himself sacrificed substantial earnings as a barrister in order to work for Congress.[13]

Even when Sinha had accepted, the appointment was not clear-cut. Morley found himself facing powerful opposition, not from the pragmatic Minto, but from the king-emperor. When Morley wrote that the appointment was necessary 'for the contentment of Your Majesty's Indian dominions', Edward VII replied: 'The King has thought it over quite as much as Lord Morley has. He remains of opinion that the proposed step is fraught with the greatest danger to the maintenance of the British empire under British rule ... As Lord Morley as well as the Viceroy recommend Mr Sinha, the King has no alternative but to agree to his appointment.' He agreed, however, with very bad grace, noting petulantly: 'Morley knows how strong my views are on subject and so does Minto, but they don't care what I say.'[14] It is hard to imagine a Mughal emperor making such an admission.

The Indian Councils Act, more popularly known as the Morley-Minto reforms, was passed by Parliament on 25 May 1909. Membership of the Imperial Legislative Council was increased from 25 to 60, in addition to the eight ex-officio members of the Executive Council. Thirty-six were officials, and five were nominated non-officials, thus ensuring a permanent majority over the remaining 27 members who, for the first time ever, were to be elected.

The electorate was still very select: general voters who qualified by virtue of the amount of municipal tax they paid or because they were university graduates of many years' standing, plus landowners, Anglo-Indians, and universities, municipal boards, and chambers of commerce, which were all given blocks of seats. There were also reserved seats for religious minorities, most importantly six for Muslims elected by the separate Muslim vote promised by Minto. In addition, Minto also promised to appoint two further Muslims, if none of the other special constituencies elected them, so at least eight of the 27 elected members would be Muslims, a far higher ratio than in the population as a whole. Muslims were also entitled to vote in the general constituencies. Reflecting their general poverty, the level of taxable income needed by a Muslim to qualify as a voter was set at 3,000 rupees, while a Hindu needed 300,000. And while a Hindu needed to have been a university graduate for 30 years to get the vote, a Muslim needed only three.[15]

The seeds planted by Sir Syed Ahmed Khan some 30 years before had borne abundant fruit, as both Morley and Minto recognized the special needs of the still backward minority community. Morley had written to Minto concerning the viceroy's promise to the Muslim leaders of a separate electorate and agreeing with him that it was not 'desirable or possible, or even conceivable, to adapt English political institutions to the nations who inhabit India'.[16] He had reinforced this during the debate in Parliament, by declaring: 'If it could be said that this chapter of reforms led directly or necessarily up to the establishment of a Parliamentary system in India, I, for one, would have nothing at all to do with it.'[17] Taken out of context, Morley's words have been misunderstood and misquoted over the years, unjustly painting one of the most progressive secretaries of state as a reactionary. What was significant, both for 1909 and for the future, was his use of the word 'nations' to describe the different peoples of India.

There were similar changes in provincial legislatures. The larger provinces – Bombay, Bengal, East Bengal and Assam, Madras, and the United Provinces – were to have 50 members on their councils, and smaller provinces 30. But the important difference was that they were all to have a majority of elected members. And in all the councils, both central and provincial, members were allowed to debate and vote on proposed legislation and budgets.

The members of the new Imperial Legislative Council took their seats in the newly gilded council chamber of Wellesley's Government House on 25 January 1910. Congress was strongly represented, for in addition to Sinha, who was there as law member of the Executive Council, the elected members included Gokhale, Surendranath Banerjea, Motilal Nehru, and Jinnah, elected as the Muslim member for Bombay, though he strongly disapproved of the principle of separate electorates. At 35 Jinnah was easily the youngest man present, but he was by no means overawed by the august company. Indeed, he was the first elected member to clash openly with the viceroy, when he spoke about a Congress-inspired resolution prohibiting the recruitment of Indian indentured labourers for South Africa. The whole of India had been shocked by news of the violent repression of peaceful protesters in South Africa, led by M.K. Gandhi. Minto's attempt to reprimand Jinnah for what he considered strong language was immediately rebuffed with the stinging retort: 'My Lord, I should feel much inclined to use much stronger language. But I am fully aware of the constitution of this Council, and I do not wish to trespass for one single moment.' Minto was struck dumb.

Having given India its first ever taste of representative government, however limited, Morley stepped down from the India Office on 7 November 1910, handing over to Lord Crewe, who had previously been colonial secretary. Minto had also come to the end of his term as viceroy during the year, so it was all change once again. As his final service to India, Morley blocked Lord Kitchener's burning ambition to become viceroy – how Curzon would have smarted had he succeeded – and appointed a Liberal career diplomat, Lord Hardinge of Penshurst – an austere, rather shy man, whose staff thought him lacking in humanity. Like Minto, Hardinge had India in his blood: his grandfather had been governor-general from 1844-8, some 30 years after Minto's great-grandfather had held the position.

Kitchener had failed because he had lost his most influential supporter, King Edward VII, who died on 6 May – in fact, Morley had offered the post to Hardinge at his funeral. The new king, George V, had visited India as Prince of Wales at the time of the partition of Bengal, and had been appalled by the racial bigotry of the Anglo-Indians. His personal attitude was much nearer to his grandmother's than his father's – in a diary entry at the time he commented: 'Evidently, we are too much inclined to look upon them as a conquered and down-trodden race and the Native, who is becoming more and more educated, realizes this.' He had also been appalled at the results of Curzon's brutal surgery in Bengal, and now that he was emperor, he was determined to do something about it. Hardinge concurred: 'A grave injustice has been done to the Bengalis, seeing that they are in a minority in both provinces, and this injustice should certainly be rectified.'[18]

The decision to reunify Bengal, and at the same time create a new province of Bihar and Orissa, was one of the best-kept secrets in British imperial history. But it was only half the story. George V had resolved to make a second visit to India, to celebrate his coronation as king-emperor with another great *durbar* in Delhi. The reunification would be announced at the *durbar*, as a surprise 'boon' to the Bengalis. So, too, would a second boon, suggested by the home member of Hardinge's Executive Council, Sir John Jenkins: the removal of the seat of government from Calcutta to the old Mughal capital, Delhi. The suggestion, intended as a 'tonic' for the rest of India, was agreed with barely a second thought. Such a move had been considered from time to time for almost a century, on the grounds of climate and geographical convenience. Now, it was doubly attractive, for it would remove the viceroy and his staff and councillors from the pressure cooker of Bengal politics – including the bomb-throwers – and from the relentless attention of British businessmen, who believed they had an inalienable right to influence the government.

On 12 December 1911, the king-emperor stood under a golden dome in the royal pavilion at the centre of the *durbar* ground in Delhi and made the announcement. The enormous throng before him, estimated at 100,000 people, stood in silence for a moment, then burst into wild and spontaneous cheering. Bengal received the news at the same moment, in a mini *durbar* on the Calcutta *maidan*. If the move to Delhi was intended as a snub to the Bengali Hindus, they did not see it in that way – after all, every Bengali knows that Calcutta is the centre of the universe, so what did it matter where the viceroy went? The Anglo-Indian box wallahs were furious, and complained long and loud, but that was no more than had been expected. They would come round eventually – and in the mean time, their discomfiture was a bonus for the civilians.

The Muslims said little about Delhi – they were too deeply shocked by the decision to reunify Bengal, something which Morley had assured them was not on the cards. Minto, back in London, spoke up for them in the House of Lords:

> We told the Musulmans that the Partition was a settled fact and we over and over again asserted that it must continue to be so. We assured the Musulman population of Eastern Bengal of our appreciation of their loyalty and our determination to safeguard their interests. I should think there could have been scarcely a Civil Servant in India who would have declared that it would not be impossible for the British Government to reverse the decision it had come to as regards the maintenance of the Partition of Bengal.

But it was all to no avail. If partition had been a 'settled fact', then so was reunification. Surendranath Banerjea led the rejoicing as he had led the campaign, proclaiming 'the triumph of British justice and the vindication of constitutional methods in our political controversies'. The Muslims saw it differently: 'No bombs, no boons,' was the new slogan they coined, bewailing the fact that concessions were only achieved through terrorism. With one move, designed to placate opponents who would never remain placated, the British had alienated their main allies in India. From that moment, the Muslims ceased believing that their future lay in helping to maintain the British presence.

In 1912 at Bankipur, the council of the ultra-loyalist Muslim League changed the aims stated in its constitution to include: 'The attainment of a form of self-government suitable to India ... through constitutional means ... by promoting national unity and fostering public spirit among the people of India, and by co-operating with other communities for the said purpose.'[19] The new clause had been urged on the League's council by a guest speaker from Congress, Mohammad Ali Jinnah, who finally agreed to join the League in 1913, on condition that his loyalty to it and to Muslim interests 'would in no way and at no time imply even the shadow of disloyalty to the larger national cause to which his life was dedicated'.[20] From the British point of view, this was disastrous: the League was actively seeking an alliance with Congress. Any policy of divide and rule was now in tatters.

While the aristocrats of the Muslim League were reluctantly reassessing their policies, other Muslims were taking a more militant line. The disillusion caused by the betrayal over Bengal coincided with a surge in pan-Islamic feeling throughout the Muslim world, which was reflected among the Muslims of India. With the Ottoman empire, the only Muslim great power, crumbling before their eyes, Muslims felt increasingly threatened. As one Muslim country after another, in North Africa, the Middle East and the Balkans, was either conquered or subjugated by Christian powers, they came to believe that there was a deliberate and concerted campaign by the west to destroy Islam in its entirety. Their fears peaked when Turkey was all but driven out of Europe in the Balkan wars of 1912-13, for the Turkish sultan was also the Caliph, the religious and civil leader of Islam, successor to the Prophet Muhammad and responsible for protecting holy places. Even Shiites, who did not recognize the Caliphate – or Khilafat as it was known in India – answered the call to join their Sunni brethren in defending it as a vital symbol of Islamic political power and spiritual values.

Like the Hindu nationalists, the new Muslim militants spoke to and for their supporters through newspapers. Several papers were started in 1911 and 1912, most notably *Comrade*, founded by Muhammad Ali, *Zamindar*, founded in Lahore by Zafar Ali Khan, and *Al-Hilal*, founded in Calcutta by Abul Kalam Azad. Both Muhammad Ali and Azad saw themselves essentially as religious leaders – both were entitled to the honorific title Maulana, signifying a man of great Qur'anic learning – but in Islam, religion and politics have always been inseparable.

Maulana Azad was the 25-year-old son of a famous family of Muslim saints and scholars, but had adopted the name 'Azad', meaning 'Free', to show that he now belonged to no sect or orthodox religious doctrine. Although born in Mecca, he was raised in Calcutta where he had become closely involved with revolutionary politics, even though it was almost entirely dominated by Hindus. He had then spent some time travelling in Iraq, Syria, Egypt and Turkey, meeting

Arab and Turkish revolutionaries. Returning to India, he launched a furious attack on the Aligarh movement, which he said had 'paralyzed the Muslims'.

In language that has an all too familiar ring 85 years later, Azad lambasted the followers of Syed Ahmed Khan as 'those heretics and hypocrites who, during the last 40 years, had co-operated with the Satans of Europe to weaken the influence of the Islamic Caliphate and Pan-Islam'.[21] Seeking an Islamic state, he wanted to organize India's Muslims into Hizbullah, the party of God — another name with familiar echoes — a separate entity in which Hindus and Britons could have no place.[22] Azad was later to become president of Congress, but at that stage in his thinking, he condemned Muslim co-operation with the Hindu-dominated organization, calling instead for a jihad, a holy war, for independence.[23]

The formal transfer of government to Delhi was to begin on 1 April 1912. During his *durbar* King George had laid the foundation stone of a fine new capital on the *durbar* site some distance north of the old city, Shajehanabad. But when a Captain Swinton of the London County Council examined the site with his practised town-planner's eyes he proclaimed it to be useless. The stone was quietly shifted, at the dead of night on a bullock cart, to a low mound called Raisina Hill, 10 miles away to the south of old Delhi.

New Delhi was intended as a visual reminder of the permanence and might of British power. It was the eighth city to be built in the area by various rulers over the centuries, in defiance of the old Indian prophecy that whoever builds a new city in Delhi will lose it. It was to be designed by Sir Herbert Baker, who was responsible for the new South African Union Buildings in Pretoria, and Sir Edwin Lutyens, the most celebrated British architect of his day, who was married to the daughter of the former viceroy, Lord Lytton. While her husband was building the Viceroy's House, Emily Lutyens occupied herself with the welfare of women labourers on the site, organizing crèches for their children.

Hardinge had specified that the new capital was to be built 'Indian style', an edict that caused trouble both for and between Baker and Lutyens, who found it difficult to interpret. Eventually, they agreed on a typical British compromise, grafting odd Indian features on to classical sandstone structures, although they still continued to quarrel over questions of detail. The disagreements were to lead to a truly monumental mistake, which mars the Indian capital to this day. The intention was for the palace to sit on top of Raisina Hill, providing an awe-inspiring vision over the entire length of the great ceremonial King's Way (now Raj Path). But arguments over the gradient of the hill left a large hump, behind which the Viceroy's House disappears entirely as one approaches from the bottom of King's Way. Lutyens and Baker blamed each other, and refused to speak for the next five years.

Baker was responsible for the two secretariats flanking the central mass of the Viceroy's House; but it was Lutyens who had the last word, ordering an inscription to be cut above the great gateway to the buildings which perfectly summed up the official British view of their imperial mission:

LIBERTY WILL NOT DESCEND TO A PEOPLE;
A PEOPLE MUST RAISE THEMSELVES TO LIBERTY;
IT IS A BLESSING WHICH MUST BE EARNED
BEFORE IT CAN BE ENJOYED

Hardinge had expected the new capital to be built immediately, or at least during his own viceroyalty. But it was not formally completed until 1931. For the moment, he and his officials had to make do with temporary offices and the buildings of the old Mughal empire, no great hardship when weighed against the steamy atmosphere – in every respect – of Calcutta. However, even as the government was congratulating itself on having distanced itself from the Calcutta bomb factories, it was sharply jolted out of its complacency.

By December, the move was complete, and another grand *durbar* was planned for Monday the 23rd, to celebrate the event. Hardinge led the procession into the old city, riding in state on the back of an elephant with his wife beside him, acknowledging the cheers of a happy crowd. As he entered the great boulevard of Chandni Chowk – 'Silver Street', once famed as the richest street in the world – an unknown terrorist, never caught despite a reward of £10,000, threw a bomb into the howdah. The man holding the ceremonial umbrella was killed outright. Hardinge survived, though badly lacerated and with a shoulder blade totally exposed. He had to undergo a series of operations to remove the screws, nails and steel gramophone needles with which the bomb had been packed, and was left permanently deaf in one ear. His self-confidence was deeply damaged. Afterwards, according to Harcourt Butler, he did 'jumpy things' occasionally. He admitted that he 'literally wept with disappointment'[24] when he realized the extent of the failure of his policies. All in all, Hardinge and his fate seem a perfect analogue for the Raj in its later years.

Fate dealt poor Hardinge further blows during the rest of his term of office. In 1914, his wife, who had survived the terrorist's bomb unscathed, died unexpectedly after surgery in London; a few months later his eldest son was killed in France, along with three of his young ADCs. Hardinge was left to govern India with only his 14-year-old daughter, Diamond, as his confidante and support.

'A Spontaneous Loyalty'

When Lord Hardinge informed the Indians that they were at war in August 1914, both the Germans and the British were surprised by their response. The Germans had confidently expected that trouble in India – as in Ireland, where they were supplying the rebels with arms – would seriously weaken the British war effort. The British had every reason to be nervous: it seemed a perfect opportunity for the nationalist movement to reassert itself after three years of quiet. Instead, as the American writer Fred B. Fisher witnessed: 'India rose to the support of the Allies with a spontaneous loyalty which stirred even the British pulse in those early days of the war, when glowing messages of support flooded into London from every corner of the Empire.'[1]

Within weeks, 290,000 fully trained and equipped troops, 210,000 of them Indian, were on their way to France and Egypt, leaving only 15,000 British soldiers to guard the whole of India. The first Indian Expeditionary Force, 28,500 Indians and 16,000 British troops, reached the western front in Flanders just in time to hold the line against the furious German assault at the first Battle of Ypres. During the month-long battle, they suffered 7,000 casualties and gained the first Indian VC, awarded posthumously to Sepoy Khudabad of the Duke of Connaught's Own Baluchis.

All told during the war 1,440,437 Indians volunteered for service – even Bengalis and other groups who had been banned from the army since 1857 flocked to the colours when the restrictions were removed. They joined up for various reasons – honour, money, adventure, duress from landlords or village headmen – but none were conscripts. And they acquitted themselves well, winning more than their share of decorations for bravery, but unfortunately losing 62,056 in battle.[2]

India provided more than just soldiers, of course. As Fred B. Fisher put it: 'Her industries leaped into unprecedented activity, to supply khaki, tents, blankets, shoes and munitions for the armies of the empire. Her farmers had to make ten seeds grow where one grew before, to produce the needed cotton, jute, wheat and foodstuffs.' Indian factories set up during the anti-British *swadeshi* movement now found themselves serving Britain, none more effectively than the new Tata Iron and Steel Works, which seized the chance to begin a dramatic expansion. By the start of the Second World War it would be the largest steel producer in the empire, far outstripping any plant in Britain itself.

India also gave Britain great sums of money towards the cost of the war: an outright gift of £100 million during the first year – worth well over £2 billion in present-day terms – was followed a year later by a loan of a further £100 million, and two years after that another £65 million was raised through public subscription. The public money was supplemented by personal contributions from wealthy individuals and the princes, who also put their private armies at Britain's disposal. The Maharaja of Gwalior spent £320,000 from his own purse to fit out a hospital ship, aptly named *Loyalty*, to accompany the Indian Expeditionary Force. Others contributed horses, camels and elephants, and gave jewels to pay for weapons and equipment. Even the chiefs of normally troublesome frontier tribes pledged their undying support.

Both Congress and the Muslim League declared their total loyalty, for was Britain not fighting for democracy? And since Indian troops were fighting and dying alongside Britons, Canadians, Australians and New Zealanders in Egypt, the Sudan, Aden, Africa and Mesopotamia, as well as in the trenches of Flanders, was it not unthinkable that Indians should be denied their rightful place alongside them in a self-governing dominion when the war was won? Indian nationalist leaders were unanimous in urging their followers to support Britain and the empire. Even 'Lokamanya' Tilak, released from his Mandalay gaol in June 1914, cabled the king emperor swearing his loyal support, and turned his oratory to helping the recruiting campaign.

Renouncing his earlier hostility, Tilak went out of his way to reassure both his compatriots and the British. On 27 August 1914, he wrote: 'The reforms introduced during Lord Morley's administration will show that the government is fully alive to the necessity of progressive change, and desire to associate the people more and more in the work of Government . . . this indicates a marked increase of confidence between the Rulers and the Ruled.' He went on to state: 'We are trying in India, as the Irish Home-rulers have been doing in Ireland, for a reform of the system of administration and not for the overthrow of Government.' Acts of violence, he now felt, had retarded rather than hastened the pace of political progress.[3]

With Bengali terrorism ended, only two small blips disturbed the atmosphere of eager co-operation in the early years of the Great War: the Ghadr movement and pan-Islamism.

The Ghadr movement, centred among the Sikhs of the Punjab, arrived from North America as the war began. It was started by a young Hindu from Delhi, Lala Har Dayal, one of the many Indian activists driven abroad by the British crackdown on dissent. A revolutionary socialist who dismissed Marxism as irrelevant nonsense, Har Dayal had won a government scholarship to Oxford, but gave it up for political reasons before sitting his finals. In 1911 he moved to San Francisco, where for a time he taught Indian philosophy at Stanford University.

Since 1904, a sizeable community of land-hungry migrants from crowded districts of the Punjab had settled on the west coast of North America, from California to British Columbia, seeking a better life. Most were Sikhs, prepared to work for what, to Americans and Canadians, were starvation wages. At first they were welcomed, but as their numbers increased, local opinion became less friendly. Ostensibly to protect fellow Indians, Har Dayal set up an organization which he called the Hindustani Workers of the West Pacific Coast. From premises in San Francisco, he also began publishing a newspaper, *Ghadr* (*Rebellion*), which within a matter of months was circulating in Indian expatriate communities all over the world. Wherever there were Sikhs, there was *Ghadr*.

From the beginning, Har Dayal was determined there should be no doubt about the purpose of his newspaper, or the movement it represented. The front page was emblazoned with the legend 'Enemy of the British Government', and the first editorial declared: 'Today there begins in foreign lands, but in our country's language, a war against the British Raj. What is our name? Ghadr. What is our work? Ghadr. Where will Ghadr break out? In India. The time will soon come when rifles and blood will take the place of pen and ink.' When he heard the news of the assassination attempt on Hardinge in Delhi, Har Dayal was delighted. 'Hail! Hail! Hail!' he proclaimed in the paper. 'Bomb of 23 December 1912. Harbinger of hope and courage, dear reawakening of slumbering souls, thou hast come just in time.'[4]

On 25 March 1914, Har Dayal was arrested by the San Francisco police and charged with anarchist activities. Released on bail, he slipped out of America, and out of the movement. Undeterred, however, the Ghadr Party in Canada decided to test the government's tough entry restrictions against Indian immigrants. They chartered a Japanese ship, the *Komagata Maru*, to bring 376 Sikhs, most of them former soldiers, from Hong Kong and the Far East to Vancouver. The local press described their arrival as an 'oriental invasion'.[5] Sir Richard MacBride, the prime minister of British Columbia, declared that to admit them would lead to 'the extinction of the white peoples' in Canada, which he said must at all costs be preserved as 'a white man's country'. Only 22 men who could prove they were normally resident in Canada were allowed to land. The others had to remain on board the ship, resisting all efforts to shift them until mid-July, when the Canadian government sent in a light cruiser and forced the *Komagata Maru* to put to sea under the muzzles of Canadian guns.

The Great War began while the *Komagata Maru* was still at sea. The ship was not allowed to land passengers at Yokohama, its home port, nor at Hong Kong or Singapore, where many of the men had their homes, but was directed on to Calcutta. Each time it reached port there were anti-British demonstrations by local Indians. But when the ship arrived at Budge Budge, near Calcutta, only the police were waiting, to board it and search for arms. They found none, which is strange since Ghadr Party members in Yokohama had given the returning emigrants 270 pistols.

The Indian government planned to send all the men to the Punjab under police escort, but 300 Sikhs refused to comply and began to march in procession to Calcutta, carrying the *Granth*, the Sikh holy book. The police, supported by an army unit, attempted to stop them, and in the ensuing clash opened fire, killing 18 marchers and wounding a further 25. Three policemen also died. Two hundred and two Sikhs were arrested and sent back to the Punjab, where they were interned. The rest managed to escape.[7]

The Ghadr leaders in America, meanwhile, had decided that the outbreak of war was the opportunity they had been waiting for. Although they were almost totally unprepared and had no arms, they believed they could overcome these minor difficulties by winning over Indian soldiers to their cause. Declaring war against the Raj, they called on their supporters around the world to return to India to join in an armed revolt. Many did return – along with thousands of loyal emigrants – but they found the police waiting for them. By February 1915, 189 had been interned and 704 restricted to their villages, where they tried to instigate a rebellion among the local population. No one in the Punjab wanted to know about rebellion, however. Local community leaders disowned the Ghadrites as 'fallen' Sikhs and criminals, and helped the police to track them down.

In desperation, the Ghadrites called in as their leader the Bengali revolutionary, Rash Behari Bose, who claimed to be the man who had thrown the bomb at the viceroy. Bose managed to impose some sort of organization on them, and turned them to inciting mutiny in the army. But the CID was watching every move. All the Ghadr leaders were arrested, apart from Bose, whose instinct for self-preservation triumphed once again. Forty-five revolutionaries were executed, and more than 200 sentenced to long terms of imprisonment.

The ruthlessness with which the Ghadr movement had been crushed was typical of the man chiefly responsible, the lieutenant-governor of the Punjab, Sir Michael O'Dwyer. O'Dwyer's harshness in the face of anything he saw as a challenge to British authority was to bear bitter fruit four years later, souring relations between the government and Indian leaders and permanently changing the course of Indian nationalism. But there was no criticism of his actions in 1915.

O'Dwyer was a sparky, clever, peppery Irishman, one of those fortunate individuals who never seem to doubt their own judgement – 'Public cares have never lost me half an hour's sleep,' he declared. And no crisis was allowed to interfere with his riding to hounds twice a week. Yet in spite of his blimpish manner, he had a first-class brain. After distinguishing himself as a linguist and as a sportsman during his two-year probationary period at Balliol College, Oxford, O'Dwyer had stayed on to take a degree. He got a first, one of only five awarded that year, after completing a three-year law course in twelve months.

In November 1885, O'Dwyer was posted to Lahore, the capital of the Punjab, where the stars of the city's intellectual and social life were John Lockwood Kipling, director of the art school and the museum, and his sparkling wife, Alice, sister-in-law of the famous painter Sir Edward Burne-Jones. O'Dwyer was not impressed: when their 20-year-old son Rudyard, then a reporter on the local *Civil & Military Gazette*, made cutting remarks about the ICS, the young O'Dwyer was only just prevented from calling him out to fight.

There was still considerable tension in the Punjab at that time, and firm government was needed to control a virile and warlike population. As Philip Mason, himself a former civilian puts it, 'it was the first article of faith that the man who is most ready to use force at the beginning will use least in the end'.[8] O'Dwyer was posted to a western district, where he became a settlement officer living and working among the Muslim peasantry, and, like most district and settlement officers, he came to regard them as his 'children', sharing their hatred of the Hindu money-lenders to whom they were always in debt. He next went to the North-West Frontier – it became a separate province during his time there – an even more strongly Muslim area, where the Pathans had an even greater hostility to Hindu money-lenders. After seven hugely enjoyable years in a variety of posts on the Frontier, he was appointed British resident in Hyderabad, the second largest princely state in India, whose predominantly Hindu population was ruled by Muslims. He followed this with a period as acting agent to the governor-general of Central India.

O'Dwyer's glittering career was crowned by his return to the Punjab in 1913 as lieutenant-governor. He brought to the position all his considerable experience, and all his considerable prejudices and preoccupations. The Ghadrites confirmed his worst fears. 'No less than 45 serious outrages had been committed by February 1915,' he wrote later, 'by revolutionaries, who were now drawing recruits from lawless elements in the population. These outbreaks ... showed how seriously the foundations of public security were being shaken in the Province.'[9] Wherever he looked, he saw insurrection, real or imagined, including an agrarian rising in March in the south-western Punjab which was in fact mainly directed against his old *bêtes noirs*, the Hindu money-lenders – with whom he now lumped Hindu politicians and all educated Indians. O'Dwyer did not like or trust educated Indians. The only Indians he did like were his children, the peasants, whom he treated rather as the Protestant Ascendancy in Ireland treated the locals: simple souls who at all costs had to be kept away from politics. Like Lady Bracknell, he did not approve of anything that tampered with natural ignorance.

O'Dwyer believed, understandably, that the Punjab had to be kept calm. Apart from being the breadbasket of India, which was exporting great quantities of wheat to Britain, the province was also the chief recruiting ground for the Indian army. Though its own population was barely 11 per cent of the national total, during the course of the war it supplied almost one third of the entire force, 446,976 men, many of them virtually press-ganged into 'volunteering'. Without that contribution, the British war effort would have been seriously impaired.

In truth, the Ghadr movement had never posed a serious, long-term threat in the Punjab. What was potentially much more dangerous, not only there but in India as a whole, was pan-Islamism, which had been further roused by Turkey's decision on 1 November 1914 to join Germany and the Central Powers against Britain, France and the Allies. This raised a terrible conflict of loyalty for the great number of Muslims in the Indian army – never before in history had Muslims fought alongside infidels against other Muslims. The British tried to resolve this difficulty by promising to respect the status of the Caliph and the holy places of Islam. After two years of fighting, however, their greed overcame their scruples, and they forgot those promises, along with others made to the Arabs, drawing up an agreement with France in early 1916 to carve up the bulk of the oil-rich Arab lands between themselves and Russia when the war was over. That agreement was a well-kept secret until Lenin revealed it after the Russian Revolution in 1917.

A high proportion of the 16,000 Indian troops of the Poona Division's 16th Infantry Brigade, who had already been shipped to Bahrain in 1914, ready to occupy Abadan and secure its oil pipelines and refinery, were Muslim. But they remained loyal to Britain, and moved with their comrades through Abadan to take Basra and advance steadily through Mesopotamia – today's Iraq – until by October 1915 they were at Kut-el-Amara, barely 100 miles from Baghdad. The Turks put mullahs in their front-line trenches, their voices ringing out across the narrow no-man's-land exhorting Muslims to remember their religious obligations and desert. A few answered the call, mainly Pathans from the tribal areas of the North-West Frontier, but the vast majority stood firm. Two units in Singapore had to be disarmed as a precautionary measure, but otherwise the hundreds of thousands of Muslims in the Indian army remained true to their salt.

Back in India, Maulana Azad and his friends did their best to arouse

Muslim passions, but their newspapers were closed down and their assets seized. Muhammad Ali and his brother Shaukat Ali were both held under close house arrest from early in the war. Azad remained free for two years, though his movements were increasingly restricted, but in late 1916 he, too, was confined under the draconian Defence of India Act. None of them would be released until the end of 1919. A fourth Muslim leader, Maulana Mahmood-ul-Hasan, went to Mecca to try, through the governor of the Hejaz, to persuade the Turkish government to invade an India depleted of British troops, through Iran and Afghanistan. No doubt the Turks would have been delighted to comply, but they were in no position to do so, and the Islamic threat to the Raj fizzled out.

During the first two years of the war, Congress was still deeply divided. Tilak, now approaching 60, his health broken by six years in the steamy heat of Mandalay prison, was eager for a reconciliation. He had abandoned his demands for direct action and now supported the Moderates' policy of seeking self-government within the empire 'by strictly constitutional means'. Tilak's role as the firebrand of Congress had been taken over by an unlikely new figure on the nationalist scene, the Anglo-Irish Annie Besant, who had succeeded her friend and guru Madame Blavatsky as president of the Theosophical Society in 1891. She tried her best to broker a *rapprochement* between Tilak and Gokhale, but without success: while Mehta was still alive, there was no chance of Tilak's being accepted back into the fold.

Although she was already 67 years old in 1914, Mrs Besant was still brimming with irrepressible energy, her appetite for attacking the establishment undiminished after 40 years of controversial causes. The estranged wife of an Anglican parson, she had been tried in England for immorality after publishing a pamphlet on birth control, and her children had been taken away from her by court order. She had espoused socialism, joined the Fabian Society and become a trade union leader, organizing the Bryant & May match girls' strike in 1888, before discovering Theosophy and moving to India, where as well as running the Society she helped found what was to become the Hindu University of India in Benares.

While Congress and the Muslim League had both put their demands for self-government on hold for the duration, Annie Besant believed the war provided the perfect opportunity to increase the pressure on Britain. The Irish Home Rule League was already doing this, and she wanted to start an Indian Home Rule movement along the same lines. For this, however, she needed Congress support. It was not forthcoming. So, in early 1915, she launched her own campaign through her two newspapers, *New India* and *Commonweal*, using the Theosophical Society's existing network to organize public meetings and conferences.

Both Mehta and Gokhale died during 1915. With their opposition removed, the annual session of Congress held in Bombay that December finally agreed to readmit Tilak and his supporters. Four months later, Tilak, afraid of losing his position as the leading proponent of self-government to a European interloper, beat Mrs Besant to the punch by starting his own Home Rule League. Mightily miffed, she followed suit in September 1916. Playing down the rivalry between them, Mrs Besant admitted that 'some of his followers disliked me and some of mine disliked him'.[10] That was putting it very mildly. There was little chance of the two leagues merging, but they agreed to work in separate, clearly demarcated parts of India, to avoid open conflicts. Tilak's group, based in Poona, confined its activities to the Marathi-speaking areas; Besant's, working initially from Madras, operated in the rest of India. Only in Bombay did they overlap.

The Home Rule Leagues flourished for the rest of the war. They achieved nothing concrete, but were hugely successful in raising political awareness throughout India by means of public meetings and newspapers. The most influential of these was the national bi-weekly *Young India*, started in Bombay by supporters of Mrs Besant. The paper took its name from the Young Italy and Young Ireland freedom movements of the early nineteenth century. After a shaky start in 1916, *Young India* gradually built up its readership, until in 1919 it was taken over by Gandhi, who swiftly made it his mouthpiece.

The government did its best to crack down on the leagues, imposing ever more stringent restrictions on Tilak and Besant, banning them from several provinces and harrying them and their supporters. Such attacks were the bread of life to the movement. On 23 July 1916, Tilak's sixtieth birthday, his supporters presented him with a gift of 100,000 rupees. As their birthday present, the authorities in Poona arrested him under section 108 of the Criminal Penal Code, charging that he had 'brought, or attempted to bring, into hatred and contempt' the Government of India. His offence was that he had made three speeches on the subject of self-government. For Tilak, this was a present worth having: 'The Lord is with us,' he declared. 'Home Rule will now spread like wildfire.'[11]

The case was heard on 7 August, before District Magistrate G.W. Hatch. This time, Tilak decided to rely on Jinnah to defend him throughout. It did him no good at first – Mr Hatch still found him guilty, binding him over to be of good behaviour for a year, against a security of 20,000 rupees. Jinnah immediately lodged an appeal in the Bombay High Court, which was very much his own turf, and on 8 November won a stunning legal success. Tilak was found not guilty and his bond was cancelled. 'A great victory has been won for the cause of Home Rule,' *Young India* exulted, 'which has, thus, been freed from the chains that were sought to be put upon it.'[12]

Thanks largely to the efforts of Jinnah, the Muslim League met in Bombay on 31 December 1915, within walking distance of the Congress tents, so that those eager for Hindu-Muslim unity could attend both. It was a controversial decision, condemned both by the British authorities, who feared a Congress-League alliance, and local Sunni Muslims, who regarded Jinnah as a heretic if a Muslim at all – 30,000 of them had attended a mass meeting to denounce both him and the League and pass a resolution protesting against holding the session in Bombay.[13]

The League was presided over by another Congress liberal, Mazhar-ul-Huq, a Bengali barrister who, like Jinnah and now Tilak, was committed to forging a joint platform to achieve self-government. Huq and Satyendra Sinha, that year's Congress president, even travelled to Bombay by the same train, comparing their presidential addresses on the way. It is said that by mistake they ended up with the wrong speeches, so that 'Lord Sinha read out the halting and hesitating address of the ever loyal Muslim, while the ever loyal Muslim read out the piquant and pungent address of the ever disloyal Bengali', with the result that at the Muslim League session 'the President was described as a man who cannot be called a Muhammadan'.[14] The story is probably apocryphal, but it reflects the mood for closer co-operation.

The League meeting, in a huge tent near the seashore in Marine Lines, was disrupted by hordes of hecklers from the public seats, including angry mullahs and maulanas who screamed abuse at Jinnah and Huq for dressing and speaking like westerners. Urdu was the only 'proper language' for Muslim League meetings, they shouted – only to be shouted down in their turn by Pushtu-speaking Pathans. The meeting quickly degenerated into a shambles. Jinnah shepherded the ladies out of the tent, and tried to persuade Bombay's police commissioner, S.M. Edwardes, who was waiting outside with 80 men and a magistrate, to intervene. Commissioner Edwardes declined – it was widely believed that he had planted the troublemakers in order to break up the meeting, as ordered by the governor of Bombay, Lord Willingdon.

But Willingdon's hopes were dashed. Huq simply adjourned the meeting until the following day, moving it to the smart Taj Mahal Hotel, where only official delegates were admitted. And there, on 1 January 1916, to loud cheers, Jinnah introduced his motion calling for a special committee to be formed to work in consultation with other 'political organizations', 'to formulate and frame a scheme of reforms ... in the name of United India'.[15] It was passed unanimously, and Jinnah was praised for his 'great work'.[16]

A committee of 71 members was appointed, representing every part of India, but the real work was done by a small working party, headed by Jinnah for the League and for Congress by an Allahabad lawyer who had gradually emerged as a leading moderate, Motilal Nehru. Motilal, already a friend and colleague within Congress, was very much a man after Jinnah's own heart. Both were highly sophisticated, successful lawyers, living thoroughly westernized lives in luxurious western-style houses. Both were essentially secular, ignoring most of the dictates of their respective religions and enjoying fine food, fine wine and good whisky. And both were utterly committed to Hindu-Muslim unity and to seeking self-government for India by strictly constitutional means. They made an excellent partnership.

Motilal Nehru came from a family of Kashmiri Brahmans, the highest of high-caste Hindus, who moved to Delhi to serve the Mughals in 1716. His grandfather, Lakshmi, took employment with the East India Company, becoming their first *vakil* (pleader) at the Mughal court. Lakshmi's son, Ganga Dhar, became a *kotwal* (chief constable) in the Delhi police force, until the great revolt of 1857 forced him to flee the city with his family and settle, penniless, in Agra. He died there four years later at the age of 34, leaving his wife six months pregnant with their third son, Motilal. Ganga Dhar had made sure his two elder sons learned English as well as Persian and Arabic, to enable them to carry on the tradition of serving the new masters of India, and they in their turn made sure Motilal did likewise. Eventually, all three found successful careers in the law, one of the few professions which were then open to a bright young Indian.

Motilal became the most successful *vakil* in the high court in Allahabad, the Hindu city at the confluence of the holy rivers Ganges and Jumna, and capital of the North-Western Provinces, as the United Provinces were known until 1901. His first brief brought him only five rupees, but his rise to fame was rapid. By his early thirties he was earning over 2,000 rupees a month, and within a few years was making seven times that amount. British judges and lawyers liked and admired him. The chief justice of the Allahabad High Court, Sir Grimwood Meares, wrote of him that

> as an advocate he had the art of presenting his case in its most attractive form. Every fact fell into its proper place in the narration of the story and was emphasised in just the right degree. He had an exquisite public speaking voice and a charm of manner which made it a pleasure to listen to him ... With his wide range of reading, and the pleasure he had taken in travel he was a very delightful companion, and wherever he sat at a table that was the head of the table and there was the centre of interest.[17]

An earlier chief justice, Sir John Edge, had even wanted to propose him for membership of the whites-only Allahabad Club. Motilal courteously declined the honour.

But for all his charm, and the uninhibited laugh which his son said 'became famous throughout Allahabad', Motilal had his darker side — an equally famous temper which could explode without warning, terrifying his children and his servants, both of whom he would thrash mercilessly for some minor transgression.

A larger-than-life character, Motilal spent money as fast as he could make it. After his first successes he moved from the crowded Chowk Mirganj area of Allahabad into a large bungalow at 9 Elgin Road, in the civil lines, where property was normally reserved for whites and Eurasians. A little while later, he bought an even grander house, I Church Road, which he named *Anand Bhavan* (Abode of Happiness). It became the first house in Allahabad to have its own indoor swimming pool, electricity and running water. Ironically for the home of a future Congress leader and founder of a great Hindu political dynasty, it had originally belonged to Sir Syed Ahmed Khan, that scourge of Indian politicians.

Motilal was the kind of figure around whom legends accrete. He was an avid fan of anything new and mechanical, and in 1904 could be seen, decked out in tweed coat and cap, proudly driving the first motor car in town. His hospitality was justly famous. Only the finest wines were served at his dinner parties and the menus would have graced the most luxurious restaurants. It was said that he had all his suits made in Savile Row – in fact only a few of them were – and that he sent his shirts to Paris for laundering: pure fantasy, but the story was good for his image.

In 1899, Motilal visited Europe for the first time, partly on business and partly for pleasure. For a high-caste Kashmiri Brahman, such a trip across 'the dark water' posed a particularly difficult religious dilemma. Two years earlier, Motilal's eldest brother, Bansi Dhar, who was so strictly orthodox that he would not even allow his children to be present when he ate, had travelled to London to attend Queen Victoria's diamond jubilee. He had regarded it as a tragedy when, in spite of all his careful precautions, he fell ill on board ship and became ritually tainted by being forced to accept food and medicine forbidden to a Brahman. On his return, he had to undergo a lengthy purification ceremony to restore his caste, the validity of which was by no means accepted by all Brahmans. Motilal was determined to have none of this 'tomfoolery' as he called it. He publicly refused to undergo any purification when he returned to India, and as a result was excommunicated. He treated the whole matter as a joke, mischievously telling an ultra-orthodox uncle who visited him: 'You may not dine with me without polluting yourself, but I suppose we could share a whisky and soda.'

Because of his aggressive stance against hide-bound Hindu orthodoxy, Motilal found himself the leader of an emancipated group of Brahmans in Allahabad. Their campaign was successful: before long, increasing numbers of Kashmiri Brahmans were travelling abroad, regardless of taboos.

While Motilal's career was going from strength to strength, in his private life he had suffered a series of domestic tragedies. He had been married while still in his teens, as tradition demanded, but his wife had died in childbirth. The child, a son, died with her. His second wife, Swarup Rani, a beautiful girl from Lahore, was described later by her son as having 'a Dresden china perfection'. It was a fragile perfection: over the years she was to suffer frequent ill-health. Their first child, also a son, died shortly after birth. The following year, Motilal's second brother, Nand Lal, also died, leaving a wife and seven children. As his eldest brother was forced by his job to live elsewhere, the 25-year-old Motilal became head of this extended family and its sole breadwinner. His responsibilities were further increased when, on 14 November 1889, Swarup Rani gave birth to another son. This one survived. His joyful parents called him Jawaharlal, which means 'precious stone' – a name the boy never seems to have liked.

'An only son of prosperous parents,' Jawaharlal Nehru confessed in his autobiography, 'is apt to be spoilt, especially so in India. And when that son happens to have been an only child for the first eleven years of his existence there is little hope for him to escape his spoiling.' Jawaharlal was 11 before his parents succeeded in producing another child. This time it was a girl. They named her Sarup Kumari. Five years after that another son was born, but he died within a month. A second daughter, Krishna, born in 1907, survived. No brother was ever to threaten Jawaharlal's position in the family. He lived in a kind of juvenile arcadia, the centre of affection of loving parents. Such adulation inevitably had its effect on his character in later life.

As an admirer of western ways, Motilal was determined that his son should be brought up by Europeans, and placed his education in the hands of a series of English governesses and private tutors. One of these was F.T. Brooks, a Franco-Irish Theosophist who had been personally recommended by Annie Besant. It was Brooks who encouraged his pupil's interest in science, rigging up a laboratory for him at Anand Bhavan.

In May 1905, when Jawaharlal was 15, Motilal took him and his mother and baby sister Sarup to England, to enrol Jawaharlal in an English public school and to consult top doctors as to the most suitable watering place for Swarup Rani. It was on the boat-train from Dover to London that Jawaharlal read in an English newspaper of the great Japanese naval victory over the Russians at Tsushima. Like so many young Indians, Nehru was excited by the news: 'Nationalistic ideas filled my mind. I mused of Indian freedom and Asiatic freedom from the thraldom of Europe. I dreamt of brave deeds, of how, sword in hand, I would fight for India and help in freeing her.'

Although none of the best English schools had any vacancies, influential English friends were able to pull strings, and a place was found for Jawaharlal at Harrow, Winston Churchill's Alma Mater. He enjoyed his time there, though at 16 he was three years older than the average new entrant. In his own words, he was 'never an exact fit', but he did well, coming top in every subject. He played the appropriate sports, including cricket and football, with more enthusiasm than proficiency, and joined the rifle club and officer training corps. He was already fascinated by politics, British as well as Indian. After the general election of 1906, with its landslide victory for the Liberal Party, he was the only boy in his form who could name all the members of Campbell-Bannerman's Cabinet. Indeed, there is little doubt that at that time he was far more politically aware than his father.

Although Motilal, aroused by the furore over the partition of Bengal, attended the Congress in Benares at the end of that year and found time to go to the Calcutta session in 1906, it was not until 1907 that he could be persuaded to become actively involved. In January of that year a group of Moderate Congress supporters met in Anand Bhavan to discuss the possibility of holding a provincial conference in Allahabad. Motilal was the obvious candidate for the chair, but he was not enthusiastic. He intended to refuse, but someone leaked the story to the press that he had accepted, and it would have been too embarrassing to withdraw. 'I have been compelled to accept,' he complained to his son in one of his frequent letters. 'It is an entirely new line for me and I have very grave doubts of being able to justify the expectations of my friends.'

Jawaharlal had no doubts about his father's ability. 'You will be as successful in the new line,' he prophesied correctly, 'as you have been in other fields.' Though he was sure his father's presidential address would be brilliant, he advised him not to be too moderate. With the instinctive shrewdness of a born politician, he pointed out that: 'Indians are as a rule too much so and require a little stirring up.'[18]

Like most Moderates, Motilal had high expectations of the Morley-Minto reforms, which he hoped would offer a steady constitutional evolution towards dominion status and self-rule. But when he read the watered-down, wishy-washy proposals he felt betrayed. These weren't reforms, he wrote to his son at Harrow, but a means of destroying the influence of the Indian educated classes in national politics. How could the creation of an Advisory Council of Notables – 'Noodles' he called them – end in anything but farce? Or an enlarged Legislative Council offer anything more than an extended provincial talking shop? He had trusted British promises and had been let down. He was also disgusted at the way some British officials did their best to exacerbate the divisions between Hindu and Muslim.

In spite of all his reservations, Motilal stood for a seat on the enlarged provincial council, and was elected. He soon found his fears had been well founded. Presided over by the lieutenant-governor and packed with British officials and Indian placemen, not only was the council powerless but its Indian members were expected to show appropriate gratitude for the wise decisions taken on their behalf by British officials. Criticism was not welcomed. When Motilal and a few others had the effrontery to question government decisions in the provincial budget – the amount of money spent on policing the United Provinces, 'the best behaved of all the provinces of India', or persistent government failure to fund education or sanitation properly – he was told to shut up and that he had no right of reply. 'The debate', he reported, 'was wound up by the Governor who patted [on the back] the *khushmadis* (sycophants) and the officials.' Undeterred by his provincial experience, however, Motilal also stood for election to the Imperial Legislative Council, taking his place in 1910 as a Congress representative in Calcutta alongside Sinha, Gokhale, Banerjea and Jinnah.

Jawaharlal left Harrow in July 1907 to go up to Trinity College, Cambridge, to read chemistry, geology and physics for the natural sciences tripos – he soon dropped physics in favour of the less arduous botany. But first he took a holiday in Dublin. His father was greatly alarmed. 'You asked me not to go near Belfast on account of the riots,' the young Nehru wrote, 'but I would have dearly liked to have been there for them.' Motilal must have been even more alarmed when his son asked: 'Have you heard of the Sinn Fein in Ireland? ... Their policy is not to beg for favours but to wrest them. They do not want to fight England by arms, but "to ignore her, boycott her, and quietly assume the administration of Irish affairs".'[19]

The years at Cambridge passed pleasantly for Jawaharlal, supported by a generous allowance from his father and with no great academic ambition. A mildly enthusiastic but hardly diligent sportsman, he put himself down for riding, tennis and the Trinity College Boat Club, where his weight of 8 stone 4 pounds made him a natural choice as cox. He joined the Magpie and Stump debating society, where members were fined if they failed to speak during a term – Jawaharlal paid frequent fines. Intellectually, he flitted frivolously from one blossom to another. He imbibed the Fabianist socialism of George Bernard Shaw and the Webbs from their own lips. He was also drawn to Bertrand Russell and John Maynard Keynes, whose lectures he often attended.

Nevertheless India and Indian politics were not forgotten. Jawaharlal's ideas were always more radical than his father's, and in his letters he was constantly criticizing his father's attitudes, sometimes to the point where Motilal threatened to cut off his allowance and call him home. But however much he disagreed with some of Motilal's over-cautious views, Jawaharlal wholeheartedly accepted his secular legacy. He was outraged by the communal, anti-Muslim flavour of Bipin Chandra Pal's nationalism when Pal came to Cambridge to speak to the Majlis, the society of Indian students. One of Jawaharlal's fellow students, incidentally, was the Muslim Saifuddin Kitchlew, who was to figure so prominently in the events leading up to the massacre in Amritsar, 10 years later.

Jawaharlal emerged from Cambridge with a lower second class degree in natural sciences and no clear idea of what he would like to do with his life. His father had originally wanted him to try for 'the greatest of services in the world', the ICS. But Jawaharlal's modest degree showed that he was unlikely to be successful in the highly competitive examinations. The next best thing was the law, and Jawaharlal duly enrolled in the Middle Temple.

The law did not prove to be particularly arduous. He ate his dinners as required, scraped through the necessary exams, and otherwise devoted himself to ice skating, golf and watching cricket at Lords. He took rooms in Holland Park, joined the Queen's Club, and socialized with friends from Harrow and Cambridge, enjoying the life of a regular man about town. He spent money like water, including large amounts on acquiring a substantial library, and when his father protested, he declared disarmingly: 'I am afraid I have no money sense.'

Jawaharlal was in no hurry to return to India, but eventually he had to face the fact that after seven years his father was not prepared to go on indefinitely financing his holiday from reality. He was told to obtain all that was needed to establish himself at the Allahabad bar: letters of commendation, particularly as to his sterling character, enrolment in the High Court in London, and purchase of a wig and gown.

Back home in India, Jawaharlal found himself 'a queer mixture of the East and West, out of place everywhere, at home nowhere'. Life in Allahabad was a bore. Even politics seemed flat. Congress was hopelessly split, many leaders were either in prison or had fled the country to avoid British repression. Dutifully, without enthusiasm, he followed his father into practice as a lawyer. His first fee was substantial: 500 rupees – a hundred times what Motilal had received for his first case – from a Sikh who employed the son in order to curry favour with the father. Unfortunately, few clients chose to follow that example, and briefs did not come as often as they might. One reason was Jawaharlal's lack of confidence: like the young Gandhi, he found it difficult to speak in open court. Gradually, however, he learned the art of advocacy, though he never took to the courtroom in the way his father had, and found the company of lawyers and officials boring.

Jawaharlal was 26 years old in 1916, when his parents decided it was time he was married. Despite his western education and his father's religious agnosticism, it would, of course, be an arranged marriage. Motilal settled on the daughter of a Delhi businessman, Pandit Jawaharmul Kaul. Her name was Kamala and she was 16 years old, tall, slim and, according to Nehru's younger sister Krishna, 'one of the most beautiful women I knew or ever had known'. She possessed great natural intelligence, but had only received the limited education of a typical Hindu girl of her class. Intellectually, a gulf always separated Kamala and Jawaharlal. Like her mother-in-law, Kamala remained obstinately Indian.

The marriage took place in Delhi on 8 February 1916. It was an auspicious day for a wedding: Vasanta Panchami, the first day of spring, when Kamadeva, the god of love, is worshipped. It is also a day sacred to Saraswati, the

Hindu Athena, goddess of learning and wisdom, but there was not much wisdom or understanding to be found in the Nehru marriage. Both husband and wife were quick tempered and they quarrelled easily. Obsessed with politics – he became joint secretary of the local branch of Annie Besant's Home Rule League that year – Jawaharlal was quite indifferent to his wife's opinions.

In November 1917, 21 months after their marriage, Kamala gave birth to a daughter. She was to be their only child: following her birth, her mother became a permanent invalid. They called the child Indira.

With Gokhale dead, Motilal Nehru was the natural choice to lead the important Congress committee to draft the pact with the Muslim League. He invited Jinnah to stay with him at Anand Bhavan, and there, during the heat of April 1916, they sat down together and drafted what they chose to call the 'Freedom Pact'. Even as they deliberated, the Easter Rising in Ireland was offering a terrible example of how the British dealt with armed rebellion, confirming that the only sensible way forward was the constitutional approach to which they were both committed. The pact they drew up was in fact a set of proposals to take the Morley-Minto reforms further and provide a government structure acceptable to both major groupings. Both sides made concessions, and inevitably both Hindus and Muslims complained that they were being asked to make more sacrifices than the other, a sure sign that the proposals were generally fair.

When he and Motilal had finished their business, Jinnah took himself away from the heat of the plains to spend two months' holiday in the hills at Darjeeling. He stayed at the summer home of a friend and client, the wealthy cotton magnate Sir Dinshaw Petit, one of the most devoutly orthodox leaders of the Bombay Parsi community. Jinnah and Sir Dinshaw's only daughter, Ruttie, a lively, intelligent and incredibly beautiful girl aged 16, fell madly in love, with a passion that totally belied Jinnah's reputation as a man of cool logic. Although he had told Jinnah he was in favour of intercommunal marriages, Sir Dinshaw was horrified at the thought of his beloved daughter marrying a Muslim, and forbade the match. But Jinnah's determination was as powerful as his fervour, and he refused to accept his old friend's rejection. He and Ruttie endured two agonizing years waiting until she reached her eighteenth birthday, when she converted to Islam and married him at his home in Bombay.

The draft pact prepared by Jinnah and Motilal was discussed by a joint meeting of Congress and League leaders in Allahabad in October 1916, and approved unanimously. In December, it was presented to the annual sessions of both Congress and the League, which were held simultaneously in Lucknow. Jinnah was elected president of the League for the first time. Congress was presided over by Ambika Charan Mazumdar, but the dominant figure was undoubtedly Tilak, who was welcomed back 'after nearly ten years of painful separation'. With his triumph in the high court still fresh in everybody's mind, Tilak was the hero of the hour – especially to the hundreds of Home Rule Leaguers who had been brought from western India by special trains to flood the Congress. There were also some 433 Muslim delegates, who had been given free admission and board and lodging. When Tilak spoke passionately in favour of the pact, the opposition simply faded away. At the League meeting, similarly, Jinnah had little difficulty in carrying all before him.

Seen in retrospect, the demands made in the Lucknow Pact, as it has become known, were eminently reasonable, not to say modest. It called for enlarged legislative councils, both central and provincial, all with majorities elected by 'as broad a franchise as possible'. In addition, half the members of the viceroy's Executive Council should be Indians, elected by the elected members of the Imperial Legislative Council. The secretary of state's council in London should be abolished, and the costs of the India Office borne by Britain rather than India. Following the *Komagata Maru* affair in Canada, and racial discrimination in South Africa, the pact demanded that 'Indians should be placed on a footing of equal status and rights of citizenship with other subjects of His Majesty the King throughout the Empire'. It made similar demands concerning the army and navy, in which 'commissioned and non-commissioned ranks should be thrown open to Indians, and adequate provision should be made for their selection, training and instruction in India'.

The great concession made by the Hindus was accepting and even extending the positive discrimination in favour of Muslims established in the 1909 Act. Muslims would have a guarantee of one third of all elected seats on the Imperial Legislative Council, well in excess of their numbers in the country, which were now about one in four. The number of guaranteed seats in provinces where Muslims were in the minority was on average to be almost double their proportion in the population as a whole. They would, however, no longer be entitled to vote in general constituencies as well as their separate ones. In Bengal and the Punjab, where Muslims were in the majority, they would have no separate electorate and fewer reserved seats than their proportion in the population, on the grounds that they did not need special consideration in those states. As a general protection for the rights and interests of all minorities, no bill or resolution concerning a community could be proceeded with in any council if three-quarters of the representatives of that community were opposed to it.[20]

Jinnah and Motilal Nehru could be justly proud of their handiwork: the Lucknow Pact was the high-water mark of the constitutional approach to the struggle for self-government, and of Hindu-Muslim co-operation. But there was a shadow, as yet unseen, waiting to fall across their achievement. By negotiating with the Muslim League, Congress had recognized it as the party representing the

Muslims of India, and in so doing would be seen by many as having tacitly accepted Syed Ahmed's theory of two nations. Jinnah and Motilal had unwittingly planted a time bomb, which would eventually destroy the unity for which they had laboured so hard.

'An Indefensible System'

By the time of the Lucknow Pact, the mood of India was already changing. The war was dragging on longer than anyone had expected, and as the death toll mounted among the Indian volunteers, disillusionment grew. In his presidential speech at the League session, Jinnah had declared that the 'united India demand must eventually prove irresistible'. He had gone on to assure his listeners that when the war was won, 'India will have to be granted her birthright as a free, responsible and equal member of the British Empire.' But the British government was already showing signs that it did not agree with him.

There was to be an Imperial War Conference in 1917, to formulate policy both for the continuation of the war and for the peace afterwards. All the white dominions would participate as a matter of course. The Indians, who were contributing so much to the Allied cause, believed they had a right to be there, too. Hardinge pressed India's claim, which he thought was entirely just. But he was ignored by a war cabinet dominated by Curzon and Kitchener, with their bitter personal memories of India. Frustrated and weary, still suffering the after-effects of the 1912 bomb, and with all his efforts to liberalize the regime sabotaged by the die-hards in Delhi, Hardinge stepped down as viceroy in 1916, and returned to Britain.

Hardinge's successor as viceroy, Lord Chelmsford, did not inspire confidence. Although he was the grandson of a distinguished solicitor-general, attorney-general and ultimately lord chancellor, he had little else to recommend him. A polished but uninspiring former cavalry captain with little knowledge or understanding of India, his political career had not been distinguished. After serving as a member of the LCC, he had been governor first of Queensland and then of New South Wales, but was subsequently turned down for the governorship of Bombay. It has been suggested that the reason Prime Minister Asquith chose him to be viceroy was that he was the only fellow of All Souls in

India at the time. Chelmsford looked every inch the romantic novelist's idea of an English gentleman – tall, slim, impeccably dressed – but remained an elegant nonentity. Lacking charm, energy and *joie de vivre*, he possessed all the charisma of a dead turbot. Indians found him difficult to communicate with and his staff found him cold, 'too much of a machine'. His five-year-old daughter, Margaret, once summed up her parents with precocious perception: 'My daddy', she said, 'works very hard and my mummy is the viceroy.'[1] It might have been better for India if she had been right.

For all his lack of distinction, however, Chelmsford was not a fool. Shortly after his appointment, he wrote to the secretary of state for India, Austen Chamberlain, stressing the need to make a definite commitment to further constitutional progress in India. The members of his council, he reported, were becoming increasingly worried about the Home Rule movement, which was proving vociferous and effective. Chelmsford suggested that India be given 'the largest measure of self-government compatible with the maintenance of the supreme authority of British rule'.[2] Throughout 1916 and 1917, the Home Rule movement was bolstered by a growing dissatisfaction with the way Britain was conducting the war. Wounded servicemen, returning to their towns and villages maimed and crippled, told how the British government had often failed to fulfil its obligations to look after Indians who had volunteered to serve overseas. The worst example had been in Mesopotamia, where the Indian army had been crushed in 1916 by a deadly combination of tough Ottoman troops, disease, and boneheaded military incompetence, and although the military situation was later retrieved, the memory of the 'Mespot disaster' lingered on.

It took until June 1917 for a royal commission to investigate the disaster and deliver a report on its causes. But when the report was published it was utterly damning. In the wave of popular outrage that followed, both in Britain and India, Rudyard Kipling spoke for millions when he derided 'the idle-minded overlings' who had been responsible for 'the slothfulness that wasted and the arrogance that slew', in his poem, *Mesopotamia*. Demanding their removal for 'the shame that they have laid upon our race', he was duly rewarded by the ritual resignation of Austen Chamberlain, and his replacement as secretary of state by Edwin Montagu.

Montagu, a tall, precise man with bald head and protruding eyes, sporting a black moustache and a monocle, had served as under-secretary at the India Office under Lord Morley, and was an even more fervent lover of India than his mentor. He had toured the country in 1913, and had been utterly bowled over by it. He felt a deep affinity with the sub-continent: as a Jew he considered himself 'an Oriental', and resolved to do everything in his power to help India and its people. In the House of Commons debate on the royal commission's report on Mesopotamia, Montagu had castigated the government of India as 'too wooden, too iron, too inelastic, too antediluvian, to be of any use for the modern purposes we have in view. I do not believe that anybody could ever support the Government of India from the point of view of modern requirements. It is an indefensible system.' A few days later, he was in charge of that system, and eager to show that he meant to do something about it.

On 20 August 1917, Montagu began his tenure of the India Office with a famous declaration:

The policy of His Majesty's Government, with which the Government of India are in complete accord, is that of the increasing association of Indians in every branch of the administration, and the gradual development of self-governing institutions, with a view to the progressive realization of responsible government in India as an integral part of the British Empire.

As a promise of freedom, Montagu's declaration was decidedly tentative, hedged in by weasel words like 'gradual development', 'progressive realization', and 'responsible government'. An accompanying clause stated that the British government alone would decide what 'responsible government' meant and when the Indians would be ready for it. But for Indian nationalists the declaration was a landmark, a clear promise of the dominion status they sought. No longer could their demands for Home Rule or independence be considered seditious.

The first opportunity to test the validity of Montagu's goodwill came immediately. In June 1917, Annie Besant and two of her Home Rule League associates had been imprisoned by the government of Bombay for 'seditious journalism'. Their internment had been the signal for a massive, nation-wide campaign of petitions and protests. Moderate leaders, including Banerjea, Malaviya and even Jinnah, who had stood aloof from the Home Rule Leagues, now joined, to demonstrate their solidarity – Jinnah, indeed, quickly became president of the Bombay Home Rule League. At a meeting of the All-India Congress Committee on 28 July, Tilak had proposed using the weapon of passive resistance or civil disobedience if the government refused to free Mrs Besant. While details of his proposals were being circulated to all the provincial committees for consideration, a thousand men signed up to march on the prison, and volunteers in Gujarat began collecting the signatures of a million peasants in support of Home Rule.

Montagu had not then been appointed, but was watching events with a lively interest. 'Shiva,' he wrote in his diary, 'cut his wife into fifty-two pieces only to discover that he had fifty-two wives. This is really what happens to the Government of India when it interns Mrs Besant.'[3]

In September, shortly after Montagu took up his new post, Jinnah made a personal appeal to the Home minister, and Mrs Besant was released. It was a good omen. In December, riding a tidal wave of emotion, she was elected president at the annual session of Congress in Calcutta, which coincided once again with the Muslim League's session.

By the time Congress and the League met, Montagu was visiting India again, something no other secretary of state had ever done while in office. Supported by a 10-man delegation, he toured the country, meeting and talking to everyone who mattered, Indian as well as British. Fearful of what his enthusiasm might lead to, his officials kept him well away from Calcutta during the meetings, pinning him safely down in Bombay, on the other side of the sub-continent. His Indian diary, dictated to a shorthand writer at all hours of the day or night during his visit, shows that their fears were well founded. 'My visit to India,' he proclaimed at the start, 'means that we are going to do something, and something big. I cannot go home and produce a little thing or nothing; it must be epoch-making, or it is a failure; it must be the keystone of the future history of India.'[4]

For all his bold words, however, Montagu was a weak man, all too ready to back down in the face of determined opposition. 'I am not the stuff to carry this sort of thing off,' he confided to his diary. 'It is one of India's misfortunes that I am alone, alone, alone the person that has got to carry this thing through.'[5] Nevertheless he persevered, though it did not take him long to discover the power of the Anglo-Indian establishment, or the ability of officialdom to obstruct his efforts.

'When I am with Mr Montagu,' wrote the commander-in-chief, General Sir Charles Munro, 'I feel that I am walking with a man who is steadily edging me towards a precipice and when he gets me near enough will push me over.' Munro's concerns were shared by most Anglo-Indians, but it comes as no surprise that Montagu's most vehement opponent was Sir Michael O'Dwyer. Reporting to Lloyd George, who had taken over from Asquith as prime minister in December 1916, Montagu complained of O'Dwyer's implacable hostility, and the way that 'he is determined to maintain his position as the idol of the reactionary forces, and to try and govern by the iron hand'.[6]

Unfortunately, O'Dwyer was one of the two men with whom Montagu had to work most closely to produce his plans for reform. The other, of course, was Chelmsford. 'The thing that alarms me in all Chelmsford's talks seems to me to be that so little has reform sunk into his mind that he seems to think everything will go on as it is,' Montagu wrote. Later, when he had persuaded Chelmsford of the virtue of his ideas for reform, he complained of another problem: 'Although he agrees, he cannot get things done.' Unlike O'Dwyer, who was never troubled by the slightest self-doubt or hesitation, Chelmsford had developed vacillation into a fine art: 'I am so afraid of putting my signature to something which will be criticized and held up to scorn,'[7] he confessed. The exasperated Montagu concurred: 'He never moves an inch without consulting his Council. He never expresses an opinion without consulting his Council. The whole time, charming man though he is, every document I show him he has to consult somebody before he expresses an opinion.'[8]

In spite of the resistance from Chelmsford, O'Dwyer and official India, Montagu managed to introduce some genuinely progressive ideas in his 300-page 'Report on Indian Constitutional Reform', many of them taken from the proposals of the Lucknow Pact. In July 1918, he presented the report to Parliament. And there it stayed. At the end of the year, the American Fred Fisher wrote: 'Although it was far from sweeping enough to satisfy even the middle ground of representative Indian opinion, Parliament found it too radical for its taste and has ever since hedged and postponed – on the ground of absorption in the war.'[9]

The truth was that there was considerable opposition to Montagu's ideas within the government, and Lloyd George was having great difficulty in getting them through. Although Kitchener was lying dead at the bottom of the ocean, Curzon and other implacable imperialists like Winston Churchill remained. Since Montagu was not a member of the War Cabinet, he was seriously outgunned. Now, it was his turn to suffer the frustrations experienced by Hardinge. He feared with some justification that the governments of Britain and India would reduce his grand plan to 'a niggling, miserly, grudging safeguard, fiddling with the existing order of things'.[10]

Montagu's watered-down proposals – the Montagu-Chelmsford Reforms as they came to be known – were hardly revolutionary, but they did mark a substantial step towards the 'responsible government' he had promised a year before. They were designed to give 'as far as possible complete popular control in local bodies', with a 'measure of responsibility' at once, leading to 'complete responsibility as soon as conditions permit'.

The centre-piece of government, the viceroy's Imperial Legislative Council, was to be replaced by two new bodies, a Legislative Assembly with 106 elected and 40 nominated members, 25 of whom would be officials, and an upper house, the Council of State, with 61 members, to represent the larger landed interests. Above this again, the viceroy's Executive Council was to have six members, three of them Indian, besides the viceroy himself and the commander-in-chief. But all these bodies remained strictly consultative. The viceroy was not answerable to any of them, only to the British government in London.

The provinces were to be given a great deal of autonomy, paving the way for federalism some time in the future. Provincial legislative councils were to be more than doubled in size, with at least 70 per cent of their members elected. But their authority was restricted by an ingenious two-level system of government known as diarchy – 'the technical term for handing over the steering wheel and retaining control of the accelerator and brake,' as Philip Mason succinctly described it.[11] Elected members were themselves to elect ministers to take charge of the 'nation-building subjects' – education, agriculture, public works, co-operative societies, and so on – over whom the governor would preside like a constitutional prime minister. But the essential departments, those dealing with revenue and law and order, were to remain under the direct orders of the governor as absolute ruler.

As a vital step towards the democratic self-government which was accepted as the ultimate goal by all but the most hardened imperialists, the franchise was to be vastly widened, with property and tax liability as the main but by no means the only qualifications. This would create over 5 million voters for the provincial councils, about 1 million for the Legislative Assembly, and 17,000 for the Council of State – tiny numbers in an adult population of some 150 million, but a significant advance towards a genuinely popular vote. In line with the proposals made in the Lucknow Pact, the separate electorates and reserved seats introduced for Muslims in 1909 were increased both in the provinces and in the centre. They were also extended to other minorities: Sikhs in the Punjab, Indian Christians, Anglo-Indians and even Europeans in other places.

Indian opinion on the report was split three ways. A survey of 29 newspapers, made by the *Indian Social Reformer*, found 11 endorsing it 'more or less warmly', nine doubtful or non-committal, and nine 'frankly opposed and disappointed'.[12] The survey was an accurate reflection of the views of the political leaders, too. Some, like Annie Besant, regarded the proposed reforms as 'unworthy of Britain to offer and India to accept', and wanted to reject them out of hand (she later changed her mind several times before eventually advocating acceptance). Others wanted to welcome them without question. Most thought they were inadequate but should be given a chance for a trial period. A joint Congress-League committee was set up – the two organizations were still capable of working together harmoniously – to co-ordinate their official response, which emerged as a qualified acceptance.

The Congress-League discussions were led once more by Jinnah, whom Montagu regarded as the most outstanding of all the Indian national leaders. 'Young, perfectly mannered, impressive looking, armed to the teeth with dialectics, and insistent upon the whole of his scheme,' he noted in his diary, adding with some satisfaction: 'Chelmsford tried to argue with him, and was tied up into knots. Jinnah is a very clever man, and it is, of course, an outrage that such a man should have no chance of running the affairs of his own country.'[13] Jinnah returned the compliment in his official reaction to the report by implying that Montagu's noble intentions had clearly been nobbled by the reactionaries. Acknowledging the effort that had been made to face the problems, Jinnah conceded that he was willing to accept the report, though 'only as a transitional stage'.

Everything seemed set for steady and peaceful progress on the road to self-government. If the rewards for India's efforts during the war were not as great as the Indian leaders had hoped, at least the reforms were a step in the right direction. They regarded the result with some satisfaction, eagerly anticipating better things to come. What was to come immediately, however, turned out to be something infinitely worse.

While the Cabinet were back-pedalling on implementing the Montagu-Chelmsford reforms, they moved more swiftly over other Indian measures. When Montagu returned from India in April 1918 on HMS *Dufferin*, one of his fellow passengers had been Sir Sydney Rowlatt, a justice of the King's Bench division. Rowlatt had been chairing a committee appointed by the government of India to look into the replacement of the 1915 Defence of India Act, a wartime emergency measure giving the government powers to deal with the revolutionary terrorism that had plagued India since 1907. Rowlatt and his committee had reviewed the situation, sitting in camera, and had drafted two bills allowing the government of India to go on bypassing the normal processes of law in dealing with activities prejudicial to the security of the state — that catch-all phrase beloved by all totalitarian regimes. The first bill laid down that for a period of three years, suspected terrorists could be arrested, detained, interned, expelled, all without warrant, charge, trial or even a stated cause. The second bill amended the Indian Penal Code to make these provisions permanent.

Almost all the Indian leaders were lawyers, many of them schooled in London's ancient Inns of Court. To them, such measures were barely tolerable in wartime but total anathema in peace, negating the very principles of British justice on which government by consent depended. The fact that the measures could even be considered damaged their faith in that supreme British quality, the sense of fair play. Was this denial of basic rights and civil liberties a fair and just reward for India's loyalty and sacrifice during the war? When the bills were presented to the Imperial Legislative Council on 6 February 1919, the Indian members condemned them without exception.

Jinnah was the most outspoken critic of the Rowlatt bills on the council. There was no precedent or parallel in the legal history of any civilized country to the enactment of such laws, he said, pointing out for good measure the folly of introducing them at such a moment, when 'high hopes of momentous reforms had been raised'. He considered it his duty, he went on, to warn that 'If these measures are passed, you will create in the country from one end to the other a discontent and agitation the like of which you have not witnessed, and it will have, believe me, a most disastrous effect on the good relations that have existed between the Government and the people.'

Chelmsford, Rowlatt and the British members clearly did not share

Montagu's high opinion of Jinnah. They chose to ignore his prophetic statement. Although the second bill amending the penal code was dropped after the committee stage, the first was duly laid before the council. There were 22 Indian members, and they opposed it unanimously. But there were 34 British members, who were prepared to rubber-stamp it. On 18 March 1919, what became known as the Rowlatt Act was passed into Law. Jinnah immediately walked out of the Legislative Council, along with two other Indian members. In his powerful and biting letter of resignation to Chelmsford, Jinnah declared:

> The fundamental principles of justice have been uprooted and the constitutional rights of the people have been violated at a time when there is no real danger to the state, by an overfretful and incompetent bureaucracy which is neither responsible to the people nor in touch with real public opinion ... In my opinion, a Government that passes or sanctions such a law in times of peace forfeits its claim to be called a civilised Government and I still hope that the Secretary of State for India, Mr. Montagu, will advise His Majesty to signify his disallowance to this Black Act.[14]

Chelmsford remained unmoved – he may even have been relieved at Jinnah's resignation, since life on the council would undoubtedly be more comfortable without that acid tongue and razor-sharp mind. But Jinnah was never one to give up a struggle easily. Little knowing how impotent Montagu had already become, he decided to sail to London to see the secretary of state personally and try to persuade him to override the Indian government.

Jinnah was planning to go to London in any case: the Muslim League had appointed him leader of a mission to plead for at least one Muslim member to be included in the delegation to the forthcoming Paris Peace Conference, where India was to have its own representation alongside Britain and the dominions. Indian Muslims feared that the Christian nations, having crushed the Ottoman empire, were about to renege on their wartime promises to the Muslims of the Middle East to protect both their interests and their holy places, and grab their lands instead.

Jinnah must have hoped to be named as the Muslim delegate to the Peace Conference, but his reputation as a difficult customer had preceded him. Although he presented his case to the British prime minister with his usual skill and energy, Lloyd George rejected all his arguments. Montagu turned out to be a man of straw, unable or unwilling to offer any practical help on either front. And doors that had previously been open to him were, since his resignation and outspoken criticisms, firmly closed in his face. So Jinnah's trip to London was a total failure politically. His only consolation was that his wife, Ruttie, gave birth to their only child, Dina, shortly after midnight on 14–15 August 1919. Had he been a superstitious man, Jinnah might have remembered it as an inauspicious omen 28 years later, when Pakistan was born at exactly the same time, day and month, for by then he and his daughter had become estranged. But the idea of 'auspicious' and 'inauspicious' days was a Hindu concept, totally alien to a Muslim, especially one whose whole approach to life was as resolutely secular as Jinnah's.

While Jinnah was sailing to England, anti-Rowlatt demonstrations were erupting all over the face of India. The demonstrations were inspired by Gandhi, and marked his emergence as a national politician. At the beginning of 1919, Gandhi was famous, even something of a hero, for his civil rights work for Indians in South Africa, and for three local campaigns in India. But his 'Indian experiment', as he described it, had barely begun. Having spent almost his entire adult life abroad, he had no power base, controlled no political organization, and did not enjoy the support of any social or political community. Within a year, however, he had become the undisputed leader of the Indian liberation movement, and had irrevocably changed both its nature and its course.

As it happened, the Rowlatt Act was never used by the Indian government: it lay on the statute book for its allotted three years, then quietly expired. But by then the damage it had inflicted was irreparable. If Chelmsford had listened to Jinnah, Motilal Nehru, and the Act's other critics, or had shown any understanding of Indian feelings, the steady and harmonious progress to self-government envisaged by Montagu might well have proceeded to a more speedy conclusion. Hundreds of thousands, perhaps more than a million, lives would have been saved, to say nothing of countless human tragedies during the following 30 years.

All that, of course, is speculation. What is certain is that without the Rowlatt Act, Gandhi could never have taken over the independence movement at the time and in the manner that he did. Gandhi's arrival would bring significant changes: he would replace the constitutional methods favoured by Jinnah, Motilal and their Moderate associates, with his own anarchistic agenda, relying on intuition more than intellect and appealing directly to the emotions of the masses. He would also turn what had been a resolutely secular political campaign into a religious crusade which sowed the seeds of destruction for a united India.

Although Gandhi was influenced by various cultures and beliefs – Christianity, Islam, Buddhism, Jainism, and Theosophy – he remained deeply rooted in his native Hinduism. It governed every aspect of his life, including his politics. 'My bent is not political but religious,' he said in mid-1919, 'and I take part in politics because I feel that there is no department of life which can be divorced from religion.'[15] Most Muslims regarded him with great suspicion, convinced that his calls for unity implied not equality but subjugation under Hindu rule, something they would fight against to the death. Over the years,

Gandhi's Hinduism would become an increasingly important factor in polarizing the two communities, helping to widen the rift between them until it became unbridgeable.

'God Bless Gandhi'

Mohandas Karamchand Gandhi was born on 2 October 1869, the year the Suez Canal was opened, in the sleepy little fishing port of Porbandar, one of the web of 200 or so tiny princely states that stretched across the Kathiawar peninsula in Gujarat, midway between Bombay and Karachi. His father, Karamchand Gandhi, was then dewan, chief minister, of Porbandar, but seven years later he moved to Rajkot as dewan to the rulers of both Rajkot and Wakaner. From his earliest years, therefore, Mohandas Gandhi was familiar with the processes of government, albeit on a minor scale, while at the same time he was insulated from direct British rule.

The Gandhis were Modh Banias, a sub-caste of the Vaishya class, the third of the four main Hindu divisions, originally composed of store-keepers and money-lenders (the name Gandhi means grocer in Gujarati). The family were devout Hindus, but not rigidly orthodox: they visited the temples of other Hindu sects and welcomed men of different faiths and traditions into their home – Muslims, Parsis and especially Jains. Monks of the Jain community called regularly and even ate with the family, and Jainism was to play a great part in shaping Gandhi's thinking.

Jainism, which started in about 500 BC as a breakaway Hindu reform movement, is particularly strong in Gujarat. It is an ascetic religion, based on the belief that everything in nature, even a rock or a stone, has a soul, and that it is wrong to destroy life in any shape or form. The eating of meat is unthinkable to Jains, who consume even vegetarian foods with great reluctance as an unfortunate necessity. Other central tenets of Jainism include the belief that fasting to death is the surest path to salvation – the founder of the faith, Mahavira, did so, though it took him 13 years.

Fasting has also always been part of Hindu tradition, both as a means of self-purification and through the practice of *dharna*. This is a means of shaming a debtor into repaying what he owes by sitting quietly at his door until satisfaction is received. Apart from the obvious social stigma involved, the debtor faces the threat of losing merit in the recurring cycle of life if the person fasting dies. *Dharna* could be turned to other purposes: in earlier times it was widely used for political ends, since it was thought to be a way of influencing the gods through self-sacrifice and the concentration of the will.

The greatest Jain influence on Gandhi was its central doctrine of *ahimsa*, non-violence. *Ahimsa* is also part of Hindu teaching, but Gandhi invested it with the more positive Jain interpretation of not simply refraining from physical violence but of actively returning good for evil. He coupled this with the search for truth, the *satya* of classical Hindu philosophy, which is indistinguishable from the concept of God.

The young Gandhi was a very ordinary child, with nothing to suggest that he might become an extraordinary man. He was timid and shy, terrified of 'thieves, ghosts and serpents', and afraid of the dark – well into his teens, he had to have a light in his room at night. His old nurse taught him to chant the name of Ram for comfort and protection, a lesson he remembered all his life, describing it as 'an infallible remedy' in times of trouble.

Modern education had recently arrived in Kathiawar with the opening of Alfred High School in Rajkot, where the young Gandhi was taught in English by three Parsis. He was no more than an adequate scholar: he managed to pass his matriculation in 1887, but failed his college examinations in Bhavnagar. He blamed this on the strain of living away from home for the first time, but his schooling had been interrupted for a whole year when he was married at the age of 13 to Kasturbai to whom he had been betrothed since he was eight. Although it was a traditional arranged marriage (Kasturbai was the daughter of one of his father's close friends), it proved to be a passionate one, and for much of his time at school, Gandhi's mind was on his wife, rather than his books.

Gandhi was also worried about his father, who had never fully recovered from injuries sustained when his carriage overturned on the way from Rajkot to Porbandar for the wedding. More seriously, he had also developed a fistula, and was now bedridden and in constant pain. Gandhi took on the role of nursemaid, reading to him, massaging his legs to relieve his pain, and generally devoting all his free time to caring for him until his father's death in 1886.

By a cruel stroke of fate, Gandhi was not with his father at the moment of his death. An uncle had offered to relieve him for a while, so that he could rest. But he was actually making love to Kasturbai when the news came that the old man had suddenly expired. For the rest of his life, he never ceased to blame himself for allowing lust to overcome his filial duty. His guilt was increased by the fact that Kasturbai had been expecting their first child at the time: the Hindu religion forbids sex during pregnancy, and when the child died soon after birth, Ghandi saw it as a judgement.[1]

Although he had failed his college exams, and was the youngest of Karamchand's three sons, Mohandas was the only one to have received an English education, so he was considered the most likely to revive the family's flagging fortunes after his father's death. They decided an English legal qualification offered the best chance of advancement, and pooled their modest resources to finance three years of study in London. Sending Mohandas to England was an enormous step for the family, and for the young man himself, since he had never set foot outside his native Kathiawar. Excited by the huge adventure ahead, he did not mind leaving his wife and recently-born first child. He sailed from India on the SS *Clyde* on 4 September 1888.

Gandhi's euphoria soon gave way to despondency on the voyage. He cried himself to sleep each night, homesick and miserable with loneliness. He missed his family, he missed India, and his shyness and poor command of English prevented him from socializing with his fellow passengers, who were all British apart from one Indian lawyer. Ill at ease with English customs, unable to use western cutlery, and still nervous of breaking the taboos on eating impure food with people from outside his caste, he avoided the dining-room and ate alone in his cabin.

Gandhi disembarked at Southampton on a cool autumn day, 27 October 1888, a pathetic little figure in a white flannel suit bought in Bombay. But it did not take him long to become thoroughly westernized. He replaced the Bombay clothes with smart suits from the Army & Navy Stores. He had an evening dress-suit made in Bond Street. High silk hat, spats, patent leather boots and silver-topped cane completed the transformation. For a while, he took lessons in elocution, dancing and the violin, but gave them up as his law studies at the Inner Temple became more demanding.

Gandhi learned a great deal more than law during his time in London. Freed from the petty constrictions of caste and locality, for the first time he was able to see himself not as a Modh Bania or a Gujarati, but as an Indian. He also became an active member of the London Vegetarian Society, a haven for unorthodox thinkers, not to mention cranks and eccentrics. He gained his first experience of committee work when he was elected to its executive council, and published his first articles in its journal.[2] Fellow members introduced him to the works of radical thinkers like John Ruskin and Count Leo Tolstoy. The Russian novelist and social reformer preached a doctrine of brotherly love, non-violent acceptance of evil, and the renunciation of wealth; Ruskin, the English art critic and moralist, was a stern critic of the industrial society.

Equally important to Gandhi's development was Madame Blavatsky's Theosophical Society, with its strong mystic elements. Gandhi never actually joined the Theosophists, but he had several friends who were members. It was through them that he began discovering the roots of his own culture through an English translation of the *Bhagavad Gita*, one of the most sacred Hindu texts, which forms part of the great classic, the *Mahabharata*. The Theosophists also introduced him to Sir Edwin Arnold's *The Light of Asia*, an account of the teachings of the Buddha, and to the Bible. He found the Old Testament hard work but was electrified by the New Testament, particularly the Sermon on the Mount.

Gandhi returned to India in 1891, to discover that his beloved mother had died while he was away: remembering the effect of his father's death on his studies, the family had kept the news from him. But that was only the beginning of his troubles. Although he was a qualified barrister and looked successful in his smart London clothes, he had neither the money nor the connections needed to set up in practice, and no knowledge of Indian law. He spent six frustrating months in Bombay trying to get started. And when he did eventually manage to get a case in Bombay's small causes court, he was too nervous to get up and cross-examine, and had to hand over the case, and his small fee, to another lawyer. In despair, he returned to Rajkot, to scrape a living drafting legal documents.

That might have been the last anyone heard of Mohandas Gandhi. However, after just over a year of drudgery, he was rescued by a Memon Muslim merchant from Porbandar, Dada Abdullah Sheth, who offered him a one-year contract to sort out various legal problems with his business in South Africa. The fee was to be £105 plus all expenses, including first-class travel. Gandhi apparently had no qualms about leaving his wife again, although she had just given birth to their second son. He sailed from Bombay in April 1893, a struggling 24-year-old lawyer with an uncertain future.

In South Africa, Gandhi was unique, the first English-educated, professional Indian, and the only one able to talk to the rulers in their own language. Even wealthy Muslim merchants had little if any formal education and could speak only the few words of English necessary for their trade. The vast majority of the 60,000 or so Indians were peasants with no education, who had been shipped in as cheap indentured labour for the sugar plantations and coal mines of Natal. It was inevitable that the erudite young lawyer should become their spokesman — there was simply no one else.

Until his arrival in South Africa, Gandhi had never encountered racial discrimination. In India, he had been a member of a privileged family living in principalities ruled by Indians. In London, he had been enrolled at the Inner Temple on an equal footing with English law students, and had met with nothing but kindness and acceptance. Yet within a few days of his arrival in South Africa, he came face to face with naked prejudice. Travelling from Durban to Pretoria, where he was to appear in court, he was thrown off the train after a white passenger objected to sharing a first class compartment with him. He spent the chilly night shivering in the waiting-room of Pietermaritzburg station, too timid to ask the stationmaster for the warm coat locked away with his luggage.

That night, however, was to see the first of many instant transformations in Gandhi. Like Joan of Arc and her voices, he was always ready to act on the inspiration of some dream or revelation. During that night, his habitual timidity seems to have been replaced by the fearlessness that marked his character for the rest of his life. Next morning, he sent a long telegram of complaint to the railway's general manager in Durban, and another to Dada Abdullah Sheth, who immediately hurried to meet the general manager. That evening, Gandhi was able to continue, in first class, to Charlestown, where the line then ended.

The stagecoach from Charlestown to Johannesburg brought another confrontation – he was beaten up by the coach leader when he tried to exercise his rights as a first class passenger. On arrival, he found all the hotels suddenly became full the moment he asked for a room. Having overcome the refusal of a first class ticket to Pretoria by quoting the railway regulations, he was only saved from being thrown out of his compartment again by the intervention of a European passenger.

The humiliations heaped upon him during that traumatic journey served only to strengthen Gandhi's new-found determination. Immediately he arrived in Pretoria, he called a meeting of the Indian population, urging them to organize themselves to fight against discrimination. His political life had begun. By the time his year's contract was up, he had not only completed his legal business successfully, but had also created the Natal Indian Congress, and persuaded the Natal government to reduce a prohibitive poll tax intended to deter Indian labourers from staying on once their indentures were complete. As an incidental, he had also established the right of Indians to travel first or second class on South African trains – as long as they were 'properly attired'.

As he was preparing to return home, the Indians of Durban begged Gandhi to help fight a bill that was about to be passed by the Natal legislature depriving them of the vote. He agreed to stay for one month. That month eventually became 20 years, during which Gandhi made only two brief visits to India. The first of these was in 1896, to collect his family, and on his return he was almost killed by an angry white mob trying to stop 600 Indians landing at Durban. He was rescued by the wife of the superintendent of police, and had to be smuggled out of the police station disguised as a constable. Typically, he refused to bring charges against those who had attacked him.

During his time in South Africa, Gandhi campaigned continuously for the rights of the Indian community, brandishing Queen Victoria's proclamation of 1858 as their Magna Carta. Oddly, he was not bothered by the oppression suffered by black and coloured people, never considering them equal to his fellow

Indians, who he believed came from a superior culture. Indeed, he shared what he saw as the Europeans' legitimate fear of being overrun by the black majority.

Perhaps because his fight was generally supported by the governments in both London and India, Gandhi's experiences never shook his faith in the British empire, which he saw as a divinely sanctioned force for India's good. Far from becoming anti-British or anti-empire, he saw himself as the champion of the empire's highest ideals, remaining unswervingly loyal and singing *God Save the Queen* with genuine fervour. He celebrated the queen's diamond jubilee in 1897 by planting a tree and distributing souvenirs to Indian children. When the Boer War started in 1899, he did his duty to Britain by raising and leading an ambulance corps of 1,100 Indians which performed valiantly in and near the front line. At the end of the war, he was proud to accept a decoration for his services to the empire.

By 1901, Gandhi decided he could return to India. The nervous, awkward young man of eight years earlier had become a confident and prosperous lawyer. He soon built a thriving practice in Bombay, and was able to live in considerable style with a large bungalow in the fashionable suburb of Santa Cruz. His activities in South Africa had made Gandhi's name well known in India, but he had few contacts there and little knowledge of the political scene. At the end of December 1901, he attended his first annual session of Congress in Calcutta, where he managed to get a resolution passed supporting the rights of the 100,000 Indians now in South Africa, and so impressed Gokhale that the Moderate leader took him under his wing as his personal protégé. Before he could start making political headway in India, however, he was called back to South Africa by an urgent telegram. The Secretary of State for the Colonies, Joseph Chamberlain, was about to pay a visit, and the Indians needed Gandhi to present their case for civil rights to him.

Chamberlain met Gandhi briefly, but declared that the imperial government did not interfere in the internal affairs of self-governing colonies. To his deep dismay, Gandhi realized that harsh new regulations had put Indians in South Africa in a worse position than ever, and that he must begin his work for them all over again. He had left his wife and children – he now had four sons – behind in Bombay, but had to send for them as it became clear that it would be some time before he could return to India. It was, in fact to be 12 years. During that time, the prosperous young lawyer in his stiff white collars and snazzy silk ties would metamorphose into the legendary Indian sage and holy man.

The catalyst again came from the west, this time in the shape of John Ruskin's book *Unto This Last*, which Gandhi read during a 24-hour train journey – first class, of course – between Johannesburg and Durban. 'It brought about an instantaneous and practical transformation in my life,' he wrote later. 'I believe that I discovered some of my deepest convictions reflected in the great book of

Ruskin.'[3] *Unto This Last* is a dense, complex book, attacking capitalism, property and modern industrial society. It propounds the moral and redemptive values of physical labour. Within a week, Gandhi was putting Ruskin's ideas into practice with his first experiment in communal living. Paying £1,000 for a 100-acre fruit farm at Phoenix, 14 miles from Durban, he moved in with his family, a few friends and the staff of the newspaper *Indian Opinion*, which he had started earlier that year.

Like so many of Gandhi's ideas, there was a practical, some might say crafty, purpose behind the Phoenix settlement: *Indian Opinion* could not survive as a normal commercial venture. But it could if it were printed, published and subsidized by a commune. Gandhi announced that he intended to retire from the law and live a life of simple self-sufficiency at Phoenix. His do-it-yourself regime there involved the family in all the lowly tasks which were forbidden to caste Hindus, such as washing clothes, cutting hair and even cleaning latrines. Within a year, however, political demands called him away to the Transvaal. He left the Phoenix settlers to get on with the farming and printing, but sent them a constant stream of instructions on cooking, diet and health, along with articles and directions for the newspaper.

For the most part, Kasturbai and the boys obeyed Gandhi's dictates without complaint – democracy had no place in his view of the family. His obsessive quest for selflessness was an extremely selfish process, especially where poor Kasturbai was concerned. One evening in 1906, having already sold all her treasured gold jewellery to help fund the Natal Indian Congress, Gandhi calmly informed her that he had decided to take a vow of *brahmacharya*, total self-control based on complete sexual abstinence. He dismissed his wife's feelings by saying 'she was never the temptress'.

Brahmacharya for a Hindu is normally part of the final stage of earthly life, when a man withdraws from worldly concerns to devote himself entirely to religion. Although Gandhi was still very much involved with politics, and was still practising law, his vow coincided with the start of a whole new phase in his life, during which he renounced all personal possessions, treated all people as his family, and devoted himself entirely to public service. His decision was triggered by his experiences leading a team of stretcher-bearers in the Zulu Rebellion that year, for which he had been awarded another medal. Having been exposed once more to the unspeakable horrors of war as he and his men tended both British soldiers and Zulu casualties whom no white men would touch, he emerged committed to a policy of positive non-violence. The doctrine of *satyagraha* was about to be born.

Satyagraha – the word was coined through a competition in *Indian Opinion* – was more than passive resistance. Indeed, Gandhi claimed it was not passive but active.

He described it as either 'soul force' or 'truth force'; 'the method of securing rights by personal suffering; it is the reverse of resistance by arms'. He was soon to have the opportunity to put it to the test. In 1906, the Transvaal government introduced a bill designed to clear Indians out of the colony by stopping immigration and harassing those already there. Indian residents were to be fingerprinted and given registration certificates which they had to carry at all times.

The Indians objected strongly. Led by Gandhi, they embarked on a peaceful protest, closing their shops in a *hartal*, organizing petitions, pickets and representations. It was all to no avail: the legislature passed the act. Gandhi, still a firm believer in the justness of the British constitution, travelled to London to lobby the secretaries of state for the colonies and India, Lords Elgin and Morley respectively. In doing so, he crossed swords for the first time with Elgin's under-secretary of state, the young Winston Churchill in his first ministerial appointment. In spite of counter-petitions from Indian Christians and Tamils in South Africa, who dissociated themselves from his mission and branded him an agitator, Gandhi returned to Johannesburg with the assurance that the act would not receive the royal assent.

It was an ephemeral victory: a few weeks later, the Transvaal became a self-governing colony, with no need to refer its legislation to London. The bill was promptly reintroduced, together with another restricting immigration for those who did not speak a European language. It became law on 1 July 1907. Gandhi and his followers refused to register, and formed what was to become the Satyagraha Association to fight it.

Gandhi had crossed the great divide, deliberately breaking the law for the first time in his life. He was arrested and sentenced to two months in gaol with hard labour. After two weeks, however, General Jan Christian Smuts, the Transvaal's colonial secretary, sent for him and offered to repeal the act and release the growing number of Indians crowding the gaol, if they agreed to register voluntarily. Claiming a moral victory, Gandhi accepted, and ordered the *satyagraha* to be lifted, to the disgust of many of his followers, who felt he had betrayed them. When he went to register, a group of Pathans set upon him, knocking him unconscious and beating him nearly to death. Once more, he refused to bring charges against his attackers.

To Gandhi's chagrin, Smuts reneged on his promise. Gandhi gathered some 2,000 followers in the grounds of the Hamidia mosque in Johannesburg, where they burned their registration certificates in a huge cauldron. It was a grand symbolic gesture, and it brought Gandhi and the other resisters further gaol sentences, which were repeated as they widened their protest against the new immigration laws by crossing the border between Natal and the Transvaal without permits.

At first, though he had urged his *satyagrahis* to regard prisons as 'His

Majesty's hotels', Gandhi was nervous of gaol, wondering how he would survive the harsh conditions. In fact, he survived very well, quickly working out a regime of cooking, exercise, prayer and study which served him well over the years. During his gaol terms in 1908-9, for example, he translated *Unto This Last* into Gujarati, discovered Henry David Thoreau's *On the Duty of Civil Disobedience*, and studied the Bible, the Qur'an, the *Gita* and other Hindu scriptural writings, together with works by Bacon, Carlyle, Emerson, Huxley, Tolstoy, Ruskin and Plato.

In 1909, plans were announced for the various South African provinces to form a federal Union. As a dominion within the empire, its constitution would have to be agreed with the British government, and Gandhi sailed off to London again to lobby for Indians' rights of citizenship within the new Union of South Africa. This time, his lobbying was even less successful – 'thankless and fruitless' as he described it. When the Union government came into being the following year, with Smuts as minister of the interior, all the racial laws of the former colonies were retained.

Sick at heart, Gandhi felt betrayed by the empire he had loved. On the return voyage from London, he gathered his thoughts into a long essay under the title *'Hind Swaraj'* (Indian Home Rule), which he published first as a series of articles in *Indian Opinion* and then as a separate booklet, which was immediately banned in India.

At first sight, *'Hind Swaraj'* appeared to be violently anti-British. In fact, like so much of Gandhi's thinking, it was both much simpler and much more complex than that; an attack not on the British Raj, but on the modern civilization it epitomized. He wanted to turn back the clock to some mythical pre-industrial golden age, with the people of India restored to a state of innocence. What Gandhi was advocating was not the violent overthrow of the British Raj, but a complete reversal of all its values and practices, including education, medicine and industrial development. He now opposed the use of English as the language of government and the law. Embracing the existing call for *swadeshi*, he said it was necessary to end the use of all imported goods, such as cloth, matches, pins, glassware, and machinery. What the Indian people could not make for themselves, he said, they could do without, as their ancestors had done.

'Hind Swaraj' was intended as a discussion paper rather than a definitive statement – Gandhi was in the process of working out his still confused ideas. For the next five years, he devoted himself to the experiment of living out those ideas in South Africa. He set up a larger commune on a 1,100-acre farm 21 miles from Johannesburg. Naming the new settlement Tolstoy Farm, he welcomed his followers there, and provided a home for the wives and children of resisters who were in prison. Men, women and children lived together as an extended family,

practising Gandhi's ideas on self-sufficiency and non-violence. They made everything themselves, grew their own food, killed nothing, not even snakes, and walked everywhere – Gandhi regularly tramped the 21 miles to and from Johannesburg to attend to his legal practice. They followed his theories on diet, sanitation, education, and even sexual abstinence. They consulted no doctors, treating anyone who fell sick entirely with diet and hydropathy. The various creeds, castes and ethnic groupings lived together in harmony.

Gandhi spent his five years at Tolstoy Farm putting his theories to the test. His attitude to diet became ever more rigorous – he would have liked to do away with food altogether, he said, reflecting the Jain influences of his youth, because it always involved violence against animal or plant life. He took a vow never to drink milk, after learning that some farmers injected hot liquids into the wombs of their cows to make them give a few more drops. But most significantly, he began fasting regularly, for a week at a time, at first as a means of self-purification, and then as a penance for the misdeeds of others.

In 1912, Gandhi's political mentor, Gokhale, visited South Africa at the behest of the viceroy, Lord Hardinge, to talk to Smuts and Prime Minister General Louis Botha, about the position of Indian immigrants. When they promised to repeal the main anti-Indian laws, it seemed that Gandhi's years of work were at last to be rewarded with success. He and Gokhale talked for days about his returning to India, his mission in South Africa accomplished. But when Gokhale went home, the promises were forgotten. The discriminatory laws remained in force, and there was worse to come: a new act was passed effectively barring all future Indian immigration, and a Supreme Court judge ruled that only marriages performed under Christian rites were legal in South Africa. On the wave of moral outrage that swept through the Indian community, Gandhi launched a new *satyagraha* campaign, declaring that he would fill the South African gaols with Indians to expose the immorality of the anti-Indian laws.

Fighting for the recognition of Indian marriages brought women into the struggle for the first time: the new *satyagraha* started with a group of 16 women from Phoenix Farm, including Kasturbai, marching illegally across the border from Natal to the Transvaal. When they were arrested, 11 women from Tolstoy Farm promptly crossed the border in the other direction. Before they in turn were arrested, they reached the coal-mining town of Newcastle, where they persuaded 5,000 Indian labourers to go on strike.

Gandhi hurried to Newcastle to take personal charge of the agitation. The employers forced the workers out of their homes, and tried to starve and beat them into submission, but they stood firm. Unable to feed and house such numbers, Gandhi decided the answer was to get them all arrested and put up in 'His Majesty's hotels'. Leading some 2,000 men, women and children on a march across the border into the Transvaal, he was arrested three times. Twice he was released, but the third time he was dragged to court in manacles and sentenced to nine months' hard labour. The ragged army, however, marched on unbowed until eventually the police rounded them up and put them on trains back to Newcastle, where they were imprisoned inside the mine compounds and brutally forced to dig coal. When news of this reached the rest of the Indian community, 50,000 labourers in mines and plantations throughout South Africa downed tools and went on strike in sympathy.

After 10 years as editor of *Indian Opinion*, Gandhi had learned a great deal about the power of the press. He had taken care to keep the papers in Britain and India, as well as nationalist leaders and the governments in both countries, fully informed of his new campaign with daily cables and statements. The march and its outcome made headlines everywhere. Gokhale toured India rousing public opinion on the issues. Lord Hardinge condemned the South African government's brutal action as 'one that would not be tolerated by any country that calls itself civilized' and called for a commission of inquiry.[4] But when the Pretoria government appointed one, Gandhi began organizing another protest march – all the commission's members were white, some of them notoriously anti-Indian.

The march never took place. Gandhi called it off when the government's survival was threatened by a strike of white railway workers on an unconnected issue. Since the whole point of *satyagraha* was to occupy the moral high ground at all times, a *satyagrahi* did not take advantage of his opponent's weakness. It was a move that disarmed his opponents and threw them into total confusion. Like many of Gandhi's actions, it also confused many of his followers, but most of them stayed loyal.

Gandhi's efforts finally bore fruit in June 1914, when, although he held no official position, Smuts negotiated an agreement with him. The £3 poll tax, registration, passes, and the system of indentured labour would all be abolished, and Indian marriages recognized. It was no more than a partial victory for Gandhi and *satyagraha* – the immigration laws remained and Indians were still not allowed to move between provinces without permits – but it was enough to enable him to leave for India with a clear conscience, 'eagerly looking forward to serving the country under Gokhale's guidance'.[5] Smuts watched him go with some relief. 'The saint has left our shores,' he declared, 'I sincerely hope for ever.'[6]

Gandhi arrived in Southampton on 6 August 1914, just two days after Britain had declared war on Germany. On 8 August, his admirers in London held a gala reception at the luxurious Cecil Hotel on the Strand, to welcome 'the hero of the South African struggle'. The principal speech, generously praising Gandhi's achievements, was made by Jinnah, who was in London as chairman of a Congress delegation to lobby the British government over a new bill for Indian council reforms.

Gandhi, however, was a sick man, suffering from piles and general exhaustion: the strain of the *satyagraha* campaign, the periods in gaol, and the prolonged fasts he had undertaken as penance for moral lapses by members of the Phoenix community, were all catching up with him. Inevitably, he insisted on treating himself with diet alone, refusing to obey the doctor's orders or to heed the pleas of Kasturbai and Gokhale to take milk and eggs to build up his strength. But despite his illness, Gandhi could not keep away from politics. His first reaction to the war had been to urge Indians to 'think imperially'. Now he went further, publishing a message to the people of India:

> The war in Europe: what is our – India's – place in it? We are, above all, British citizens of the great British Empire. Fighting as the British people are at present in a righteous cause for the good and glory of human dignity and civilization ... our duty is clear: to do our best to support the British, fight with our life and property.

To many of Gandhi's admirers, this call to arms was a bewildering volte-face from one so dedicated to the practice of non-violence. His response was typically Gandhian: the path of *ahimsa* was rarely an easily discernible one, he told them, since men were inevitably involved with violence simply by living. Moreover, it would be cowardly for a *satyagrahi* such as himself not to take part in a war he had done nothing to prevent, particularly since in London he enjoyed the protection of British arms.

Gandhi followed his usual custom and offered to raise an Indian field ambulance corps. Some 80 men volunteered, and all went well until the British army appointed Colonel R.J. Baker, a former member of the Indian Medical Service, as commanding officer. Baker insisted on treating the volunteers as a regular army unit, and refused to recognize Gandhi as the unofficial but *de facto* leader. Outraged, Gandhi launched a personal *satyagraha* campaign against Baker, but this petered out when his health broke down again. The India Office managed to effect a compromise, and the unit went into action nursing a contingent of wounded Indian troops brought over from France. By that time, however, Gandhi was suffering a severe attack of pleurisy. Friends and doctors advised him to leave the cold and damp of the London winter and seek a warmer climate. For once in his life, Gandhi was happy to take their advice.

The voyage from England on the SS *Arabia* served as an excellent convalescence. On 11 January 1915, Gandhi stepped ashore in Bombay, fit again in body and mind, wearing a white cotton dhoti, shawl and turban, having forsworn western clothes for ever. To the huge crowd that welcomed him on the Apollo Bunder he declared 'I propose to remain in India and serve the motherland for the rest of my days.'[7]

The failed barrister who had sailed away from that same quay in 1893 was now a celebrity, with a growing reputation among the masses as a holy man. Wherever he went, crowds gathered round him eager for *darshan*, the reflected holiness that can be absorbed simply by seeing or being close to a holy person, object or place. In the New Year's honours list he had been awarded a Kaiser-i-Hind gold medal for public service, and both the governor of Bombay and the viceroy arranged to meet him informally.

Among the many receptions held in Gandhi's honour, the Gurjar Sabha (the Gujarat Society), threw a garden party at Jehangir Petit's palatial home where its chairman, M.A. Jinnah, made another speech lauding the man and his achievements. Jinnah's speech, like most of the others, was in English. Gandhi chose to respond in Gujarati, pointedly telling his audience that he preferred to speak to them in their own tongue. If Jinnah was annoyed by this implied criticism, he must have been furious when Gandhi went on to remark that he was 'glad to find a Muhammadan not only belonging to his own region's Sabha, but chairing it'.[8]

Deliberately drawing attention to Jinnah's minority religion at a mixed gathering in the house of a leading Parsi was patronizing, if not actually insulting. Since Gandhi never spoke carelessly, it is hard to avoid the conclusion that he was seeking to score points against a man whom he instinctively recognized as a potential rival for power. Jinnah made no public comment, either at the time or later, but the exchange set the tone of their future relationship.

After a brief visit to his family in Rajkot, Gandhi hurried off to Poona, to see Gokhale. Both Gandhi and Gokhale were keen that he should join the Servants of India Society, but the members of the SIS strongly disagreed with Gandhi's hatred of the modern world, his anarchistic beliefs and extra-constitutional methods, and they refused to accept him. Gokhale himself had been highly critical of Gandhi's booklet, *'Hind Swaraj'*, which among other things had attacked him and the other Congress Moderates. He thought it was crude and ill-informed, showing how out of touch Gandhi was with Indian life and thought: he recommended that before speaking in public or taking any active part in politics, Gandhi should spend a year getting to know India. Gandhi agreed.

But first, Gandhi had to attend to the needs of 20 of his fellow *satyagrahis* from Phoenix Farm, who had returned directly to India when he went to London. They were living in the settlement run by the poet Sir Rabindranath Tagore as a centre of arts and learning, at Santiniketan in West Bengal, about 40 miles north of Calcutta. Gandhi and Tagore quickly established a mutual admiration society — it was Tagore who bestowed on Gandhi the title 'Mahatma' (Great Soul), which was soon taken up throughout India. After less than a week, however, Gandhi's stay at Santiniketan was cut short by the sad news that Gokhale had suddenly died. He and Kasturbai left immediately for Poona, where Gandhi again tried and failed to persuade the Servants of India Society to accept him as a member.

Gokhale had promised to fund the new *ashram* Gandhi wanted to set up for his followers. Now that he was dead, Gandhi would have to look elsewhere for support. Ahmedabad, the principal city of his native Gujarat, was known as the Manchester of India because of its cotton mills, and various wealthy mill-owners were eager to follow the ancient Hindu tradition of giving charity to a holy man, particularly one of their own. With their backing, Gandhi set up the Satyagraha Ashram in May 1915, on a 150-acre site by the banks of the Sabarmati river, on the outskirts of the city. However when he took in a family of untouchables, a teacher from Bombay and his wife and daughter, most of the mill-owners withdrew their support. A number of *satyagrahis* also deserted, including, briefly, Kasturbai and Gandhi's cousin, and Lieutenant Maganlal. Shrugging aside this misfortune, Gandhi prepared to move the *ashram* into the untouchable quarter of the city, where the remaining members would support themselves by doing the work of untouchables. They were saved at the last minute by an anonymous donation of 13,000 rupees, a vast amount of money in 1915 – the story is that a stranger drove up in a big car one day and simply handed the money over. The donor turned out to be Ambalal Sarabhai, the young owner of one of the biggest cotton mills in Ahmedabad.

With the *ashram* secure, Gandhi set off on a tour of India, to get to know the people – and for them to get to know him. In stark contrast to his early experiences in South Africa, he insisted on travelling third class on the railways, often to the acute distress of poor Kasturbai, who did not enjoy the squalor, stench and overcrowding. In this way, Gandhi covered the length and breadth of India, from the Bombay presidency to the United Provinces, Delhi, and Calcutta, from Burma to Madras. When he stepped down from the train, he walked, reaching remote villages never visited by the westernized élite.

Gandhi was received with rapturous enthusiasm everywhere. In Calcutta, the friend in whose house he was to stay collected him from the station in a carriage, but before they could set off, a crowd of young men unhitched the horses and insisted on pulling the carriage themselves. Their leader was a 21-year-old Marwari merchant who had already made a small fortune buying and selling textiles, Ghanshyamdas Birla. It was the first time G.D. Birla, a follower of Tilak and the revolutionary terrorists, had met Gandhi, and he found his message of non-violence disconcerting. Nine years later, the young businessman struck up a lasting relationship with Gandhi, becoming his principal financial supporter for the rest of his life.

When his year of touring was up, Gandhi remained on the political sidelines. He attended conferences, made the occasional speech on social or religious matters, but took no part in either of the two Home Rule Leagues or in the business of Congress. He did, however, propose a successful motion at Lucknow in December 1916, calling for the abolition of indentured labour, which took poor Indians abroad under conditions close to slavery. He saw this not as a political but a moral issue, and mounted a national campaign which succeeded in extracting a promise from the viceroy that the system would be ended.

Gradually, however, Gandhi found himself drawn into affairs that were increasingly political. He presided at conferences against the English education system, and drew up elaborate plans for 'a big educational scheme'[9] including a national school in Gujarat based on the teaching methods he had developed at Phoenix and Tolstoy Farms. He made speeches calling for the adoption of an Indian national language, advocating the Hindi spoken by both Hindus and Muslims in the north.

Gandhi finally became a hero to India's masses during 1917 and 1918, through three campaigns on behalf of peasants and workers. The first was in support of indigo farmers in Champaran, a district of Bihar in the foothills of the Himalayas, close to the border with Nepal. The location may have been remote, but the issue was a suitably emotive one for launching Gandhi on to the national scene. The indigo industry had been notorious for its appalling conditions ever since it had been introduced to Bihar by British entrepreneurs in the eighteenth century, wiping out the traditional indigo industry in Gandhi's native Gujarat in the process. Now, the industry in Bihar was being wiped out by cheap synthetic dyes from Germany. The planters were trying to cover their losses by demanding hard cash from tenant farmers instead of the indigo which they were obliged to plant on 15 per cent of their land in lieu of rent.

The farmers hired local lawyers to fight the landlords but got nowhere, until in desperation one of them travelled to the Lucknow session of Congress to seek help. Having tried and failed to interest other prominent figures, the representative turned to Gandhi, who at first was extremely reluctant – only after the farmer had followed him around the country, pestering him for weeks on end, did Gandhi agree to go to Champaran.

The news that the champion of the poor was coming to their aid was received with excitement in Champaran. Growing crowds waiting to see Gandhi along the way often spilled on to the track, stopping the train. Gandhi made the last nine miles to the indigo villages on the back of an elephant, escorted by a jubilant throng. When he arrived, he was met by police and served with a notice ordering him out of the district. To their astonishment, he refused to go.

In a packed courtroom, with thousands of supporters waiting outside, Gandhi calmly informed the magistrate that he was deliberately disobeying the law and was ready to suffer the penalty. It was, of course, exactly what he had planned for. The bewildered magistrate postponed sentence until he had consulted higher authority, releasing Gandhi in the mean time on bail of 100 rupees. When Gandhi gleefully said he did not have the money, the magistrate told him to go anyway. It was a sensible decision – Gandhi had taken care to keep the viceroy, the press and all his influential friends informed of events by telegram, and his arrest was already big news throughout India.

Horrified at the prospect of playing into Gandhi's hands by making a martyr of him, the viceroy leaned on the lieutenant-governor of Bihar, who swiftly issued a sharp rebuke to the commissioner of the division for his 'serious mistake of judgement', and ordered him to drop the charges against Gandhi, and to 'provide all possible facilities for the conduct of his investigations'.[10] Gandhi's first, one-man satyagraha in India had been a success. When the viceroy ordered an official commission of inquiry to be set up, he was given a seat on it.

Gandhi stayed in Champaran for several months. While he and his devoted band of volunteers obtained testimony from some 8,000 farmers, he introduced the villagers to his ideas on health, diet and sanitation, and opened schools, clinics and soup kitchens throughout the area. The result of the inquiry was a complete vindication for Gandhi and the farmers. But it was not the peace with honour that Gandhi claimed. The whole system of land tenure was to be reformed, and the planters and landlords were to pay back the rents they had illegally extorted. To everyone's surprise, however, Gandhi recommended that they should refund only 25 per cent of the money. In his view, the principle was more important than the amount, and a compromise would prevent permanent ill-feeling. No one had asked the peasant farmers how they felt about getting only a quarter of the money owing to them, and they were understandably bitter. Both sides were soon conducting what amounted to a guerrilla war against each other.

When Gandhi and his followers moved on, there was no one in Bihar able or willing to carry on his social teachings and the villagers quickly reverted to their old ways. Filth and squalor returned, schools and soup kitchens closed, clinics were deserted. In the event, the whole Champaran affair was soon to become academic, for with the final collapse of the indigo market the planters began selling up and leaving. Within a decade there were none left.[11]

However illusory it may have been, Gandhi's triumph in Champaran made him a national figure: he had taken on the might of the empire, and won. The nationalist Amrita Bazar Patrika trumpeted: 'God bless Gandhi and his work. How we wish we had only half a dozen Gandhis in India to teach our people self-abnegation and selfless patriotism.'

The British were bemused. 'We may look on Mr Gandhi as an idealist, a fanatic, or a revolutionary according to our particular opinions,' reported W.H. Lewis, a young ICS man in Bihar, 'but to the raiyats [farmers] he is their liberator, and they credit him with extraordinary powers. He moves about in the villages asking them to lay their grievances before him, and he is transfiguring the imaginations of masses of ignorant men with visions of an early millennium.'[12]

In October 1917 Gandhi was elected president of the Gurjar Sabha, his first institutional position, and was invited to preside over a Gujarat political conference. In November, he was invited to meet Montagu during his tour of India. Montagu was not impressed. He described Gandhi as a social reformer, who 'dresses like a coolie, forswears all personal advancement, lives practically on the air, and is a pure visionary. He does not understand details of schemes.'[13] Montagu's view of Gandhi was both perceptive and obtuse: he failed to grasp that what he saw as weaknesses were in fact Gandhi's strengths, and that the reason Gandhi did not understand details was because he chose not to.

Back home in Ahmedabad, there was trouble at the mill, or rather the mills, for a wages dispute by workers in the city's cotton mills was threatening to escalate out of control. Gandhi's reputation was already so high that everyone looked to him to solve the problem: Ambalal Sarabhai, the leading mill-owner who had rescued the *ashram*, asked Gandhi to intervene on behalf of the employers; Ambalal's sister Anasuya, who had become a voluntary social worker, approached him on behalf of the mill hands, who had no organization and no leaders; and finally, the British collector asked Gandhi to mediate. Gandhi persuaded both sides to agree to arbitration, but he could not control the workers. When they began to go on strike, the owners, who were having problems with shortages of coal and raw materials because of the war, took the opportunity of looking them out.

Gandhi began to organize the workers, leading daily prayer meetings under a pipul tree on the banks of the Sabarmati river, and publishing a news sheet every morning. He got them to take a solemn pledge that they would not go back to work without the 35 per cent rise that he considered fair, that they would not beg, steal, loot or damage property, and that they would use no violence against employers or blacklegs. However after three weeks, the workers' resolve began to weaken. Stung by what he regarded as justifiable taunts 'that it was all very well for us who had motors at our disposal and plenty of food to attend their meetings and advise staunchness even unto death,'[14] Gandhi hit on a powerful new weapon, or rather an old weapon to be used in a new way. 'While I was still groping and unable to see my way clearly, the light came to me,' he wrote later. 'Unbidden and all by themselves the words came to my lips.'[15] The words that came to his lips were that until either the employers agreed to pay the 35 per cent, or the workers themselves called off their strike, he would fast.

Gandhi's opponents condemned the fast as moral blackmail against his mill-owner friends. The Ahmedabad police dismissed it as a stunt, a theatrical gesture made at a time when a settlement could not be far off. Gandhi agonized as always about the moral and religious aspects: a fast, he decided, was permissible in pursuit of a 'creative idea', but not for private gain or to coerce or intimidate an opponent. In this case, he convinced himself his fast was not intended to coerce the owners but to persuade the workers not to break their solemn vows.

Understandably, the mill-owners found it hard to appreciate the distinction: they were just terrified of the consequences should anything happen to Gandhi. Within three days, they agreed to arbitration, and the weavers returned to work. The arbitrator, a local academic, deliberated with care, then awarded a 35 per cent increase, which most of the mills were already paying anyway. The only real winner was Gandhi.

In Champaran and Ahmedabad, Gandhi had successfully tried out two of the weapons that were to form the basis of his armoury in the national independence struggle: civil disobedience and the fast. He had not yet tried out the third in India, the mass *satyagraha* that he had developed in South Africa. Even while he was concluding the campaign in Ahmedabad, however, he was presented with a perfect opportunity. Crop failures caused by a drought in 1917 were causing great hardship to the local peasant farmers, members of the tough Patidar caste, in Kheda, a rural district not far from Ahmedabad. The problem was exacerbated by outbreaks of cholera and the plague, and there was a serious threat of famine. The revenue code provided for total remission of land tax when crop yields fell below 25 per cent of normal, and the Patidars had applied to the government for remission. The Gurjar Sabha had supported the campaign, which had been ably led by Sardar Vallabhbhai Patel, a prominent young Gujarati lawyer, himself a Patidar from Kheda. However all their appeals and petitions had been rejected.

Gandhi, aided by members of the Servants of India Society, investigated the situation in some 50 villages and found the Patidars' claims were justified. He reported this to the Bombay government and requested an official inquiry. When the government refused, and pressed for immediate payment in full, Gandhi launched a *satyagraha* at a meeting of some 5,000 Patidars.[16] The richer farmers, who could afford to pay, took a vow that they would not do so until the government agreed to suspend collection from the poor.

For almost four months, the Patidars stood firm, refusing to pay even though the government seized cattle and household goods, and attached standing crops. By June 1918, they were almost exhausted, and Gandhi later admitted that he was 'casting about for some graceful way of terminating the struggle', when he learned that because of the government's need for calm and support during the war, it had secretly instructed local officials not to collect tax from those who really were too poor to pay. There was to be no public announcement, which might jeopardize the entire revenue system, but since the outcome was more or less what Gandhi had been demanding, he called a halt to the *satyagraha*. As far as the Patidars were concerned, he had triumphed again.

The campaigns in Champaran, Ahmedabad and Kheda boosted Gandhi's prestige, both locally and nationally. But in April 1918, while still leading the Kheda Patidars' fight against the government, he risked alienating his entire following by accepting an invitation from the viceroy to take part in a conference on India's contribution to the war effort. The war in France was at a critical stage, and Britain needed all the support it could raise. There were already some 800,000 Indian combatants in the British army, but more were needed. Gandhi offered to help recruit them, at a price: 'I recognize that in the hour of its danger we must give, as we have decided to give, ungrudging and unequivocal support to the empire of which we aspire in the near future to be partners in the same sense as the dominions overseas,' he wrote to the viceroy on 30 April. 'But it is the simple truth that our response is due to the expectation that our goal will be reached all the more speedily.'[17]

On the question of non-violence, he was able, as always, to convince himself that there were times when violence was justified, though he would never commit it himself. Indeed, he believed that only those who were courageous enough to use violence could practise true *ahimsa*, and that *satyagraha* must be a weapon of the strong and not the weak.

Gandhi's reasoning was beyond most people, and his supporters and detractors both condemned his decision as at best inconsistent and at worst hypocritical. Undeterred, he chose to start recruiting in Kheda, where his stock should have been highest. He met hostility everywhere. Of his previous helpers, only Sardar Vallabhbhai Patel and one or two lesser lights stood by him as he tramped through the district's 600 villages, usually on foot since no one would lend them carts. Gandhi had hoped to recruit at least 20 men from each village, but of the few hundred he eventually signed up only about 100 were local, and none of those was a Patidar.

Undermined by physical and emotional exhaustion, Gandhi's health failed again. Already weak, in mid-August he contracted dysentery, but insisted on carrying on until he collapsed, delirious with a high fever. The faithful Patel helped the Sarabhais to take him back to Ahmedabad, where they nursed him in their comfortable home. Convinced that this was the end, Gandhi wanted to die in his own *ashram*, and had himself carried back there. But even in the face of death, he refused to take the nourishing foods his doctors and Kasturbai tried to press on him. The only compromise he was prepared to make was to drink goat's milk, when Kasturbai managed to persuade him that the vow he had taken in South Africa applied only to cow's milk. Even that left him struggling with a deep sense of guilt, but it undoubtedly helped him survive. By the time he had recovered enough to return to public life, the war was over and the time of reckoning had arrived.

II

'A Himalayan Miscalculation'

The end of the First World War left India seething with discontent from many different causes. There was disillusion with the meagre rewards being offered by Britain for India's support during the war. There were swingeing new taxes on excess profits. The upheaval of changing from a wartime to a peacetime economy had brought rampant inflation, widespread shortages, a disastrous slump in the textile trade, and a wave of industrial disputes with mill-owners. There was the terrible death toll from the influenza epidemic, which Gandhi and his followers saw as a cosmic indictment of western civilization and British rule. There were Hindu fears over a new marriage bill, which threatened traditional practices, and Muslim fears over the dismemberment of the Turkish empire, which threatened the holy places of Islam. The list went on and on.

In such an atmosphere, the Rowlatt Bills provided a convenient focus for all the various grievances. The textile industry might have been in the doldrums, but the rumour mills were working overtime spreading the most horrendous stories. The anti-terrorist legislation proposed by the Bills would hardly affect ordinary Indians, and few really understood what was involved, but the Bills were seen as an insult to Indian honour, and defeating them became a matter of national pride.

The young men of the Home Rule Leagues held protest meetings in various towns and cities. But these were local affairs, run by local leaders. They needed someone with enough clout and charisma to weld them together into a national campaign. But who? Tilak had left for London in the autumn of 1918 to pursue a personal libel action, and would be away for most of 1919. Annie Besant had turned respectable since her term as Congress president, and was dithering over whether to accept the Montagu-Chelmsford reforms. Other leading radicals were too rooted in their own communities to command a genuinely popular following. In desperation, the young men turned to Gandhi.

B.G. Horniman, the British editor of the liberal *Bombay Chronicle* who was vice-president of Mrs Besant's League, had already called for a *satyagraha* campaign, both in his newspaper and at a public meeting on 16 February 1919. Many of the young men of the movement begged Gandhi to lead it. Although he was still bedridden and not fully recovered from his collapse, Gandhi allowed himself to be persuaded.

The anti-Rowlatt action would be Gandhi's first attempt at a national campaign – indeed, it would be the first truly national campaign ever launched against the British government. To co-ordinate it, Gandhi formed the Satyagraha Sabha, with himself as president, Horniman as vice-president, and various prominent Home Rulers such as Jamnadas Dwarkadas and the diminutive but doughty poetess, Sarojini Naidu, on its committee. The Sabha effectively took over both Home Rule Leagues, making use of their existing networks to print and distribute leaflets and posters, organize meetings and recruit supporters. Those who joined had to take a pledge:

> . . . in the event of these Bills becoming law and until they are withdrawn, we
> shall refuse civilly to obey these laws and such other laws as a Committee to
> be hereafter appointed may think fit and we further affirm that in this
> struggle we will faithfully follow truth and refrain from violence to life,
> person or property.[1]

Gandhi began by informing the viceroy that he would start recruiting signatories if the government did not change its position. Two days later, he launched an intensive publicity campaign, using all his skills in manipulating the press, and all the resources of the Home Rule Leagues. Despite his frail physical condition, he set off on a whirlwind tour of India to whip up support, set up local committees, and make public speeches – though these usually had to be read for him, because of his weakness. The results were disappointing. Even in the Bombay Presidency, the movement's stronghold, fewer than 800 people had signed the pledge by mid-March, and support elsewhere was decidedly patchy.[2] There was stiff opposition from many senior Indian political figures, who saw Gandhi as a naive Gujarati upstart playing with fire by trying to mobilize the masses. It was a fear shared by many of his disciples – committed to non-violence, they were troubled at the idea of using *satyagraha* against measures designed to control terrorism. The campaign seemed doomed before it began.

Then, during the night of 18 March 1919, when the Rowlatt Act became law, Gandhi's voices spoke to him once more. 'The idea came to me in a dream,' he recalled later, 'that we should call upon the country to observe a general *hartal*. *Satyagraha* is a process of self-purification, and ours is a sacred fight, and it seems to me to be in the fitness of things that it should be commenced with an act of self-purification. Let all the people of India therefore suspend their business on that day and observe the day as one of fasting and prayer.'[3] With typical lack of forethought, he immediately issued his call for a nationwide *hartal* on 30 March. When his lieutenants pointed out that there was no hope of organizing any sort of national event in a mere 11 days, he agreed to put it off for one week, until 6 April. How the *hartal* was to be observed was left to local leaders – Gandhi gave them no guidance.

There was, inevitably, more than a little confusion. Two cities, Delhi and Amritsar, staged their *hartals* on the original date, 30 March. In Amritsar, the *hartal* was a success 'beyond expectation'. But in Delhi, there was trouble during the morning when a crowd trying to force a refreshment seller at the main railway station to close his stall clashed with police and troops in the mistaken belief that two of their number had been arrested. Things got out of hand and the troops were forced to open fire in self-defence, killing eight and wounding about a dozen. Surprisingly, the chief commissioner allowed a mass meeting to go ahead later in the afternoon and even attended it himself. It passed off without incident, as did the funerals of the dead men next day. The situation had been successfully defused, and shops began opening normally again on 1 April.[4]

Ignoring the warning signs from Delhi, Gandhi pressed on with his call for a general *hartal* on 6 April. It was taken up in varying degrees throughout India. In Bengal, including Calcutta, and central and southern India, the response was poor. In Bombay, where Gandhi himself led thousands in prayer and purification by bathing in the sea, four-fifths of the shops closed. And in the United Provinces, the Punjab and Bihar almost all large towns came to a standstill, though most people simply stopped work and took no part in fasting, prayer or purification. A second *hartal* in Delhi, held despite appeals against it by the Satyagraha Sabha itself, passed off peacefully, with the Hindu leaders being invited to speak in the city's main mosques. Amritsar, too, held a trouble-free second *hartal* with Hindus, Muslims and Sikhs taking part in complete harmony.[5]

The peaceful nature of the *satyagraha* demonstrations failed to assuage the Anglo-Indian diehards, particularly in the Punjab. Sir Michael O'Dwyer was about to retire after six years as lieutenant-governor, and seemed to relish the prospect of a final show-down before he left. The fact that in the principal cities of Lahore and Amritsar order had been maintained not by authoritarian force but by the educated Indians whom he so despised, did nothing to improve his temper. The following day, he used his farewell speech to his legislative council in Lahore to issue a warning that was so imperious it is hard to believe it was not a deliberate challenge:

I have already said publicly that the Punjab repudiated what is or was known during the war as passive loyalty. It will repudiate even more emphatically the veiled disloyalty which while hiding itself under the cloak of passive resistance leads on its dupes into open defiance of authority and the penalties which such open defiance entails.

The Government of this province is, and will remain, determined that public order which was maintained so successfully during the war shall not be disturbed in time of peace ...

The recent puerile demonstrations against the Rowlatt Acts in both Lahore and Amritsar would be ludicrous if they did not indicate how easily the ignorant and credulous people, not one in a thousand of whom knows anything of the measure, can be misled. Those who want only to mislead them incur a serious responsibility ... Those who appeal to ignorance rather than to reason have a day of reckoning in store for them.[6]

Dwyer ordered armed police and troops on to the streets of Lahore and Amritsar. For two days the two sides glowered at each other. On 9 April 1919, in both cities, British residents and officials were alarmed to see Muslims joining in the Ram Naumi festival celebrating the birthday of Lord Rama the semi-divine hero of Hindu mythology. The religious occasion had been turned into a political show of unity which the Anglo-Indians found most worrying. But although the crowd of 20,000 in Lahore was truculent and aggressive, there was still no violence; in Amritsar there was even a carnival-like atmosphere, with marchers pausing to cheer the uneasy deputy commissioner, Miles Irving, while their bands played *God Save the King*. Within a few hours, however, the situation was to change dramatically.

O'Dwyer heard that Gandhi had been invited to Delhi by the Hindu leader of the movement there, to mediate between the authorities and the people; he was also proposing to visit Lahore. O'Dwyer promptly issued an exclusion order banning him from the Punjab, and persuaded the Indian government to do the same for Delhi. To get to Delhi by train, Gandhi would have to pass through part of the Punjab, and O'Dwyer planned to seize him and deport him to Burma. Wisely, the viceroy countermanded this, and ordered that Gandhi simply be confined to the Bombay presidency. So, early in the morning of 10 April, Gandhi was taken off his train at the first railway station in the Punjab, and put on the next train back to Bombay.

The news of Gandhi's 'arrest' reached Bombay long before he did, and as it spread through the city, protesters began taking to the streets. Throughout the night and most of the next day shops and markets were closed and crowds roamed the city chanting slogans: '*Hindu-Mussulman ki-jai!*' and '*Mahatma Gandhi ki-jai!*' (*ki-jai*, like *vive*, means 'long live', 'hurrah for' or 'victory to'). But there was little violence or serious damage, and calm was restored when Gandhi himself arrived on the scene and persuaded the mob to disperse, rebuking them severely and threatening to undertake a personal *satyagraha* against them if they did not behave properly.

In Ahmedabad, home of the *satyagraha* movement, things were much worse. Many of the city's mills had been on strike for the preceding two weeks, and 5,000 disgruntled workers were easy meat for troublemakers. On 10 April they attacked two European weaving masters who were alleged to have unwisely declared 'Damn Gandhi!' when asked to get down from their vehicle, provoking a disturbance in which an Indian policeman was killed and several rioters injured. *Satyagrahis*, led by Vallabhbhai Patel and Kasturbai Gandhi, managed to quieten things down that evening, but next day there were 'hell fires', as the official report put it. The mischief makers had been active during the night, spreading further rumours, including one that the workers' beloved Anasuyabehn Sarahbhai had also been arrested.

The mob was soon out of control in a full-scale riot, attacking any European they saw, burning down some 51 government and municipal buildings, cutting telegraph wires and smashing lights, looting houses, shops, temples and liquor stores, stripping Indian police constables of their uniforms, and murdering a British police sergeant. Graffiti appeared on the walls of wrecked police stations: 'The British Raj is gone. The King of England is defeated and *swaraj* is established.' 'Kill all Europeans. Murder them wherever they be found!' Before order was restored, 28 rioters had been shot dead and at least 123 wounded. A horrified Gandhi arrived next day, Sunday 13 April. He went straight to the commissioner, Mr Pratt, who at once gave him permission to hold a mass meeting, lifting the curfew so that people could attend.[7]

'Addressing the meeting,' Gandhi wrote later, 'I tried to bring home to the people the sense of their wrong, declaring a penitential fast of three days for myself, appealed to the people to go on a similar fast for a day, and suggested to those who had been guilty of acts of violence to confess their guilt.'[8] How many actually confessed or even fasted is not known, but certainly there was no more trouble in Ahmedabad.

There was trouble in Delhi, however, where a new *hartal* lasted eight days, but there was little damage or violence, except for a riot on 17 April in which two men were killed. The most worrying aspect of the situation was that the *satyagraha* leaders lost control after the first day, and were powerless to call off the action, which was taken over by various local groups with their own agendas. Gandhi, of course, was banned from going to Delhi himself, so was unable to work his personal magic there.

Thanks to O'Dwyer's exclusion order, Gandhi was unable to work any magic in the Punjab, either. Within an hour of news of his arrest reaching Lahore, the city had closed down in a spontaneous *hartal*. It began quite peacefully, but when a number of protesters began heading towards the civil lines, O'Dwyer saw

1. The start of British rule in India, 12 August 1765: the Mughal emperor Shah Alam gives Robert Clive the right for the East India Company to collect revenues from Bengal, Bihar and Orissa, 'from generation to generation, for ever and ever'.

2. Lord Macaulay introduced English education to India, believing that Indians would eventually demand self-rule on 'the proudest day in British history'.

3. Allan Octavian Hume, retired British official, founder of the Indian National Congress in 1885.

4. The first Indian National Congress, Bombay, 1885. Hume is seated centre, next to his friend William Wedderburn (with black beard) who was twice elected Congress president.

5. Mentor of both Gandhi and Jinnah: Gopal Krishna Gokhale, moderate nationalist, Congress leader and founder of the Servants of India Society, which refused membership to Gandhi.

6. The smart young attorney: Mohandas Karamchand Gandhi and his staff pose proudly outside his law office in Durban, South Africa, in the mid 1890s.

7. Foundation of a dynasty: the successful lawyer Motilal Nehru with his wife Swarup Rani and young son, Jawaharlal, who wears a very English sailor suit and Eton collar.

9. Described by Edwin Montagu as 'a little, rough Irishman', Sir Michael O'Dwyer distrusted all educated Indians and ruled the Punjab with an iron fist.

8. A most superior person: Lord Curzon, viceroy 1898-1905, boosted Indian nationalism by disastrously dividing Bengal.

10. Brigadier-General Rex Dyer destroyed Indian trust in British justice and changed the course of Indian nationalism with the Jallianwala Bagh massacre in 1919.

11. Annie Besant, Theosophist and 1917 Congress president, with early Salt Tax fighters in 1923.

12. Edwin Montagu (left) Liberal secretary of state and author of the Montagu-Chelmsford reforms of 1919, with the wartime Chancellor of the Exchequer, Reginald McKenna.

13. Gandhi Day, Delhi, 26 July 1922, with Khilafat flags and bundles of British cloth for burning.

14. Two viceroys for the price of one: Lord and Lady Reading (left) with Lady and Lord Willingdon, then governor of Madras, in 1923.

15. Black Flag processions everywhere greeted members of the Simon Commission, including future premier Clement Atlee, the man who would give India independence.

16. Perfect Indian Englishmen – princely Indian delegates to the Imperial Conference in London, 1930.

17. Lord Irwin takes tea at his farewell party in 1931 with Mrs F. H. Mehta, wife of a Parsi Congress leader.

18. Gandhi, with Sarojini Naidu, 'the merriest rebel ever to come out of Girton', leads the march to the sea in 1930 to defy the Salt Tax Law.

19. A year later, in 1931, Gandhi was the sole Congress representative at the round-table conference in London.

20. Gandhi and Subhas Chandra Bose were still on good terms when Bose was elected Congress president for the first time in 1938, but Sardar Vallabhbhai Patel (right) was not amused.

21. The stiff-necked Lord Linlithgow and his wife at a viceregal garden party in Delhi, shortly before he offended Congress by announcing without consultation that India was at war.

red. Fearing an invasion of the European quarter, he sent out troops and police with orders to drive them back behind the walls of the old city. When the students at the head of the crowd refused, explaining that their intentions were entirely peaceful and that they only wanted to show their sorrow at the Mahatma's arrest, the police opened fire at point blank range. Eight marchers dropped dead. The rest scattered. Elsewhere, police confronted other crowds with less success, and before long the city was out of control. All police were withdrawn. O'Dwyer called on the local community leaders to exert their authority, but no one would listen to them.

From 11 to 14 April 1919, the only real power in Lahore was held by the 50 members of the People's Committee, elected at a packed meeting of Muslims, Hindus and Sikhs at the great Badshahi mosque. The very name of the People's Committee, with its overtones of red revolution, was enough to horrify O'Dwyer. Before things could go any further, he called in the army. A military force under Colonel Frank Johnson marched through the streets to the Badshahi mosque, where they broke up a meeting, then opened fire on demonstrators, killing 10 and wounding 27. Martial law was proclaimed, and within a couple of days everything had apparently returned to normal.

Elsewhere in the Punjab, however, things were far from normal. In Amritsar on the morning of 9 April, shortly before the Ram Naumi procession was due to start, Deputy Commissioner Irving called a meeting at his bungalow to discuss the situation with the commander of the local garrison, the two chief police officers and Lieutenant-Colonel Henry Smith, the civil surgeon. Aware of the menacing undertones in the city, and warning the police and military to stand by for possible trouble, Irving was growing increasingly nervous. He had already sent a report to the Punjab government requesting an extra company of troops, but since there seemed little more that he could do, he set off to view the procession from a balcony.

Lieutenant Colonel Smith, who was rabidly anti Indian and saw Bolshevik conspiracies everywhere, was far from satisfied with Irving's attitude. Immediately he left the deputy commissioner's bungalow he set off on the two-hour road journey to Lahore, to see O'Dwyer, a man after his own heart. Smith was convinced the *hartals* and the whole *satyagraha* movement were part of a revolutionary conspiracy, which was about to raise the red flag all over India. The only way to deal with it was with 'prompt force', before it got out of hand. This coincided exactly with O'Dwyer's own views: there would have to be a day of reckoning, and the sooner the better.

O'Dwyer sent Smith back to Amritsar with an order for Irving to arrest the city's two Indian leaders: Dr Saifuddin Kitchlew, a Muslim lawyer who was a member of Lincoln's Inn, a Cambridge graduate and a PhD of Munster University; and Dr Satyapal, a Hindu doctor who had qualified at Lahore Medical

College and served during the war in the Indian Medical Service. Irving had already been instructed to silence them both by banning them from speaking in public, but O'Dwyer now wanted them removed from the scene altogether. Whether he was deliberately provoking the confrontation he must have known would follow remains an unanswered question.

Smith handed Irving his orders at 7.00 p.m. that evening, when there were already disquieting signs such as the burning of stalls that were being set up for the coming horse fair and Baisakhi celebrations. Next morning, Kitchlew and Satyapal were invited to the deputy commissioner's bungalow, as though for consultation. They were immediately arrested and whisked away to Dharmsala, a hill station 100 miles away, with a military escort disguised as a hunting party. Word of their disappearance quickly spread throughout the city, shortly before the news arrived of Gandhi's arrest. By 11.30 a.m. a great crowd began advancing through the city towards Irving's bungalow, demanding to know what had become of their local heroes.

According to the Indian version of events, the crowd was sorrowing and peaceful – the men had removed their turbans and shoes in the traditional sign of mourning. The British, however, saw the crowd as a menacing mob, which had thrown off its turbans and shoes to be ready for battle. Whichever is the correct version, a battle is what they got. As the masses marched through the city, their numbers growing all the time to an estimated 40,000, their mood became more excited and aggressive. Stones rained down on police and troops sent to head them off, and the troops opened fire. Three or four people were killed, and several wounded, and in no time the demonstration had become a full-scale riot. The mob, now in a fury, headed for the commercial heart of the city where they destroyed the telegraph exchange offices, smashed and looted shops and burned down the town hall, a Christian church and school, and two of the three European banks, murdering the managers and burning their bodies. During the day, as the violence raged throughout the city, a total of five European men and at least 25 Indians were killed.

But what really inflamed Anglo-Indian tempers was an attack on a white woman, an unpardonable offence in the eyes of the British male. Even though the woman in question was a missionary and therefore much 'lower' down the social scale than a proper memsahib, she was still a sacred being. Miss Marcia Sherwood had worked in Amritsar for the past 15 years as a medical missionary. She was also superintendent of the five local church schools for girls. When she heard of the rioting, she set off immediately on her bicycle to ensure that all the schools were locked and the girls sent home to safety. Unfortunately, on her way she ran into a mob, which chased her into Durga Koti Lane, knocked her from her bicycle, beat her and left her for dead. A local Hindu shopkeeper saved her life at the risk of his own, picking her up from the gutter and hiding her in his house. By this time, the remaining European women and children were being ferried either to the railway station or to the old Gobind Garh fort, where they were defended by a mixed force of British and Indian troops, strengthened by a detachment of Gurkhas whose train had fortuitously stopped at Amritsar.

During the night, military reinforcements promised by O'Dwyer began arriving. But the fire had already gone out of the demonstrations, and there was no further trouble. The next day, Friday 11 April, an eerie calm had descended on the city. When a group of local Indian lawyers asked Irving for permission to bury or cremate their dead, he agreed, provided there were no large processions: no more than four friends or family could accompany the bodies to the burning ghats or burial grounds. At 9.00 p.m. Brigadier-General Reginald 'Rex' Dyer, with his brigade major, Captain F.C. Briggs and a Captain Bostock, arrived by road from Dyer's brigade headquarters at Jullundur. By midnight, he had persuaded Irving to hand over the city to his control.

Rex Dyer was a classic product of the Raj, whose attitude to political Indians made O'Dwyer look like a watery liberal. Born in India 54 years earlier, only five years after the end of the great revolt, Dyer was a third generation Anglo-Indian, with all the combined prejudices of both the British box wallahs and the military. His father was a successful brewer; his mother, Mary, was the archetypal memsahib. When her husband once told a story at the dinner table which included his lighting a cigarette from a Burmese girl's cheroot, she cut him off abruptly by declaring: 'That sort of looseness is what has peopled Simla with thirty thousand Eurasians!' Naturally, she forbade her young family from mixing with any Indians apart from servants.

Educated in India and Ireland, Dyer followed his mother's wishes by enrolling as a medical student at the Royal College of Surgeons in Dublin, but found he could not stomach the blood and stink of the dissecting room, so switched to Sandhurst and the army. Over the years, his military career blossomed modestly. He finally made his name in 1916, leading 150 men into the arid Sarhad region on the Baluchistan-Persian border, to suppress 3,000 tribesmen who were colluding with a German mission plotting to launch a Muslim invasion of India from Afghanistan. During the campaign, he took the opportunity to promote himself from colonel to brigadier-general: 'I ... advised Simla that the rank was necessary for my purpose,' he wrote later. 'The reply came back, "You are a general."'[9] For his success, he was also made Companion of the Order of the Bath.

Although immensely popular with his junior officers and, apparently, with his men – Dyer loved his sepoys as much as O'Dwyer loved his peasants – he had an increasingly uncertain temper, which was exacerbated by recurring health problems. He suffered from arteriosclerosis, from the effects of a lifetime of chainsmoking and from the illnesses common among Anglo-Indians – heat-stroke, sun-stroke, fevers, and malaria. He also suffered from the residue of a succession of sporting accidents, most of which seem to have involved concussions with their inevitable consequences. The last of these was in 1917 when his horse fell on him as he was jumping a trench – with superhuman strength, he had managed to hold up the entire weight of the horse until help arrived. He was sent back to England to recuperate, 'the wreck of a man, only able to crawl a few steps with the help of two sticks'.[10] In spite of being in constant pain, he forced himself to walk again and even to sit astride a horse. Astonishingly, he managed to bluff an army medical board into passing him fit for duty, and by April 1918 he was in command of the garrison at Jullundur.

This was the man who, on Sunday 13 April 1919, marched a detachment of Indian troops into the Jallianwala Bagh and turned a dusty, crowded garden into a killing field.

Irving, who had been asleep in his bungalow while Dyer was massacring the crowd in the Jallianwala Bagh, informed O'Dwyer about it that evening. O'Dwyer reported it to the viceroy, denying responsibility by pointing out that Irving, his own civil subordinate, had not been present and that the troops were under the command of General Dyer. He gave the estimated death toll as 200 – there seems to have been no attempt to establish how many people had really been killed until much later. O'Dwyer called on the viceroy to declare martial law in the Punjab, in the face of civil unrest – what Dr Satyapal was to call O'Dwyer's 'apparition' of rebellion. The viceroy agreed.

One of the immediate effects of the declaration of martial law was a complete clamp-down on information. As B.G. Horniman put it: 'From the beginning, every newspaper in the Province was placed under pre-censorship by the Government and nothing, either by comment or report of events, could be published without being submitted for official approval and sanction.'[11] Despite this, news of the massacre spread rapidly throughout the Punjab, sparking trouble in several places next day.

At Gujranwala, a town of about 30,000 inhabitants, 36 miles from Amritsar, the body of a dead calf was found hanging from a railway bridge shortly before 7.00 a.m. – no one was quite sure what it meant, except that it clearly meant trouble. Crowds of Indians were soon astir. They stoned a train, set fire to a couple of railway bridges, the railway station, the telegraph office, the post office, the local dak bungalow, the district court and an Indian Christian church. They attacked the superintendent of police, a Mr Heron, who ordered his men to fire on them.

Appeals for help from Gujranwala left O'Dywer in a predicament: he could not send large numbers of troops without seriously depleting the garrisons in Lahore and Amritsar, where the army was already overstretched, and in any case it would take them several hours to get there. So, he turned to the Royal Air Force, who very promptly sent a flight of three BE2c aircraft, each armed with a Lewis machine-gun and carrying ten 20-pound bombs. They were under the command of Captain D.H.M. Carberry, who had flown the reconnaissance mission over Amritsar for General Dyer two days earlier. His instructions from the general staff of I6 Division were that he should not bomb the town 'unless necessary', but that any crowds in the open were to be bombed, and that any gatherings near local villages were to be dispersed if they were heading to or from the town.

Carberry arrived over Gujranwala at 3.I0 p.m. He dropped his first three bombs on a party of I50 people in the nearby village of Dhulla, who looked as though they were heading for the town. One bomb fell through the roof of a house and failed to explode; two fell near the crowd, killing a woman and a boy and slightly wounding two men. The rest of the crowd fled back to the village, encouraged by 50 rounds from the Lewis gun 'to ensure they dispersed effectively'.

A few minutes later, Carberry dropped two bombs — one of them a dud — and fired 25 rounds at a crowd of about 50 near the village of Gharjakh, without causing any casualties. Returning to Gujranwala, he attacked a crowd of about 200 in a field near a large red building on the north-western outskirts of the town. The building turned out to be the Sikh Khalsa High School and Boarding House. Carberry dropped one bomb which landed in the courtyard, and followed up with 30 rounds of machine-gun fire: a sweet-seller was wounded by a bullet, a student was hit by a bomb splinter, and a small boy was stunned. In the town itself, Carberry dropped four bombs — two of which failed to explode — and fired between I00 and I50 rounds at crowds in the streets. His two fellow pilots appeared to have had less of an appetite for blood. One fired 25 rounds at a group of 25–30 people — who were later said to have been busy harvesting — without hitting anybody; the other, according to the official report, 'took no action'.

The total casualties reported by Colonel A.J. O'Brien, the deputy commissioner of Gujranwala, were II killed and 27 wounded. Carberry, who seems to have been made of the same stuff as Dyer, later claimed that from the altitude of 200 feet at which he had been flying, 'I could see perfectly well and I did not not see anybody ... at all who was innocent.' When asked why he machine-gunned crowds even after they had been dispersed, he replied: 'I was trying to do this in their own interests. If I killed a few people, they would not gather and come to Gujranwala to do damage.' His idea was 'to produce a sort of moral effect upon them'.[12]

Back in Amritsar, all was quiet. But the spectre of 1857 still haunted the British lines. Having delivered his own moral lesson, Dyer was now concerned with inflicting punishment on all Indians for the unspeakable attack on British womanhood. He instituted various ordinances intended to degrade and humiliate them, beginning with what became known as the 'crawling order': all Indians, regardless of age or status, who wished to pass along the street where Miss Sherwood had been attacked were forced at bayonet point to crawl on their bellies. Since it was the residents of that street who had saved her from certain death, it was a bizarre way of rewarding them for their humanity and courage. Meanwhile, at the end of the street, a platform and a large wooden triangle were erected, where selected Indian men who might have been involved in the attack were publicly flogged, without the inconvenience of a trial.

British troops committed numerous acts of religious sacrilege, deeply offending local opinion. The Congress inquiry into the events found that: 'Sacred pigeons and other birds were shot. The Pinjarapole, a sacred house for the care of animals which was just at the end of the lane, was defiled. The wells in the lane were polluted by soldiers easing themselves near them.'[13]

Martial law brought out that peculiar combination of silliness and sadism that so often raises its head when British officialdom is affronted. Under Martial Law Number 7, for example, any Indian carrying an open umbrella was required to close and lower it whenever he passed a British officer.

At Kasur, a Captain Doveton invented a whole range of what were called 'fancy punishments', the kind of indignities often inflicted on small boys by other boys at public schools. If an Indian failed to salaam to a European in the street he was forced to skip with a rope or rub his nose in the dirt. Others were made to write poems. Doveton had a group of men flogged in front of a number of prostitutes because they had visited the brothel during the hours of curfew. He also had an entire wedding party flogged, including the priest, since they numbered more than 10 and therefore constituted an illegal gathering. There is even a suggestion that Doveton had Indians whitewashed, though this was explained as being the result of their having been forced to carry blocks of limestone.

Another official, Mr Bosworth Smith, seems to have delighted in ripping off women's veils and then spitting on them and calling them 'flies, bitches, she-asses and swine'. He also demonstrated an unhealthy fondness for whipping all and sundry, even for supposed offences that were not punishable by whipping.

These punishments were not confined to Amritsar or Lahore, but spread throughout the Punjab. In some towns and villages, crops in the fields and goods in the shops were seized. In Lahore itself, Colonel Johnson confiscated some 800 tongas and motor cars belonging to Indians. He restricted rail travel, and filled the gaols with people arrested without charge. The number of public floggings became so great that Johnson had to be ordered to stop them. Most of them were carried out in the market place, where Europeans, including many of those tender memsahibs whose honour was being protected, stood by urging the floggers to strike harder.

*

News of the true extent of the massacre in Amritsar, and what was going on elsewhere in the Punjab, leaked out only slowly. Censorship was highly effective, travel was restricted, and for the first four days after the Jallianwala Bagh shooting, no telegrams were allowed to be sent from the city. It was largely thanks to B.G. Horniman that the truth emerged, when he defied the censors and published in the *Bombay Chronicle* an unofficial report that had been smuggled out of the Punjab. The government of India, which had been trying to get rid of this thorn in its side for years, promptly had Horniman arrested and deported back to the UK. Unfortunately, of course, it had no power to muzzle him once he was home. In London, he immediately began a campaign attacking not only the military handling of the Amritsar disturbances but 'the whole conduct of the Punjab over a series of years', and the man responsible for the chaos, Sir Michael O'Dwyer.

Already aghast at the events in Bombay and Ahmedabad, Gandhi was mortified when he read the reports from the Punjab. On 18 April, blaming himself for what he described as 'a Himalayan miscalculation' in asking people to disobey the law before they were properly prepared for *satyagraha*, he abandoned the civil disobedience campaign. He still believed passionately in *satyagraha*, but acknowledged that a great deal needed to be done in educating the people before it could be safely used as a mass weapon. As it happened, he was presented with the perfect opportunity for doing this when Horniman was deported, for he was able to take over control of the bi-weekly *Young India*, and of the weekly Gujarati journal *Nava Jivan*. Under his editorship, the magazines grew rapidly in importance and circulation, spreading his teachings just as *Indian Opinion* had done in South Africa.

In a little over a month, Gandhi had established himself as a national figure with his own political platform, poised to challenge the existing order at all levels. Political leaders and officials alike still did not really know what to make of him, or how his idiosyncratic ideas could be harnessed. Chelmsford summed up the feelings not only of the British but also of most educated Indians when he wrote to Montagu on 9 April:

Dear me, what a d....d nuisance these saintly fanatics are! Gandhi is incapable of hurting a fly and is as honest as the day, but he enters quite lightheartedly on a course of action which is the negation of all government and may lead to much hardship to people who are ignorant and easily led astray.[14]

On 30 May 1919, Rabindranath Tagore wrote to Chelmsford formally relinquishing the knighthood he had received after winning the Nobel Prize for Literature in 1913. His eloquent letter, which was widely circulated throughout India, complained of 'the enormity of the measures taken by the Government in the Punjab for quelling some local disturbances', of the 'insults and sufferings undergone by my brothers', and of the way the 'universal agony of indignation ... has been ignored by our rulers, possibly congratulating themselves for what they imagine as salutory lessons'. 'The time has come,' he concluded, 'when badges of honour make our shame glaring in their incongruous context of humiliation, and I for my part wish to stand shorn of all special distinctions by the side of those of my countrymen who, for their so-called insignificance are liable to suffer a degradation not fit for human beings.'[15]

The viceroy, unable as usual to make a decision, passed the letter to Montagu, who sensibly passed the buck back to him, advising him to do nothing. Chelmsford told Tagore that he could not relieve him of his knighthood, and did not propose to make any recommendations to the king-emperor. Whatever the official protocol, in the eyes of Indians the deed was done – an Indian had thrown an honour back in the face of the Raj.

What had provoked Tagore's gesture was O'Dwyer's final act of contempt. Lesser offences were dealt with by summary courts, which could hand out on-the-spot punishments like whipping and flogging. But for 'waging war against the king', the sentences the lieutenant-governor and his officials wanted – hanging, transportation for life, long terms of imprisonment with hard labour – could only be imposed by higher courts or by courts martial. To handle these cases quickly and quietly, special martial law commissions were set up, which were held in camera, with limited legal representation, restricted cross-examination of prosecution witnesses, and no right of appeal. Eight hundred and fifty-two men, with ages ranging from 11 to 115, were tried by the commissions. Five hundred and eighty-one were convicted, of whom 108 were sentenced to death and 264 to transportation for life and forfeiture of all goods.

Unfortunately for O'Dwyer, the men he was really determined to nail, Doctors Kitchlew and Satyapal, could not be tried under martial law provisions: they had been under arrest 100 miles away from Amritsar when martial law was declared, and could therefore not have taken any part in the disturbances. There would be little chance of getting a conviction in the high court, where all the normal safeguards of the law would apply. O'Dwyer, however, had a breathtakingly simple answer: he bullied Chelmsford into backdating the start of martial law from 13 April to 30 March.

The two doctors, along with 13 other Amritsar leaders, were duly tried by a martial law commission. Both were sentenced to transportation to a penal colony for life, plus forfeiture of all property. Of the other defendants, five were acquitted, while the rest received varying prison sentences. Gandhi was one of the defence witnesses, but was not allowed to say anything about the aims and principles of *satyagraha*. The prosecution case relied almost entirely on the dubious evidence of an informer, Hans Raj, a police spy and *agent provocateur* who had actually played a large part in organizing the meeting in the Jallianwala Bagh. Besides being granted immunity, Raj was rewarded at the end of the case with a large sum of money, and moved to safety in Mesopotamia.

The judge, Mr Justice Broadway, declared that O'Dwyer had been right: the riots had indeed 'constituted a deliberate and most determined waging of war'. By then, O'Dwyer had retired to England in a glow of self-satisfaction. He had been replaced as lieutenant-governor by Sir Edward Maclagen, a more reasonable soul, but O'Dwyerism lived on, and there was general rejoicing at the judgement among Anglo-Indians, not only in the Punjab but throughout India. For Indians, however, the whole process was insupportable. Motilal Nehru wrote to Chelmsford requesting a stay of execution for the men who had been condemned to death, announcing that he was briefing no less a personage than Sir John Simon, the former solicitor-general, attorney-general and home secretary, to appeal to the Privy Council in London.

Chelmsford and the machine in India had taken care to keep Montagu in the dark as much as possible, sending him only the most scanty information about the affair. But now the lid was off at last, and with a political row boiling up in Parliament, Montagu was forced to act. In the best parliamentary tradition, he decided to play for time by appointing a committee of inquiry. It took a while before a suitable chairman could be found – no politician could be persuaded to take hold of such an obviously hot potato – but eventually he settled on Lord Hunter, a senator of the College of Justice in Edinburgh, who had been solicitor-general for Scotland in the Asquith government.

The Hunter Committee – officially 'The Committee to Investigate the Recent Disturbances in Bombay, Delhi and the Punjab' – consisted of four Britons and three Indians, in addition to Hunter himself. It began its sessions in Delhi on 29 October 1919, and moved to Lahore on 11 November, to spend two months painstakingly receiving evidence and examining witnesses. Dyer appeared before it on 19 November, giving a full, frank and totally unrepentant account of his actions. O'Dwyer, equally unrepentant, returned to India to give evidence on 15 and 16 January 1920, as the last witness before the committee retired to Agra to sift through the evidence it had heard.

By then, there had been significant developments in London. Despite Horniman's attempts to publicize what had been going on in the Punjab, the British public had heard very little. Disasters in India, whether natural or man-made, were never of much interest back home, and in any case the disturbances had been overtaken by more newsworthy events in Afghanistan during May. Upset at the way both Hindus and Muslims were being treated in India, the ruler had threatened to assert his independence from British control and even to mount attacks on the North-West Frontier. Troops had been rushed to close the Khyber

Pass and bring the Amir to heel in a short, sharp local war. In the face of such competition, almost the only reference to the Amritsar massacre in the national press had been one short paragraph in *The Times*.

With the opening of the Hunter Committee's inquiry, however, the *Daily Express* had managed to get the full story of the Jallianwala Bagh shooting, and splashed it across its pages on 13 December 1919 as a scoop under the headline: '2,000 INDIANS SHOT DOWN. General's Terrible Remedy to Curb Rebellion.' Other papers picked up the story, and a great deal of heat was generated with awkward questions being hurled at Montagu in Parliament. Some of the heat was removed on 23 December when Kitchlew, Satyapal and the others convicted by the martial law commission were released under an amnesty for political prisoners announced by the king to mark the introduction of the Montagu-Chelmsford reforms. The king hailed the reforms as beginning 'a new era'. But the situation remained decidedly uneasy.

It took the Hunter Committee until 8 March to prepare its draft report for submission to the government of India, and it was the end of May before the report was ready for publication. The Indian members of the committee had stopped speaking to Lord Hunter after he had shouted at them in a temper: 'You people – you want to drive the British out of the country!'[16] Although they agreed with the report's criticisms of the Punjab government and condemned the riots, they insisted on including a minority report rejecting the idea that the riots had constituted a rebellion. In an even more damning indictment of O'Dwyer's regime, they contrasted what had happened in the Punjab with Delhi, where 'a difficult situation was handled with tact and restraint', with Ahmedabad, where the administration 'acted with discretion and judgment which must be acknowledged', and with Bombay, whose government 'displayed to our mind creditable statesmanship'.[17]

A high-powered Cabinet committee, chaired by Montagu, discussed the Hunter Report and accepted it in its entirety. The committee concluded that 'His Majesty's Government repudiate emphatically the doctrine of "frightfulness" upon which Brigadier-General Dyer based his action.' Dyer's action, it said, was a 'complete violation' of the principle of minimum force, which remained the 'prime factor' of government policy, adding that the crawling order 'offended against every canon of civilised government'.[18] This was not a universally popular interpretation. Dyer had been relieved of his command and sent back to England on sick leave, but when Churchill, on behalf of the Cabinet, tried to force the Army Council to dismiss him, he met stiff opposition. In a particularly savage debate, the House of Commons condemned Dyer by 230 votes to 129, with many government supporters abstaining. 10 days later, however, the House of Lords decided by 129 to 86 that Dyer had been treated unjustly.

Conservatives throughout Britain joined Anglo-Indians in vociferous support for their hero. On the same day as the Commons debate, the *Morning Post*, which described itself as 'The Empire's Senior Daily', launched a fund to raise money for 'the man who saved India'. Contributions poured in from all quarters, reaching a grand total of £26,317/4s/10d, the equivalent of about £573,000 today.[19] Along with the money, Dyer was presented with a jewelled sword, inscribed 'To the Saviour of the Punjab'.

This apparent vindication of Dyer was the final straw for many Indians who had previously been favourably disposed towards Britain and the empire. What had begun as a suspicion was confirmed beyond all doubt. 'I realized then, more vividly than I had ever done before, how brutal and immoral imperialism was and how it had eaten into the souls of the British upper-classes,' wrote Jawaharlal Nehru.

Nehru, in fact, had already been converted from his pro-British leanings by an extraordinary personal experience. When the Indian government had refused to release Kitchlew, Sityapal and other prisoners to appear as witnesses before the Hunter Committee, Congress had declined to co-operate with the committee. It had launched its own inquiry, initially under the direction of Motilal Nehru, interviewing hundreds of people and gathering evidence throughout the Punjab. Jawaharlal had always been highly sceptical of a Congress dominated by Moderates – including his father, who was to be president that year – but he was incensed by the Jallianwala Bagh massacre and offered his services as an assistant. Any doubts he may have had were overcome by the fact that his hero, Gandhi, was a member of the Congress committee. Returning from gathering information in Amritsar on 19 November 1919, he joined the night train from Lahore to Delhi. What happened then was described by Nehru himself in his autobiography:

The compartment I entered was almost full and all the berths, except one upper one, were occupied by sleeping passengers. I took the vacant upper berth. In the morning I discovered that all my fellow passengers were military officers. They conversed with each other in loud voices which I could not help overhearing. One of them was holding forth in an aggressive and triumphant tone and I soon discovered that he was Dyer, the hero of Jallianwala Bagh, and he was describing his Amritsar experiences. He pointed out how he had the whole town at his mercy and had felt like reducing the rebellious city to a heap of ashes, but he took pity on it and refrained. He was evidently coming back from Lahore after giving his evidence before the Hunter Committee of Inquiry. I was greatly shocked to hear his conversation and to observe his callous manner. He descended at Delhi station in pyjamas with bright pink stripes, and a dressing gown.[20]

Dyer's display of arrogance that morning was enough to demolish what remained of Nehru's faltering faith in the British empire. From then on, he had no qualms about following the line that an equally disillusioned Gandhi had already decided upon after the trauma of the Jallianwala Bagh.

'When a Government takes up arms against its unarmed subjects,' Gandhi wrote, 'then it has forfeited its right to govern. It has admitted that it cannot rule in peace and justice ... nothing less than the removal of the British and complete self-government could satisfy injured India.' For the rest of his life, he observed a 24-hour fast on the anniversary of the massacre. 'Plassey,' he observed, 'laid the foundation of the British empire. Amritsar has shaken it.'

'The Very Brink of Chaos and Anarchy'

Until he was nearly 30, Jawaharlal Nehru lived in the shadow of his dominating, larger-than-life father. Although politically shrewder than Motilal, he was, unlike him, a prey to indecision and doubt. So far, he had always done what his father wanted, mostly out of love but a little out of fear, too. But by 1919, he was ready to cast off one father figure in exchange for another: Motilal was to be replaced by Gandhi.

Jawaharlal was not religious. He had been educated as a scientist, and it was the idea of an economy organized along scientific lines that attracted him to socialism. It was astonishing that he should succumb, intellectually and politically, to a traditional Hindu godman. But he was dazzled by this extraordinary little nut-brown man who seemed to have stepped straight out of the Middle Ages, by his ideas and intelligence and by his sheer magnetism. 'I was bowled over by Gandhi straight away,' Nehru wrote later. When Gandhi announced the Satyagraha Sabha, Jawaharlal was one of the first to sign up and take the vow of civil disobedience.

Like most Moderates, Motilal was appalled at the idea of *satyagraha*. As a lawyer, the idea of deliberately disobeying the law shocked him profoundly. What good would it do, he wanted to know, if hundreds of hitherto blameless young Indians were sent to gaol? More to the point, he dreaded the thought of his only son winding up behind bars. 'It seemed to him preposterous that I should go to prison,' wrote Jawaharlal. For several days, father and son went out of their way to avoid raising the issue. They treated each other with almost unnatural consideration. Jawaharlal learned later that his father had even taken to sleeping on the floor to see what prison might be like for his son.

Things could not go on like that, so Motilal invited Gandhi to Allahabad to discuss his dangerous influence on his son. They had several long talks – from which Jawaharlal was banned – before Gandhi emerged to advise the young Nehru 'not to precipitate matters or do anything to upset father'. He refused to take Jawaharlal back with him to the Sabarmati Ashram, telling him his relationship with Motilal was more important. Clearly, Gandhi had no wish to alienate Motilal at that critical time.

The 1919 session of Congress was held that December in Amritsar – a fortuitous choice of location, decided long before the massacre. In recognition of his work in the Punjab, Motilal was elected president, and had the pleasure of steering through the acceptance of the Montagu-Chelmsford reforms. It was a notable victory for Hindu-Muslim unity: Jinnah was elected president of the Muslim League and simultaneously obtained its approval of the new Act. It was also a notable victory for the Moderates – even Gandhi had joined in urging Congress to co-operate with the government in implementing the reforms. It was, however, to be their last victory. Motilal might have been the president, but Gandhi was undoubtedly the star of the Amritsar Congress. During the next 12 months, he would change the political agenda out of all recognition, carrying not only Jawaharlal but also Motilal with him.

1920, in fact, proved to be a watershed year for both Nehrus. In May, while Motilal was away from home conducting a major court case, Jawaharlal's wife and mother both fell ill. Their doctor advised a change of air, so Jawaharlal took them off to the hills, to stay at the Savoy Hotel in Mussoorie. By coincidence, the Afghan delegation negotiating the peace treaty after the short Anglo-Afghan war was staying at the same hotel. The local CID were immediately suspicious. What was the young Nehru up to? Was he a Congress emissary, secretly trying to influence the Afghans? In no time, a charming superintendent of police appeared, with an official letter demanding an undertaking from Nehru that he would not communicate with the Afghans. Nehru had not met the delegation, and had no intention of doing so, but he was certainly not going to be ordered off by some policeman. He refused. Whereupon, the superintendent served him with an externment order, banning him from Mussoorie. 'Greatness is being thrust upon me,' Nehru wrote to his father on 14 May. He returned to Allahabad in a rage.

When Motilal learned what had happened, he wrote a magisterial letter to his friend of 30 years, the governor of the United Provinces, Sir Harcourt Butler. Within two weeks, the order was withdrawn. But Motilal was growing increasingly worried about the political direction his son was taking. He wrote to him, warning that any further political excesses would 'mean the final break-up of the family and the upsetting of all public, private and professional work. One thing will lead to another, and something is sure to turn up which will compel me to follow you to the gaol or something similar.'[1] By then, however, Jawaharlal had been drawn into another affair, one which was to have as powerful an effect on him as his encounter on the train from Amritsar with General Dyer.

As Jawaharlal was kicking his heels in Allahabad, some 500 peasants from the rural Jaunpur and Pratapgarh districts were camped on the banks of the River Jumna. Led by a Maharashtra Brahman holy man, Baba Ramachandra, they had come hoping to see Gandhi, who they believed would be returning home from a Congress meeting in Benares via Allahabad, where he would naturally stay at Anand Bhavan. They wanted his help with their fight against corrupt landlords, the taluqdars, who were bleeding them dry with excessive rent demands, impossible interest charges, and arbitrary evictions. Gandhi, in fact, was still in Benares, but Jawaharlal happened to be at home. He was a lawyer, he was available, and above all he was a Nehru. The peasant leaders turned to him, asking him to visit their districts to see conditions for himself. Toiling through remote districts in the hottest part of the year was not an appealing prospect, but as he recalled in his autobiography, 'They would accept no denial and literally clung to us. At last I promised to visit them two days or so later.'[2]

Thus it was that for the first time in his life Jawaharlal Nehru came face to face with the real India, peasant India, Gandhi's India. The villages were all well off the beaten track, far from railways and roads, and he was touched to discover that thousands of men and women had turned out to make roads overnight by hand, so that he and his companions could drive through in his car. What he saw during that visit came as a profound shock, a revelation that changed his life. He returned home 'filled with shame and sorrow, shame at my own easy-going and comfortable life ... sorrow at the degradation and overwhelming poverty of India. A new picture of India seemed to rise before me, naked, starving, crushed, and utterly miserable. And their faith in us ... embarrassed me and filled me with a new responsibility that frightened me.'[3]

The young Nehru had at last found a cause he was prepared to die for. Kisan sabhas (peasant associations), were being set up all over the country in the first genuinely grass-roots political movement in India. Nehru took up their fight against oppression, corruption and injustice. For the next two years, he became one of the leaders of what threatened at times to become a full-scale peasants' revolt throughout the whole of central India. He soon came to the attention of the Indian as well as the provincial government. Every move he made was followed, noted and reported. Nervous as always of anything that smacked of Bolshevism, they marked him down as a potentially dangerous revolutionary. Nehru did not manage to achieve an immediate success: despite the struggles, the peasants would go on suffering at the hands of their landlords for more than 25 years. But one of his first acts when he became prime minister of India in 1947 would be to abolish the taluqdar system.

While Nehru was following his personal road to Damascus among the peasants of Pratapgarh, the political climate elsewhere in India remained stormy. In parallel with the peasants' *kisan sabhas*, industrial workers were forming highly politicized labour unions, which were organized into the All-India Trade Union Congress under the leadership of Lala Lajpat Rai during 1920. In the first half of that year alone, there were some 200 strikes, involving over a million workers. The Indian Communist Party was formed in the same year. Many young Indians found its doctrine of violent revolution more attractive than Gandhi's *ahimsa*, but perhaps because of the Mahatma's unique charisma, or because Russian-style communism was incompatible with India's religious nature, it was never a threat to Congress.

At the end of May, the situation was aggravated still further by publication of both the Hunter Committee's report and the peace treaty which the Allies intended to impose on Turkey. Although the Hunter report was generally fair and thorough, condemning both Dyer's actions and the Punjab government's handling of the situation, most Indians, including Gandhi, dismissed it as a whitewash. Dyer's vindication by the House of Lords and the orchestrated public support for him in Britain rubbed salt into wounds that were still raw. But it was the older running sore, the future of the Islamic caliphate – known in India as the Khilafat – that provided Gandhi with the immediate excuse to launch a new campaign against the Raj.

The British prime minister, David Lloyd George, had assured Indian Muslims that when Turkey was defeated Britain would respect the sultan's position as caliph, the spiritual leader of Islam and protector of the holy places. But that had been during the war, when Britain needed the loyalty of Indian Muslims. Now the war was won, and it was clear that Lloyd George was about to renege on his promise and join the French prime minister Clemenceau in dismantling the Ottoman empire and dividing up its territories, including many of the holy places, between Britain and France. To the British government, the treaty was a purely political issue between the Allies and Turkey, and had nothing to do with religion, or with India. Indian Muslims, however, saw it as a deliberate attempt by the Christian west to destroy the power of Islam.

Faced with an almost insuperable problem, the Muslims did what Indians always did – they formed a committee. To begin with, the Khilafat Committee involved only a small minority of Indian Muslims, mostly younger, educated men from the north and a few wealthy merchants in Bombay. The Muslim League seemed disinterested. Jinnah, true to his secular beliefs, remained aloof. But anything that had a religious base, and could be turned into a weapon against the Raj, had a natural appeal for Gandhi. Reasoning that his support would place Muslims in his debt, strengthen Hindu-Muslim unity against the British, and above all harness Muslim energies to his campaign for *swaraj*, he threw himself wholeheartedly into this new cause.

It started badly: Gandhi's efforts to persuade both Hindus and Muslims to observe a 'Khilafat Day' *hartal* in October 1919 were a failure. But he persevered. In Delhi on 23 November he urged the first national Khilafat conference to adopt the tactic of 'non-co-operation' with the Raj. It was the first time he had used the term and, as with so many of Gandhi's pronouncements, even he was not clear exactly what he meant by it. But the delegates resolved to make a start by taking no part in the forthcoming victory celebrations, and by boycotting British goods.

At the end of December, the Khilafat Committee gained new strength when Muslim activists who had been interned or imprisoned during the war – most notably the brothers Muhammad and Shaukat Ali and Abul Kalam Azad – were released under the general amnesty for political prisoners. In March 1920, Muhammad Ali led a deputation to London, to warn the government that Muslims were bound to obey their Holy Prophet, who with his dying breath had commanded them never to surrender control of the Arab lands containing their holy places to any non-Muslim. They could therefore never accept the proposed British and French mandates over Iraq, Syria and Palestine. Their arguments failed to move Lloyd George: when Muhammad Ali demanded justice for Turkey, the prime minister replied that Turkey would indeed get full justice: 'Austria has had justice, Germany has had justice – pretty terrible justice, why should Turkey escape?'[4]

Muhammad Ali and his deputation returned to India empty-handed and bitter to join Gandhi in preparing the Khilafat movement for battle. In the mean time, the Turks themselves had rather upset the apple cart by deposing their sultan and making it clear that the only territory they were interested in retaining was the oil-rich Mosul region and those parts of Thrace and Anatolia which had been ceded to Greece. But such minor inconveniences were not allowed to spoil what promised to be a good fight.

With the return of the Ali brothers and Azad to the scene, the Khilafat campaign began to turn into the popular mass movement that Gandhi wanted. All three were *maulanas*, learned men, and thus automatically commanded the respect of believers, and all three were capable of arousing the masses with fiery rhetoric, appealing directly to their emotions and religious fervour. Like Gandhi, they placed their trust in God and gave little thought to the consequences of their actions.

Azad is generally credited with inciting thousands of Muslims in Sind and the North-West Frontier to abandon their homes and join a *hijrat*, a religious emigration, to Afghanistan, by declaring that India had become *dar-ul-harb*, an accursed land in which it was a sin for a Muslim to live, because of the disregard for the law of Islam shown by the British government. Eighteen thousand Muslims made the trek across the Khyber Pass in August alone. They had been told that the Afghans would welcome them with open arms and fertile fields. But no one had told the Afghans – horrified by this influx, they turned them back without food or funds. When they finally staggered back to their villages, the migrants found their Hindu neighbours had grabbed their property – a situation that did little for Hindu-Muslim unity.[5]

Throughout 1920, Gandhi continued to press the Khilafat Committee to launch a national campaign of non-co-operation. On 9 June at a meeting in Allahabad, they unanimously agreed, and asked him to lead it. Among the invited guests observing the meeting were Motilal Nehru, Sir Tej Bahadur Sapru and Annie Besant, three pillars of the Congress establishment. Gandhi knew that they and the other Moderate leaders would never have supported his ideas. But by side-stepping Congress and launching his campaign through the Khilafat Committee, he was throwing down a challenge which they could not afford to ignore. He was duly rewarded when Congress called a special session to be held in Calcutta in September 1920 to consider the idea of non-co-operation. Jinnah followed suit by calling a simultaneous meeting of the Muslim League.

Gandhi kept up the pressure on Congress by going ahead without it. On 22 June, he wrote to the viceroy, warning him that unless the injustices imposed on Turkey were not removed by 1 August, he would mount a national campaign of non-co-operation, asserting the right recognized 'from time immemorial of the subject to refuse to assist a ruler who misrules'.[6] Ninety influential Muslims signed a similar letter to the viceroy. There was no response from the government – Chelmsford was determined not to get involved, and Montagu was helpless in the face of Lloyd George's hostility to Turkey. So, the campaign was officially launched.

By another of those fortuitous coincidences that ran through Gandhi's career, Tilak died in the early hours of 1 August. As an orthodox Brahman, the Lokamanya had been strongly opposed to any Congress involvement with a Muslim campaign. Since he was the only man who could have been a rival to Gandhi as a populist national leader, and probably the only man who could have turned Congress against him, his death removed that danger. In fact, by a strange irony it actually helped the campaign's launch: the nationwide hartals and processions to mourn his passing merged inextricably with those to mark the start of non-co-operation, which would otherwise have been fairly insignificant.

Gandhi marked the start of the campaign with a suitably dramatic gesture, publicly returning his Kaiser-i-Hind gold medal and his medals from the Boer and Zulu wars. He then set off on a whirlwind tour of the country, to drum up support before the all-important Congress session in September. The Khilafat movement may have been important to him in its own right, but it was even more valuable as a tool to help capture Congress. He had already extended his power base by taking over the presidency of the Home Rule League, at the invitation of Motilal Nehru. But he arrived in Calcutta knowing he faced powerful opposition from all the heavyweights of the Congress old guard.

Motilal and Jinnah, joint leaders of the constitutionalist group, joined forces with C.R. Das, Annie Besant and the Hindu Mahasabha leader, Madan Mohan Malaviya, agreeing that they would accept the idea of non-co-operation, but not Gandhi's programme, which they saw as fraught with dangers. Jinnah pursued this line in a passionate presidential speech to the League, bitterly denouncing the Raj and the British government. But when the first round of the battle was fought in the Congress subjects committee, all the Muslims present apart from Jinnah himself voted for Gandhi. Feelings ran high: at one point, Shaukat Ali had to be physically restrained from striking Jinnah.[7] Gandhi refused to compromise in any way: if Congress refused its support, he announced, he would simply continue without it. The outcome was in doubt until the last minute, when a surprise defection helped sway the voting in Gandhi's favour: Motilal Nehru changed sides, taking with him enough members to carry the motion, which scraped through by 144 votes to 132. Motilal never explained his sudden change of heart. But his letters make it clear that he felt he would lose his son, who was more dear to him than life itself, if he continued to oppose Gandhi.

Once Gandhi had cleared that first hurdle, there could be no doubt about the result in open Congress, for this was a Congress unlike any other before it. There were nearly 6,000 delegates and 15,000 observers. Special Khilafat trains had brought thousands of Muslim workers from Bombay and Madras, to vote for whatever Gandhi proposed. Anyone who paid the price of admission to the Congress tent was allowed to vote. One of Gandhi's opponents later told Dr B.R. Ambedkar, leader of the untouchables, that 'a large majority of the delegates were no others than the taxi-drivers of Calcutta who were paid to vote for the non-co-operation resolution'.[8] But such objections were meaningless in the face of the revolution that was transforming Congress from an élite middle-class debating society into a popular mass movement.

Gandhi appeared to have quite forgotten his 'Himalayan miscalculation' of 18 months before. Amid scenes of wild enthusiasm, he promised that if his programme was followed, swaraj would be achieved within a year. Doubters like Besant, Pal, Das or Jinnah were dismissed contemptuously when they tried to voice their fears about launching non-co-operation before the masses had been trained in its principles.

Gandhi's programme of 'progressive, non-violent, non-co-operation' had a familiar ring to anyone who remembered the swadeshi campaign of 1905. Many of its seven points covered the same ground: surrender of titles, honours and nominated positions; a boycott of official and semi-official functions; withdrawal of children from government schools and colleges, which were to be replaced by national schools and colleges; boycott of British courts by both lawyers and litigants; no recruitment for military, clerical or labouring service in Mesopotamia; boycott of the forthcoming elections to the reformed councils by both candidates and voters; and a boycott of foreign goods. The resolution was passed by 1,886 to 884. But the disquiet of many delegates was indicated by 3,188 abstentions.[9]

Annie Besant denounced Gandhi's movement as 'a channel of hatred'. Gokhale's successor as head of the Servants of India Society called him 'fanciful'. And Ferozeshah Mehta's disciple, Sir Dinshaw E. Wacha, the Parsi leader of the National Liberal Federation, spoke for many when he complained of 'the wrongs this madman is now inflicting on the poor country in his mad and arrogant career'. 'The vast unthinking multitudes,' he said, seemed willing to follow 'like a flock of sheep, this unsafe shepherd who is bringing the country on the very brink of chaos and anarchy'.[10]

Gandhi's bandwagon, however, was now rolling inexorably. From Calcutta he and Jinnah went on to a Home Rule League meeting in Bombay. Gandhi took the chair, and immediately proposed changing both the name and the constitution of the League, to bring it into line with his own ideas. Henceforth, it would drop its English title and be known more appropriately as the Swaraj Sabha. And he wanted its main goal, 'Attainment of self-government within the British Commonwealth ... by constitutional methods', changed to 'To secure complete *swaraj* for India according to the wishes of the Indian people'. When Jinnah demurred, Gandhi told him anyone who could not accept the majority's decision was free to resign. Only 61 out of 6,000 members were at the meeting, which had been called at short notice, but two thirds of them voted for Gandhi. Jinnah, with his 18 supporters, left the meeting, and the League which he had once led.

In his letter of resignation, while condemning government policy as 'the primary cause of it all', and pledging to continue to work 'for the early attainment of complete responsible government', Jinnah made no bones about his feelings for Gandhi:

> Your methods have already caused split and division in almost every institution that you have approached hitherto ... not only amongst Hindus and Muslims but between Hindus and Hindus and Muslims and Muslims and even between fathers and sons ... your extreme programme has for the moment struck the imagination of the inexperienced youth and the ignorant and the illiterate. All this means complete disorganisation and chaos. What the consequence of this may be, I shudder to contemplate ... I do not wish my countrymen to be dragged to the brink of a precipice in order to be shattered.[11]

Gandhi's triumph over the Moderates was completed in December at Nagpur in central India, where he was midwife to the birth of the revolutionary new Congress that had been conceived in Calcutta four months earlier. He had spent much of the year preparing a new constitution for the Congress – busy lawyers like Jinnah, Motilal and Das simply did not have the time to spend on such a project – and he presented it to the 14,500 delegates to great acclaim. With the November elections over, and their boycott no longer a contentious issue, previous opponents like Das, Lajpat Rai and Motilal had now swung into line behind him. Indeed, Lajpat Rai seconded his motion on the new constitution, which began by changing Congress's main object to 'the attainment of *swaraj* by the people of India by all legitimate and peaceful means'. Das was persuaded to propose the main resolution on non-cooperation.

Once again, only Jinnah had the nerve to question Gandhi's wisdom. Other former Congress stalwarts, some of them former presidents, who could not stomach the Mahatma's radical policies, stayed away, among them Pandit Madan Mohan Malaviya, Surendranath Banerjea, Bipin Chandra Pal, Tej Bahadur Sapru and C. Sankaran Nair. When he urged caution in the subjects committee, Jinnah was accused of 'a want of courage'. But it must have taken great bravery to stride to the dais and speak against Gandhi that day. When he tried to introduce a reasoned and logical argument he was howled down with cries of 'shame, shame' and 'political imposter'. The boos and hisses and catcalls grew more and more violent – especially when he refused to refer to Gandhi as 'Mahatma', insisting on calling him plain 'Mr Gandhi' – until he was eventually driven from the platform, and from the tent. He gathered up Ruttie, and left Nagpur by the next train, his political career in ruins. He did not even bother to attend the Muslim League session, knowing full well that it, too, was in the hands of his opponents.[12]

Gandhi's new Congress was a more streamlined, efficient and representative organization than before. For the first time, it was to have a working committee of 15 members as a year-round permanent executive, selected by the 350 members of the All-India Central Committee. India was to be divided into areas defined by natural linguistic boundaries rather than those of the British provinces, each entitled to send a number of delegates to national Congress sessions based on the size of its population. Congress was to have local committees organized right down to district and village levels. And the annual membership fee was reduced to four annas – one quarter of one rupee – to enable the poor to become full members, thus ensuring mass involvement and a regular income. And where before English had been the lingua franca, Congress was now to conduct its affairs in Hindi wherever possible. The new era had begun.

As the old stars began to fade with the eclipse of their cosy political world, a new generation of Congress leaders began to emerge, names that would become increasingly familiar over the next quarter-century as the freedom struggle ran its course. One of the brightest new hopes was a young Bengali Kayastha, 23-year-old Subhas Chandra Bose, the son of a successful barrister from Cuttack, near

Calcutta, whose attitude to the British was summed up in one of his letters home from Cambridge University saying 'What gives me the greatest joy is watching the whiteskins serving me and cleaning my shoes.'[13]

In his teens, Bose had come under the influence of the teachings of Swami Vivekananda, who sought to combine 'muscular Hinduism' with western scientific ideas and preached what has been described as a form of 'bastard socialism'. Bose had a brilliant mind, and came fourth in the ICS examinations in London in July 1920. This guaranteed him a place as one of the heaven-born, and lifelong prestige, power and security at the very heart of the Raj. But to his father's fury, he turned down the chance of a glittering career in the ICS: after Jallianwala Bagh, he felt no patriotic Indian should serve the British.

Returning to Calcutta to work under C.R. Das, Bose became principal of the National College there, one of 800 schools and colleges set up throughout the country to replace boycotted government institutions. Soon, although he was six years younger than Jawaharlal Nehru, he was sharing the leadership of the *kisan sabhas* and the youth movement with him. The two men were to be political rivals for the next 20 years.

Other youngsters in their twenties and thirties who began their rise to prominence in Congress at this time included the future president of India, Rajendra Prasad, Mahadev Desai, J.B. Kripalani and the Muslims M.A. Ansari and Maulana Abul Kalam Azad. Slightly older, but still young enough to see the movement through to independence and beyond, were Gandhi's Gujarati disciple Vallabhbhai Patel, and Chakravarti Rajagopalachari, the Madras lawyer with whom Gandhi had been staying when he had the dream telling him to launch his first *satyagraha* campaign against the Rowlatt Act. Patel would become India's deputy prime minister, and Rajagopalachari its only Indian governor-general.

Gandhi had promised *swaraj* during 1921, and he believed he could achieve it through non-co-operation. As soon as the Congress session at Nagpur had given him its blessing, he was off on the campaign trail through the towns and villages of India. Hindus and Muslims everywhere took up the call, fired by the two key words, '*swaraj*' and 'Khilafat'. *Swaraj* was clear enough, but out in the boondocks, few people of either faith had much idea what Khilafat meant. However, as it sounded like '*khilaf*', which is Urdu for 'against', they were happy to assume it meant they should oppose the government.[14]

As the year progressed, so did the movement. With so many prominent Congressmen depending for their livelihoods on education and the law, the working committee had sensibly watered down the original resolution to allow the boycotts in these areas to be introduced gradually. But even so, they gathered momentum as the months passed. The boycott of schools and colleges was successful in most areas, apart from Madras and the south. The Ali brothers literally laid siege to Syed Ahmed's Muslim University at Aligarh. They did not succeed in closing it down, but did achieve a large number of defections from both students and staff, who founded a rival Muslim National University. The law courts boycott was less successful. Although several hundred lawyers stopped practising, at least for the moment, the business of the courts went on virtually unchecked. Nevertheless the lawyers who did withdraw included many famous, high-profile figures, among them C.R. Das, Saifuddin Kitchlew, Vallabhbhai Patel, C. Rajagopalachari, and, of course, Motilal Nehru, all of whom sacrificed their hugely profitable legal practices.

Motilal, in particular, set an example that would have been hard to fault. He took his younger daughter Krishna out of school, resigned from the United Provinces council, and closed down his law firm. But that was not enough. He had never been one for half measures, and having pledged his allegiance to Gandhi, he was determined to go the whole hog. He sold his horses, carriages and motor cars, cut down his army of servants to just one, and replaced his Savile Row suits with a *kurta*, the long *khaddar* shirt, pyjamas and a Ghandi cap. Instead of the finest quality cloth from Lancashire and Yorkshire, he wore homespun *khadi*. He gave up his wine cellar and changed his diet, as he told Gandhi in a letter during the summer of 1921:

> The brass cooker ... has taken the place of two kitchens ... one square meal of rice, dal, vegetable, sometimes *khir* [a milk and rice savoury] in the middle of the day that of breakfast, lunch and dinner 'à l'Anglaise' ... the *shikar* [hunt] has given place to long walks, and rifles and guns to books, magazines and newspapers (the favourite book being Edwin Arnold's *Song Celestial* which is undergoing its third reading). 'What a fall, my countrymen!' But, really, I have never enjoyed life better.[15]

Jawaharlal took quite easily to this sudden change. Perhaps more surprising was the reaction of the women in the household, his wife and mother, who had to exchange silk saris for homespun *khadi*. Far from being dismayed, they were both delighted at a return to the traditional Indian lifestyle which neither had ever wanted to abandon. Across the country, many other Congressmen's wives and families felt the same, for, to a large extent, women had not become as westernized as their husbands.

Few title-holders returned their honours, even fewer government servants actually resigned, and the boycotts in education and the law may have been patchy. But in one area at least, the campaign was a huge success: the boycott of foreign cloth reduced imports from Lancashire during 1921 by almost 50 per cent. Gandhi started it off by personally supervising a great ceremonial bonfire of imported finery. Across the country, volunteers went from house to house collecting clothes made of foreign cloth, and everyone would gather to consign them to the flames. At every small station where his train stopped for a few minutes on his nationwide tour, Gandhi persuaded the assembled crowd to discard at least their headdress on the spot, piling them into a heap on the ground and setting fire to them.[16] Shops selling foreign cloth were picketed until their owners agreed to give it up. *Khadi* became the uniform of the nationalist movement. When students he was addressing in Madurai complained that it was too expensive, Gandhi replied that the answer was to wear less – and promptly discarded his own *dhoti* and *kurta* in favour of a loin cloth, with a cotton shawl for cold weather.

To supplement the new *swadeshi* movement, Gandhi promoted the idea of hand spinning, not only for its benefits in producing homespun yarn but also as a symbolic act representing an individual's commitment to the cause. He himself took a vow to spin for at least half an hour every day. In the great recruitment drive that raised Congress membership to about 5 million, Congressmen collecting funds and enrolling new members were also expected to distribute *charkhas*, the simple spinning wheels that became the Congress symbol.

Although it was not part of the Congress programme, a vigorous temperance movement sprang up, picketing toddy shops and bringing the sale of liquor almost to a halt in many provinces. This brought an unexpected bonus for the movement, by reducing the revenue from excise duty so severely that several provinces were soon in financial trouble. In Madras, the governor reported in February 1922 that his government's finances were 'really desperate'.[17]

Despite all the agitation openly aimed at overthrowing the Raj, the government of India steadfastly refused to intervene. For all his apparent insouciance, Chelmsford had been profoundly shocked by the events of 1919, and was determined to see that such tragedies should not happen again. He was also determined that the reforms which bore his name alongside that of Montagu should be brought into effect. Since the Moderates and Liberals who had left Congress, together with a number of other groups, were prepared to work the reforms, it was important to do nothing that would drive them into the arms of Congress – as a new wave of harsh repression would certainly have done. As early as February 1920, the government decided on 'a policy of abstaining as far as possible from interference, in order to avoid making martyrs of fanatical leaders or precipitating disorders'.[18]

Chelmsford stuck by his decision in the face of all the provocation from non-co-operators and Khilafatists, and the continuing howls of outrage from Anglo-Indians. 'The one great principle,' his home member, Sir William Vincent, told the legislative assembly in January 1921, 'is to promote the progress of this country towards responsible government and at the same time to preserve public tranquillity.'[19] When the more diehard governors, led by the lieutenant-governor of Burma and former home member, Sir Reginald Craddock, called for sterner measures they were put firmly in their place. And when the chief of the general staff protested about the Home Department's soft policy on the Khilafat campaign, which was seriously threatening the loyalty of the army, he was slapped down by Chelmsford in no uncertain manner for interfering in political matters. The policy was under constant review, but it was still in place – and Gandhi and the Khilafat and Congress leaders were still free – when Chelmsford came to the end of his term in April 1921 and sailed back home to England, where he was to become first lord of the Admiralty in 1924 and warden of All Souls in 1932.

Chelmsford's replacement was Rufus Isaacs, Marquess of Reading, a distinguished lawyer who had been solicitor-general, attorney-general, lord chief justice and special envoy to the USA. The Liberal Lord Reading quickly confirmed that he intended to continue the policy of non-interference, but it was not long before his resolve was severely tested. The Ali brothers were becoming more belligerent by the day, and were only saved from arrest by the intervention of Gandhi, who after several personal interviews with the new viceroy in mid-May, persuaded them to apologize and promise to abjure violence as long as they were associated with him.

In July, Muhammad Ali finally overstepped the mark when, in a speech at the All-India Khilafat Conference, he said that if the Afghans were to invade India, Muslims would help them against the British. This was bad enough, but he and his brother then went on to propose a resolution 'that it is in every way religiously unlawful for a Mussulman at the present moment to continue in the British Army or to induce others to join the army and it is the duty of Mussulmans ... to see that these religious commandments are brought home to every Mussulman in the army'.[20] Such direct incitements to desertion and disloyalty were too much for the military to stomach. Lord Rawlinson, the commander-in-chief, declared that the time had come for action. Reading and his council were forced to agree, especially since there was evidence that Shaukat Ali had already been interfering with the army. Even so, it was two months before the Ali brothers and four of their colleagues, including Azad, were arrested, tried and sentenced to upwards of two years' imprisonment.

As soon as the Ali brothers were charged, Gandhi led Congress and Khilafat leaders across the country in publicly repeating their words, and then publishing them in a printed manifesto. But the government had been expecting this, and refused to take the bait. They made no more arrests, created no more martyrs. Guided by Vincent and the law member of his council, Sir Tej Bahadur Sapru, Reading was content to bide his time and wait for Gandhi to make a more serious mistake, or for the movement to run out of steam, as they believed it surely would.

Already, non-co-operation was beginning to fragment into local issues.

Many of them were long-standing grievances or labour and property disputes which had little or nothing to do with the national campaign, but were fanned into flame by the propaganda and the general atmosphere. At the same time, the first cracks were already appearing in the wall of Hindu-Muslim unity as Muslims who had never been wholly convinced by Gandhi's insistence on non-violence became steadily more militant and more difficult to control. At the Khilafat Conference, the *maulanas* had recited verses from the Qur'an referring to a jihad and to killing infidels – which Malaviya and others were quick to point out could apply to Hindus as well as the British.[21]

In August 1921, the cracks widened into a breach on the Malabar coast in the deep south, where a fanatical Muslim group known as Moplahs rose in a jihad against their Hindu landlords and the British, killing both indiscriminately. When a British regiment was sent in to restore order, some 3,000 Moplahs arrived by train for a pitched battle. Others declared their own Khilafat kingdom, and at Tirur a mob of 10,000 set fire to the police station and the courts and seized all the arms and ammunition. They sacked Hindu homes, destroyed their temples and raped the Hindu women. By the time the rising was put down, an estimated 4,000 Moplahs and almost 100 British troops had been killed.[22] Since the deaths and thousands of injuries were the result of an open rebellion, there was no outcry, even though the toll was more than 10 times that of the Jallianwala Bagh. But many Anglo-Indians were quick to draw comparisons, asserting that Dyer's firm action in Amritsar had prevented a tragedy of similar proportions in the Punjab.

During the rising, the Moplahs forcibly converted thousands of Hindus to Islam – Hindus on the Congress subjects committee were shocked when a *maulana* who was a member of the committee refused to condemn this, arguing that it was a voluntary change of faith, not a forcible conversion, if the Hindus had become Muslims to save themselves from death.[23] It is hardly surprising that Hindus began to retaliate. Malaviya's Hindu Mahasabha joined with the Arya Samaj to mount a campaign to 'reconvert' and 'purify' low-caste Hindus who had become Muslims. Inevitably, tensions increased and communal rioting broke out, the prelude to a decade of unprecedented intercommunal hatred and violence. In the next five years alone, there were no fewer than 112 major communal riots, mostly in the northern cities.

As 1921 moved towards its end with still no sign of the *swaraj* that Gandhi had promised within the year, many supporters were becoming disillusioned and the movement was showing clear signs of winding down. Something had to be done before it disintegrated altogether. Gandhi decided to move to the next stage in his plan: active civil disobedience. He announced to the AICC in Delhi that he intended to start a trial campaign in one district on 23 November, and if this was successful would extend it throughout India. The district he chose was Bardoli, near Surat in his native Gujarat.

Gandhi's timing was perfect. The Prince of Wales was due to arrive in Bombay on 17 November for a 246-day goodwill tour of India, and Reading did not want to see the royal progress disrupted, or the prince's thunder stolen. But there was little he could do about it. Congress boycotted the visit and called a highly successful *hartal* on the day the prince arrived, not only in Bombay but also in a number of other northern cities. But there were problems in Calcutta, where the police clashed with Congress supporters and lost control of the centre of the city, and even worse trouble in Bombay itself, which was to have unfortunate effects both immediately and in the long term.

The royal party included the prince's second cousin, the 21-year-old Lord Louis Mountbatten, as his personal ADC. It was Mountbatten's first visit to India, and his future attitude to the sub-continent was undoubtedly influenced by his experiences then, not the least of which was having his proposal of marriage accepted by the glamorous and extremely rich Edwina Ashley in the Viceroy's House in February 1922. However Mountbatten's other experiences in India were less romantic, stamping the fear of uncontrolled communal violence firmly in his mind. Twenty-six years later, when he and Edwina were the occupants of the Viceroy's House, that fear was to play a crucial part in his decision-making.

Almost all Bombay's Hindus and Muslims stayed away for the prince's arrival, but the city's Parsi and Eurasian communities were eager to demonstrate their loyalty. They joined enthusiastically with the Europeans to welcome the royal visitor. As the prince stepped ashore, Gandhi was addressing a crowd of some 60,000 only a few hundred yards away, before going on to supervise a great bonfire of British cloth. His message, as always, was one of non-violence and communal harmony, but when the crowds leaving his meeting met Parsis and Eurasians returning from welcoming the prince all ideas of non-violence were forgotten. Hindus and Muslims united to fall upon the loyalists with unbridled ferocity. The rioting and looting that followed continued for five days – workers in the city's textile mills had staged a strike to coincide with the *hartal*, and there were 140,000 of them free to roam the streets wreaking havoc. By the time the disturbances had burnt themselves out 59 people had been killed and countless others injured.

Gandhi was shattered: the *swaraj* he had seen in Bombay, he said, 'has stunk in my nostrils'.[24] He went on a five-day fast to expiate the sins of his followers, which he ended after three days, when community leaders promised to make amends to the victims and their families. But his hopes of a peaceful campaign of civil disobedience had been dashed again, and he called it off. The doubters had been proved right: the Indian masses were not yet ready for *satyagraha*.

The violence had finally made Reading decide that the time had come to take action against the non-co-operators. The Prince of Wales was due in Calcutta on 24 December, and any more violent disorder there had to be prevented at all costs. Immediately the Bombay riots had been quenched, provincial governments were told that the policy of non-intervention was ended. Most political meetings were banned. So, too, were organizations such as the Congress National Volunteers – squads of activists who wore uniforms, drilled and often acted as a parallel police force, marshalling and trying to control demonstrations and other activities. Their members, particularly those in charge, were to be arrested.

Among the first to be pulled in were the more prominent leaders, including C.R. Das in Bengal, Lajpat Rai in the Punjab, and of course the two Nehrus in the United Provinces. For Jawaharlal, it was the first of nine sentences which would confine him to gaol for a total of 3,262 days over the next 24 years: this time, he was released on 3 March 1922, but was arrested again shortly afterwards and given another 18 months, of which he served eight. During the next two months over 30,000 people were arrested in India as a whole, and of the top leadership of the non-co-operation movement, only Gandhi remained free – the government judged that arresting him was still too dangerous, and in any case, Reading needed someone to negotiate with.

There was a very real danger for the government that its new wave of repression would drive the Liberals and Moderates back into the Congress camp, which would have been disastrous. Malaviya had been urging the viceroy for some time to call a round-table conference with Gandhi and the Moderates. In mid-December, Reading agreed, promising at the same time to release the political prisoners, end the repressive measures, and even grant 'full provincial autonomy' if Gandhi would call off the non-co-operation movement, and in particular the *hartal* in Calcutta on 24 December. At first, Gandhi agreed. But he quickly changed his mind, wiring Malaviya: 'Non-co-operation can cease only after satisfactory result conference. In no case have I authority decide for Congress.'[25] His 'private notes' made at the time give a more complex, perhaps more revealing, reason for his decision: 'I am sorry,' he wrote, 'that I suspect Lord Reading of complicity in the plot to unman India for eternity.'[26]

There is little doubt that if Gandhi had agreed to attend the conference, the Moderates would have joined forces with him to achieve substantial constitutional concessions. Reading was prepared to give full responsible government to the provinces, despite the doubts of London and most of the senior governors. He told Montagu: 'I ... was prepared to act on my own responsibility if the proper assurances had been forthcoming.'[27] This would have been not merely a step but a giant leap towards self-government, advancing the eventual transfer of power by a full 15 years. But it was not to be.

The royal visit to Calcutta passed off without incident. Four days later at a stormy annual session of Congress in Ahmedabad, Gandhi came under attack both from those who wanted to seek an accommodation with the government and those who wanted more militant action immediately. But in the end, as always, Gandhi carried the day. His rejection of Reading's offer was confirmed, and he was given dictatorial powers over non-co-operation. He announced that the postponed campaign of 'offensive civil disobedience' in Bardoli would go ahead.

Although they had been upset by Gandhi's intransigence, some of the Moderates were still hoping to find some way of bringing Gandhi and Reading together, to achieve the positive constitutional advances they knew were possible. Jinnah and Malaviya called an all-parties conference in Bombay for mid-January 1922, which was attended by some 300 leaders from all of India's major parties – excluding, of course, those Congressmen who were in prison. Gandhi attended 'informally', after Congress had agreed to postpone the start of civil disobedience until the end of the month. The motions calling for a round-table conference were passed unanimously. But then Gandhi threw another spanner in the works by refusing to take part. Obsessed with putting full-scale *satyagraha* to the test, he decided that a conference 'for devising a scheme of full *swaraj* [is] premature. India has not yet incontestably proved her strength'.[28]

Gandhi had handed the moral and strategic advantages back to Reading and the government, who could now sit back and watch his support falling away in all directions. Even those in prison, whose release he had demanded, were horrified at his rejection of such a golden opportunity. C.R. Das, always a reluctant ally, urged him to seize the moment, and began rethinking his position when he refused. Soon, it would be safe to arrest him. All that Reading needed now was for Gandhi to provide the right excuse. He did not have to wait long.

At the start of February, Gandhi wrote threatening mass civil disobedience if all his demands were not met at once. Reading naturally declined to oblige. Gandhi moved to Bardoli, to supervise the start of the campaign. He called on the rest of the country to stay calm, but on 5 February, what began as a minor disturbance in the remote village of Chauri Chaura in the United Provinces, blew up into a major incident and changed everything. An altercation between the local police and the tail-end of a Congress and Khilafat procession ended with a mob of 2,000 burning alive 22 policemen and government officials trapped inside the police station. It took two days for the news to reach the outside world. When it did, a shattered Gandhi called off his campaign and withdrew to fast, emerging to announce that 'God has been abundantly kind to me. He has warned me the third time that there is not yet in India that truthful and non-violent atmosphere which and which alone can justify mass disobedience ... God spoke clearly through Chauri Chaura.'[29]

Those followers like the Nehrus who had not been alienated by Gandhi's refusal to negotiate were shattered by this new about-face. They had been preparing for this battle for 18 months, and now their general had deserted them.

If one unfortunate incident was enough to stop him, then all the British had to do in future was to provoke such incidents and all threats of *satyagraha* would be meaningless.

The pressure from London and the governors for Gandhi's immediate arrest was now enormous, but Reading, on the advice of Sapru, kept his nerve for another month, and was rewarded by seeing what remained of the non-co-operation movement crumble into total collapse. When Gandhi was arrested on 10 March 1922, there was not a single incident in the whole of the country. A week later, he pleaded guilty to 'bringing into hatred or contempt ... the Government established by law in British India', and was sentenced to six years' simple imprisonment. The non-co-operation campaign was finished. The Raj had survived three years of its most dangerous crisis since the great revolt of 1857, but it would never be quite the same again.

'A Butchery of Our Souls'

Gandhi was released from prison in Poona on 5 February 1924, to be operated on for appendicitis. Although he had served only two years of his sentence, he was not sent back to prison. There was no need. The movements he had led were dormant if not dead, and there seemed little chance that they could be revived. In fact, they had been in a bad way long before his arrest: many Indians as well as Anglo-Indians believed he had used the Chauri Chaura incident as a convenient excuse for calling off non-co-operation before it turned into a débâcle, and that by arresting him, the government had rescued him from political ignominy.

The world had not stood still during the two years Gandhi had been in gaol: there had been developments – some welcome, some which he disliked intensely – both in government and in Congress. There had even been some progress towards self-government, under the intelligent guidance of Lord Reading, who had shown himself to be one of that rare sub-species, the listening viceroy. Reading was always prepared to lend a sympathetic ear to Indian aspirations, even while determined to keep them under control. In doing so, however, he unwittingly brought about the downfall of a secretary of state who was also prepared to listen, Edwin Montagu.

On 1 March 1922, Reading sent a telegram to Montagu urging a revision of the harsh terms of the Treaty of Sèvres, which was causing so much bitterness among Indian Muslims and adding fuel to the Khilafat fires. Later in the day, he telegraphed Montagu again, asking for permission to publish his recommendations. Montagu gave his consent at once, without waiting to consult his Cabinet colleagues. Some of them were furious, none more so than Lord Curzon, now foreign secretary, who claimed that the disclosure had weakened his hand in the negotiations he was about to begin for a revision of the treaty after Turkey's victory in its two-year war with Greece. Montagu was forced to resign. Two years later he was dead.

Montagu was replaced at the India Office by the innocuous Lord Peel. Reading, however, remained as viceroy, and in 1923, he fulfilled three of the most cherished dreams of the early Congressmen: ICS entrance examinations were held in New Delhi as well as London, with the avowed object of equalizing the numbers of British and Indian members; the first Indians began training as commissioned officers for the army; and India was given fiscal autonomy, freed from London at last. As additional bonuses, the costs of the India Office were to be borne by the British government, and the Indian army was to be used solely for the defence of India except in dire emergency, and even then only with the consent of the government of India and the payment of all costs by Britain.

Another long overdue advance was the establishment of a Tariff Board in New Delhi, which set about abolishing the excise duty on Indian cotton. But this notable victory for Indian industry came with a nasty sting in its tail: to make up the lost revenue, the tax on salt was reintroduced and then doubled, imposing what Motilal Nehru and others described as a 'cruel burden' on the poorest section of society; the peasants and landless labourers, for whom salt was vital.

Without Gandhi's charismatic presence, Congress had begun to disintegrate amid communal squabbles and factional infighting. Das and Motilal Nehru, released from their own prison sentences in 1922, joined in planning a new strategy which would at least give them something positive to do. They proposed that instead of continuing to boycott the councils, nationalists should seek election and then sabotage them from within by obstructing all business, 'either mending or ending' them, as Das put it succinctly. In Gandhi's absence, these two elder statesmen were the undisputed leaders of Congress: Das became president and Motilal secretary at the annual session in Gaya that December. But they were not strong enough to carry Congress: even in his absence, Gandhi's influence remained all-pervasive. His most faithful disciples, Vallabhbhai Patel, C. Rajagopalachari and Rajendra Prasad, led the opposition to the proposals, which were rejected by a majority of almost two to one.

Motilal and Das promptly resigned their offices, and founded their own 'Congress-Khilafat Swaraj Party', splitting Congress into 'pro-changers' and 'no-changers', those who remained true to Gandhi's programme of boycott and non-co-operation. The split threatened to destroy Congress, but eventually a compromise was reached, and a special session in September gave its consent to Congressmen taking part in the November elections. Motilal and Das were among those elected to the Central Legislative Assembly, taking their seats on 31 January 1924 along with another 40 Swarajists, 23 independents and Liberals, and 36 official nominees. They did well in provincial and municipal elections, too, taking effective control of Bengal, the Bombay presidency, and the United Provinces, but losing out in Madras and the Punjab, where communal elements held sway.

In the cities the Swarajists were even more successful: Das became mayor of Calcutta, with Subhas Bose as his chief executive officer, Vallabhbhai Patel became mayor of Ahmedabad, Vithalbhai Patel president of Bombay Corporation, Rajendra Prasad of Patna and Jawaharlal Nehru of Allahabad. It was the younger Nehru's first experience of public office and he acquitted himself well for a year until the pressures of trying to combine local and national politics became too much. He resigned to devote himself to his duties as general secretary of the All-India Congress Committee, the position he had held since mid-1923.

In the Central Assembly, Jinnah, who had been elected unopposed to the Bombay Muslim seat from which he had resigned in 1919, bounced back to something like his old political self. He started by calling together the other 23 independent members immediately after the viceroy's opening address, and somehow managed to persuade them to bury their many differences and work together on his programme of basic reforms. He then went to Motilal and Das, and persuaded them to bring their 42 Swarajists into a solid Nationalist bloc which would always outvote the 36 official members. Similar deals soon followed in provincial and municipal councils.

The new Nationalist coalition within the Assembly was quick to show its teeth, forcing through a resolution calling for a round-table conference, 'with due regard to the protection of the rights and interests of important minorities', to 'take steps to have the Government of India Act revised with a view to establish fully responsible government in India'.[1] Reading, dismayed by Jinnah's political coup in welding together so many disparate interests and individuals, had no option but to appoint a Reforms Inquiry Committee – which, though chaired by the Home member, Sir Alexander Muddiman, was always referred to as 'the Jinnah Committee'.

Jinnah was riding high again. He had no desire to rejoin a Congress dominated by Gandhi, but his successes in the Assembly enabled him to recapture the Muslim League. Muhammad Ali had been elected president of the League the previous December, but it was Jinnah who presided over a special session in May, calling for a renewal of Hindu-Muslim unity, which he described as 'the one essential requisite condition to achieve *swaraj*.[2] Demanding a return to the constitutional path to self-government, he denounced as failures both non-co-operation and the Khilafat movement, which had been dealt its *coup de grâce* two months earlier not by the British but by a Muslim hero, the new Turkish president, Mustafa Kemal, when he abolished the Caliphate.

In a burst of renewed energy, the League backed Jinnah's resolution to work for *swaraj*, which it defined as a federal union of virtually autonomous provinces, with central government responsible for only the minimum number of areas 'of general and common concern'. Separate electorates would remain, since joint electorates were 'a source of discord and disunion'. Religious freedom was to be guaranteed for all. To prepare for the great day, several committees were appointed – one to draft a new constitution for India, one to liaise with the Central Khilafat Committee, another to stimulate 'internal solidarity among the Mussulmans of India'. They all seemed to be chaired by Jinnah. And to cap his triumph, he was appointed 'permanent' president of the League for the next three years.

Unfortunately, at about the same time as Jinnah was firing up the Muslim League for a constitutional campaign, Gandhi was reasserting his own authority on Congress. He started with a public statement condemning council entry. Motilal tried to argue with him, but Gandhi could be more stubborn than virtually anybody in India, apart from Jinnah. Motilal did eventually manage to persuade Gandhi that since so many Swarajists had been elected to so many councils and so many offices, it would be invidious and even dishonourable to demand their withdrawal. For many of them, it might also have proved an unbearable strain on their loyalty to Congress, a pragmatic point which could not have escaped Gandhi. In return, however, Motilal was forced to agree that his Swarajists would start a blanket obstruction of government legislation.

As Gandhi must have anticipated, the new tactics sounded the death knell for the Nationalist coalition, since Jinnah and his independent colleagues insisted on judging every issue on its merits. The coalition began to crumble, and so did the Swaraj Party, helped on its way by Reading's refusal to allow any debate on the recommendations of the Jinnah Committee when it reported towards the end of the year – a pertinent reminder to the elected members, both at the centre and in the provinces, of how illusory their power actually was. Not only could the viceroy and the governors veto legislation or resolutions passed in council, they could also 'certify' legislation that had been rejected, including budgetary grants.

Clearly feeling that he needed to do still more to bring Congress to heel, Gandhi decided that he would be president that year, for the one and only time. In a fascinating example of his political wiles, he wrote to Motilal, who was now his only rival for the leadership since Das had fallen mortally ill, offering to use his influence to have Motilal elected president. As though it were an afterthought, he casually mentioned that several prominent Congressmen were 'insistent' that he himself should become president, though he was, of course, most reluctant. 'The only condition that would make me reconsider my position,' he wrote, 'would be your desire that I should accept.' Motilal took the heavy hint, and Gandhi was elected.

When Jinnah heard that Gandhi was to be president, he immediately moved the Muslim League's annual session away from Belgaum, where Congress was due to meet in December, ending the practice of simultaneous sessions which he personally had started in the heady days of 1915. The clash of personalities and ideologies between two leaders who sought the same end but by different means was achieving what the British had failed to do; driving a wedge between their two organizations that could only widen as the years passed.

The final collapse of both the Khilafat campaign and non-co-operation left the young men of India frustrated and angry. One of the most ominous developments was the revival of revolutionary terrorism, much of it inspired and encouraged by Soviet Russia, which even set up a training camp for Indians in Tashkent. In Cawnpore, one group formed the Hindustan Republican Army (or Association), based on the IRA, dedicated to overthrowing colonial rule through armed revolution. It lasted barely a year. Its first 'action' was a botched train robbery, after which the authorities struck fast and hard, hanging or deporting all the members except one, who escaped to join other would-be revolutionaries from northern India five years later in a re-formed, renamed but equally ineffective Hindustan Socialist Republican Army.

Bengal naturally had its own brand of terrorism, which turned out to be no more efficient. Its downfall came when a young terrorist called Gopinath Saha set out to assassinate the hated police commissioner of Calcutta, Charles Tegart, but bungled it by shooting and killing the wrong man, a British businessman called Ernest Day. Not surprisingly, the police reacted strongly, rounding up all the usual suspects under a newly promulgated ordinance. Among those caught in the net were many Congressmen, including the authorities' pet hate, Subhas Chandra Bose.

Bose made no secret of the fact that he rejected Gandhian non-violence: 'Give me blood,' he once said, 'and I promise you freedom.' In fact, he was always immune to Gandhi's charm, never calling him 'Bapu' (Father) like Jawaharlal Nehru and most Congressmen, but choosing instead the more formal, 'Ghandiji' or 'Mahatmaji'. There was always a certain coolness between the two men, which Gandhi must have found unsettling – he was used to winning people over through his warmth and humanity, ensnaring political associates in a web of affection as well as respect. Most people, however irritated they might become with him, were loath to wound. But Bose had no such scruples.

There was a certain snobbery in Bose's attitude – in Bengal his Kayastha sub-caste was considered second only to the Brahmans, and he looked down on Gandhi both because he was a Bania, a trading caste, and because, through his life style and his actions, he had deliberately tried to turn himself into a poor peasant. As an intellectual, Bose was also scornful of Gandhi's political tactics. Gandhi, he wrote later, 'did not have a clear idea of the successive stages of the campaign [to bring about Indian independence]'. Nehru often made the same criticism – but stayed loyal because, as the late Frank Moraes put it, 'he was susceptible to Gandhi's blandishment and blarney'.[3]

The British accused Bose of conspiring to plan terrorist attacks. It was alleged that he and another man had planned to throw a bomb in the Calcutta council chamber — a most unlikely charge, considering Bose's position as the council's chief executive — that he had smuggled arms, and, most seriously, had been involved in planning the assassination attempt on Tegart. Bose's involvement was never proven, and he indignantly denied all charges. Nevertheless, he was arrested under Regulation III of 1818 and carted off to Alipore Central Gaol, 'a vast collection of barracks between the Calcutta Zoo and the race course'.[4] After about seven weeks he was shipped to the prison in Mandalay where Tilak had languished for so many years.

In some ways, Bose was at his belligerent best in gaol. Energetic and bloody-minded, he wrote endless letters to the chief secretary of the Burmese government pointing out that the law under which he had been detained did not permit any 'hardship savouring of punishment', and quite clearly he was suffering hardship. He complained, too, that his treatment ought to have accorded 'with my rank and station in life'. When the prison authorities refused to allow him to receive money from well-wishers to enable him and some of his fellow inmates to celebrate the festival of Saraswati in style, he wrote attacking their 'arbitrary infringement of religious rights'. Saraswati, incidentally, is the Hindu goddess of poetry and music, the wife of Brahma, and notoriously disputatious.

On 18 February 1926, Bose organized a mass hunger strike in Mandalay prison; four days later the inmates of Insein prison joined in. The authorities began to force-feed prisoners, with all the dangers that implied. Both the government of India and Congress were alive to the risks — indeed, the Congress leaders were so concerned that they sent Shaukat Ali to persuade Bose to end the strike. By then, the Burmese government wanted rid of Bose at any cost, particularly when he was diagnosed as suffering from TB. The problem was, what to do with him? The Bengal government wanted him kept in gaol, any gaol, anywhere — except Bengal. New Delhi, on the other hand, worrying lest his TB prove fatal, suggested he be offered a passport to go to Switzerland for a cure. In the end, Bose got exactly what he had always wanted: he returned home to Calcutta, two and half years after he had been arrested, with all charges withdrawn.

While Bose had been in prison his political mentor, C.R. Das, had died in June 1925. Combined with his own extraordinary wilfulness, the loss of Das's support and guidance at a particularly critical moment in his career meant that sooner or later Bose was bound to end up in the political wilderness. At the time of Bose's release, however, it was Congress that was in the wilderness. The accord with the Muslim League was totally defunct. Das was dead, and several other leading figures, most notably Lajpat Rai and Malaviya, had jumped ship to follow their communal consciences through the Hindu Mahasabha. The Ali brothers and many of their Muslim supporters had also departed to stir the bubbling cauldron of communal strife, and what remained of the Khilafat movement had finally expired amid accusations of fraud and embezzlement. Motilal Nehru had had enough of the struggle to keep his Swaraj party alive, and pulled it out of the legislatures. And Gandhi had withdrawn from active politics, to concentrate on spiritual matters and the social problems of India, especially what he described as 'the curse of untouchability'. While untouchability remained, he declared, there could be no true *swaraj*. For those supporters who were bewildered by his withdrawal, he had a typically Gandhian response: the six years' imprisonment to which he had been sentenced should have continued until February 1928, and although the British had released him, he felt that he was morally bound to abstain from active politics until that date.

The nationalist movement was disheartened and in total disarray. The only thing that could revive it was a new issue that would reunite the various factions in fighting for a single cause. With typical ineptitude, the British government provided just such an issue.

The 1920s had brought as much political turmoil to Britain as they had to India. While trying to fight off its hangover after the Great War, the nation was wracked by the twin migraines of Ireland and labour relations, which forced India's problems into the background. In Ireland, a much smaller group of nationalists than existed in India had succeeded in driving out the British by resorting to the violence that Gandhi and his followers abjured. The result for Ireland, however, had been civil war and partition on religious lines, setting an ominous precedent for India. Meanwhile, in Britain waves of strikes in the docks, transport and above all the coal mines, heralded the beginning of the workers' long battle for social justice.

The split in Congress had been mirrored by a near fatal split in the British Liberal Party, with Asquith and Lloyd George heading opposing factions. When the ruling Conservative-Liberal coalition collapsed in October 1922, the ensuing general election brought the Tories back to power under Andrew Bonar Law, with Labour as the main opposition party. Five months later, suffering from an incurable cancer of the throat, Bonar Law resigned, without naming his successor. This was the moment for which Lord Curzon had been preparing all his life, the culmination of all his dreams and ambitions. Everyone expected the king to send for him. India held its breath – his appointment as prime minister would have a profound effect there. But the Tory Party cabal moved in an even more mysterious way than usual and it was the phlegmatic, pipe-smoking Midlands ironmaster, Stanley Baldwin, who went to Buckingham Palace and on to 10 Downing Street. Curzon remained as foreign secretary, never to scale his ultimate peak. India breathed again.

The political upheavals in Britain continued. Baldwin made the mistake of calling a snap general election in November 1923, which produced a stalemate and a minority Labour government, under Ramsay MacDonald. For India, this should have been good news: for the first time ever, Britain had a government that was actively opposed to imperialism, at least in theory. But MacDonald's government lasted only nine months, before Baldwin and the Tories were back in power, this time with a huge majority.

After his election victory in 1925, Baldwin was faced with paying off his political debts. But as always there were only so many Cabinet posts available, and a number of political heavyweights competing for them; men like Curzon, Austen Chamberlain, twice chancellor of the exchequer and a former party leader, Winston Churchill, who had deserted the Liberals and crossed the floor for the second time as a 'Constitutionalist', and the great lawyer F.E. Smith, now Lord Birkenhead and a former lord chancellor. Two of them, Curzon and Chamberlain, had strong connections with India – Chamberlain had been Montagu's predecessor as secretary of state. Neither of them was offered the India Office. Curzon accepted the post of lord president of the council, which he was to hold for only a few weeks before he died at the age of 66. Austen Chamberlain became foreign secretary; his younger half-brother, Neville, became health secretary at the same time, his first important office.

Churchill's only personal experience of India had been as a subaltern in the 4th Hussars in 1896, though his father, Lord Randolph, had been secretary of state in 1885–6. Nevertheless, for a brief time, he was considered for the post. Tom Jones, the assistant Cabinet secretary, was one of those who was horrified at the prospect. 'For heaven's sake do not do that,' he wrote to Baldwin. 'I have seen him lose his head at critical moments during the Irish business.' Instead, Jones proposed Birkenhead: 'He has better judgment than Winston and it will keep him pretty well occupied.' This was an important consideration, since Birkenhead had the reputation of being a great political intriguer. Birkenhead was delighted at the prospect of overseeing the government of some 320 million people. Churchill was equally delighted to be offered one of the great offices of state as chancellor of the exchequer, although he had only just rejoined the party and was accurately described by Leo Amery, then colonial and dominions secretary, as 'a brilliant talker and military strategist who is frankly incapable of understanding finance or the meaning of Empire development'.[5]

One of Birkenhead's first tasks was to appoint a new viceroy to replace Reading, whose term of office ended in 1926. He chose a 45-year-old high Tory MP, Edward Wood, who carried the courtesy title of Lord Irwin as the eldest son of the second Viscount Halifax, a wealthy Yorkshire landowner. He was also the grandson of Sir Charles Wood, an official whose Indian Education Despatch of July 1854 had led to the establishment of the three presidency universities and the funding of many vernacular mission schools. Cadaverously tall, and born with a withered and handless left arm, Irwin still managed to ride to hounds as MFH, and to shoot grouse and pheasant on the vast family estates. However, he was also a fellow of All Souls, a devout Anglo-Catholic, and the biographer of John Keble, one of the founders of the early nineteenth-century Oxford Movement. In 1938, as Lord Halifax, he was to earn opprobrium in the history books as the foreign secretary who accompanied Neville Chamberlain to Munich to appease Hitler. But between 1926 and 1931, his conciliatory instincts were used to better effect in India.

Although he was a true-blue Tory, Irwin was by no means a reactionary as far as India was concerned, publicly declaring that constitutional progress would lead naturally to dominion status. In private, however, he added that he thought it 'wholly improbable whether now or in the near future'.[6] His doubts must have increased very soon after he arrived in India, when the worst communal rioting yet seen erupted in Calcutta. The city was brought to its knees for six weeks during April and May, with more than 100 people killed and well over 1,000 seriously injured before the madness finally burned itself out.

Under section 84-A of the Government of India Act of 1919, a statutory commission was to be appointed within 10 years to examine how the Montagu-Chelmsford reforms were working in practice. At various times Indian leaders had tried to speed up the process, but without success. In Britain, however, still reeling from the effects of the 1926 general strike, the political situation was looking increasingly unsettled. There was a strong possibility that by 1929, when the commission was due, there would be a Labour government in power. Ramsay MacDonald was already promising India immediate dominion status, a prospect that Birkenhead, who believed it 'frankly inconceivable that India will ever be fit for Dominion self-government'[7] found quite appalling. He wrote to Irwin about his fears, saying that the Conservatives must not 'run the slightest risk that the nomination of the Commission should be in the hands of our successors'.[8] There was only one sure way of forestalling this disaster, and Birkenhead took it – he appointed the commission himself, bringing forward the date on which it was to start work to November 1927, a full two years before it was required by the legislation.

Birkenhead's first choice as chairman of the commission was the Lord Chief Justice, Lord Hewart, but Hewart's judicial duties prevented him from accepting. Looking around for someone of sufficient weight who had no major commitments, his choice fell on Sir John Simon, a personal friend and one of the most successful lawyers of the day, who had been solicitor-general, attorney-general and in 1915–16 home secretary. Simon was ostensibly a Liberal, which was calculated to impress Indian politicians who might not have been aware that his views had moved steadily further to the right – he had recently denounced the general strike as illegal, for instance. He also had some experience of India, having spent some months there the year before on a major legal case. What was perhaps more to the point for Birkenhead was that he had returned saying that Indian reform should proceed 'very slowly indeed'.[9]

'The work of chairman', Birkenhead wrote to Irwin, 'requires a man of great subtlety, acuteness, quickness, industry and tact. Simon possesses all these qualities to a remarkable degree.' He went on to add that he had 'every reason . . . to believe that his views upon the fundamentals of the matter are very largely in agreement with my own'.[10] What he did not add, though it might have counted as an extra qualification, was that Simon was famous for his use of 'judicious indecision'. Birkenhead offered him the job during a round of golf at the Tadmarten course near Banbury. Simon was flattered and agreed at once – 'I am very much gratified that you should think of me in [this] connection,' he wrote in his letter of acceptance.[11]

Birkenhead chose to make it a Parliamentary commission, because this meant its members had to be either peers or MPs: there would be no Indian representation whatsoever. As it happened, there were actually two Indians sitting in the British Parliament at that time, Lord Sinha and Shapurji Saklatvala, but neither seems to have been considered – an odd decision since Sinha in particular had a most distinguished record. As Sir Satyendra P. Sinha, he had been the first Indian ever appointed to the viceroy's executive council as law member back in 1909 over the objections of King Edward VII; he had been president of Congress in 1915; he had been Parliamentary under-secretary for India under Montagu in 1919; and in 1920, elevated to the British peerage, he had become the first Indian provincial governor, of Bihar and Orissa. Nevertheless, he was not considered suitable for membership of the commission.

Although he had urged the inclusion of at least two Indian members, Irwin now agreed that excluding them would prevent the commission's becoming too large and unwieldy – if there were Hindus on it there would also have to be Muslims and Sikhs, and the sheer numbers, not to mention the clash of religious views, would complicate and delay any decision. In fact, Birkenhead feared that Indians might combine with Labour MPs in the commission to produce recommendations that would not be acceptable to the Conservative Party.

The Labour Party's position on India was clear. Its annual conference in 1925 had accepted India's right to equal status with the existing white dominions. The following year its left-wing component, the Independent Labour Party, had gone a stage further by coming out in favour of total independence. At first, the party's national executive refused to participate in Birkenhead's commission unless Indians were included. But Ramsay MacDonald persuaded them to change their minds provided a committee set up by the Indian legislature agreed to consult with the commission. Even then, MacDonald had difficulty finding two suitable members. In the end, he settled on Vernon Hartshorn, a former South Wales miner and ex-postmaster-general, and the 44-year-old Major Clement Attlee, MP for Stepney and MacDonald's own PPS. Ironically, Attlee had been educated at Haileybury, the successor to the old East India Company's college and probably the most imperialist of all English public schools.

The other four members of the seven-man committee were Conservatives, carefully chosen to produce a 'sober' report which would do nothing to precipitate dominion status. Lord Burnham was the owner of the *Daily Telegraph*; Lord Strathcona was vice-chairman of the party and a close friend of Baldwin; George Lane Fox was a foxhunting Yorkshire landowner and the brother-in-law of Lord Irwin; and Edward Cadogan was son of the Earl of Cadogan. None of them could boast any great knowledge of India.

Indian reaction to the all-white commission surprised everyone by its sheer ferocity. The country as a whole was outraged. Protest meetings were held in towns and villages all over India. The *Bengalee*, usually a moderate newspaper, wrote that while 'not prepared to accuse Lord Birkenhead of calculated insult to India ... his contempt for Indians and their co-operation ... is intense and real'.[12] The more forthright *Bombay Chronicle* caught the Indian mood in a two-word headline on 9 November: 'Boycott It.' Most shades of Indian opinion were united in condemnation – even the ultra-loyal Sir Tej Bahadur Sapru, leader of the extreme right, to whom the viceroy looked for support, believed the British had insulted Mother India. He also complained about the quality of the commission: in his view only Sir John Simon was a person of consequence; all the others, he considered, were mediocrities.

There were some in India who were happy to work with the commission: the Scheduled Caste Federation, the Indian Christians, the Parsis, and other minorities. The Indian Legislative Assembly resolved to have nothing to do with it, though the Council of State decided to co-operate. But the larger groups and organizations, the National Liberal Federation, the Hindu Mahasabha and Congress, were united in their determination to boycott. Congress called on all its members to co-operate with other political parties to make the work of the commission impossible.

Anger and resentment over the Simon Commission dominated the annual session of Congress at Madras in December 1927. Riding on the tide of discontent, Jawaharlal Nehru managed to get a last-minute resolution passed calling not for dominion status but for complete independence – an important step for Congress. Nehru's motion was late because he had literally just stepped off a ship at Madras as the session began. Jawaharlal had spent over 20 months in Europe, having been forced to take his ailing wife Kamala to Switzerland in March 1926, when, having given birth to a premature son who died after two days, she was diagnosed as suffering from tuberculosis.

During Kamala's treatment, Jawaharlal had taken a small flat in Geneva and installed the nine-year-old Indira in an exclusive girls' school, while he spent his time improving his own political education. Although Switzerland has always been perhaps the most deeply bourgeois country in the world, it has always provided a haven for political exiles – it was only nine years since Lenin and 32 comrades had left Bern in the famous sealed train to Petrograd. There was also a regular traffic in political notables visiting Switzerland: Geneva housed the League of Nations and many of its subsidiary agencies, not least the International Labour Organization. All this gave Jawaharlal, released from the day-to-day concerns of Congress, the opportunity to meet revolutionary thinkers, confirming and hardening his socialist beliefs.

When Kamala's health at last began to improve, Jawaharlal began to travel to other parts of Europe. In Berlin, he met a number of Indian communists, including Virendranath Chattopadhyaya – more conveniently known as Chatto – a Marxist revolutionary who scorned Gandhi's non-violence and mysticism. It was Chatto who persuaded Jawaharlal to go to Brussels, to take part in the Comintern-sponsored International Congress against Colonial Oppression and Imperialism, a subject which was naturally dear to his heart. Congress agreed that he should be its official representative, and sent him £500 to cover his expenses. It was money well spent.

This was Nehru's first appearance on the international stage, but he quickly became one of the stars of the conference. His success was crowned with his appointment as honorary president of the League against Imperialism and for National Independence, the setting up of which was the conference's main object. The other members of the executive committee were Albert Einstein, Romain Rolland, the French author and biographer of Gandhi, the former British Labour leader George Lansbury, and China's Madame Sun Yat-sen. But the main benefit Nehru derived from his 10 exhausting days in Brussels was meeting like-minded nationalists from various parts of the world, including Chinese, Arabs, Persians, Indonesians, Koreans, Mexicans, South Americans, and both black and white Americans and South Africans. There were also sympathizers from various European nations, including several leading members of the British Labour Party and Harry Pollitt, leader of the British Communist Party – Nehru, however, was always sceptical of British socialists. He was more impressed by a young Vietnamese called Nguyen Ai Quoc, whom he was to welcome to Delhi in 1954 under his adopted name of Ho Chi Minh ('he who enlightens').

After Brussels, Motilal arrived from India to join his family for a holiday, his first in Europe for 19 years. He was concerned, like many of his fellow

Congressmen, that Jawaharlal was becoming too much under the influence of the Comintern. As always, Jawaharlal was able to convince his father that he had nothing to worry about. He then persuaded him to join him in a trip to Moscow, where they had both been invited to join the celebrations for the tenth anniversary of the Russian revolution. They were just too late for the main event on 7 November, but there were plenty of banquets and receptions to be enjoyed, and they were personally received by the Soviet president, Kalinin. Motilal may have had reservations about the Soviet system, but his son was deeply impressed by the achievements of the past 10 years in Russia – or at least what he could see of them in a hectic three-day visit. He returned home full of enthusiasm and hope. What was more, he was now able to present himself to Congress as a young man of international stature and outlook.

The Muslim League was split in two over the issue of boycotting the Simon Commission. A minority, mostly from the Punjab and led by Sir Muhammad Shafi, former law member of the viceroy's council, broke away and held a separate annual session in Lahore, where they voted to welcome the commission and to co-operate fully with it. But the majority followed Jinnah to Calcutta, where the main resolution declared the commission and its procedures unacceptable, concluding: 'It [the Jinnah League] therefore resolves that the Musulmans throughout the country should have nothing to do with the Commission at any stage or in any form.'[13]

The resolution was carried unanimously, and Jinnah was re-elected permanent president for another three years. In his triumphal address, he declared 'a constitutional war' on Britain. 'Jallianwala Bagh was a physical butchery,' he thundered, 'the Simon Commission is a butchery of our souls. By appointing an exclusively white commission, Lord Birkenhead has declared our unfitness for self-government.' Among the honoured guests in Calcutta were Sarojini Naidu, Annie Besant and even Mohan Malaviya, the Hindu Mahasabha leader. For a moment, it seemed that the spirit of the Lucknow Pact was returning. 'I welcome the hand of fellowship extended to us by the Hindu leaders from the platform of the Congress and the Hindu Mahasabha,' Jinnah continued. 'This is indeed a bright day; and for achieving this unity, thanks are due to Lord Birkenhead.'[14]

From Calcutta, Jinnah hurried back to Bombay, to chair the committee organizing the boycott of the Simon Commission. His young legal assistant, M.C. Chagla, was its secretary. He recalled later that 'Jinnah was firm as a rock as far as the question of the boycott of the commission was concerned. Proposals were made that the boycott should be only political and not social. Jinnah would not agree and did not give an inch. He said a boycott was a boycott and it must be total and complete. We had a mass meeting at the Chowpatty sands.'[15]

Birkenhead, who always seemed to prefer confrontation to agreement, was unmoved by the furore. Contemptuously dismissing the threat of boycott, he challenged Indian politicians to write their own constitution. 'Let the malcontents ... produce their own proposals,' he wrote to Irwin, adding that Indians were 'quite incapable of surmounting the constitutional and constructive difficulties involved'. And even if they were able to overcome these difficulties, he believed that any opposition to the British government simply could not hold, since 'a unity which can only survive in an atmosphere of generalisation would disappear at once'.[16]

Two weeks later, Birkenhead wrote to Irwin again, offering him what he clearly thought was a masterly game plan:

> I should advise Simon to see at all stages important people who are *not* boycotting the Commission, particularly Moslems and the depressed classes. I should widely advertise all his interviews with representative Moslems. The whole policy is now obvious. It is to terrify the immense Hindu population by the apprehension that the Commission having been got hold of by the Moslems, may present a report altogether destructive of the Hindu position, thereby securing a solid Moslem support and leaving Jinnah high and dry.[17]

The policy of divide and rule had never been put more baldly. However, although it may have worked before, this time it was doomed to failure.

'A Year's Grace and a Polite Ultimatum'

The Simon Commission landed at Bombay to begin the first of its two planned visits to India on 3 February 1928. Despite torrential rain, demonstrators had turned out in their thousands. A few from the minority groups were there carrying leaves and flowers to welcome the British politicians, but they were vastly outnumbered by protesters carrying black flags and banners inscribed 'SIMON GO BACK'. The city was closed down in a *hartal*: shops and offices were shuttered, and the streets were deserted apart from the demonstrators. Gandhi wrote to 'tender my congratulations to the organizers for the very great success they achieved ... It did my soul good to see Liberals, Independents and Congressmen ranged together on the same platform'.[1] Was it deliberate that he failed to mention the Jinnah League?

All the other major cities and towns staged *hartals* at the same time, with black flag processions and rallies. In Madras, demonstrators clashed violently with police, who opened fire, killing one of them. The commission moved on to Delhi, where its reception was as hostile as that in Bombay; Calcutta and Madras were only slightly less so. Nowhere could they escape the protestors – their train from Bombay to Poona was escorted by young Maharashtrans waving black flags at them from a lorry on the road which ran alongside the track for most of the 70 miles between Poona and Lonavala. In Lucknow, the local Muslim League leader, Choudry Khaliquzzaman, conceived the brilliant notion of painting 'Go Back Simon' on kites and balloons and floating them over the official reception organized by the taluqdars in the Kaiserbagh gardens.[2] Only in country districts were the commissioners reasonably well received.

Simon put a brave face on what was clearly becoming a public relations disaster. One of the members of the commission who was close to him, George Lane-Fox, noted that he was on the verge of despair. The Labour members, Clement Attlee and Vernon Hartshorn, managed to make secret contact with at least one senior Congressman – unnamed but said to be the vice-chairman – but he proved to be 'quite impossible and not co-operative'.[3] Yet when they met some of the Indian members of the viceroy's council of state, men who were eager to co-operate with them, Attlee found them a singularly unimpressive bunch.

When he first arrived in India, Attlee had broadly supported Irwin's plans for a future constitution that would increase democracy. But he was soon having second thoughts – like many before him, he found India too big and complex for neat, Westminster-inspired solutions. 'The more he studied the situation, the more puzzled he became,' wrote the Indian journalist Durga Das, press officer to the commission, who became friendly with Attlee as he accompanied the members round the country.[4] At that point, Attlee felt that the main stumbling block to a political solution was not the communal question but the princely states. How could hundreds of princedoms, ranging in size from mere dots on the map to the size of France, be fitted into a parliamentary democracy? How could the princes, most of them medieval autocrats, be brought within a parliamentary institution? At this stage, Attlee seems to have favoured some form of federation for India, but the terms under which the commission was set up did not permit it to propose any solution but the Westminster model. He told Das that the whole inquiry 'had raised more question marks than it had answers to'.[5]

While the Simon Commission was struggling to come to terms with India's complexity, the Indians themselves were taking up Birkenhead's challenge to write their own constitution. An All-Parties Conference chaired by Dr Ansari, that year's Congress president, met in Delhi on 12 February. Almost all the political leaders of India were there – the two Nehrus, Lala Lajpat Rai, Malaviya, Jayakar, Jinnah – but Gandhi, who set little store by constitutional planning, pointedly stayed away. The conference was not a success. After 10 days of bickering and wrangling it broke up without agreeing on anything, not even the basic aim of the proposed new constitution. Delegates were split between those who favoured dominion status and those, like Jawaharlal Nehru, who demanded nothing less than complete independence. They eventually settled for a fudge, calling simply 'for the establishment of full responsible government', but after that it was downhill all the way. Jawaharlal gave up after a week. 'The strain was too much for me and I fled to avoid riot and insurrection!' he told Gandhi.[6]

Inevitably, the biggest bone of contention was the question of safeguards for the Muslim minority. The Hindu Mahasabha wanted to do away with separate electorates entirely, without substituting any other form of protection. Jinnah himself had drawn up proposals the year before for removing separate electorates, which he had never regarded as anything more than a temporary but necessary measure. He had actually managed to persuade most leading Muslims to accept in their place guaranteed numbers of seats for minorities, which would include

Hindus in Muslim majority provinces. He also called for not less than one third of the seats on the Central Legislature to be reserved for Muslims, to be elected by a general vote, even though this meant they could be Congressmen or Khilafatists and not just members of the Muslim League. Congress had endorsed these proposals in 1927, but now backed off, under pressure from the Mahasabha, and the opportunity for an acceptable compromise was lost.

Jinnah had to stay in Delhi after the conference broke up, to attend the budget sessions of the Assembly. Depressed by the chaos into which Indian politics was again descending, he approached the viceroy with two suggestions for ending the impasse over the Simon Commission, promising to 'take the brunt of the attack in India' if either was accepted. Irwin liked his ideas, and reported them to Birkenhead. 'One was by turning Simon's Commission into a Mixed Commission,' he wrote, 'and the other was by establishing a twin Indian Commission with parallel authority.[7] If Jinnah had been depressed by the attitudes of his Indian colleagues, however, he must have been even more so over Birkenhead's response. It was a flat refusal even to consider the suggestions: 'It does not do', Birkenhead pontificated to Irwin, 'to take these people too seriously; indeed I find it increasingly difficult to take any Indian politicians very seriously.'[8]

Rejected by all sides, Jinnah must have felt that he had reached another nadir in his life. But there was worse to come. He went wearily back to Bombay, only to find that Ruttie had moved out of their home and taken up residence in the Taj Mahal Hotel. The great romantic love story, it seemed, was over. In April, Ruttie left for Paris, with her mother. A month later, Jinnah sailed for London. For once, he had no official business, but he needed to get away from India, and he enjoyed meeting old friends in England, including Lord Reading and Ramsay MacDonald, whom he had known since 1913 when they had both been members of the Royal Public Services Commission. While he was visiting Ireland as a guest of another eminent friend, the Labour politician Fenner Brockway, he received word that Ruttie was dying. He dashed to Paris, made new hospital arrangements for her, and she survived. But there was to be no reconciliation. They returned separately to India.

Shortly after Jinnah had left India for London, some of those who had attended the All-Parties Conference in February met again in Bombay, under the chairmanship of Ansari. On 18 May, they appointed a sub-committee to draft their own constitution, one that would be acceptable to all shades of Indian opinion – a tall order by any standard. Motilal Nehru was chairman, and Jawaharlal secretary. Their brief was to produce a draft report by 1 July, but by the end of June they were still deadlocked over the minorities question. As Ansari wrote to Gandhi: 'The Sikhs would have no reservation of seats at all. The Mahasabha people would allow reservations for the minorities, but not the majorities. The Congress and the Muslim proposal was for a reservation of seats both for the majorities and the minorities.' The committee's problems were further complicated by the fact that the young Turks of the Congress Party, Jawaharlal Nehru and Subhas Bose, refused to accept anything less than total independence as the basis for the draft constitution.

In fact, dominion status was total independence in all but name. Under pressure from South Africa, the Irish Free State and finally Canada, all of whom were determined to establish the fact of their individual sovereignty beyond doubt, the 1926 Imperial Conference had officially defined the constitutional relationship between Britain and its dominions:

> They are autonomous communities within the British Empire, equal in status, in no way subordinate one to another in any aspect of their domestic or external affairs, though united by a common allegiance to the Crown, and freely associated as members of the British Commonwealth of Nations.

The definition included Britain itself. And the phrase 'freely associated' implied that any member state was free to dissociate as and when it chose. The older Congress leaders, most notably Motilal and Gandhi, the supreme pragmatist, were prepared to accept the reality under whatever label. But the younger men feared that their integrity would be compromised by the semantics of colonialism, and refused to accept it.

Despite the tensions between the two camps, the committee pressed on with preparing what was to be known as the Nehru Report – a fitting title, since it was drafted by Motilal personally, with help from Jawaharlal though he still rejected its basic premise. It was not a fully fledged constitution but a blueprint from which professional parliamentary draftsmen could create a practical political document. Its essence was that India should become a federation, with a bi-cameral central parliament which would be sovereign. Following the pattern already established by Congress, provincial boundaries were to be redrawn along linguistic lines. As in Canada and Australia, there would be a governor-general representing the Crown, but he would be no more than a figurehead. Among other things, the draft contained a declaration of rights, and provided for universal adult franchise, equal rights for women, an independent judiciary, freedom to form labour unions, and dissociation of the state from religion in any form.

Apart from the question of dominion status, none of these provisions was particularly contentious. But when it came to the question of minorities, every word was loaded with trouble. The report rejected not only the idea of separate electorates, but also of weightage for minorities. Seats would be reserved for Muslims at the centre and in those provinces where they were in a minority, but for no other group except the non-Muslims in the North-West Frontier Province.

'A minority must remain a minority,' the report stated, 'whether any seats are reserved for it or not.' The only significant concession to Muslim interests was a proposal to create two new Muslim majority provinces by giving the NWFP full provincial status and separating Sind from Bombay. But this was matched by the creation of a new Hindu province in the south.

Motilal believed in secular, democratic constitutional government, seeing the Muslim problem as a cultural and religious matter: 'If the fullest religious liberty is given, and cultural autonomy provided for, the communal problem is in effect solved, although people may not realize it.' Once alien authority and intervention were withdrawn from India, he wrote, people would start thinking in terms of the larger economic and political problems. In such a climate, political parties based mainly on economic grounds were a natural outcome.[9]

The draft report was approved by most members of Motilal's committee on 21 July – the Muslim Shuaib Qureshi disagreed, but his views were summarily overruled.[10] Sir Tej Bahadur Sapru suggested six or seven small verbal changes, then declared it to be 'A1'. But when the All-Parties Conference reconvened in Lucknow on 10 August, there were so many conflicting views that it proved impossible to reach a decision. Significantly, however, with Jinnah still absent in London, his young assistant, M.C. Chagla, accepted the report on behalf of his faction of the Muslim League. Jinnah was furious when he returned, but there was little he could do as he found himself outvoted and increasingly isolated. He could only watch helplessly as his League quarrelled, fragmented and eventually disintegrated over the issue.

The Simon Commission returned to India in October 1928 for a second visit that was to last six and a half months and take it to every province, including Burma. Overwhelmed by the sheer size of India and the complexity of what he described as 'an amazing patchwork of races and creeds', Simon confessed to Irwin that he was 'feeling appalled at what is in front of us'.[11] Birkenhead had concluded that Simon was no nearer a constitutional solution to the India problem than when he had begun. By then, however, Birkenhead was losing interest, beset by his own personal problems: he was almost bankrupt and his drinking had become an embarrassment to everyone. Neville Chamberlain confided to his diary that 'F.E. never goes to [the India Office] and his officials are "fed up" with him.'[12] In October, despite a recent declaration that he felt it his 'duty to remain at the India Office for the next 18 months', he resigned. Lord Peel was wheeled out yet again as a stop-gap replacement.

In India, the commission continued to take evidence, this time with the assistance of a seven-man Indian Provincial Committee and a nine-man Central Committee. The Congress-led boycott, however, remained in force, and the ubiquitous 'Simon Go Back' demonstrations were even bigger than before. In

Lahore on 30 October, Lala Lajpat Rai, Malaviya and local Sikh and Muslim leaders headed a march of several thousand protesters carrying placards and black flags towards the railway station where the commission's special train was due to arrive. They were stopped some 200 yards from the station by barbed wire and wooden barricades. The police, led by the young Superintendent Scott, began wading into the crowd, beating the leaders with metal-tipped lathis. Many collapsed, among them Dr Satyapal, one of the heroes of Amritsar in 1919. Scott, wielding his own heavy knobbed stick, struck Lajpat Rai twice on the chest. A constable joined in with his lathi. The aged Lion of the Punjab was more shocked than physically injured, but he had long suffered from heart disease: when he collapsed and died 18 days later, few Indians believed the beating was not to blame.

Lajpat Rai's death provoked a wave of anger throughout India. The revolutionary terrorists of the Hindustan Socialist Republican Army avenged his death by assassinating a police officer called Saunders in Lahore, proclaiming in a poster: 'We regret to have had to kill a person but he was part and parcel of that inhuman and unjust order which has to be destroyed.'[13]

India declared a day of mourning for the Lala on 29 November, which happened to be when the commission was due in Lucknow, capital of the United Provinces, the Nehrus' home territory. For some days, Jawaharlal had been preparing Congress supporters in the city for a demonstration on a truly grand scale, with full dress rehearsals on 26 and 28 November which provoked police lathi charges. On 29 November, Jawaharlal was charged and beaten by mounted police while on his way to a mass meeting. The situation was defused, and the police escorted him to the meeting in safety. But the next day they charged the main demonstration with increased savagery, and Jawaharlal and his nearest supporters, including the future chief minister of the province, Govind Ballabh Pant, were only saved from serious injury by university students who shielded them with their own bodies.

It was a painful experience for Nehru, though he tried to play it down – 'Injuries severe but not serious. Hope survive the British Empire,' he cabled anxious friends in London. But it immediately increased his stature as a hero throughout India. Gandhi sent his love, and added portentously: 'It was all done bravely. You have braver things to do. May God spare you for many a long year to come and make you His chosen instrument for freeing India from the yoke.'[14] Whatever God might decide, Gandhi had already decided to make Jawaharlal his chosen instrument. On his advice, the younger Nehru had, like Gandhi himself, spent most of 1928 touring India, promoting both the cause of independence and his own claims to national leadership. He was to continue the campaign throughout 1929.

Motilal was elected president of Congress for the second time in Calcutta in 1928, a fitting tribute to his many years of service. But his election marked the end of an era: he was to be the last of the old guard. From then on, the new generation, led by Jawaharlal and Subhas Chandra Bose, would take over completely – the two young lions had already jointly started their own Independence for India League. Only Gandhi, then in his sixtieth year, remained.

The Calcutta Congress was hosted with great show by Subhas Bose. The Nehru Report was naturally the main item on the agenda, but Jawaharlal and Bose threatened to split Congress by refusing to support it. The bone of contention was once again the question of dominion status or complete independence, and both men threatened to resign from Congress over it. Gandhi, emerging from his non-active state, brokered a compromise with a resolution that if the British government failed to accept a constitution based on dominion status within a year, Congress would adopt *purna swaraj*, complete independence, as its aim. To achieve it they would launch a nationwide campaign of non-violent non-co-operation, including a general refusal to pay taxes.

Jawaharlal accepted the decision, but commented derisively that Congress had given the British 'a year's grace and a polite ultimatum'.[15] Polite the ultimatum may have been, but there was no doubt about its seriousness as far as the British were concerned. Gandhi would have preferred to give them more time – two years, perhaps – to make up their minds. He warned Congress that they would concede nothing until they felt the full weight of the proposed sanctions, and in order to make this threat convincing, Congress would first have to put its own house in order and impose some discipline on its followers.

Bitter experience had taught Gandhi how dangerous it was to launch a non-co-operation campaign without long and careful preparation. He spent most of the next 12 months travelling ceaselessly across India, spreading the word, building his own following and trying to educate the people and their local leaders in the basic tenets of non-violence.

The Calcutta Congress renewed Gandhi's appetite for politics, bringing him back into the nationalist mainstream. For Jinnah, it had the opposite effect, confirming his belief that the Hindus were determined to deprive Muslims of the safeguards they had won at Lucknow in 1916. Throughout the autumn, he had resisted all attempts by Motilal, Ansari, Azad and Chagla to discuss the proposals with him, claiming that he could not speak until he had a mandate from his League members. In fact, he was temporizing frantically as he tried in vain to persuade his own followers to reject the Nehru Report. It was not until 27 December that they decided to appoint 23 delegates to accompany him to the All-India National Convention called by Congress, which had already been meeting for five days. He had not been able to persuade them to reject the report outright, but they had agreed to table three basic amendments: to retain separate electorates, to reserve one third of the seats in the Central Legislature for Muslims, and to vest residuary powers in the provinces rather than central government.

When Jinnah tried to put the amendments to the convention, he was contemptuously dismissed by the Hindu Mahasabha's M.R. Jayakar as representing only 'a small minority of Muslims'.[16] Deeply wounded, he made what was to be his farewell speech to Indian nationalism. He still pleaded that 'Hindus and Muslims should march together until our object is attained', and he reminded his audience that: 'We are all sons of this land. We have to live together. We have to work together ...' But he went on: 'If we cannot agree, let us at any rate agree to differ, but let us part as friends.'[17] On the last day of 1928, he left Calcutta by train for Delhi, to attend a meeting of the anti-nationalist All-Parties Muslim Conference presided over by the Aga Khan — its members were those very Muslims, the aristocrats and *maulanas* and imams, whom he had fought and reviled for the past 30 years.

It was a time of great emotional crisis for Jinnah, which must undoubtedly have influenced his thoughts and his actions. The trauma of the breakdown of his marriage was eclipsed by a greater tragedy when his beloved Ruttie finally lost her long battle with tuberculosis. She died in her suite at the Taj Hotel on 20 February 1929, her twenty-ninth birthday. During her last few weeks, Jinnah had visited her every evening when he was in Bombay, but he was in his New Delhi apartment when the end came, and so was denied the comfort of a final farewell. As her coffin was lowered into the grave two days later, 'he broke down suddenly and sobbed and wept like a child for minutes together'.[18] For once, the mask had slipped, the iron self-control faltered. 'That was the only time,' recalled Chagla, who was at the graveside, 'when I found Jinnah betraying some shadow of human weakness'.[19]

Within days of the funeral, Jinnah was back in Delhi, berating Motilal in the assembly over his report, which he insisted was 'not acceptable to the Muslims'. But until he could refute the charge made by Jayakar that he represented only a small minority of Muslims, his words carried little weight. He called a meeting of the League for 30 March, and spent virtually the entire preceding night closeted with the main Muslim dissenters, trying to hammer out a formula which they could all support. By morning, he had drafted a resolution which at least some of them agreed with. But all hopes of resurrecting a united front evaporated next day, when the meeting at the Rowshan Theatre in Old Delhi, and with it the Muslim League itself, broke down into dozens of warring factions.

Jinnah's resolution was never presented to the members, so was never debated or accepted. But it was endorsed by the Jamiat Ulama-i-Hind, the highest Islamic authority in India, and during the next decade and a half its 14 points — deliberately tailored to echo the famous 14 points proposed by US President Wilson in 1917 as a basis for ending the First World War — were to remain the definitive statement of policy for Jinnah and his supporters. They were the rock on which the ship of Hindu-Muslim unity, which Jinnah had spent so many of his early years helping to build, would eventually founder. Because of their later importance, it is worth recording them here:

1. The form of the future Constitution should be federal with the residuary powers vested in the Provinces.

2. A uniform measure of autonomy shall be granted to all Provinces.

3. All legislatures in the country and other elected bodies shall be constituted on the definite principle of adequate and effective representation of minorities in every Province without reducing the majority in any Province to a minority or even equality.

4. In the Central Legislature, Mussulman representation shall be not less than one third.

5. Representation of communal groups shall continue to be by means of separate electorates as at present; provided it shall be open to any community, at any time, to abandon its separate electorate in favour of a joint electorate.

6. Any territorial redistribution that might at any time be necessary shall not in any way affect the Muslim majority in the Punjab, Bengal and the North-West Frontier Province.

7. Full religious liberty, i.e. liberty of belief, worship and observance, propaganda, association and education, shall be guaranteed to all communities.

8. No Bill or resolution or any part thereof shall be passed in any legislature or other elected body if three-fourths of the members of any community in that particular body oppose such a Bill, resolution or part thereof on the ground that it would be injurious to the interests of that community or in the alternative, such other method is devised as may be found feasible and practicable to deal with such cases.

9. Sind should be separated from the Bombay Presidency.

10. Reforms should be introduced in the North-West Frontier Province and Baluchistan on the same footing as in other Provinces.

11. Provision should be made in the Constitution giving Muslims an adequate share, along with other Indians, in all the Services of the State and

in local self-governing bodies having due regard for the requirements of efficiency.

12. The Constitution should embody adequate safeguards for the protection of Muslim culture and for the protection and promotion of Muslim education, language, religion, personal laws and Muslim charitable institutions and for their due share in the grants-in-aid given by the State and by local self-governing bodies.

13. No Cabinet, either Central or Provincial, should be formed without there being a proportion of at least one-third Muslim Ministers.

14. No change shall be made in the Constitution by the Central Legislature except with the concurrence of the States constituting the Indian Federation.[20]

The ill-fated Simon Commission sailed for home on 13 April 1929 from Bombay, a city which had been torn by intermittent Hindu-Muslim communal riots for several weeks, leaving many dead. It was a sobering last impression for the British politicians to take away with them, one which would have a marked effect on their final report, and on Attlee's future attitude to India. They arrived in London just in time for the death throes of the Conservative administration. Parliament was dissolved on 10 May, a general election was held on 31 May, and on 7 June Ramsay MacDonald became prime minister for the second time, at the head of a minority Labour government with the support of Lloyd George and his 60 Liberal MPs. As secretary of state for India, he appointed William Wedgewood Benn.

The change of government was good news for India, since both Labour and the Liberals were publicly committed to constitutional progress. Although a Tory, Irwin remained as viceroy, but would shortly travel back to London for instruction from his new bosses. Jinnah hurried to Simla for a 'long personal talk' with him – if his own people would not listen to him, maybe the British would. He urged the viceroy to press MacDonald and Wedgewood Benn to make a strong statement confirming that they intended to confer dominion status on India, and suggested that they should call a round-table conference in London to draft a constitution. He then wrote to his old friend MacDonald, suggesting the same things and outlining the political situation in India as he saw it. He warned that there was no point in waiting for the Simon Commission's report: 'So far as India is concerned, we have done with it,' he wrote.[21]

Arriving in London, Irwin went straight to the India Office to see the new secretary of state and present Jinnah's suggestions to him. Irwin recalled that Wedgewood Benn 'was disposed to concur', but was worried about upsetting

Simon by appearing to go behind his back. Eventually, with a little help from Lord Reading, Irwin persuaded Simon to agree to both suggestions – as long as it could be made to appear that the ideas were his.[22]

The Nehrus and Gandhi did not visit Irwin before he left for London. Quite apart from their determination not to be seen to co-operate with the Raj, they were far too occupied with other matters. If Motilal's presidency of Congress had marked the end of the old era, what could be a more fitting start to the new than the election of Jawaharlal to succeed him? The provincial Congress committees unanimously wanted Gandhi to take the throne, to steer them through what would undoubtedly be troubled waters ahead. But the shrewd Mahatma knew that he had no need of any official position. He was in effect a permanent 'super president', holding the strings of power. His puppet was to be Jawaharlal, who knew that the position would impose serious constraints on him: 'I have seldom felt quite so annoyed and humiliated,' he complained in his autobiography.[23] But the old dictator was not to be denied, and in any case, as a born politician, Nehru was acutely aware that when power beckoned it had to be seized.

The provincial Congress committees were not pleased. If they could not have Gandhi, their next choice was the reliable right-winger Vallabhbhai Patel, but although Patel was also a protégé, Gandhi rejected him. On the face of it, this could be seen as a desire not to favour a fellow Gujarati. But Subhas Chandra Bose for one saw a deeper reason: 'It was essential,' he wrote, 'that he should win over Jawaharlal if he wanted to beat down the Left Wing opposition and regain his former undisputed supremacy over the Congress.' Once Jawaharlal was elected, Bose noted, 'it was clear that the Congress would be dominated by the Mahatma and the President would be a mere dummy'.[24]

There may have been an element of sour grapes in Bose's attitude – Gandhi undoubtedly wanted to cash in on Jawaharlal's popularity among youth and labour movements, knowing that his election would bind them closer to Congress. Bose, of course, was also active and popular in the same areas, but he was not Motilal's son. Motilal, of course, was the one person whose delight at the choice of Jawaharlal was pure and unalloyed – to him it was an even greater prize than his own election as president.

Jawaharlal may have been a reluctant candidate, but he felt no compunction about hitting the campaign trail throughout India. As a committed socialist, he supported the Indian Trade Union Congress, and despite being, in his own words, 'a newcomer and a non-worker', he was elected its president at the end of 1928.[25] Like so many Indian political organizations, the TUC was soon riven by internal squabbles, and fell apart a few months later – but it added a valuable new constituency to Jawaharlal's power base. 1928 had been a year of unprecedented labour disputes and strikes, and the unrest continued into 1929.

On 20 March, the government clamped down on Communist labour leaders, arresting 31 of them and marching them off to Meerut in the UP to face trial for conspiracy. Both Nehrus became heavily involved in the defence committee, Motilal as its chairman.

On 8 April 1929, Bhagat Singh and Batukeswar Dutt of the Hindustan Socialist Republican Army, the men who had assassinated the police officer in Lahore to avenge the death of Lala Lajpat Rai, threw two bombs from the public gallery on to the floor of the Central Legislative Assembly. No one was seriously hurt: the bombs were intended, as leaflets thrown at the same time declared, 'to make the deaf hear'.[26] But the two men were arrested, as they desired, along with dozens of their supporters. Visiting them in gaol in Lahore, and helping to organize their defence, made further claims on Jawaharlal's time. Then a number of them went on hunger strike to protest against their treatment as political prisoners. One of them, a delicate young man named Jatindranath Das, died after 61 days of fasting, creating a national sensation and more public exposure for Jawaharlal.

Gandhi, meanwhile, was buzzing around the sub-continent like a wasp in a jam factory, preparing the ground for the civil disobedience campaign he knew he would be launching when the 'year's grace and polite ultimatum' expired at the end of December. At times, particularly in the UP, Jawaharlal shared the platform with him, which did the younger man's image no harm at all.

Although the *satyagraha* was not due to begin yet, there was no reason why the policy of non-co-operation and boycott should not be continued and even stepped up. Gandhi persuaded the Congress leadership to form yet another committee, the Foreign Cloth Boycott Committee, and personally started the campaign by once more lighting a great bonfire of imported cloth in Bombay. He then set off for a visit to Burma, which was followed by a six-week tour of the Andhra districts of the Madras Presidency covering no fewer than 319 villages, and then by similar tours in the hills and plains of the UP. Everywhere he went, the smell of burning cloth mingled with the smoke of dung fires, symbolizing his coming revolution.

It was mid-August before Ramsay MacDonald could reply to Jinnah's personal letter — it had taken until then for him to assuage Simon's wounded pride and assure himself of Liberal support for the proposals. Jinnah had every reason to be pleased with the result, for the prime minister told him that 'the report of the Simon Commission . . . was never intended to be anything more than advice given for the guidance of the Government' and that 'the suggestions which you make in your letter will be pondered over with a desire to use them in every way that circumstances allow'. He promised an announcement 'very soon'.[27]

Irwin returned to India on 25 September 1929, and also wrote to Jinnah confirming that the British government was prepared to announce dominion status as its aim for India, and the calling of a round-table conference. The official statement appeared on the front page of every Indian newspaper on 1 November. Jinnah and 18 other political leaders, including the poetess Sarojini Naidu, Bhulabhai Desai, Chagla, and the two Dwarkadas brothers, met and issued a joint statement welcoming the announcement unreservedly. In New Delhi, however, 30 other leaders, including Gandhi, met under the chairmanship of Motilal and issued their own response, which was that they accepted the viceroy's declaration, subject to certain conditions. Among these were that there should be 'a predominant representation of Congressmen at the conference', and a general amnesty for all political prisoners. But the most important condition was that 'the Conference is to meet not to discuss when Dominion Status is to be established, but to frame a scheme of Dominion Constitution for India'.[28]

This 'leaders' manifesto' as it became known, represented a personal triumph for Motilal in reconciling many diverse attitudes. But some of those present still had serious misgivings, among them Jawaharlal, who wrote:

> That manifesto was a bitter pill for some of us. To give up the demand for independence, even in theory and even for a short while, was wrong and dangerous ... So I hesitated and refused to sign the manifesto (Subhas Bose had definitely refused to sign it), but, as was not unusual with me, I allowed myself to be talked into signing. Even so, I came away in great distress, and the very next day I thought of withdrawing from the Congress presidentship, and wrote accordingly to Ghandiji ... A soothing letter from Ghandiji and three days of reflection calmed me.[29]

At Westminster, the government's announcement raised a storm of protest. The Labour government was forced on to the defensive and Wedgewood Benn attempted to make out that it was merely a 'restatement' of Montagu's 1917 declaration, and thus no radical change of policy. But the diehards, led by Churchill and Birkenhead, were not placated. Heated debates in Parliament did nothing to increase Indian confidence in British promises. Any lingering trust which Indian nationalists may have had in British good faith was destroyed when Birkenhead stood up in the House of Lords and abandoned all pretence by declaiming:

> What man in this House can say that he can see in a generation, in two generations, in a hundred years, any prospect that the people of India will be in a position to assume control of the Army, the Navy, the Civil Service, and to have a Governor-General who will be responsible to the Indian Government and not to any authority in this country?[30]

Irwin was astonished at the 'violent political explosion' at Westminster, which was followed inevitably by another in India – equally violent but of a more physical nature. On 23 December 1929 a bomb exploded under the viceroy's train just outside New Delhi, as he was returning from a viceregal tour. The dining saloon was damaged and one of his servants hurt, but he narrowly escaped injury.

At 4.30 that same afternoon, Irwin met an invited delegation consisting of Gandhi, Motilal Nehru, Jinnah, Sapru, and Vithalbhai Patel, the president of the Central Legislative Assembly. The meeting could not start earlier, as it was a Monday, and ever since the Jallianwala Bagh massacre Gandhi had kept Mondays as a day of silence, communicating only through scribbled notes until sundown.

Irwin, and indeed Jinnah, who had spent some two months preparing the ground for this meeting, had high hopes that they could make real progress towards a round-table conference, the purpose of which, as Irwin said, 'was to thresh out the problems which arose out of His Majesty's Government's definite declaration of policy'. Their hopes were soon dashed against the stone wall of Congress obduracy. Gandhi and Motilal flatly refused to discuss any conference that was not guaranteed to result in immediate dominion status. They saw no difficulties in the way of this, Motilal told the viceroy, 'But if there were any, they could be solved after the central point was admitted; India could solve them for herself.' Gandhi was at least prepared to admit that 'the lack of unity' did present a difficulty, but Motilal refused to recognize any 'Muslim problem'.[31]

Irwin refused to accept any preconditions for the proposed conference. It was to be an open and frank discussion of the problems that needed to be solved before India could be granted dominion status. He could not prejudge its findings, or commit the British government to anything in advance. This, of course, was not acceptable to Congress, and the meeting broke up. The participants went their separate ways – symbolically, Gandhi and Motilal travelled in one car, Jinnah, Sapru and Patel in another. The parting of the ways which Jinnah had spoken of exactly a year before was now complete. Bitter, angry and disillusioned, he turned his back on his former colleagues in Congress, abandoning all hopes of a *rapprochement*.

Motilal and Gandhi went straight to that year's Congress in Lahore, where the Nehru family watched proudly as Jawaharlal rode through the streets on a white charger, leading what was effectively his own coronation procession. At just over 40 years of age, he was not the youngest-ever president – Gokhale was only 39 when he was elected in 1905 – but he was undoubtedly the most glamorous. And he was, as always, very conscious of his destiny. 'The whole atmosphere was electric and surcharged with the gravity of the occasion,' he recalled later. 'Our decisions were not going to be mere criticism or protests or expressions of opinion, but a call to action which was bound to convulse the country and affect the lives of millions.'[32]

There was only one issue that mattered at the 1929 session of Congress. The year's grace was over, the polite ultimatum had expired, now was the time to declare *purna swaraj*, complete independence, as Congress's only goal, and to embark on a campaign of civil disobedience. The main resolution was passed by a huge majority – surprisingly there were some, though 'barely a score, out of many thousands', who voted against – at the stroke of midnight on 31 December.[33] Jawaharlal took great delight in leading a procession to the banks of the Ravi river and raising the tricolour flag of Indian nationalism to shouts of '*Inquilab zindabad!*', 'Long live the revolution!'.

January the twenty-sixth was chosen as Independence Day and a declaration written by Gandhi was read out in towns and villages all over India:

We believe that it is the inalienable right of the Indian people, as of any other people, to have freedom and to enjoy the fruits of their toil and have the necessities of life, so that they may have full opportunities of growth. We believe also that if any government deprives a people of these rights and oppresses them, the people have a further right to alter it or to abolish it. The British government in India has not only deprived the Indian people of their freedom but has based itself on the exploitation of the masses, and has ruined India economically, politically, culturally, and spiritually. We believe, therefore, that India must sever the British connection and attain *purna swaraj* or complete independence.

... We hold it to be a crime against man and God to submit any longer to a rule that has caused this fourfold disaster to our country. We recognize, however, that the most effective way of gaining our freedom is not through violence. We will therefore prepare ourselves by withdrawing, so far as we can, all voluntary association from the British Government, and will prepare for civil disobedience, including non payment of taxes. We are convinced that if we can but withdraw our voluntary help and stop payment of taxes without doing violence, even under provocation, the end of this inhuman rule is assured.[34]

'A Mad Risk'

The success of Independence Day, on 26 January 1930, when huge crowds in towns and villages throughout India had gathered to take the pledge of independence solemnly and entirely without incident, led Gandhi to believe that all his work of educating and preparing the people for *satyagraha* was bearing fruit. The time was ripe for action, with little fear of another Chauri Chaura. But what form should that action take? For once, Gandhi made no claim that his voices had spoken to him, but with or without them he settled on the perfect answer: salt. 'Salt suddenly became a mysterious word,' Jawaharlal Nehru recalled later, 'a word of power. The Salt Tax was to be attacked, the salt laws were to be broken. We were bewildered and could not quite fit in a national struggle with common salt.'[1]

Gandhi was probably the greatest exponent the world has ever seen of what might be described as symbolic politics. He had an extraordinary flair for dramatizing political issues through easily comprehensible yet potent images which even the simplest peasant could understand. The Salt Tax was just such an issue. The manufacture and sale of salt was one of the three original monopolies established for the East India Company by Clive, back in 1765 – the others were tobacco and betel nuts – and had long been subjected to a heavy tax, which, since salt is one of the staples of life, no one could avoid paying. Even those living by the ocean were forbidden to pick up lumps of natural sea salt for their morning rice, on pain of heavy fines. 'There is no article like salt outside water by taxing which the State can reach even the starving millions, the sick, the maimed and the utterly helpless,' Gandhi wrote. 'The tax constitutes therefore the most inhuman poll tax the ingenuity of man can devise.'[2]

On 2 March, Gandhi wrote a personal letter to the viceroy, warning him that he was about to start a new campaign:

Dear Friend,

Before embarking on civil disobedience and taking the risk I have dreaded to take all these years, I would fain approach you and find a way out. My personal faith is absolutely clear. I cannot intentionally hurt anything that lives, much less fellow human beings, even though they may do the great wrong to me and mine. While, therefore, I hold British rule to be a curse, I do not intend to harm a single Englishman or any legitimate interest he may have in India ...

He had hoped, he said, that the proposed round-table conference might furnish a solution. 'But when you said plainly that you could not give any assurance that you or the British Cabinet would pledge yourselves to support a scheme of full dominion status,' then the conference was a complete waste of time. He was aware, he continued, that in order to defend its Indian interests Britain would use 'all the forces at her command', including physical force. This was why he had decided that India must evolve non-violent force, 'enough to free herself from that embrace of death'. 'I know that in embarking on non-violence, I shall be running what might fairly be termed a mad risk, but victories of truth have never been won without risks.' What he sought was 'no less than to convert the British people through non-violence and thus make them see the wrong they have done to India'.[3]

Gandhi ended his letter by telling the viceroy exactly what he planned, as a good satyagrahi was bound to do:

On the 11th day of this month, I shall proceed with such workers of the Ashram as I can, to disregard the provisions of the salt laws ... It is, I know, open to you to frustrate my design by arresting me. I hope that there will be tens of thousands ready, in a disciplined manner, to take up the work after me, and, in the act of disobeying the Salt Act to lay themselves open to the penalties of a law that should never have disfigured the Statute-book.[4]

The viceroy's reply was brief: it expressed his regret 'at Mr Gandhi's contemplating a course of action which was clearly bound to involve the violation of the law and danger to public peace'. Privately, he dismissed Gandhi, remarking that in India 'all problems are 90 per cent psychological and 10 per cent rational'. The battle lines were drawn.

Gandhi's hopes for tens of thousands of followers were amply fulfilled. In another masterly stroke, he chose to open the campaign by leading a march from his Sabarmati Ashram south to the village of Dandi on the Gujarat coast, a distance of 241 miles. There, he proposed to make salt by boiling up deposits left by the tide on the mud flats. The march began 6.30 a.m. on 12 March 1930. Gandhi, staff in hand, led 79 *satyagrahis*, including men from almost every region and religion in India, in his progress to the sea. It turned into something, akin to a religious procession, like Peter the Hermit leading the Children's Crusade. Crowds lined the way. They sprinkled the roads with water to lay the dust and strewed green leaves in the path of the pilgrims. They festooned their villages with flags and banners. Men and women paid homage to the Mahatma by spinning yarn on their *charkas* as he passed.

At first, the British authorities ridiculed 'Mr Gandhi's somewhat fantastic project', observing that India was still in 'the kindergarten stage of political revolution'. The idea that the Raj could be brought down by a half-naked native 'boiling sea-water in a kettle' was clearly absurd. But the march caught the imagination of the nation, leaving the British, as Gandhi had predicted, 'puzzled and perplexed'. It took him 24 days to reach Dandi, and news of his progress and reports of his speeches were printed and broadcast nationally and internationally every day. Soon, the whole of India, and indeed the whole world, was waiting expectantly for the final act of the drama.

While Gandhi was marching, Congress leaders completed their preparations for the campaign. Not least among these were arrangements for deputies to take over both locally and nationally as elected leaders were arrested. Jawaharlal nominated his father to stand in for him as president when the time came, having failed to persuade Gandhi to do so. Motilal had already struck the first blow in the new campaign by resigning his seat in the Central Assembly and persuading most of the other Congress members to follow suit. From the special session of the AICC in Ahmedabad called to finalize plans, the leaders hurried back to their provinces to organize the next stage and, as Sarojini Naidu put it, 'to pack up our toothbrushes for the journey to prison'.[5]

The two Nehrus broke their journey home to meet Gandhi for a few hours at Jambusar. As well as giving him details of the AICC meeting, Motilal informed him that he was changing the name of his mansion in Allahabad from Anand Bhavan, the Abode of Happiness, to Swaraj Bhavan, and giving it to the nation. He had already built a new, much smaller Anand Bhavan alongside it for himself and the family. He handed the old house over to Congress as soon as he returned home; half of it was converted into a hospital for Congress volunteers injured in the civil disturbances that were erupting in the city. Jawaharlal had little time to spend in either house: he was constantly on the move. During the first four days of April alone he made no fewer than 22 speeches at meetings attended by some 250,000 people.

With immaculate timing, Gandhi arrived in Dandi on 5 April, ready to make the decisive move the next day, the anniversary of the first national *satyagraha* and the first day of National Week, which was celebrated every year to commemorate the events of that week in 1919 which culminated in the Jallianwala

Bagh massacre. At 5.30 a.m. on 6 April, Gandhi led a crowd of supporters into the sea for a ritual cleansing. Police and officials had deliberately stayed clear, having thwarted Gandhi's original plan by stirring the salt deposits into the mud. Undaunted, he simply bent down and picked up a lump of salt from the beach, to a jubilant cry of 'Hail, law-breaker!' from Sarojini Naidu. It was the signal for the start of civil disobedience.

Across India, hundreds of thousands of supporters began making their own salt. The fact that most of it was totally unusable was quite irrelevant, all that mattered was that they were breaking the law. *Satyagrahis* also organized raids on salt works. At Dharasana in Gujarat the raid was led by Imam Sahib, an elderly follower of Gandhi who had been with him in South Africa, Gandhi's son, Manilal, and Sarojini Naidu, who instructed the crowd before they went into action that they must not use violence under any circumstances. 'You will be beaten but you must not resist,' she told them. 'You must not even raise a hand to ward off blows.'

Half a dozen British officials backed by 400 police armed with lathis guarded the salt pans. The leaders of the salt raiders were arrested while the rank and file were brutally beaten up. An American journalist, Webb Miller, watched with a growing sense of outrage. 'The spectacle of unresisting men being methodically bashed into a bloody pulp sickened me so much I had to turn away,' he reported. 'The western mind finds it difficult to grasp the idea of non-resistance. I felt ... a sense of helpless rage and loathing almost as much against the men were were submitting unresistingly to being beaten, as against the police wielding the clubs.'[6] By 11.00 a.m., 320 protesters had been injured and two killed.[7]

Salt marches were staged in various parts of the country, and the movement spread rapidly into other areas of resistance. The foreign cloth boycott was virtually complete and shops selling it were picketed; British schools, colleges, law courts and other institutions were boycotted; anti-tax campaigns flared up in Bengal, Bihar, Gujarat and the UP. Local officials resigned their posts, including 300 in Gujarat alone.

Gandhi particularly called for the picketing of liquor shops, and shrewdly asked women to play a leading role. His own wife, Kasturbai, was first in the line in Ahmedabad. In Allahabad, Jawaharlal's wife, Kamala, and his sister, Krishna, had joined in the drill sessions organized by Jawaharlal as part of the volunteers' training programme, wearing men's clothes. Now, they threw themselves into the movement with great enthusiasm, as did his mother, Swarup Rani. Kamala, who had been sickly and delicate for so long, amazed her husband when she 'forgot her ill-health, rushed about the whole day in the sun, and showed remarkable powers of organization'.[8] Throughout India, other women did the same, emerging from the seclusion of centuries to play prominent and public roles in the struggle. It was, according to Jawaharlal, the most striking aspect of those exciting days.

The arrests began early in the campaign. Vallabhbhai Patel was among the first to be gaoled, on 7 March, before Gandhi had even set out from Sabarmati, on the orders of local officials acting on their own initiative. Jawaharlal was arrested in Allahabad on 14 April and sentenced the same day to six months' imprisonment. He was quickly followed by numerous other Congress leaders, but the campaign continued unabated, with reserves stepping in every time a leader was imprisoned.

Gandhi was finally arrested at three-quarters of an hour after midnight on 5 May, in a village three miles from Dandi, sparking off a tidal wave of protest, with strikes, hartals, and the burning of public buildings throughout India. Fully aware of the dangers of putting him in front of a judge, the authorities had resurrected an obscure regulation — Bombay Regulation XXV of 1827 — which gave them the power to hold him without trial. The order was served by the district magistrate from Surat, accompanied by two police officers and 30 constables, who gave him 25 minutes to pray and gather his belongings into two khadi satchels, then took him by lorry to the familiar surroundings of Yeravda Central Gaol. There, he settled down to his usual prison routine of praying, spinning and reading, treating the prison as if it were his own ashram. Nothing the authorities could do disturbed him.

Although he was in prison, Gandhi saw no reason why he he should not continue negotiating with the viceroy. Less than two weeks after he arrived in Yeravda, he was writing to his 'dear friend' setting out his terms and conditions for calling off the civil disobedience campaign. These were 11 demands, which he had sent to Ramsay MacDonald back in January, before starting the campaign. They began with total prohibition of alcohol; abolition of the Salt Tax was number four on the list. Others included cutting 50 per cent off land revenue, military expenditure, and the salaries of the highest grade civil servants; a protective tariff on foreign cloth; an amnesty for all political prisoners; abolition or 'popular control' of the Criminal Intelligence Division of the police; and — amazingly for Gandhi — issuing firearms licences 'for self-defence, subject to popular control'.[9] He received no response from Irwin.

Despite the fact that Gandhi was committed to non-violence above all else, there were others in Congress who, in the words of maulana Abul Kalam Azad, regarded ahimsa as 'a matter of policy, not of creed'. Their view was that if independence could be won without violence, so much the better; but if it could not, then force would have to be used. There was renewed revolutionary terrorist activity in the Punjab, the UP and Bihar, but inevitably, the main centre was Bengal, where it flourished again between 1930 and 1932. During that time, 22 officials and 20 non-officials were murdered, including three British magistrates in one district alone. Two inspectors-general of the police were killed, and unsuccessful attempts were made on the lives of two governors.

The most active of the 'revolt groups' was led by a young schoolteacher called Surya Sen, who was Congress secretary in Chittagong, East Bengal. Five of the others in his group were also members of the district Congress committee. Styling themselves the Indian Republican Army, Chittagong Branch, they staged a rebellion with 65 men on the night of 18 April 1930. While the bulk of the force concentrated on disrupting telephone and telegraph systems and the railway, Surya Sen and six others captured the police armoury, and another group of 10 took the Auxiliary Force armoury. They seized a number of Lewis guns and Lee Enfield .303 rifles but couldn't find any ammunition, which was a severe setback.

Knowing that they couldn't defend themselves, they held a brief parade outside the police armoury, where Surya Sen raised the national flag, took a military salute, and proclaimed a provisional revolutionary government. Then they left town in a hurry and took to the hills. Four days later, they were surrounded by several thousand troops. In the shoot-out that followed, they claimed to have killed 80 soldiers, for the loss of 12 of their own men, before splitting up and escaping into the neighbouring countryside. Despite having their villages burnt by government forces, local peasants, most of them Muslims, sheltered Surya Sen and his men for three years. Sen was captured on 16 February 1933, tried, and hanged on 12 January 1934. Most of his men were captured and sentenced to long terms of imprisonment.[10]

Most Muslims followed Jinnah's lead and had nothing to do with civil disobedience. There were exceptions, of course, the most notable being Khan Abdul Gaffar Khan, 'the Frontier Gandhi', a Pathan nationalist and passionate believer in the doctrine of non-violence. An impressive figure, tall, gaunt and with the air of an Old Testament prophet, he dreamed of uniting the Pushtu-speaking people of the North-West Frontier into an independent state stretching from Baluchistan to the Hindu Kush – a dream that was political anathema to the British, and, 20 years later, to the Pakistan government, too.

Gaffar Khan's followers, the Khudai Khidmatgars, Servants of God, were popularly known as Red Shirts, for the obvious reason. They seem to have been rather less Gandhian than their leader: when the British arrested him for inciting civil disobedience, they protested in typical Pathan style. For over a week, they took over the city of Peshawar, before the authorities sent in armoured cars and aircraft, killing hundreds of tribesmen. At one point, they called out two platoons of the 18th Royal Garhwal Rifles, a Hindu regiment, but the troops refused to fire on the Muslim demonstrators and even handed over their weapons to the crowd.

The Simon Commission Report was published at last in June. The main thrust of its conclusions and recommendations was that the existing dyarchy should be replaced with a constitution giving wider powers to provincial governments, with ministers responsible to the legislatures. But at the same time, it left the levers of power – defence, internal security, and the protection of minorities – in the hands of the governors, and, of course, ultimately in the hands of 'the actual and active Head of Government', the viceroy. Dominion status, never mind independence, was still as far from becoming reality as it had ever been. Simon saw future political advancement as a gradual evolution, a series of slow stages leading to some as yet unspecified goal.

As far as the Indians were concerned, the British had reneged yet again on the promise of self-government which they had been making for at least 12 years. In Britain, the report found favour with Conservatives, most of whom believed that it had at least laid to rest the ghost of self-rule for the time being. The viceroy, on the other hand, bewailed the 'amazing lack of imagination' revealed by Simon.[11] It was Beatrice Webb, never the wittiest of women, who summed up the whole farrago most succinctly: she said that the report assumed that 'the British are born rulers and the Indians born to be ruled'. Which was precisely how the Indian nationalists saw the report.

At the end of June, Jawaharlal was joined in Naini prison, near Allahabad, by his father and two other leading Congressmen. Motilal was in very poor health by then – his chronic asthma had developed into advanced fibrosis of the lungs, which was aggravated by the damp conditions of the gaol in the rainy season. But he declined the prison governor's offer of better accommodation, preferring to stay in a cramped and leaky cell alongside his son. His arrest marked a new development in the conflict with the government, which had now proscribed the Congress Working Committee, putting all its members under threat of immediate arrest. By then, the numbers of Congress prisoners had swelled to between 60,000 and 90,000, but still the civil disobedience campaign continued.

Irwin announced that the round-table conference would be held in London that autumn. But while Gandhi and the other Congress leaders remained in prison they would not be able to take part, and the conference would be little more than a hollow sham. With the backing of the Central Assembly, Sir Tej Bahadur Sapru and M.R. Jayakar offered to act as intermediaries, hoping to persuade Gandhi at least to give the conference his blessing. The Nehrus and the Congress secretary, Dr Syed Mahmud, were taken by train from Naini to Yeravda for an extraordinary meeting inside the prison with the viceroy's two emissaries together with Gandhi, Vallabhbhai Patel, Sarojini Naidu and another Congress committee member, Jairamdas Doulatram.

After three days of talks, it became clear that there was no common ground. The Congress leaders said they could not endorse the round-table conference without the approval of the banned Working Committee. They refused to make any concessions in their minimum demands – and in fact added new ones: the right of India to secede at will from the empire, plus full self-government, including defence and finance. And the British government must accept all of Gandhi's 11-point plan.[12]

Congress was not alone in opposing the round-table conference: in Britain, there was considerable and noisy hostility from many Conservatives. Birkenhead had died on 30 September, but Churchill continued to lead the fight against any concessions to Indian opinion. Since he had left the Exchequer, India had become his main obsession, outweighing even disarmament. He had fulminated against Irwin's declaration on dominion status, now he charged MacDonald with encouraging 'false hopes' among Indian politicians. It was wrong, he declared, 'to lure and coax' them to a conference 'with vague phrases about dominion status in their lifetime'.[13]

In spite of all the objections, the conference was opened in London by King George V on 12 November 1930. It was chaired by the prime minister himself, and attended by representatives of all the main political parties in Britain, and all the principal interests in India, apart from Congress. There was an interesting omission on the British side, too: MacDonald had not invited Sir John Simon to take part, thus effectively consigning his report to history's dustbin. When, later in the conference, Lord Peel, leader of the Conservative delegation, argued that the government should implement the report and nothing more, Jinnah firmly declared that the report was 'dead'.

In the absence of Congress, it was left to Jinnah, the spokesman for the 16 Muslim delegates, to cut through the flannel and the polite platitudes of the opening speeches and demand that British promises be translated into action. With his inimitable sense of theatre, he ended his speech by looking around at the assembled guests and telling them: 'I must express my pleasure at the presence of the Dominion Prime Ministers and representatives. I am glad they are here to witness the birth of a new Dominion of India which would be ready to march with them within the British Commonwealth of Nations.'[14]

For all the talk, there could be little hope of the conference reaching any meaningful decision without Congress involvement, and it is hardly surprising that it ended without accomplishing much. What was surprising was that all the Indians – Hindus, Muslims, princes and businessmen – agreed on the idea of an All-India federation. They were also unanimous in wanting dominion status at once, though none of them could agree on how to achieve it. The British government agreed only to limited autonomy for the provinces and the gradual introduction of that old and ill-defined chestnut 'responsible government'. On that note, the conference ended.

Back in India, the cause of Muslim separatism was taking a significant step forward. Jinnah, still nominally permanent president of the Muslim League, had asked Dr Muhammad Iqbal, a distinguished Urdu poet and philosopher from the Punjab, to preside in his absence over the annual meeting, in Allahabad. Iqbal, though educated at the universities of Heidelberg, Munich and Trinity College, Cambridge, and called to the bar at Lincoln's Inn, remained an Islamic mystic. He had his own vision of the future for India's Muslims, which he unveiled to the poorly attended meeting. 'I would like to see,' he told them, 'the Punjab, the North-West Frontier Province, Sind and Baluchistan amalgamated into a single State. Self-government within the British Empire, or without the British Empire, the formation of a consolidated North-West Indian Muslim State appears to me to be the destiny of the Muslims, at least of North-West India.'[15]

Two years after Iqbal's speech, a small group of Indian Muslims in Cambridge, calling themselves students though they were all in their thirties, were inspired to follow in his footsteps. In a four-page pamphlet entitled *Now or Never*, published in January 1933, Choudhry Rahmat Ali and three others went one step further: they defined the 'fatherland' they sought and gave it a name, 'Pakistan, the land of the pure' (*Pak* is an Urdu word meaning ritually pure). The name, which Rahmat Ali claimed to have arrived at with divine guidance, is a convenient acrostic: P for Punjab, A for Afghania (the North-West Frontier Province), K for Kashmir, S for Sind and Tan for the last part of Baluchistan. Rahmat Ali added Kashmir, which Iqbal had thought it expedient to omit, but neither included Bengal in their proposed fatherland. Rahmat Ali, however, added a map of India showing three independent Muslim nations joined in a triple alliance. They were Pakistan in the north-west, Bang-i-Islam consisting of Bengal and Assam in the north-east, and Usmanistan in the south, a renamed Hyderabad – Usman was the family name of the nizams.

There was one other significant difference between the two proposals. Iqbal foresaw his north-west state remaining in an all-India federation. Rahmat Ali and his friends had other ideas: 'These provinces should have a separate Federation of their own,' they wrote. 'There can be no peace and tranquillity in the land if we, the Muslims, are duped into a Hindu-dominated Federation where we cannot be the masters of our own destiny and captains of our own souls.'[16]

At the time, few people took much notice of either idea for a separate Muslim state. The official aim, which Jinnah pursued rigorously, was for autonomous provinces within a loose Indian federation, and most Muslims dismissed any other suggestion. But the Hindu leaders in Muslim majority provinces were alarmed at what they saw as a new pan-Islamic movement posing a military threat to India. They began a nationwide campaign against it, calling on the British to crush any such movement before it began. It was the best publicity the Pakistan idea could possibly have hoped for. Most Muslims still dismissed it as speculative and impractical, but the seed had been planted.

As for Jinnah himself, conditions were far from right for his own political ambitions. When he left Bombay for London in October 1930, it was not just to take part in the round-table conference. Disillusioned and in despair at the situation in India, he intended to stay in London for good. He kept on his house on Malabar Hill, but wound up his Bombay legal practice and acquired chambers in King's Bench Walk in the Inner Temple – whose treasurer, coincidentally, was Sir John Simon. Simon expressed himself 'very glad to have so distinguished a man within our boundaries ... He need not trouble about recommendations, as, of course, I know all about him ...'[17] Jinnah sent for his sister Fatima and his daughter Dina, found a villa in eight acres of garden and pasture on Hampstead's West Heath Road with a splendid view over the open heath, and settled down to devote himself entirely to appeals before the Privy Council, the highest court in the empire.

In his speech winding up the first round-table conference, Ramsay MacDonald had promised federation and 'the greatest possible measure of self-government' for the provinces. He ended by hoping that what had been achieved might enable those who had refused to co-operate in the conference so far to take part in the future. With the prime minister's blessing, Irwin released Gandhi and the rest of the Congress leadership on 25 January 1931. Setting the tone of reconciliation, he told the Central Legislative Assembly: 'No one can fail to recognize the spiritual force which impels Mr Gandhi to count no sacrifice too great in the cause, as he believes, of the India he loves.' He was imposing no conditions, he said, 'for we feel that the best hope for the restoration of peaceful conditions lies in discussions being conducted by those concerned under terms of unconditional liberty ... I am content to trust those who will be affected by our decision to act in the same spirit as inspires it.'[18]

After a brief stop in Bombay, where he received a rapturous welcome from huge crowds, Gandhi hurried straight to Allahabad, where Motilal was close to death. Motilal had been released on 8 September because of his health, but had apparently recovered after a spell in hospital. It proved to be only a brief respite: the fibrosis in his lungs had formed a tumour on the right side of his chest. His condition was deteriorating rapidly.

In the early morning of 25 January, Jawaharlal was discharged from Naini prison – as it happened, only a few hours before he would have been released anyway – so that he could hurry home to his father's bedside. He had completed his original six-month sentence in October but had been arrested again after only five days for disobeying an order forbidding him to make public speeches, and was sentenced to two years' solitary confinement. His wife, Kamala, was released on the same day from gaol in Lucknow, where she had been imprisoned, to her great delight, on 1 January.

Motilal rallied a little, and although he could barely speak managed to hold court to a succession of old friends visiting in twos and threes from Working Committee meetings in the old house next door. 'There he sat,' Jawaharlal recalled in his autobiography, 'like an old lion mortally wounded and with his physical strength almost gone, but still very leonine and kingly.' On 4 February, his doctors, one of them another former Congress president, M.A. Ansari, decided he was well enough to be taken to Lucknow, where deep X-ray treatment was available. Gandhi and a large party of friends followed in another car. In the event, the journey proved to be too much. Exhausted, Motilal passed peacefully away in the early morning of 6 February 1931.

Word spread quickly through Lucknow, and huge, grieving crowds gathered to watch as the procession of cars set off for Allahabad. Jawaharlal sat in an open car at its head, dazed and hardly aware of what was happening, alongside the body of his father wrapped in the forbidden national flag, and with another big flag flying above it. That same day, after some ceremonies at home, the body was carried through a great concourse of people to the Ganges, where Jawaharlal performed the son's duty of lighting the sandalwood pyre. His own description of the final events cannot be bettered:

> As evening fell on the river bank on that winter day, the great flames leapt up and consumed the body which had meant so much to us who were close to him as well as to millions in India. Ghandiji said a few moving words to the multitude, and then all of us crept silently home. The stars were out and shining brightly when we returned, lonely and desolate.[19]

Among the thousands of messages of sympathy to Jawaharlal and Swarup Rani was a heartfelt note from the viceroy and Lady Irwin.

At almost exactly the time of Motilal's death, most of the Indian delegates to the round-table conference disembarked from their ship at Bombay. A group of them, led by Srinivasa Sastri, Sir Tej Bahadur Sapru and M.R. Jayakar, went at once to Allahabad to pay their respects to the Nehrus and report on the conference to the Congress Working Comittee. After some discussion, they persuaded Gandhi that he should grasp the olive branch offered by Irwin, and write to him suggesting they meet for a frank talk.

Irwin accepted eagerly − his time in India was running out, and he desperately wanted to end his viceroyalty in just over two months' time with a positive achievement. He must also have been aware that his successor, Lord Willingdon, would be less sympathetic to Indian aspirations: there can be little doubt that Irwin had been genuine in appealing to Gandhi, when ordering his release, to co-operate in placing 'the seal of friendship once again upon the relations of two peoples, whom unhappy circumstances have latterly estranged'. To the diehards, among whom Willingdon must be counted, such talk was almost treasonable. The *Daily Mail* spoke for them in a typical tub-thumping editorial: 'Without India, the British Commonwealth would fall to pieces. Commercially, economically, politically and geographically it is our greatest imperial asset. To imperil our hold on it would be the worst treason any Briton could commit.'

One who agreed wholeheartedly with the *Daily Mail* was Winston Churchill. He had already resigned from the Tory shadow cabinet over Baldwin's support for Indian constitutional progress and the release of the Congress prisoners, committing himself to the political wilderness where he would languish until 3 September 1940. The announcement of the Gandhi-Irwin talks drove him into paroxysms of rage. 'It is alarming and nauseating,' he told the Conservatives of West Essex, 'to see Mr Gandhi, a seditious Middle Temple lawyer, now posing as a fakir of a type well known in the East, striding half naked up the steps of the Viceregal palace, while he is still organizing and conducting a defiant campaign of civil disobedience, to parley on equal terms with the representative of the King-Emperor.'[20]

The talks between Irwin and Gandhi began on the afternoon of 17 February 1931 and dragged on until 7 March. Nehru and the other members of the Working Committee all gathered in Delhi, where they met Gandhi every day for interminable arguments on every point discussed at his meetings with the viceroy. There were eight such meetings in all, and they attracted world-wide press attention, particularly in the USA. Gandhi displayed all his usual mastery in handling the media: he even had his secretary, Madeleine Slade, the daughter of an English admiral now known as Mira Behn, bring his food, his dates and hot milk to the viceregal palace every day in what he called his 'gaol pot', a memento of his stay in Yeravda prison.

Irwin and Gandhi were both deeply religious men as well as politicians. Irwin's staff joked that it was 'a meeting of saints', while Sarojini Naidu called them 'the two Mahatmas'. In fact, there was little that was spiritual about their negotiations: they went at it like a couple of Kashmiri carpet-sellers. Irwin described Gandhi as 'a relentless bargainer', but in the end it was the viceroy who emerged triumphant, having won the battle of words and given away very little in return. Gandhi agreed to call off the civil disobedience campaign, which was running out of steam anyway, and agreed that Congress would take part in the next round-table conference.

In return, Irwin agreed to release all political prisoners not convicted of violent offences, to waive all fines which had not already been collected, to return confiscated lands which had not already been resold, and to deal leniently with government employees who had resigned. The soldiers of the Royal Garhwal Regiment who had refused to fire on unarmed Indians in Peshawar were not included in the amnesty, and Irwin refused Gandhi's demand for an inquiry into police brutality. On the Salt Laws, Gandhi won only meagre concessions, allowing villagers on the coast to make salt for their own use, and the right to peaceful and non-aggressive picketing.

The pact was not popular with Indians, and Gandhi faced severe criticism from many of his own followers. Nehru and Patel both believed that by ending the civil disobedience campaign he had laid down their strongest weapon and got very little in exchange. Certainly, in their eyes, the cause of independence had not been advanced. Many others thought that before signing the pact, Gandhi should have demanded a reprieve for Bhagat Singh and two other young men who were under sentence of death for conspiracy and throwing the bomb in the assembly. While they understood his refusal to condone violence, they could not understand why he did not extend this to the violence committed by the state in taking lives. But Gandhi stood firm. The three men were hanged on 23 March, six days before the annual session of Congress, and became martyrs. For once, it was Gandhi who faced black flag demonstrations all along his route to Karachi.

Although the British authorities believed they had won the duel with Gandhi, the Gandhi-Irwin Pact which was signed on 5 March 1931 achieved very little for them, either. It was only a truce, a provisional agreement rather than a final settlement. But Gandhi was playing to a wider audience. It was not lost on other Indian leaders, including Jinnah, that while they had played the game according to British rules, had gone to London and returned virtually empty-handed, Gandhi had emerged from prison to negotiate face to face with the viceroy himself.

Gandhi pulled the final trick by insisting to his fellow Congressmen that he should be their sole representative to the second round-table conference which was to take place in London that same year. Understandably, there were serious misgivings about this, especially among the 150 Congressmen who had applied for the 16 places allocated by the government. Nehru was particularly put out at being excluded, even though he regarded the conference as a device to let Britain off the hook. He stormed off to Ceylon to nurse his wounded pride and take a much-needed rest. But as always there was method, however devious, in Gandhi's madness. James Millar of the Associated Press of America had asserted to the Indian journalist Durga Das that the government's only reason for holding the talks so soon after the first round-table conference was to force Gandhi and Congress to take part in the next one. There, it was fondly hoped, the differences between the Congress leaders would be exposed for all to see, thus diminishing Gandhi's stature as a national leader. By going alone, Gandhi demolished any such hopes and enhanced his stature immeasurably.

By the time the second round-table conference was due to start, there was a new viceroy in India and a new government in London. There was also a new Congress president. Gandhi had finally decided to reward Vallabhbhai Patel for his loyalty by giving him his turn on the throne at Karachi in March 1931 – Nehru had decided during his term of office to change the date of the annual Congress session from December, because poorer members could not afford to buy the extra clothing needed to keep warm in northern cities during the cold weather. Patel was a very different character from Nehru, with a very different political philosophy: he was a man of the right, with no time for socialism. But little changed within Congress. Like everyone else, Patel found himself doing Gandhi's bidding.

The new viceroy, Lord Willingdon, was an old India hand and, though nominally a Liberal, was much more reactionary than the high Tory Irwin. As Freeman Freeman-Thomas – he had somewhat bizarrely opted to hyphenate his surname with his Christian name – he had enjoyed an undistinguished but blameless career at Westminster as an MP, first for Hastings and then for Bodmin. In 1913, as a reward for 10 years of party loyalty on the back benches, he had been appointed governor of Bombay, where his high-handedness and undisguised contempt for Congress and all it stood for had brought him into bitter conflict with local Indian politicians, and in particular with Jinnah. On a personal level, he had earned Jinnah's undying enmity when he insulted Ruttie at a dinner-party by calling for a wrap to cover her dazzling but revealing Paris gown. Jinnah swept his wife out of the house, and bore a grudge against Willingdon for the rest of his life. Following Bombay, Willingdon had been appointed governor of Madras, and in 1926 was made governor-general of Canada. Returning to India at the age of 64, he was the oldest man ever to hold the post of viceroy.

A keen cricketer – he had captained both Eton and Cambridge – Willingdon cut an elegant figure with his I Zingari tie and beautifully tailored grey suits. He reminded Malcolm Muggeridge, who was then assistant editor of the Calcutta *Statesman*, of 'an old beau in a Restoration comedy. I half expected him to take a pinch of snuff and flick his handkerchief.'[21] He possessed great charm and, as far as his political masters were concerned, the virtue of not being overburdened with ideas. Edwin Montagu once dismissed him as 'such a good fellow and such a stupid fellow'.

The truth was that Willingdon was essentially lazy. At the end of his term, his successor, Lord Linlithgow, is said to have found sheaves of official papers unsigned. Willingdon had never bothered to read them. Once, slightly tipsy, he told Malcolm Muggeridge, '[Irwin] was a very bad viceroy, I'm quite a good one. Yet he'll be remembered and I'll be forgotten.' In the second part of his statement at least, he was correct.

Unlike her husband, Lady Willingdon was lively to the point of being overwhelming – 'so vulgar and full of vitality' was how Malcolm Muggeridge saw her. The vicereine's overbearing ways extended even to architecture. Deciding to 'improve' the Viceroy's House in Delhi, she had many of the rooms repainted in her favourite colour, mauve. The result was then embellished with a design described by one visitor as looking like 'wild duck falling into Dorothy Perkins roses'. Lutyens protested against the desecration of his masterpiece. 'I told her,' he said, 'that if she possessed the Parthenon she would add bay windows to it. She said that she did not like the Parthenon.'[22]

Britain's Labour government fell on 24 August 1931. The majority of Ramsay MacDonald's cabinet resigned in protest at his and the chancellor's decision to cut unemployment benefit as part of their emergency economic strategy. The great world depression, which had been looming since the Wall Street crash in 1929, was now raging out of control throughout Europe. The collapse of the German banking system, and Germany's inability to continue paying war reparations, had led to a run on the pound which swallowed one quarter of Britain's gold reserves in two months and threatened to destroy sterling completely.

MacDonald formed a new National Government to address the crisis and try to balance the budget. The all-party coalition that had effectively existed over India now became official. Although MacDonald remained prime minister, his new government was dominated by Conservatives. Sir Samuel Hoare, of the famous banking family, known as 'Slippery Sam' to his opponents, became the new secretary of state for India. Malcolm Muggeridge, who interviewed him shortly afterwards, described him succinctly: 'neatly attired, sleek, with white kid tops to his boots, he felt himself to be in charge of India's destiny'.[23] In Hoare's hands, the official policy on India remained unchanged.

The second round-table conference went ahead as planned, against a background of unrest and uncertainty, in Britain as much as in India. On the day the conference opened, there was a mutiny by 12,000 Royal Navy sailors on 15 ships of the Atlantic Fleet at Invergordon in protest against pay cuts. Five days later, the economic crisis reached its zenith when Britain was forced off the gold standard and sterling was devalued by a massive 30 per cent. Throughout Britain there were strikes and demonstrations, clashes between Communists and Oswald Mosley's Fascists, and even a riot in Battersea by 5,000 unemployed workers. After three weeks of the conference, MacDonald called a general election. It took place on 27

October 1931, and resulted in the biggest landslide ever known, virtually wiping out the Labour Party in Parliament. Even MacDonald had left the party and stood as a National Labour candidate. Although his National Labour splinter group had only 13 seats against 473 Tories, he continued as prime minister of the coalition National Government, and so continued to chair the round-table Conference, too.

Gandhi had sailed from Bombay on 29 August 1931 aboard the P&O steamer *Rajputana*. His tiny staff consisted of Mahadev Desai and Pyarelal Nayar, his secretaries, Mira Behn, his English secretary and interpreter, and his son Devadas. Typically, they all travelled second class, with cabins in the bowels of the ship, though Gandhi himself seems to have slept on deck throughout the voyage, claiming a small area in the stern where he spun and prayed and held court.[24] Also on board were Sarojini Naidu, representing not Congress but Indian women, Madan Mohan Malaviya for the Hindu Mahasabha, and G.D. Birla, Gandhi's friend and greatest benefactor, who would represent the Indian business community. None of them felt the need to rough it.

The party arrived in London on 15 September, having finished the journey by train from Marseilles, where they had been besieged by crowds of French students hailing Gandhi as 'the spiritual ambassador of India'. More crowds turned out for him when the train pulled into the Gare de Lyon in Paris. Someone even brought along a white goat to supply the Mahatma with fresh milk, but the French police would not allow it on to the platform. To avoid the embarrassment of a similar welcome at Victoria Station, the British authorities sent an official car to meet Gandhi at Dover. Much to their annoyance, his staff had to travel to London by train.

In London, Gandhi insisted on staying at Kingsley Hall, a mission for the poor in Bow, among the slums of the East End. Muriel Lester, who ran the mission, had stayed at the Sabarmati Ashram during a visit to India, and had offered to put him up when he came to London. Since the conference was being held at St James's Palace, some eight miles west of Bow, it was hardly the most convenient address from which to commute each day, so a house was rented at 88 Knightsbridge and there Gandhi's staff established their headquarters. He, however, was driven every day from Bow to St James's. There was a further complication when British summer-time came to an end: all clocks and watches were put back one hour – except Gandhi's. He decided it was bad for watches to keep changing them, so he got up in the morning an hour earlier than he need have done, which meant that Mira Behn and anyone else staying at Kingsley Hall had to follow suit.

As usual, Gandhi had his own agenda. In his personal diary, Birla recorded: 'The only person Gandhi is really interested in seeing in London is Winston Churchill because of his hostile attitude to India. He has no desire at all to meet people like Bernard Shaw.'[25] Gandhi saw the trip to Britain as an opportunity to proselytize people, to spread his ideas among East End housewives, Lancashire mill-workers and others who had been directly affected by his policies of *swadeshi* and boycott. He genuinely believed that he could convert the British to the doctrine of non-violence, seeking like some Hindu Saint Columba to convert the heathen as well as win freedom for his country. In the event, he did meet Bernard Shaw, Charlie Chaplin and various other celebrities. He also visited Oxford colleges and northern mill towns. Surprisingly, when he did visit Lancashire, he was warmly welcomed by the very people he had helped to put out of work.

For much of the time, Gandhi appeared to be revelling in playing the role of the half-naked fakir. When he was invited to Buckingham Palace to take tea with the king, reporters asked if he intended to go in his usual dress. 'Some go in plus-fours,' he quipped merrily, 'I shall go in minus-fours.' After the event, he silenced his critics by telling them 'The king was wearing enough for both of us.'

Gandhi did not confine his preaching to the workers. At an early meeting with Hoare, he told the secretary of state he 'should be ashamed of the atrocities and injustice your race has imposed on the Indian people'. On the opening day of the conference, when MacDonald began by welcoming 'My Hindu and Muslim friends', Gandhi interrupted, telling him 'There are only Indians here.' MacDonald, an experienced politician well used to hecklers, was not thrown. He began again: 'My Hindu friends ... and others.'[26] In his own opening speech, Gandhi repeated the call for independence, speaking of India being held 'not by force but by a silken cord of love' and declaring that he still aspired to be a citizen, 'not in the Empire, but in a Commonwealth'.[27] When he addressed the House of Commons on 28 September, he told the members that what India wanted was an equal, not a subordinate relationship.[28] Sometimes the preaching bore fruit in unexpected ways. After one committee meeting, MacDonald 'came up to Gandhiji with folded hands and expressed his desire to visit his Sabarmati Ashram as an act of expiation'.[29]

The journalist Durga Das travelled to London to cover the conference for the Indian press. There, he met up with Clement Attlee again. In the period between his membership of the Simon Commission and the second round-table conference, Attlee had spent much time thinking about India. Besides the Simon Report, he had also studied the Nehru Report and the report on the first round-table conference. His conclusions were depressing: the Tories, he told Dass, would stop at nothing to prevent India's advance to self-rule. They would exploit anything, even the grievances of the Muslims, in order to prevent the march of Congress.[30]

When Das made contact again with Jinnah, whom he had known for a number of years, he was given much the same message. Jinnah was bored with his London practice, however profitable it was. He would have liked a seat on the Judicial Committee of the Privy Council, but even that would probably not have brought relief. In truth, he missed politics, and longed to return to the arena. He even considered seeking a seat in Parliament as a Labour MP, but recognized that there was not much chance of that now – he had upset Ramsay MacDonald too much by his uncooperative line at the first conference. He complained to Das: 'I seem to have reached a dead end. The Congress will not come to terms with me because my following is very small. The Muslims do not accept my views, for they take their orders from [the local] district commissioner.' He would take part in the forthcoming conference, but was dismissive about its prospects: 'What can you expect from a jamboree of this kind? The British will only make an exhibition of our differences.'[31]

In the end, Jinnah was proved to be absolutely right, though the British hardly needed to stir themselves to reveal the differences – the Indians managed to display them perfectly well on their own. The Muslims and the various other minorities – the Sikhs, Indian Christians, Eurasians, the British business interests and the Depressed Classes – were all agreed on one thing: that they should all have separate electorates. Congress, of course, was opposed to the very idea. And when the minority groups jointly demanded that this question be settled before any other business was done, the conference was clearly doomed.

Gandhi might have been persuaded at least to consider separate electorates for most of the groups, despite Congress's official line. But for one group he refused even to contemplate it. The group was the euphemistically titled 'Depressed Classes', or 'Scheduled Castes', polite labels for the untouchables. To Gandhi, India's 50 million untouchables were an indivisible part of Hinduism, even though he had described the concept of untouchability as its greatest blot. He saw any attempt at separating them from other Hindus as another example of British 'divide and rule' policy.

Not surprisingly considering their appalling treatment at the hands of caste Hindus, the untouchables themselves saw things differently. They had only recently emerged as a force on the political scene, due to the efforts of one remarkable member of their community, Dr Bhimrao Ramji Ambedkar, who was representing them at the conference. Just 40 years old, Ambedkar had somehow managed to escape from the ghetto of untouchability to study law in London and achieve a doctorate at Columbia University, New York. Now, he demanded the justice for his people which he knew the Hindus would never grant voluntarily. If a separate electorate was desirable for Muslims, who would always remain a minority in India as a whole, then it was essential for the untouchables if their voice was to be heard at all. Gandhi claimed to represent the untouchables 'in my own person'. Ambedkar, though grateful for all Gandhi's efforts on behalf of untouchables, would have none of this.

And so, the conference failed. The Muslims were pleased that MacDonald, at the end, conceded their demands for a new province of Sind and for full governor's status for the North-West Frontier Province. But communalism, the bugbear of every attempt at constitutional progress, had struck again. The minorities naturally saw the British government, which had listened sympathetically to their pleas, as their ally, and Congress as their adversary. They were happy to leave the government to settle the question of minority representation.

16

'Civil Martial Law'

When Gandhi returned to Bombay, empty-handed, on 28 December 1931, he found Nehru back in gaol and the country once more in political turmoil. Nehru had been arrested two days earlier, while on his way to meet Gandhi, for disobeying an order confining him to Allahabad. With him was the UP provincial Congress president, Tasadduq Sherwani. In that morning's newspapers, which they received as they boarded the train, they had read of the arrest of Abdul Ghaffar Khan, his brother Dr Khan Sahib, and other Congress leaders in the North-West Frontier Province. The government had clearly decided the Gandhi-Irwin truce was over and it was time to clamp down again.

The situation was tense all over India, but especially so in the UP, NWFP and Bengal. In the UP, Nehru had been leading a no-tax, no-rent campaign for the peasants and tenant farmers, who were suffering severe hardship as the great depression destroyed the market for their produce. In the NWFP, Gaffar Khan's Red Shirts were threatening rebellion and had already restarted civil disobedience. In Bengal, the terrorists were active again: two girl students assassinated a British magistrate, and a Muslim police inspector was shot dead in Chittagong, provoking massive Hindu-Muslim communal rioting. There had also been violent riots in several gaols and detention camps in the province. In all three provinces a series of far-reaching government ordinances had banned virtually all political or public activity.

Gandhi sent off a telegram to the viceroy:

I was unprepared on landing yesterday to find Frontier and United Provinces Ordinances, shootings in Frontier and arrests of my valued comrades in both, on the top the Bengal Ordinance awaiting me. I do not know whether I am to regard these as an indication that friendly relations between us are closed, or whether you expect me still to see you and receive guidance from you as to the course I am to pursue in advising the Congress. I would esteem a wire in reply.[1]

But Willingdon was not Irwin. There could be no personal pact with him, as there had been with the previous viceroy. He would not agree to any interview unless Gandhi first undertook not to try to discuss recent events in the three troubled provinces, the ordinances, or the arrests. Not knowing what else he was expected to talk about, Gandhi and the Working Committee called on all Indians to resume civil disobedience.

The months of truce had given the government a much needed breathing space in which to consider its options and make its plans for dealing with any renewal of the struggle with Congress. The officials had used the time well. Everything was ready. All they needed was the order to proceed. It was given on 4 January 1932. Early that morning, Gandhi and Vallabhbhai Patel, that year's Congress president, were arrested and gaoled without trial as state prisoners. That same day, Nehru and Sherwani were tried in Naini prison under the UP Emergency Powers Ordinance. Sherwani was given six months' rigorous imprisonment and a fine of 150 rupees. For exactly the same offence, Nehru got two years and 500 rupees or an extra six months for non-payment. Tongue in cheek, the Muslim Sherwani asked the magistrate 'if his smaller sentence was due to communal considerations'.[2]

A whole raft of ready prepared new ordinances was issued, giving far-reaching powers to magistrates and the police in what officials had labelled 'civil martial law'.[3] 'Civil liberty ceased to exist,' Nehru wrote later, 'and both person and property could be seized by the authorities. It was a declaration of a kind of a state of siege for the whole of India.' Even Samuel Hoare, in the House of Commons, was forced to admit that 'the ordinances we have approved are very drastic and severe. They cover almost every aspect of Indian life.'[4]

The ban on all public meetings or processions was made nation-wide. Newspaper censorship was tightened. Congress itself was never outlawed – this would have been seen as an attempt to crush the nationalist movement *per se*, which could have antagonized the government's moderate allies – but almost all its activities were banned. So, too, were all manner of other organizations – *kisan sabhas*, peasant unions, youth leagues, students' associations, national universities, schools and colleges, *swadeshi* concerns, libraries, even hospitals – the list of proscribed organizations ran into several thousands. One of the hospitals closed was that in the Nehrus' old house, Swaraj Bhavan, which was itself confiscated by the government. The number of prisoners, including 'detenus' as the Indian government called political prisoners held without trial, soared again. By May, there were 36,000 Congress members behind bars. All told, some 70,000 people were convicted during the renewed campaign.[5]

Most people went to gaol willingly – a prison sentence was almost an essential qualification for any active Congressman. Even beatings could be accepted as a badge of courage. But what really hurt was the seizure of their property. Since property was defined as ranging from buildings to bank accounts, the Indian middle classes soon lost their enthusiasm.

For once, Gandhi had met his match. Willingdon may not have been the brightest of viceroys, but his was not the only new appointment in India. His inner cabinet, the Executive Council, had a new Home member, Sir Harry Haig. Haig had previously been secretary of the Home Department, a position from which he could only offer advice. Now he had executive power, and quickly proved himself to be a master of the political game. His strategy was bold, simple and effective. It consisted of two strands: shutting down Gandhi and Congress by refusing any talks or negotiations until they called off civil disobedience, and at the same time pressing ahead as quickly as possible with constitutional reforms. This was designed to reassure the government's supporters and the services that it was being tough with Congress and not rewarding it for breaking the law; that it was determined to go on governing the country; and that real progress towards self-government could be made without any help from Congress.

Gandhi was nonplussed. Every effort he made to talk to the viceroy met with a flat rejection. His messages went unanswered. The government refused point blank to bargain with him in any way. Desperately, he sought some new issue which would grab the imagination of Indians as the Salt Tax had done, and restore him to the moral high ground. For months he racked his brain for some suitable issue. Then, on 16 August 1932, Ramsay MacDonald announced his decision on electoral representation for the minorities.

MacDonald's Communal Award confirmed separate electorates and reserved seats in provincial legislatures for Muslims, Sikhs, Europeans, Indian Christians, and Anglo-Indians, a term which had now come to mean Eurasians rather than the British living in India. There were also reserved seats for women (divided communally), for labour, commerce and industry, planting, mining and landholders. But what really upset Gandhi was that for the first time the untouchables were given both reserved seats and a separate electorate.

Gandhi had his issue. He had long been concerned with what he considered the disgraceful blot of untouchability. He had started calling untouchables *Harijans*, children of God, as a way of encouraging a fresh approach to them, and he had, of course, set a sterling example by including them in his various communities, despite deep-rooted objections even from his own wife and family. Now, if he championed their full integration into Indian society, as opposed to any further separation, he might be able to force the government to deal with him, and thus open the door again for negotiations on other issues.

After writing to MacDonald: 'I have to resist your decision with my life,' he began a fast unto death on 20 September 1932.

The government allowed him to make a statement to the press from his cell. It read: 'My life, I count of no consequence. One hundred lives given for this noble cause would, in my opinion, be poor penance done by Hindus for the atrocious wrongs they have heaped upon helpless men and women of their own faith.'[6] There was a certain exasperation among other Congressmen at what they saw as a distraction from political issues but it produced an immediate emotional response, putting Gandhi back in the spotlight. Rabindranath Tagore sent him a telegram of support: 'It is worth sacrificing precious life for the sake of India's unity and her social integrity ... Our sorrowing hearts will follow your sublime penance with reverence and love.'[7] But he never offered to join the fast himself.

The British looked on with cool interest. Haig announced that Gandhi would be released from prison for the duration of the fast – an offer which Gandhi refused. As his condition worsened, Malaviya and other Hindu leaders started frantic negotiations with the untouchables' leader, Ambedkar. The authorities provided full facilities for them to visit Gandhi, and after four days a deal was cobbled together. The text was cabled to two English sympathizers in London, who took it to MacDonald. He accepted it readily – the terms of the Communal Award already provided for its amendment if the parties concerned agreed among themselves.

Ambedkar had driven a hard bargain. Untouchables would give up their separate electorates and vote jointly with Hindus. But in return they would have almost double the number of reserved seats promised by MacDonald: the total number in provincial councils was increased from 81 to 148, and in the Central Assembly 18 per cent of the seats would be reserved for untouchables. The extra seats would come from the 'general non-Muhammadan' places – in other words, from the Hindus. Since the lists of untouchable candidates for election would be chosen by a separate ballot of untouchables the difference seems fairly esoteric, but it was enough to satisfy Gandhi that Hinduism had been preserved intact, and he broke his fast.

On the tide of emotion following the Yeravda Pact, the following week was celebrated throughout India as Untouchability Abolition Week. The Hindu Leaders' Conference passed a resolution: 'That henceforth, amongst Hindus, no one shall be regarded as an untouchable by reason of his birth, and those who have been so regarded hitherto, will have the same right as other Hindus in regard to the use of public wells, public schools, public roads and other public institutions.' Temples that had always been closed to untouchables, even in the holy city of Benares, the fount of Hindu orthodoxy, were opened to them. This egalitarian atmosphere didn't last, of course. Before long, caste Hindus were abandoning the temples opened to untouchables, and taking their children out of the schools. But it was a start.

The government was delighted. 'We think,' Willingdon cabled Hoare on I November, no doubt following advice from Haig, 'there may be definite advantages in Gandhi getting involved in untouchability. It will rouse strong feelings on both sides and will divert attention from strictly political issues and civil disobedience.'[8] Gandhi was offered all the facilities he needed to run his campaign against untouchability from gaol. He was even allowed to start a newspaper, *Harijan*, editing it from his cell. But there were strings: he had to promise that nothing he wrote or said 'shall have any reference to civil disobedience or matters outside removal of untouchability'.[9] It was a masterly stroke from Haig, effectively removing Gandhi from the head of the civil disobedience movement, and at the same time making sure he had something to keep him occupied. When Gandhi asked shortly afterwards to take part in some Hindu-Muslim negotiations he received a very frosty response.

Without Gandhi's leadership, the civil disobedience campaign was rapidly fizzling out. The number of Congressmen in gaol was diminishing as their sentences ended, and when some of them tried to light the fires again, there was little response. Jamnadas Dwarkadas caused a stir when he publicly renounced civil disobedience, saying Gandhi had already abandoned it despite the sacrifices made by so many of his followers. Others followed suit. Haig's carrot-and-stick policy was working well, so far. The stick had been much in evidence – but where was the carrot? And was it succulent enough to do the trick?

A third round-table conference in London in November 1932 was a bigger wash-out than the first two. Only 46 delegates attended. There was no Gandhi, of course, nor Nehru, nor Jinnah, who had not even been invited. None of the major princes bothered to attend – their initial enthusiasm for federation had waned as they began to appreciate the disadvantages of allowing democracy to intrude into their private fiefdoms. When the conference ended on Christmas Eve, Hoare had little of any importance to announce in his closing speech: Muslims would be guaranteed one third of the total seats in the Central Assembly, though they made up only a quarter of the population; and Sind would be made into a separate, predominantly Muslim, province. Shortly afterwards, as a counterbalance, it was decided to divide Orissa and Bihar into two separate, Hindu-majority provinces.

The failure of the conferences was not allowed to interfere with the government's plans. Its White Paper on the new Indian constitution was published in March 1933, and a month later a joint select committee of both houses of Parliament was set up 'to consider the future government of India'. The chairman was the Tory Lord Linlithgow. Attlee was the leading Labour representative. The White Paper made no mention of dominion status, but

Attlee's speech in the Commons clearly reaffirmed the party's policy: self-government and self-determination, leading to an equal partnership in the British Commonwealth, if that was what the Indians themselves wanted. He did not, however, mention any time scale.

The lure of real power, at least in the provincial governments, formed the basis of the second half of Haig's dual policy. It was soon seen to be bearing fruit. 'There is a large body of Congressmen,' he noted on 18 March, 'thoroughly alarmed at the possibility of being left out of the new constitution, and anxious to take part in the elections and strive for power, though continuing to denounce the actual provisions of the constitution.'[10] A few weeks later, he met Jamnadas Dwarkadas at Bombay railway station, the first meeting between a Congressman and a government official for 18 months.

Dwarkadas was seeking a way of calling off civil disobedience without losing face. He said he believed the vast majority of Congressmen wanted to end it in their own interests, 'but the young men would feel this was a humiliation and a disgrace'. He went on to confirm Haig's belief that 'the majority of Congress would gladly come into the new constitution and work it, though they might profess to begin with a desire to wreck it'. Would the government release the remaining prisoners if civil disobedience was called off?, he asked. Haig was adamantine: there was to be no deal, no movement, no concessions. All he would say was that he would welcome Congress co-operation in working the new constitution.[11]

Gandhi, according to government reports, was 'becoming impatient at his continuing eclipse in the political world'. What would he do to regain attention? The answer came at the beginning of May: his voices had spoken again, and they had told him he must undertake another fast, lasting 21 days. It was to have nothing to do with civil disobedience, he announced, but would be for 'self-purification', directed solely against the existence of untouchability. Once again, however, Haig outmanœuvred him. On the day Gandhi began his fast, he was released from prison 'on grounds of humanity connected with a definitely non-political development'.

Wrong-footed and confused, Gandhi insisted on continuing his fast in a mansion in Poona, where he announced that he was suspending civil disobedience for six weeks, but would start it again if the government failed to release the remaining political prisoners. The government publicly reminded him that his release had nothing to do with the civil disobedience campaign, and that its policy was unchanged. He completed his fast without incident, extended the suspension of civil disobedience for another six weeks, then high-handedly announced that, as a mass movement, civil disobedience was at an end. Only days before he had persuaded a gathering of 150 Congressmen in Poona – regarded as an 'informal meeting' and therefore allowed by the government – to vote for it to continue, much against their will. Now, in another piece of pedantic hair-splitting, he declared that this was not a surrender: mass civil disobedience was ending, but individual civil disobedience would go on.

The confusion was compounded when Gandhi first decided to send members of his Sabarmati Ashram to conduct a series of individual fasts unto death in various parts of India, then decided instead to lead another Dandi-like march. He was arrested again after making a defiant statement, sent back to Poona, released on a restriction order which he promptly disobeyed, arrested again and returned to his old cell, for another year's imprisonment. This time, however, when he demanded all his old privileges to work against untouchability, he was refused. The end game was approaching, and Haig and the government were showing no mercy.

In desperation, Gandhi started another fast as a protest. After five days, he was in a serious condition. Determined that he should not die in a British gaol, the government released him and suspended his sentence unconditionally. Somewhat forlornly, he tried to gain what little moral advantage was left by announcing that he would not offer civil disobedience again until the 12 months of his latest sentence had expired.

Congress was still in serious disarray. Many members were furious with Gandhi for what they saw as his abject surrender. The left wing, led by Subhas Bose, called for his suspension, insisting that he had failed as a political leader and that Congress needed 'radical reorganization'. Other left-wingers formed a Congress Socialist Party, with a strongly Marxist line, within Congress. A group of orthodox Hindus, led by Malaviya, broke away, calling themselves Congress Nationalists, repudiating MacDonald's Communal Award in its entirety. Another group, headed by Ansari, Asaf Ali, Satyamurti and Bhulabhai Desai, started creating a new Swarajist Party to contest the forthcoming elections, reopening the old divide over council entry. Never was it more clear that Congress was not a party but a movement, an umbrella sheltering several distinct parties which in other times, other circumstances, would have been enemies rather than allies.

Nehru had been released from prison slightly early in August, in order to visit his mother, who was seriously ill. As bewildered and exasperated as everybody else by Gandhi's actions, he called a meeting in Allahabad of 80 of his left-wing supporters, who resolved to continue the struggle and to work for a socialist transformation of Indian society. He did everything he could to block the efforts of other Congressmen to have civil disobedience officially abandoned, but was then removed from the scene again when he was arrested for making fiery speeches in Bengal. In February 1934 he received his seventh prison sentence, two years' imprisonment to be served in the steamy, oppressive surroundings of Alipore gaol, near Calcutta, where conditions were far more rigorous than in Naini, his usual prison in the UP.

Gandhi, depressed and defeated, considered leaving Congress and politics altogether, something which many of his critics in the movement would have welcomed. Instead, he filled the time during which he had forsworn political action with a '*Harijan* tour' of most parts of the country.

From early November till the end of July 1934, he covered over 13,000 miles, campaigning, teaching, preaching the removal of untouchability in all its forms and practices, and collecting money for the cause. His Congress critics, led by Subhas Bose, decried his tour as a diversion from nationalist issues. His Hindu critics were more vociferous: they met him with black flags and inflammatory leaflets; they disrupted his meetings and burnt portraits of him; in Poona, they even tried to kill him, throwing a bomb at a car they believed he was travelling in, injuring its seven passengers. Many of the untouchables themselves, and especially their leader, Dr Ambedkar, distrusted him. Ambedkar disagreed violently with Gandhi's defence of the caste system, believing that only the destruction of caste itself could bring about the emancipation of the untouchables.

Gandhi, being Gandhi, was not deterred. He pressed on regardless, breaking off only to announce at the beginning of April that from then on everyone but himself should abandon even individual civil disobedience. He was persuaded, largely by the right-wing Tamil Congress leader Rajagopalachari, who had previously been a staunch no-changer, to agree to Congressmen standing in the elections to the Central Legislative Assembly at the end of the year. In May, a full meeting of the AICC, readily approved by the government, confirmed Gandhi's decision and decided that the Swarajists should stand as official Congress candidates. 'Gandhi,' Willingdon crowed to Hoare, 'has in effect capitulated ... At present our policy has triumphed.'[12]

The feeling of triumph must have seemed even greater in October 1934, when Gandhi resigned from Congress because of his disagreement with both the socialists and the right-wingers. 'For me to dominate the Congress in spite of these fundamental differences is almost a species of violence which I must refrain from,' he wrote. But any gloating by the British was short-lived. In yet another example of his baffling logic, he declared that his resignation from Congress was 'only to serve it better in thought, word and deed'.[13] And no matter what he said, even though he was no longer a member, he would always dominate it.

Haig's dual policy seemed to have paid off on both fronts. The civil disobedience movement appeared to be finished, and Congress was returning to the constitutional path to self-government. On 6 June 1935, the government issued an official communiqué announcing the withdrawal of all proscriptions against Congress activities. But the government's victory proved to be pyrrhic. In the past,

Congress had often struggled to win seats, but when the elections were held – still under the provisions of the old 1919 Act – Congress emerged with 44 seats, and Malaviya's Congress Nationalists with 11. The government and its supporters – Europeans, officials and nominated members – also mustered a total of 55. The balance was held by the 22 independents, all but three of whom were Muslims. The Muslim League as such did not put up any candidates.

Now it was Congress's turn to crow over what G. D. Pant called 'This national triumph'.[14] 'These brilliant Congress victories fill me with delight,' Gandhi wired to the Madras Congress leader S. Satyamurti.[15] Willingdon's immediate response was less sanguine: 'Singularly unfortunate,' he cabled to Hoare, 'A great triumph for little Gandhi.'[16] He complained bitterly that his own old province of Madras, which had 'gone over body and soul to Congress' had 'let us down very badly indeed'. But within a month, he was putting a brave face on it: 'Altogether I am really much more hopeful than I have been for some time, and I am beginning to believe more and more that it is a good thing we have got so many Congress people into the Assembly.'[17]

The surprise leader of the Muslim independents in the new Central Assembly was Jinnah. Since beginning his voluntary exile, he had built up a successful legal practice in London which was earning him at least £2,000 a month, a vast income at that time, plus considerable respect – though not enough to gain the place he coveted on the Privy Council's judicial committee. He missed the fire and brimstone of active politics, but for nearly four years he rejected the many pleas he received from his former colleagues in the Muslim League to return and preside over it again. 'There is no room for my services in India,' he wrote, adding, 'there is no chance of doing anything to save India till the Hindus realise the true position.'[18] He was sorely tempted when he was told that Sir Ibrahim Rahimtoola, who now represented his old constituency in the Central Assembly, was planning to retire, and the seat was his for the asking. But it took a beautiful young woman to change his mind. She was the newly married wife of the 37-year-old Nawabzada Liaquat Ali Khan, an Oxford-educated minor nobleman from the UP, who had been one of Jinnah's most fervent supporters in the League for several years.

Liaquat and his begum were on their honeymoon when they called on Jinnah in Hampstead during the summer of 1933. The dazzling young woman reminded him irresistibly of Ruttie as she had been at the time of his own marriage, glowing with youthful vitality and appealing to him with the same idealistic enthusiasm. Always vulnerable to flattery, his defences were breached by her adoring hero-worship. When Liaquat begged: 'You must come back. The people need you. You alone can put new life into the League,' he listened. Liaquat continued to press him, returning to Hampstead for long discussions while walking together across the heath. Others added their voices, and gradually Jinnah began to be persuaded.

When Jinnah returned to Bombay for a four-month business trip at the beginning of 1934, the pressure on him to stay was immense. The League was still hopelessly split into two main groups, who would have nothing to do with each other. But their two leaders were both prepared to stand down and bring their factions together if Jinnah would become president again. Liaquat and the others who had pleaded with him in London were right: Jinnah was the only man who could reunite the tattered remnants of the League. Indeed, a sudden rash of deaths among the older generation of Muslim leaders meant he was virtually the only one left. Finally, he agreed. But he had time for only one meeting of the League's council before he had to sail back to London at the end of April.

Jinnah was still in London when he was elected unopposed for his old Bombay Muslim seat. He returned to India in December to take up his position as leader of the independents in the assembly. His first statement on resuming the League presidency back in March had been an appeal to Congress to accept MacDonald's Communal Award and join forces with the Muslims to fight the rest of the White Paper. 'Can we even at this eleventh hour bury the hatchet, and forget the past in the presence of imminent danger?' he had asked.[19] Now, almost the first thing he did on arriving in New Delhi was to meet that year's Congress president, the Bihari lawyer Rajendra Prasad, for 'heart-to-heart' talks in an effort to resolve the communal deadlock. It was no use. Prasad might have been disposed to listen, but Malaviya and his Congress Nationalists refused even to consider Jinnah's case for Muslim safeguards, and the talks ended fruitlessly. Another opportunity – perhaps the last – to heal the wounds and make a fresh start had been lost.

Nevertheless, when Jinnah led the attack on the White Paper in the first major debate of the new assembly, the Congress members did not oppose the first part of his motion accepting the Communal Awards 'until a substitute is agreed upon between the communities concerned', but merely abstained; only the Congress Nationalists and three others voted against. For the rest of Jinnah's motion, rejecting almost everything else in the White Paper, Congress members were solidly behind him, inflicting a major defeat on the government. It was, as Jinnah accepted, only a 'paper victory' which the British government could and probably would ignore. But it showed he was back on the Indian political scene with a vengeance.

On 2 August 1935, eight years after the appointment of the Simon Commission, the British Parliament passed the new Government of India Act, which turned out to be the longest piece of legislation in its history. For the Indians, it was a grave disappointment, though hardly a surprise. Jinnah had been right – all their representations both in and out of the Delhi assembly, had been ignored. There was no suggestion of the country's ever achieving dominion status, self-rule or independence; at most there would be some degree of self-government at the provincial level.

In essence, the Act was a series of compromises. It sought to achieve a balance between the demands of the minorities and the majority, between British and Indian economic interests, between the Tory and Labour parties, neither of which was disposed to grant India full independence. It was vast and complex, and much of it was never to be brought into operation. It was unwanted, unloved and unworkable. Nehru described it as 'a machine with strong brakes but no engine', and a 'charter for slavery'. Jinnah dismissed it as 'thoroughly rotten, fundamentally bad, and totally unacceptable'. And yet, some of its provisions were so well drafted that they were later considered suitable for inclusion in the constitution of independent India.

There had been some 2,000 speeches, totalling 15.5 million words, in the debates on the Bill in both houses of Parliament, many of them against it for various reasons.[20] Churchill and his diehard cronies had opposed it because they felt it gave away too much to the Indians; for them, any constitutional advance, however minor, was too much. Attlee criticized the Bill because it gave away too little. The legislation, he said, was 'deliberately framed so as to exclude as far as possible the Congress Party from effective powers in the new Constitution ... Anyone reading through this Bill is struck not by what is conceded but by what is withheld.' He doubted if it would be accepted in India. He was right. Virtually all shades of opinion in India were unanimous in rejecting the Act. Only the pro-British National Liberal Federation and the Hindu Mahasabha supported it. While most Indians were in favour of federation, they all opposed it in the form that the Act sought to impose.

Lord Linlithgow, the Act's principal architect as chairman of the Joint Parliamentary Commission, made no bones about the government's intentions. 'We thought,' he wrote later, 'that was the best way ... of maintaining British influence in India. It is no part of our policy ... to expedite in India constitutional changes for their own sake, or gratuitously to hurry the handing over of controls to Indian hands at any pace faster than that which we regard as best calculated, on a long view, to hold India to the Empire.'[21]

The new Act, decried by Churchill with his usual overblown rhetoric as 'a gigantic quilt of jumbled crochet work, a monstrous monument of shame built by pigmies',[22] was designed to promote and maintain the unity of India. It proposed an all-India federation with a two-chamber assembly at the centre, including for the first time not only the provinces of British India but also the princely states. It would not include Burma, however, which was to be separated from India again – to the private relief of all those who, like Subhas Bose, had been imprisoned in

Mandalay over the years. The viceroy, as governor-general, would retain personal control over the usual sensitive areas – defence, ecclesiastical affairs, foreign affairs and the tribal areas – and would have special powers to safeguard the country's financial stability, the services, commerce, the minorities, and the maintenance of 'peace and tranquillity'.

The accession of the princely states was to be voluntary, and the federation would only come into existence when enough states had joined to fill half the number of seats allotted for them in the upper chamber. The extra weightage both they and the Muslims had been given meant that Congress could never secure more than about one third of the total number of seats, and thus could never dominate the assembly. Unfortunately for the government's plans, however, most of the princes had now gone cold on the idea. The viceroy sent out three senior officers of the political service to persuade them. They visited each prince in turn, and failed with every single one. Trained to treat the rulers, however petty, with undue deference, they simply could not bring enough pressure to bear in order to force them into compliance. So, federation never came into being, and a major chance of preserving the unity of India died with it.

The second major part of the Act, however, giving full autonomy to the 11 British provinces, went ahead as planned. Out went dyarchy, and in came elected ministers responsible to elected legislatures, controlling all provincial government departments. Governors were no longer absolute rulers, but to all intents and purposes constitutional monarchs bound by the decisions of their ministers. All the separate electorates and reserved seats were retained, but the overall franchise was vastly extended from the 7 million of 1920 to some 36 million property-owning voters, 6 million of whom were women and over 3 million untouchables, representing 30 per cent of the entire adult population of British India.

It was by any standards a major step forward. The liberal elements in Britain could claim that the experience of self-government in the provinces was a wonderful way of training and preparing Indians for the full responsibility of independence, when that day eventually came. Others, more cynically, saw it as a way of putting off that evil day. Most Indians regarded provincial self-government as a sham, since the governors retained so many special 'safeguarding' powers by which they could overrule their assemblies. In the last resort, under section 93 of the Act, if a governor was satisfied that the government of his province had broken down, he could dismiss it and rule directly.

One of the hidden agendas of provincial autonomy for the British was the hope that it would undermine Congress as a national organization by creating powerful provincial leaders – the provincial governments were to be equal to the central government, and independent of it in most respects. Never one for concealing his motives, Linlithgow wrote: 'Our best hope ... is in the potency of

Provincial Autonomy to destroy the effectiveness of Congress as an All-India instrument of revolution.'[23]

In fact, Linlithgow and his colleagues hoped that the Act would split Congress so severely between right and left that it would destroy itself as an effective political force. Once the left was isolated, it could then be crushed. Certainly Nehru, Bose, the Congress Socialists and the Communists were all violently opposed to supporting the Act in any shape or form. To Nehru, boycott was the only option. But Nehru was in prison and Bose was in Europe, having been released from his own gaol sentence to go abroad for TB treatment. Most of the Congressmen who were free were eager to grab their first real chance of power, and would resist any attempt to deprive them of it.

Surprisingly, Gandhi was in favour of accepting the Act, largely on the advice of the industrialist G.D. Birla. Birla had been active in London throughout the passage of the Bill, lobbying intensively and acting as an intermediary between Congress and the British government, and reporting everything back to Gandhi regularly. Birla summed up the predicament admirably when he wrote, after meeting the under-secretary of state, R.A. Butler: 'To me, it was already evident that the English in London sincerely believed that a great step forward towards India's self-government was about to be taken as soon as the Bill became law, whereas in India there was an equally genuine feeling that it would be a great step backwards.'[24] Birla reported that Butler was intelligent, charming, but demoralized, and had told him: 'We feel disheartened when we think that this Bill, for which we sacrificed our health, our friends and our time, is supposed to be a retrograde step.'[25]

In a 45-minute talk with Birla on 26 June, Lord Lothian, the Parliamentary under-secretary, made a powerful plea for understanding. 'I agree with the diehards that it has been a surrender,' he told him.

You who are not used to any constitution cannot realise what great power you are going to wield. If you look at the constitution it looks as if all the powers are vested in the Governor-General and the Governor. But is not every power here vested in the King? Everything is done in the name of the King but does the King ever interfere? Once the power passes into the hands of the legislature, the Governor or the Governor-General is never going to interfere. ... The Civil Service will be helpful. ... Once a policy is laid down they will carry it out loyally and faithfully.

The only real threat, he said, would be military control: 'You have got every other thing.' Apologizing for the graceless language of the Bill, he explained: 'We could not help it. We had to fight the diehards here. You could not realise what great courage has been shown by Mr Baldwin and Sir Samuel Hoare. We did not want to spare the diehards as we had to talk in a different language. Besides this, the other great difficulty was Lord Willingdon. He has great distrust of the Mahatma and he is not a very brainy man.'

On 4 September 1935, Nehru was released from prison, five and a half months before the end of his sentence, to fly to his sick wife's side at a clinic in Badenweiler, in the German Black Forest. He had been moved from prison in Bengal to Naini the previous July, to be near her, and had been released for three weeks in August, as her condition deteriorated. When Kamala was taken to a sanatorium in the hills at Bhowali, he had been moved to the tiny district gaol at Almora, near by, and was allowed to visit her once or twice a month – though Hoare, in London, had decreed two or three visits a week. Now, however, her condition was hopeless. Nehru was with her when she died on 28 February 1936. It was a tragic end to a love that had grown stronger over the years. Separated so often and for so long by politics and prison, they had only grown really close during the last few years, when Kamala herself had become active in the independence movement. Nehru had her body cremated in Switzerland, and carried her ashes back to India when he returned. For the rest of his life, he kept part of those ashes always with him, even in gaol, to be mingled with his own when he died.

During Kamala's last illness, Nehru had, largely at her insistence, visited London to arrange for publication of the autobiography which he had written in prison. He was also able to settle Indira into an English school at Badminton, near Bristol, where she was to prepare for entrance to Somerville College, Oxford – like so many politicians, before and since, Nehru did not allow his beliefs to interfere with his daughter's education. While in England, he had resisted pressure to spend a weekend with Lord Lothian, the under-secretary of state for India, and Lord Halifax, the former Lord Irwin, knowing that they wanted to try to persuade him to accept the new Act. But he had found time to meet a number of influential friends, most of them fellow socialists. What he saw of the rise of fascism and Nazism in Europe had reinforced his own commitment to socialism.

Shortly before Kamala died, Nehru had received word from India that Gandhi had chosen him to succeed Rajendra Prasad as Congress president in 1936. Although supposedly devoting himself to the untouchables, the old fox had moved with all his customary adroitness to neutralize the threat to Congress unity by putting the leading rebel on the throne. It was now Nehru's responsibility to hold Congress together, rather than split it apart. Gandhi's ploy worked, but only just. Very soon, there was serious in-fighting among the members of the Working Committee, many of whom had been forced on Nehru by Gandhi, who refused to let Nehru pack it with his own supporters. Nehru's socialist beliefs offended the Moderates and right-wingers – among other things, he called for an end to all private property, 'except in a restricted sense' – and a group of them, including such notables as Patel, Rajagopalachari, Prasad, Kripalani and S.D. Dev, actually resigned from the committee. Nehru's response was to write a long letter to Gandhi, complaining bitterly of their lack of loyalty, accusing them of regarding him as 'an intolerable nuisance', and threatening to resign himself.[25]

Gandhi stepped in and knocked the two sides' heads together. He called the right-wingers to his *ashram* at Wardha, lectured them severely, and persuaded them to stay. He then laid down the law to Nehru: 'I am firmly of opinion that during the remainder of the year, all wrangling should cease and no resignations should take place ... If they are guilty of intolerance, you have more than your share of it. The country should not be made to suffer for your mutual intolerance.'[27] Gandhi had little time for Nehru's brand of socialism, which he purported not to understand. 'How I wish you would put your foot down on "insane" programmes,' he scolded him, 'and save your energy for the common good.'[28]

Socialism apart, the biggest bone of contention threatening to split Congress was whether or not to fight the elections to the new provincial legislatures, and whether Congressmen should accept office as ministers. All the old arguments of boycott and non-co-operation were revived, with Nehru leading the fight for a total boycott. He demanded instead a constituent assembly in which Indians would draw up their own constitution. His bemused opponents asked 'Where is this assembly, Jawaharlal?' and threw out his resolutions. When the wrangling became intolerable, Gandhi produced a compromise formula: Congress would contest the elections, but the decision over whether they would accept office or pursue the old policy of wrecking the assemblies from within was to be decided after the elections. With much grumbling, the Congressmen agreed, and prepared to launch a massive campaign for 1937. To avoid disruption, and possibly to make sure Nehru could not change his mind, Gandhi proposed that he should continue as president for another year.

'The Empty Fruits of Office'

While the Congressmen argued among themselves over the 1935 India Act, there had been important changes in Britain. On 7 June 1935, Ramsay MacDonald's failing health had forced him to resign as prime minister, and Baldwin moved back into Downing Street. In October, Attlee became leader of the Labour Party. And on 16 November Baldwin called a snap general election, which swept the Tories back into undisputed power. The days of the National Coalition Government were over. On 21 January 1936, the political climate in London was unsettled again when King George V died, coincidentally only two days after the death of the Poet Laureate of the Raj, Rudyard Kipling.

One of Baldwin's first changes was to move Sam Hoare from the India Office to the Foreign Office. As it happened, he did not last long there, being replaced by Anthony Eden on 18 December after making a pact with French premier Laval to appease Mussolini over his aggression in Abyssinia. Hoare was replaced as secretary of state for India by the second Marquess of Zetland, a sporting peer who was a steward of the Jockey Club.

Zetland was a tall, slim, bespectacled figure, wearing one of those peculiarly Edwardian moustaches that were once thought to inspire confidence in bank managers. He was born in Yorkshire 58 years earlier, though the family originally hailed from Scotland and still retained estates there. Educated at Harrow and Trinity College, Cambridge, he had a less than glorious academic career – he had left Cambridge without a degree – but he had at least been master of the university drag hounds. He knew India well, having started his career on the personal staff of Lord Curzon, returning later as governor of Bengal. In spite of this background, he was becoming steadily more liberal towards India as he grew older. Unfortunately, however, he was a political lightweight carrying little influence in Cabinet – his under-secretary of state, R.A. Butler, whose family had long connections with India, looked on him as something of a figure of fun.

There was also a new viceroy. Lord Linlithgow was sent out to New Delhi in April 1936 to supervise the implementation of the India Act for which he had been mainly responsible. Linlithgow, then aged 48, was a Scot, the son of the first governor-general of Australia. Born with the courtesy title Lord Hope and always known to his intimates as 'Hopie', he was a former deputy chairman of the Conservative Party, an elder of the Church of Scotland, and a devotee of English music-hall. He had a great theoretical knowledge of India: before chairing the joint Parliamentary select committee on the Act, he had been chairman of a royal commission on agriculture in India. But he once admitted to his private secretary that he had never set eyes on an Indian rupee.[1]

Linlithgow had a reputation for coldness and pomposity. The accusation of pomposity was unjust: it was an impression given by his height of six feet five inches, and by his being literally stiff-necked, thanks to a bout of childhood polio. His handsome wife, Doreen, daughter of an ancient baronetcy, was herself almost six feet tall, so together they made a imposing couple. But they were not above breaking into song, often joining in the chorus of *The Roast Beef of Old England* as the band played them into dinner.[2]

Linlithgow's reputation for coldness appears to have been more deserved. Although he was an affectionate father of five, he seems to have been unable to demonstrate much warmth and humanity away from the family circle. He might have appeared in a more favourable light had he been a good public speaker, but he was not. And, most seriously, he lacked ease of manner in even the simplest human relationships, particularly with Indians. Willingdon, whatever his failings as an administrator, had made personal friendships with many Indian princes who shared his Eton and Cambridge background, though he had little sympathy for the Congress leaders, many of whom were from lower castes, like the Modh Bania Gandhi. But 'Hopie,' according to Lord Halifax, 'did not get on terms with anyone'.[3]

Not surprisingly, Linlithgow's relations with men like Gandhi, Nehru and Patel were distant and unsatisfactory. Nehru described him as 'heavy of body and slow of mind, solid as a rock and with a rock's lack of awareness'.[4] G.D. Birla, who had had long and generally amicable discussions with him in London, damned him with faint praise as 'not brilliant but capable and sound'. He was, Birla said, without imagination but was well-intentioned. Linlithgow, however, at least had the sense to recognize the importance of Gandhi as a political force. 'The more I see of him,' he wrote, 'the more I am convinced that he is the only man in [Congress] who can deliver the goods.'

Gandhi was not interested at that time in delivering anything. Above all, he was not interested in the viceroy's new constitution, once it became clear to him that the British had no intention of relinquishing power in the foreseeabe future. He would not actively oppose the new constitution, since it undoubtedly offered some benefits, nor would he oppose the idea of Congress taking an active part in the elections to the new provincial assemblies that were due to take place in 1937. But he remained convinced that independence could only be achieved through *satyagraha*.

While other Congressmen mounted a mammoth election campaign – in 130 days Nehru covered over 50,000 miles, some for the first time by air, making speeches to more than 10 million people – Gandhi did not make a single speech. He spent his time tramping from village to village, preaching the need for peasants to take part in what he called his Constructive Programme. This phase of the programme stemmed from the decision of the Bombay session of Congress in 1934 to authorize the formation of the All-Indian Village Industries, a project close to Gandhi's heart. It combined his two great passions, arousing the masses through social education and attacking the roots of untouchability. He was convinced that any reform of untouchability was dependent on overcoming the grinding poverty of the villages: because of the decay of village industries, untouchables were slipping ever deeper into hopeless misery.

Gandhi's programme was in essence a form of do-it-yourself rural socialism, owing more to William Morris and Leo Tolstoy than to Marx and Lenin. His message to the peasants was that salvation lay in their own hands: only by their own efforts could they achieve the goal of a decent life for themselves and their families. They must educate their children. They must clean up their filthy streets and backyards, which meant they must stop defecating there and build proper latrines. As with an earlier reformer, Florence Nightingale, latrines were at the very centre of Gandhi's thinking; he had long been fascinated by their construction and design. But latrines held a deeper significance for him than simply hygiene, vital though that was. If human excrement could be dealt with sanitarily, then there would be no need for untouchables to dispose of it. Remove the need for untouchables, and untouchability itself would wither.

Gandhi's attempt to change village India was, as he put it, 'a plodder's work', slow and laborious. Many of his political colleagues regarded the whole project as a waste of time and energy, inappropriate in the modern world. They suspected that he wanted to turn the clock back to some fantasy Vedic India. To some extent this was true, but there was also a hard core of political common sense in his campaign. Eighty-five per cent of all Indians lived in villages, and rural poverty had been increasing since the end of the world war. Gandhi and his disciples offered peasants simple, practical ways in which they could help themselves. Weaving, mat-making, woodcarving, and so on, however primitive and inexpert the results, helped to rouse villagers from the terrible lethargy of destitution. Until they were awakened, they could never join Gandhi's *satyagraha* shock troops. 'Swaraj,' he told the impatient left-wingers of Congress, 'can only come through an all-round consciousness of the masses.'[5]

Gandhi drove home his message to Congressmen by staging Congress's golden jubilee session, in December 1936, not in a great city but in the Maharashtra village of Faizpur. The 100,000 delegates were housed in a 'bamboo city' designed by the famous painter Nandalal Bose to Gandhi's own specification: 'This Congress will be for villagers and not for townsfolk,' he decreed. 'Its setting should be made by village artisans out of materials commonly available in the village.' Even the traditional entrance of the president on a magnificent horse was countrified: Nehru arrived instead on a 'beautifully designed and decorated chariot drawn by six pairs of bullocks'.[6]

There were none of the amenities to which city-dwelling Congressmen were accustomed. They were given peasant food to eat: unpolished rice, bread made from hand-ground flour. And to complete the culture shock which Gandhi imposed on them, they had to do their own sweeping, scavenging and washing – he took particular pleasure in putting the Brahmans in charge of sanitation. 'We want this contact with villagers to grow,' he lectured them in his closing speech. 'Your Constituent Assembly can meet anywhere you like, but the real Constituent Assembly will be in the villages like Faizpur.'[7]

While the powerful Congress machinery drove the election campaign as smoothly as was possible in India, the Muslims were struggling to mount any sort of co-ordinated effort. Although Jinnah had managed to reunite the two main shards of the shattered League, other groups which had broken away remained obstinately apart. And the League still represented only a pitifully small proportion of India's Muslims: there was a great deal of truth in the charge that what remained of the League represented mainly landlords, aristocrats and lawyers – a middle-class pressure group rather than a broadly based national party.

There are no reliable figures available for 1936–7, but we do know that during the years 1931–3, the League's annual expenditure was less than 3,000 rupees, and that in 1927, membership had fallen to a mere 1,330.[8] The famous 1930 session in Allahabad when Iqbal called for a separate Muslim state, could not even raise its quorum of 75 members – another poet, Hafiz Jalandhari, entertained those who had turned up with a reading of his work while the organizers scoured the city enrolling new members to make up the numbers.[9]

One of the main problems was separate electorates: because Muslims were already guaranteed a proportion of seats in every assembly, they felt no need to form strong, disciplined political entities. By 1936, they had already won their political battle – the British had handed it to them on a plate with MacDonald's Communal Award. On the whole, this made them unadventurous, intellectually lazy, and given to bickering among themselves. The arrival of provincial autonomy worked against the all-India League in exactly the way the British had hoped it would destroy Congress as a national party: each province had its own party or more often parties, each with its own leaders, representing local Muslims and their local concerns and interests.

This was the situation facing Jinnah when he was once again elected permanent president in April 1936, at the League's first meeting for two and a half years. It was not a promising position with barely nine months to go before the provincial elections. Despite an almost total absence of any organization, however, he decided the League should contest the elections. Banging the nationalist drum again, he called on all his followers to 'stand shoulder to shoulder' with Congress and other Hindu-majority parties. He invited those parties to join with the League in finding 'such minimum measure of agreement as would enable us to act together ... to draft a Constitution for India'. 'Constitutional agitation', he declared, was the only sound way to force the British to grant their demands, since 'armed revolution was an impossibility, while non-co-operation had been tried and found a failure'.[10]

Jinnah was given the authority to set up a Central Parliamentary Board to run the election campaign, with affiliated boards in all the provinces, but time was against him. Choosing members from all over India was not too difficult – there were, after all, few suitable candidates. But persuading them to work together was a different matter, particularly when he insisted on forming a common platform with Congress, and therefore the Hindus. It was not until the first week of June that he was able to assemble 54 prominent Muslim politicians to begin planning the campaign. In the mean time, the Calcutta industrialist Mirza Abol Hassain Ispahani – the Muslims' equivalent of the Hindu G.D. Birla – was given the task of reorganizing the League's finances and raising half a million rupees to cover election costs and setting up a country-wide secretariat.

The men Jinnah gathered on to his Parliamentary Board were a varied bunch. They ranged from the ultra-conservative Muhammad Iqbal to the radical Bengali Hussain Shaheed Surhawardy; from the young Raja of Mahmudabad, the biggest Muslim landlord in Lucknow with an annual income from property of some 2 million rupees, to the leader of the peasants' and tenants' party in Bengal, Fazlul Haq, who wanted to abolish landlords without compensation. Somehow, Jinnah managed to bind them all together, for a while at least. Fazlul Haq, for example, quarrelled with rival leaders in Bengal, and even the normally faithful Liaquat stormed off to England in the middle of the campaign after Jinnah had overruled him and formed an alliance with other Muslim parties in the UP, Liaquat's own province.

There were great differences of opinion in Congress, too. It was, as has been said, not so much a party as a movement, a collection of people often holding totally opposed political, racial and religious views. Fascists sat with socialists and anarchists, communists with capitalists; members of the Arya Samaj who demanded a return to the purity of Vedic Hinduism sat alongside thousands of Muslims like the future Congress president Maulana Azad, who did not feel at home in any of the Muslim parties. Christians, Hindus and Sikhs, Parsis, pagans, Buddhists and Jains — the whole fantastic *mise-en-scène* of India was reflected in Congress. They were united — in so far as that was possible — by their desire for independence. Members of the Muslim League, on the other hand, had only their religion in common. And when that religion itself was not under threat, it served more to divide than unite them. Even with the charismatic Jinnah as a figurehead, it would take a major shock to galvanize them into concerted action. As it happened, that was precisely what they were about to get.

The provincial elections in January and February 1937 proved to be a triumph for Congress. It contested 1,161 out of a total of 1,771 seats — 1,585 in the provincial assemblies and 186 in the upper houses of the six provinces with a bicameral system. It won 716 seats, 494 of them in just five of the 11 provinces, where it achieved clear majorities. In three others it became the largest single party. In Bombay, though it polled 65 per cent of the vote, it missed an overall majority by only two seats, winning 86 out of 175, but could still form a government with Dr Ambedkar's Independent Labour Party, which had won 13 of the 15 seats reserved for untouchables. It was in a minority only in Bengal, the Punjab, Sind and Assam, where it was still the largest single party with 35 of the total 94 seats. All told, Congress was said to have polled about 15 million out of a total of 35 million votes cast.[11]

The Congress leaders were understandably cock-a-hoop. Immediately after the elections, Nehru wrote jubilantly to his friend Sir Stafford Cripps, former solicitor-general in the first Labour government, and co-founder of both the Socialist League and the new weekly journal the *Tribune*, describing how they had won against all the odds: 'We had all the government apparatus and all other vested interests against us and all means, fair and otherwise, were employed to defeat us.' Nehru was referring to apparent British efforts to influence the elections. In the UP, for instance, he believed they had supported the Nawab of Chhatari's National Agriculturist Party.

The Nawab, a large, jovial figure sporting a magnificent handlebar moustache, had been governor of the UP from 1933 until 1937, a symbol of the increasing Indianization of government. No doubt the British entertained hopes that the combination of the Nawab's faithful peasantry and fear of Nehru's socialism would drive orthodox Hindus to the right. But if they had been trying to influence the elections they failed miserably: the NAP managed to win only 13 seats in Agra and 12 in Awadh. Other landlord-dominated parties, such as the Justice Party in Madras, fared no better. Nor did most of the communal parties: the Hindu Mahasabha won only seven seats in the whole of India — two in Bengal, one in the Central Provinces, and four in Sind — while the Congress Nationalists succeeded in winning just two, one each in the Punjab and Bombay.

The real loser in the elections was the Muslim League. It won only 108 of the 485 seats reserved for Muslims, with only 4.4 per cent of the total Muslim vote, a devastating result for a party claiming to represent the whole of Muslim India.[12] Interestingly, it was in Hindu majority provinces that the League did best — in Bombay, for instance, it won 20 of the 29 Muslim seats, while in the UP the League and its allies captured 29 of the 35 seats they contested. Every Congress Muslim but one failed miserably, and even he was elected only with League support. But in the Muslim majority provinces, it was a dismal picture for Jinnah and his men. In the Punjab only two out of seven League candidates for the 84 Muslim seats succeeded, in Bengal 38 out of 117, and in Sind a mere three out of 33.

The seats where the League failed were not lost to Congress, apart from in the NWFP, where Abdul Gaffar Khan lived up to his name as the Frontier Gandhi by delivering his 15 seats *en bloc*, but to local parties and politicians. In Sind, a new province with only an embryo political organization, there was barely a Muslim party at all: most of the seats were filled by feudal landlords, a tradition which still survives. Assam, too, was highly personalized and confused, with independents and three other parties fighting the League for the Muslim seats.

In the Punjab and Bengal, the victorious parties fought on economic policy rather than Muslim communalism. The Unionist Party led by Sir Sikander Hayat Khan in the Punjab was only marginally defined by religion, representing local farming interests, which included Hindus and Sikhs. In Bengal, Jinnah made valiant efforts to unite Fazlul Haq's Krishak Proja Party with the Nawab of Dacca's United Muslim Party under the League's banner, but it was hopeless from the start. The Nawab's party represented big landlords, lawyers and businessmen, while the radical and populist KPP represented their tenants, poor peasants and small landholders. Haq finally broke with the League over Jinnah's refusal to include in its election manifesto a commitment to abolish the Permanent Settlement system of land ownership in Bengal — a policy more suited to Nehru and Congress than the League.

The Congress landslide resurrected an old, familiar problem for the movement: it was now in a position to form the governments in seven of British India's 11 provinces, but should it do so? Nehru and his comrades were still against taking office, which they regarded as a dishonourable compromise with the Raj. They had agreed to take part in the elections only to enter the assemblies and wreck the new constitution from within. They were not alone in this resolution — Cripps wrote congratulating Nehru on the Congress victories, but hoping he would not 'partake of the empty fruits of office which can do nothing but poison the pure and free spirit of the Congress'. A few days later, Cripps told a crowded meeting in London: 'I want the Congress Party to succeed in wrecking the constitution because I want Congress to demonstrate that British imperialism has created new designs for the exploitation of the working class in India and Britain alike.' He hoped Nehru would persuade Congress not to accept office, because there was 'no greater danger then getting entangled in the imperialist machinery of government'.[13]

At its first meeting after the elections, at Gandhi's Wardha *ashram*, Nehru persuaded the Working Committee to confirm his view with a clear resolution:

> The Congress has entered the legislatures not to co-operate with the new Constitution or the government but to combat the Act and the policy underlying it, as this Act and policy are intended to tighten the hold of British imperialism in India and to continue the exploitation of the Indian people. The immediate objective is to resist the introduction and working of the federal part of the Act, and to lay stress on the nation's demand for a Constituent Assembly.

Nehru's satisfaction was short-lived. The Maharashtra Provincial Congress Committee met in Poona on 8 March and decided against taking office, but that same day their newly-elected assembly members held their own meeting and resolved to accept. They also passed a resolution nominating K.F. Nariman, the Bombay city Congress leader, as premier. In other provinces, too, elected members clamoured for office, in some cases simply for the sake of holding power, but also because they were eager to start putting promised social and agrarian reforms into practice.

As the prospect of fatal divisions loomed, Gandhi stepped in to save the day. Under pressure from Patel and Rajagopalachari, he drafted a new resolution, which was passed by a substantial majority of the full AICC on 18 March. It was a typical piece of Gandhian double-think: after confirming Congress opposition to the constitution and demanding its withdrawal, it ended by 'authorizing and permitting' the acceptance of office, 'in pursuance of this policy'. In other words, Congress was committed to wrecking the constitution at the same time as working with it.

As with so many of Gandhi's resolutions, the sting came in the tail. Ministries would not be accepted 'unless the leader of the Congress Party in the legislature is satisfied and is able to state publicly that the Governor will not use his special powers of interference or set aside the advice of ministers.'[14] This was a sop for Nehru, but it did little to ease his wounded feelings. As a democrat he was bound to accept the AICC's decision, but he took it badly. He returned to his house in Delhi, 'threw himself on a bed and, on the point of tears, talked of resignation after the way Gandhiji had sabotaged his resolution'.[15]

A three-man Parliamentary Committee consisting of Patel, Azad and Rajendra Prasad was appointed to control the selection of ministers in the Congress provinces. But first, they demanded assurances from the governors that they would never use the powers of intervention given to them in the constitution. The governors quite rightly replied that that was impossible, as it would have been contrary to their statutory duties, particularly where the protection of the interests of minorities was concerned. The provincial Congress leaders refused to accept office, leaving the governors with only two options: to impose direct governor's rule under section 93 of the Act, or to appoint caretaker governments from the minority parties. Obviously, the use of section 93 would have given Congress a great propaganda weapon, so the minority parties were invited to form governments.

The stalemate continued for nearly three months, despite efforts from both sides to find a compromise. Lord Lothian came closest, with letters to *The Times* and to Nehru as early as 9 April, proposing the typically English solution of suck-it-and-see. 'You do not want to be bound by undertakings nor does the Governor,' he wrote to Nehru.

> 'Why don't you adopt the traditional course of taking office, passing your legislation and challenging the Governor to interfere? If he does not interfere, you will have assumed full responsibility, and within a very few weeks or months, the parliamentary system will be in full operation in the provinces, and with every month that starts, interference, unless the ministry plays the fool, will become more difficult. If he does interfere, you will have a far better wicket to bat upon from your own point of view than you have today.'[16]

Lothian's advice was good, pragmatic medicine, but taking it was more difficult for the Indians than the British. Finally, it was Linlithgow who broke the deadlock on 22 June 1937 with a surprisingly brave statement, which had brought him to the verge of resignation when the government in London got cold feet. In essence, it made it clear that governors were not entitled to intervene at random, but only within the narrowest possible limits, and that they were bound to do everything in their power to avoid or resolve conflicts. He concluded with a personal pledge: 'I am convinced that the shortest road to that fuller political life which many of you so greatly desire is to accept this Constitution and to work it for all it is worth ... You may count on me, in face of bitter disappointment, to strive untiringly towards the full and final establishment in India of the principles of parliamentary government.'[17]

Guided by Gandhi, the Working Committee decided that the viceroy's assurances satisfied their demands. They gave the go-ahead for Congress governments to be formed in Madras, Bombay, the Central Provinces, Bihar, Orissa and the UP. The NWFP followed soon afterwards; the government in Assam was replaced by a Congress-led coalition in October 1938. It was a victory for Patel and the pragmatists over Nehru and the idealogues. Unfortunately, however, it did not bring peace to the Indian political scene, but opened the door to further in-fighting within Congress, and an increasingly bitter conflict with League Muslims and other minorities.

In Bombay, the local party's choice of Nariman as premier without consulting the Parliamentary committee had infuriated Patel, who was responsible for the province along with Madras, the CP and Sind. In 1933, Nariman had led a move to abandon civil disobedience, and the following year he had let Congress down by withdrawing at the last minute from the elections to the Central Legislative Assembly. Patel did not want him now, and replaced him with B.G. Kher. Unfortunately, Nariman was a Parsi, while Kher was a Hindu, like Patel and the overwhelming majority of the local party. The aggrieved Nariman accused Patel of religious discrimination and demanded an inquiry. This was conducted by a distinguished Parsi lawyer, who found against Nariman, but the damage had been done. The accusation of Patel's Hindu communalism passed into legend, strengthened in later years by Azad in his autobiographical but often unreliable book *India Wins Freedom*.[18]

A similar situation arose in Bihar, this time involving a Muslim. There was some feeling in the province that the general-secretary of the AICC, Syed Mahmud, a dear friend of Nehru since their days together at Cambridge, should be made premier. When he was not, it was rumoured that Rajendra Prasad, who was responsible for Bihar, Orissa and Assam, had vetoed his appointment in favour of a Hindu, Sri Krishna Sinha. In fact, Mahmud was never seriously in the running for the premiership, though he was said to nurse a private hope. Prasad claimed in his autobiography that he ruled out Mahmud because 'he was not so well known in Bihar ... he had been working outside the province'.[19] But he admitted that there had been 'a feeling among Muslims, particularly among non-Congress Muslims ... that Dr Syed Mahmud was ignored only because of his being a Muslim'.

Mahmud himself made no complaint, and received some consolation by being given a seat in the provincial cabinet. But some 'distinguished complainants' went to Azad, who had overall responsibility for Muslim representation in Congress ministries. He dismissed their charges, saying that if he had been in Prasad's place he would probably have done the same. Once again, however, the damage had been done.

Whether or not there was any truth in the accusations of Hindu communalism, many Muslims were all too ready to believe them. Their sensibilities had already been aggravated by a campaign within Congress, led by Gandhi personally, to make Hindi, written in the Devnagrahi script, the official language of India. Muslims believed the Hindus intended to destroy their version of the northern Indian language, Urdu, with its Arabic script, and impose the Hindu version on them in its place. Other communities with their own languages and scripts, from Punjabi in the north to Bengali in the east and Tamil in the south, were also violently opposed to the use of Hindi and insisted on retaining English as the lingua franca. But for the Muslims the threat to Urdu had a darker significance: they regarded their language and its script as a vital part of their religious identity, and saw any attack on Urdu as an attack on Islam. They were upset, too, by other aggressive acts by Hindus. In October 1936, for instance, Hindus in Bombay had erected a temple alongside a mosque, provoking a riot that lasted for five days, bringing the entire city to a halt and leaving 60 dead and some 500 injured.

During the build-up to the elections, Jinnah and Nehru had indulged in a slanging match that had become increasingly personal. But for both of them, and most certainly for Jinnah, that was simply part of the cut and thrust of electioneering. Despite his taunts, Jinnah continued to seek co-operation, claiming that his nationalist views had not changed since he had first joined Congress 33 years before. 'We have made it clear,' he said, 'and we mean it that we are ready and willing to co-operate with any group or groups of progressive and independent character, provided that their programme and our programme are approximately the same.'

At the same time, Jinnah demanded equality for the League, vigorously asserting its independence: 'I warn my Hindu friends and the Congress to leave the Muslims alone. We are not going to be the camp followers of any party or organization.' Nehru asserted: 'There are only two forces in the country, the Congress and the government ... To vote against the Congress candidate is to vote for the continuance of British dominion ... It is the Congress alone which is capable of fighting the government.'[20] Jinnah was quick to retort: 'I refuse to line up with the Congress. There is a third party in this country and that is the Muslims. We are not going to be dictated to by anybody.'[21]

Nehru's response was crushing. He described Jinnah's views as 'medieval and out of date' and 'communalism to the nth power'. 'What does the Muslim League stand for?' he asked. 'Does it stand for the independence of India, for anti-imperialism? I believe not.' He derided the League as representing only 'the higher reaches of the upper-middle classes' and added cuttingly: 'May I suggest to Mr Jinnah that I come into greater touch with the Muslim masses than most of the members of the Muslim League? I know more about their hunger and poverty and misery than those who talk in terms of percentages and seats in the councils and places in the state service.'[22] It was a savage attack, even to the stress on the word 'Mr', a mark of British identity. Such taunts were a grave mistake – Jinnah never forgot nor forgave an insult; they served only to fire his resolve for revenge.

For the moment, however, revenge could wait. There were more practical matters to be dealt with first – including the very survival of the League after the electoral disaster. With no chance of forming a government in any province, its only hope of achieving any degree of power was by sharing with Congress. Jinnah wasted no time before flying a kite. 'The Constitution and policy of the League,' he declared in a statement given immediately the election results were known, 'do not prevent us from co-operation with others. On the contrary it is part and parcel of our basic principle that we are free and ready to co-operate with any group or party from the very inception, outside or inside the legislature, if the basic principles are determined by common consent.'[23]

A stream of similiar offers of co-operation followed, but Nehru and the Parliamentary committee remained deaf. The Congress high command, and Nehru in particular, were adamant that Congress should not share power with anyone, anywhere. Under the new constitution governors had been instructed that they must see that important minorities – which in effect meant Muslims – must be adequately represented in provincial governments. But there was nothing to say that they must come from the League, and Congress was determined to find Muslim ministers from within its own ranks.

In Bombay, the chief minister designate, B.G. Kher, asked Jinnah 'to give him two members of his Muslim League to join the Ministry'.[24] But his move, which recognized the strength of the League in Jinnah's home territory, was vetoed by Azad and Patel unless the two League ministers agreed to join Congress and accept its discipline. Jinnah was so put out by this that he even appealed to Gandhi, through Kher, to lend his weight to negotiations for a nation-wide Hindu Muslim accord. Gandhi responded: 'I wish I could do something but I am utterly helpless. My faith in unity is as bright as ever, only I see no daylight out of the impenetrable darkness and, in such distress, I cry out to God for light.'[25]

In the UP, Nehru's home province, the League had scored an even bigger success than in Bombay. The League and Congress had campaigned on very similar platforms during the election, and had even canvassed on behalf of each other's candidates. Both had seen the British-supported National Agriculturist Party as their chief opponent. The accord was cemented by the fact that several of the UP League's leading members had belonged to Congress, and remembered Hindus and Muslims working in harmony during the Khilafat campaign.

The League in the UP was jointly led by Nawab Ismail Khan and Choudry Khaliquzzaman, a product of Aligarh Muslim University and a direct descendant of the first Caliph of Islam. Khaliquzzaman, another personal friend of

Nehru, had been a Congressman for 20 years before forming his own Muslim party, the aptly named Unity Board, which he had merged with the League in 1936. One of his greatest friends was a provincial Congress leader, Rafi Ahmed Kidwai, an ebullient character who had been Motilal Nehru's private secretary until his death, when he attached himself to Jawaharlal and became one of his principal aides. Rafi, himself a Muslim, had been one of the founders, with Subhas Chandra Bose, of the Congress Socialist Party. With such closely entwined personal and political relationships, it was only natural that there should have been talk of a Congress-League understanding. But it was not to be.

There were six ministerial portfolios in the UP, under the premiership of G.B. Pant. The understanding was that two of them should go to Khaliquzzaman and Ismail Khan, in return for their support during the elections, and their refusal to help the British by accepting office during the interim period when Congress was arguing about whether or not to form governments. Unfortunately, another of the six seats would have to go to Rafi, which meant that three seats would be occupied by Muslims, even though one of them was a leading Congressman. Despite all Nehru's protestations that Congress was strictly non-communal, such a proportion was too much for Congress Hindus to swallow in a province where Muslims made up only 16 per cent of the population.

Talks to try to find a way out of the impasse dragged on until July, but there was little chance of success, particularly when Azad managed to persuade the powerful Jamiat-ul-Ulama to desert the League and join Congress, 'unconditionally'. Jinnah was livid – 'This is war to the knife,' he snapped. The Jamiat had been one of the UP League's most important constituents, and its defection reduced the pressure on Congress to do a deal. 'We came to the conclusion,' Nehru wrote, 'that we should offer stringent conditions to the UP Muslim League group and if they accepted them *in toto* then we would agree to two ministers from their group.'[26] Nehru's 'stringent conditions' amounted, in fact, to an ultimatum. As he wrote: 'This was the winding up of the Muslim League group in the UP and its absorption in the Congress. This would have a great effect not only in the UP but all over India and even outside.'[27] The conditions were delivered by Azad and Pant, neither of whom could have been surprised when Khaliquzzaman and Ismail Khan rejected them indignantly.

The resentment at the League's exclusion from the UP government and the way in which it was done left scars that were never to heal – in the eyes of many observers, this was where the seeds of partition in India were truly sown. Muslims like Khaliquzzaman who had previously been sympathetic to Congress and more than willing to work alongside it were permanently alienated. From then on, Jinnah could count on their support in building a new, powerful League to protect them against what they saw as the arrogance and insults of Congress and the threat of a Hindu Raj. And if that protection meant the creation of their own Muslim state, then so be it.

For all its general success, Congress had failed to attract Muslim voters: outside the NWFP, it had won only 11 of the 58 reserved Muslim seats which it had contested. Nehru's reaction was to mount a 'Muslim mass contact' movement, designed to attract lower-class Muslims to join Congress by stressing its economic and social aims. It was, of course, designed to eliminate the League by reinforcing Congress's claim to speak for all Indians, regardless of religion. Jinnah knew that the only way he could respond to this challenge was by uniting the existing Muslim parties into one League which could then set out to capture the masses for itself, and the only way to achieve that was by playing the communal card for all it was worth.

In the process, Jinnah would have to become a good Muslim, something which was alien to his essentially secular mind. At that year's League session, which opened on 15 October in Lucknow, with its memories of his triumph in uniting Hindus and Muslims back in 1916, he discarded his Savile Row suits for the *sherwani*, the long black Punjabi coat. To top it, he borrowed a black Persian lamb cap which contrasted most elegantly with his white sideburns – it was to become as much a trademark as the white cotton 'Gandhi cap' favoured by the Congress leaders.

However beneath the smart black cap worn at a jaunty angle, the face was becoming pale and drawn, and the thin frame was regularly racked by what he dismissed as 'a smoker's cough, a touch of bronchitis'. It was, in fact, something far more deadly, but he could not afford to display any sign of weakness at this critical time. Nor did he for the remaining 11 years of his life. His sister, Fatima, already his housekeeper and constant companion, became his nurse and protector.

Jinnah had spent the months before Lucknow travelling throughout India, sometimes on legal business, sometimes on political business, but always showing himself to the people and talking to local Muslim leaders, trying to persuade them to join him in the gigantic task he had set himself. At his invitation, they came to Lucknow, prepared to trade, and by the time of the opening speeches, the deals had already been done. If Congress could be a broadly based umbrella organization, then so could the League. The two most important, and most widely differing, provincial leaders – the radical Fazlul Haq, now premier of Bengal, and the reactionary Sir Sikander Hayat Khan, premier of the Punjab – both agreed to enter the League fold, bringing their parties with them. The premier of Assam, Sir Muhammad Saadullah followed suit. The alliance with Sir Sikander was to remain an uneasy one, but the Punjab was vital to any scheme of Muslim unity, and the League needed his Unionist Party in order to gain a foothold there.

The new spirit of the League was evident even before Jinnah arrived in

Lucknow. As his train from Bombay steamed into Cawnpore, its first stop in the UP, his compartment was mobbed by a vast crowd of excited Muslims. According to an eye witness, Jinnah was visibly moved, and 'spoke a few soothing words to pacify their inflamed passions. Many Muslims, overcome with emotion, wept tears of joy to see their leader who, they felt sure, would deliver them from bondage.'[28] When he arrived in Lucknow, he was greeted by 'a small army of volunteers', who drew him and his sister through the streets in an open carriage by the light of flaming torches. Populism had never been his style — he had always avoided anything that smacked of demagoguery. But now the actor-manqué was prepared to play a new role, a combination of Gandhi and Nehru for India's Muslim masses. His supporters responded enthusiastically by giving him a title to match Gandhi's Mahatma. They began speaking of him as their 'Quaid-i-Azam!', their 'Great Leader'.

Jinnah's presidential speech at Lucknow was a resounding call to arms. He denounced Congress for pursuing a policy which he described as 'exclusively Hindu' and for demanding 'unconditional surrender' as the price for co-operation. He called on Muslims to organize and equip themselves 'as trained and disciplined soldiers' to fight against the 'forces which may bully you, tyrannize over you and intimidate you'. It was only, he declared, 'by going through this crucible of the fire of persecution . . . that a nation will emerge, worthy of its past glory and history, and will live to make its future history greater and more glorious not only in India, but in the annals of the world. Eighty millions of Musulmans in India have nothing to fear. They have their destiny in their hands . . . There is a magic power in your own hands.'[29] It was all stirring stuff, and it worked. It electrified the 5,000 members present in the great tent in Lucknow, who rose to their feet as he finished to acclaim him with wild cheers.

Within three months of the Lucknow conference, the League had established over 170 new branches nation-wide. Ninety of them were in the UP, with 100,000 new members in that province alone. The explosion of League strength was marked by overwhelming successes in the first three by-elections, where Congress candidates were all but wiped out: Nehru's mass contact campaign had failed utterly. By the spring of 1938, when the League met again in Calcutta, Jinnah was able to state with full justification: 'Within less than six months we have succeeded in organizing Musulmans all over India as they never were during the last century and a half.'

The League's remarkable turn-around was achieved largely through blatantly communal appeals from the leadership. The old Khilafat campaigner, Shaukat Ali, led the way, losing no opportunity to raise the war cry 'Islam in danger!', which was always guaranteed to produce a reaction in Muslims. But the cause was helped by the blunders of Congress leaders, particularly at local and district level. While the high command continued to proclaim its high-minded non-communal ideals, the lower ranks were overwhelmingly filled with Hindus who were determined to favour their own people. Having been starved of power for so long, they had no inclination to share it with anyone, thus bearing out Adlai Stevenson's neat reversal of Lord Acton's dictum, that while all power corrupts, lack of power corrupts absolutely. As with every new government, they found it hard to resist the temptations of nepotism, the need to find the wife's useless brother a job, to repay favours received. Congressmen were only human – they rewarded friends with contracts or lucrative positions and punished their enemies by withholding them.

To those who lost out, it seemed that local Congressmen's actions were blessed by the high command, which forbade any alliances with non-Congress groups or individuals. This applied to everyone, of course, but to Muslims it appeared to be directed specifically against them.

The old charge that Congress Raj meant Hindu Raj seemed to be borne out as accusations of anti-Muslim activities in Congress provinces mounted. Muslims complained that the Congress song *Bande Mataram*, which they regarded as both idolatrous and anti-Muslim, was imposed on them as a national anthem; that their children were made to sing it in school every morning, and to salute the Congress tricolour, with Gandhi's *charka* at its centre, which was adopted as a national flag. Some said that their children were made to pay homage and sing hymns of praise to Gandhi's portrait, a doubly obnoxious practice for any Muslim. What was more, the schools themselves were reorganized on Hindu lines in some provinces, as *Vidya Mandirs*, 'temples of learning', whose very name was seen as a deliberate affront. No provision was made for separate Muslim schools, or for the teaching of Urdu. Congress governments attempted to ban the traditional right of Muslims to sacrifice cows or to eat beef, while at the same time sanctioning offensive activities such as the playing of music in front of mosques. The list went on and on – it appeared that there was no end to anti-Muslim bias and discrimination in the Congress provinces.

Some of the charges were undoubtedly justified. Equally, there can be no doubt that many of them were exaggerated, sometimes deliberately, sometimes simply as part of the growing hysteria of the time. But whatever the truth, the result was the same: the rift between the two main communities grew ever wider as distrust between them swelled and festered. Both League and Congress regularly accused each other of being fascist or Nazi.

Throughout 1938, Jinnah conducted desultory negotiations, mainly by correspondence, with Gandhi, Nehru and Subhas Bose, who succeeded Nehru as Congress president in February 1938. But they always foundered on the rock of Jinnah's insistence that Congress should recognize the League as having sole authority to represent Muslims; Congress, for its part, insisted that it alone spoke for all Indians, and that the League was simply one of a number of Muslim communal organizations. Finally, on 16 December 1938, the Congress Working Committee emphatically closed the door by declaring both the League and the Hindu Mahasabha as communal organizations and forbidding any Congress member to belong to either.

Two months earlier, the League had acknowledged that it, too, had come to the end of that particular road. The conference of the Sind Muslim League held in Karachi in October, passed a portentous resolution:

> This Conference considers it absolutely essential in the interests of an abiding peace of the vast Indian continent and in the interests of unhampered cultural development, the economic and social betterment, and political self-determination of the two nations known as Hindus and Muslims, to recommend to All-India Muslim League to review and revise the entire question of what should be the suitable constitution for India which will secure honourable and legitimate status due to them, and that this conference therefore recommends to the All-India Muslim League to devise a scheme of Constitution under which Muslims may attain full independence.[30]

For the first time, Hindus and Muslims had been officially described by the League as two separate nations. In December 1938, the All-India League gave its approval for Jinnah to start 'exploring a suitable alternative to the government of India Act, 1935, which would safeguard the interests of Muslims and other minorities'. And in March 1939, it set up a committee to examine various schemes 'for dividing the country into Muslim and Hindu India'.[31] The seeds which Iqbal and Rahmat Ali had planted in 1930 and 1933 were suddenly growing at an alarming rate.

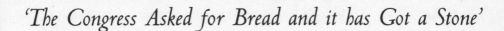

18

'The Congress Asked for Bread and it has Got a Stone'

Nehru's view of the 1937 election results and the establishment of Congress governments in the provinces was understandably emotional: 'There was a sense of immense relief as of the lifting of a weight which had been oppressing the people,' he wrote. 'There was a release of long-suppressed mass energy which was evident everywhere.'[1]

The exhilaration was real enough for most poor Indians, many of whom rushed eagerly into the 'sacred precincts' of the provincial secretariats to see for themselves what they believed they had inherited. 'They went into the Assembly Chamber, where the sessions used to be held; they even peeped into the Ministers' rooms,' Nehru recalled. 'It was difficult to stop them for they no longer felt as outsiders; they had a sense of ownership in all this, although it was all very complicated for them and difficult to understand.'[22]

To the surprise of many on both sides, Congress and the British, the new system worked. As Philip Mason, then a young deputy commissioner, put it, 'There was enough Congress idealism, there was enough British goodwill.'[3] The goodwill from officials was not all British, of course: by 1937, 540 of the 1,300 members of the ICS were Indians and within two years they would reach the promised parity. From then on, in fact, they would be in an increasing majority.[4] Congress premiers found that governors and civil servants, both British and Indian, were ready to guide and advise them in a courteous and friendly manner, and most of them soon formed harmonious working partnerships. One of the closest, and most unexpected, was between G.D. Pant and the redoubtable Sir Harry Haig, who was now governor of the UP. There were hiccups from time to time, of course, but for over two years these were generally settled quickly and amicably.

With one notable exception, the officials made no attempts to block Congress policies, though in the way of civil servants everywhere, they sometimes tried to modify them, if only to make them more workable. The exception involved the release of political prisoners and 'detenus', which was naturally the first priority of every Congress government. Most of them were freed almost immediately, but there were problems over those convicted of crimes of violence. By February 1938, there were 15 such prisoners left in the UP and 23 in Bihar, who could only be released with the consent of the governors concerned. The governors refused, on the instructions of the viceroy. The ministries promptly threatened to resign, whereupon the viceroy agreed that the governors would consider each case individually. The threats of resignation were withdrawn, and by the end of March, all the prisoners were free. Lord Lothian's 'suck-it-and-see' advice had been proved right in its first major test. In non-Congress provinces, meanwhile, political prisoners remained in detention.

The new governments quickly discovered that although their civil servants did as they were told, their own power was limited by three things: the constitution, finance, and the orders of the Congress high command at the centre. But within these limitations they pressed on as quickly as they could. They removed press censorship and bans on formerly illegal political organizations — apart from the Communist Party which was proscribed by the central government. They passed new industrial relations legislation. They introduced prohibition in selected areas. They brought in measures for the advancement of untouchables. They organized mass literacy campaigns and introduced a new scheme of compulsory basic education along Gandhian lines. And perhaps most important of all, they made a start on the huge task of agrarian and social reform. District officers found the emphasis of their work had suddenly changed. Their priorities had always been keeping public order, dispensing swift justice, assessing and collecting taxes and maintaining accurate land records. Now they had to concentrate on promoting rural development, setting up co-operative banks, and working with village committees.

Gandhi had urged the new ministries to try to govern without using the police or the army. This soon proved to be impossible, but to everyone's relief, the police accepted their new masters, and the curbs they imposed on police powers, without demur. At first, many Congressmen could not resist the opportunity of settling old scores with those who had harrassed them for so long. But even here they somehow reached a *modus vivendi*, as they realized how much they depended on the services. This was particularly true where communal troubles were concerned: in the two years from October 1937, there were no fewer than 85 serious outbreaks of rioting, resulting in some 2,000 casualties, including about 170 deaths.[5] And when trouble began, Congress ministers were as ready as anyone to use force to restore order. Indeed, as Philip Mason recalls, governors often found themselves in the anomalous position of having to restrain their ministers: "'Why don't they shoot sooner?" was the question one Governor was constantly asked by his Premier.'[6]

The Congress ministries had made an impressive start, but after the first flush of enthusiasm, the stresses and strains began to show. Many provincial leaders resented the dictatorship of the centre, which they saw as negating the principles not only of provincial autonomy but also of democracy itself: in the Central Provinces, the premier was forced to resign after disagreeing with the high command, though he still commanded support in the Assembly. Local parties operated as parallel governments alongside their elected representatives, pursuing their own projects and even giving orders to officials and district officers. Ministers did not take kindly to such interference, nor to agitation by their own supporters – Congressmen had become addicted to a diet of protest, and many of them found it impossible to kick the habit even when their own people formed the government.

Along with the factional and personal bickering, corruption grew alarmingly at local levels. The lure of jobs, power and money began to attract self-seeking chancers to the party, undermining the high moral tone struck by the Congress leadership. Nehru complained that Congress was 'developing very rapidly on Tammany Hall lines', and that 'We are sinking to the level of ordinary politicians who have no principles to stand by and whose work is governed by a day-to-day opportunism.'[7]

Almost from the beginning of the Congress ministries, the division deepened between the left and right of the Congress party. In both Bombay and Madras, the new governments instructed the CID to report on Communists and other left-wing Congressmen. As early as July and October 1937, the Madras government prosecuted two Congress Socialist leaders for making inflammatory or seditious speeches, sentencing the second, S.S. Batliwala, to six months' imprisonment. In the row that followed, Nehru rounded furiously on the Madras premier, Rajagopalachari. 'Do you mean to say,' he demanded, 'that if I come to Madras and make a similar speech you would arrest me?' 'I would,' Rajagopalachari replied calmly.[8] Rajagopalachari was at the opposite end of the political spectrum from Nehru – the governor of Madras, Lord Erskine, later described him as 'too much of a Tory even for me'[9] – but eventually he was forced to give in. Batliwala was released, and allowed to go round the Madras presidency making more speeches. The ill-feeling between the two wings of the party remained.

Nehru, still ambivalent over the whole question of taking office, grew more and more depressed as the months passed. 'The Congress ministries are tending to become counter-revolutionary,' he complained to Pant in November 1937. 'If this is a likely contingency then the sooner we are out of office the better. I am quite clear that we are better out than in unless we can go ahead much faster than we have been doing.'[10] Personally, he was convinced that he would be better out. There were moves within Congress to draft him for a third term as president, which he scotched by writing an anonymous article for the influential *Modern Review* attacking both his own character and this threat to democracy:

> By electing him a third time we shall exalt one man at the cost of the Congress and make people think in terms of Caesarism ... In spite of all his brave talk, Jawaharlal is obviously tired and stale ... we have a right to expect good work from him in the future. Let us not spoil that and spoil him by too much adulation and praise ... We want no Caesars!'[11]

The device worked. Subhas Bose was elected president in his place, for the next annual session at Haripura.

Although the weight of presidential responsibility had been lifted from his shoulders, Nehru's health and spirits had suffered from the strain of non-stop work. He was further depressed in January 1938 by the sudden death of his mother. With Indira away in England, Anand Bhavan was empty and soulless, and by the end of April he decided he must get away. 'For months past I have felt that I could not function effectively in India as things were going,' he wrote to Gandhi, who had also been seriously ill for several weeks. 'I have carried on of course as one can always carry on. But I have felt out of place and a misfit.'

Nehru's disillusionment even embraced his relations with Gandhi – he found it difficult to discuss anything with him at length, he said, not only because he did not want to tire him but because: 'I have also felt that such discussions do not yield any worthwhile results.' He announced that he was sailing for Europe on 2 June, and did not know how long he would be away. He needed the trip, he said, 'to freshen up my tired and puzzled mind'.[12]

As Nehru himself admitted, 'Europe was hardly the place for peaceful contemplation or for light to illuminate the dark corners of the mind.'[13] It was 1938, after all, with Hitler and Mussolini in the ascendant and the French and British governments desperately trying to dodge the looming threat of war by appeasing them. War was already raging in Spain, a civil war between left and right that had been tearing the country apart for two years. It was to Barcelona that Nehru went first, at the invitation of the Republican government. He spent five days in the city, watching the bombs fall every night, visiting the front line, meeting generals and politicians and 'comrade soldiers', and admiring the courage and determination of people 'doing something worthwhile'.

Nehru was an international figure now, and much in demand. His time in Britain was taken up with a mad whirl of meetings, speeches, dinners, discussions, with friends old and new. He accepted an invitation from Linlithgow, then on home leave, for a chat, during which Nehru told the viceroy that he gave England 10 years at the outside before India was independent. He argued – and naturally disagreed – with Zetland over Spain as well as India. He spent a weekend in Norfolk with Lord Lothian, who invited Lady Astor, General Ironside and Tom Jones, former deputy-secretary of the Cabinet and close friend of Baldwin. He lunched and dined with Paul Robeson and his wife Eslanda, talking not about music but about the National Negro Congress. He met Ivan Maisky, the Soviet ambassador in London, who gave him an official invitation to visit Moscow. He sat in the visitors' gallery of the House of Commons and heard Neville Chamberlain, who had replaced Baldwin as prime minister the year before, announce that he was going to Munich next day to parlay with Herr Hitler over the Czechoslovak problem.

Nehru had just visited Prague, to see the situation in Czechoslovakia for himself: he also revisited his old haunts in Geneva, and Paris, which he found particularly distressing. 'This was the Paris of the Revolution,' he wrote, 'the symbol of liberty the world over.' And yet it 'did not even protest over-much' at the betrayal of the Czechs.[14]

For five months, Nehru toured Europe and Britain, observing the political scene and preaching the cause of Indian independence. But in all his travels, one meeting was to prove more important than all the rest. This was a weekend in a mellow Cotswold stone house in Gloucestershire called 'Goodfellows', the home of his friend Sir Stafford Cripps. Cripps invited Attlee and other leaders of the Labour Party to what was essentially a concentrated seminar with Nehru. According to Attlee, the basis of his policy on India when he became prime minister was laid down during that weekend.[15]

Nehru returned home, with Indira, in November, after a short stop-over in Egypt to confer with the leaders of the Wafd Party, who were also intent on removing the British from their country. He was soon back in the thick of Indian politics on two fronts. The first was the growing ferment in 'those relics of the Middle Ages', the semi-feudal princely states, which he described as 'Britain's fifth column in India'. After presiding over the All-India States' Peoples' Conference at Ludhiana, he had no doubts over what needed to be done about them. 'They cannot remain as feudal enclaves in a democratic India,' he wrote. 'A few large ones may become democratic units in a federation, the others must be completely absorbed. No minor reforms can solve this problem. The States system will have to go and it will go when British Imperialism goes.'[16]

Nehru's second activity was the chairmanship of a new National Planning Committee. As an uncritical admirer of the Soviet Union and the system which he fervently believed had given fresh life to Russia, he was convinced that India needed a fully planned economy, and that 'any effective planning must involve a socialization of the economic structure'. In the way of all planning committees, it grew rapidly until it embraced almost every activity in the country, with no fewer than 29 sub-committees labouring to produce outline schemes to be put into effect in a free India.[17]

While this was going on, Congress was once again plunged into internecine turmoil. Subhas Bose decided that he would stand for a second term as president – Nehru had had two terms, so why shouldn't he? However, responsibility had failed to mellow his radical views, as Gandhi had hoped when he reluctantly approved his candidacy the first time, and now he was seen as a liability. Since he seemed to have no real policy, apart from wanting to get rid of Gandhi and all he stood for, it was hardly surprising that Gandhi, Patel and the rest of the Congress high command did not want him again. When he insisted on standing, it became clear that the presidential election would be contested for the first time in Congress history – though two years earlier Gandhi had only dissuaded Patel at the last minute from running against Nehru.

Gandhi's first choice as new president was Azad – it would be a good move to elect a Muslim at that time – but the Maulana declined the honour. None of the other leading figures was prepared to risk his reputation in a fight, either, so Pattabhi Sitaramayya, the Congress historian, was put up instead. To everyone's amazement, Gandhi's blessing was not enough. Bose defeated both Sitaramayya and the party machine to win by 1,580 votes to 1,377.

The 1939 session of Congress at Tripuri was the stormiest since the clashes between Tilak and Gokhale more than 30 years before. The militant Bose wanted Congress to issue an immediate ultimatum to the British, giving them six months to clear out or face total civil disobedience. Gandhi and the other leaders said this was impossible, knowing that neither Congress nor the Indian people were ready. Bose rounded on them, branding them as 'rightists' who were ready to come to an understanding with the British government, and in effect labelling them cowards and collaborators. They promptly resigned from the Working Committee, without which Congress could not function.

Bose had believed he had the support of his fellow Bengali politicians, but when it came to a straight choice between him and the Mahatma there was no contest. They deserted him. Left with no friends and no influence, Bose did as he had often done in moments of stress – he lost his nerve and took to his bed with a mysterious illness, probably psychosomatic in origin. Nehru tried to mediate between him and the other leaders but it was hopeless as the rift became more and more personal.

Gandhi at that time was involved in a campaign to force the princely states to introduce civil liberties. He had been away in his home state of Rajkot, where he had started a fast in protest against the autocratic methods of the dewan

– the position his own father had held 60 years before, but which, like so many others, was now filled by a retired British officer. Once back at Wardha, however, he turned the screw on Bose. 'Taking all things into consideration,' he wrote, 'I am of the opinion that you should at once form your own cabinet, formulate your own programme definitely and put it before the forthcoming AICC. If the Committee accepts the programme all will be plain-sailing . . . If on the other hand your programme is not accepted you should resign and let the Committee choose its President.'[18] Recognizing defeat, Bose resigned. The reconstituted Working Committee appointed Rajendra Prasad in his place.

    Bose continued to rail against those who had unseated him. For a time this was tolerated, but when he made a public call for an all-India protest against various decisions by the AICC, the Working Committee finally lost patience. They removed him from the presidentship of the Bengal Provincial Congress Committee and barred him from holding any office for three years. Defiant to the end, Bose and his brother Sarat set up their own party, the Forward Bloc, dedicated to militant action against the British. In emulation of Mussolini's 'Duce', Hitler's 'Führer' and maybe even Jinnah's 'Quaid-i-Azam' (all meaning leader), Bose invested himself with the same title in Bengali: 'Netaji'.

While Congress was involved in its latest bout of self-mutilation, the Muslim League was consolidating its new-found strength. As a counter to Nehru's successful and highly publicized visit to Europe, Jinnah decided to send his own emissaries to put across the Muslim point of view. The men he chose for this important mission were two members of the League's Working Committee, Abdur Rahman Siddiqi from Calcutta and, more significantly, Choudry Khaliquzzaman, still smarting over his treatment at the hands of Congress in the UP. One of their more controversial tasks was to establish the credentials of Jinnah and the League with the German and Italian governments – Jinnah thought too many foreign governments believed that only Gandhi and Nehru spoke for India. But their main business, of course, was in London.

    On 14 March 1939, Khaliquzzaman and Siddiqi called on Colonel Muirhead, who had replaced R.A. Butler as under-secretary of state for India. They found him most helpful. 'We have got great sympathy for you but we do not know how to help,' he told them. By way of reply, Khaliquzzaman walked over to a map of India hanging on the wall and pointed to the provinces in the north-west and east. The colonel took their point. 'Yes,' he agreed, 'that is an alternative. Have you talked about it to Lord Zetland?'[19]

    Muirhead arranged for the two men to meet the secretary of state on 20 March, the day before they were due to sail for home. They began, Zetland told Linlithgow, by talking 'a little vaguely about the Palestine problem and then they turned to what they obviously wished to discuss with me, namely, the position of the Muslim community in India'. Khaliquzzaman said Muslims would not agree to federation if it meant Hindu domination. Zetland asked if they had an alternative suggestion. They were vague about the details, he told the viceroy, but 'what was in their minds was a federation of the Muslim Provinces and States in North-West India, a further federation of Bengal and Assam and possibly Bihar and Orissa in the East, and a further federation, or possibly more than one, of the other provinces and States in the remaining part of India'. Whatever the practical difficulties of such a policy – and Zetland's impression was that it had not been well thought out – 'I gathered from them that many Muslims were thinking along these lines.'[20]

Khaliquzzaman, in his own account of the meeting, says he suggested partitioning 'the Muslim areas from the rest of India and proceeding with your scheme of federation of the Indian provinces without including the Muslim areas, which should be independent from the rest'. He also told Zetland that the Muslim League intended to announce its demand for partition at its next annual session, to be held in Lahore in March 1940. He was sufficiently encouraged by Zetland's reaction to assure Jinnah, when he was back to India, that he was certain the British would 'ultimately concede partition'.[21]

Zetland was still flogging the dead horse of federation as laid down in the 1935 Act, but even he was beginning to have doubts. After his meeting with the two League men, he wrote gloomily to Linlithgow that he was 'becoming steadily confirmed in my view that it will be the Muslims rather than the Congress that will provide the biggest obstacle to the early achievement of the Federation'. Linlithgow, as one of the principal architects of the Act, still refused to accept this unpalatable truth. He did not see, he said, how the Muslims could possibly 'torpedo the Federation scheme', unless they could 'discover means to prevent a sufficient number of [princes] from acceding'.[22] It came as a nasty shock to him when a conference of princes and their ministers passed a resolution declaring that the present terms of the federal offer were unacceptable. But that shock was as nothing compared to the crisis that was about to be unleashed in India, and which was entirely the fault of Linlithgow himself.

On 3 September 1939, the official Gazette of India carried a portentous announcement by the viceroy:

> I, Victor Alexander John, Marquess of Linlithgow, Governor-General of India and ex-officio Vice-Admiral therein, being satisfied thereof by information received by me, do hereby proclaim that war has broken out between His Majesty and Germany.

That bald statement, followed by a viceregal broadcast, was the first any Indian heard of the fact that he was now at war with a country he and his compatriots knew nothing about and which, as far as they could see, did not threaten them directly in any way. The white dominions of Canada, Australia, New Zealand and South Africa were entitled to decide for themselves whether or not they should go to war alongside Britain. 'Not so in India,' commented Nehru, 'and it hurt.'[23] In strictly constitutional terms, India did not have a choice – but it was singularly obtuse and maladroit of Linlithgow not even to have consulted the Indian leaders until after the event.

It was not as if Linlithgow had not been warned of Indian feelings. Three weeks earlier, the Congress executive had publicly condemned fascist aggression, but had added: 'The past policy of the British Government as well as recent developments, demonstrated abundantly that this government does not stand for freedom and democracy and may at any time betray these ideals. India cannot associate herself with such a government or be asked to give her resources for democratic freedom which is denied to her and which is likely to be betrayed.'[24] Congress provincial governments were told 'to assist in no way in war preparations', and Congress members of the Central Legislative Assembly were ordered to stay away from its next session in Delhi. As a result, they were unable to vote or even protest against a new Defence of India Bill giving the government emergency powers. The Bill was passed unanimously, without a division – but it raised uncomfortable echoes of the First World War and the Rowlatt Act that followed.

To the dismay of the Congress leaders, there was another echo of the First World War which was equally unwelcome. When war was declared, thousands of young Indians flocked to the recruiting stations, eager to swell the ranks of an army that had been allowed to fall to fewer than 200,000 men during the 1930s, with constant cuts in the defence budget. Most of them were turned away – at that point the government saw no external danger to India and was more concerned with using its manpower to provide material and food. But their willingness to serve undermined Congress's stand, and helped maintain the British delusion that the Indians loved them.

In a slightly belated effort to mend fences, Linlithgow invited Gandhi, Jinnah and the chancellor of the Chamber of Princes to come and see him next day. Gandhi was first. In a two-hour conversation he said that the very thought of the possible destruction of the Houses of Parliament and Westminster Abbey produced a strong emotional reaction in him, and that he was 'in favour of India giving full and unconditional support to Britain'.[25] He did, however, point out that he could not speak for Congress. Although he stood for non-violence, he said he had supported the recruitment of his fellow countrymen in the First World War and he would do so again. In return, he begged the viceroy to use all his efforts to encourage the Muslims to co-operate with Congress.

With the best will in the world, Linlithgow was not able to deliver the Muslims to Congress: the only man who could do that was Jinnah, whom he saw next. Jinnah welcomed the war as an ideal opportunity to pursue his personal goal of separate Muslim states within a loose Indian federation. He was furious to learn from Linlithgow that Sir Sikander Hayat Khan, the premier of the Punjab, jealous at not being invited to meet the viceroy himself, had already volunteered his support for the British without demanding anything in return, 'whatever Jinnah and his friends might say'. All Sir Sikander had asked, apparently, was that 'nothing should be done to inflate Jinnah or make him more difficult to deal with'.[26] Linlithgow could not afford to make an enemy of Sir Sikander, since the Punjab was the major source of Muslim recruitment for the Indian Army, providing 52 per cent of the entire force. But the Punjab was only one province, and he needed Jinnah's support for recruitment elsewhere, and for the general co-operation of Muslims in the war effort.

Jinnah was prepared to promise Muslim support, but in return he wanted the viceroy's assurance that something would be done to clip Congress's wings. To begin with he wanted amendments to the constitution, which he thought favoured Congress too much. The experience of provincial autonomy had shown how 'Hindus' behaved when they were in a majority. Linlithgow asked if he wanted the Congress ministries sacked immediately. 'Yes,' replied Jinnah. 'Turn them out at once. Nothing else will bring them to their senses. Their object ... is nothing less than to destroy you British and us Muslims. They will never stand by you.'[27]

Linlithgow turned to a speech Jinnah had recently made stating that he no longer believed in democratic government for India. How was India to achieve self-government, he asked, if not by democratic means? Jinnah insisted that parliamentary democracy could not work where there was a permanent majority and a permanent minority. The only viable political solution for India, he believed, 'lay in partition'.

Linlithgow's third interview, with the chancellor of the Chamber of Princes, must have come as a great relief. The princes not only promised unconditional support but even offered to make financial contributions to the war effort amounting to more than twenty lakhs (2 million) rupees, then worth about £150,000.

Linlithgow had been 'profoundly moved' by Gandhi's sympathy for England, and reported to Zetland that his attitude 'could not have been better'. He hoped that the Mahatma would be able to 'keep things on the right line' with the Congress Working Committee.[28] But the viceroy knew that Gandhi was no longer the force in Congress that he had been. The pressure from the left was increasing all the time, and the man the British would have to deal with in the future was Nehru, for whom Linlithgow had little time.

Nehru, as it happened, was in China as a guest of Chiang Kai-shek when war was declared, but hurried back to India at once. His first public statement on arriving home must have given the viceroy both fresh hope and new anxiety, as he declared: 'In a conflict between democracy and freedom on the one side and fascism and aggression on the other our sympathies must inevitably lie on the side of democracy ... I should like India to play her full part and throw all her resources into the struggle for a new order.'[29] The big question was, what exactly did Nehru mean by 'the new order' – and which struggle was he talking about? Many Congressmen wanted to know, too.

One Congressman who had his own answers was Subhas Chandra Bose. Despite the débâcle of his second presidential term, Bose was still an important figure in Congress, and as such was invited to the special Working Committee meeting at Wardha from 10 to 14 September 1940, to help decide Congress policy on the war. He spoke with considerable passion, declaring that this was India's golden opportunity. There could be no question of supporting either side in the European war, since both were imperialists fighting for colonial possessions. A Britain at war meant a weak Britain, – now was the time to launch the final struggle for independence with a great new non-co-operation movement. The argument of Bose and his socialist allies was a powerful one. But there were many others who were enjoying power for the first time in their lives, and they were not eager to give it up. As so often in the past, Congress could not make up its collective mind.

Gandhi was alone in pressing for unconditional – though strictly non-violent – support for Britain. Others were prepared to fight, but only in return for freedom. They agreed with Nehru, who had written earlier in the year: 'We are not going to line up under Chamberlainism; we are not going to throw our resources in defence of empire. But we would gladly offer those very resources for the defence of democracy, the democracy of a free India lined up with other free countries.'[30] It was all very difficult, and very confusing.

In the end, Gandhi threw in his lot with Nehru, and the rest of the Working Committee fell into line. On 14 September they agreed on a statement drafted by Nehru. It was a long and rambling statement, wordy, worthy, and full of righteous indignation. While condemning fascism and Nazism, it declared that 'the issue of war and peace for India must be decided by the Indian people' – they could not fight for freedom for others while they were not free. This principle, the statement added, also applied within India itself – the offers of the princes to support the cause of democracy in Europe would be more fitting if they introduced democracy in their own autocratic states. Indians were eager to help in every way, but first they wanted a quid pro quo. The statement invited

... the British Government to declare in unequivocal terms what their war aims are in regard to democracy and imperialism and the new order that is envisaged, in particular how these aims are going to apply to India and be given effect to in the present. Do they include the elimination of imperialism and the treatment of India as a free nation whose policy will be guided in accordance with the wishes of her people?[31]

If Congress could use the situation for bargaining, then so could the Muslim League. The League's Working Committee met immediately after the Congress statement was issued, and agreed on its own demands. They were simple enough: the British must recognize the League as the sole voice of Muslim India; the 1935 constitution must be revised in the light of the experience of provincial autonomy; the present scheme for federation, 'which must necessarily result in a majority community rule, under the garb of democracy', must be dropped; and no declarations on constitutional change should be made without the consent and approval of the League.

Linlithgow was faced with political deadlock. Congress was demanding immediate freedom on its own terms. Jinnah and the League were demanding a veto on those terms. Seeking a way out of the impasse, the viceroy embarked on a frenetic round of talks with Indian political leaders. Over the next month, he invited no fewer than 57 of them to meet him individually in Simla. They ranged from Gandhi and Nehru to Ambedkar and Jinnah, plus the Sikhs and a clutch of princes. The only thing they were all agreed on was their opposition to the 1935 scheme of federation – Congress because the scheme did not give it enough power, all the others because it gave Congress too much. The Liberals, the Hindu Mahasabha, the untouchables and the Parsis joined together to remind the viceroy that Congress and the League did not represent everyone in India, and that to accept Congress's claim to be the only national party would be 'a death-blow to democracy'.

On 17 October, Linlithgow finally made his long-promised statement. It was a grave disappointment to just about every section of Indian opinion. It dodged the main question of Britain's war aims by simply referring everyone to the prime minister's statement. It claimed that provincial autonomy had been a success but confirmed that the idea of federation had been shelved for the duration of the war. All it offered was a reiteration of the old pledge of dominion status at some unspecified time in the future, and a vague promise that at the end of the war the government would be 'very willing to enter into consultation' on possible amendments to the 1935 Act. As for India's part in the actual conduct of the war, the viceroy announced that he would be setting up a 'consultative group' consisting of representatives of all the major political parties and of the princes, over which he would personally preside. The rather nebulous purpose of this group was 'the association of public opinion in India with the conduct of the war and with questions relating to war activities'.[32]

Linlithgow could not have believed that this vapid statement, forced on him by the government in London, would satisfy Congress. Perhaps he never intended that it should. Soon afterwards he told Zetland: 'I am not too keen to start talking about a period after which British rule will have ceased in India. I suspect that day is very remote and I feel the least we say about it ... the better.'[33]

Gandhi, who had worked so hard to persuade both the viceroy and his own Congress colleagues to agree, reacted sadly. 'The Indian declaration shows clearly that there is to be no democracy for India if Britain can prevent it,' he said. 'The Congress asked for bread and it has got a stone.' The Congress Working Committee agreed. It met at Wardha on 22 and 23 October and condemned the viceroy's statement out of hand as nothing but a repetition of the old imperialist policy. Since supporting Britain in any way would be seen as an endorsement of that policy, the Working Committee ordered all Congress governments to resign by the end of the month. Obediently, but in many cases reluctantly, they did so, and in seven Congress provinces the governors took over direct rule under section 93 of the Act. In Assam, Congress had ruled only in coalition, and when its ministers resigned the other members of the coalition took control. The Muslim governments of Bengal, the Punjab and Sind, meanwhile, carried on as normal.

Many Congressmen wanted to start an immediate campaign of civil disobedience, but Gandhi squashed this at once. This was not the time, and in any case Indians were not ready — there was no way civil disobedience could be prevented from sliding into violence. Instead, he joined Nehru, Prasad and Jinnah in a last attempt to find a solution. It proved to be in vain, and only served to boost Jinnah's position — the Congress leaders went to *him* at *his* new house in Delhi, 10 Aurangzeb Road, and were driven to the Viceroy's House in *his* Packard car, for the first-ever joint meeting with the viceroy. Jinnah had at last been accorded full status as an equal.

When it was clear that the joint talks had failed, Jinnah produced another masterly stroke by calling for a national 'Day of Deliverance and Thanksgiving' on Friday, 22 December 1940, 'as a mark of relief that the Congress regime has at last ceased to function'. To avoid any charge of inciting communal disturbances, he appealed to his followers for calm: 'Let there be no *hartals*, processions or any such demonstrations, but let a spirit of humility and a mood of reflection prevail. There is relief and gratitude in our hearts, not joy and triumph.'[34]

Jinnah's proclamation catalogued Muslim grievances against the Congress governments, which 'have done their best to flout the Muslim opinion, to destroy Muslim culture, and have interfered with their religious and social life, and trampled upon their economic and political rights'.[35] Congress naturally denied the charges, and offered to investigate them, but other minorities rushed to give their support. Dravidians in the south, the All-India Depressed Classes Association, various Anglo-Indian groups, Ambedkar and his Independent Labour Party; all joined in celebrating Jinnah's Day of Deliverance.

Among those who watched the Day of Deliverance celebrations with real regret was Sir Stafford Cripps, who had been in India since 7 December. Cripps had no official status – he was not even a member of the Labour Party at that time, having been expelled earlier that year for trying to set up a popular front with the Liberals – but although he was often regarded as a tiresome maverick, he still commanded respect in Parliament. He had persuaded the Foreign Office to give him its unofficial backing for a personal mission to study the situations in India, China and the Soviet Union, and to try to explain Britain's position to their political leaders. India came first, in every way. Having cast himself in the role of India's champion, he had spent much time since Nehru's visit to his country house working on detailed proposals for its independence. He took the draft with him, hoping to get Indian leaders to approve it. If they did, the government had promised to consider it seriously.

Cripps's plan was a development of the ideas floated during Nehru's weekend at Goodfellows. Under it the government would reiterate the promise of dominion status, which he defined as meaning 'complete self-government and absolute liberty to terminate partnership in the British Commonwealth of nations'. A constituent assembly of some 2,000 members from all parties and those states that wished to take part would be elected 'immediately the war is over, or before that time if opportunity occurs'. A majority of three-fifths would be needed to carry any vote. The British government would accept and respect the decisions of the assembly, which would be incorporated into a treaty between Britain and the new United India. This would include provisions for the protection of minorities, and would last for a set period of transition – 15 years was suggested – during which finance, defence and other details would be settled.

Cripps and his private secretary Geoffrey Wilson landed in Allahabad on 7 December. Nehru welcomed Cripps warmly, as a friend, but he had certain reservations about his plan. 'There are some desirable features in it,' he wrote to Mahadev Desai, Gandhi's secretary and editor of *Harijan*, 'but I think it suffers from two or three fatal defects.' As for Cripps himself, while he was 'thoroughly straight and his abilities unquestioned, his judgement is not always to be relied upon'.[36] In other words, he didn't always say exactly what Nehru wanted him to. What was worse, he suffered from the English disease of seeking to solve problems by compromise.

Nehru had arranged a hectic schedule for Cripps, and for the next 18 days, he spun through India talking, listening, and lecturing by day and travelling by night. In Delhi he met a number of political leaders including Birla and Liaquat

Ali Khan who each told him that Hindus and Muslims would have to be separated in some way. Birla related the situation to business, where 'you cannot carry on with an unsatisfactory partner'. Liaquat told him:

> Unless a constitution could be devised which would make it impossible for one community to rule by itself, it would never bring peace to the country ... The Muslims had three thoughts. These were (I) Partition, but not on the lines of the Muslim empire; (2) Free and independent states, with a federation of the Hindu and Muslim Provinces and a Confederation of the two; (3) Dominion Status for each of the Provinces, with a federation at the centre to which should be given only such powers as the Provinces agree to give, and giving the Provinces the right to opt out.[37]

In Lahore, Cripps first met with Sir Sikander, who airily asserted: 'Half a dozen people could settle the communal question in principle in half an hour,' and insisted that a constituent assembly 'would do more harm than good'. The Hindu Mahasabha, whose leaders Cripps met later that day, presented a very different picture. 'First settle our differences,' they told him, 'then get rid of the British. If you make it an essential condition of a settlement that you must have the consent of the Muslim League as represented by Jinnah, you make it impossible.'[38]

In Bombay, Cripps addressed 1,000 members of the Civil Liberties Union in the Opera House, met the governor, trade union leaders and various government officials, and talked to Ambedkar, who gave the impression of being 'somewhat embittered by the experiences through which he himself and his people had passed'. To him *swaraj* meant more domination and molestation of the untouchables by the Hindus. He shocked Cripps with a drastic solution: the government should provide new land for the untouchables, to which they would all be moved.[39]

Then Cripps called on Jinnah at his home on Malabar Hill. Jinnah was naturally suspicious of his motives and his impartiality, since he was being 'shepherded around the country by the Congress'. But after Cripps had managed to put his mind at rest, Jinnah treated him to a detailed lecture on the history and distribution of the Muslims in India, and outlined his own plans firmly and clearly. He promised, however, to consider Cripps's proposals on their own merit, and they parted with mutual respect, if not warmth. As a local wit commented in the *Bombay Chronicle*: 'I am given to understand on great authority that the smile on the faces of Mr Jinnah and Sir Stafford Cripps in the pictures published in the local press is not an indication of Sir Stafford's reaction to the Muslim leader, but purely the answer to a photographer's prayer, "Smile, please!"'[40]

The highlight of Cripps's tour came at Wardha, when he met up again with Nehru, who took him for a 90-minute talk with Gandhi over a simple meal of bread and fruit – which suited the strictly vegetarian Cripps perfectly. Gandhi was not impressed with his visitor, whom he thought 'lacked humility'. For his part, Cripps thought Gandhi 'shrewd and clever'. Next day, they met again, to discuss the Mahatma's reaction to Cripps's proposals in greater detail. Basically, what the old man had to say was: 'HMG must make up its mind whether it trusted Congress, and, if it did, must rely on Congress and the Constituent Assembly to safeguard the minorities, as, of course, they must.'[41] In other words, 'leave everything to us'.

On 22 December, as Jinnah's Day of Deliverance was being celebrated by the minorities throughout India, Cripps finally met the viceroy in Calcutta. Having spent the best part of three weeks in India, he felt he knew the answers to all its great problems, and so had no qualms about giving Linlithgow the benefit of his knowledge. The Muslims, he said, should be made to put down in writing exactly what their minimum demands were; Congress should then be made to put down in writing exactly how far they were prepared to go to meet them. It would then be up to the viceroy to 'bridge the difference by negotiation'.[42] It was as simple as that.

The visiting politician who became an instant expert on India was hardly a new phenomenon – Kipling had satirized the breed a full 50 years earlier with his fictitious Member for Lower Tooting. Cripps was a particularly fine specimen, but Linlithgow did actually take notice of what he had to say. Less than three weeks later, in a speech at the Orient Club in Bombay, he did as Cripps had suggested and made an unequivocal declaration that the British government's goal for India was 'full Dominion status ... of the Statute of Westminster variety' – in other words, independence in all but name. He went on to say that he was prepared to expand his Executive Council by adding 'a small number' of Indian political leaders.[43] Had he made such an announcement three months before, it might just have been enough to prevent the Congress walk-out. Instead, it was another case of too little, too late.

'A Landmark in the Future History of India'

✧✧

The 1940 session of Congress was held in the Bihar village of Ramgarh on 19 and 20 March. In an effort to woo and reassure Muslims, Gandhi had finally persuaded Maulana Azad to stand as president. And to further the cause, Azad chose three other Muslims, including 'the Frontier Gandhi', Abdul Gaffar Khan, to join him on the 14-strong Working Committee. He also brought Nehru back on to it. No one knew it then, of course, but it was to be the last election for six years, during which time Azad and his committee were to remain in office.

There was only one resolution at Ramgarh, and it consisted of just three paragraphs. The first called for the start of civil disobedience, but only when the organization and the people were ready; the second declared that Congress would accept 'nothing short of complete independence', rejecting 'dominion or any other status within the imperial structure'; the third called again for a 'constituent assembly elected by adult suffrage'. Its final sentence was an unequivocal blast aimed at the Muslim League and its allies: 'India's constitution must be based on independence, democracy and national unity, and the Congress repudiates attempts to divide India or to split up her nationhood.'[1]

The League's response came four days later in Lahore. Jinnah was a sick man – he had collapsed on his way to the Central Legislative Assembly in Delhi barely a week earlier, suffering from what had been diagnosed as pleurisy. But he rose from his bed and travelled to the Punjab capital, in a train festooned with garlands and green flags bearing the League's crescent and star emblem. Whatever the state of his health, he was determined to preside over a session which, he told newsmen at the station, 'is going to be a landmark in the future history of India'.

Lahore was seething with unrest after clashes two days earlier between Sir Sikander Hayat Khan's police and a paramilitary Muslim organization known as the Khaksars – the name literally means 'humble workers' – wielding razor-sharp spades. At least 30 Khaksars had been killed, and two British police officers wounded, one of whom died in hospital, while the other, Superintendent D. Gainsford, had his nose chopped off. A curfew was in force, and there was some doubt whether the League session could go ahead: the Khaksars were as hostile to the League as they were to Hindus and Sikhs, and bands of them were still at large. Jinnah helped to calm the situation by visiting wounded Khaksars in hospital and speaking to each of them individually. The effect may have been only temporary – the Khaksars tried several times to assassinate him during the next few years – but at least the historic session could start as planned the following day.

Sixty thousand delegates crammed into the enormous tent on 22 March 1940, and an overflow of at least 40,000 more filled the surrounding Minto Park. It was a far cry from the time only 10 years before, when the organizers had had to scour Allahabad to raise a quorum of 75 to hear Iqbal proclaiming his vision of a separate Muslim state. Now, everyone knew Jinnah was about to declare the same thing, and the vast crowd had come to hear him do it. As he entered the park at 2.25 p.m., he was greeted with a thunderous roar of '*Quaid-i-Azam Zindabad!*' ('Long live the Great Leader!'), and '*Pakistan Zindabad!*' The same voices, minutes before, had been chanting '*Sikander Hayat Khan Murdabad!*' ('Death to Sikander Hayat Khan!'). Sir Sikander survived, but his hopes of supplanting Jinnah were dead.

After beginning his presidential speech in Urdu, Jinnah switched to English for the benefit of the newsmen present – his words were directed not to the crowd in Minto Park but to the world, and specifically to Britain. Few of his audience understood what he was saying, but after a few mutterings, they listened in silence for two hours, totally enraptured by his presence and his presentation. He challenged Gandhi to come to him 'as a Hindu leader proudly representing your people and let me meet you proudly representing the Muslims'. He demanded of the British that 'as soon as circumstances permit, or immediately after the war at the latest, the whole problem of India's future Constitution must be examined *de novo*, and the Act of 1935 must go once and for all'.[2]

It was a masterly performance, perhaps his greatest, combining humour with passion, cool logic with dramatic effect. And like all great performances it built steadily to a climax, saving the best for the end:

> It has always been taken for granted mistakenly that the Musulmans are a minority, and of course we have got used to it for such a long time that these settled notions sometimes are very difficult to remove. The Musulmans are not a minority. The Musulmans are a nation by any definition ... If the British Government are really in earnest and sincere to secure the peace and happiness of the people of this Subcontinent, the only course open to us all is to allow the major nations separate homelands, by dividing India into "autonomous national States".[3]

Jinnah had not used the word Pakistan once. Nor was it mentioned in the resolution that was passed by acclamation the next day. It was the Hindu newspapers which labelled it the 'Pakistan Resolution' as they raised an outcry against what they saw as the first move towards the vivisection of Mother India. The resolution's all-important third paragraph stated:

> ... no constitutional plan would be workable in this country or acceptable to the Muslims unless it is designed on the following basic principles, viz., that geographically contiguous units are demarcated into regions which should be so constituted, with such territorial readjustments as may be necessary, that areas in which the Muslims are numerically in a majority, as in the North-Western and Eastern zones of India, should be grouped to constitute Independent States in which the constituent units shall be autonomous and sovereign.[4]

The wording of the resolution was deliberately vague. This was partly because the League's Subjects Committee, and specifically Fazlul Haq and Sir Sikander, had not been able to agree on which of the half-dozen versions of partition to support. Sir Sikander still wanted a loose federation for the whole of India, united by a minimal central government; Haq wanted two independent Muslim states, one of them, of course, his own Bengal; some favoured a single, sovereign Muslim state with two wings; others variations on a federal grouping of autonomous Muslim provinces. Every point of the resolution was open to different interpretations, and Jinnah took great care not to clarify any of them until the last possible minute, seven years later. As a shrewd politician he intended to keep all his options open, hoping to put himself in a powerful bargaining position for future negotiations.

It was only to be expected that Congress and the Hindus would react angrily to the League's resolution. Only slightly more surprising was the condemnation heaped upon it by other Muslim nationalist groups, who met in Delhi in April under the banner of the Azad Muslim Conference. They announced their support for Congress in its struggle for complete independence, and disputed the League's claim to speak for all Indian Muslims. But their protestations rang increasingly hollow as the League's strength continued to grow.

The Pakistan Resolution and the success of the Lahore session had torpedoed once and for all the Congress claim to speak for the whole of India. Now, exasperated and alienated by Congress's intransigence, the British turned to the League for support in the war effort. Early in April, Linlithgow warned Zetland that 'it would be politically unfortunate' to reject the Pakistan scheme, which 'might be pressed' after the war.[5] He then wrote a friendly letter to Jinnah, assuring him that there would be no repetition of the Turkish problem of the

First World War: 'His Majesty's Government are in friendly and sympathetic relations with all Muslim powers to some of whom indeed they are bound by alliance.'[6] Zetland, meanwhile, told the House of Lords that a united India could only be achieved through agreement between the Indian communities, and that Britain could not force a constitution on the Muslims.

Zetland's April speech was his swan song as secretary of state. A month before, on 13 March, he had been wounded by a gunman who had invaded the fortnightly meeting of the Royal Society for Asian Affairs at Caxton Hall, Westminster. Zetland had been in the chair at the meeting, at which Sir Percy Sykes had lectured on 'Afghanistan: the Present Position'. The hall had been packed with old India hands, among them Lord Lamington, one-time governor of Bombay, and two former lieutenant-governors of the Punjab, the 84-year-old Sir Louis Dane, and his successor, Sir Michael O'Dwyer. The meeting was just breaking up when a dark-skinned man wearing a suit and a trilby hat pushed his way to the front. Coming up behind O'Dwyer, he pulled out a revolver and shot him twice at point blank range. He then hit Dane in the right forearm and Lamington in the right hand, before firing a fifth shot at Zetland, which fortunately only grazed the right side of his rib cage. Before he could fire again, the gunman was tackled by a Miss Bertha Herring, a hefty lady in her sixties, who brought him crashing to the floor. Several men then found the courage to fling themselves on him and hold him until the police arrived. O'Dwyer died a little while later. Zetland, though not seriously injured, was understandably shaken.

The assassin turned out to be a Sikh named Udam Singh, who had been wounded in the Jallianwala Bagh massacre as a child. It had taken him almost precisely 21 years to exact vengeance on the man many people believed carried the ultimate responsibility for the Amritsar killings. After trial at the Old Bailey, Udam Singh was found guilty of the murder of O'Dwyer, and was hanged at Pentonville. He went willingly to his death, certain of his place as a Sikh martyr. His remains were returned to Amritsar for reburial in 1974, a fitting postscript to a black chapter in the history of the British in India.

The 'phoney war' in Europe ended abruptly on 9 April 1940 when Hitler invaded Denmark and Norway. On 7 May, after a disastrous month of fighting and confusion in Norway, a prominent Tory back-bencher, Leo Amery, rose in the House of Commons and assailed Neville Chamberlain with the words Oliver Cromwell had used to the Long Parliament on 20 April 1653: 'You have sat too long here for any good you have been doing. Depart, I say, and let us have done with you. In the name of God, go!' Three days later, as Hitler's armies crashed across the frontiers of the Low Countries, Chamberlain finally went. After an abortive attempt by the old guard and the king to put Lord Halifax into Downing

Street, Winston Churchill took over as prime minister, promising nothing but 'blood, toil, tears and sweat'.

Churchill moved swiftly to form a national government. Among his many changes, he appointed Attlee as his deputy prime minster, sent Cripps, who was still vigorously pressing for a firm promise of independence for India, as special envoy to Moscow, and removed Zetland from the India Office. Zetland was not only suffering from the after-effects of being shot, but was also seriously at odds with Churchill over India: 'Winston's approach to the Indian problem differs so fundamentally from my own,' he wrote in his last letter to Linlithgow, 'that my inclusion in his government was scarcely possible; I should indeed only have ended up being an embarrassment to him.'[7] The man Churchill chose to replace him was Leo Amery.

Amery was an ebullient little man, only five feet four inches tall but a fine athlete in his youth and still an enthusiastic mountaineer at the age of 65. He had, like so many prominent Britons of his generation, been born in India, in his case at Gorakhpur in the North-Western Provinces as the UP was then known. His father had been an official in the Indian Forest Department, his mother was a Hungarian, hence the name Leopold. However, again like so many, he was brought home to England at an early age, never to return to the sub-continent. He was educated at Harrow, where he was a contemporary of Churchill. At their first encounter, Churchill pushed him, fully clothed, into the swimming pool. Amery retaliated. After that they got along reasonably enough, though they were never close friends. Unlike Churchill, Amery shone academically, coming top in the school examinations and going on to Oxford, where he was later elected a fellow of All Souls, the epicentre of the British establishment, at the age of 24. His closest friend there was John Simon, who was elected at the same time.

Amery was an unabashed imperialist all his life. But his was 'a radical imperialism ... of free and equal partnership in the Commonwealth'.[8] In his early years he became an ardent disciple of Sir Alfred (later Lord) Milner, foreseeing, as he wrote to Simon in 1897, 'the [British] Imperialist running the whole world on sound economic and self-government principles'.[9] Shortly before the Boer War he went to South Africa, where Milner had been appointed high commissioner, to see his ideas being put into practice. There, he formed a lifelong friendship with Jan Smuts, and an admiration for the Boers which survived the war. He must also have been aware of the activities of Gandhi at that time, though we do not know what he thought of them. After serving as a war correspondent for *The Times* from 1899 to 1902, he returned to London to continue working for the newspaper as a leader writer and as the editor and principal author of its massive seven-volume *History of the War in South Africa*.

In 1911, Amery entered Parliament as the Conservative member for

South Birmingham (Sparkbrook), a seat which he held continuously until 1945. He had a distinguished Parliamentary career, holding office in the first Baldwin government as First Lord of the Admiralty and colonial secretary, but joined Churchill in the wilderness throughout the 1930s, supporting him over rearmament, though not over India. But although he undoubtedly had a brilliant mind, Amery lacked political weight: he was too fussy, too garrulous, to command the respect his intellect deserved. It was a surprise, and a severe disappointment, only to him that he was not offered something grander, such as the Exchequer, or Defence, in May 1940.

Amery regarded the India Office as a second-rate post, unworthy of his talents, his experience, and his loyalty. But he swallowed his pride, and accepted the offer out of a sense of 'public duty'. At least he was in the Cabinet, 'inside the fortress' as he put it,[10] and it was not long before he realized that he had taken responsibility for one of the major issues of the time. It was, all the same, a curious appointment for Churchill to make: although Amery was on the hard right of the Tory Party, he was no diehard where India was concerned. 'L [Linlithgow] will I think be a bit startled by my radical views,' he confided to his diary.[11] Those views, diametrically opposed to Churchill's as well as Linlithgow's, were that India should become independent within the Commonwealth as soon as possible.

From the moment he had taken office, Amery began trying to persuade Linlithgow – who had served under him at the Admiralty in 1923 – to go along with his ideas. He wanted a committee of 'representative' Indians to be invited to consider India's future, believing that freedom after the war should be promised during the war, and that the Indians themselves should decide its form and timing. Britain, he believed, must now say to India: 'We are prepared to implement immediately after the war any agreement which you may by then have reached among yourselves.'[12] To this end, Linlithgow should seek a reconciliation with Gandhi and the Congress leaders, especially Nehru and Vallabhbhai Patel, something the viceroy found distasteful in the extreme.

Amery's aims, however, were not entirely altruistic. At the end of May, with the war situation in Europe becoming more disastrous every day, he told Linlithgow: 'My whole conception is that of India humming from end to end with activity in munitions and supply production and at the same time with the bustle of men training for active service of one sort or another, the first operation largely paying for the cost of the second.'[13]

One might imagine that Churchill would have been delighted with such a vision, but he was not. 'Winston', Amery recorded in his diary, 'hates the idea of Indians producing anything for themselves in the way of defence.'[14] But Churchill's disapproval of that was as nothing compared with his response to the idea of promising them independence. As Amery warned Linlithgow, Churchill 'reacts instinctively and passionately against the whole idea of any government for India other than that which he knew forty years ago'.[15]

Churchill's views on India and the Indians were if anything hardening. His patience was further tested by what he saw as the disloyalty of Congress and Gandhi's dangerous attitude to the war. Gandhi had written to Linlithgow on 26 May offering 'to go to Germany or anywhere required to plead for peace ... I do not believe Herr Hitler to be as bad as he is portrayed. He might even have been a friendly power as he still may be.'[16] That letter, with its echoes of appeasement, had been bad enough. But now, when Britain's back was against the wall, he infuriated his British friends and foes alike by publishing an 'Appeal to Every Briton' to 'accept the method of non-violence instead of that of war'.

It was barely a month since Churchill had stirred the House of Commons and the country after the 'colossal military disaster' of Dunkirk by declaring: 'We shall defend our island, whatever the cost may be, we shall fight on the beaches, we shall fight on the landing grounds, we shall fight in the fields and the streets, we shall fight in the hills; we shall never surrender.' Gandhi's was a very different message:

> No cause, however just, can warrant the indiscriminate slaughter that is going on minute by minute ... I want you to fight Nazism without arms or with non-violent arms. I would like you to lay down the arms you have as being useless for saving you or humanity. You will invite Herr Hitler and Signor Mussolini to take what they want of the countries you call your possessions. Let them take possession of your beautiful island, with your many beautiful buildings. You will give all these but neither your soul, nor your minds. If these gentlemen choose to occupy your homes, you will vacate them. If they do not give you free passage out, you will allow yourself, man, woman and child, to be slaughtered, but you will refuse to owe allegiance to them ... This process or method which I have called non-violent non-co-operation is not without considerable success in India ... I know of no single case in which it has failed. I am telling His Excellency the Viceroy that my services are at the disposal of His Majesty's Government, should they consider them of any practical use in advancing the object of my appeal.[17]

The viceroy declined Gandhi's services with commendable courtesy. Churchill, for once, mercifully managed to keep silent. The members of the Congress Working Committee dissociated themselves from Gandhi's views: 'The Indian National Congress is a political organization pledged to win the political independence of the country. It is not an institution for organizing world peace.'[18]

But they were still influenced by the Gandhian dictum of not taking advantage of an opponent's misfortunes. Even left-wingers like Nehru were reluctant to embarrass Britain at such a critical moment, and Rajagopalachari was able to frame a resolution that Congress would take an active part in the war effort in return for a provisional national government 'without delay'. As a measure of good faith, he even suggested that the Muslim League should nominate the prime minister.

There was little chance of Churchill or any other British politician accepting the Congress offer. However, Amery recognized Indian sympathy for Britain's position, and increased his pressure on Linlithgow to make a firm promise of independence immediately after the war, and to appoint Indian political leaders to his Executive Council at once. Linlithgow had finally, and with great reluctance, consented when Churchill discovered what was going on. He erupted in a blind rage, charging Amery with encouraging revolution in India and with misleading the Cabinet. The row between them was so intense, with Amery giving every bit as good as he got, that Sir Alexander Cadogan of the Foreign Office left the Cabinet room in embarrassment.[19]

Churchill told Amery that at that moment of crisis, 'all our thoughts should be devoted to the defence of our Island and to the victory of our cause'.[20] But he still found time to intervene personally with the viceroy, to read all the private correspondence between Amery and Linlithgow, and to rewrite the draft declaration they had prepared.

It was Churchill's version, therefore, that Linlithgow announced on 8 August, and which became known as the 'August Offer'. The clarity of Amery's prose and the precision of his promises had been replaced by obfuscation, a combination of Churchillian wind and Linlithgow's grandiloquence. Gone were Amery's pledges that Indians would decide for themselves the timing and form of independence. Gone was any mention of the guarantee of equality within the Commonwealth. There was a vague promise that Indians should draw up their own constitution some time after the war, but no indication of when or how. The only concessions to Indian opinion were an enlarged Executive Council and the setting up of a War Advisory Committee including Indian representatives. 'The whole thing,' Nehru wrote scathingly, 'is fantastic and absurd and has not even the merit of decent phraseology about it.'[21]

When Congress unequivocally rejected the August Offer as 'a direct encouragement and incitement to civil discord and strife' and 'proof of the British Government's determination to continue to hold India by the sword', the door was closed to any further discussion.[22] Linlithgow had already intimated that he was ready to drop his careful policy of not taking sides if the League agreed to enter the Executive Council while Congress refused. Now, Amery told the House of Commons that if Congress refused to play its part in the government of India, 'the Viceroy would of course go ahead with those who were prepared to work with him and with each other'.

Many of the provisions in the August Offer, including the expanded Executive Council and the War Advisory Committee, had been suggested by Jinnah after a meeting with the viceroy at the end of June. The most significant of them was the pledge: 'It goes without saying that they [HMG] could not contemplate transfer of their present responsibilities for the peace and welfare of India to any system of government whose authority is denied by large and powerful elements in India's national life.'[23] In effect, the Muslims were being given a veto on future constitutional progress.

The majority of the League's Working Committee wanted to accept the offer as it stood, but Jinnah persuaded them to sit tight. The League, he claimed later, had accepted the August Offer 'in principle', though the details were not satisfactory.[24] His price for full co-operation was that the League should be recognized as the sole representative of Indian Muslims and have total parity with Congress in all councils and discussions. And if Congress chose not to enter the government, then the League should be taken into full and equal partnership with the British in the running of the country. He also demanded the right to veto Congress's entry into the Executive Council before the end of the war. Naturally, these terms were not acceptable to the viceroy, but Jinnah was careful to leave the door open for further discussions, and further concessions. Conscious as always of the strength of his bargaining position, he never refused co-operation – he simply did not offer it.

With both major parties refusing to play, the viceroy shelved his plans for an expanded Executive Council, and for the setting up of a War Advisory Committee. Only the minority parties – the Liberals, the Sikhs and the Scheduled Castes – had accepted the August Offer. Even the Hindu Mahasabha, which had at first approved, had withdrawn its support after being refused its demand for three times as many seats as the League.

Faced once again with political stalemate, Congress needed to do something positive to revive its flagging fortunes. Having forsworn power it was drifting aimlessly. The Working Committee was splitting into various factions, with Nehru at one end and Rajagopalachari and Patel at the other. Only one man was capable of reviving and uniting them, and it was not President Azad, who was never the most charismatic of leaders. At the end of September 1940, they invited Gandhi to come back and lead them in the new campaign of civil disobedience which had been authorized at Ramgarh.

Anyone who had been hoping for a great popular movement of non-co-operation was in for a grave disappointment. Gandhi still had no wish to embarrass the British. He also knew that the Indian people as a whole were not ready for peaceful civil disobedience, and that a mass movement would either fail to take off or deteriorate into communal violence. So, he inaugurated a curiously low-key action, calling not for immediate independence but for freedom to speak out against the war. In a personal meeting on 27 September, Linlithgow pointed out that in Britain itself conscientious objectors were absolved from the duty of fighting, and even allowed to profess their faith in public, but not to try to persuade soldiers and munitions workers to quit their posts. He could not offer Gandhi more. It was a fairly esoteric difference, but it was enough. Gandhi had his cause – or his excuse – for mounting his campaign. After suspending *Harijan*, refusing to continue publishing under censorship, he considered starting a fast 'unto death', but was dissuaded by Nehru and G.D. Birla. Instead he announced the beginning of 'individual' *satyagraha*.

Gandhi's plan was for hand-picked Congressmen to court arrest, one at a time, by making anti-war speeches after first informing the authorities. The first was one of Gandhi's oldest disciples from his Wardha *ashram*, Acharya Vinoba Bhave. He was arrested on 21 October 1940 after three days of speech-making, and sentenced to three months' simple imprisonment. The next in line was Nehru, who had been kicking his heels in idleness for months, and to fill the time, had taken up spinning again after a gap of four years. He was arrested on 31 October after making three speeches. As usual, he refused to offer any defence, and was sentenced to sixteen months' rigorous imprisonment for each speech, a total of four years. Even Churchill was shocked by the severity of the sentence, and Amery instructed Linlithgow to make sure Nehru was not treated like a common criminal. The viceroy, however, took care to see that he was denied special privileges, and that his 'rigorous imprisonment' was not relieved by sympathetic gaolers.

Azad, Rajagopalachari and other members of the Working Committee took their turns, followed by lesser figures, both nationally and locally. By the end of the year, more than 400 Congressmen, including 29 former ministers, were in prison. In April 1941, the rank and file members of Congress were enlisted, and by the middle of the year the number of *satyagrahis* in gaol peaked at about 14,000. After that it dwindled rapidly – few were eager to seek rearrest once they had been released. Soon the campaign fizzled out altogether. There had been about 20,000 convictions in all, a relatively low figure considering the total membership of Congress. The movement had failed to ignite the public imagination, partly because censorship squashed news of the arrests, but even more because the general public did not understand or sympathize with the issues. Most ordinary Indians were only too happy with the money and jobs created by the booming war industries and the demand for greater food production.

British officials remained unimpressed by the campaign. The journalist Durga Das, visiting Delhi to report on the 1941 Budget sessions in the Central

Legislative Assembly, found them relaxed, complacent even. Civil disobedience, they told him, was having remarkably little effect. As one bureaucrat observed to him, if the price of having Congress on board was a national government, they were better off without them: 'Why do we need a National Government,' he asked. 'We are getting all the supplies we need for our war effort.'[25]

While Congressmen were doing their duty by trooping non-violently to gaol, their renegade former president was advocating a very different line of attack. Unlike Gandhi and Nehru, Subhas Chandra Bose had no scruples about attacking Britain while she was down: in his eyes, that was exactly the right time to strike. Simultaneously with the Ramgarh Congress session, he had held an 'Anti-Compromise Conference', where he had bitterly attacked the Congress leaders, and Gandhi in particular, as being all talk and no fight. The British, he claimed, 'have ceased to take the Congress seriously'.[26] Throughout the spring and early summer he revelled in Britain's difficulties, hailing each set-back in the war and continuing to call for action, violent if need be.

Bose was walking a tightrope, but somehow he managed to remain free. Even when most other leaders of his Forward Bloc were imprisoned in April, he was not arrested, maybe because the Bengal government considered it too risky. Not only were his own followers likely to react violently, but the local Muslim League might also have seen it as a direct threat – since breaking with Congress, Bose had managed to forge links with some of the most important Muslim leaders in Bengal, especially the mayor of Calcutta, Abdur Rahman Siddiqi, and M.A.H. Ispahani, leader of the League in the Calcutta Corporation and Jinnah's principal financier.

But Bose's immunity could not last for ever. When Siddiqi told him of the fall of Paris, he is said to have danced round the office, his face lit up with joy, convinced that Britain was finished. 'England,' he cried, 'will accept defeat and surrender by 16 July.'[27] In an editorial in his newspaper Forward Bloc on 15 June, he forecast that a great anti-British alliance would emerge. 'Since both Germany and Italy – and perhaps Soviet Russia – now regard Great Britain as public enemy number one,' he wrote, 'it is also likely they have a plan of carving up the British Empire. In this task they may invite Japanese help and co-operation.' He thought such an alliance was bound to founder on old enmities: Germany and Russia would inevitably quarrel over the Balkans. But whatever happened, he declared, India could only gain from the downfall of Britain.[28] Bose had finally overstepped the mark. On 2 July 1940, he was arrested and imprisoned once again in Calcutta's Presidency Gaol.

For some time, Bose had been playing with the idea of making a grandstand gesture that would place him centre stage once more. Seeing himself in the role of a Mazzini or a Sun-Yat-Sen, a leader in exile, the king over the water, he planned to make a dramatic escape from India to the Soviet Union. His plan was forestalled by his arrest, but it was not abandoned, merely shelved. Nearly five months later, he revived it, encouraged by news from Ispahani that the Forward Bloc's financial backer, Lala Shankarlal, had been to Tokyo and made contact with the Japanese foreign minister and the German, Italian and Soviet ambassadors. On 29 November, he went on a hunger strike. Within a week, his health was giving cause for alarm, and the authorities decided they had no alternative but to release him, at least temporarily. On 5 December, he was taken by ambulance to the family home on Elgin Road. On 16 January, disguised as a Muslim in wide pyjamas, a long coat and a black fez, he slipped quietly out of the house and away from the watching police: he had become Mohammed Ziauddin, travelling inspector for the Empire of India Life Assurance Company.

After several days spent in hiding 'in rather humiliating circumstances' in Peshawar, an Afridi guide was found to lead Bose and his companion, Bhagat Ram Talwar, across the frontier into Afghanistan. Partly on foot, partly using the ubiquitous Afghan truck system, they finally reached Kabul on 27 January. No one was expecting them, least of all the Russians, who were extremely suspicious and who made it clear they did not want him. Bose turned instead to the German ambassador, Dr Hans Pilger, whom he had met previously. Pilger recognized him, but was worried that he might turn out to be a British agent, so contacted Berlin for instructions.

Berlin was not particularly interested in Bose, until Pietro Quaroni, the Italian ambassador in Kabul, reported to his government: 'According to Bose, India is morally ripe for revolution; what is lacking is the courage to take the first step. Bose says that if 50,000 men – Italian, German or Japanese – could reach the frontiers of India, the Indian army would desert, the masses would uprise and the end of English domination could be achieved in a very short time.' He concluded that Bose was 'intelligent, able, full of passion; and without doubt the most realistic, maybe the only realist, among Indian national leaders'.[29]

Hearing this, the Germans changed their minds and decided perhaps they did want Bose after all. On 18 March 1941, leaving Bhagat Ram Talwar to return alone to India, Bose left Kabul for the Soviet border, where he caught a train via Bokhara and Samarkand to Moscow. From there, he was flown to Berlin, arriving on 2 April.

One week after his arrival in Berlin, Bose submitted the first of many memoranda to the German Foreign Ministry. Entitled 'Plan for Co-operation Between the Axis Powers and India', it included a 'Declaration of an Independent India', with proposals for setting up a Free India Government in Berlin along the lines of the French and Polish governments in exile in London. On 29 April, he met the Nazi Foreign Minister, Joachim von Ribbentrop, in the Hotel Imperial in Vienna.

Ribbentrop was at his most bombastic and evasive. The war was virtually over, he declared. England was finished – unless it accepted the Führer's terms. These were simple: provided the British allowed Germany to rule Europe, they could keep their empire. When Bose pointed out that this meant the status of India would not change, Ribbentrop argued that England was too far gone even to worry about India. Bose pressed him on the possibility of recruiting Indian prisoners of war to fight the British, but Ribbentrop was non-committal – the Führer had not sanctioned any such development.

However unsatisfactory the meeting with Ribbentrop proved to be, the foreign minister was generous with money. He granted Bose a personal allowance of 12,000 Reichsmarks, and allotted 1 million Reichsmarks for propaganda against the Raj. He also provided him with a luxurious home at 6-7 Sophienstrasse, which lies between Viktoriaplatz and Augustaplatz in Berlin's fashionable west end district of Charlottenburg. The British, meanwhile, had no idea where Bose was. There were rumours that he had escaped by freighter to Japan, and even as late as September 1941, he was thought to be hiding out in Bangkok.

In October 1941, the Zentralstelle Freie Indien (the Free India Centre) was opened at 10 Lichtensteinallee in the Tiergarten diplomatic quarter. But it was all front and no substance: for the moment at least, the Nazis had no idea what to do with their new brown-skinned ally. They would not even allow Bose to live under his own name. Joseph Goebbels, the propaganda minister, insisted that he 'remain camouflaged' as Orlando Mazzotta, the name under which he had left Kabul on a false Italian passport, until he had met and been accepted by Hitler. Hitler, however, was in no hurry – he had other things on his mind.

With Congress out of the picture and the League sitting on the fence, there was little or no constitutional progress during 1941, though Amery was determined not to let things drift. As he told Lionel Curtis, a friend from his South African days: 'It is no good our sitting back and saying "When you [Indians] have agreed, we will think about doing something."'[30] He sent Reginald Coupland, Professor of the History of the British Empire at Oxford and a fellow of All Souls, to India to examine and write a report on the problem in order to find a way of breaking the communal deadlock. He also persuaded the viceroy to appoint another, younger, fellow of All Souls, H.V. Hodson, as his constitutional adviser to work on possible reforms. Both did sterling work, but the results of their labours were too scholarly, too carefully balanced, to be taken seriously by most Indians.

Time after time, Amery repeated his message that Britain could not give India its independence until the two main parties could agree on what they wanted. It may have been a convenient excuse – ignoring as it did the attitude of the prime minister among others – but it was true for the men of goodwill in the

British government. In a speech to the House of Commons on 22 April, Amery said Sir Tej Bahadur Sapru and his Indian Liberals, who joined with the Hindu Mahasabha and the various minority parties to demand an immediate national government, should concentrate instead on bringing about an agreement between Congress and the Muslim League.[31]

Gandhi described Amery's speech as an insult to Indian intelligence. He admitted that 'there is unfortunately an unbridgeable gulf between the Congress and the Muslim League', but said this was a 'domestic quarrel' caused by the British. Once the British left, the Indians would soon find their own 'home-made solution'. 'It may not be scientific; it may not be after any Western pattern; but it will be durable,' he went on. 'It may be that before we come to that happy state of affairs, *we may have to fight amongst ourselves*. But, if we agree not to invite the assistance of any outside Power, the trouble will last perhaps a fortnight.'[32] It was a line that Gandhi was to go on repeating in various forms for the next six years. To Muslim ears, it sounded ominously like a threat.

Jinnah naturally took full advantage of the fears induced in Muslims by Gandhi's pronouncements. He collapsed again on his way to the League's annual session in Madras in April, but recovered sufficiently to electrify the delegates with another two-hour speech. 'Since the fall of the Mughal Empire,' he began, '... Muslim India was never so well organized and so alive and so politically conscious as it is today. We have established a flag of our own, a national flag of Muslim India ... We have defined in the clearest language our goal about which Muslim India was groping in the dark, and the goal is Pakistan.' That, he said, had been the five-year plan of the past. What they now needed was another five-year plan for the future.[33]

For the government, Jinnah had another message:

Please stop your policy of appeasement towards those who are bent on frustrating your war efforts and doing their best to oppose the prosecution of the war and the defence of India at this critical moment ... You are not loyal to those who are willing to stand by you and sincerely desire to support you; you placate those who have the greatest nuisance value in the political and economic fields ... If the Government want the whole-hearted co-operation of Muslim India, they must place their cards on the table.[34]

In the middle of 1941, Britain's war situation was still deteriorating. Hitler had overrun Yugoslavia and Greece, and successfully invaded the Soviet Union. In the Middle East, the Iraqis were openly courting the Axis powers, while the Grand Mufti of Jerusalem had called for a revolt in Palestine. And in north Africa, early British victories over the Italians had been reversed by Rommel, whose German army corps was fast threatening to cut the umbilical cord between Britain and India; the Suez Canal. Hitler was creeping ever closer to India.

For the government of India, the pressure of work caused by the war had increased so much that the viceroy decided he could wait no longer before expanding his Executive Council. On 21 July 1941, without consulting either Congress or the League, he announced five new ministerial portfolios, all of which were to be filled by Indians. This increased the overall size of the Executive Council from seven to 12, eight of whom were now Indian – for the first time ever, Indians were in the majority, though the all-important portfolios of defence, finance and home affairs remained safely in British hands.

In London, Amery told the House of Commons that the new members were as representative of public opinion as was possible, given the refusal of Congress and the League to co-operate. He also described the move as an earnest indication of the British government's desire to transfer a steadily increasing share of power to Indian hands.[35] At the same time, Linlithgow created a new consultative body, the National Defence Council, with 30 members drawn from as many parts of Indian national life as possible, including representatives from the princely states. Five of those invited to be members were prominent Muslim Leaguers: Begum Shah Nawaz, the Nawab of Chhatari, and the premiers of the Punjab, Bengal and Assam, Sir Sikander, Fazlul Haq and Sir Muhammad Saadullah.

Indian reaction to the new moves was mixed. Gandhi issued a statement saying that they changed nothing as far as Congress was concerned. The Hindu Mahasabha welcomed them as a step in the right direction, but suggested that a Sikh should be included in the Executive Council. Jinnah, although he had been informed in advance about the NDC, was furious that the government had gone over his head in inviting the three Muslim premiers. Backed by his Working Committee, he insisted that they resign from the NDC. With great reluctance, they did so – though Haq also resigned from the Working Committee at the same time, as a protest against the president's 'arrogant and dictatorial conduct'.

Always a maverick, Haq went on to split with his provincial League colleagues in Bengal, and was finally expelled from the League altogether in December 1941, after forming a new provincial ministry with Bose's Forward Bloc and the Mahasabha. The Begum Shah Nawaz was expelled for five years, when she refused to resign from the NDC, as was Sir Sultan Ahmed, the new law member of the Executive Council. Jinnah was increasing his authority and imposing discipline over the League with every step. He confirmed it at the end of October by pulling out all League members from the Central Legislative Assembly for the entire session.

On 9 August 1941, Churchill and President Roosevelt met aboard the American cruiser *Augusta* in Placentia Bay, Newfoundland. It was their first face-to-face meeting, apart from a brief encounter back in 1919, though they had corresponded regularly for two years. Essentially, the occasion was symbolic, but at the same time the military staffs who accompanied the two leaders were there to decide how American defence production was to be allocated between the USA, Britain and the Soviet Union, and in this respect it was highly successful.

Churchill, as was his wont, wanted to conclude the three-day conference with some ringing declaration of Anglo-American unity. Roosevelt refused to be bounced into any public commitment – America, after all, was still neutral. In the end, they agreed to issue an eight-point declaration of peace aims that became known as the Atlantic Charter. This proclaimed both parties' dedication to democracy, freedom of the seas, general disarmament and, within limits, free trade – Churchill, who at heart was still a Liberal free-trader, seems to have missed the significance of this blatant American attempt to undermine and eventually destroy Imperial Preference and the Sterling Area.

Churchill also failed to appreciate the hidden meaning behind article III of the Charter, affirming that the two countries 'respect the right of all peoples to choose the form of government under which they will live and they wish to see sovereign rights and self-government restored to those who have been forcibly deprived of them'. The Indians and other colonial peoples, however, spotted it immediately, and greeted it with great enthusiasm.

Amery was quick to realize the implications – which were brought home forcibly to him by a Burmese delegation headed by their premier, U Saw, which happened to be in London at that moment. Citing article III, they demanded self-government immediately, without waiting for the end of the war. Amery stuck to his guns, repeating the promise of independence after the war, and U Saw and his colleagues left for home in a very disgruntled mood.

Amery prepared a lengthy statement for Churchill to make, explaining that the Atlantic Charter had nothing to do with India or the rest of the British empire. But Churchill ignored it, and made his own statement on 9 September, baldly declaring that it was intended to apply only to Europe, and did nothing to change British policy towards India, or its 'responsibilities to its many creeds, races and interests'. This abrupt denial naturally caused great resentment in India, and not only in Congress circles. Even the Central Legislative Assembly protested, passing a motion without division, recommending that the Charter should be applied to India.

The new Executive Council, with its Indian majority, was in place by October, and was soon pressing the viceroy to make a conciliatory gesture to Congress by freeing those civil disobedience prisoners who were still in gaol, including Azad and Nehru. Some officials, notably the governor of the UP, Sir Maurice Hallett, were uneasy at the idea of releasing Nehru, believing it would upset the Muslim League. But the councillors insisted, despite the objections of Churchill, who wanted all the Congressmen kept locked up indefinitely. When he was overruled by his own War Cabinet, he snapped peevishly: 'I give in. When you lose India, don't blame me.'

Nehru, Azad and the others were released on 4 December 1941. Three days later, the Japanese attacked Pearl Harbor. The day after that, they bombed the Philippines, Guam, Midway, Wake, Hong Kong and Singapore, occupied the International Settlement in Shanghai and landed troops in Malaya and Thailand. Like it or not, the Indians now found themselves at war on two fronts, one of which threatened them directly.

20

'A Post-dated Cheque on a Bank that is Failing'

In December 1941 and the first few months of 1942, victory followed victory for the Japanese in the Pacific and South-east Asia. Only a dogged four-month defence in the Philippines by General Douglas MacArthur's US forces slowed them down, tying up thousands of troops who would have been used elsewhere. British prestige in India was reduced still further as one imperial bastion after another crumbled before the invaders. Malaya's fate was sealed only three days after Pearl Harbor, when two British capital ships, the battleship *Prince of Wales*, on which Churchill had voyaged to meet Roosevelt four months earlier, and the battle-cruiser *Repulse*, were sunk off Kuantan by torpedo bombers of the Japanese navy's First Air Group. On that same day, the Japanese-trained Burma Independence Army, led by Aung San, marched across the border from Thailand. With a strength of only 2,300 men, it was barely even a token force, but the government of India watched aghast as it rapidly gained support from the Burmese people. A month later, Burmese premier U Saw was arrested for communicating with the Japanese.

It was not only the British who were worried that Indians might follow the Burmese example. So, too, were many Congressmen. Azad and Rajagopala-chari were so concerned that they managed to persuade the Congress Working Committee to offer full co-operation against the Japanese in return for a national government at once and a firm promise of freedom immediately after the war. Gandhi, who refused to contemplate any involvement in any war, promptly resigned his leadership. Spurred on by this small but significant shift in the Congress position, Sir Tej Bahadur Sapru and a group of leading Moderates sent a message to Churchill calling for 'some bold stroke of far-sighted statesmanship', which would 'rouse [India] on a nation-wide scale to the call for service'.[1]

But Churchill was in no mood to listen. And why should he? As he told Attlee, the Indian Liberals 'have never been able to deliver the goods. The Indian troops are fighting splendidly, but their allegiance is to the King Emperor.'[2] Linlithgow, wedded to his 1935 Act, dismissed the Indian moves, saying it was 'important not to let ourselves be hypnotised by Rajagopalachariar [sic] and his appearance of reasonableness and plausibility'. In a telegram to Amery on 21 January he offered his usual advice: do nothing, the British are the rulers, the British must be seen to rule. 'Further transfer of power,' he warned, 'would give marked encouragement to quisling activities. Recent report from military authorities in Eastern India is to the effect that there is a large and dangerous Fifth-column in Bengal, Assam, Bihar and Orissa.' In the event of an invasion, he was afraid the local population would regard the Japanese as liberators:

India and Burma have no natural association with the Empire, from which they are alien by race, history and religion, and for which as such neither of them have any natural affection, and both are in the Empire because they are conquered countries ... which hitherto it has suited to remain under our protection.[3]

The viceroy's cynicism was justified by at least one unnamed Congress leader, who told the Chinese generalissimo, Chiang Kai-Shek, who was visiting Delhi in early February to try to persuade Indian leaders to support the war against Japan: 'Let nobody imagine that it can make any possible difference to us whether it is the Japanese or the British who rule India.'[4]

The Japanese had calculated that it would take them 100 days to overrun Malaya and capture Singapore. In the event, General Yamashita's three divisions completed the job in 70. Singapore fell on 18 February 1942. It was the most humiliating British defeat since the retreat from Kabul, and the shock waves reverberated throughout the empire. Nowhere were they felt more strongly than in India – among the 130,000 men taken prisoner during the Malayan campaign were no fewer than 60,000 Indians.

Singapore and Malaya were under the control of General Sir Archibald Wavell, who had been commander-in-chief in India since 21 June, when Churchill had switched him and General Sir Claude Auchinleck after the north African disasters in Wavell's previous command as commander-in-chief for the Middle East. He had been appointed supreme commander of Allied forces in the south-west Pacific on 30 December 1941, responsible for an area stretching from India to the Philippines and including Australia and the Dutch East Indies, all of which were under threat from the seemingly unstoppable Japanese.

Until that time, the main theatre of war had been in the western desert and the Middle East, with the result that no resources were available for India. And to make matters worse, Wavell's forces had been stripped of their most able officers – his ADC, Major Bernard Fergusson, later recalled that 'even the scrapings of the barrel were meagre'. In contrast to the brilliant staffs who had supported him in Palestine and Cairo, Wavell 'was now being served by a second XI of staff and subordinates. One or two quite ordinary officers shone like jewels in comparison with those about him.'[5] Churchill, who disliked Wavell, described his task as having 'to bear a load of defeat in a scene of confusion'. It was an accurate description.

Many Indian nationalists rejoiced at Britain's misfortunes. But none crowed louder than Subhas Chandra Bose, who was finally allowed by the Germans to break cover and start broadcasting under his own name on Azad Hind (Free India) Radio, the Japanese network beaming anti-British propaganda into India. 'The fall of Singapore means the collapse of the British empire,' he told his listeners, 'the end of the iniquitous regime which it has symbolized and the dawn of a new era in Indian history.' He denounced those Indians who had collaborated with the British, and declared that 'the vast majority of the Indian people' were with him in the struggle for freedom.[6] His followers, particularly in Bengal, were stirred to action by the sound of his voice. A wave of terrorism swept the province, to continue spasmodically until the end of the war.

With the Japanese at the very gates of India and refugees swarming out of Calcutta in fear of an invasion, the need to rally the Indians became acute. Attlee recognized that there was little chance of anything positive coming from the viceroy. In a strong memo to Amery, he condemned Linlithgow's 'defeatist' telegram of 21 January as helping to explain his past failures, then continued:

> Now is the time for an act of statesmanship. To mark time is to lose India. A renewed effort must be made to get the leaders of the Indian political parties to unite. It is quite obvious from his telegram that the Viceroy is not the man to do this ... His mental attitude is expressed ... when he talks of regaining lost ground after the war ... A representative with power to negotiate within wide limits should be sent to India now, either as a special envoy or in replacement of the present Viceroy, and ... a Cabinet Committee should be appointed to draw up terms of reference and powers.[7]

Attlee's views were supported by increasing pressure from the United States and China as well as from India and Britain. For a few days, Churchill considered going to India himself, but to the immense relief of both Amery and Linlithgow, he changed his plan to making a broadcast, then was persuaded – largely by the viceroy's determined opposition – to abandon this, too, in favour of sending a mission. On 26 February 1942, he followed Attlee's advice and set up an India Committee of the Cabinet.

The new committee was chaired by Attlee, who in addition to his position as deputy prime minister had also been appointed secretary of state for the dominions in a government reshuffle a week earlier. Atlee was joined on the committee by Amery; Simon, now translated to the upper House as a viscount and lord chancellor; Sir John Anderson, former governor of Bengal and a stern opponent of centralization in India; Sir James Grigg, a former finance member of the viceroy's Executive Council who believed Linlithgow was too soft on Congress; and Sir Stafford Cripps.

Cripps, newly returned from his successful stint as ambassador in Moscow, had replaced Attlee as lord privy seal and Churchill as leader of the House of Commons, but his interest in India was as keen as ever. Almost the first thing he said to Churchill when he came back from Russia was: 'This Indian problem must be solved.' As soon as he entered the War Cabinet, Churchill asked him to start drafting his ideas.[8]

It was only natural, given the presence of both Cripps and Attlee, that the committee's starting point should be the plan cooked up during Nehru's weekend with them at 'Goodfellows' and subsequently developed by Cripps in his 1939 visit to India. What is surprising is that it was accepted by the rest of the committee with only one significant addition: Amery successfully pressed for the right of any 'dissident province' to opt out of a united India, though not to stop the other provinces framing a new constitution. As Amery privately admitted, this was 'the first public admission of the possibility of Pakistan', but it was vital if they were to retain Muslim co-operation.[9] Cripps and the others agreed readily.

It was Churchill, attending the first meeting ex officio, who caused the problems, as Amery confided to his diary:

What really killed the whole discussion was Winston's complete inability to grasp even the most elementary points ... After one had spent ages explaining the effect of enabling a province to stand out he still harked back to the iniquity of any body on which there was a Congress majority, as if a majority mattered in such a case.

He seems quite incapable of listening or taking in even the simplest point but goes off at a tangent on a word and then rambles on inconsecutively ...

Certainly a complete outsider coming to that meeting and knowing nothing of his reputation would have thought him a rather amusing but quite gaga old gentleman who could not understand what people were talking about.[10]

In fact, as Amery later admitted, Churchill was not so much gaga as highly emotional, hating the idea of having to submit to American pressure almost as much as he hated any idea of Indian independence. Later that year, in a memorable speech at the Mansion House celebrating the turning point of the war in North Africa, he would declare: 'I have not become the King's First Minister in order to preside over the liquidation of the British Empire.' Now, he regarded the proposals to be made to India as little more than window dressing, a display of good intent for the benefit of Roosevelt and the Americans, which could not possibly succeed – or be allowed to succeed.

The committee's draft declaration of policy, completed on 7 March 1942, finally answered the questions of how and when India would achieve full independence:

> His Majesty's Government ... have decided to lay down in precise and clear terms the steps which they propose shall be taken for the earliest possible realization of self-government in India. The object is the creation of a new Indian Union which shall constitute a Dominion, associated with the United Kingdom and the other Dominions by a common allegiance to the Crown, but equal to them in every respect, in no way subordinate in any aspect of its domestic or external affairs.

There would be provincial elections immediately after the war, following which the entire membership of all the lower houses would elect a constituent assembly based on a system of proportional representation, to draw up a new constitution for India, 'unless the leaders of Indian opinion in the principal communities agree upon some other form before the end of hostilities'. The Indian states would be invited to take part, appointing a number of members in proportion to their total population. British interests and obligations, including those to minorities and the princely states, would be covered by a treaty between the British government and the Indian constituent assembly.[11] At long last, this was a clear and unequivocal promise that the Indians would decide their own future immediately after the war was won.

First, however, the war had to be won – and to many Indians that was looking more and more unlikely. The day after the draft declaration was finished, the Burmese capital, Rangoon, was abandoned to the Japanese. To British consternation, increasing numbers of Burmese were supporting the invaders. Spurred on by fears that many Indians might do the same, Cripps volunteered to take the proposals to India personally, to discuss them with Indian leaders before they were published – the British government had at last learned that it was fatal to spring any form of *fait accompli* on the Indians. They were, however, imposing a *fait accompli* on Linlithgow, who was distinctly unhappy at being rushed into something with which he did not agree. Wavell and all the provincial governors joined him in condemning the 'local option' allowing provinces and states to stand out. They believed this would provoke communal trouble, particularly with the

Sikhs, who would be upset at the prospect of a separate Punjab under Muslim control. Wavell feared that this would cause serious damage to the services and their ability to wage war.

Churchill soothed Linlithgow's wounded pride by explaining his real purpose in backing the operation. 'It would be impossible,' he wrote, 'owing to unfortunate rumours and publicity, and the general American outlook, to stand on a purely negative attitude and the Cripps mission is indispensable to prove our honesty of purpose ... If it is rejected by the Indian parties for whose benefit it has been devised, our sincerity will be proved to the world.'[12] Linlithgow got the message, and withdrew his threatened resignation. He was still unhappy at having Cripps interfering in his patch, regarding him as a meddling dilettant with highly suspect political aims. But now that he understood what Churchill was about, he knew he would have the prime minister's backing in seeing off the threat. All he had to do was give Cripps enough rope, and wait for him to hang himself.

Linlithgow's suspicions were well founded, for Cripps was planning to spring his own *fait accompli* on Churchill and the British government. He accepted that it would be impossible during the war to push through the full independence demanded by Congress. But he believed that he could achieve the vital first step of creating a national government by completely Indianizing the viceroy's Executive Council and turning it into a representative Cabinet, with the viceroy's role reduced to that of a constitutional monarch. There was, of course, no mention of this in the draft, but the final paragraph was ambiguous. It stated that, while the British government must retain responsibility for defence, 'His Majesty's Government desire, and invite, the immediate and effective participation of the leaders of the principal sections of the Indian people in the counsels of their country, of the Commonwealth and of the United Nations [the Allies].'[13] 'Effective participation' was a phrase that allowed Cripps plenty of room for manœuvre.

Cripps arrived in Delhi on 23 March 1942, with what H.V. Hodson described as 'a substantial entourage' headed by Amery's India Office secretary, Frank Turnbull, and joined by Professor Sir Reginald Coupland as constitutional adviser. 'There is no time to lose,' he told reporters at his opening press conference, 'and no time for long discussions. I am sure that in the circumstances of today the leaders of the main parties and interests in India will be ready to make quick decisions.' Just how quick those decisions would have to be came as a shock to everyone. Cripps proposed to stay for just two weeks, in which time he believed he could crack the nut that had defeated some of the best brains in both Britain and India over the previous quarter of a century.

Cripps's bold move was in part a political gamble with an enormous personal prize in view — nothing less than the key to 10 Downing Street, where he believed he could do a better job than Churchill by applying scientific methods to the war effort. His aide, the young Welsh socialist David Owen, was by no means alone in his thinking, when he told Coupland, 'If he brought this settlement off, Cripps would certainly replace Winston.'[14] The prospect was not as preposterous as it seems in retrospect: Cripps, though an independent MP, was enjoying great popularity in Britain since his high-profile ambassadorship to Moscow. A Mass Observation poll asking 'If anything should happen to Mr Churchill, whom would you like to succeed him as Prime Minister?' showed Cripps closing fast on Churchill's heir-apparent, with 34 per cent to Anthony Eden's 37. Attlee ran a poor third with only 2 per cent.[15]

The question of succession was not entirely hypothetical: Churchill's health was not good at that time, he faced danger every time he flew off on one of his many visits to America or the fighting fronts, and his position was threatened by the continuing series of British military disasters. When the fall of Tobruk in June of that year brought yet more speculation about Churchill's future, Cripps even asked Ramsay MacDonald's son Malcolm, home on leave from his position as high commissioner in Canada, to sound out other members of the Cabinet about his taking over. MacDonald wisely declined.[16]

By chance, Cripps had arrived in Delhi on 'Pakistan Day', the second anniversary of the Lahore resolution, and he could not have failed to be impressed by the mile-long procession of Muslims marching through the streets of the city. Nor could he have failed to note that Jinnah's rousing speech at the mass meeting that followed in Urdu Park was directed as much at him as at the 50,000-strong audience. Cripps, Jinnah said, was a friend of Congress, who had enjoyed the hospitality of Nehru, but there was no need for Muslims to be afraid on that score, as he had not come in a personal capacity. However, he warned, 'If any scheme or solution which is detrimental to the interests of Muslims is forced upon us ... we shall not only not accept it but resist it to the utmost of our capacity. If we have to die in the attempt we shall die fighting.'[17]

Linlithgow, though courteous as always, took pains to distance himself from Cripps and his mission – a point that was emphasized by housing him not in the Viceroy's House but in a bungalow some way away at 3 Queen Victoria Road. He started his first meeting with Cripps by firing a warning shot over defence, which he said was for him to deal with. A day or two later he put up another warning signal when he threw back a draft plan for an all-Indian Executive Council, apart from the commander-in-chief and the viceroy himself, with the curt comment: 'That's my affair.'[18]

After three days spent talking to the viceroy, the commander-in-chief, various officials and each member of the Executive Council individually, Cripps began presenting the draft declaration to Indian political and communal leaders, starting with Congress and the Muslim League. The Congress Working

Committee had decided that Azad and Nehru would represent it, but Nehru was ill with a fever and for the first meeting on 25 March, Azad was accompanied by another Muslim, Asaf Ali. Their only immediate objection was, perhaps inevitably, to the defence clause. Jinnah, who followed them, had no difficulty with defence – he was more interested in the first part of the document. Cripps thought he seemed pleasantly surprised at how far it went towards meeting the Pakistan case. Their meeting was 'extremely cordial'. 'On the whole,' Cripps noted, 'I was hopefully impressed by his general attitude and his lack of pernickity criticism of phrases and words which I had rather expected. His only substantial suggestion was for clearer wording regarding the second dominion.'[19]

With the two major parties briefed, Cripps plunged into three days of meetings with other parties and interests. Representatives of the Chamber of Princes, the Indian TUC, the Anglo-Indians, the European business community, the Liberals, the Scheduled Castes, followed each other in and out of the bungalow in Queen Victoria Road in quick succession. The Sikhs came on 27 March, and demanded their own province carved out of the Punjab – the governor of the Punjab had already told Cripps that they were troublesome, and that 'if there were a hint of secession they would concentrate on getting ready to fight the Muslims'. With the Hindu Mahasabha delegation, Cripps was barely able to get a word in. Its leader, Savarkar, 'spent most of his time lecturing me upon the principles of majority determination and of fallacies in the document'. Savarkar wanted to accept the first part of the declaration, reject the opt-out provisions, and have two defence advisers, one Hindu, one Muslim, as he said the two sides did not trust each other.

For all the long line of political leaders trooping in to see him, Cripps knew that there was one man who counted more than any of them. Gandhi at that time was not even a member of Congress, and represented no one but himself, but Cripps persuaded him to leave his Wardha *ashram* and travel to Delhi for a meeting. He arrived in the early afternoon on 27 March, and Cripps hurried from the bungalow personally to open the door of the car that had brought the old man from the railway station. They greeted each other warmly, though Cripps was a little put out when Gandhi claimed not to remember anything of their political discussions in 1939 on which much of the present scheme was based, only their conversations about vegetarianism.

Gandhi was not encouraging. After studying the declaration briefly, he said: 'Why did you come if this is what you have to offer? If this is your entire proposal to India, I would advise you to take the next plane home.'[20] He went on to predict that Congress would reject it on three grounds: the inclusion of the Indian states in the proposed constituent assembly, the opt-out provisions, and, he added rather vaguely, the defence question. After two and a quarter hours of discussion, he left, strongly urging Cripps not to publish the declaration.

Cripps should have realized that without Gandhi's imprimatur his mission was already doomed. But he pressed on, encouraged by a further meeting with a 'most urbane and pleasant' Jinnah: it was, Cripps noted, 'quite clear from his whole attitude that his committee had already accepted the scheme in principle'. This was confirmed later in the day by Sir Sikander Hayat Khan, who said they were ready to start working out the details, especially on defence. Rajagopalachari, too, was encouraging, suggesting ways of redrafting the defence clause to make it more palatable to his Congress colleagues. He wanted Indian leaders to be able 'to give some clarion call to the Indians which would stimulate them from their present defeatist attitude'. But Azad was not so easily swayed – he spent a full hour and a half arguing about the defence issue, unwilling to accept that British troops could not be put under an Indian C-in-C, and that two separate commands simply would not work.

By the end of his first week in India, Cripps had already shown the draft declaration to so many people that it was pointless trying to keep its contents secret any longer. On Sunday 29 March he held another press conference, at which he released the full text and answered journalists' questions. Cripps's press conferences, held every other day, were something quite new for India: Coupland wrote:

Nobody would have imagined ... that such direct and open personal relations could be established between the British Government in London and the Indian public six thousand miles away; that a British Minister would himself discuss and defend 'high policy' with that public's representatives and be ready to answer forthwith and forthright any kind of question. No wonder that there was talk that night of a breath of fresh air in Delhi.[21]

To the viceroy, who had always conducted negotiations in the strictest secrecy, it must have felt more like an icy blast.

Linlithgow could not have found much comfort, either, in what Cripps had to say to reporters. When he was asked why the British government was still only promising dominion status, Cripps replied that the constituent assembly would be completely free to decide for itself whether or not to remain in the Commonwealth. It would be free to do exactly what it wanted. It could declare that it did not want a governor-general. It could start with its own declaration of independence – at last, a British minister had said the magic word. And there was more: he went on to announce his own idea that the new Executive Council should function as a Cabinet, a suggestion that infuriated Linlithgow, who had specifically warned him off this area.

It was not all good news for the nationalists, however: defence remained a vexed question. 'It would be dishonest', Cripps went on, 'to say that an Indian

Defence Minister would be responsible for the defence of India.' But for the most part, the British felt justified in believing they had gone as far as any reasonable person could expect in the middle of an all-consuming war. Indeed, many of them believed they had gone much too far. The declaration, however, and Cripps's assurances, cut little ice with Gandhi, who was still in Delhi, staying at Birla House. When he was asked what he would tell the Congress Working Committee to do, he replied: 'My advice will be, this is a post-dated cheque. Accept or leave it as you like.' In the next day's papers, journalistic licence had both embroidered and shortened his answer to: 'This is a post-dated cheque on a bank that is failing.' Whoever coined it, it was a brilliant phrase that said it all, and Gandhi was in no hurry to disown it.

After the press conference, Nehru joined Cripps for breakfast, the first time they had met during this visit. Cripps thought he seemed 'tired and not well', having only just left his sickbed, but that his attitude as they discussed the proposals in general and the defence issue in particular was 'mild and conciliatory'. Nehru, on the other hand, recalled later that he had been 'profoundly depressed' when he first read the proposals, 'and that depression was largely due to the fact that I had expected something more substantial from Sir Stafford Cripps as well as from the critical situation that had arisen'.[22] It was only the first among several significant misunderstandings which were to dog Cripps's mission.

So far, Cripps had managed to stay detached and professional in his dealings with all the Indian parties, but with the arrival of Nehru, he became more and more involved with Congress. That Sunday morning he went with Nehru to Birla House, where there was a great gathering of Congress people. Azad took them straight in to see Gandhi, then Cripps spent three and a half hours with various Congressmen, discussing details of the draft and the revisions he had already made to the original.

The Congress Working Committee was once again deeply divided. Gandhi and his close disciples were against any involvement in the war under any circumstances. Rajagopalachari, Azad and their supporters, who had always regarded non-violence as little more than a useful tactical device, were eager to co-operate in the war effort, provided they had real responsibility and power. A third group, led by Vallabhbhai Patel, approached the subject as hard-nosed politicians who saw the war as an opportunity of gaining their long-term objectives. Nehru hovered unhappily between them all, torn between his respect for Gandhi and his own desire to join the fight against Fascism.

Next day, Cripps made a broadcast on All-India Radio, explaining the declaration and his hopes directly to the Indian people. But those hopes took a knock when Nehru came to dinner, looking 'more serious and more worried about the Indian situation' than Cripps had ever seen him. According to Cripps, Nehru implied that 'the Working Committee would not accept, largely, though he did not say so precisely, due to the influence of Gandhi. I gathered that he was doing his utmost to gain support for acceptance, but felt he was fighting a losing battle. Non-violence meant dissociation from any involvement in war effort.'[23]

Nehru was right. On 2 April, the Working Committee formally rejected the proposals in a long resolution, which Nehru and Azad took to Cripps. At first glance, it looked conclusive, but on closer inspection it was clearly a negotiating document. The ritual demand for complete independence for the whole of India was qualified by the claim that 'only the realisation of present freedom would light the flame which would illumine the hearts of millions and move them to action'. The inclusion of representatives of the states in the proposed constituent assembly was objected to only because they would be nominated by the princes and not elected by their peoples. And while the provincial opt-out provisions were condemned as 'a severe blow to the conception of Indian unity and an apple of discord likely to generate growing trouble in the provinces', the document recognized the principle that some form of self-determination must be allowed to the Muslims – an enormous concession for Congress to make.

Having dealt somewhat airily with the future, the resolution finally got down to business in its penultimate paragraph, stating baldly that 'it is the present that counts, and even proposals for the future are important in so far as they affect the present'. What Congress wanted was effective power now, and the essence of that power lay in the provisions for defence:

> At any time defence is a vital subject; during war time it is all important and covers almost every sphere of life and administration. To take away defence from the sphere of responsibility at this stage is to reduce that responsibility to a farce and a nullity, and to make it perfectly clear that India is not going to be free in any way and her Government is not going to function as a free and independent government during the pendency of the war.

To make their unspoken invitation to negotiate quite clear, the two Congress leaders told Cripps they did not intend publishing their resolution for the moment, adding that if any change were made to the draft declaration, 'they would naturally reconsider their attitude to the new document'.[24]

Amery was delighted by Cripps's optimistic report that day. 'Everyone admires manner in which you have discharged your difficult mission,' he telegraphed, 'and effect of our proposals has been most beneficial in USA and in large circles here.'[25] As far as Amery and Churchill were concerned, Cripps's mission had served its purpose, and he could come home. Cripps, however, had other ideas. Ignoring a warning from Amery that he could not make any changes on defence without Cabinet approval, he began negotiating in earnest on that very point. First, he arranged for Azad and Nehru to talk to Wavell as soon as the commander-in-chief returned to Delhi in two days' time. No doubt Cripps hoped that the C-in-C would be able to explain the difficulties involved in transferring defence to Indian hands, enabling them to understand the British position more clearly.

On Saturday, 4 April 1942, Cripps took Nehru and Azad to meet Wavell, but after making the introductions he left them to it. Wavell, a grizzled and rather daunting figure with a glass eye, was notoriously taciturn, but that day he excelled himself. General G.N. Molesworth, deputy chief of the general staff, who was present, described what happened next:

> When tea was cleared away, Wavell asked the Indian leaders to open proceedings, and Pandit Nehru spoke for some time. Briefly he wanted the Defence Member to be an Indian in place of the Commander-in-Chief, who would become an executive adviser ... When he had finished, I imagined that some discussions, and perhaps bargaining, would take place ... To my intense astonishment, Wavell said, 'If that is your case, there is nothing more to be said.' There was dead silence. After a pause Wavell stood up and the Indian leaders rose to take their leave.[26]

In spite of Wavell's abrupt dismissal of the Indian case, Cripps persevered. Defence was the only issue on which there was any room for negotiation, and to his mind it offered the greatest rewards. If he could swing the Congress Working Party, he told Churchill in a lengthy telegram, the pacifists would probably be forced out, leaving Azad, Nehru and Rajagopalachari in undisputed command. 'I am satisfied that if once they come in they will go all out to maximise Indian resistance to Japan and will fight with courage and determination to galvanise the Indian people to action. They have told me that there would be no question whatever of any separate peace and I am certain this can be relied upon.'[27]

Linlithgow and Wavell were both utterly opposed to handing over defence to an Indian minister, or to any measure that gave the impression that Indian members of a 'Cabinet' would be able to overrule the commander-in-chief. But that same day, Cripps managed to persuade them to agree to split the defence portfolio into two departments. They saw 'no very serious risks in handing over to an Indian member of Council a portfolio of Defence Co-ordination, with limited powers'. They even agreed to give him the title defence minister and make the commander-in-chief war minister, if it would make the offer more attractive to Congress.

The new minister would be responsible for press relations, demobilization and post-war reconstruction, petroleum supplies, amenities and welfare of troops and their dependants, canteens, certain non-technical educational institutions, stationery, printing and forms for the army; also reception, accommodation and social arrangements for all foreign missions. He would also take over some areas with an indirect bearing on defence, such as scorched earth policy, evacuation from threatened areas, signals co-ordination and economic warfare.[28] It was not a particularly inspiring list, and Congress saw through it immediately, rejecting it out of hand as making the position of the Indian defence member 'almost ludicrous'.

With stalemate approaching, a new player suddenly appeared on the scene. Colonel Louis Johnson, a former US assistant secretary of war, had arrived in Delhi on 3 April at the head of a five-man technical advisory mission to find out how America could help in developing India's production of war materials for the Allied armies in the Far and Middle East. Johnson, senior partner in what he described as 'the largest law office south of Philadelphia', based in Clarksburg and Charleston, West Virginia, was also to be the special representative of the president in New Delhi, with the rank of 'minister plenipotentiary', a significant American move which placed India on the same diplomatic plane as Canada, Australia, New Zealand and South Africa. The appointment had been made very quickly, and Johnson's briefing by the State Department was at best sketchy – he felt 'that he had not been given any very positive information about anything'. Nevertheless, he was keen to try to 'do' something with the nationalists. He was told he probably could, but that it must be done with the utmost care.[29]

Linlithgow invited Johnson to lunch on 5 April, Easter Sunday, together with Cripps. The two men hit it off instantly, and Cripps recognized this fellow liberal lawyer as a potential ally. So, too, did Nehru, who was quick to seize the advantages of enlisting what he believed would be the powerful support of President Roosevelt's personal envoy. Linlithgow and his officials were horrified by the intervention of a man whom Hodson described as 'completely ignorant both of Indian problems and personalities and of the structure of government in India'.[30] They became more and more irritated as he threw himself with blind enthusiasm into his chosen role as intermediary between Cripps and Congress, shuttling to and fro between 3 Queen Victoria Road and Birla House at all hours of the day and night with drafts and redrafts of the defence provisions.

The inevitable explosion came on the evening of 8 April, when the viceroy discovered that Cripps and Johnson had been so carried away that they had made their own proposals to Congress without consulting him beforehand. Linlithgow complained bitterly to Amery and Churchill, who responded by delivering a sharp rap to Cripps's knuckles. Amery reprimanded him for making proposals to Congress without the prior knowledge and approval of the viceroy and commander-in-chief, and told him he must bring the whole matter back to the Cabinet's plan which he had gone out to urge on the Indians. Churchill told him he 'must not commit us in any way' and that the Cabinet would not come to any decision until it had the 'independent and unprejudiced' opinions of the viceroy and commander-in-chief. The prime minister then thundered – wrongly, as it happened – that 'Colonel Johnson is not President Roosevelt's personal representative in any matter outside the specific Mission dealing with Indian munitions and kindred topics ... The President would be very vexed if he, the President, were to be drawn into the Indian situation. His message to me ... was entirely opposed to anything like US intervention or mediation.'[31]

Cripps replied in great detail and with a very aggrieved tone, setting out exactly how the offending formula had been arrived at, with the approval of the viceroy and the C-in-C. He ended: 'I am sorry that my colleagues appear to distrust me over this matter, and I am quite prepared to hand the matter over if they would rather someone else carried on the negotiations ... Unless I am trusted I cannot carry on with the task.' But Cripps's protestations were too late: the truth was, he had been rumbled. His mention of negotiations was a mistake, allowing Amery to fire back: 'It was certainly agreed between us that there were not to be negotiations but that you were to try to gain acceptance with possibly minor variations or elaborations of our great offer which has made so powerful an impression here and throughout the United States.'[32]

The Congress negotiators were bemused next day when, instead of offering further concessions, Cripps returned abruptly to the basic terms of the original declaration with a new proposal drafted by Linlithgow. Whereupon, the whole house of cards which he had built up over the previous three weeks collapsed. Congress formally rejected the proposals, giving as their main reason not the defence issue but the lack of any offer of an immediate national government, with the viceroy responsible to an all-Indian Cabinet. Gandhi had taken no part in the final discussions – he had hurried home to Wardha on the previous Saturday, having received news that Kasturbai was ill – but his very absence was eloquent, and the result was exactly as he had forecast to Cripps nearly three weeks before. Jinnah, who had been biding his time for the Congress decision, immediately followed suit on behalf of the Muslim League: he could not afford to risk alienating mass opinion by openly supporting the British.

'There is clearly no hope of agreement,' Cripps cabled London at 10 minutes to midnight on 10 August, 'and I shall start home on Sunday.' His next message, barely 12 hours later, was more upbeat: 'My own view is that despite failure the atmosphere has improved quite definitely. Nehru has come out in a fine statement for total war against the Japs; Jinnah has pledged me the unwavering support of the Muslims and the Sikhs and other minorities will be on the whole relieved and I hope to some extent reassured. The real difficulty has been the internal stresses in Congress itself ...'[33]

Churchill raised no objections to Cripps's returning to London at once.

He is said to have put on 'an act of sham tears and sorrow' to Roosevelt's envoy, Harry Hopkins, who was with him at Chequers when Cripps's message arrived, but did not really trouble to conceal his pleasure.[34] When Roosevelt urged him to postpone Cripps's departure until a 'Nationalist government' could be set up, saying that American public opinion was blaming Britain for the breakdown by unreasonably withholding self-government from the Indians, he replied that he would treat the cable as 'purely private' and say nothing to the Cabinet.[35]

'Leave India to God — or to Anarchy'

The failure of the Cripps mission was a turning-point for many in India. Most Congressmen, and certainly Azad, were bemused by Cripps's sudden departure: knowing nothing of the telegrams flying to and from London, they had assumed that the talks so far had been the normal limbering up for the start of serious negotiations. The result was serious disillusionment, particularly when Cripps broadcast a farewell message putting all the blame for the breakdown on Congress. The Congress newspapers, which had treated the declaration as a fair basis for negotiation while talks were still in progress, suddenly changed their tune. Taking their lead from Gandhi's *Harijan*, they now denounced it as an affront to the country, an insult to Indian intelligence and final proof of Britain's naked imperialism.[1]

Britain's stock was sinking fast, with an increasing number of Indians believing she could not win the war in the east — and who could blame them, as disaster followed disaster during the whole of April. Along with the continuing reverses in Burma, powerful Japanese naval forces moved into the Indian Ocean at the beginning of the month. On Easter Sunday, carrier-based aircraft attacked Colombo, the capital and chief port of Ceylon, causing considerable damage and sinking six British ships, including three warships and a submarine depot ship, in less than an hour. Shortly afterwards, Japanese aircraft spotted two British cruisers, the *Devonshire* and the *Cornwall*, and sank them both with terrifyingly accurate dive-bombing.

A second Japanese naval force appeared in the Bay of Bengal the following day. Fifty-five merchant ships in east-coast Indian ports were ordered to sea, but within a few hours 20 of them were at the bottom of the ocean, while Japanese submarines went into action in neighbouring waters to bring the total tonnage sunk that day to a staggering 92,000. The Japanese then bombed the Indian ports of Vizagapatam and Kakindada, which lie between Calcutta and Madras. As these first bombs fell on Indian soil, civilians fled in panic. 'I know ... that even if a few hundred Japanese soldiers had landed on the East Indian coast the whole of South India could become depopulated,' wrote Nirad C. Chaudhuri.[2] Three days later, the first Japanese naval group turned its attentions to the Royal Navy base at Trincomalee on Ceylon's north-east coast, wiping out almost half of the defending aircraft and setting fire to at least two ships before sinking two tankers, a corvette, the carrier *Hermes* and the Australian destroyer *Vampire*, which were at sea near by.

The two Japanese admirals then turned their ships round and headed back to the Pacific. Their Indian raids had been devastating, but were never to be repeated – though no one could know that at the time. Indian reaction, particularly in Bengal, was an inevitable combination of fear and *Schadenfreude*. According to Chaudhuri: 'There was not only panic but also a good deal of eager expectation of more humiliation for the British.'[3]

Indian doubts and fears were heightened by Japanese propaganda broadcasts from Tokyo and Bangkok. The Japanese prime minister, General Hideki Tojo, had told Indians in early March that one of Japan's war aims was to free them from Anglo-Saxon rule. While the Cripps talks were in progress, he followed this up with a warning that the Indians would suffer heavy losses if they remained under British military control. A week later, it was the turn of Rash Behari Basu, the old Bengali revolutionary who had claimed he was responsible for the assassination attempt on Lord Hardinge back in 1912 and who briefly led the Ghadr revolt in the Punjab in 1914 before fleeing to safety in Japan. Basu was now leader of the Indian Independence League in east and south-east Asia. He assured his fellow countrymen that the Japanese would not invade India if they drove out the British themselves.

Gandhi was among those influenced by the Japanese broadcasts, and by those of Subhas Bose from Berlin. Shortly afterwards, he began a series of articles in *Harijan* demanding the withdrawal of all foreign troops from Indian soil – not only British but also the Americans who were just beginning to arrive. He was bitterly critical of America for failing to prevent the war: 'If she had really wished to do so, she could have brought about peace.' Amazingly, considering Pearl Harbor, he thought she need not have entered the war at all: 'America could have remained out. Even now she can do so ...'[4]

From demanding the withdrawal of British troops, Gandhi progressed to demanding the immediate withdrawal of all the British. 'The presence of the British in India is an invitation to Japan to invade India,' he wrote. 'Their withdrawal removes the bait. Assume, however, that it does not; free India will be better able to cope with the invasion.'[5] Shrugging aside fears of complete lawlessness and even civil war if the British did go, he announced that he was not asking them to hand over the administration to Congress or any other person or party. The message he had for them was simple: 'Leave India to God — or to anarchy.'

With the war situation in the Mediterranean and north Africa as well as Burma growing more critical every day, the British had little patience for Gandhi's demands. Wavell was more concerned with the problems of trying to defend India from the Japanese with an air force that was 'quite inadequate'. It was, he cabled Churchill on 14 June, 'deficient in numbers, in reserves, in range, in hitting power and in training'.[6] In response, Churchill lashed out with an angry memo to Amery: 'If Gandhi tries to start a really hostile movement against us in this crisis, I am of opinion that he should be arrested, and that both British and United States opinion would support such a step. If he likes to starve himself to death,' he concluded hopefully, 'we cannot help that.'[7]

By no means all of the leading Congressmen agreed with Gandhi's views. Nehru had pledged to organize guerrilla warfare against the Japanese if they did invade. Others, most notably Rajagopalachari, wanted to go even further. Rajagopalachari wanted to create a national front, to mobilize the country for active defence. When the Working Committee met in Allahabad at the end of the month, he brought two resolutions passed by his members in Madras, one calling for Congress to return to government in the provinces, the other calling for it and the Muslim League to settle their differences and form a national government together. Always a realist, he knew that Congress would first have to acknowledge the League's claims to represent Muslims and for the right of provinces to secede. In his view, this was a price worth paying in the present emergency. Few of his colleagues agreed: they threw out his motions, forcing him to resign from Congress in order to continue his campaign for a *rapprochement* with the League.

Gandhi had decided to take up the reins of Congress again, and the members as always responded dutifully to his commands. When Azad called for fresh talks with the British with Roosevelt acting as mediator — something which Cripps had favoured[8] — Gandhi brought him to heel by threatening to remove him as Congress president. Nehru stood out against him for a while, but eventually they reached a compromise. Nehru abandoned his plans for guerrilla war and agreed to support only non-violent resistance, in exchange for Gandhi dropping his demand for the withdrawal of foreign troops.

The resolution that was passed by the Working Committee at Wardha on 14 July 1942 after nine days of heated discussion was an intriguing mix of Nehru and Gandhi. It attacked Nazism and Fascism as well as imperialism, and actually invited Allied forces to stay 'in order to ward off and resist Japanese or other aggression, and to protect and help China'. The Indian people's resistance, however, was to be limited to offering 'complete non-violent non-co-operation to the invading forces'. But the nub of the resolution was a demand for an immediate end to British rule, with the threat of mass action under Gandhi's leadership if they did not. The Indian press seized on this with glee. The headlines everywhere compressed it into one memorable phrase, which was to be become the slogan of the new movement: 'Quit India!' Gandhi declared that this would be his last campaign and his biggest, and that it would either end British rule or end him.

Outside Congress, the new move was universally condemned. Jinnah, naturally, led the opposition, describing the Quit India resolution as 'blackmailing the British and coercing them to concede a system of government ... which would establish a Hindu raj immediately under the aegis of the British bayonet'.[9] Jinnah had some unlikely bedfellows, including the newly legalized Communist Party, the Hindu Mahasabha, the All-India TUC, the All-India Students' Conference, the Scheduled Castes, the Sikhs, all the other minorities, and even Nehru's peasant organizations, the *kisan sabhas*, which held rallies in hundreds of villages. On a practical level, industrial production of war materials continued to rise, and army recruitment figures reached a new peak of 70,000 volunteers during the month of May.

Ignoring the hostile reactions, Gandhi and Nehru pressed on. On Friday, 7 August the full AICC met in Bombay to ratify the Working Party's decision. It was the middle of the monsoon season, but some 7,500 delegates braved the heavy rains to converge on the Gowalia Tank in the heart of the city, where an area of 30,000 square feet had been roped off and covered with a double tarpaulin to keep everyone reasonably dry. The Quit India resolution was put to the meeting next day and passed by a huge majority – the only votes against coming from the 13 Communist members.

Gandhi spoke for two hours, in English and Hindi, beginning typically by praising the Communists for their courage in voting against the resolution and then castigating them for their lack of judgement. The time for talking to the British, the time for pacts and agreements, he said, was past, though 'the actual struggle does not commence at this moment. You have only placed all your powers in my hands. I will now wait upon the Viceroy and plead with him for the acceptance of the Congress demands.'

Gandhi thought the process was likely to take two or three weeks, but he assured his audience that he would not strike any bargains. He would tell the viceroy: 'Nothing less than freedom.' He gave detailed instructions to all sections of the community on what they were to do, then concluded with a personal exhortation: 'Here is a mantra, a short one, that I give you. You may imprint it on your hearts and let every breath of yours give expression to it. The mantra is: "Do or Die." We shall either free India or die in the attempt; we shall not live to see the perpetuation of our slavery.'[10]

The viceroy's answer did not take two or three weeks. It did not even take 24 hours. The AICC meeting had conveniently assembled all the Congress leaders in Bombay, and before dawn next morning the police swooped, arresting them under Section 26(i)(b) of the Defence of India Act, which allowed for detention without trial. Linlithgow had planned to deport them all, especially Gandhi, to Aden or east Africa, but was persuaded not to do so by his Executive Council, which he had enlarged in July without further consultation. Eleven of its 15 members were now Indian, and they reminded him that Gandhi was nearly 73 and would almost certainly fast to death if he were taken from India. If he were to die overseas, whether from fasting or some local disease, the effect on world-wide, never mind Indian, opinion would be much more serious than if he died in India. The British would be regarded as little better than the Nazis.

It was decided that Gandhi would be confined in the Aga Khan's summer palace outside Poona as a state rather than a security prisoner, which meant that he would be allowed certain additional privileges. He took with him a small retinue consisting of his secretary Mahadev Desai, his English acolyte Mira Behn, the physician Sushila Naiyar, sister of his other secretary and *Harijan* editor Pyarelal, and Sarojini Naidu. Kasturbai was not originally included, but forced the government's hand that evening by threatening to make a speech to a protest meeting, whereupon she was arrested and sent to join her husband. Nehru, Azad, Patel and nine other senior members of the Working Committee were imprisoned 70 miles away in the less salubrious surroundings of Ahmednagar Fort, an ancient monument that had been converted into a gaol during the First World War. All Congress committees were banned, and local leaders throughout India were rounded up and locked away.

Strict press censorship muffled news of the arrests, but nothing could keep them secret for long. The protests began in Bombay, where at least nine people died in clashes with police on the day of the arrests. Ahmedabad and Poona followed. Twenty-four hours later, the trouble had spread to Delhi, the UP and Bihar, and for the next six weeks there were disturbances over much of northern India. Gandhi's pleas for non-violence were ignored as mobs took to the streets. In the first week, according to official estimates, 250 railway stations and over 500 post offices were damaged or destroyed, 150 police stations attacked, 59 trains derailed, and many bridges and government godowns destroyed. Railway lines were torn up, telegraph wires were torn down.

As usual, there was little trouble in the south. Perhaps more surprisingly, Bengal and the NWFP remained comparatively calm. After Bombay, the worst violence was in Bihar and the eastern UP, traditionally the main centres of migrant labour for South-east Asia and now suffering the loss of money sent home by those working abroad. For two weeks the government completely lost control of large areas in this region. At Fatwa, near Patna, two Royal Canadian Air Force officers were killed at the railway station and their bodies paraded through the town; at nearby Monghyr the crews of two RAF planes which crashed during August were beaten to death by villagers. In retaliation, the viceroy authorized the machine-gunning of rioters by aircraft; the RAF carried out at least six such operations, resulting in an unknown number of deaths.

'I am engaged here,' Linlithgow informed Churchill at the end of August, 'in meeting by far the most serious rebellion since that of 1857, the gravity and extent of which we have so far concealed from the world for reasons of military security.'[11] Many British, seeing disturbing similarities with the events of 85 years before, panicked and over-reacted, stamping out the unrest with a brutality they might not normally have employed – even the old Emergency Whipping Act was resurrected and put to liberal use in Bombay. But there were two significant differences from that earlier revolt: this time the authorities had had plenty of time to prepare themselves, and the troops stood firm. The would-be revolutionaries had chosen a bad time to rebel, for the army had never been stronger. Some 57 battalions were available for internal security duties, and because of the war situation the loyalty of the Indian troops was never in doubt: they joined the police with a will to restore order on more than 60 occasions.

After a month, the fires of revolt were burning out. The Home department of the government reported that, excluding Bihar where there was no way of reliably estimating the numbers killed by aerial strafing, at least 340 Indians had been killed and 630 wounded. The 'true total', they added, had to be 'considerably higher'.[12] Other estimates put the 'true total' at about 2,500. On the police side, there had been 28 deaths.

By the end of September, the back of the revolt had been broken; by the end of the year it was all over. There had been 60,000 arrests, with 26,000 convictions; 18,000 people had been detained under the Defence of India Act. With all its leaders locked away indefinitely, Congress had been emasculated and the independence movement put on ice. Although spasmodic terrorist and guerrilla activity rumbled on for another two years or so, there would never again be a major physical challenge to the Raj.

The British and their supporters could now govern India and conduct the war against Japan without hindrance. Freed from Congress propaganda and pressure, recruitment boomed, with the strength of the armed forces reaching 2 million, all of them volunteers. India's war industries also flourished, supplying not only the country's own needs but those of other war theatres: Tata's works at Jamshedpur became the biggest single producer of steel in the entire empire, turning out more than 1.5 million tons a year; the cotton mills were all working to full capacity and beyond; and Bombay's chemical and pharmaceutical industries expanded dramatically. By the end of 1943, the supply of electric power had risen by 45 per cent from its pre-war level. Many new industries opened up for the first time, including the building of locomotives, automobiles and bicycles, all of which had previously been imported. As with any boom, anywhere, prices and inflation rocketed, bringing fortunes for the fortunate, and misery for the masses. But

India's industrial base received the vital boost which it needed to support an independent country.

By the beginning of 1943, the tide of war everywhere had turned in the Allies' favour. In north Africa, in the Atlantic and the Pacific, in Russia, in South-east Asia, the Axis forces had been stopped. The threat of invasion had been lifted from India when the 14th Indian Division began an advance into Burma to recapture the port of Akyab on the Arakan coast, 90 miles south-east of Chittagong. Maybe the British were not winning yet, but at least they had stopped losing. 'India should be entering upon 1943 in much better mood than she began in 1942,' Amery wrote to Linlithgow.[13]

For Gandhi, however, nothing had changed. On New Year's Eve, he wrote to the viceroy: 'I must not allow the old year to expire without disburdening myself of what is rankling in my breast.'[14] What rankled, in fact, was Linlithgow's blank refusal to engage in any kind of meaningful discussion. 'Convince me of my error or errors and I shall make amends,' Gandhi wrote. If not, he said he would have to 'crucify the flesh by fasting'. Linlithgow asked if this meant Gandhi wanted to dissociate himself from the policy of last summer; if so he had only to say so and the viceroy would reconsider. Gandhi responded by blaming everything that had happened on the government, which had 'goaded the people to the point of madness'. He ended by announcing that he would begin a 21-day fast on 9 February.[15]

No one was quite sure what Gandhi hoped to achieve by his fast. He was making no demands, and indeed made it quite clear that it was not to be a fast unto death. He claimed that it was 'for the service of God'. His previous fasts had always had clear and specific political aims, but to some of his friends and followers this one smacked of an attempt at moral coercion. Others felt that he was simply being perverse — Kasturbai once observed to the superintendent of prisons that 'he always mischiefs'.[16] However they interpreted it, the Delhi government was in a quandary. Gandhi was old and in poor health: it was extremely doubtful if he could survive a three-week fast. If he died, who would be blamed, and what would the consequences be? Certainly, if he died in custody, the government would take the blame and the riots that would follow would make the events of the previous August seem like a tea-party.

Linlithgow remained implacable. 'I have never wavered,' he wired Amery, 'that Gandhi, if he desired to do so, should be allowed on his own responsibility to starve to death.'[17] To the viceroy's amazement, his Executive Council did not agree — they were unanimous in wanting Gandhi released as soon as he began to fast, and threatened to resign en masse. The War Cabinet in London backed Linlithgow: Amery reported that they were 'greatly disturbed' at the prospect of releasing Gandhi 'on a mere threat to fast'.[18] Churchill was more than disturbed —

he was positively vitriolic. As far as he was concerned, it didn't matter if all the Executive Council resigned: 'We could carry on just as well without them and this our hour of triumph everywhere in the world was not the time to crawl before a miserable little old man who had always been our enemy.'[19]

In the end, the viceroy turned to the tactic used so successfully against Gandhi by Sir Harry Haig during the civil disobedience campaign in 1932 and 1933. He announced that Gandhi would be released from detention for the duration of his fast, and could return to his *ashram* to be looked after by his followers. Gandhi politely refused the offer: 'I shall be quite content,' he wrote, 'to take my fast as a detenu or prisoner. The impending fast has not been conceived to be taken as a free man.'[20] Linlithgow was satisfied, and relieved – Gandhi had clearly taken the responsibility for his life on himself. Only three members of the Executive Council resigned, and the viceroy had little difficulty in replacing them.

There was a general feeling among those in the Aga Khan's palace that this time the Mahatma would not survive his self-imposed ordeal. And indeed halfway through the fast it looked as if the worst might happen, when he became very weak and drowsy and seemed on the verge of slipping into a coma. However, watched over not only by three of his own physicians but also by three British doctors, including the surgeon-general, he surprised everyone by coming through successfully, professing to have achieved a state of inner peace and illumination in the process. Medical opinion was that he would be incapacitated for several months, as though he had suffered a severe illness. But as usual, all fasting seemed to do was give him renewed energy to continue his battle with the Raj.

The one undoubted winner in the 'Quit India' stakes was Jinnah. By the spring of 1943, his position as leader of India's Muslims had become almost unassailable. Previously, only two men had posed any sort of threat, Sir Sikander Hayat Khan in the Punjab and Fazlul Haq in Bengal. Sir Sikander, the arch-advocate of a united Punjab, with Muslims sharing power with Hindus and even Sikhs in his Unionist Party, had died in December 1942; his successor, Khizar Hyat Khan Tiwana, had neither the experience nor the personality to pose a challenge to the Quaid-i-Azam. Any scheme for Pakistan depended on the partition of the Punjab, the one province with roughly equal numbers of Hindus and Muslims. Sir Sikander would never agree to a division, but now that he was gone there was no one to stand in Jinnah's way. Although it was the Unionist Party and not the League which governed, Khizar was committed to supporting Jinnah's Pakistan policy.

In Bengal, Haq, who had been premier since 1937, was finally forced out in March 1943 by an alliance between the League and the European members of the legislature. He had always been a mercurial and unreliable ally, the more so since his resignation from the League in 1941 to form a coalition government with Mahasabha, Congress and Forward Bloc members. Now, Muslims who had previously supported him were crossing the floor of the legislature in droves to give the League undisputed control in Bengal. The other three provinces claimed for Pakistan: Assam, Sind, and the North-West Frontier Province, had come over to Jinnah's camp during the last few months, with more than a little help from their British governors.

At the League's annual session, held in Delhi in April 1943, Jinnah was re-elected president for the eighth time. Dressed in an elegant white *sherwani*, with a gold pin engraved with the letter 'P' in his collar, he attacked Gandhi. Jinnah challenged Gandhi to write to him directly, so that an agreement could be reached over the issue of Pakistan. A British agent watching the proceedings reported a change in Jinnah's manner: 'He has become more aggressive, more challenging and more authoritative. The reason appears to be consciousness of power lately acquired and of certain old injuries which can now be avenged therewith.'[21] Jinnah concluded by saying that the war could last another three years, and during that time they must 'put our house in order ... the fight being inevitable, we must make our preparations flawless'.[22]

Gandhi read the reports of the Delhi speeches in *Dawn*, Jinnah's English-language Muslim daily, and wrote to him at once, suggesting a meeting rather than correspondence. But the British Cabinet refused to allow the letter to be delivered. Amery suggested to Linlithgow that he should see Jinnah himself, but Linlithgow dismissed the idea. He also dismissed Jinnah: '... his threats do not cause me any sleepless nights! ... Jinnah is not in as strong a position as Gandhi and Congress, and he is never likely to be ... since he represents a minority ... that can only hold its own with our assistance ... His curse is personal vanity which at his age he is not likely to shake off.'[23]

Linlithgow's time as viceroy was finally coming to an end. He had ruled for seven and a half years, longer than any other viceroy or any other governor-general apart from Lord Dalhousie who had held office from 1848 to 1856. His original five-year term had been extended twice, largely because of the difficulty of finding a suitable replacement. Even as late as April 1943, he was asked to hang on just a little longer, as Churchill and Amery riffled desperately through the list of possible candidates. But by late summer he was preparing to lay down his burden, convinced that he had done a good job. Amery seemed to agree: 'It looks as if India had never been so quiet politically as it is at this moment.'[24] Linlithgow said he believed India to be 'in pretty good trim ... The leaders of the revolt ... have neither programme nor policy. The Working Committee are in gaol and forgotten ... Gandhi is equally out of the way of doing mischief, and so long as he maintains his present point of view I trust he will so remain.'[25]

There were many in India who did not share Linlithgow's self-satisfaction, particularly those living in east Bengal. A Japanese counter-attack in Arakan in March and April had driven the Indian army back to its starting point, resurrecting fears of invasion. Meanwhile, the people were enduring both daily Japanese air raids and the looming threat of famine. India's population had grown by over 50 million in the previous 10 years, and most of this growth had been in the Punjab and Bengal. The fertile Punjab, with the aid of vast new canal irrigation schemes, had no difficulty feeding the new mouths. Bengal, where landholdings were traditionally small and harvests unreliable, was another matter. The eastern part of the province had long depended on supplies of rice from Burma and South-east Asia, which had been cut off with the Japanese advance. At the same time, rice-growing areas near the border were taken out of production as part of the scorched earth policy designed to deny food to the invaders. When the invaders didn't come, the result was that food was denied to the local people instead.

In the sure and certain expectation of huge profits as shortages enabled them to force prices up, local merchants began buying up and hoarding grain which should have remained in villages for both food and seed. In the bad old days, district officers would have requisitioned stocks and put them into famine relief stores, but those authoritarian times were over. Fazlul Haq's provincial government, hamstrung by a lethal combination of incompetence and corruption, had done nothing to stop the profiteers. The situation was aggravated by a government order to seize and destroy all country boats to prevent their falling into Japanese hands, totally ignoring the fact that the waterways were the only means of transport for the local population. The railways, which might have brought in grain from other parts of the country, were unable to do so because of their military commitments – for the government of India, guns came before rice and wheat.

Linlithgow might have been expected to have visited the stricken region, and at the very least to have offered his sympathy. But he refused, in spite of pleas from his wife, who seems to have had a better sense of public relations than her husband. Instead, he stayed aloof in Delhi and Simla, blaming everything and everyone but himself for an immense human tragedy which had been caused entirely by human error and human greed and which could have been prevented, or at the very least alleviated, by firm and intelligent action. All in all, it was a fitting indictment to his period as viceroy, which had been marked from its beginning by a total lack of understanding or regard for the Indians.

A week before his departure, Linlithgow granted an interview to the Indian journalist Durga Das. His own words revealed the reasons for his failure to engage with the Indian leaders more clearly than any amount of analysis could ever do. 'India,' he said, 'could not hope to become free for another 50 years.' Since the country was new to Parliamentary institutions, it would require a leavening of British officials and Europeans to ensure that everything functioned successfully. However, 'With the advent of air-conditioning, it was now possible for Britons to settle down in areas like Dehra Dun, and when there were some 6 millions of them to buttress a democratic administration India might expect to make substantial progress towards self-government.'[26]

Linlithgow's replacement as viceroy was Wavell – a choice that surprised Wavell himself as much as everyone else. He was already a field marshal, having written to Churchill on 20 August 1942 asking to be promoted, probably the first general in the British army ever to make such a request. It was completely out of character, and in his letter he pointed out that he 'had never before asked for anything for myself'. He felt a field marshal's baton might help to impress the Americans and Chinese in the forthcoming negotiations on the war in Burma, which were clearly going to be difficult. But he admitted with his habitual honesty that there was a personal element, too, now that his military career was approaching its end: 'I confess that I should like to enjoy prestige as long as possible ... Gingerbread is always gingerbread, but may I have it with gilt on please?'[27] Overruling objections from the War Office, Churchill granted his wish.

Wavell's promotion to the highest rank did not make it any easier to deal with the Chinese, or with the American General 'Vinegar Joe' Stilwell. Nor did it produce a victory in Burma. In April 1943, the new field marshal was recalled to London for talks with Churchill. The prime minister, Wavell noted in his diary, 'was far from cordial; and ... very critical and even unpleasant about the Arakan operations'. The successes of Orde Wingate's Chindits, special units operating deep in the jungle behind enemy lines, was forgotten. 'I pointed out,' Wavell wrote, 'that [the Arakan operations] would never have been undertaken at all if I had had shipping available for a direct assault on Akyab, and that I had at least kept the Japanese busy for a whole campaigning season without much encouragement from home and entirely on my own initiative.'[28]

Perhaps impressed by Wavell's refusal to be brow-beaten, Churchill decided he would accompany him and the chiefs of staff to Washington, to discuss plans with the Americans. Wavell was told that Eden wished to see him at the Foreign Office before they left, but Amery insisted that he must see him first. Amery said that Churchill was pressing Eden to become the next viceroy, and that Eden wished to discuss it. Amery wanted Wavell to persuade him to accept, as he thought he was the best man for the job. So, it transpired, did Wavell. He did his best, but Eden had his eyes on the premiership should anything happen to Churchill, and in any case he felt he could not risk being out of British politics for five years.

After Eden, the list of candidates for the post read like a register of the great and the good. Churchill's favourite was Sir Miles Lampson, then ambassador to Egypt, who had just humiliated King Farouk by imposing a pro-British government on him; but both Amery and Linlithgow protested that he would be an unmitigated disaster in India. Amery favoured Sir Samuel Hoare, then ambassador in Spain, but Churchill refused even to consider him – as secretary of state, Hoare had opposed him over the 1935 India Act. Others included Sir John Anderson; Sir Roger Lumley, the governor of Bombay; the Duke of Devonshire; R.A. Butler; Lord Halifax; Lord Cranborne; Sir Archibald Sinclair; Oliver Stanley; Oliver Lyttelton; and even Lloyd George's son, Gwilym, then minister of fuel and power. Cripps was notably absent from the list. So, too, was Attlee, who would have been ideal but who could not be spared from his job as deputy PM: 'God forbid!' was Attlee's own reaction to the possibility. Amery is believed to have suggested Lord Louis Mountbatten, who was then chief of combined operations, but Mountbatten was favourite for the job of supreme allied commander, South-east Asia.

One name that was never on the list was that of Wavell, who did not expect, or want, to be considered for the post of viceroy. 'I had seen enough of the business of the government of India,' he wrote, 'to convince me that I had no inclination or capacity for that sort of work.'[29] What he did want, was to be supreme commander, South-east Asia. 'Without vanity,' he wrote, 'I could consider that I was the obvious choice ...'[30] Unfortunately, Churchill did not: militarily speaking, he regarded Wavell, in his newly acquired American slang, as a 'busted flush'. He could not forgive what he saw as Wavell's malign influence on the Indian army, accusing him of 'creating a Frankenstein by putting modern weapons in the hands of sepoys'. Indeed, Churchill's main purpose in making him viceroy, as Amery told Linlithgow, who received the news of his successor without enthusiasm, was to dispense with him as a military commander.[31] Churchill saw Wavell as a stopgap, an ex-soldier who would keep the peace and keep an eye on the Indian army. Amery knew better. He took a mischievous delight in noting that 'Wavell may ... prove more radical before long than most politicians.'[32]

Little knowing what was in store, Wavell drove up to London from his home in Winchester on 14 June 1943 to dine alone with Churchill at Number 10. Churchill came straight to the point: he wanted Wavell to give up his appointment as C-in-C India and accept the post of viceroy and the peerage that went with it. 'You will have to become a civilian and put off uniform,' he told him.[33] Wavell, who always went 'where I was told during the war without protest', could hardly turn down the honour, in spite of his misgivings. His only proviso was that he must consult his wife, Queenie, since it was a job that weighed almost as heavily on the vicereine as on the viceroy himself. Two days later, Queenie gave her consent.

As a military commander, the shy, rather inarticulate Wavell had always liked to put his thoughts down on paper for his chief of staff, to clarify his own thinking and make his subordinate aware of his intentions. In this case, his chief of staff was his private secretary, Evan Jenkins. Wavell's note to him, dated 20 August 1943, possessed a luminous common sense which inevitably doomed it to oblivion. In it, he mapped out a scenario, a possible way out of the impasse, which would have fulfilled all of Churchill's deepest fears.

Wavell's idea was to invite 10 distinguished Indian politicians and businessmen to the Viceroy's House in New Delhi, and address them somewhat as follows: 'I have collected you here, gentlemen, to debate the problem of India's future and to advise me on the solution to the present deadlock.' He would point out that they were 'a body small enough to deal with really important questions ... It is my experience that any body larger than this is too unwieldy to arrive at a decision. I believe that a vital decision in matters of government – and I am asking you to make a vital decision for India – can be arrived at only by a few selected men of wisdom and good will, not by counting votes.'

The men Wavell proposed to invite were: Gandhi; Nehru; Jinnah; Ambedkar, leader of the untouchables; V.D. Savarkar, leader of the Hindu Mahasabha; the Jam Saheb of Nawanagar, chancellor of the Chamber of Princes and one of the two Indian representatives in the War Cabinet and the Pacific War Council; his fellow representative, Sir A. Ramaswami Mudaliar, member without portfolio of the Executive Council; Sir Mohammed Zafrullah Khan, a supreme court judge; and either G. D. Birla or the head of Tata, to represent Indian business interests. He confessed to being a little doubtful about Savarkar and Birla or Tata, but it was an impressive list by any standard. He would tell them that he was fully aware that neither Sikhs nor Anglo-Indians nor the British were represented, but felt that any further enlargement of the original group would hinder decision-making. He would say that he hoped, therefore, that the members of the group would bear in mind their friends and do right by them.

Wavell intended to make it clear that he had no axe to grind, no political career to make, and little knowledge of politics; that his only aim was to redeem the British pledges of self-government as soon as possible, 'and to do my best for the Indian people'. The present government in India, he would say, 'is prepared to govern and able to do so ... until some better government, that is equally prepared and able to govern, can be formed'. First, however, the war would have to be won, and then the British 'must be satisfied we are handing India over to a government that can govern and enforce its decisions ... We do not intend simply to abrogate government and leave India to chaos.'

It would be up to the 10 'wise men' to create their 'own procedures and methods of debating the problem of India's future and advising me on it'. The only condition Wavell would lay down was that the meetings be held 'in *purdah*', so that neither press nor political allies could influence them. He wanted them free of any outside influence during their discussions. Whatever they might come up with, he did not want them simply to regurgitate old political slogans such as 'Quit India' or 'Immediate Declaration of Pakistan'. He believed that the Cripps proposals still held good, and 'may serve as the basis for your discussions'. But they might like to look at other, different systems of government, such as the Swiss cantonal system, the American federal system, and others. He would have his staff prepare notes on them all.

What he required from them, he would say, was 'a practical programme to give India self-government as soon as possible after the conclusion of hostilities, and to secure in the mean time the best government to carry the war to a successful conclusion, to deal with the many and urgent day-to-day problems of India, and to prepare for self-government after the war'. He would end by reminding them that 'no political progress has ever been made without the spirit of compromise'. It was a brave statement of faith. Wavell invited Evan Jenkins's comments. They were that the scheme stood only a one in five chance of success, but that it should not be ignored for that reason.[34]

On a less elevated plane, before his departure for India Wavell regularly attended Cabinet meetings and held a series of talks with politicians and 'experts' on India, which left him depressed and angry. Lord Lytton, governor of Bengal from 1922 to 1927, spent half an hour telling him how inconsiderate it was of viceroys to visit Calcutta near Christmas, because it 'stole the limelight from the Governor just at the time of all the big social events'. Lord Reading, Lytton complained, had been particularly inconsiderate about this when he was viceroy. Wavell's reaction was predictable: 'I don't like limelight or Calcutta or big social events,' he confided to his journal. 'As far as I am concerned the new Governor can have them.'[35]

William Phillips had replaced Louis Johnson as the US representative in India barely a month after the end of the Cripps mission, when Johnson had been invalided home with a severe sinus infection. Now visiting London, Phillips told Wavell that both the president and US opinion wanted the Indian political deadlock sorted out as soon as possible. This, of course, ran contrary to Churchill and the Tory diehards, who wanted to 'put the whole constitutional and political business into cold storage' for the duration of the war. When Wavell suggested in Cabinet that the British ought to make a sincere attempt at political progress no matter what the difficulties, Churchill 'worked himself up into a tirade against Congress and all its works and then digressed into the dangers of the Indian army becoming politically minded and anti-British'. 'The more I see of politicians,' Wavell concluded glumly, 'the less I respect them.'[36]

Wavell's last meeting with Churchill was bad tempered and angry. Churchill 'indicated that only over his dead body would any approach to Gandhi take place'. Wavell believed that Churchill now probably regretted having appointed him to the job, having always disliked and mistrusted him. His conclusions were that 'the Cabinet is not honest in its expressed desire to make progress in India'; and that 'very few of them have any foresight or political courage'.[37]

Before he left for India, Churchill gave Wavell a written directive. It was, Wavell noted, 'mostly meaningless, i.e. it exhorted me to get on with the war, to improve the lot of the Indian, to make peace between Moslem and Hindu', and at the end indicated that political progress was not ruled out. Amery — who at a Cabinet meeting earlier had passed a note to Wavell saying that Churchill 'knows as much about India as George III did of the American colonies' — observed: 'You are wafted to India on a wave of hot air.'[38]

Wavell arrived back in India on 17 October 1943, and dined with Linlithgow at the Viceroy's House two days later. Linlithgow was gloomy about the future for India. He did not believe any political progress was possible while Gandhi was alive, and even then he thought the British would probably have to stay for a further 30 years — which was at least an improvement on the 50 years he had previously thought necessary. The problems, he said, 'were the stupidity of the Indian and the dishonesty of the British'. 'We shall not be able to get away with it much longer,' he observed. As for the famine that was now raging in Bengal, Linlithgow was dismissive. In July, he said, he had expected the death toll to be up to a million or even one and a half million, but it looked as if they were getting off better than he had thought possible.[39] In that, he was to be proved disastrously wrong — but by that time he had gone, exchanging India's myriad problems for a more mundane and ordered existence as chairman of the Midland Bank. No reliable figures were possible, but the best estimate of the famine death toll during the 12 months from July 1943 to June 1944 is around 3 million.

Faced with a problem, Wavell's instinct as a soldier was to make his own reconnaissance and then do something about it. In marked contrast to Linlithgow, who revelled in pomp and circumstance and always travelled about India in the long, white viceregal train with literally hundreds of retainers, Wavell believed in moving fast and light. Six days after being sworn in as viceroy, he piled a handful of staff into an airplane and flew to Calcutta to study the famine for himself. He spent three hectic days talking to ministers and officials. He went round the streets at night to see how the destitutes were sleeping, and in the day to see them being fed. He also spent a day in the Contai district of Midnapore, which was one of the worst affected areas. Those in charge did not impress him with any sense of urgency: he thought the acting governor, Sir Thomas Rutherford, 'had no fire in him'.

The director general of the Indian Medical Service, Lieutenant-General Sir J.B. Hance, also aroused the new viceroy's ire when they met in New Delhi on

1 November. Not everyone who dies in a famine starves to death: general malnutrition leaves people weak and a prey to many diseases. In Bengal that year, deaths from starvation peaked in September and October, but cholera, malaria, dysentery and the ubiquitous fevers all took their toll. Smallpox, too, played its part, though that tended to strike mostly in the spring. Wavell asked Hance about the supply of medicines in Bengal, to which the general replied, 'with an air of conscious rectitude', that he was going down there on 8 November to see for himself. 'Why in a week's time?' demanded Wavell. 'Why not tomorrow or the day after?' Hance explained that he had to attend a meeting of the Sanatorium Committee in Simla. Wavell, as he put it in his journal, 'gave him to understand in very clear terms that sanatoriums in Simla could wait but the Bengal famine would not'.

Committed to the need for famine relief, Wavell realized that, though he could not work miracles and produce food out of thin air, he could at least keep up the pressure for aid both in India and London. Writing an official letter to his friend, the Chief of Imperial General Staff, Field Marshal Sir Alan Brooke, he added an unofficial postscript in his own hand: 'Our food problem is acute, so please support me.' And, in Churchill's own phrase, he 'badgered' the prime minister and the British government mercilessly for grain shipments. Amery backed him, but Churchill commented callously that despite the famine, Indians would continue to breed 'like rabbits'. Wavell got his shipments only by threatening to resign, provoking Churchill to describe him as 'the greatest failure as a Viceroy that we have ever had!'[40]

'The Two Great Mountains have Met – and not even a Ridiculous Mouse has Emerged'

Frustrated and disillusioned after nearly two years in Germany, Subhas Chandra Bose sailed from Kiel in a U-boat on 8 February 1943. His government in exile remained little more than a fantasy, and his efforts to create an Indian Legion from prisoners of war had so far produced a mere dozen men: by the end of the war, it would claim to have swelled to 2,500, but even so was too insignificant to leave any mark on history. All that Bose had to show for his efforts was a number of broadcasts, which had at least kept his name alive in India. The German defeat at Stalingrad finally convinced him that Germany was going to lose the war, and that he would be better off with Britain's other enemy, Japan. In any case, there were far more Indians in South-east Asia than there were in Europe, including 60,000 prisoners of war, and Rash Behari Basu's Indian Independence League appeared to be flourishing.

The U-boat made rendezvous with the Japanese submarine I-29 in the Mozambique Channel off Portuguese East Africa on 26 April. The following day Bose and his faithful assistant Abid Hasan transferred to it for the rest of their epic 93-day voyage to Singapore. From there, they were flown to Tokyo, where Bose met Prime Minister Tojo on 10 June. The meeting was astonishingly successful, so successful that Tojo called another four days later, impressed by Bose's passionate conviction as he urged him to liberate India. On 18 June, Bose watched in the Japanese Parliament as Tojo pledged his country's support for the Indian freedom struggle. The following day, Bose spoke to over 60 Japanese and foreign newsmen, declaring in typically melodramatic mixed metaphors: 'The enemy that has drawn the sword must be fought with the sword. Civil disobedience must develop into armed struggle. Only when the Indian people receive the baptism of fire on a large scale will they qualify for their freedom.'[1]

Bose returned to Singapore on 2 July, to be greeted ecstatically by the Indian community. He formally took charge of the Independence League from the 60-year-old Basu, who after 28 years in Japan was totally out of touch with the new generation of Indians – he had, after all, left India when Jinnah was the bright new hope of Congress, Gandhi was recruiting soldiers for the British, and Tilak and Ghokale were at loggerheads. The India he remembered was the one before the First World War.

Bose also took command of the newly reconstituted Indian National Army, the INA, naming himself supreme commander, and letting it be known that he would like all Indians to use the title he had adopted in Bengal, 'Netaji'. 'The role of India's Führer is what Subhas Chandra Bose will fill,' explained Abid Hasan.[2]

The INA was the brainchild of Gianni Pritam Singh, a Sikh priest who had joined the Bangkok branch of the Independence League in 1939, and a Japanese intelligence officer, Major Iwaichi Fujiwara. During the invasion of Malaya, they began approaching captured Indian soldiers and offering them freedom if they defected to the Japanese side. Their biggest catch to begin with was Captain Mohan Singh, an ardent nationalist and an Indian commissioned officer in the I/14 Punjab Regiment. Two days after the fall of Singapore, Mohan Singh and Fujiwara addressed a gathering of Indians in the city park. Fujiwara told them: 'The independence of India is essential for the independence of Asia and the peace of the world ... Japan is willing to give all-out aid and assistance to Indians in East Asia to achieve their aspirations.'[3] Singh told them he was forming the *Azad Hind Fauj* or Indian National Army, and called for volunteers.

The number of soldiers and civilians coming forward gradually grew from a trickle into a flood. Soon 25,000 of the 60,000 captured troops had joined the INA. Some were genuine nationalists; some were opportunists out to better their lot and save their skins (one fifth of those who remained loyal to the British failed to survive to the end of the war); some saw joining the INA as giving them the chance to escape and return to their own lines; but most, as Philip Mason, then secretary to the Indian War Department and later author of a classic history of the Indian army, put it, 'were puzzled, misinformed, misled, and on the whole believed that the course they took was the most honourable open to them'.[4] They had been told that they had a choice between digging latrines for the Japanese, or becoming soldiers again, in the service of an independent India. It is hardly surprising that many proud professional soldiers chose the chance to take up arms.

By the end of 1942, Mohan Singh had fallen out with his Japanese masters over policy matters and also with his own officers because he tended to promote Sikhs, even those of junior rank, into senior positions over the heads of more experienced officers from other communities. In December, the Japanese arrested Mohan Singh, and disbanded the INA – only to reform it six months later on the arrival of Subhas Bose, who saw it as his spearhead for a revolutionary war in India.

On 21 October 1943, Bose established the Provisional Government of Azad Hind (Free India), with himself as head of state, prime minister, war minister and foreign minister, in addition to his position as supreme commander; two days later, he declared war on Britain and the USA. Units of his army paraded in front of the Singapore municipal buildings, where they were reviewed by Tojo and Field Marshal Count Terauchi, commander of Japanese forces in South-east Asia. In spite of Japanese objections, Bose also raised a women's battalion, the Rani of Jhansi Regiment, named after the nineteenth-century Indian heroine who died in battle fighting the British in 1868. To live up to his new position as leader and military man, Bose gave up wearing civilian clothes in favour of a military style uniform, though – like Hitler's – without badges of rank. There is something faintly comic and scoutmasterish about the pictures of him in uniform – khaki tunic, forage cap, riding breeches and boots, and spectacles.

'Thirty million dollars and 300,000 men' was what Bose declared he wanted – an army powerful enough to take on the British in India. But his plans were becoming less practical as they became more grandiose. Even though many of the original volunteers had changed their minds, he dreamed of expanding his 13,000-strong force not just to 300,000 but to 3 million men. When his men crossed the border, he claimed, 'a revolution would break out, not only among the civil population at home but also among the Indian army which is now standing under the British flag'.⁵ It was pure fantasy. Even if he could have doubled the original force – which was by no means certain – it is doubtful if the Japanese could have equipped them at that stage in the war.

Bose aimed at all costs to get himself and at least part of his army into India, preferably Bengal, where they could carve out a small territory of Azad Hind. He was such a hero to the Bengalis that, as Ian Stephens, editor of the *Calcutta Statesman* observed, he would only have to parachute on to the *maidan* beside the Hooghly river in Calcutta, and 90 per cent of the population would rise up and follow him. Bose hoped that the Japanese would take Chittagong, the first port in Bengal, but the Japanese generals felt it would be too vulnerable to attacks from both the sea and the air: with Japanese naval and air strength dwindling, they would find it impossible to defend. Instead, in January 1944, they ordered an invasion across the Indo-Burmese border into Manipur, 'to capture strategic areas near Imphal and in North-Eastern India'.⁶

To be close to the impending action, Bose immediately moved his headquarters to Rangoon, where he was welcomed by the entire Burmese Cabinet as a head of state. This pleased him greatly, but the high point for him was a trip to the Andaman Islands in the Bay of Bengal. He renamed the islands 'Shahid'

(Martyr), raised the flag of Azad Hind and appointed the first Indian chief commissioner, Lieutenant-Colonel Loganadhan of the INA. The nearby Nicobars he renamed the Swaraj Islands. The whole thing, of course, was a propaganda exercise, which Bose exploited to the full. Loganadhan soon discovered that his new role was purely advisory – the Japanese navy had no intention of relinquishing its hold over the islands. Bose did manage to achieve one practical result at that time: getting wind of a proposed air raid on Calcutta, he convinced the Japanese that the political consequences of bombing the city would far outweigh any temporary military advantage, and he managed to persuade them to abandon the plan.

On 7/8 March, Lieutenant-General Renya Mutaguchi, commander of the Japanese 15th Army, crossed the Chindwin river and then the Indian border with 100,000 men. His orders were to take Imphal and Kohima in Manipur, and then drive north-eastwards to Dimapur, the nearest railhead and supply base in Assam. It was important that Imphal should fall before the end of April, when the monsoon rains would turn the terrain into a swamp. At first, Field Marshal Count Terauchi, commander of the Japanese forces in Burma, refused to have anything to do with the INA, his lack of faith compounded by the fact that only 12,000 of its 25,000 men were found to be fit for combat. His doubts were further intensified by a mutiny among its troops in Singapore – Bose panicked, and the Japanese were needed to restore discipline.[7]

Under pressure, Terauchi finally agreed to accept 3,000 men, and as a result the Subhas Brigade was formed from the INA 1st Division. Unfortunately, however, the brigade was barely trained and totally ill-equipped, with no artillery, mortars or communications equipment, and only an inadequate number of machine-guns. The medical service was risible: five medical officers with limited medical supplies and no surgical instruments, to look after 3,000 men. Bose was forced to raise money from Indian sympathizers in South-east Asia in an attempt to make good some of the deficiencies. His slogan was 'Total Mobilization' and the cry 'Give your all for the cause, even if your are left a pauper'. But it was a hopeless task.[8]

By the end of March, the Japanese were close to success. But the British and Indians hung on. General Bill Slim airlifted the 5th Indian Division into Imphal and ordered the British 2nd Infantry Division down from the north to relieve Kohima. The rains came, and the Japanese were bogged down. More INA men were sent in, but their involvement in the fighting round Imphal never came to more than 8,000 men. The Japanese commanders on the ground did not trust their fighting qualities, so they set them to road-building, repairing bridges, extinguishing jungle fires, driving bullock carts, and performing all the 'duties of a labour battalion'. Even when they got a chance to prove themselves, they had little luck. In mid-May, Lieutenant-Colonel Shah Nawaz Khan was warned that his brigade was going into action at last. He was ordered to the Kohima sector, to support the Japanese 31st Division. After a long march up the Kabaw valley, he and his men arrived just in time to meet the 31st Division in full retreat.

The Gandhi and Azad brigades of the INA, under the overall command of Colonel (later Major-General) Mohammad Kiani, were ordered to march with all speed to Palel. They were told Imphal had fallen, or would do so in a few hours, and if they wished to take part in the celebrations they should leave their equipment behind and press on as fast as possible, with each man carrying only a blanket, his rifle and 50 rounds of ammunition. When they got to Imphal, however, they found it had not fallen and they were expected to charge suicidally against British forces who were well dug in and well equipped. The Gandhi Brigade in particular suffered heavy casualties.

Imphal did not fall. The besieged British and Indian troops there and at Kohima held on, sustained by an incredible airlift operation while the Japanese ground supply lines were all but washed away by the monsoon. What had seemed a certain defeat for the Allies was transformed into a major victory. It was the turning-point of the war in South-east Asia. By mid-July, the Japanese were back at the Chindwin, having lost over 60,000 men. Some 6,000 INA men had surrendered during the campaign, including many who had taken the first opportunity to cross the lines in the hope of rejoining the British Indian army.

Bose sent some INA personnel by submarine to Baluchistan, to raise a rebellion, but on arrival they gave themselves up.[9] Yet nothing deterred Netaji. He continued broadcasting to the Indian people, beginning each speech with the old mutineers' slogan from 1857, which he had adopted as his own: 'Delhi chalo!', 'On to Delhi!' Whatever happened, he declared, the INA must continue advancing into India. 'As soon as all our preparations are complete,' he said, 'we shall launch a mighty offensive against our enemies once again.' He was, in Colonel Fujiwara's words, 'inclined to be unrealistic'.

Gandhi's time in the Aga Khan's palace had not been happy, despite the luxurious surroundings. His faithful friend and secretary, Mahadev Desai, had died early in the detention, and Gandhi had presided over the funeral rites. Desai was a great loss, but there was an even greater one to come. At the beginning of 1944, Kasturbai had begun to grow increasingly feeble. Her health had been giving cause for concern for some time: she had become depressed and had developed a cough which she did not seem able to shake off. When she asked for permission to consult her usual doctor, the government delayed needlessly and only later permitted Dr Dinshaw Mehta to attend her. She grew worse and expressed a wish to see a traditional Ayurvedic doctor. Again, permission was delayed. As her condition deteriorated, so members of the family were allowed in to nurse her, while other relatives visited her daily. The crisis came on 22 February 1944: it was clear that she was dying. Gandhi held her in his arms. As her breathing began to change, he asked her: 'What is it?' 'I don't know what it is,' she answered – and died.

No doubt fearing public disorder, the inspector-general of prisons refused Gandhi's request for the body to be handed over to the family for a traditional cremation. So Kasturbai's remains were cremated in the grounds of the palace on the same spot as Mahadev Desai's had been. Gandhi waited beside the funeral pyre until it had burned down to a pile of ashes. When the time came for the bones to be collected, Kasturbai's bangles were found intact among the ashes – a good omen according to Hindu lore, meaning her soul had gone straight to heaven.[10]

Gandhi was more deeply affected than he had ever expected to be. 'With Ba it was as if a part of Bapu departed,' Mira Behn wrote to Amrit Kaur later. 'Such things we went through in that Palace. Things that are branded on one's memory with burning fire.'[11] To those who saw him, including his doctors, he seemed to have lost the will to survive. He did, however, manage to summon up the energy to continue arguing with Wavell by post.

Shortly before, Gandhi had written to the viceroy trying to convince him that the Congress leaders were completely innocent of the charges under which they had been arrested, and that 'Quit India' did not have 'the sinister and poisonous meaning attributed to it without warrant by the Government of India'. Kasturbai had died a few days later, and Wavell sent his sincere condolences. He also sent a copy of his first major speech as viceroy, an address to a joint session of the Central Legislature on 17 February 1944, which he felt stated his own position clearly. After expressing his hopes for India's future, he had acknowledged 'how much ability and high-mindedness' Congress contained. 'But,' he had gone on, 'I deplore its present policy and methods as barren and unpractical.' He would welcome its leaders' co-operation 'in solving the present and future problems of India', but he could not release them until they had forsworn their policy of non-co-operation and obstruction, 'not in sackcloth and ashes – that helps no one – but in recognition of a mistaken and unprofitable policy'.[12]

Gandhi replied with a detailed criticism of the speech, and for a few weeks they batted the argument backwards and forwards. Gandhi's response to Wavell's appeals for co-operation was to turn the issue on its head: wasn't it high time, he asked, for the viceroy to co-operate with the people of India through their elected representatives, rather than expecting co-operation from them? India, he said, was one vast prison containing 400 million souls, and the viceroy was their sole custodian.[13]

The correspondence ended abruptly in April, when Gandhi suffered a severe attack of malaria. On the 28th, Wavell was informed that Gandhi's blood pressure had suddenly dropped dangerously low. On 4 May, while he was touring

Sikkim, the viceroy was woken at 2.30 a.m. with a telegram saying that Dr B.C. Roy and the surgeon general of Bengal, Major-General R.H. Candy, were both so worried about Gandhi's condition that they wanted to release him the following day. He was anaemic, and suffering from kidney and blood pressure problems which could cause cerebral or coronary thrombosis. He also had hookworm and amoebic dysentery.

Although he did not trust Gandhi or his doctors, Wavell cabled Amery, recommending unconditional release at once and warning that 'serious difficulties would result if Gandhi died in detention' — he had been rather surprised to discover that there was no official plan for action should the old man 'hand in his checks'. He said he agreed with the doctors' opinions that 'Gandhi was unlikely to be an active factor in politics again'.[14] Churchill took this to mean that Gandhi was actually dying, and gave his consent, though he stipulated that Wavell must not start any negotiations with him.[15]

Gandhi was released on 6 May, and was taken to recuperate at Juhu, a beach resort north of Bombay, where today many of India's film stars live. He started by observing two weeks of silence by the seaside, then returned to Poona, to stay as a guest in the house of an old English friend, Lady Thackersey. As other friends and colleagues visited him, his spirits began to rise again, and he appeared to be recovering quickly — so quickly, in fact, that Churchill accused him of having faked his illness. Amery told Wavell he was reminded of what Lord Byron had once written in a letter: 'My mother-in-law has been dangerously ill; she is now dangerously well.' He hoped 'that this is not going to be true of our old friend Gandhi'.[16] It was not: a few weeks later, Wavell told the prime minister that Gandhi was still far from well, and was incapable of prolonged physical or mental effort.

Even Gandhi himself now realized that age and the years of hardship he had imposed on his body were taking their toll. Nevertheless, he found it impossible not to take an active part in the freedom struggle. On 17 June, he wrote to the viceroy suggesting that they meet as soon as he was well enough, and also asking to be allowed to meet the imprisoned Working Committee, to try to formulate a fresh approach to the problem. Only too well aware of Churchill's orders, Wavell sought permission from Amery to talk to Gandhi. It was refused. Reluctantly, therefore, he had to turn down both requests, but said that if Gandhi came up with a 'definite and constructive' proposal, he would be glad to consider it.

The only definite and constructive proposal Gandhi could come up with, over a month later, was remarkably like the demands made by Congress to Cripps in 1942 for an immediate national government in return for co-operation in the war effort. The only notable change matched the changing war situation — now that the British were winning, Gandhi was prepared to leave defence in their hands, and settle for Indian control of civil matters. Since the demands were much the same as those of 1942, Wavell gave much the same answer: the British could not agree to a national government until the Indians themselves could agree on how it was to be formed.

While Gandhi was involved in his long-range dialogue with Wavell, one man was doing his best to square the circle for everybody concerned. Rajagopalachari had been allowed to see Gandhi during his fast the previous year, and had persuaded him then to accept a formula designed to bridge the gap between Congress and the League. In April 1944, he approached Jinnah with it. The idea was that the League should endorse the Congress demand for independence and co-operate with it in forming an interim national government, and in return Congress would accept the principle of Pakistan. After the war there would be a plebiscite in the areas of the north-west and north-east where Muslims were in an absolute majority, allowing the people to vote on whether or not they wanted to separate from India. If they did decide to separate, a sovereign state would be set up, 'without prejudice to the right of districts on the border to join either state'. Essential common subjects such as defence, commerce and communications, would be dealt with by mutual agreements. Any transfer of population would be entirely voluntary. The terms of the formula would become binding when Britain transferred power.[17]

Scenting a famous victory, Jinnah immediately began raising the stakes. If Gandhi was prepared to concede so much already, how much more could he be forced to give under pressure? Jinnah told Rajagopalachari that he could not commit himself on the formula until he had placed it before his Working Committee – as though they might oppose anything he had decided. If it had Gandhi's blessing, he complained, then Gandhi himself should have offered it, now that he was no longer a prisoner. Just over a week later, Gandhi took the bait. He wrote to Jinnah in their joint mother-tongue, Gujarati: '... I have not written to you since my release. But today my heart says that I should write to you. We will meet whenever you choose. Don't regard me as the enemy of Islam or of the Muslims of this country. I am the friend and servant of not only yourself but of the whole world. Do not disappoint me.'[18] Jinnah was then in Kashmir, trying to ease the pain in his failing lungs with pure mountain air, but he replied with triumphal hauteur: 'I would be glad to receive you at my house in Bombay on my return which will probably be about the middle of August.'[19]

The League Working Committee met on 30 July in Lahore, to discuss Rajagopalachari's formula and the talks with Gandhi. Jinnah's opening speech was that of a lawyer rubbishing his opponent's case at the start of a civil trial. The formula, he told them, was 'a parody and a negation of, and intended to torpedo, the Muslim League's resolution of March 1940'. In conceding the terms of the formula, he said, Gandhi was offering 'a shadow and a husk, a maimed, mutilated, and moth-eaten Pakistan', and 'trying to pass off as having met our Pakistan scheme and the Muslim demand'. The only clear merit he saw in the formula – and he did not underestimate its significance – was that at last Gandhi 'has at any rate in his personal capacity accepted the principle of Pakistan'.[20]

The significance of Gandhi's acceptance was not lost on the rest of India's body politic. As the Liberal leader Srinivasa Sastri told a public meeting in Madras on 13 August 1944:

> Mr Jinnah, so far as the formula goes, has triumphed. He has got the principle of Pakistan admitted by those who have the greatest influence with the Congress and with the country ... Four years ago he got from Lord Linlithgow a declaration in which it was emphatically stated that no changes would be made in the future constitution of India, unless beforehand the Muslim community had been consulted, and they had also agreed to the changes. Mr Jinnah can also pride himself on that point. He has got two great points – one from the regular Viceroy of India and the other from the unofficial 'Viceroy'. The third thing is that Mahatmaji against the old claim of the Congress has, without using these words, accepted the position of the League as the only representative of the Muslims.[21]

Jinnah's success could be measured in the vehemence with which the announcement of his talks with Gandhi, and Rajagopalachari's formula itself, were greeted by the Hindu press and by the Mahasabha, whose leader, Savarkar, cabled a warning to Amery: 'Hindu-sabhites can never tolerate breaking up of union of India their fatherland and holyland.'[22] But while they denounced Jinnah as an inflexible and truculent negotiator who was never satisfied with the generous offers made by the Hindu leaders, they reserved their deepest anger for Gandhi, whom they saw as the betrayer of *Bande Mataram*, Mother India. They would never forgive him for apparently opening the door to partition. For the more extreme members, their hatred would continue to fester over the next four years.

The League Working Committee gave Jinnah its unanimous approval for the talks with Gandhi, and they began at his luxurious house on Malabar Hill on 9 September. They went on until the Id holiday, which fell on 23 September that year, by which time it was clear that there could be no agreement. It had, in fact, been clear since the 14th, but the two ageing, ailing leaders – Jinnah was now almost 68 and his health, like Gandhi's, was steadily growing worse – continued to argue fruitlessly, more in the hope of scoring points off each other than of coming to any positive conclusions. They kept no record of their meetings, but wrote each other lengthy letters virtually every day, confirming what had been said and raising new points. At the end, on 27 September, the correspondence was published.

Much of the time during the talks was spent, as always, in arguing over detail. What exactly did each clause of Rajagopalachari's formula mean? What exactly was the independence which the League was being asked to support? What form was the 'provisional interim government' intended to take? Was the formula really, as Gandhi claimed, only giving 'substance and shape' to the Lahore resolution? And what, in fact, did the Lahore resolution really mean, since it made no mention of Pakistan? Who was to decide the exact nature of the proposed plebiscite in the Muslim majority areas, and who was to be allowed to vote? Jinnah – aware of the fine balance in the Punjab and Bengal – insisted that it should be restricted to Muslims alone; Gandhi wanted Hindus and Sikhs to have a say in their own future, too.

Behind the lawyers' pettifogging lay two immutable blocks to any understanding, and it was as a result of these that the talks broke down. The first was the question of nationhood. 'I find no parallel in history,' Gandhi wrote on 15 September, 'for a body of converts and their descendants claiming to be a nation apart from their parent stock. If India was one nation before the advent of Islam, it must remain one in spite of the change of faith of a very large body of her children.'[23]

To Jinnah, this was fighting talk: by no means all Muslims were converts from Hinduism, especially in the most northerly areas, where there could be no doubt that they were racially distinct from southern Indians. Muslims and Hindus, he blasted back at Gandhi, were

two major nations by any definition or test of a nation. We are a nation of a hundred million and, what is more, we are a nation with our own distinctive culture and civilisation, language and literature, art and architecture, names and nomenclature, sense of values and proportion, legal laws and moral codes, customs and calendar, history and traditions, aptitudes and ambitions. In short, we have our own distinctive outlook on life and of life. By all canons of international law, we are a nation.[24]

Gandhi, however, saw other dangers in admitting this. 'The more I think about the two-nation theory,' he wrote, 'the more alarming it appears to be. Once the principle is admitted there would be no limit to claims for cutting India up into numerous divisions, which would spell India's ruin.'[25]

The second major block was the all-important question of timing. Gandhi insisted that independence must come first, and that the Indians themselves should then decide on the question of the division of India, through their provisional government. For Jinnah, this spelt disaster:

It would ... be a Hindu majority government which would, when it becomes a permanent Federal Government, set up the post-war Commission for demarcating frontiers and arranging the plebiscite. I am asked to agree, before the plebiscite and therefore before I know what Pakistan will be, to making arrangements on Defence, Finance, Foreign Affairs, Commerce, Customs, Communications, etc, as a condition of our being allowed to have any kind of Pakistan at all; and it will be a 75 per cent Hindu majority government with which we shall have to agree ... This is not independence. It is a form of provincial autonomy subject as always in the most vital matters to an overwhelmingly Hindu federal authority.[26]

In short, he was being asked to trust Congress and the Hindus to act with goodwill towards the League and Muslims once the British had left – and trust and goodwill had been in short supply for many years.

Wavell summed up the result with his usual perspicacity:

I must say I expected something better ... The two great mountains have met and not even a ridiculous mouse has emerged. This surely must blast Gandhi's reputation as a leader. Jinnah had an easy task, he merely had to keep on telling Gandhi he was talking nonsense, which was true, and he did so rather rudely, without having to disclose any of the weaknesses of his own position, or define his Pakistan in any way. I suppose it may increase his prestige with his followers, but it cannot add to his reputation with reasonable men.[27]

While Gandhi and Rajagopalachari retired to lick their wounds, others in India continued to search for a solution. The end of the war could not be far off now, and this added urgency to their efforts. That old Liberal campaigner Sir Tej Bahadur Sapru revived his Non-Party Conference, which resolved on 19 November 1944 to appoint a 'Conciliation Committee' to search for a way out of the communal and political problems. It laboured until the beginning of April 1945, before producing a set of proposals which might have been acceptable to Congress but which failed to satisfy the League on almost every count, recommending no division of India 'in any form or shape', no provincial opt-outs, and the abolition of separate electorates.

Wavell, meanwhile, was itching to get something moving, pleading with the government in London for 'a change in spirit' and begging in vain to be allowed to include representatives of the major parties in his Executive Council. He also called for the prime minister to make a declaration confirming that Britain intended to give India self-government as soon as possible. But when Amery actually put a 'revolutionary' proposal to the India Committee at Christmas 1944 for a unilateral declaration that India would be given 'full and unqualified independence within the Commonwealth' on either VE Day or VJ Day, Wavell was among those who opposed it. He believed it would be fatal to bypass Gandhi, Jinnah and the Congress leaders, and that it would be disastrous to leave all constitutional questions entirely to the Indians alone. Ironically, Amery's only supporter was, as he put it, 'the ever useful Cripps', who defended him when he had his most violent row yet with Churchill.

For the immediate future, Wavell favoured reaching understandings with the Congress right and the League, which might help in 'bringing about a more reasonable frame of mind in the Congress High Command, and so paving the way towards ending the deadlock'.[28] He was encouraged when his general plan was taken up by Bhulabhai Desai, Congress leader in the Central Assembly, and Liaquat Ali Khan, *de facto* leader of the League in the Assembly, who agreed that a Congress-League coalition at the centre was both desirable and possible. Unofficially, Gandhi had given his blessing to Desai, and Jinnah his to Liaquat.

Desai and Liaquat drafted and initialled a pact, under which their two parties would each hold 40 per cent of the seats in an interim national government, with 20 per cent reserved for the other parties and groups. Their government would work under the terms of the 1935 Act, though the viceroy should not use his powers to override its decisions. Its first task would be to release the imprisoned members of the Congress Working Committee – but not until the government was up and running: if the Committee were released beforehand, as Desai told Wavell, it would wreck the negotiations.[29] Wavell was enthusiastic – this could be the breakthrough that everyone was searching for. But, like every other approach he made to London, it was blocked by Churchill, who was deeply suspicious of 'this new, sudden departure'.[30] He wanted Wavell to get assurances and guarantees on just about everything from everyone concerned, including Jinnah, before he would even consider it.

To complicate matters, Jinnah now publicly repudiated the Desai-Liaquat pact, disclaiming all knowledge of it. But Desai told V.P. Menon, the viceroy's constitutional adviser and the only Indian official on his personal staff, not to take this too seriously: once the plan was accepted, he said, Jinnah would take part. 'I remember,' Menon wrote later, 'his quoting a Gujarati proverb to the effect that one might grumble about the food, but one would eat it all the same.'[31] Desai had good reason for optimism, as Jinnah's position was slipping badly during the spring of 1945. As Wavell released more and more provincial Congressmen from detention and allowed them to take up their old seats in the assemblies on promises to co-operate in the war effort, the ministries in the NWFP, Assam, Sind, Bengal and the Punjab all fell, one after the other. With no provincial government left under its control, the League now desperately needed a share in government at the centre, and Jinnah could not afford to lose the chance of parity with Congress.

Wavell had been pressing for some time to be allowed to return to London for face-to-face discussions. He was, as Menon noted, 'more concerned to know the mind of His Majesty's Government than that of Jinnah or Desai'.[32] For months the government stalled, but eventually Wavell's persistence ground down both Churchill and Attlee, who was equally hostile to the viceroy's negotiating with Indian political leaders during the war. Accompanied by Menon and Sir Evan Jenkins, Wavell left for London on 22 March – the day after British and Indian forces in Burma had reopened the road to Mandalay. The government, however, was understandably more preoccupied with the death throes of Nazi Germany and the problems of feeding the peoples of liberated Europe than with the constitutional problems of India. Wavell was kept hanging around for several weeks.

It was not until late April, when Attlee had left for the San Francisco conference to set up the new United Nations Organization, that Wavell was able to make any headway. Even then, he still had to contend with Churchill, who somehow blamed him for Britain's sterling debt to India, which was now enormous: 'As usual,' Amery noted in his diary, 'he poured contempt on Wavell and talked rubbish about abolishing landlords and money-lenders.'[33]

Wavell argued that the government of India could not carry on as it was. With 11 Indians to four Europeans on the Executive Council, the British no longer had the power to control events, and it was difficult for the viceroy to veto clearly expressed Indian opinion. The situation, he said, was deteriorating both in the political sphere and in administration. The ICS was largely moribund, and was coming apart rapidly – having begun the war with only a light administration, it had had to try to cope with a huge increase in its workload and many new problems, with no increase in personnel. After eight years without home leave, the civilians were all very tired. Many were due for retirement, it was almost impossible to find replacements, and as a result the administrative machine was now a pretty poor one. Something had to be done, and quickly, before everything broke down.

The governors, Wavell said, agreed unanimously that a move forward must be made before the end of the war. They all approved of the Desai-Liaquat pact, which followed Wavell's own thinking, and he wanted to put it or something like it into operation as soon as possible. The security and prestige of Great Britain in the east depended on finding some solution or making progress. And looking to the future, he added: 'If we want India as a Dominion, we must now treat her much more like a Dominion.'[34]

By the end of April, relations between Wavell and Churchill were so bad that Amery had to step in and warn the prime minister that if he forced the viceroy's resignation, he, Amery, would resign, too. Suddenly, however, everything changed. Churchill became incredibly friendly towards Wavell, and agreed to all his requests. The reason was not hard to see: the war in Europe ended on 8 May 1945, Churchill would have to go to the country very soon, and he and the Tories could not allow India to become a general election issue.

Wavell arrived back in Delhi on 4 June, to a buzz of excitement. Amery had made a brief announcement that the viceroy had been empowered to make proposals on forming an interim government, and everyone was eager to know the details. Ten days later, in a broadcast on All-India Radio, Wavell told them. At the same time, Amery made a complementary statement to Parliament in which he declared that the proposal owed everything to Wavell's initiative and 'his deep sympathy with India's aspirations'.[35] There were only about 30 MPs in the House, as Wavell's son-in-law, who had gone to the Commons gallery to hear the announcement, wrote and told him. It showed, Wavell observed glumly in his journal, 'the measure of interest taken in the Indian problem at home'.[36] The statement was Amery's last speech in the House as secretary of state: Parliament was dissolved the following day, after a record-breaking nine and a half years, though ministers would remain in office as a caretaker government until the final results of the general election were known.

Wavell began his broadcast by saying that the proposals he had been authorized to place before Indian political leaders were 'designed to ease the present political deadlock and to advance India towards her goal of full self-government'. Indian leaders were to be invited to help form a new Executive Council 'more representative of organised political opinion'. It would include 'equal proportions of Caste Hindus and Moslems', and would be 'an entirely Indian Council, except for the Viceroy and the Commander-in-Chief, who would retain his position as War Member'. Even the vital portfolios of finance, home and external affairs would be in Indian hands, and members would be selected by the viceroy 'after consultation with political leaders'. The final veto would remain with the viceroy, but, in a conscious echo of Linlithgow's 1937 declaration, Wavell stressed that 'it will of course not be exercised unreasonably'.

The main tasks of the new Executive Council, Wavell said, were: first, to ensure the utter defeat of Japan; second, to carry on the government of British India until a new constitution could come into force; third, to find a long-term solution to India's problems. To help in forming the new Council, he proposed to call a conference in Simla consisting of the leaders of Congress and the Muslim League, including Gandhi and Jinnah; current provincial premiers and those who had been premiers before the imposition of governor's rule under Section 93; leaders of the Scheduled Castes, Sikhs, the Nationalist Party, and the European group in the Central Assembly; altogether a total of 21 men. Orders had already been issued, he said, for the release from detention of the remaining members of the Congress Working Committee; decisions about releasing other prisoners who had been involved in the 1942 disturbances would be left to the new central and provincial governments.[37]

The proposed conference was not quite Wavell's cherished dream of locking 12 Indian wise men in a room and telling them not to come out till they had answers to the questions that were bedevilling the road to independence. But it seemed as close as he was likely to get. It was not long, however, before he began to realize that his hopes had been simplistic, to say the least. The various participants wasted no time in taking up their positions. 'Gandhi and Jinnah,' he complained in his journal on 16 June, 'are behaving like very temperamental prima donnas, and the latter is publishing his telegrams in the Press before I even receive them; Gandhi at least had the courtesy to ask whether I agreed to publication.'[38] Gandhi began by issuing a press statement condemning the use of the term 'Caste Hindus' in Wavell's broadcast as offensive, inaccurate, and opposed to 'the modern tendency in Hinduism ... to abolish all caste distinctions' – itself a piece of wishful thinking. Jinnah for his part, through an editorial in his daily paper, *Dawn*, planted his standard by declaring that 'the League could not participate in [an] Executive Council in which non-League Muslims were included'.[39]

Wavell went up to Simla for the conference on 22 June 1945, and two days later had separate interviews with Azad, Gandhi, and Jinnah. Azad came first, accompanied by Govind Ballabh Pant, the ex-premier of the UP, who acted as his interpreter: although the Congress president understood English, he was shy of speaking it. Wavell describes their meeting as 'quite friendly', but nothing new emerged from it. After lunch, he was closeted for nearly two hours with Gandhi, the first time they had met.

Gandhi was at his most tortuous and prolix. For over half an hour he lectured Wavell on 'the history of the Congress, British rule in India, British character, the qualities of a good soldier, and many other more or less related subjects'. Finally, however, he got down to the business in hand. In his view, all political prisoners should have been released, not merely the Congress Working Committee – Wavell thought so, too, but had been unable to convince the Cabinet. On the vexed question of parity between Congress and the League, Gandhi said he was prepared to accept this, in spite of considerable Congress opposition, provided Congress was permitted to nominate Muslims or members of the Scheduled Castes for the Executive Council. Wavell agreed.

When Wavell asked if he proposed to attend the conference in person, Gandhi pointed out that he was not a member of Congress, and in any case he thought his presence would be 'undesirable'. But he would remain in Simla, if he could be of any service to the viceroy, and on that note they ended their talk. Wavell found Gandhi friendly, but had the impression that he was 'perfectly prepared to go back at any time on anything he had said'.[40]

After Gandhi came Jinnah. Wavell found him more direct but thought his manners far worse. Jinnah told him he was afraid that Muslims would always be in a minority on the Council, because when it came down to it, the other non-Muslim minorities such as the Sikhs and the Scheduled Castes would inevitably vote with the Hindus, leaving Muslims at the mercy of Congress. He repeated his claim that the League had the right to nominate all Muslim members of the new Council. Wavell refused to give any guarantees about this: it was a matter for negotiation. When Jinnah learned that Gandhi would not be attending the conference, he declared that 'it was another trick of Gandhi's, he pretended not to belong to Congress when it suited his book, but when necessary appeared as the Dictator of Congress which everyone knew he was'. At the end of the interview Jinnah avoided giving any indication as to whether the League would attend the conference or not. Wavell formed the impression that he was having problems with his fellow League members; he found Jinnah 'rather depressed and not sure of his position'.[41]

The conference opened the following morning in the grand ballroom of Viceregal Lodge. Azad accepted that the British proposals were designed to achieve an interim settlement only, and that any final settlement would have to come later. But he warned that Congress would not agree to anything, however temporary, that prejudiced its role as a national party representing all castes and all religions. Jinnah interjected with his oft-repeated argument that Congress represented only Hindus, a view vehemently objected to by the Muslim Dr Khan Sahib, Congress premier of the NWFP. Wavell deftly averted a row by persuading everyone to agree that, if nothing else, Congress clearly represented its members. Jinnah then insisted that the League would 'not agree to any constitution except on the fundamental principle of Pakistan'.[42]

Day two passed in a much more friendly atmosphere. With the two major players having established their positions, the conference could get down to the practical issues involved in setting up a new government: the general principles under which it would operate, and its actual composition. Discussions went on all day, and continued between the various parties after the conference had adjourned. But the following day, Wednesday 27 June, it became clear that no progress had been made overnight: Congress and the League were deadlocked. After three-quarters of an hour of verbal skirmishing, Wavell called a halt for two days, to allow time for progress to be made behind the scenes.

That afternoon, at 5.30 p.m., Jinnah returned to Viceregal Lodge for tea with Wavell and his wife, Queenie. Afterwards the two men remained closeted together until 7.15 p.m., discussing the perennial problem of Muslim representation. Jinnah wanted the Council to consist of 12 Indian members, plus the viceroy and the commander-in-chief: 5 Hindus, 5 Muslims, 1 Sikh, 1 Scheduled Caste. This, he thought, was the only composition under which the Muslims would not be outvoted on every issue.

The problem, as always, was who should choose the Muslim members. Jinnah insisted that they must all be nominated by the League. The viceroy, however, wanted one of them to be a non-League Muslim from the Punjab. In Jinnah's opinion, this posed a deadly threat both to the League and to Pakistan, for the Punjab was at the very heart of the Pakistan concept. If Punjabi Muslim leaders saw that they could obtain the prizes of high office outside the League, they would have no need to join it. They would remain with Khizar Hyat Khan's Unionist Party, which was committed to a united, multi-communal Punjab that could not become part of Pakistan. What was more, such a representative on the Executive Council was quite likely to vote with Hindus and Sikhs rather than with League Muslims. Once Jinnah knew that this was what Wavell intended, the conference was doomed.

When the delegates reconvened on 29 June, it was obvious that agreement was further away than ever. Seeking to salvage something from the wreckage, Wavell tried a new tack: he asked all the parties to send him their lists of suitable candidates, from which he would personally select an Executive Council, to be put to a reconvened conference on 14 July. Azad and the other party leaders all agreed, readily. Jinnah, of course, refused — and went on refusing, despite all Wavell's efforts to persuade him. Finally, on 9 July, Wavell sent his own list, including four Muslim League members, to Amery in London. 'I hope,' he wrote in his journal, 'the Cabinet will back me up and will not haver or delay.'[43]

The Cabinet did not keep Wavell waiting, but cabled him next day giving general approval. Being 'rather pernickety',[44] however, they insisted that he saw Jinnah first, to tell him the Muslim names and try to persuade him to put them forward as his party's list. Wavell did as he was told, but found Jinnah in an uncompromising mood: 'He refused even to discuss names unless he could be given the absolute right to select all Muslims and some guarantee that any decision which the Muslims opposed in Council could only be passed by a two-thirds majority — in fact a kind of communal veto. I said that these conditions were entirely unacceptable, and the interview ended.'[45]

The conference met again as planned on 14 July, but only to be formally abandoned. Wavell made no attempt to revive it, though V.P. Menon had been told by Hossain Imam, the leader of the League in the Council of State, that there were serious divisions in the League Working Committee over rejecting the viceroy's offer. Menon had asked Liaquat Ali Khan to speak to Jinnah the previous night, but had heard nothing more from him. Instead, as though to prove his obduracy, Jinnah next day claimed parity in the Council *'with all other parties combined. If he really meant this,'* Wavell noted, 'it shows that he had never at any time an intention of accepting the offer, and it is difficult to see why he came to Simla at all.'[46]

But whatever he thought about Jinnah in private, Wavell studiously avoided blaming him in public for the breakdown. Like the decent, honourable man that he was, he chose to take the blame on his own shoulders. 'I wish to make it clear that the responsibility for the failure is mine,' he told the delegates in his closing address. 'The main idea underlying the Conference was mine. If it had succeeded, its success would have been attributed to me, and I cannot place the blame for its failure upon any of the parties.'

What Wavell could not say was that he was under strict instructions from London not to embarrass Jinnah. The Cabinet, Amery had told him bluntly, were 'afraid of the whole onus of failure being thrown on Muslims'.[47] In fact, much of the onus lay on the India Committee of the Cabinet itself: Lord Simon, Sir James Grigg and R.A. Butler in particular had made no secret of their wish that the conference should break down, and Churchill had only agreed to it in the first place because he had been assured that it would fail.[48] Amery had little doubt who was to blame. In almost his last day as secretary of state, he noted with some bitterness: 'The immediate wrecker was Jinnah, but the real wrecker ... was Winston.'[49]

Wavell's hands had been tied from the beginning. He had been forbidden from calling Jinnah's bluff at a time when Jinnah had shown his vulnerability by more than once appealing to him, 'in a high state of nervous tension': 'I am at the end of my tether ... I ask you not to wreck the League.'[50] Far from wrecking the League, the British had rescued it, immeasurably strengthened Jinnah's personal position, and made Pakistan virtually inevitable.

22. Leo Amery, Tory secretary of state, battled with Churchill on India's behalf throughout the Second World War.

23. Happiness for Nehru and Gandhi is to be together again after being freed from gaol to resume the struggle for freedom.

24. Mission of hope: Sir Stafford Cripps (right) talks with Congress president Maulana Azad during the Cabinet Mission's visit in 1946, watched by Asaf Ali and A.V. Alexander.

25. Mission deadlocked: political leaders join the British ministers at Viceregal Lodge, Simla, in a desperate effort to achieve agreement. The tall figure on the left is the 'Frontier Gandhi', Abdul Gaffar Khan.

26. Mission of despair: Indian leaders arrive at London airport in a cold December, 1946, for fruitless talks with Attlee. Left to right: Liaquat Ali Khan, Jinnah, Baldev Singh, Pethick-Lawrence.

27. Police use tear-gas in their efforts to halt the Calcutta killings of 1946. Over 5,000 Hindus and Muslims were slain in communal savagery following Jinnah's call for a day of 'direct action'.

28. The outgoing viceroy, Lord Wavell, greets his successor, Lord Mountbatten, and Lady Mountbatten on the steps of the Viceroy's House, 22 March 1947.

29. Enthroned in splendour: the last viceroy and his consort.

30. 'A rose between two thorns': Jinnah's prepared quip misfired when photographers placed him between Mountbatten and Edwina.

31. The new government of Pakistan was deprived of most modern facilities, even for moving its furniture and equipment into the former Sind Assembly buildings.

32. Meanwhile, Muslims awaiting transport to Pakistan took refuge in camps in Delhi and in the great Jama Masjid (above), where thousands lived for weeks in appalling conditions.

33. Riots in the Punjab left thousands dead and devastation reminiscent of the war-time Blitz in Amritsar and other towns.

34. In Calcutta, meanwhile, Suhrawardy (left) joined Gandhi's 'one-man boundary force' to prevent communal violence in Bengal.

35. Free at last! While the Punjab was engulfed in murder and mayhem, the citizens of Calcutta, traditionally India's most violent city, celebrated independence in joyous harmony.

36. 'The light has gone out of our lives and there is darkness everywhere.' Gandhi, assassinated by his own people, lies in flower-bedecked state, mourned by millions but especially by his 'walking sticks', his beloved great-nieces.

23

'Patriots not Traitors'

Because of the vast number of men and women still serving overseas whose votes had to be collected and sent back home, the results of the British general election were not declared until 26 July 1945, three weeks after polling day. Both Attlee and Churchill had expected the Tories to win by about 70 seats. But to the surprise of everyone except the opinion pollsters, whose predictions were still regarded as little better than reading tea-leaves, Labour were swept into power by a landslide: they had a majority of 180 over the Tories and 146 over all others combined. Churchill was out. Attlee was the new prime minister, so unprepared that he had not even talked to his family about the possibility of a move to Downing Street from their modest home in Stanmore.[1] In India, nationalists greeted the news with enthusiasm, and Azad immediately cabled Attlee: 'Hearty congratulations to the people of Great Britain on the results of the election which demonstrate their abandonment of the old ideas and acceptance of a new world.'[2]

    The Tories' last landslide defeat, in 1906, had brought the ageing Lord Morley to the India Office. 1945 brought the 74-year-old Frederick Pethick-Lawrence, an equally well-intentioned old-Etonian lawyer, Fabian idealist, and sincere believer in Indian independence. He had just been elevated to the peerage as a baron, after serving as a back-bench Labour MP in 1923–31 and 1935–45. Together with his wife, a former suffragette, he had first visited India in 1926–7, where he had become a lasting friend of Gandhi and other Congress leaders. He had been a member of the round-table conference and was a founder of the India Conciliation Group, set up at Gandhi's suggestion after the second conference in 1931 – Cripps's stepmother was another active member of this influential group. He was trusted and respected by Indian nationalists, and by appointing him Attlee was sending them a clear signal of good intent. His double-barrelled name, incidentally, came from adding his wife's family name, Pethick, to his own:

inevitably, the sharper wits in India changed it to 'Pathetic-Lawrence', a cruel label which stuck.

In many ways, Morley and Pethick-Lawrence were very similar, but there were vital differences in their situations. This time there was no vacillating Minto in the Viceroy's House and no obstructive ICS machine determined to thwart any efforts at liberalization. This time the viceroy was leading the way, and the government at home, taking over a nation exhausted and reduced to near penury by the war, had no stomach to continue ruling an unwilling India. Though some Labour leaders, most notably the new foreign secretary Ernest Bevin, were emotionally upset at the idea of leaving, the intellectual wing of the party believed the time had come to fulfil its long commitment to Indian independence. It had been part of the general election manifesto, and would be included in the king's speech at the opening of Parliament. Pethick-Lawrence's brief, therefore, was to prepare the way for the earliest possible hand-over of power.

Attlee's new India Committee was markedly different from Churchill's. The diehards and the old India hands were gone. Besides Attlee himself, Pethick-Lawrence and Cripps – back in the Labour Party and the Cabinet as president of the Board of Trade – the other members were all sympathetic to Indian aspirations. They were Lord Stansgate (the former William Wedgwood Benn, secretary of state for India, 1929–31), Ellen Wilkinson, the current minister of education, and Lord Listowel, the postmaster-general. Though Attlee was firmly in control, Cripps was the driving force: his 1942 plan formed the basis of the new government's policy for India, and he had every hope that without Churchill's malevolent interference he could make it work.

The idea of elections for India was on everyone's mind. With the unanimous backing of all the governors, Wavell pressed hard for permission to announce them. Cripps had been pressing for them ever since the breakdown of the Simla conference. Nehru and Congress wanted them, to re-establish their mandate to represent all Indians. And Jinnah was already publicly clamouring for them, to prove to Congress and everyone else that the League really did now represent the Muslim nation. When Japan surrendered on 14 August, bringing the war in the east to a sudden end, there was no longer any need to think about interim solutions: it was time to move on to a permanent constitutional settlement. Wavell was told to announce elections to both provincial and central assemblies, and to fly back to London at once for consultations. He left Delhi on 24 August, accompanied as usual by the redoubtable V.P. Menon and Sir Evan Jenkins.

Before he left, Wavell had cabled a warning to Pethick-Lawrence:

Party attitudes have hardened since 1942, and Jinnah now seriously demands immediate grant to Moslems of right of self-determination and separation of Moslem majority provinces from rest of India by plebiscite of Moslems only. Moslems are most unlikely to co-operate in or to recognise any constitution-making body unless this right is conceded ... I am clear that it would be most unwise for H.M.G. to announce their long term intentions in any detail until they have formed definite conclusions on Pakistan issue.[3]

It was good advice, based on bitter experience, but it took Wavell three weeks of argument to make the India Committee in general and Cripps and Attlee in particular understand just how much things had changed since 1942. Above all, he tried to impress on them that 'we had to face the Pakistan issue and bring its real implications into the light before we could get any further'.[4] This was not a welcome view to Attlee, who, as he later admitted to his biographer, Kenneth Harris, was still underestimating Jinnah and the League.[5]

With his usual distrust of politicians, Wavell suspected that the prime minister had his own agenda. After an hour's talk with him on 4 September he noted that Attlee 'made it clear, without intending to do so, that the Cabinet was thinking more of placating opinion in their own party and in the USA than of the real good of India ... They are obviously bent on handing over India to their Congress friends as soon as possible ... I may have to decide whether to refuse to be a party to their plans to quit India, or to go back and try to keep them out of disaster as much as possible.'[6] He chose to go on, though he did not find it easy. Having spent the previous two years trying to push the old government to move more quickly, he now found himself trying to hold the new one back. It would be fatal, he told them, to think they could simply impose the old Cripps offer, or any other British solution, for that matter. The Indians must decide for themselves.

Finally, through dogged persistence, Wavell won the day: the elections would be held first, and only then would he meet the parties' representatives to discuss setting up a constitution-making body. He returned to India well satisfied with the result. But Cripps was thoroughly peeved at being balked, and whereas Churchill had regarded Wavell as a dangerous radical, Attlee now thought him an old-fashioned reactionary. Neither Cripps not Attlee would ever forgive him for spoiling their party.

Back in India, Wavell made an announcement on 19 September confirming what had been decided in London. 'His Majesty's Government', he began, 'are determined to do their utmost to promote in conjunction with the leaders of Indian opinion the early realisation of full self-government in India.' After the elections, he said, the government hoped that political leaders in all the provinces would accept ministerial responsibility. As a first step towards setting up a constitution-making body, he would meet representatives of the provincial legislative assemblies to find out whether they would accept the 1942 Cripps offer, or if not, what alternative scheme they would prefer. He would also talk to the Indian states about their involvement. In the mean time, he would form a new Executive Council 'which will have the support of the main Indian parties'.[7] Attlee backed up the statement in a broadcast that same day, but gave the game away by saying that the government was acting in the spirit of the Cripps offer.

Neither of the main Indian parties reacted favourably. Congress complained that the proposals were 'vague and inadequate' and refused to believe that this was not just another piece of temporizing by perfidious Albion. 'It is the same old story,' Patel wrote to G.D. Birla next day, 'and you can hardly distinguish between a Labour Prime Minister speaking and a Conservative with the exception of some plain and direct expressions of the Conservative Prime Minister.'[8] Jinnah repeated his old line that the League would not accept any solution that did not include Pakistan. The truth was that both parties were already electioneering.

Nehru and Congress used the election campaign to whip up anti-British feeling. At first, their main plank was condemnation of the repression of 1942. They erected martyrs' memorials to those who had been killed, and started relief funds for their dependants. Atrocity stories proliferated, as did demands for inquiries and the punishment of those responsible. And then, just as the atmosphere was reaching its most explosive, the British themselves lit the blue touch-paper: they decided to put the former officers of the INA on trial in Delhi. Nehru had never supported the INA, and before the end of the war with Japan had declared, in Bose's own city of Calcutta, that he would oppose him even at the head of his army. However when the British handed out such an opportunity, how could Nehru possibly fail to seize it? The INA had never achieved much during its life, but now that it was dead, it was to make a striking contribution to the Indian freedom movement.

At the end of the war, the British Indian army had taken 23,000 INA prisoners. Technically, they could all have been shot for desertion and mutiny, but not even the British were that stupid. They divided the men into three categories: 4,000 'whites', who were judged to have genuinely intended to escape from the Japanese and rejoin the British Indian army, and were restored to their former privileges; 13,000 'greys', who were judged to have been misled, were released without charge, but forfeited their pay and allowances for the time they were prisoners of war; but the remaining 6,000, officers, senior NCOs and those responsible for murder and other brutalities, were marked as 'black' and held for trial. These men were a source of controversy, but fortunately for all concerned, the British were spared the hottest potato of all. Subhas Chandra Bose, Netaji, was not among the prisoners.

Let down by Hitler and Tojo, Bose had turned to his earlier hero. 'There is one man in Europe who holds in his hands the destinies of the European nations for the next few decades,' he declared in his last broadcast on 25 May 1945. 'That man is Marshal Stalin.' The struggle for Indian independence, he said, now lay in association with Soviet Russia.[9] Three days after the Japanese surrender, on 17 August, he and seven of his staff flew out of Saigon, heading for Russia, via Manchuria. Their transport was an overloaded, decrepit Japanese bomber with a crew so inexperienced that the captain was not even a qualified pilot. As they took off again the next afternoon, after refuelling at Taipeh in Formosa, there was a loud explosion and the port engine fell off. The plane caught fire and nosedived into the ground. Astonishingly, Bose survived the crash, and managed to climb out of the wreckage, with his clothes ablaze. Badly burned and with appalling head injuries, he was rushed to a Japanese military hospital, but died shortly afterwards. On 20 August, his body was cremated and the ashes taken to Tokyo, where they were left in the keeping of Buddhist monks of the fiercely nationalistic Nichiren sect.

Bose had been a failure as a conspirator, as a military leader, as a revolutionary. But whatever his shortcomings, he never lacked courage, and he still casts a long shadow over Indian politics, even today. He set out to create a myth, and he succeeded – so much so that some Indians, mostly Bengalis, do not believe he died at all. They say he is in Russia, or is living as a hermit in the Himalayas, and that one day, like King Arthur or the Emperor Barbarossa, he will awake from his long sleep and emerge to claim his kingdom.

Without Bose, the INA trials were always likely to be *Hamlet* without the prince. None of the captured officers were men of any political significance, and from the beginning there were grave doubts about the value of bringing them to court. But Wavell, as a soldier, was faced with a dilemma: what would those soldiers who had remained loyal think if he did not punish those who had, as he saw it, betrayed their trust, their honour and their comrades? Praising the 70 per cent of those who 'under pressure and punishment, under hardships and want, stood firm' he pointed out: 'As proof of what they endured as a price of their loyalty to their ideals of a soldier's duty, I will tell you this: the 45,000 Indian prisoners of war who stood firm are estimated to have lost about 11,000 or one quarter of their number, from disease, starvation and murder; the 20,000 who went over to our enemy's side lost only 1,500 or $7\frac{1}{2}$ per cent.'[10] Of those 1,500, incidentally, only two officers and 150 other ranks were actually killed in action.

Wavell's decision to try the INA men was supported by General Sir Claude Auchinleck, who had returned as C-in-C when Wavell was appointed viceroy. Nothing could have shown more clearly that though they were both transparently honest and honourable men, they lacked political nous. Auchinleck promptly compounded Wavell's blunder in holding the trials at all, by deciding to hold them in public in the Red Fort in Delhi. Senior officials felt it would be wiser to hold them in some remote town where they could perhaps be hushed up. The Red Fort, they pointed out, was far too handy for the politicians and lawyers of Delhi; it also had unfortunate associations with pre-British glories and with the great revolt of 1857, only 90 years before. But 'the Auk', as Auchinleck was universally known, was cut from the same cloth as Wavell, and always refused to stoop to subterfuge in any shape or form. 'Once it was decided that the trials could not be held in secret,' he wrote later, 'it would have been wrong to tuck them away somewhere where defence counsel, relations, etc, could not conveniently attend, and the Red Fort was the most convenient place from nearly every point of view.'

It seemed that just about everybody objected to the INA trials for one reason or another. Many British officers felt that the men should never have been brought back to India, but should have been dealt with by summary courts-martial in forward areas. Congress and the Indian nationalists thought they should not be tried at all, and certainly not by the British. At its first post-war session in Bombay on 21 September, the AICC called for clemency: 'It would be a tragedy if these officers were punished for the offence of having laboured, however mistakenly, for the freedom of India.'[11] Privately, however, Asaf Ali confessed that although Congress 'would lose much ground in the country' if it failed to take up their cause, when the party came to power it would certainly remove them from the army and might even put 'some of them on trial'.[12]

For the moment, however, there were elections to be fought, beginning with those for the Central Legislative Assembly, and no party could afford to miss the opportunity presented by the trials. Congress led the way, setting up INA relief funds and providing a panel of eminent defence lawyers led by Bhulabhai Desai and including Sir Tej Bahadur Sapru and Nehru, who put on his barrister's wig and gown for the first time in 25 years. Jinnah did not offer his services, but the League joined the outcry, for the majority of the INA prisoners were Muslims. As the politicians toured the country, they all found the issue a valuable stick with which to beat the British. It soon became difficult to tell the difference between an INA rally and an election meeting.

As the time approached for the trials, the British handed the nationalists yet more ammunition by agreeing to use Indian troops to help restore French and Dutch colonial rule in Indo-China and the Dutch East Indies, the future Indonesia. Wavell had seen the danger in this move and had opposed it vigorously, but he was overruled by Mountbatten as supreme allied commander.[13] And so the anti-imperialist cause, and the rising political temperature, were given another boost. The situation was further aggravated by sharp increases in unemployment and prices throughout India, and a new food crisis as crops failed in Bombay and Bengal and Madras was devastated by a cyclone.

The first three INA officers to be tried were charged with waging war against the king-emperor, murder, and abetting murder. They were a Hindu, a Muslim and a Sikh – an example of British even-handedness which inevitably backfired by unifying all three creeds against them. 'Quit India' slogans began to appear on walls in all the major towns and cities, pamphlets proclaiming 'Patriots Not Traitors' circulated widely, and posters threatening 'Death to 20 English Dogs' for every INA man sentenced were pasted all over Delhi. At a public meeting in Benares the threat was voiced that 'if INA men were not saved, revenge would be taken on European children'.[14] When the trials began on 5 November, the actions were stepped up even further with the declaration of an 'INA Week', culminating in 'INA Day', involving protest marches, hartals and public meetings.

On 21 November, after relatively minor disturbances in Bombay, violence erupted in Calcutta when a combined demonstration by Forward Bloc, Congress, the League and Communist students clashed with police. A lathi charge was met with brickbats and stones, whereupon the police opened fire, killing two students and wounding 33. Calcutta Corporation employees were already on strike for more pay, and many of them, especially Communist-led transport workers, took to the streets in support of the students. Sikh taxi-drivers and workers at many factories joined in. Cars, buses and lorries were set on fire, barricades thrown across streets, trains stopped by crowds. It took two days to restore order, by which time police had been forced to open fire 14 times, killing another 33 people and injuring some 200. Seventy British and 37 American soldiers were also injured, and 150 police and army vehicles destroyed.[15]

Congress leaders were horrified at the events in Calcutta. Subhas Bose's brother Sarat refused to talk to the students, Patel condemned the 'frittering away' of energies on 'trifling quarrels' with the police, and the Working Committee strongly reaffirmed its faith in non violence. Gandhi began a more or less friendly dialogue with Richard G. Casey, the governor of Bengal – Wavell was still refusing to meet Gandhi, whom he distrusted profoundly, describing him later as 'an unscrupulous old hypocrite'. Casey reported after his first meeting that: 'His political reasoning lacked realism and balance. However there was no sign of senility.'[16]

The British, too, were horrified at the strength of Indian reaction to the trials, and were beginning to realize just how serious a mistake they had made. Reports poured in to New Delhi from the provinces similar to that from Sir George Cunningham, governor of the NWFP, warning that 'every day that passes now brings over more and more well-disposed Indians to the anti-British camp'. Cunningham suggested that the trials should be abandoned, since with each day the issue was becoming 'more and more purely Indian versus British'.[17] The director of the Intelligence Bureau noted that 'sympathy for the INA is not the monopoly of those who are ordinarily against Government', and that it was 'usually the case that INA men belonged to families which had traditions of loyalty'.[18]

To Wavell's astonishment, Indians in the armed forces were also sympathetic to the INA 'traitors'. Soldiers and airmen, often in uniform, attended INA support meetings and contributed money to the defence fund. By late November, Auchinleck, who was being kept informed daily of the effects of the trials on army personnel, was reporting to Wavell that 'the general opinion in the Army (as opposed to that of certain units who have particular reason for bitterness) is in favour of leniency'.[19] Many British officers disagreed with him. General Sir Geoffrey Scoones, GOC-in-C Central Command, wrote a stiff letter to Auchinleck saying: 'Leniency will not attain our immediate objective ... We may be blamed for lack of moral courage ... and the armed forces will get confused.'[20] Others, such as Major C.W. Cockin, said they believed it was wrong for British officers to judge the INA men's conduct, and that the trials should be put into cold storage until an Indian government was formed.[21] This was precisely what most Indian officers thought, and there were now far more of them than there were British officers, whose numbers had shrunk to less than 4,000 from a pre-war figure of 11,000.

On 1 December, Auchinleck announced that the charge of waging war against the king would be dropped for all defendants, and that further trials would only be for murder or brutality against other POWs. But this did little to calm Indian passions. Bhulabhai Desai warned that if any of the accused were executed it was likely to cause an armed revolution, which Congress might support. The first trial finished at the end of December. The three men were sentenced to cashiering, forfeiture of pay and allowances, and transportation for life, but Auchinleck immediately commuted the sentences of transportation, and there was no trouble from the Indian people.

There was trouble, however, from an unexpected source – from British officers, who broke with military tradition and publicly criticized their own C-in-C. Auchinleck responded with cold fury. He called for reports from all formation commanders, then wrote them a long memorandum which in their own language 'tore them off a strip' in no uncertain fashion. It was a truly remarkable document, which illustrated the immense changes that had already taken place, not only in the army but in Britain's entire relationship with India. It was a document that one could never imagine Linlithgow, for example, and certainly not Churchill, even contemplating. Its purpose, Auchinleck said, was 'to remove the feelings of doubt, resentment and even disgust which appear to exist in the minds of quite a number of British officers, who have not the knowledge or the imagination to be able to view the situation as a whole, or to understand the present state of feeling in India'.[22]

'It should be remembered,' Auchinleck's memorandum continued, '... that every Indian worthy of the name is today a "Nationalist", though this does not mean that he is necessarily "anti-British". All the same, where India and her independence are concerned, there are no "pro-British" Indians. Every Indian Commissioned Officer is a Nationalist and rightly so, provided he hopes to attain independence for India by constitutional means.' He castigated British officers who 'forget, if they ever knew, the great bitterness bred in the minds of many Indian officers in the early days of "Indianization" by the discrimination, often very real, exercised against them, and the discourteous, contemptuous treatment meted out to them by many British officers who should have known better'.

The VCOs – viceroy commissioned officers, a category equivalent to warrant officers in the British army – had been shattered, Auchinleck reminded his commanders, by the terrible tragedies of Singapore and Hong Kong, which must have seemed to them and the rank and file 'to be the end of all things and certainly of the British "Raj", to whom the Army had been used for so many years to look as its universal provider and protector ... It is quite wrong to adopt the attitude that because these men had taken service in a British-controlled Indian Army, therefore their loyalties must be the same as those of British soldiers ... They had no real loyalty or patriotism towards Britain as Britain, not as we understand loyalty.'

Officers, because of their superior education, experience and knowledge of the world, presented a much more difficult problem: 'There is no excuse for the regular officers who went over, beyond the fact that the early stages of "Indianization" ... were badly mismanaged by the British Government of India, and this prepared the ground for disloyalty when the opportunity came.' However, he stressed that 'No Indian officer must be regarded as suspect and disloyal merely because he is what is called a "Nationalist", or in other words – a good Indian!'[23]

There were 14 more trials of INA men, resulting in prison sentences, before they were called off altogether in the face of increasingly vociferous demands for a general amnesty. The first sentence was passed on 11 February 1946, when a man called Rashid Ali was given seven years' rigorous imprisonment for murder. Calcutta exploded again, starting with a protest march led by Muslim League students which was joined by Congress and Communist student organizations, and workers both Muslim and Hindu. The following day, the city was paralysed by a Communist-led general strike and a massive rally was held in Wellington Square. It took the police and the army two days to put down what became known as 'the almost revolution', after numerous street battles in which 84 were killed and 300 injured.[24]

Around the same time as the INA upheavals, there were violent clashes in many other parts of India for various reasons, including rising prices and cuts in rations as food shortages increased. Railway and postal workers were striking all over India, and in Allahabad a mob of 80,000 stormed ration centres. Even British servicemen caught the mood of unrest, as RAF ground and maintenance units at Dum Dum airfield near Calcutta, and at several other stations throughout India, mutinied in mid-January, demanding early demobilization. The situation could easily have turned ugly – the local army commander moved troops and artillery into the area – but a British MP visiting India with a Parliamentary delegation defused it by promising that he would take up the men's case when he got home, and they soon returned to work. Their brothers in the RIAF, however, were inspired to stage their own mutiny, demanding equal privileges with the RAF. They were quickly and painlessly subdued, but in early February there was more trouble in an India Pioneer unit in Calcutta and in various centres at Jubbulpore in the Central Provinces.

On 8 February 1946 came the first sign of trouble in the Indian navy, at HMIS *Talwar*, a shore-based signals training school in Bombay, when a number of ratings were charged with catcalling at women of the WRINS. They were acquitted, but discipline and morale were already uncertain, and a rash of slogans appeared on the walls of the establishment: 'Quit India', 'Revolt Now', 'Kill the British White Bastards'. The dissatisfaction simmered for 10 days, before boiling over on the morning of 18 February over the poor quality of the food. The mutineers began by refusing breakfast. From then on things escalated rapidly. Soon there were chants of 'The British must go!', and more slogans appeared. The arrest of one rating for scrawling 'Quit India' on a wall, intensified the friction.

A central strike committee was formed, which drew up a list of 40 grievances to be presented to the flag officer in Bombay, ranging from complaints about racial insults and discrimination to demands for equal pay with British naval personnel, the release of all the INA prisoners and the withdrawal of all Indian troops from Indonesia – which was in fact already under way. Since *Talwar* was a signals establishment, there was no way the authorities could stop the mutineers informing the rest of the navy what was happening. The result was that the mutiny soon spread to 78 ships and 20 shore establishments, including a cookery school and two demobilization centres, eventually reaching as far afield as WT stations in Aden and Bahrain.

Bombay, the home of the RIN, remained the focal point, with 22 ships in the harbour, as well as both Castle and Fort naval barracks, taken over by mutineers. A mass meeting on shore turned into a nationalist demonstration march, with much shouting of slogans, and the mutineers calling themselves the Indian National Navy, or the INN, in imitation of the INA. Some flags were burned including a number of White Ensigns and the Stars and Stripes flying outside the US Information Service office: they were replaced by Congress, Muslim League and 'Jai Hind' flags. In the bay, HMIS *Narbada* trained its guns on the Yacht Club, just back of the arch of the Gateway of India. Soon, the whole city came to a standstill as the civilian population showed its support with strikes, *hartals*, barricades, street battles and the destruction of police stations, post offices and other official buildings, while shopkeepers provided the mutineers with free food and drink.

In Karachi, the other main centre of confrontation, mutineers took over the corvette HMIS *Hindustan*, plus one other ship and three shore establishments. On 20 February the *Hindustan* fired on troops on shore with an Oerliken cannon and the ship's main armament, a four-inch gun. The troops did not reply at first, but the following morning opened fire on the ship with mortars and howitzers. After two hours, the mutineers surrendered: they had lost six dead and 25 wounded.

For the British the events in Bombay and Karachi once again revived memories of 1857. For the more politically aware – including many leading Congressmen – there were even closer echoes of the mutiny of the Black Sea fleet in the first Russian Revolution of 1905, immortalized by Sergei Eisenstein in his film classic *Battleship Potemkin*. That, too, had started with complaints about inedible food, and ended with the shooting of civilian sympathizers on the Odessa steps. Congress joined the League in condemning the mutineers and the strikers, and made no complaint when Wavell and Auchinleck acted firmly to suppress the mutiny. General Sir R.M. Lockhart, GOC Bombay, had 'ample force available', Wavell reported to London, and 'if ships open fire they will have to be sunk'.[25] When Muslim seamen turned to Jinnah for advice, he told them to return to their ships and lay down their arms. Gandhi scolded them for setting 'a bad and unbecoming example for India'. Nehru quickly declared himself 'impressed by the necessity for curbing the wild outburst of violence'.[26] Sardar Vallabhbhai Patel hurried to Bombay and went out to the ships in person to persuade the mutineers to surrender, having done a deal with Auchinleck that they would not be punished and their grievances would be examined.

Persuading the citizens of Bombay was another matter, however – it took two army battalions to restore order. Significantly, they were not British troops but local Marathas. They moved into the city on 23 February with bren gun carriers and tanks, while a flight of Mosquito fighter-bombers roared over the port, and the British light cruiser *Glasgow* and other Royal Navy warships trained their guns on *Talwar* and the other Indian ships which had gone over to the mutineers. Official casualty figures were 228 civilians killed and 1,046 injured.[27]

The events in Calcutta, Bombay and Karachi, together with lesser upheavals in various other towns and cities, had started more or less spontaneously, but they had been orchestrated and encouraged by the Communists, socialists and the Forward Bloc. Congress leaders had opposed the disturbances, for the very good reason that they were about to assume power as the legitimate government of India, and had no wish to inherit a revolutionary situation, or rebellious and indisciplined armed forces. They were as pleased as Wavell and Auchinleck that the army had remained rock solid throughout.

The results of the central elections had been announced at the beginning of the year, revealing a marked polarization along communal lines. Both Congress and the League had triumphed in their own spheres: Congress won 91.3 per cent of the vote in the general constituencies, utterly trouncing the Hindu Mahasabha, the Nationalists and other parties; the League won 88.6 per cent of the total Muslim vote and every single Muslim seat. The new assembly was made up as follows (previous figures in brackets): Congress 57 (36), Muslim League 30 (25), Independents 5 (21), Nationalist Party 0 (10), Akali Sikhs 2 (0), and Europeans 8 (8).

The provincial elections were still in progress, with the campaigns generating increasing heat. The anti-British unity shown during the INA demonstrations soon evaporated into communal disputes and rioting, especially in the Punjab. The pattern of Congress activity was being set for the vital following years: Nehru was the front man, the star who travelled thousands of miles to address rallies and whip up enthusiasm in towns and villages; but the man who organized and controlled the party machine was Patel. Patel had by then supplanted Gandhi as the main link with Birla and the other rich businessmen who financed the party. While they saw the value of Nehru's charisma, they distrusted his socialism and were much more comfortable with Patel's right-wing politics. Like him, they saw the emergent Communists as the chief enemy, now that the British had conceded the principle of early independence. For the League, Jinnah combined both roles, refusing to allow Liaquat or his other lieutenants to see the viceroy or anyone else at the top without him, not trusting them to resist giving even an inch over Pakistan.

'The day is not far off when Pakistan shall be at your feet,' a jubilant Jinnah had told student supporters after the central election success.[28] The provincial results were far less decisive: the League won just two provinces, Bengal and Sind, and even in those was able to form ministries only with the support of the Europeans. Congress in contrast was able to form ministries not only in Bihar, the UP, Bombay, Madras, the Central Provinces and Orissa, but also in Assam and the NWFP, two of the provinces claimed by Jinnah for Pakistan. In the NWFP, Abdul Ghaffar Khan and his brother Dr Khan Sahib won 19 Muslim seats for Congress against the League's 17. Perhaps the most disappointing result for Jinnah was in the all-important Punjab, the P in Pakistan, where, although the League leaped dramatically from two to 79 of the 86 Muslim seats, Khizar Hyat

Khan and his rump of seven Unionists were able to hang on to power for another year by forming a coalition with Congress and the Sikhs in the 175-seat legislature. Overall, however, the League had won 442 out of 509 Muslim seats, almost 87 per cent of the total, in the 11 provinces. It was a giant vote of confidence for Jinnah and Pakistan, and a truly remarkable turn-around since the disasters of 1937.

With the new provincial assemblies in place, Wavell was ready to fulfil his promise to consult them about setting up a constitution-making body, and to form a new Executive Council based on party lines. But he was stopped in his tracks by a decision made by the Cabinet in London, which was announced on 19 February 1946, the day after the RIN mutiny began: Cripps was returning to India to search for a new solution.

24

'We are on the Threshold of a Great Tragedy'

The widespread violence surrounding the INA trials convinced Attlee that he had to do something quickly to reduce tension in India. In early December 1945, Pethick-Lawrence assured Indians of 'the British people's urgent desire' to see India rise quickly to the full and free status of an equal partner in the British Commonwealth. On New Year's Day, 1946, he broadcast a personal message telling them their battle was won: 'The problem now is a practical one. It is to work out a rational and acceptable plan of action. It must be a plan under which authority can be transferred to Indian control under forms of government which will willingly be accepted by the broad mass of India's people – so that the new India will not be torn and rent by internal strife and dissentions.'[1] It was a fine aim – but more easily said than done.

To back up the pious words, Attlee sent an all-party Parliamentary delegation of eight MPs and two peers to India, to meet Indian political leaders and learn their views at first hand. The delegation, headed by Professor Robert Richards, a long-serving Labour MP who had been under-secretary of state for India in 1924, arrived in India on 5 January 1946, and spent a month touring the country talking to just about every political leader. Its members were received everywhere 'with cordiality and friendliness', according to V.P. Menon, and no doubt they learned a great deal as the provincial election campaigns raged around them. But they had no authority and no purpose apart from trying to mend fences and gather information which the governments of both India and Britain already knew.

The one definite conclusion the delegation brought back to London was that the 1942 Cripps plan was a dead letter. Attlee, however, was convinced that it had come so near to success that it was worth trying to develop and modify it until it was acceptable, though he had no illusions about the difficulties involved. 'It was clear to me,' he wrote in his autobiography, 'that the problem could not be handled by a Secretary of State and a Viceroy, however able they might be.' In truth, he had little faith in Wavell, and had only appointed Pethick-Lawrence as a benign figurehead while he and Cripps dictated policy. Apart from himself, which was clearly impossible, there was only one man for the job, and that man, of course, was Cripps. Cripps would go out to India again, accompanied by Pethick-Lawrence and A.V. Alexander, who had retained the position as First Lord of the Admiralty which he had held in Churchill's government. By sending no fewer than three senior Cabinet ministers for an indefinite period while the government was faced with enormous problems at home, Attlee was showing just how serious he was about reaching an early settlement.

The third man in the Cabinet mission, Alexander, was a Co-operative socialist and party stalwart whom Attlee trusted implicitly. He was an affable fellow, fond of playing the piano and singing into the small hours at social gatherings or when work was done. He had never been to India before, and regarded his role in the three-man mission as 'ballast'. But in fact his presence emphasized the importance the government placed on the defence aspects of Indian independence. Britain was still a world power, with world responsibilities, and India was a vital link in the chain between the Middle East and South-east Asia, protecting British interests from Suez to Singapore and beyond. It was essential to the security of those regions that a free India should remain friendly – it would be disastrous if a left-wing Congress government chose to ally itself with Soviet Russia. For that reason alone, as well as a myriad others both practical and emotional, it was important not to offend Congress by taking the obvious way out of the problem and giving Jinnah his Pakistan there and then.

From the British viewpoint, the defence question was one of the most powerful arguments against the creation of Pakistan. India's two most vulnerable frontiers had always been the north-west and the north-east, the routes taken by invaders since time immemorial. Both would be in Pakistan. But would an independent Pakistan be capable of defending them without the co-operation of India? British experts were extremely doubtful, arguing that even if 'the Commonwealth substantially provided the Navy and Air Force, [Pakistan] would go bankrupt in the anarchical sense of being unable to pay its services'.[2] The chiefs of staff concluded that:

... should India become divided into two or more self-governing and independent parts, her defence problem will be very greatly increased; further, without a single common defence authority for the whole country, the defence of India will be jeopardised ... It is of very great importance that there should be co-ordinated machinery for defence of geographical India, and that there should be a single common defence authority with whom His Majesty's Government could deal.[3]

In marked contrast to 1942, when his rushed visit to India had been fraught with misunderstandings back home, Cripps drafted a clear and well thought-out directive which was approved by the Cabinet as a whole. The purpose of the mission was 'to secure agreement amongst the Indian leaders as to the method of arriving at the new constitutional structure for India and the setting up of an interim Executive'. Together with the viceroy – another important difference from the last time – it was to 'discuss and explore all possible alternatives without proceeding upon any fixed or rigid pre-conceived plan'.[4]

The idea was to mediate, not to impose British solutions, and the government would accept whatever the Indian leaders agreed, subject to only four conditions: protection of the minorities either in the constitution or by treaty; provision for the defence of India and the Indian Ocean area; no transfer of British paramountcy over the states to an Indian government; and a satisfactory financial settlement between India and Britain. An independent India would choose for itself whether or not to remain in the Commonwealth, or to have a defence treaty with Britain. None of Britain's own needs would be treated as 'essential' to an agreement. In effect, the mission had virtual plenipotentiary powers to achieve the best solution possible.

Cripps, Pethick-Lawrence and Alexander – promptly christened 'the Magi' by Wavell – arrived in New Delhi at noon on Sunday, 24 March 1946. It was exactly four years and a day since Cripps's last arrival, and the difference between the two visits could hardly have been more marked. For a start, the three Cabinet ministers spent their first two nights in the Viceroy's House, before moving into the house of the military secretary at 2 Willingdon Crescent, within the viceregal grounds. Their offices remained in the south-east wing of the Viceroy's House. Wavell played a full part in their discussions, sitting on Pethick-Lawrence's left at the centre of a circular table throughout. Cripps sat alongside Pethick-Lawrence, and Alexander next to Wavell. They spent their first week examining the implications of the provincial election results and talking to members of the existing Executive Council and the governors, who had all been brought to Delhi to meet them.

Each of the three ministers had brought his own team of advisers and assistants. Pethick-Lawrence had Sir William Croft, his deputy under-secretary of state, the brilliant Frank Turnbull of the India Office, who had accompanied Cripps in 1942, and a political ADC. Alexander had only a political ADC, who had so little to do that he soon became bored and 'browned off'. Cripps took two hand-picked personal assistants, Major J. McL. 'Billie' Short and Major Woodrow Wyatt, and a private secretary, George Blaker. Short was a former officer in the 5/11 Sikhs, who had returned to the Punjab in the early part of the war as civil liaison officer and now worked for the Ministry of Information. He had written several valuable papers on India and the possibility of a modified form of Pakistan. Wyatt, a newly-elected Labour MP who had been a member of the Parliamentary delegation, had also served in India, but his contacts were mainly Muslim. In particular, he had 'an old friend ... who is quite close to Jinnah'.[5] She was the beautiful young Mumtaz 'Tazi' Shah Nawaz, granddaughter of the late Sir Muhammad Shafi, who had been president of the League when Jinnah first joined it in 1913. Wyatt called on Jinnah at his home in New Delhi three days after arriving in India, and reported to Cripps that the Muslim League appeared to be solidly behind their Quaid-i-Azam.

With Short and Wyatt providing behind-the-scenes liaison with the Sikhs and Muslims, Cripps worked hard at cementing his own contacts with Congress and Gandhi. He was aided unofficially by two of the leading lights of the India Conciliation Group, Horace Alexander (no relation to A.V. Alexander) and Agatha Harrison. Miss Harrison was visited regularly at the YWCA by the Rajkumari (Princess) Amrit Kaur, one of Gandhi's secretaries, who came for a bath every morning while she was living with Gandhi in the New Delhi sweepers' colony. Each day, she told Harrison the Mahatma's thoughts and feelings, which Harrison passed on to Cripps. To Cripps this was a particularly valuable contact: he believed he had made the mistake in 1942 of not paying enough attention to Gandhi, and was determined to do better this time.

Cripps was denied, for the time being, his personal contact with Nehru, who was at that time away in Malaya, meeting political leaders and investigating conditions for the local Indian population. Nehru had wanted to visit Burma and Indonesia, to meet the leaders of the freedom movements there, but had been refused permission. Wavell had allowed him to go to Malaya and Singapore, but local officials decreed that his movements would be strictly limited, and no official transport would be provided. Suddenly, however, the doors of Singapore were thrown open, through the personal intervention of Lord Louis Mountbatten (as he still was: he became a viscount two months later, having turned down a barony as being beneath him).

Mountbatten, who was still supreme commander in South-east Asia, based in Singapore, insisted on treating Nehru as though he were already prime minister of an independent India. He entertained him at Government House, and lent him his personal official car and driver. When Nehru visited the Indian YMCA forces' canteen, Mountbatten and his wife, Edwina, went with him, sitting alongside him in the open car. It was a typical piece of Mountbatten grandstanding, and it produced the required result: an incipiently anti-British Indian mob turned into an exuberantly pro-British crowd. They burst into the canteen behind Nehru and the Mountbattens, knocking Edwina over in their enthusiasm and threatening to trample her underfoot. Nehru and Mountbatten linked arms and charged the crowd to try to rescue her, but she managed to crawl between people's legs to the far end of the room, where she climbed on to a table and shouted that she was all right. Nehru gazed at her in admiration. 'That was,' he recalled many years later, 'an unusual introduction for us.'[6]

Nehru continued his tour without incident, speaking everywhere of Asiatic unity, and denigrating Jinnah and the whole concept of Pakistan. In Malaya he was given two national flags which the INA had used in action, one of which had been planted on Indian soil at Kohima. He wrapped them carefully in paper and took them home with him when he returned to India at the beginning of April.[7]

Back in Delhi, the Cabinet mission had made a promising start. Cripps had met Jinnah privately for an hour on the morning of Saturday 30 March, and reported that: 'He was calm and reasonable but completely firm on Pakistan.'[8] Obsessed with the importance of Gandhi, Cripps even managed to persuade Jinnah to agree to meet him. Cripps himself met Gandhi next day, hurrying to pay his respects as soon as the Mahatma arrived from Wardha to stay among the untouchables in the sweepers' colony, a collection of hutments built by the municipality around the temple of Balmiki in Reading Road. The rest-hut of the temple had been converted into Gandhi's living-room, complete with all modern conveniences, including electricity, fans, telephone and bathroom. It was there that the British journalist James Cameron claimed he was told by Sarojini Naidu, 'the merriest Hindu rebel who ever came out of Girton', 'Ah, if the Mahatma only knew what it costs *us* for him to live the simple life.'[9] Cripps and Pethick-Lawrence had invited Gandhi to come to Delhi early so that they could talk to him before his formal meeting with the mission on 3 April. They now begged him to stay on afterwards, to be on hand for consultation.

At the formal meeting, Wavell was 'horrified at the deference shown' to Gandhi by Cripps and Pethick-Lawrence. They stood up when he entered, 'naked except for a *dhoti* and looking remarkably healthy', and later, 'when he expressed a wish for a glass of water, the Secretary was sent to fetch it himself, instead of sending for a *chaprassi*; and when it did not come at once Cripps hustled off himself to see about it'. In Wavell's eyes, the interview itself was 'a deplorable affair', with Pethick-Lawrence showing 'his usual sloppy benevolence to this malevolent politician'. Pethick-Lawrence confirmed the viceroy's worst fears by ending the meeting with a little speech of 'penitence for Britain's misdeeds in the past!'[10]

Gandhi pooh-poohed the idea of meeting Jinnah again, saying he had already spent 18 days talking to him in 1944. He was willing to accept the truncated Pakistan which he had conceded then, but beyond that Pakistan was 'an untruth', 'a sin which he ... would not commit'. He reiterated his belief that the two-nation theory was dangerous – all Indian Muslims, he said, were converts, 'all descendants of Indian-born people'. Sticking to the idea of independence first, with the constitution to be drawn up later, he demanded an 'absolutely national' government immediately, even if it meant asking Jinnah to lead it: 'Let Mr Jinnah form the first Government and choose its personnel from elected representatives in the country ... If he does not do so then the offer to form a Government should be made to Congress.' In the mean time, he would apply an 'acid test of British sincerity': Britain should abolish the Salt Tax, release all the remaining prisoners who were still in gaol for violent offences in 1942, and dismiss Ambedkar, the untouchables' leader, from the government.[11]

Gandhi stressed the fact that he was speaking as an individual and not on behalf of Congress, of which he was not even a member. He referred the mission to the 'authorized representatives' of Congress. In fact, Azad had met the mission that morning, and he had told them much the same as Gandhi in terms of independence and an immediate national government – though without the suggestion that Jinnah should lead it.

Although Azad was still president of Congress, the thoughts he presented were largely those of Nehru, who had prepared notes for him and Patel in mid-March, before leaving for Singapore. The essence of his plan was for a federal government 'with fully autonomous Provinces with residuary powers vested in the units themselves'. There would be two lists of federal subjects, one compulsory, including such areas as defence, foreign affairs and communications, the other optional. Once the constitution was settled, by all provinces and states, certain clearly defined areas, as opposed to provinces, would be able to stand out: this would allow the non-Muslim majority areas of the Punjab and Bengal to opt out of the opt-out if they chose. Cripps was quick to see the potential in this, and pressed Azad to consider developing the plan so that there might be a sub-federal grouping of Muslim provinces – in other words, Pakistan in all but name. Azad took the suggestion on board, but said he would have to consult his Working Committee before going any further.[12]

Jinnah arrived for his first official interview next morning at 10 o'clock. He stayed for a full three hours, the first two of which he spent lecturing the mission on Indian history and the differences between Hindus and Muslims. Most of the remaining hour was spent with Cripps exercising his noted lawyer's examination skills, trying to break Jinnah down and force him to reveal the details of his concept of Pakistan, and how it would be defended. He failed. For once, he had met his match, and when Jinnah left, all that he had revealed was that he was still committed to an undefined but totally sovereign Muslim state.

Among Muslims, the bandwagon of Pakistan was now rolling, giving Jinnah the problem of keeping it under control. All the newly-elected League members of both provincial and central legislative councils gathered in Delhi in early April to take a solemn vow, 'in the name of Allah, the Beneficent, the Merciful' that 'the safety and security, and the salvation and destiny of the Muslim Nation, inhabiting the Subcontinent of India lies only in the achievement of Pakistan ... and, believing as I do in the rightness and justice of my cause, I pledge myself to undergo any danger, trial or sacrifice which may be demanded of me'.[13]

One after another, the provincial leaders rose amid thunderous applause, each to sound his own call to arms. From Bengal, H.S. Suhrawardy, who moved the pledge resolution, declared: 'We do not intend to start a civil war, but we want a land where we can live in peace ... I have long pondered whether the Muslims are prepared to fight. Let me honestly declare that every Muslim of Bengal is ready and prepared to lay down his life.' Turning to Jinnah, who sat on the presidential throne, impassive and immaculate in cream silk *sherwani*, white *shalwar* and his trade-mark fur cap, he cried theatrically: 'I call upon you to test us.'[14] From the UP, Khaliquzzaman vowed: 'We will lay down our lives for Pakistan.' The Nawab of Mamdot declared: 'If the stalwart soldiers of the Punjab could defend Britain against Nazi aggression, they can also defend their own hearths and homes.' The Pathan leader Khan Abdul Qayyum Khan from the NWFP rose to cry: 'Thank God, we have one flag, one leader, one platform and one ideal, Pakistan, to fight for. We are only waiting for the final order to do whatever is considered necessary for the attainment of Pakistan.'

As the emotional temperature soared, more and more delegates clamoured to add their own battle cries. Only a few older, wiser heads held back, men like Sir Firoz Khan Noon of the Punjab, the former defence member of the Executive Council, who warned: 'Neither the Hindus nor the British know yet how far we are prepared to go in order to achieve Pakistan. We are on the threshold of a great tragedy.'[15]

Jinnah acknowledged the passions of his members, telling them: 'We have done wonders. In five years our renaissance has been a miracle of achievement. I begin to think it has been a dream.'[16] 'What are we fighting for?' he asked them rhetorically. 'What are we aiming at?' It was a good question. The obvious answer was 'Pakistan' – but what exactly did he mean by Pakistan? As always, even at this crucial stage, Jinnah took great care not to define it too clearly, keeping all his options open for as long as possible. This was to be his strategy throughout his talks with the Cabinet mission.

For seven weeks the mission laboured on, interviewing no fewer than 472 people in 181 formal meetings, though everyone knew that there were really only three or four men who counted. Wavell thought it was a waste of time talking to so many minor politicians. It imposed a heavy strain on the ministers and himself, and kept the two important parties waiting impatiently, while the real business lost momentum.

The only important minorities apart from the Muslims were the 6 million

Sikhs and the 60 million untouchables, the Scheduled Castes. The Sikhs, represented by Master Tara Singh and two others, were strongly opposed to partition and pressed for a separate Sikh state or province within India if the Punjab went to Pakistan. Unfortunately, however, they disagreed among themselves on just about everything else. Because of this, and the fact that they were comparatively few, and were mainly concentrated into one area of the Punjab around Lahore and Amritsar, the ministers failed to take them seriously. It was to prove a tragic and costly mistake, perhaps the most serious in British India since the introduction of cartridges greased with animal fat 90 years before.

Like the Sikhs, the Scheduled Castes were also split into two distinct groups. One, led by Ambedkar, claimed the untouchables were a distinct religious minority and opposed the whole idea of a constituent assembly, which would be dominated by caste Hindus: they wanted the new constitution to be drawn up by experts under British or perhaps American guidance. The other group, the All-India Depressed Classes League led by Jagjivan Ram, held that untouchables were Hindus, but needed help and protection to improve their lot. Faced with such a welter of confusion, the mission decided that Wavell was right, and that they would have to concentrate on trying to solve the Hindu-Muslim problem before they could do anything for anybody else.

By 10 April, Cripps had concluded that there were only two possible solutions that stood any chance of acceptance by both Congress and League, and he prepared a memorandum setting out his ideas. Plan A was based on a combination of Azad's proposals and a suggestion made by Sir Frederick Burrows, a former railwayman and union official who had been appointed governor of Bengal in February. It provided for an all-India union of three parts – the Hindu majority provinces, the Muslim majority provinces, and the Indian states – with a central government controlling a minimum number of subjects such as defence, foreign affairs, communications and the protection of minorities. Plan B was for the partition of British India into Hindustan and Pakistan, with the states free to choose federation to either, or to remain independent. However, since Pakistan was based solely on religion, it followed that non-Muslim areas in the relevant provinces should be excluded – which meant that most of the eastern Punjab and virtually the whole of west Bengal, including Calcutta, would go to Hindustan, leaving Jinnah with what he had earlier described as 'a moth-eaten Pakistan'.[17]

Plan B would obviously raise difficulties over the defence of the sub-continent, and since this was an important element of the mission's directive from the Cabinet, the two alternative proposals had to be referred back to London before they could be presented to Congress and the League. Pethick-Lawrence cabled them to Attlee on 11 April, pointing out that if no agreement was reached 'we risk chaos in India and no scheme of Defence will then be of any value'.[18] The mission planned to see Jinnah first, on 16 April, 'in the hope of persuading him to get down to discussions with the Congress',[19] and then Azad. Then, on Good Friday, 19 April, they aimed to leave for five days' well-earned rest in Kashmir, while Congress and the League considered the proposals. The Cabinet gave its approval: they preferred plan A, but would reluctantly accept partition rather than risk chaos.

Azad, meanwhile, had been following Cripps's suggestion to develop his own ideas, and after much argument had managed to persuade the Working Committee and Gandhi to accept them. He came to see Cripps privately on 15 April, to ask what the mission would be proposing to Jinnah so that he could advise him in advance on the probable Congress reaction. That same day, he issued a lengthy public statement, setting out his personal objections to the idea of Pakistan, and outlining his proposed solution, which, he claimed, 'secures whatever merit the Pakistan scheme contains while all its defects and drawbacks are avoided'. It was a powerful and passionate cry for unity and understanding, designed to cut the ground from under Jinnah's feet:

I have considered from every possible point of view the scheme of Pakistan as formulated by the Muslim League. As an Indian I have examined its implications for the future of India as a whole. As a Muslim I have examined its likely effects upon the fortunes of Muslims of India ...

I have come to the conclusion that it is harmful not only for India as a whole but for Muslims in particular ...

Such a division of territories into pure and impure is un-Islamic and is more in keeping with orthodox Brahmanism ... a repudiation of the very spirit of Islam. Islam recognises no such division and the prophet says 'God has made the whole world a mosque for me.' ...

Let us consider dispassionately the consequences which will follow if we give effect to the Pakistan scheme. India will be divided into two States, one with a majority of Muslims and the other of Hindus. In the Hindustan State there will remain three and a half crores [35 million] of Muslims scattered in small minorities all over the land. With 17 per cent in the UP, 12 per cent in Bihar and 9 per cent in Madras, they will be weaker than they are today in the Hindu majority provinces. They have had their homelands in these regions for almost a thousand years and built up well known [sic] centres of Muslim culture and civilisation there.

They will awake overnight and discover that they have become alien and foreigners. Backward industrially, educationally and economically, they will be left to the mercies of what would become an unadulterated Hindu raj ...

Two states confronting one another, offer no solution of the problem of one another's minorities, but only lead to retribution and reprisals by introducing a system of mutual hostages. The scheme of Pakistan therefore solves no problem for the Muslims. It cannot safeguard their rights where they are in a minority nor as citizens of Pakistan secure them a position in Indian or world affairs which they would enjoy as citizens of a major state like the Indian Union.

Azad blamed the hostility of 'certain communal extremists among the Hindus' for the popularity of the Pakistan idea among Muslims. 'With simple though untenable logic,' he wrote, 'they argued that if Hindus were so opposed to Pakistan, surely it must be of benefit to Muslims.' This, he believed, had created 'an atmosphere of emotional frenzy' especially among the younger and more impressionable Muslims, which made reasonable appraisal impossible. After briefly outlining the main features of what he now described as 'the Congress formula' – which was virtually indistinguishable from the Cabinet mission's plan A – he described it as 'the only solution ... which allows room for development both to the provinces and to India as a whole'. He concluded:

I am one of those who considers the present chapter of communal bitterness and differences as a transient phase in Indian life. I firmly hold that they will disappear when India assumes the responsibility for her own destiny ...

Differences will no doubt persist, but they will be economic not communal. Opposition among political parties will continue, but it will be based, not on religion but on economic and political issues. Class and not community will be the basis of future alignments, and policies will be shaped accordingly. If it be argued that this is only a faith which events may not justify I would say that in any case the nine cores [90 million] of Muslims constitute a factor which nobody can ignore and whatever the circumstances, they are strong enough to safeguard their own destiny.[20]

The mission met Jinnah again at 11.00 a.m. the next day Wavell, Cripps and Turnbull had all prepared notes on how to handle him, but in the end he still outwitted them. Pethick-Lawrence began by telling him he had little chance of getting 'the full and complete demand for Pakistan': he could not have both the whole territory and full sovereignty. It was a question of choosing either plan A or plan B. Which did he prefer – a small but sovereign Pakistan, or a larger Pakistan within an all-India union? In a trice, Jinnah turned the meeting on its head. Suddenly, he was cross-examining the three ministers, with a stream of searching questions about the details of the two plans. When they in turn tried to pin him down on exactly what he wanted he simply told them that the area involved could be discussed once the principle of Pakistan had been conceded. As usual, he refused to commit himself until he had heard what Congress had to say. And it was on that note that the meeting finished, with Pethick-Lawrence suggesting that

Jinnah should think it over and let them know his position after they returned from Kashmir.

It was Alexander, the only non-lawyer of the three ministers and the most sympathetic to the League, who realized what Jinnah was about. 'I came to the conclusion,' he wrote in his diary that night, 'that he is playing this game, which is one of life and death for millions of people, very largely from the point of view of scoring a triumph in a legal negotiation by first making large demands and secondly insisting that he should make no offer reducing that demand but should wait for the other side always to say how much they would advance towards granting that demand.'[21]

Alexander was absolutely right. Jinnah was a lawyer first, second and last, and his whole life revolved around winning whatever case he was fighting. Back in 1942, a young Muslim friend, Wajid Ali, had asked him one evening after dinner: 'Quaid, tell me how you have bamboozled the Mussulmans. You enjoy yourself in the evening, you are not a scholar of Urdu, you don't practise your religion – how do you manage to be their leader?' Jinnah replied, 'Have I ever told you that I am your leader as a Mussulman? I am an advocate, pleading the cause of Mussulmans, taking the part of Mussulmans, fighting their fight. Nothing more, nothing less.'[22] For Jinnah, that statement still held good. Now, with the biggest and most important case of his life nearing its conclusion, he could not allow himself to weaken – any concession made in advance was a bargaining point given away to the other side.

The five days they spent in Kashmir, away from the searing heat of Delhi, were supposed to be a holiday for the Cabinet mission. Certainly, they found the cool climate refreshing, so much so that Cripps was later moved to write a poem to the beauty of Kashmir's mountains and lakes. But inevitably they found it impossible to stop working, and they returned with a new proposition to put to the Indian leaders: an interim government should be formed immediately; this would then set up an all-India commission made up of elected members of both the central and provincial assemblies, which would be charged with determining the constitutional provisions for the protection of minorities, and also whether or not British India should be partitioned into two sovereign states.

The commission would be given 30 days to decide. If by that time they had failed to agree, then Muslim members of the assemblies in Sind, the NWFP, the Punjab, Bengal, and the Sylhet district of Assam, would vote on whether or not they wanted their provinces to be separated from the rest of India. They would need a 75 per cent majority for separation. Non-Muslims in districts adjoining the main part of India – most notably east Punjab and west Bengal – would themselves be able to vote for their districts to be separated from the provinces and to join India.

It was an ingenious attempt to break the deadlock, though as V.P. Menon and Wavell both perceived, it would ultimately give Jinnah nothing more than the moth-eaten Pakistan which he had already rejected. Cripps found Jinnah 'in an unreceptive mood' when he put the plan to him at his house. Jinnah did, however, promise to lay the proposal before his Working Committee – if Congress accepted it. Encouraged by this positive sign, which he regarded as 'provisional, very provisional, acceptance', Cripps went to see Nehru privately, to sound him out. Nehru turned the idea down flat. Amazingly undeterred, Cripps went back to Jinnah's house that same evening, told him what had happened, and offered him plans A and B once again. This time, Jinnah agreed to put plan A – a larger Pakistan within a loose all-India Union – before his committee, again on condition that Congress was 'prepared to consider it'.[23] This was highly promising: for the first time, it seemed Jinnah was prepared to consider something less than a fully sovereign Pakistan.

The following morning, the mission and Wavell considered their next move. Since Congress had officially rejected plan A, although it was based on their own proposals, they agreed that they would say nothing about it to Azad when he came for a prearranged meeting that morning. Instead, Cripps would visit Gandhi that night, to try and persuade him to talk to Jinnah. Azad, however, surprised them all by taking the initiative. He told them he thought he could get the Working Committee to agree to a three-tier system, with Muslim and non-Muslim provinces forming their own sub-federations, each with its own legislature, and a loose federal government at the centre. He authorized Cripps to tell Jinnah that 'he was confident that Congress would go as far as that'.[24] He proposed that four representatives from each of the two parties should meet with the mission at Simla, away from the heat of Delhi, to thrash out an agreement. When Cripps put the proposal to Jinnah that evening, he, too, agreed to put it to his Working Committee. This was progress indeed.

What Azad did not tell the mission was that he was operating without authority either from his Working Committee or from Gandhi. He did not tell them, either, that he had already spent an hour that morning with Gandhi, who was becoming increasingly concerned about his sympathy for the Muslim cause and his eagerness to reach a settlement even if it meant conceding some form of Pakistan. Gandhi had insisted he should step down as president of Congress. He had agreed to do so, but was maintaining his traditional right to name his successor. He chose Nehru, with whom he had been working closely and who had supported him during all the arguments in the Working Committee, rather than Patel, who took a far more hardline Hindu attitude to the sacred unity of India.

Gandhi must have been severely torn between his love for Nehru, his anointed but wayward successor, and Patel, his devoted disciple. But when Patel threatened to stand for election against Nehru, Gandhi intervened as he had done in the past. Patel withdrew, and Nehru took over as president the following month, though Azad continued to lead the negotiations while the Cabinet mission remained in India.

The viceroy, the ministers and their aides flew to Ambala early in the morning of Wednesday 1 May 1946, then drove the remaining 93 miles over the winding mountain roads to Simla. The Congress delegation was already there: Azad, Nehru, Patel and Abdul Ghaffar Khan – two Hindus and two Muslims. So, too, was Gandhi, persuaded by Cripps, who still desperately wanted his blessing. He was, nevertheless, full of serious misgivings, and had not forgiven Azad for going behind his back in approaching the mission without first obtaining his approval. Although the delegations themselves were small, the whole of political India seemed to have decamped to Simla, followed by a large press corps. There was little chance of sitting down to discuss the issues in peace and quiet, but at least it was cooler than Delhi, which was suffering unusually hot weather that year.

Gandhi was given what James Cameron called 'a rather commonplace furnished bungalow called Chadwick at the end of a five-mile track',[25] which had been the wartime residence of the governor of Burma, Sir Reginald Dorman Smith. Gandhi had arrived there with an entourage of 15, but immediately sent them all back to Delhi. He replaced them with Horace Alexander, Agatha Harrison and a young Tata executive, Sudhir Ghosh, who acted as his private channel of communication with Cripps, much to the annoyance of Wavell. He also invited Patel and Ghaffar Khan to move in with him, but significantly did not ask Nehru and Azad – they had to journey out to Chadwick early each morning for their daily conference. Since all cars except the viceroy's were banned in Simla, Nehru avoided the politically unacceptable transport of a rickshaw pulled by four sweating coolies, by hiring 'a gay little piebald pony', on which he trotted briskly up and down the steep hilly roads. Azad, who was neither a horseman nor a socialist, settled for a rickshaw.

The talks got off to a bad start. They were due to begin on 2 May, but Jinnah kept everyone waiting for three days, claiming pressure of work in Delhi. When he did come, he brought with him Liaquat, Ismail Khan from the UP, and Abdur Rab Nishtar from the NWFP, but he might just as well have come alone, for both the policies and the tactics he pursued were strictly his own. When the two teams eventually met on Sunday, 5 May – which happened to be Wavell's 63rd birthday – Jinnah refused to shake hands with Azad or Ghaffar Khan, whom he had castigated as 'Congress show-boys' and traitors to the Muslim cause.

The two sides began arguing at once, unable to agree on anything, it seemed. And they continued arguing for the next seven days, sometimes all together, sometimes with each other, sometimes with the mission, sometimes leaving Nehru and Jinnah to battle it out alone. Should there be a central legislature and if so what should its powers and responsibilities be? Should the provinces be allowed to form themselves into groups, and if so should those groups have their own legislatures? Should the constitution-making body be set up before or after a decision on groupings, and therefore on Pakistan? Should there be one constitution-making body or two – one for Hindustan and one for Pakistan? Should the League be given parity with Congress in any interim government? Round and round they went, in ever-decreasing circles, getting nowhere.

Through it all, Cripps flitted busily from Viceregal Lodge to the various delegates' bungalows, frantically trying to build bridges. He argued, he reasoned, he drew up lists of points for discussion – but even those were dismissed by Gandhi as offering 'worse than Pakistan'. Wavell noted that Gandhi 'seemed quite unmoved at the prospect of civil war ... I think he had adopted Patel's thesis that if we are firm the Muslims will not fight.'[26] It was a dangerous assumption, especially as Jinnah was already having difficulty holding back his more militant members, who were ready to launch a full-scale jihad if they were refused their Pakistan. Despite this, however, it was Jinnah who showed the first sign of movement, intimating that given enough safeguards he might be prepared to consider accepting groupings of autonomous provinces within a loose union. But Gandhi and Patel were not, and by Sunday 12 May the gap between the two parties was still so wide that Pethick-Lawrence had no alternative but to admit failure and close the conference.

And so, the politicians and officials and advisers and newsmen all trooped back down the mountain, back into the baking oven that was Delhi, to start all over again. Jinnah stayed behind in Simla to recuperate, exhausted and ill after the strain of the conference had brought on a recurrence of his chronic 'bronchitis'. Everything seemed to be back to square one, and the mission was forced to take matters into its own hands and announce its own solution. It had some difficulty persuading the Cabinet in London to drop its quibbles and caveats – basically, the government was worried at what Churchill and the Tory opposition might say. But when Cripps and Pethick-Lawrence, tired and edgy after the strain of the last few weeks, threatened to resign, Attlee agreed to give them a free hand.

The mission published and broadcast its plan on 16 May. It rejected a sovereign Pakistan as impractical and unworkable, creating enormous economic, military and administrative difficulties: with two geographically separated halves seven hundred miles apart, 'the communications between them both in war and peace would be dependent on the goodwill of Hindustan'. And in any case, it would not solve the communal problem, since there were large non-Muslim minorities in the Punjab and Bengal. Any 'radical partition' of those provinces would be 'contrary to the wishes and interests' of a very large proportion of the population, and in the Punjab would leave 'substantial bodies of Sikhs on both sides of the boundary'.

What the plan proposed was essentially Azad's three-tier scheme, with provinces, groups of provinces, and a minimal union government at the centre consisting of representatives from both the provinces and the Indian states. The big difference was that in place of two groups there were now three, described as A, B and C. Group B was to include the Punjab, Sind, the NWFP and Baluchistan. Group C would be Bengal and Assam. Group A would include everything else. There was to be a constituent assembly elected by the provincial legislatures on a single transferable vote system of proportional representation for India's three major communities, Muslim, Sikh and 'General' – which included everyone else from untouchables and Christians to Hindus. The representatives of each group would also be responsible for drawing up constitutions for the provinces in that group. The new constitutions, both local and national, would run for 10 years, after which any province could vote to have them reconsidered at 10-yearly intervals. Until the new national constitution was agreed, the country would be run by an interim government consisting entirely of 'Indian leaders having the full confidence of the people' – including the war member, the position that had caused so much trouble in 1942.

As for the states, the existing relationship between the crown and the rulers would clearly be impossible after independence. 'Paramountcy,' the mission statement said, 'can neither be retained by the British Crown nor transferred to the new Government.' This was a neat way of getting Britain off a particularly tricky hook: the states' future 'must be a matter for negotiation during the building up of the new constitutional structure'.

It was a complex and imaginative proposal which, the mission told the Indian people, 'will enable you to attain your independence in the shortest possible time and with the least danger of internal disturbance and conflict'. Since there was 'small hope of peaceful settlement by agreement of the Indian Parties alone' it was perhaps the last chance of any form of union without 'violence, chaos, and even civil war'. The statement concluded with a deeply-felt plea:

We therefore lay these proposals before you in the profound hope that they will be accepted and operated by you in the spirit of accommodation and goodwill in which they are offered. We appeal to all who have the future good of India at heart to extend their vision beyond their own community or interest to the interests of the whole four hundred millions of the Indian people ... we look forward with you to your ever increasing prosperity among the great nations of the world, and to a future even more glorious than your past.[27]

Press and public reactions to the mission plan were generally favourable, though the Sikhs and the untouchables were violently opposed to it. The two main parties remained silent: both had been consulted during the drafting and had seen it before publication. Gandhi, however, welcomed it. 'Whatsoever the wrong done to India by British rule,' he announced next day, 'if the statement of the Mission was genuine, as he believed it was, it was in discharge of an obligation they had declared the British owed to India, namely, to get off India's back. It contained the seed to convert this land of sorrow into one without sorrow and suffering.'[28]

Much encouraged by Gandhi's statement, Cripps and Pethick-Lawrence went to see him the following day. They spent three hours with him at the Balmiki temple, during which time he shifted his position from satisfaction to extreme scepticism. His criticisms centred on the question of whether or not acceptance of the plan by either party would be binding or simply a recommendation to the proposed constituent assembly. If the assembly was to be free and sovereign, then it could not be bound by any previous decisions, and should be free to throw out any or all of the details of the plan, no matter what had been agreed beforehand.

For the next few days, Gandhi indulged in a flurry of correspondence with the mission, splitting hairs, raising esoteric questions, shifting and changing in his most exasperating fashion. As Wavell reported later to the king:

Gandhi ran entirely true to form: his influence is still great; his line of thought at any given moment and on any particular issue is as unpredictable as ever; he never makes a pronouncement that is not so qualified and so vaguely worded that it cannot be interpreted in whatever sense best suits him at a later stage ... My distrust of this shrewd, malevolent, old politician was deep before the Conference started; it is deeper than ever now.[29]

The mission itself split in two, with Alexander joining Wavell in increasing hostility to Gandhi, while Cripps and Pethick-Lawrence clung with increasing desperation to their faith in him. That faith was severely dented, however, on 20 May, when they received a letter that seemed to turn the clock back to the dark days of 1942:

I would put on record my conviction that Independence in fact would be a farce, if the British Troops are in India even for peace and order within or danger from without ... If the position about the Troops persists, 'Independence next month' is either insincere or a thoughtless cry. Acceptance of 'Quit India' by the British is unconditional, whether the Constituent Assembly succeeds or fails ... As to the Interim Government, the more I think and observe, the more certain is my feeling that a proper

National Government responsible in fact if not in law, to the elected members of the Central Legislative Assembly should precede the summons for the election of members of the Constituent Assembly.[30]

'I have never seen three men more taken aback [than] by this revelation of Gandhi in his true colours,' Wavell noted in his diary that night. 'Cripps and Secretary of State were shaken to the core, while Alexander's reactions were pure John Bull at his most patriotic and insular ... If it were not so tragic and dangerous, it would also have been amusing to see the sudden change in the three men.'[31] Alexander was convinced that 'Gandhi had two objects – to humiliate the British Government and to promote a policy of scuttle, and secondly, to secure power without a constitution coming into being and so to abandon the just claims of the Muslim League'.[32] Wavell agreed, adding that Congress also wanted to displace the princes before any constitution was made. After a break to allow tempers to cool – Alexander and Wavell both wanted to tell Gandhi he had to 'take it or leave it' on the plan – they agreed to send a calmer, more reasoned reply which Cripps had prepared, reaffirming that 'independence must follow not precede the coming into operation of the new Constitution, and that paramountcy must remain until independence'.[33] Gandhi dismissed the mission's letter as being 'in the best imperialistic style which I thought had gone for ever'.

The Congress Working Committee's initial response to the plan was not hopeful. Jinnah, however, seemed quite positive, but stressed that he needed to consult his Working Committee, and that it would be a month before he could get any decision. Trying to rush things, he said, could be fatal – feelings among the extremists in the League were running so high that a wrong move could spark off a jihad, which he would be unable to control. He also needed time to recover his strength before returning to the fray in Delhi. He finally agreed to cut short his rest and recuperation in Simla by a week, bringing forward the meeting of the Working Committee to 3 and 4 June, with a full council meeting the following day. He begged not to be hurried further, 'as it would take time to persuade his people to accept the proposals'. This was the most promising sign yet.

Pethick-Lawrence had shown his age a day or two before by fainting in the heat, and Cripps had been suffering from dysentery ever since he returned from Simla. They agreed to take a few days' holiday, starting on 21 May, but that same day Cripps collapsed and was taken into the Willingdon Hospital. Tests showed that his dysentery was not amoebic, but he was suffering from the combined effects of overwork and heat exhaustion. His wife was flown out from England to be with him for the rest of his stay in India.

By the time Cripps was discharged from hospital on 3 June, after 10 days of enforced rest, matters were moving ahead. Woodrow Wyatt had seen Jinnah in Simla and had elicited from him the view that the League would accept the mission's plan – as the first step on the road to Pakistan. Wavell had got much the same impression when he met Jinnah on his return to Delhi on 2 June. And indeed that was what happened. Uniquely, Jinnah persuaded his council to agree 'by a large majority', even before Congress reached any decision. One of the factors which made this possible was that he had extracted a promise from Wavell that if the League accepted and Congress did not, then he would invite the League to form a government. Immediately he had won over his committee, Jinnah began detailed talks with the viceroy about positions in an interim government.

In truth, Jinnah had probably got exactly what he always wanted. He had the promise of a big Pakistan in all but name, with self-governing status for Muslim provinces within a loose federal union: this would remove the doubts over defence and the economic viability of a separate state. He would also have a position of authority and power in the government of all-India, which would enable him to give some protection to the millions of Muslims in the Hindu-majority provinces. The idea of Pakistan had served its purpose by uniting the Muslims, revitalizing the League and providing him with a powerful bargaining position: it was possible that even to Jinnah, it may never have meant more than that. Like any good negotiator, he had always known that he could not achieve a hundred per cent of the claim for Pakistan. Perhaps it was now time to lay it quietly aside and settle for 95 per cent, with added benefits. Persuading his dangerously volatile members to accept what he saw as a notable victory was his final triumph.

The struggles with and within Congress proved much more difficult. Agreement on the composition of an interim government broke down constantly on the old rock of including Congress Muslims. Twice, the mission believed it had reached agreement with the Working Committee after tortuous negotiating sessions, and twice Gandhi scuppered it. But after three weeks of heated argument, Azad and Nehru finally managed to pull the Working Committee away from him. Even Patel joined them when the committee passed a resolution on 25 June to accept the Cabinet mission plan, albeit with serious reservations about 'the limitation of the central Authority ... as well as the system of grouping of Provinces'.[34] And on that apparently happy note, the three ministers packed their bags and staggered back to Britain on 29 June, believing their mission was accomplished.

'If India Wants Her Blood-bath She Shall Have It'

Cripps, Pethick-Lawrence and Alexander believed they could feel satisfied with what they had achieved in three months of tortuous negotiations. Certainly, they had left the viceroy and the Indian political leaders a basic framework around which the future of India could be built. But there was too much that had been left unresolved, too much that could be interpreted in different ways. All the Indian leaders apart from Azad were barristers, and barristers make their living by interpreting the law as it suits their cause. They immediately began doing just that with the plan. Wavell, by contrast, was not a lawyer but, as he was fond of saying, a plain soldier, and he was soon out of his depth.

Things began promisingly enough, with Azad persuading the AICC to ratify acceptance of the plan by a massive majority on 6 July 1946, in spite of vehement opposition from the Congress socialists. It was Azad's final act as president, before he handed over to Nehru, a fitting climax to six turbulent years in office. The following day, however, in his speech wrapping up the session, Nehru acknowledged the strong criticisms from the left wing by assuring them that Congress had not in fact accepted any plan, either short or long term. 'We are not bound by a single thing,' he told them, 'except that we have decided to go into the Constituent Assembly.'[1] At a press conference three days later, he underlined this astonishing statement by saying that the Constituent Assembly would be a sovereign body, free to do whatever it chose. 'In regard to the minorities,' Nehru went on, 'we accept no outsiders' interference in it – certainly not the British Government's.' He dismissed the idea of grouping, which he said would probably never happen: the NWFP, Bengal and Assam would all reject it. He envisaged a much more powerful central government than that which had been proposed. Congress, he concluded, regarded itself as free to change or modify the Cabinet mission's plan exactly as it pleased.[2]

Azad was mortified by this demolition of the plan on which he had pinned so many hopes. For ever afterwards he would blame himself for having nominated Nehru as his successor, rather than Patel who would never have committed such a political blunder – Patel, in fact, condemned Nehru's remarks as 'emotional insanity'. But Azad was deluding himself if he thought he had really been responsible for the choice of Nehru, or that Nehru was now speaking entirely for himself. Nehru may have uttered the words, but the thoughts behind them were exactly what Gandhi had told Cripps and Pethick-Lawrence at the Balmiki temple. Now, however, Gandhi advised Nehru that the statement 'did not sound well' and needed 'some explanation'. Changing his stance yet again, he wrote: 'It must be admitted that we have to work within the limits of the State Paper.'

The effect of Nehru's words on Jinnah was entirely predictable. Jinnah had risked everything in persuading the League to accept something less than a sovereign Pakistan, and now he had been made to look a fool, something he could never forget or forgive. He called on the British government to condemn the Congress about-face, but both Pethick-Lawrence in the Lords and Cripps in the Commons only fudged the issues. In trying to avoid offending Nehru and Gandhi, they destroyed what was left of Jinnah's faith in British fair play. He was, in any case, already becoming disillusioned, as the wrangling over the proposed interim government grew more and more bitter. Even Wavell had reneged on his promise to call on the League to form an interim government if Congress refused to take part: he had also gone back on commitments over its composition and the perennial question of including Congress Muslims. He appeared to be caving in to Congress demands.

Pethick-Lawrence wanted to see an interim government formed as soon as possible, and on 22 July, on his orders, Wavell wrote to both Nehru and Jinnah setting out proposals for a government of 14 ministers: 6 from Congress (including one representative of the Scheduled Castes), 5 from the Muslim League, and 3 representing the other minorities. The League would have no veto on Congress Muslim nominees, and would have an 'equitable' rather than an equal share of the most important portfolios. Nehru replied next day, rejecting the proposals as inadequate, and demanding total freedom of action for any government, with the viceroy acting purely as a constitutional head. Jinnah kept the viceroy waiting until the League's All-India Council had met at the end of the month.

Seeing themselves as betrayed from all sides, the League's Council met in Bombay on 27 July in a highly-charged atmosphere. Four-hundred and fifty members crammed into a sweltering hall to hear Jinnah tell them how the League had 'made concession after concession ... because of our extreme anxiety for an amicable and peaceful settlement which will lead not only Hindus and Muslims but also other communities inhabiting this sub-continent to the achievement of freedom'. The League, he declared, was 'the only party that has emerged from these negotiations with honour and clean hands'. Congress, by contrast, had 'done the greatest harm to the peoples of India by its pettifogging, higgling attitude [with] no other consideration except to down the Muslim League'.

'Throughout these negotiations,' Jinnah went on, 'the Cabinet Mission were under terror and threats of the Congress.' They had gone back on their plighted word over the interim government, and 'today are cowed down and paralysed'. Cripps, 'that ingenious juggler of words', had put 'a fantastic and dishonest construction' on paragraph 8 of the statement of 16 June to evade the formation of an interim government. 'I am sorry to say,' he continued, dredging up the deepest condemnation he could heap on anyone, 'that Sir Stafford debased his legal talents.'[3]

For two days, the League's Council and Working Committee debated more than a dozen resolutions which had been tabled to decide 'what steps' the League should take. Sir Firoz Khan Noon spoke with his usual quiet reason amid the furore: 'The best for us is frankly to admit that we made a mistake in accepting a Union of some sort proposed in the Scheme and go back to our Pakistan ideal. The path of wisdom lies in the total rejection of the constitutional proposals ... let there be one guiding beacon before us – a fully sovereign, separate state of Pakistan.' One after another, amid roars of approval, the khans and mullahs and maulanas pledged their undying support for Pakistan, and to rise in revolt 'if the Quaid-i-Azam will only give his word'.

The Quaid-i-Azam did not give his word. But he went a good way towards it when the Working Party put up two resolutions on 29 July, one withdrawing the League's acceptance of the Cabinet mission's plan, the other laying out the course to be followed in its place:

> whereas it has become abundantly clear that the Muslims of India would not rest contented with anything less than the immediate establishment of an Independent and fully sovereign State of Pakistan ... the time has come for the Muslim nation to resort to Direct Action to achieve Pakistan, to assert their just rights, to vindicate their honour and to get rid of the present British slavery and the contemplated future Caste-Hindu domination.[4]

The Council gave instructions for the preparation of 'a programme of direct action ... to organize the Muslims for the coming struggle to be launched as and when necessary'. It also called on Muslims, 'as a protest against and in token of their deep resentment of the attitude of the British' to renounce all titles 'conferred upon them by the Alien Government'.[5]

After both resolutions had been passed unanimously, Jinnah told the meeting:

We have taken a most historic decision. Never before in the whole life-history of the Muslim League did we do anything except by constitutional methods and constitutional talks ... Today we have said goodbye to constitutions and constitutional methods. Throughout the painful negotiations, the two parties with whom we bargained held a pistol at us; one with power and machine guns behind it, the other with non-co-operation and the threat to launch mass civil disobedience. This situation must be met. We also have a pistol.[6]

The Working Committee set 16 August as 'Direct Action Day', on which there would be a 'universal Muslim *hartal*'. Congress had proved that civil disobedience could be effective: now it was time for the League to use the same weapon.

Next day, Jinnah wrote to the viceroy, formally refusing the offer of 22 July to take part in forming an interim government. This could have come as no surprise to anyone, but it was still a blow to Pethick-Lawrence and Wavell: with communal tension and labour unrest growing daily, it was urgent that there should be a representative government as soon as possible. Pethick-Lawrence urged the viceroy to meet Jinnah and try to persuade him to join 'even now'. Wavell, however, chose not to take the League's determination or Jinnah's anger seriously, clearly believing that the Muslim leader needed to be put in his place. He wired back that there was 'no indication of any immediate attempt at a mass movement'. 'If I send for Jinnah at once,' he said, 'it will be regarded as a panicky reaction to a threat and will put up Jinnah's stock.'

Wavell did, however, see Nehru, and tried to convince him that the League's stance was a direct reaction to his own statements. This, he said, was an opportunity for Nehru to show real statesmanship by giving the League the assurances needed to bring it into the government and the constituent assembly. Nehru replied that he did not see what assurances he could give. He evaded the issue by suggesting that any dispute over the interpretation of the Cabinet mission's statement could be referred to the Federal Court.

Although both viceroy and secretary of state were reluctant to see a government dominated by one party alone, they were prepared to go ahead with Congress if the League still refused. On 6 August 1946 Wavell invited Nehru to 'submit to me your proposals for the formation of an Interim Government ... It will be for you to consider whether you should first discuss them with Mr Jinnah.' Since the viceroy had earlier refused to ask Jinnah to form a government on the grounds that he needed the participation of both parties, this was twisting the knife with a vengeance. Naturally, Jinnah rejected Nehru's approach. He also rejected a long, wordy Congress statement which attempted to reassure the League and the other minorities. He did, however, offer to meet Nehru to see if the two of them could resolve the deadlock. The two presidents met at Jinnah's Bombay house on Malabar Hill, but although their talk was amicable it was fruitless. Nehru left to begin forming his government. It was the evening of 15 August 1946, just a few hours before the start of Jinnah's 'Direct Action Day'.

Jinnah had issued a statement explaining that Direct Action Day was

for the purpose of explaining to the Muslim public all over India the resolutions that were passed by the Council of the All-India Muslim League on the 29th July at Bombay ... and not for the purpose of resorting to direct action in any form or shape; therefore, I enjoin upon the Muslims to carry out the instructions and abide by them strictly and conduct themselves peacefully and in a disciplined manner and not to play into the hands of the enemies.[7]

Throughout most of India, Muslims obeyed Jinnah's instructions and the *hartals* passed off peacefully. There was some trouble in Sind, but nothing serious. In Bengal, however, and particularly in Calcutta, things quickly got out of hand, thanks largely to the chief minister and leader of the League in Bengal, Hussain Shaheed Suhrawardy. Wavell, who had first encountered Suhrawardy during the Bengal famine, when he had been accused of black market dealings in grain intended for the starving, described him as 'one of the most inefficient, conceited and crooked politicians in India, which is saying a good deal', and as 'a self-seeking careerist with no principles'.[8] Shortly before Direct Action Day, Suhrawardy threatened to declare Bengal an independent state, withholding all revenues, if Nehru was allowed to form a central government.

On Tuesday, 13 August, Suhrawardy announced a three-day public holiday starting on the Friday, Direct Action Day itself. Why he did this is not clear. One explanation is that, fearing communal violence, he hoped to direct the wrath of the mob away from public offices and departments. Whatever its purpose, the result was to release Muslims to take part in meetings and marches – and mischief. On the Friday, Suhrawardy planned to address a mass meeting on the *maidan*, the public open space in the centre of the city, by the Ochterlony monument. This was a 165-foot obelisk of uncertain architectural pedigree topped by a mini Byzantine dome, erected in 1828 in honour of the victor of the Nepalese war, Sir David Ochterlony, a Scot born in Boston, Massachusetts.

Direct Action Day dawned hot and sticky in Calcutta – it was the monsoon season, with a temperature of 88°F and 91 per cent humidity. At daybreak Muslim workers from the Howrah jute mills began pouring across the Hooghly river, heading for the *maidan*. By 7.30 a.m. reports began reaching the British military HQ in Fort William that Hindus were erecting barricades on the Tala and Belgachia bridges to prevent them entering the city. Fearing trouble,

Brigadier J.P.C. Mackinlay confined his troops to barracks pending orders from the local government – which meant Suhrawardy. The orders did not come.

Communal clashes had already started in Maniktala, a north-eastern suburb on the way to the airport, and were spreading to other areas, with looting of shops and arson attacks. 'Weapons employed appear to have been chiefly brickbats,' the governor of Bengal, Sir Frederick Burrows, reported later to Wavell, 'but in a number of cases shot guns have been used by members of both communities and some cases of stabbing have been reported ... A marked feeling of panic, especially among Hindu traders in north Calcutta, has been feature of situation since early in the day and has given rise to many wild reports far exceeding actualities ... Disturbances so far have been markedly communal and not, repeat not, in any way anti-British.'[9]

Intelligence reports reaching Lieutenant-General Sir Francis Tuker, GOC-in-C Eastern Command, said that Suhrawardy himself had told the huge Muslim crowd at the Ochterlony monument that 'he would see how the British could make Mr Nehru rule Bengal', and that 'Direct Action Day would prove to be the first step towards the Muslim struggle for emancipation'. He had urged the crowds to return home early, and said that he had arranged with the police and military not to interfere with them. Whether this promise of immunity was meant as an invitation to loot and kill is hard to say – but a number of well-known Muslim goondas (gangsters) were among the crowd, and they needed no second bidding. When the meeting ended, they set off into the narrow streets of the city and soon Hindu shops and houses were being looted and burned. Hindu goondas soon retaliated. At 4.15 p.m., Fortress HQ sent out the code-word 'Red' to indicate that there were incidents all over Calcutta.[10]

A curfew was imposed that night, and at 8.00 p.m. the 7th Battalion of the Worcestershire Regiment and the Green Howards were called out of their barracks in the north of the city to maintain it. They found fires burning, homes and shops sacked, and dead bodies everywhere. Calcutta was beginning to look like a battlefield. But that was only the beginning: at dawn next day the killing began again. A train, the 36 Down Parcel Express, was stopped and looted outside the city and its crew butchered. No one, Hindu or Muslim, was safe. The Sikhs, the city's drivers and mechanics, joined the fray that afternoon as motorized cavalry, charging through the Muslim quarters slaying indiscriminately and without mercy. The city had gone berserk. 'It was unbridled savagery,' General Tuker noted, 'with homicidal maniacs let loose to kill and kill and to maim and burn. The underworld of Calcutta was taking charge of the city ... The police were not controlling it.'[11]

On the third day, Sunday, 18 August, Wavell recorded in his journal that Calcutta was 'as bad as ever and the death toll mounts steadily. Sarat Chandra Bose rang up in the afternoon with a message of protest ... that the police were favouring the Muslims against the Hindus'. Sarat Bose's charge was true, but it did not alter the fact that, as Burrows reported, 'the casualties are higher amongst the Muslims'. Azad called in person to protest about the feebleness of the Bengal ministry's response to the killings. Although they had apparently expected trouble, they had been 'too late in enforcing a total curfew, and the troops had not been called out soon enough'. Wavell had a soft spot for Azad, whom he had always found easier to deal with than Jinnah, and sympathized with his fears for what might happen in places like Cawnpore and Lucknow, where there were high concentrations of both Muslims and Hindus in the populations.[12]

By the Monday, the stench of decomposing corpses in Calcutta was overpowering. There were dead bodies lying in the streets, some piled high on abandoned handcarts. One journalist out with a military patrol came upon about 50 bodies in two heaps in Upper Chitpore Road. The vultures had started feeding on them – he noticed they seemed to prefer human flesh, ignoring the carcass of a dog lying nearby. The British military commander wanted to start burning the bodies to prevent an outbreak of cholera, but was accused of flouting both Muslim and Hindu religious sensibilities. Nevertheless, the problem was so acute that the Bengal government offered troops five rupees for every body delivered to either the Muslim burial grounds or the Hindu burning ghats. They worked through the day and night, clearing the rotting piles of humanity.

The British continued to move troops into the city. By 19 August, there were four British battalions, with one more due, two Indian battalions, with two more on the way, and a British armoured car squadron. Soon the total number of troops had reached about 45,000, and gradually they restored some kind of order. 3,468 of the bodies found in streets and houses were identified and accounted for by 27 August, but no one had any idea how many had been thrown into the murky waters of the Hooghly and carried out to sea. Figures for those injured varied from 13,000 to 16,000. The most reliable estimates are that about 20,000 were killed or injured during those three days of carnage.

Meanwhile, anyone who could get out of Calcutta fled the city in any way they could. Lines of refugees jammed the roads leading out of town, and Howrah railway station became a seething mass of those desperate to get aboard a departing train. Within a week some 110,000 people had left, while another 100,000 were refugees within the city, having been driven out of their homes and workplaces and forced to find shelter elsewhere.

On 2 September, the Calcutta stock exchange reopened. The killings still went on, but by then they had become sporadic, often with several days between incidents – nine people were killed and 54 injured in another riot on 14 September. Normality was returning, but slowly – the racing correspondent of *The Statesman*, the city's leading newspaper, complained of the poor attendance at the Tollygunge autumn meeting on 29 September, due to 'the present uneasiness in

Calcutta'. Nevertheless, 'the racing was very enjoyable ... and those who lost heavily on such favourites as Playtime, Sweetheart, Pladda Light and Gypsy Moon, will look forward to better luck in the near future'.[13] The near future, however, brought no better luck on the communal scene. The Great Calcutta Killings, as they came to be called, set off a chain reaction through much of northern India, heralding a year of bloody violence.

The Calcutta killings had barely been halted when, on 24 August, Wavell announced the names of the interim government, which was to take office at the beginning of September. Nehru had wanted to put non-League Muslims into all five Muslim seats, but the viceroy, still hoping that Jinnah would agree to join, appointed only three of them, leaving two places vacant. A week later, in Simla, one of Nehru's three, Sir Shafaat Ahmad Khan, was stabbed seven times in an assassination attempt by two young Muslim League fanatics.

As soon as he had announced the new government, Wavell flew to Calcutta to see the situation for himself. He spent 18 hours touring the city and talking to the police, military and government officials. After snatching a few hours' sleep, he was out again, visiting relief centres, which, he noted 'brought home to one the misery caused by this communal frenzy'.[14] He returned to Delhi more than ever convinced that agreement between the League and Congress was vital if further catastrophes were to be prevented.

On 27 August 1946, Wavell summoned Nehru and Gandhi to the Viceroy's House and told them in graphic detail what he had seen and heard in Calcutta. He then presented them with the draft of a formula which he believed might be enough to bring the League into both the interim government and the constituent assembly : though elections to the assembly had been completed by the end of July, Muslims and Sikhs were boycotting it. The formula laid down that, 'in the interests of communal harmony', Congress would accept the intention of the Cabinet mission's statement of 16 May that the proposed grouping of provinces into groups A, B and C was compulsory until the new constitution came into force, after which the elected legislature of any province could vote to opt out of the group in which it had been placed.[15] He told the Congress leaders that such a formula was the only chance of a peaceful transfer of power, and that he could not call a constituent assembly until the point was settled.

Gandhi and Nehru, however, still insisted on treating the Cabinet mission's statement as a legal document to be examined and interpreted and argued over. When Gandhi began picking at its legal inconsistencies, Wavell's patience ran out. Still emotional after the horrors of Calcutta, he snapped that he was 'a plain man and not a lawyer', that he knew perfectly well what the mission meant, and that compulsory grouping for constitution-making was the crux of the plan. Nehru snapped back that Congress would not bend before the League's blackmail. Gandhi, according to a shocked Wavell, thumped the table and declared 'If India wants her blood-bath, she shall have it!'[16]

That night, Gandhi cabled Pethick-Lawrence in London that the viceroy was 'unnerved owing to the Bengal tragedy' and needed to be assisted by 'an abler and legal mind', or 'the repetition of the Bengal tragedy would be a certainty'. Attlee had been pressing the viceroy to accept a political or legal adviser since the start of the Cabinet mission. 'He had obviously been told that I receive nothing but official advice and that my political judgement is therefore unsound, i.e., not sufficiently pro-Congress,' Wavell wrote acidly. 'I think my judgement is better than HMG's and shall say so, and tell him that if HMG don't like it, their duty is to find another viceroy, as I will not be a figurehead.' He had stuck with that position, and Attlee was indeed now starting to think of finding a replacement.

Gandhi may well have been aware of Attlee's doubts through his secret contacts with Cripps and Pethick-Lawrence. Largely at Cripps's insistence, Tata had agreed to send Sudhir Ghosh to London, officially as their representative but unofficially as an agent of the Congress Working Committee. Wavell was even forced, under protest, to secure a priority air passage for him. Wavell's suspicions of Ghosh, whom he regarded as 'a snake', were confirmed when the Intelligence Department reported on a tapped phone conversation between Ghosh and Patel about his efforts to persuade Pethick-Lawrence to dismiss the League government in Bengal and institute governor's rule under section 93. Wavell complained to Attlee that he could not be 'responsible for affairs in India if some members of your Government are keeping in touch with Congress through an independent agent behind my back'.[17] Attlee warned Cripps that Ghosh was causing trouble, but it was left to Pethick-Lawrence to apologize to Wavell. Later he told Cripps that he was disturbed at letters Ghosh was writing in 'an attempt to undermine our confidence in and support for the Viceroy'.[18]

Nehru had his own representative in London: his close personal friend Krishna Menon (no relation to V.P. Menon), a graduate of the London School of Economics, a barrister of the Middle Temple, and a left-wing Labour member of St Pancras Borough Council. As head of the India League, Menon had been Congress's unofficial ambassador in London since the 1930s, and had built up a formidable range of contacts, including a close relationship with Cripps. He was able to back up the letters which Nehru was writing to all his influential friends in Britain, describing Wavell as a weak man who had lost all flexibility of mind and who, in wishing to appease Jinnah, was leading India to disaster. Nehru described the viceroy's principal advisers, Sir Francis Mudie, previously Home member of the Executive Council and now governor of Sind, and George Abell, who had replaced Sir Evan Jenkins as the viceroy's private secretary, as 'English mullahs', rabidly pro-Muslim. Ironically, at the same time Jinnah was announcing that Wavell had 'struck a severe blow to the Muslim League and to Muslim India' by inviting Nehru to form a government, 'and he has only added insult to injury by nominating three Muslims who, he knows, do not command either the respect or the confidence of Muslim India'.[19]

Without mentioning his cable to Pethick-Lawrence, Gandhi wrote a strong letter to Wavell next day, which he insisted should be shown in full to the government in London. He accused the viceroy of using 'minatory' language at their meeting, going on: 'As representative of the King you cannot afford to be a military man only, nor to ignore the law, much less the law of your own making. You should be assisted, if necessary, by a legal mind enjoying your full confidence.' Wavell should not, he said, have threatened to delay calling the constituent assembly until Congress accepted the formula he had presented to them. If that was the viceroy's attitude he should not have invited Nehru to form a government, and should now rescind his decision and form a different administration which enjoyed his full confidence. Gandhi, as always, blamed the communal troubles entirely on the British presence, and repeated his demand for the immediate withdrawal of the British army, leaving its peace-keeping role to Congress. 'Quit India,' he said, was unconditional.

Gandhi's letter was, of course, not intended for Wavell, who regarded it as 'abusive and vindictive', but for Attlee. And it had the required effect. Attlee chose to ignore Wavell's assertion in his covering note that the letter proved Jinnah's suspicions were justified. 'It is to my mind convincing evidence,' Wavell wrote, 'that Congress always meant to use their position in the Interim Government to break up the Muslim League and in the Constituent Assembly to destroy the Grouping scheme which was the one effective safeguard for the Muslims.'[20]

Most of the officials at the India Office agreed with Wavell's assessment. In a sharp and impressive analysis, Frank Turnbull concluded that the present problems stemmed from the Cabinet mission's refusal to take Wavell's advice and stand firm on the question of grouping. It was now clear, he wrote, that Congress had intended all along to follow its own interpretation, and that in forming the interim government as planned 'we are in fact turning India over to Congress control'. The permanent under-secretary, Sir David Monteath, added that he could 'hardly escape the conclusion that the Mission have been diddled'.[21]

Attlee and Pethick-Lawrence chose not to listen. With Cripps away recovering in a Swiss clinic for the crucial period from 7 August to 10 September, the decision was left to the harassed prime minister and the weary secretary of state. They chose to override the viceroy and instruct him not to press the grouping argument but to go ahead with inaugurating the interim government and the constituent assembly. He was 'not to take any steps which are likely to result in a breach with the Congress without prior consultation with us'.[22]

On 2 September 1946, Wavell swore in the new ministers. It was an historic occasion: the first representative government in the entire history of India. It was not yet the whole hog, as Nehru acknowledged by softly adding '*Jai Hind*' (Victory to India), to the end of his oath, but it was a giant last step but one. Nehru, as vice-president of the Executive Council under the viceroy, was to all intents and purposes the prime minister and foreign secretary of India. Patel was home member, in charge of the police and internal security. Defence, with responsibility for the army, went to the solitary Sikh member, Baldev Singh. At his prayer meeting that morning, Gandhi declared: 'The door to *purna swaraj* has at last been opened.'

The Muslims, of course, were less pleased. As it happened, the Id holiday fell on 29 August that year, and in his annual message Jinnah called on Muslims to 'rally round the Muslim League ... and be determined and prepared to face the worst as a completely united and great people with our motto: unity, faith and discipline. God is with us and we are bound to succeed.'[23] Millions of Muslims marked the eve of the new government's inauguration by flying black mourning flags from their homes.

In Bombay, the black flag demonstration turned into a communal riot. Troops were called out promptly and a curfew was imposed, but 35 people were killed and 175 injured that night, with 200 more dying in sporadic violence over the next week. During the next six weeks, there were more than 6,000 arrests in the city. The Bombay killings, however, were nothing like the apocalyptic scenes in Calcutta: in place of near civil war there were stabbings, sudden, nasty and secretive, producing a remarkably even death toll during September of 162 Hindus and 158 Muslims.[24] There were disturbances in Ahmedabad and Karachi, too, but on a lesser scale.

Bombay had been divided between Muslims and Hindus from about the end of 1945. According to the journalist, novelist and film producer Khwaja Ahmad Abbas: 'Trams passing through Bhendi Bazaar would empty at Crawford Market at the southern end, and at Byculla Bridge at the northern end. No Muslim would venture into Gurgaum or Kalvadevi, Lal Bagh or Parel or Dadar.' He described a typical Bombay killing at the time, which he witnessed from his office balcony opposite Harkisandas Hospital:

It was a 'Hindu' area, and a *goonda* spied a man in a *kurta* and *pyjama* [traditional Muslim dress] walking by the side of the road. He followed him, and taking him to be a Muslim, stabbed him in the back. The knife pierced some vital spot and the man lay dead. The *goonda* wiped the blood from the knife on the clothes of the victim, and as he was doing it, a doubt seemed to cross his mind. So he tugged at the *pyjama* cord, unfastened it, saw that the man was not circumcised, and then ... said 'Mistake ho gaya' ('I've made a mistake').[25]

Nehru broadcast to the nation on 7 September 1946. 'India, this old and dear land of ours,' he intoned, 'is finding herself again through travail and suffering. She is youthful again with the bright eyes of adventure, and with faith in herself and her mission.' The interim government, he said, was only one part of a larger scheme which included the constituent assembly, which would soon be meeting to decide on a constitution for a free and independent India. Holding out a sop if not an olive branch to the League, he said Congress was perfectly willing to sit in the assembly in sections, which would then consider the formation of groups. He and his colleagues, he said, were seeking agreement not conflict, and he appealed to the League to enter the assembly as equals and partners, with no binding commitments, in the hope they could resolve their differences and difficulties.[26]

Nehru's words were encouraging enough for Wavell to continue working for a *rapprochement* between Congress and Jinnah, which would enable the League to take its place first in the interim government and then in the constituent assembly. But they were not encouraging enough to make him stop working on a contingency plan for a British withdrawal in the event of a total breakdown not only of negotiations but of public order. He and a team of officials led by George Abell had been preparing such a plan since early April. They had discussed it with the Cabinet mission, and Wavell had worked on the details with Pethick-Lawrence, Alexander and Auchinleck while Cripps was in hospital in New Delhi. They had concluded that it would be best for the British to withdraw from the Hindu provinces and hand them over to Congress, while remaining in the Muslim provinces to protect them until they had sorted out their own constitution. It was possible that simply announcing this might be enough to make Congress see sense. Cripps disagreed. He believed it would be better to announce a date for a complete British departure, and if there had been no agreement by that time, to hand over the central government to Congress.

The proposals had been discussed in June by the full Cabinet, with the chiefs of staff and Auchinleck, who had rejected it as unthinkable. But with the renewed violence and the threat of a civil war which the British would be unable to extinguish, Wavell returned to the attack. On 8 September he sent a revised plan to Pethick-Lawrence, with a request for an immediate decision. He said that both the civil administration and the army were in such bad shape that the British could not go on governing India for more than 18 months. They must therefore be ready to complete their withdrawal by 31 March 1948, and to start pulling out of Madras, Bombay, the Central Provinces and Orissa 12 months before that. An announcement of this should be made on 1 January 1947, unless the constituent assembly was already set up and running smoothly, in which case the announcement could be delayed until the end of March 1947.

Wavell did not get his immediate decision. Pethick-Lawrence refused to believe Britain could not go on governing India after March 1948. Attlee, Cripps and Alexander all rejected the plan for their own reasons – Attlee later remarked, revealingly, 'That was what Winston would certainly quite properly describe as an ignoble and sordid scuttle and I wouldn't look at it.'[27] The rest of the Cabinet went along with them, reluctant to face the loss of international prestige for Britain, and the weakening of the Commonwealth defence system in the Middle and Far East. Alexander even persuaded the Cabinet to agree that the administration in India should be bolstered by recruiting more British civil servants with a guarantee of 15 years' employment. In the end it all came down to pride: Britain must not be seen to leave India under 'circumstances of ignominy after there had been widespread riots and attacks on Europeans. It must be clear that we were going freely and not under compulsion.'[28]

Attlee told Wavell at the end of September that his 'Breakdown' plan was unacceptable. The time might well come when the British would have to withdraw, but if so they would leave the whole of India at once, and as quickly as possible. Giving early notice would do more harm than good. There was already a military plan for the protection and evacuation of Europeans; he would not consider anything more. He instructed Wavell to go on working for a political settlement.

Wavell did as he was told, but went on trying to convince Attlee and the Cabinet that time was running out – there could be a total breakdown as early as I January 1947. It was essential to set a final date for withdrawal. He failed to persuade them, but he did succeed, after two weeks of byzantine negotiation, in persuading Jinnah to bring the League into the government. In itself, that was a considerable achievement – but it would have been impossible if Jinnah had not decided that the League was missing a great opportunity by not joining.

Jinnah did not take office himself. Perhaps he couldn't bear the idea of playing second fiddle to Nehru, perhaps by then he was simply too ill. It was left to Liaquat to lead the League's ministers: after much haggling and threats of resignation from Patel, he was given the finance portfolio, a position of considerable power with great potential for disruption and obstruction. The other League members, who were all given lesser posts, were surprisingly second-rate: they were probably chosen by Jinnah less for their abilities than for their reliability in opposing Congress. Other, more able men such as Nazimuddin, were left out because they were more likely to reach an accommodation with Congress in order to achieve agreement. Bizarrely, one of the League's nominees was in fact an untouchable, Jogendra Nath Mandal, a Scheduled Castes minister in the League government of Bengal, chosen by Jinnah as a petulant protest against the inclusion of a nationalist Muslim, Asaf Ali, by Congress. The other two Congress Muslims – the wounded Sir Shafaat Ahmad Khan, and Syed Ali Zaheer – were dropped, together with Subhas Chandra Bose's brother, Sarat. The new government consisted of:

Congress

Jawaharlal Nehru	External Affairs and Commonwealth Relations
Vallabhbhai Patel	Home, Information and Broadcasting
Rajendra Prasad	Food and Agriculture
C. Rajagopalachari	Education and Arts
Asaf Ali	Transport and Railways
Jagjivan Ram	Labour

Muslim League

Liaquat Ali Khan	Finance
I.I. Chundrigar	Commerce
Abdur Rab Nishtar	Communications
Ghazanfar Ali Khan	Health
J.N. Mandal	Legislative

Minorities

John Matthai (Indian Christian)	Industries and Supplies
C.H. Bhaba (Parsi)	Works, Mines and Power
Baldev Singh (Sikh)	Defence

The League's entry into the interim government might have been expected to lower communal tension. But even as the new ministers were preparing to take their places, a new wave of terror broke out in the Noakhali and Tippera districts of east Bengal, on one of the mouths of the Ganges about 70 miles south of Dacca and 140 miles east of Calcutta. The area had a long history of agrarian unrest, partly because of the economic circumstances of the two communities: almost all the peasants were Muslims while landlords, traders and the professional classes were almost entirely Hindu. The violence was mainly directed at property, with pillage, arson, rape, and forcible conversion and marriage far outweighing murder. There were only around 300 deaths, but the loss of property amounted to tens of millions of rupees.

There had been some signs of organization in the Calcutta killings, but in Noakhali and Tippera the violence appeared to be entirely orchestrated, under the direction of one of the few Muslim landlords in the area, Ghulam Sarwar, an ex-Congressman who had recently defected to the League. The trouble involved not only imported Muslim *goondas* but also armed squads of Muslim National Guards, the paramilitary arm of the League. The National Guards, in common with the Hindu Mahasabha's offshoot, the RSSS (Rashtriya Swayamsevak Sangh, 'National Personal Service Society'), the Sikhs' Shiromani Akali Dal, the Congress Volunteers and various smaller private armies, had been suppressed during the war but were revived in September 1946 when the Defence of India Rules lapsed. Their joint membership rocketed to over 400,000 by the end of the year, with the three largest claiming about 100,000 each, a disturbing portent of civil war.

How far the National Guards were operating under their own initiative is open to question. Suhrawardy declared that the League had nothing whatever to do with the disturbances, and local League members certainly helped to restore order.[29] But as the flow of terrified Hindu refugees out of the affected areas became a torrent, it was hard to avoid the suspicion that this was a deliberately engineered transfer of population with the connivance of the provincial government – what we would now call 'ethnic cleansing'. The central leadership of the League, meanwhile, resolutely refused to make any statement condemning the events in east Bengal. Two of Jinnah's nominated ministers in the central government actually made belligerent speeches, one of them claiming that what had happened was part of the battle for Pakistan.

Gandhi, typically, tried to take all the guilt for Noakhali and Tippera on himself. 'There has been some flaw somewhere in my *ahimsa*,' he told Congressmen. If this had not been so, he told a Swiss friend later, 'we would have been spared the humiliating spectacle of weak brother killing his weak brother thoughtlessly and inhumanly'.[30] He went to Noakhali, to try to bring peace by his presence. Azad added his *maulana*'s voice: 'I would make a special appeal to Muslim brethren in East Bengal. Islam enjoins that the protection of one's neighbour is one's religious duty.'[31]

Thousands of those neighbours ended up seeking safety in Hindu-majority areas of Bihar and the UP, bringing with them harrowing tales of Muslim atrocities. Some Hindu organizations, especially the Hindu Mahasabha and the RSSS, seized on these to fan the flames of retribution. Trouble began in Patna on 25 October 1946, when a *hartal* called in sympathy with Hindu victims in Noakhali degenerated into an anti-Muslim riot. Over the next few days, roving Hindu mobs swept through the whole of Bihar province, slaughtering at least 7,000 Muslims – the worst death toll for any incident since 1857, dwarfing even the Calcutta killings. The governor, Sir Hugh Dow, reported that 75 per cent of the casualties were women and children.

The Congress ministry in Bihar, with the full support of the interim government, did its best to put a stop to the massacres. Police opened fire 23 times by the end of the month, and nine battalions of troops were sent in to restore order. The ministry insisted that they should shoot to kill, and Nehru wanted to send in aircraft to bomb the mobs into submission. He was prevented from doing anything by Wavell, who told him it was a provincial matter and that any interference from the centre could make things even worse. Utterly distraught, Nehru was close to resigning. 'What is the good of forming the Interim Government of India,' he wrote to the viceroy, 'if all that we can do is to watch helplessly and do nothing else when thousands of people are being butchered?'[32]

In the hope of being able to do something personally, Nehru travelled to Patna, the capital of Bihar, on 3 November. From the Circuit House there, he wrote to Indira, telling her that 'after a few minutes of mental conflict' he had decided to stay on:

> The immediate need was here in Bihar, and all else became secondary. We have heard ghastly stories here and what we have seen is pitiful enough. Stories of Noakhali, etc., bad as they were, became more and more exaggerated as they spread from mouth to mouth and inflamed the Hindu peasantry. For the last week or more the idea of revenge for Noakhali spread – a queer idea of revenging themselves on innocent people for others' faults. They have been terribly cruel – the lust for murder is a horrible thing and to it is added arson and looting. No one knows exactly how many people have been done to death ... Patna is full of refugees – miserable weeping men, women and children. Mass misery has a curious numbing effect.[33]

No sooner had an uneasy peace been restored in Bihar than the trouble spread to the UP, with more death and destruction as Hindu pilgrims at Garhmukteswar massacred some 1,000 Muslims at a local fair. Despite tight censorship, news of the killings spread throughout India, fuelling further bitterness. When Nehru made a visit to the NWFP, hitherto a Congress bastion held by Abdul Gaffar Khan, he was met by hostile tribal demonstrations and was lucky to escape with his life when they tried to stone him.

Gandhi was mortified by the violence, which shattered his belief in the innate peacefulness of the Hindus. He begged the refugees to return to their homes, and called for a Hindu and a Muslim in each village to accompany them and guarantee their safety. Starting in the Muslim village of Srirampur, he toured east Bengal, walking barefoot to atone for what had happened. In seven weeks he covered 116 miles and visited 47 villages – protected, it must be said, by a discreet police presence. The Mahatma, however, was beginning to lose faith not only in Hindus but also in his own purity of spirit. If his spirit was pure, he asked, how was it that he had failed? So he began his last experiment in *bramacharya*, proving his purity by sleeping naked with young female disciples – in the midst of murder and chaos, and at the age of 77, he was testing himself to see whether he got an erection.

The interim government never worked as a proper coalition, for the Muslims were simply not interested in co-operation. They refused to accept Nehru's leadership, treating him merely as external affairs member and operating as a separate bloc under Liaquat. Patel realized too late that he had made a grave mistake by refusing to step down as home member and insisting that Liaquat take finance instead. As finance member, Liaquat could interfere with every other department, controlling its operations by controlling the purse strings, and obstructing whatever he disagreed with. Wavell found this state of affairs extremely tiresome, but he was soon facing a still more intractable problem. Having at last got the League into the government, he now had to try to persuade Jinnah to enter the constituent assembly.

Both the British government and the Congress leaders were insisting that the assembly be called on 9 December, as planned. Nehru told Wavell that he thought the first session would last about 10 days, while procedures were discussed and committees appointed; the assembly would then be reconvened in about April 1947, to begin making real decisions. Jinnah refused to talk about the assembly until the British government gave a clear and unequivocal confirmation of the Cabinet mission's intentions, or until Congress gave guarantees that it would abide by the mission's interpretation of its statement on grouping. Pethick-Lawrence, like most politicians, seemed to find it impossible to give a straight answer. And even if he had, Congress would not have accepted it unless it said what they wanted to hear. 'No law-giver can give an authoritative interpretation of his own law,' was Gandhi's elliptic pronouncement.

Wavell warned Pethick-Lawrence that India was on the brink of civil war, and that announcing the constituent assembly might push it over the edge. But he felt the risk must be taken. On 20 November, he issued invitations for 9 December. Jinnah publicly refused, saying that the League stood by its withdrawal from the Cabinet mission plan. Liaquat told the viceroy the League members of the interim government were ready to resign whenever he wanted them to. It was back to square one again.

In a last attempt to produce some sort of agreement between the Indian parties, Pethick-Lawrence suggested two members of each should travel to London to discuss with the British government the problems of making the constituent assembly work. Wavell agreed, but added a Sikh representative. On 26 November, he invited Jinnah and Liaquat for the League, Nehru and Patel for Congress, and Baldev Singh for the Sikhs. Even this, however, turned into a test of the viceroy's patience. Jinnah and Liaquat agreed, but Nehru, Patel and Baldev Singh all refused. Attlee then sent a personal plea to Nehru, and he and Baldev

Singh changed their minds and decided to go. Thereupon, Jinnah changed his mind, and decided he would not go. Only Patel remained constant in his refusal.

'What an impossible set of people they are!' an exasperated Wavell noted in his journal that night. 'I sent Ian Scott off to see Liaquat; and by midnight he returned to say that ... Liaquat had agreed to come with us to Karachi tomorrow to see Jinnah and try to persuade him to come.' Next morning, when the rest of the party boarded the aircraft at Delhi's Palam airport, Wavell was relieved to see that Liaquat was 'dressed for Europe'. When they landed at Karachi, Jinnah finally appeared, though 'rather late' – he had been swayed by a personal telegram from Attlee at midnight.

In fact, all the fuss was pointless. Four days of wrangling and bickering in London produced nothing but confirmation that the three sides – Congress, the League and the British government – were unable to agree on anything. On 6 December, Nehru and Baldev Singh flew back to India, for the opening of the constituent assembly. Jinnah and Liaquat stayed on in London at Claridges: they had no wish to be in Delhi when the assembly met. Wavell stayed, too, to continue his battle with the government.

The British government tried to put a gloss on its failure to reach a settlement by saying the Indian representatives had to consult their colleagues before they could agree to anything. It then tried to placate both sides by first declaring that the League's interpretation of the Cabinet mission plan, with compulsory grouping of provinces, was correct and should be accepted by all parties to the constituent assembly, then saying that Congress was free to refer the question of grouping to the Federal Court, as Gandhi and Nehru had demanded all along. It was a peculiarly ham-fisted piece of equivocation, which only succeeded in alienating everybody still further.

The constituent assembly met as planned on 9 December, with 73 empty Muslim seats, and it elected Rajendra Prasad as its president. Nehru proposed what came to be known as the Objectives Resolution, which began: 'This Constituent Assembly declares its firm and solemn resolve to proclaim India as an independent and sovereign republic.' The assembly was then adjourned until 20 January. By the time it met again, Congress had compounded the general confusion by first agreeing to abide by the British – and therefore the League's – interpretation of the mission plan, and then immediately nullifying this by saying there must be no compulsion on any province or any part of any province, and that the rights of the Sikhs in the Punjab must not be jeopardized in any way. On hearing this, the League immediately abandoned its plans to enter the assembly and instead demanded that the British government should dissolve it, since clearly neither Congress nor the Sikhs nor the Scheduled Castes accepted the Cabinet mission plan. Congress in turn demanded that the viceroy sack the League members of the interim government, since the League had clearly rejected the plan and was now actively opposing the government in which they sat. If the League members were allowed to stay, Patel declared, then the Congress members would leave.

From April 1946, Wavell had had two plans for the emergency evacuation of British civilians and eventually of the British army, province by province: one, in the event of the Indian army becoming unreliable, was labelled 'Madhouse'; the other, in the event of its becoming actively hostile, was called 'Bedlam'. He must have felt he was living in both in January and February 1947. The situation was not helped by his fraught relations with the British government, which refused either to accept his plan for a withdrawal by stages, or to decide on 31 March 1948 as the final date for the transfer of power. The gap between them was now so wide that when Attlee called him back to London for 'a review of the situation', he refused, suspecting that 'the idea is to get me home and force my resignation'.[34]

In this, at least, he was right. When he refused again, he was told to make no further plans relating to the transfer of power until he had been home for discussions. A week later, Attlee sent him a letter by courier. He received it while having breakfast with George Abell. He opened it, read it, then continued eating his egg. After five minutes' silence – nothing unusual for Wavell – Abell asked if it was anything important. Wavell looked up. 'They've sacked me, George,' he said. There was another long pause, then he added, 'They were quite right, I suppose.'[35]

'Possible New Horror Job'

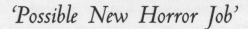

In his diary for 17 December 1946, King George VI recorded: 'Attlee told me that Lord Wavell's plan for our leaving India savours too much of military retreat and that he does not realise it is a political problem and not a military one. Wavell has done very good work up to now, but Attlee doubts whether he has the finesse to negotiate the next steps when we must keep the two Indian parties friendly to us all the time.' Attlee had come to the conclusion that the situation could only be saved by drastic action. 'Two things were necessary,' he recalled in his draft autobiography. 'One was to make the Indians feel their responsibility by announcing that we were definitely clearing out within a definite period, the other was to find the man to put this through.'[1] He now believed he had found that man: the king's second cousin, Lord Mountbatten. The king agreed – but would Mountbatten?

Attlee chose Mountbatten for purely pragmatic reasons. One of these was his undoubted 'star' quality – his rank, his royal connections, his perceived military record – which Attlee believed would impress the Indian princes: some of them had looked down on Wavell because he was a mere soldier. Ever since his time on the Simon Commission, Attlee had seen the princes as an obstacle to political progress in India; Mountbatten's role was to dazzle them. But of course there were other reasons, too: in Burma, which Mountbatten had ruled for a while as supreme commander, he had shown himself to be sympathetic to, and able to work with, native leaders, whereas old Burma hands returning from wartime exile in India were still trapped in the colonial past and unable to adapt to new conditions. Mountbatten, Attlee wrote, 'had an extraordinary facility for getting on with all kinds of people'.

In the weeks before the arrival of Wavell and the Indian leaders, Attlee had been in close touch with Mountbatten over Burma, which was demanding immediate independence even more vociferously than India. He had been impressed with Mountbatten's grasp of the situation, and with his eagerness to recommend that power should be handed over at once to the former rebel and resistance leader, U Aung San. When the newly-returned governor of Burma, Sir Reginald Dorman-Smith, disagreed, Attlee summarily dismissed him, replacing him with a Mountbatten protégé, Brigadier Sir Hubert Rance, who had been chief civil affairs officer in Burma in the post-war military administration.

In fact, Dorman-Smith was not quite such a colonial blimp as Mountbatten painted him – he was not opposed to Burmese independence, only to rushing headlong into it without adequate preparation for a stable democratic regime, following free elections. In many respects, the results of Mountbatten's haste may be seen in Burma's subsequent troubled history. But that, of course, is hindsight, and could not have been obvious at the time to a prime minister anxious to relieve his country of troublesome colonial burdens.

On Wednesday, 18 December 1946, the day after he had spoken to the king, Attlee invited Mountbatten to 10 Downing Street to discuss his future. He began by asking whether his heart was still set on resuming his naval career. Mountbatten said it was: he had retired as supreme commander, South-east Asia, at the end of May and was now attending a senior officers' technical course at Portsmouth, in preparation for taking command of the First Cruiser Squadron in the Mediterranean. What Attlee may not have realized was the personal significance of this appointment to Mountbatten.

For much of his life, Mountbatten was driven by a burning need to redress the wrongs done to his father, Prince Louis of Battenberg, when he was hounded out of the Royal Navy at the beginning of the First World War because he was a German. 'Ever since that disgraceful episode,' he once told General Sir Philip Christison, the British commander in Indonesia, 'I have lived determined to get to the top and vindicate his memory. Nothing and no one; I repeat, nothing and no man, will ever be allowed to stand in my way.'[2]

Mountbatten aimed to emulate his father's successes, and then to complete the career out of which he believed his father had been cheated. Prince Louis had commanded the Second Cruiser Squadron in 1905, a post which Mountbatten's new appointment matched closely enough. The next step was to become C-in-C Mediterranean Fleet. After that, he planned to work his way up to first sea lord; the position his father had been forced to resign in 1914. Becoming viceroy of India had many attractions, but it was not part of his plan.

Mountbatten was born Prince Louis Francis Albert Victor Nicholas of Battenberg on 25 June 1900, at Frogmore House in the Home Park of Windsor Castle. Despite having such a plethora of names to choose from, however, he was always known as 'Dickie' – to avoid confusion with his many British, German and Russian relatives. In the female line, his descent was spotless: his mother was

Princess Victoria of Hesse, daughter of Queen Victoria's third child, Princess Alice, and Grand Duke Louis IV of Hesse and the Rhine. The male line, however, was somewhat tarnished. His father, Prince Louis of Battenberg, was the son of Prince Alexander of Hesse-Darmstadt, who was supposedly the son of Grand Duke Louis II of Hesse, but who was actually fathered by the Grand Duchess's court chamberlain, the handsome Baron von Grancy, with whom she lived openly after separating from her extremely ugly husband. Louis II was persuaded to accept paternity 'for the honour of his crown and family'. He was required to do the same thing again a year later, on the birth of a daughter, Marie, who later married the Tsarevitch of Russia.

Prince Louis, Alexander's son, had set his heart on becoming a sailor, and since neither Hesse nor Germany then had a navy, he was sent to Britain in 1868, at the age of 14, to serve in Queen Victoria's. His fellow officers resented his fast track to advancement, but eventually he earned their respect by hard work and decency, though marrying the Queen's granddaughter in 1884 certainly did his career prospects no harm.

By 1911, Prince Louis had become second sea lord, but with Anglo-German tensions increasing, the voices of prejudice were growing louder. Horatio Bottomley's paper, *John Bull*, greeted his promotion with the headline 'SHOULD A GERMAN "BOSS" OUR NAVY? Bull-dog breed or Dachshund?' the following year he was appointed first sea lord, and the press campaign intensified. By 1914, he had become an embarrassment to the royal family. King George V, in Prime Minister Asquith's words, was 'a great deal agitated about Louis of Battenberg's position' and upset by letters complaining of 'the German spy' in the Admiralty.[3] Not wishing to discomfit the king further, Louis resigned. 'Dickie', at the time a naval cadet at Osborne, is said to have wept at the news of his beloved father's humiliation, and suffered brutal bullying from fellow cadets. The experience left him with a life-long obsession, and a ferocious determination to get even.

In June 1917, the king decided to change the royal family's name from Prince Albert's Saxe-Coburg-Gotha to something completely English. He chose Windsor. The various royal relatives were expected to do something similar. Prince Louis chose a straight English translation of Battenberg: he considered Battenhill, but settled for the more euphonious Mountbatten. In return for surrendering his titles of prince and serene highness, he was rewarded with the Marquessate of Milford Haven. His elder son, George, became the Earl of Medina; Dickie, as the younger son, took the courtesy title Lord Louis Mountbatten, which he retained until he was created viscount in 1946.

Mountbatten served as a midshipman in various ships and a submarine during the final three years of the First World War, which he ended as a sub-lieutenant. In 1919, he was sent, with other young officers whose education had been interrupted by the war, to Cambridge, where he spent most of his time cultivating the friendship of his distant cousins Bertie and Harry – the future King George VI and Duke of Gloucester – who had taken a house just outside the town. He persuaded Bertie to get him an invitation to accompany the Prince of Wales on the tour he was to make of Australia and New Zealand, leaving in March 1920. During the seven months they were away, he built such a close relationship with the future king, that the prince decided he should accompany him on his tour to India, the following year.

In September 1921, shortly before he left for India, Mountbatten was shattered by the sudden death of his father from a heart attack. A few days later, there was another death, almost equally significant for Mountbatten: that of Sir Ernest Cassel, the multi-millionaire financier who had been King Edward VII's personal banker and friend. Cassel left an immense fortune for those times, £7.5 million, £2,900,000 of which went to his 19-year-old granddaughter, Edwina Ashley, along with several houses, including the penthouse at Brook House in Park Lane. The will specified that she would inherit on her 28th birthday or when she married, whichever was the sooner. Mountbatten was already smitten with Edwina, whom he had met at Mrs Vanderbilt's ball at Claridges the previous October. Now, she seemed even more attractive to the penurious 21-year-old sub-lieutenant, who had only about £300 a year from his naval pay plus the same amount from a family trust. At his suggestion, she followed him to India, where he proposed to her in a sitting-room in the Viceroy's House in New Delhi.

Edwina and Mountbatten were married on 18 July 1922 at St. Margaret's, Westminster. It was the wedding of the year: he was a charismatic, good-looking young semi-royal; she was a society millionairess; the Prince of Wales was best man. The marriage meant that money was no longer a problem for Mountbatten – Edwina's income from her fortune brought in £60,000 a year, or more than £1,150 a week, at a time when the weekly wage of a bank clerk, for instance, was between £3 and £4.

Though it lasted 38 years, the Mountbatten marriage was not particularly happy once the first romantic flush had worn off. Mountbatten's obsession with himself and his career soon began to bore Edwina. After the birth of two daughters, whom Mountbatten adored, Edwina travelled, and in the course of time took numerous lovers. Mountbatten later confessed to Sir Robert Scott: 'Edwina and I spent all our married lives getting into other people's beds.'[4] This was undoubtedly true of Edwina, but Mountbatten does not seem to have been particularly interested in sex. Although he enjoyed two lengthy liaisons with women, no one could ever have come between him and his one great and abiding love: himself (or at least his vision of himself as his father's successful *alter ego*).

While Edwina pursued her rackety social and sexual life throughout Europe and the USA, Mountbatten made steady progress in his naval career. He escaped the axe which chopped 350 lieutenants from the navy, and in 1924 found his true forte when he was sent on a year-long signals course at Portsmouth. Always fascinated by modern technology and by gadgets of every kind, he threw himself into this new speciality with his usual energy and enthusiasm, emerging top of his intake. By 1931, he was fleet wireless officer to the Mediterranean Fleet, which was then the biggest single maritime unit in the world. Many regarded him as the outstanding signals officer of his generation. Certainly he embraced the latest technology and did much to bring the navy's communications into the modern world. Others, less kindly, felt that for all his energy, his effect was to increase the proliferation of paper rather than improve overall efficiency.

Specialization, particularly in technical areas, was not the way to the very top, however, and after two and a half years Mountbatten moved back into general duties. He commanded two destroyers in the Mediterranean, then returned to London for a tour of duty in the Air Division of the Admiralty, a job he had set up for himself while visiting the capital for the funeral of George V. With his 'best friend' now on the throne as Edward VIII, the future was looking increasingly rosy. The abdication crisis proved only a temporary blip: Edward forsook the throne – and Mountbatten promptly forsook Edward, hitching his star immediately to the new king, George VI. He was promoted to captain at the end of June 1937, exulting in his diary: 'Promoted at 37.0. Average age 42–5. Some Lt Cdrs to Cdr over 37!'[5]

On 27 June 1939, Captain Lord Louis Mountbatten took command of the newly completed HMS *Kelly*, which was to be his flagship as commander of the eight-strong Fifth Destroyer Flotilla. Under Mountbatten's command, *Kelly* lived dangerously. One scrape followed another, helping to establish her captain's reputation for heroism – and borderline competence. Within days of the declaration of war she was in action just outside Portsmouth harbour, depth-charging a U-boat which turned out to be a shoal of fish. Two months later, she was almost capsized by a huge wave while steaming at a suicidal 28 knots through a heavy Arctic sea; all the boats, davits and guard rails on the starboard side were washed away, together with one sailor, who was drowned. Soon afterwards, Mountbatten sailed the ship into the middle of a British minefield in the Tyne estuary, where she struck a mine and had to be towed back to port for repairs lasting 11 weeks.

After only nine days back at sea on convoy escort duty, *Kelly* collided with another British destroyer, damaging both vessels. Another six weeks in dry dock followed, after which came an episode of genuine heroism as Mountbatten took *Kelly* and the rest of his flotilla into a Norwegian fjord under heavy attack from German dive-bombers, to help rescue the ill-fated Anglo-French military force.

On 9 May 1940, Mountbatten's recklessness led to *Kelly*'s most famous incident, while escorting the cruiser *Birmingham* off the Dutch coast. Strictly against orders, he signalled the *Birmingham* using an Aldis lamp, which attracted the attention of the enemy. Within minutes, *Kelly* was hit by a torpedo which blew a 50-foot hole in her starboard side, killing 27 crew and wounding dozens more. But she did not sink, and Mountbatten succeeded in bringing her home to the Tyne. The final report blamed Mountbatten, and the C-in-C Home Fleet recorded witheringly 'that owing to a series of misfortunes – mine, collision, torpedo – *Kelly* had only been at sea 57 days during the war'.[6] But Mountbatten's luck held: the navy needed a public relations triumph, and the saga of the valiant *Kelly* and her dauntless captain was ideal material.

The fictionalized story of HMS *Kelly* was filmed by Noël Coward, a close friend of the Mountbattens, as *In Which We Serve*, with Coward playing the intrepid captain. As a depiction of British stiff-upper-lip valour, it was wonderful propaganda for the navy – and even better propaganda for Mountbatten's own image. He saw it 12 times and never tired of it. Other naval officers were less enthusiastic. As a naval commander, his personal courage and leadership were never in question: his seamanship and judgement, however, were. His peers regarded him as 'no better than second rate', while one former Canadian commander has described him as 'quite the worst ship handler I ever saw'.

It took six months to repair *Kelly* and make her seaworthy again. During that time, Mountbatten had succeeded in having one more ship blown from under him due to yet another disastrous blunder. 'Maddening to be put out of action but lucky to escape with 50 killed and bow and stern blown off,' Mountbatten recorded insouciantly.[7]

Kelly was back at sea early in December, despite the slight initial setback of ramming another ship on the way out of dock, which meant more repairs on her bow. Four months later, she was sunk by Stuka dive-bombers during the battle for Crete. Nine officers and 127 ratings perished. Mountbatten was trapped on the bridge as the ship went down, but managed to escape underwater. For once, Mountbatten himself was blameless, and showed great heroism in helping survivors to reach the liferafts and then keeping up their morale during the long hours before they were rescued. But even then he could not resist gilding the lily, claiming that the German aircraft had machine-gunned the helpless men in the sea, though none of the other survivors had any such memory.

Churchill may not have been aware of the generally poor opinion of Mountbatten's seamanship, but he was impressed by his ideas and his flair – so impressed that, on 4 March 1942, in the face of considerable opposition, he appointed him chief of Combined Operations. Mountbatten was still only a junior captain, but he was to be given the acting ranks of vice-admiral, lieutenant-general and air marshal, so that he would be able to command men of all three services. The first sea lord, Admiral Sir Dudley Pound, objected forcefully, but was overruled by the prime minister. King George VI greeted the news with great enthusiasm.

As chief of Combined Operations, Mountbatten was responsible for a number of small and daring cross-Channel raids, many of them successful, by British commandos. Then, six months after he had taken over, he launched Operation Rutter, a large-scale raid on the heavily fortified port of Dieppe. Everything that could go wrong at Dieppe did go wrong. There was no agreed chain of command, resulting inevitably in serious confusion. Enigma signals revealing the presence of German naval patrols in the area were ignored, with the result that the force was spotted and the vital element of surprise was lost. In all, nearly 1,000 men were killed in the raid and 2,000 taken prisoner. It was, by any reckoning, a total disaster.

In fact, the Dieppe raid was more of a political than a serious military operation, designed as a grand gesture to placate the Russians and Americans who were exhorting Churchill to do something to relieve German pressure on the eastern front. For Churchill, it had served its purpose – if only to prove that an early cross-Channel invasion was impossible – and he was duly grateful to the man who had been responsible for it. In 1943, he proposed Mountbatten as the supreme Allied commander, South-east Asia. President Roosevelt had the veto over any such appointment, but agreed to Mountbatten, whom he had met, and been charmed by, the previous year. In the Admiralty, the news was greeted with incredulity. 'I think most people in the Service ... just laughed,' said Admiral Cunningham later.[8]

Mountbatten's new appointment took him back to India, which was, after all, providing most of the troops under his command. But he chose not to set up his headquarters in Delhi, or any other Indian city, where he might have had to face competition from two field marshals – Wavell and Auchinleck – and other senior officers of quality and experience. Also, there was the fact that as viceroy, Wavell would always have precedence over him. Instead, he established only a small rear HQ in Delhi, which he visited every few weeks, and set up his main camp at Kandy, in Ceylon, where he soon built his own empire with a staff of 8,000 and every modern convenience imaginable. And there, safely removed from any direct action, he saw out the rest of the war without creating any fresh disasters.

With his generals, particularly Sir Oliver Leese and William Slim, the legendary commander of the 14th Army, taking care of strategy and tactics under Auchinleck, Mountbatten was able to indulge in what he did best – diplomacy, politicking, morale boosting, and above all public relations. He played no part in the campaigns that recaptured Burma – though this did not inhibit him from styling his viscountcy and later earldom 'of Burma'. The chief of the Imperial

General Staff, Field Marshal Sir Alan Brooke, who had earlier regarded Mountbatten as 'an over-promoted nuisance as Chief of Combined Operations'[9], recorded in his diary at the end of the war: 'Seldom has a Supreme Commander been more deficient of the main attributes of a Supreme Commander than Dickie Mountbatten.'[10] This was the man to whom Attlee was to entrust the dismantling of the Raj.

Mountbatten's own words are never the most reliable source of evidence – he habitually embellished events and conversations, giving different versions to different people as the fancy took him. His official biographer, Philip Ziegler, writes that 'his vanity, though child-like, was monstrous, his ambition unbridled. The truth, in his hands, was swiftly converted from what it was to what it should have been. He sought to rewrite history with cavalier indifference to the facts to magnify his own achievements.'[11] His achievements, by any standards, were considerable, as were his qualities – he had great warmth and social skills, a quick mind and incredible energy, in addition to a remarkable self-confidence which made him a natural leader. But his successes never seem to have been enough to satisfy his insatiable thirst for personal glory, something which needs to be remembered when reading his recollections and reports.

Mountbatten claims that when he was called to see Attlee at Number 10 on 18 December 1946, he had no idea what the prime minister wanted. He arrived, however, to find him sitting in the Cabinet room with Cripps, which should have given him some inkling. In a tape-recorded interview with the authors of *Freedom at Midnight*, he says 'it all started in a very friendly, relaxed way, talking about India'. It was only as 'they began asking more and more searching questions, what did I think ought to be done, how would I approach the thing,' that the penny dropped. 'I said, "Good God, Mr Prime Minister, I have a very, very, very uneasy unpleasant feeling that you're trying to suggest – no you can't be – are you trying to suggest that you're going to ask me to relieve Archie Wavell?"' When Attlee said he was – 'You weren't supposed to guess so soon' – Mountbatten says he replied: 'You ought to have your head examined, I wouldn't dream of going out. In Wavell you've got a man who's taciturn, he's silent, but first class. His whole loyalty is for India, the British. You couldn't have a better man ... I wouldn't dream of taking over from him. It's out of the question. It isn't even worth discussing.'[12]

Edwina, who had been looking forward to sun and wine and the good life in the Mediterranean, summed up the Mountbattens' joint reaction succinctly: 'Possible new horror job,' she wrote in her diary. Mountbatten did, of course, agree to take over as viceroy, but only after six weeks of hard bargaining. Pushing his royal connections to the limit as always, he first insisted on seeing the king, which he did on 20 December. Again, there are several different versions of the interview as remembered by Mountbatten: what they all have in common is an emphasis on his reluctance to take on a task which everyone agreed was impossible. This presented his eventual 'success' as yet another personal triumph, another victory in the face of certain disaster.

Mountbatten returned to Downing Street with a list of conditions – he wanted to choose his own personal staff while keeping on Wavell's; he wanted complete control of the honours list for India; he wanted the four-engined York aircraft, MW 102, which he had had as supreme commander, as well as the viceroy's existing two-engined Dakota. Attlee agreed to everything. There was one nasty moment when Cripps volunteered to go with Mountbatten as his chief of staff – Cripps was almost the only man guaranteed to overshadow him in India. Mountbatten scotched it by saying it was 'too great an honour' and suggested that Cripps would be more valuable back home, possibly in the India Office. 'You certainly had a brainwave in asking Cripps to take on the I.O.,' the king wrote, congratulating him. 'I should never relish the idea of having him on my staff or staying in my house.'[13] In the event, Attlee decided Cripps would be still more valuably employed in managing the mounting crisis in British industry and the desperate coal shortage which threatened to bring the entire country to a standstill.

What Mountbatten wanted most, however, was to be sure that if he did become the last viceroy he would be able to get back into the navy afterwards. 'I've just been appointed commander of the First Cruiser Squadron,' he said. 'I'd like to have that appointment again or else a comparable one. I'd like it guaranteed, certain. Can you arrange this?' Attlee, according to Mountbatten, immediately sent for the first lord of the Admiralty and the first sea lord, and put the question to them. 'Of course, Mr Prime Minister, anything you say, certainly,' said the first lord. The first sea lord, however, Admiral Sir John Cunningham, who knew Mountbatten well, demurred. Clearly, he did not want him back at any price. Attlee settled the matter in his usual dry manner. 'I wasn't asking your approval,' he rasped. 'I was asking your accord, do you understand?'

There were two other important demands which Mountbatten claims were granted. One was that he should have full plenipotentiary powers – 'The decisions must be mine and mine alone, on the spot.' He says Attlee agreed,[14] but there is no record of this anywhere. It is most improbable that a prime minister like Attlee would consider handing over to someone as politically inexperienced as Mountbatten total responsibility for such a monumental task, which carried with it the potential for bringing down the government if things went wrong. Certainly, Mountbatten was given a more or less free hand to open discussions and settle details, but anything vital had to be referred back to London for a decision.

The second demand Mountbatten claims he made was for a time limit to be set and announced for the handing over of power. Wavell, of course, had been pressing for a time limit for some months, and the subject had been discussed several times in the India Committee before Mountbatten was offered the viceroyalty. Cripps had suggested that Parliament should be asked 'to hand over power in India not later than 31 March 1948', following Wavell's report that Britain would not be able to hold India later than that, 'and possibly not for so long'.[15]

   While Mountbatten was away skiing in Switzerland over the Christmas period, the committee advised the Cabinet 'that an early announcement of our intention to withdraw was the most hopeful means of inducing the Congress and the Muslim League to come to an agreement'. It considered that by the end of January the League would have finally decided not to enter the constituent assembly, and that the government should then make its announcement on the transfer of power. Attlee, wishing to retain the maximum room for manœuvre, was against setting a precise date at this stage, and amended 31 March to 'an appointed day which will not be later than the first half of 1948'.

   The Cabinet was deeply divided over this issue, with Bevin, who was at heart an old-fashioned imperialist, leading the opposition to an early withdrawal, which he believed would have serious repercussions in Egypt, Palestine, and the Middle East, not to mention Malaya, Ceylon and Britain's African territories. But in the end Attlee and Cripps prevailed, and the other ministers agreed that a statement should be made. They also agreed that Wavell should be replaced, a decision that was made easier by his stubborn refusal to do as he was told and come home to be sacked.

   The decision to set a deadline was enough to persuade Mountbatten to accept the position. He wrote to Attlee on 3 January 1947:

> It makes all the difference to me to know that you propose to make a statement in the House, terminating the British 'Raj' on a definite and specified date; or earlier than this date, if the Indian Parties can agree a constitution and form a Government, before this. I feel very strongly that I could not have gone out there with confidence, if it had been possible to construe my arrival as a perpetuation, at this moment, of the viceregal system, or of our imposing our nominee to arbitrate in their affairs.[16]

   In his letters and conversations with Attlee over the next few weeks, Mountbatten consistently pressed for an actual date to be announced. He was astute enough to accept that setting a deadline was essential to any sort of political success. It was also entirely in character for him to want that date to be as early as possible – he would steer India like he did every ship he commanded, at full speed ahead, whatever the dangers, whatever the conditions of weather and water. And what was the point of racing, if there was no finishing line to aim for?

   There was, perhaps, another reason why he was so keen on a time limit.

His mother was not the only one who warned him gloomily, 'You'll be there for years, if you come back at all.' Mountbatten always insisted: 'Well, I'll be back in a few months.' For him, his period as viceroy was to be no more than a temporary pause in his headlong dash for the position he really craved: that of first sea lord. He was anxious to get back to the navy, back on the escalator – it can scarcely be described as a ladder – which would carry him to that goal. And, to use his own words, nothing and no man would be allowed to stand in his way.

While he was still negotiating with Attlee, Mountbatten began recruiting his personal staff. For the sake of continuity and their wealth of experience, he intended to keep on all Wavell's staff, including George Abell as private secretary, but with so much to be done in so little time, he wanted to supplement them with his own men. As he had shown during the war, both at Combined Operations and SEAC, he liked to fill his hive with as many people as possible – the more there were, the bigger the buzz.

First, and most important, Lord Ismay volunteered to go with him as his chief of staff. Ismay, christened Hastings but known to everyone as 'Pug', had been steeped in Indian affairs since his birth in 1887 at Naini Tal in the UP. By that time, his family were already very old India hands – his great-grandfather had been military secretary to the viceroy Lord Hastings, after whom Pug was named; his father had been a member of the viceroy's Legislative Council and later chief judge of the Mysore court. Ismay had spent his early days in the army with the 21st (Sam Browne's) Cavalry, seeing active service on the North-West Frontier. After secondment to the King's African Rifles in east Africa and then to the Somaliland Camel Corps, with whom he won a DSO in operations against the 'Mad Mullah', he had passed through the Indian staff college at Quetta. He then spent five years in the heart of Whitehall as assistant secretary to Sir Maurice Hankey in the Committee of Imperial Defence, before returning to India as military secretary to Lord Willingdon. During the war, he had been Churchill's chief of staff, staying on in the same role with Attlee.

Ismay had retired at the end of 1946, a full general and with a peerage, and was looking forward to a long and well-earned holiday in Australia and New Zealand, when he received the call from Mountbatten. 'The idea of emerging from my new-found retirement and getting involved in the last chapter of the story of British rule in India was singularly unattractive,' he wrote in his memoirs. 'On the other hand, I owed so much to India that it was my bounden duty to lend a hand, if I was wanted.'[17] He was very much wanted – the new viceroy could not have found a better qualified chief of staff, though his view of India did tend towards the romantic.

Mountbatten asked Ismay to approach the second key figure for his team, Sir Eric Miéville, whom he wanted as principal secretary. Miéville had been private secretary to Lord Willingdon, and then assistant private secretary to the king for several years before becoming 'something in the city'. His attitude to India was far less romantic than Ismay's, but he, too, was prepared to drop everything and go back to assist in the final act.

The other central members of the entourage were four men who had worked closely with Mountbatten during the war, and on whom he knew he could rely for unswerving loyalty and support. Collectively and somewhat derisively dubbed 'the Dickie Birds' by the rest of the staff, they were: Captain Ronald Brockman, RN, Mountbatten's naval secretary since 1944, who was to be his personal secretary; Lieutenant-Colonel Vernon Erskine-Crum, of the Scots Guards, who was to be conference secretary; Lieutenant-Commander Peter Howes, previously Mountbatten's flag-lieutenant and now his senior ADC; and Alan Campbell-Johnson, a former RAF Public Relations Officer who had been, as he puts it, 'part of the Mountbatten machine' since July 1942, when he had joined his staff at Combined Operations HQ. Campbell-Johnson was to be press attaché, a post unknown to all previous viceroys and certainly to Wavell, whose aversion to any form of publicity had contributed to his downfall. For Mountbatten, Campbell-Johnson's role was vital. Like some medieval Celtic chieftain he always took with him his own bard, recorder of his victories and apologist for his defeats.

With his team already signed up, Mountbatten formally accepted the office of viceroy on 11 February 1947. Wavell received his letter of dismissal two days later, having been kept totally in the dark for six weeks. On 20 February Attlee made his statement in the House of Commons, announcing Britain's intention to leave India not later than June 1948, come what may. 'It is therefore essential,' he continued, 'that all parties should sink their differences in order that they may be ready to shoulder the great responsibilities which will come upon them next year.'[18] He also announced that Wavell would be replaced by Mountbatten in March, giving as an excuse that Wavell's appointment had been a wartime one, and that this 'new and final phase in India' was an appropriate moment to end it. For his devotion to duty during a very difficult period, Wavell was to receive an earldom.

With his notice of dismissal so publicly served, Wavell was left to work out the remaining month of his viceroyalty as what we would now call a lame-duck administration. The situation in India, however, remained volatile. The storm centre had by then moved from Bengal and Bihar to the Punjab, where the thunder clouds of communal tension had been building steadily for months.

Ever since the provincial elections, the Muslim League in the Punjab had been running a civil disobedience campaign, based on the Congress movements of the 1920s and 30s, against the government of the Unionist Khizar Hyat Khan, who was hanging on to power by an unstable alliance with Congress and the Sikhs' Akali Dal Party. With the situation already tense, news of the troubles in Calcutta, Bombay, Noakhali, Bihar and the UP had raised communal passions to a critical level. Minor disturbances in Amritsar and other locations were successfully quelled by firm action, but Sir Evan Jenkins, who had been appointed governor of the Punjab in April 1946, reported that an atmosphere of civil war was developing, with all communities arming themselves for a struggle which seemed inevitable.[19]

In January 1947, Khizar tried to ban the two main private armies – the League's National Guards and the Hindu RSSS – fearing that their existence would encourage the Sikhs to reform their own Akali Sena, which had been disbanded in 1940. The National Guards, who had been put on a 'war footing' the previous October, ignored the ban and went on parading the streets of Lahore in uniform. But when more than a thousand steel helmets were found in their headquarters, the general commanders were all arrested. The League immediately launched full-scale 'direct action'. Khizar panicked and withdrew his ban on the National Guards next day, but it was too late. Muslims at mass meetings in Lahore and other cities screamed for his immediate resignation.

Khizar responded at midnight by arresting all the provincial League leaders and banning all public meetings, which provoked more riots and angry demonstrations in every district of the Punjab. The Hindus warned Khizar that if he failed to suppress the Muslim agitation they would take matters into their own hands. Master Tara Singh called on the Sikhs to get ready to fight. 'The extreme arrogance of the demonstrators,' Jenkins reported, 'had alarmed the non-Muslims to the point of hysteria.'[20]

Attlee's statement on 20 February 1947 came at precisely that moment, increasing the pressure on Khizar. After 10 days of vacillation, he resigned. Jenkins went through the motions of inviting the leader of the League in the Punjab, the Khan of Mamdot, to form a government, but he knew it was a forlorn hope – both Hindus and Sikhs refused to co-operate with the League, which still did not have an overall majority. He was left with no alternative but to take over the administration himself, imposing governor's rule under Section 93. This started fresh rioting, more violent than ever, which spread from Lahore to other towns and cities throughout the Punjab, with stabbings and killings everywhere. Mobs of young League supporters rampaged through the streets, trying to pull down the Union Jack and hoist the Muslim League flag in its place.[21] The unrest was exacerbated by a severe food crisis, rising inflation and a deteriorating economic situation. A rash of strikes for more pay in the public services added to the government's problems. Jenkins clamped down hard, sending in the army and police to stop the fighting.

As a brief and uneasy peace was restored in the Punjab, the troubles spread to the neighbouring NWFP, where for some time the League had been organizing demonstrations to try to bring down the Congress ministry. Unruly mobs surrounded the Peshawar house of the Congress premier, Dr Khan Sahib, throwing stones and breaking windows while police stood by and 'refused to obey orders and open fire'.[22] Dr Khan raised the stakes by calling some 7,000 armed Red Shirts to Peshawar. The governor of the NWFP, Sir Olaf Caroe, believed the only answer was to impose direct rule then call new elections, which the League would now almost certainly win, but he was forced to wait and struggle on as best he could. Meanwhile, the League was mounting another civil disobedience campaign on the other side of the country in Assam, where it was already fomenting trouble by bringing in large numbers of Muslim immigrants from east Bengal in an attempt to swing the communal balance in its favour.

By this time, Congress leaders were starting to think that the Muslim provinces were more trouble than they were worth. In the Punjab, both Hindus and Sikhs began to favour partition of the province as their only safeguard. Even Patel was beginning to see the partition of India itself as something other than an unthinkable vivisection. This was largely thanks to V.P. Menon, who had managed to persuade Patel that a united India under the Cabinet mission plan was impossible and that since Jinnah would never give up his demand for an independent Pakistan, it would be better to divide the country than to destroy it through civil war. In an argument designed to appeal to the hard-nosed politician in Patel, he pointed out that if Congress agreed to partition, Jinnah could hardly expect to get the non-Muslim parts of the Punjab, Bengal and Assam.

Equally skilfully, Menon had convinced Patel that it would be best for everyone, but especially for Congress, if power were transferred to two central governments on the basis of dominion status. By accepting dominion status, he suggested, Congress would ensure a peaceful hand-over and win the friendship and goodwill of Britain. This would avoid the endless trouble that could be caused by the senior British officials who occupied most of the higher levels of the civil service, and whose co-operation was essential to a smooth transition. Even more important was the goodwill of British officers in the Indian armed forces, whose help would be vital in the early days of the new state.

Dominion status, he continued, would not affect the Indian government's power to amend its own constitution, and therefore would have little practical effect on the nation's sovereignty – and in any case India could walk out of the Commonwealth at any time she chose. Finally – and this was a point that was to have particular significance for Patel and Menon in the near future – dominion status would help to reassure the princes, and make them more willing to come to the negotiating table.

Patel had bought Menon's package, and promised him that if dominion status meant power could be transferred at once, he would make sure Congress accepted it. While Patel was still with him, Menon dictated an outline plan, which he sent, with Wavell's consent, by special messenger to Pethick-Lawrence in London. Menon had been corresponding with the India Office about such an approach for some time, but Pethick-Lawrence and the British government were still committed to the Cabinet mission plan.

Nevertheless, the ground had been broken with Patel and Congress. Nehru and the Working Committee under Acharya Kripalani, the former general secretary of Congress who had been elected president at Meerut in November 1946, went on trying to persuade the League to join the Constituent Assembly and to co-operate in preparing for the early transfer of power promised by Attlee. But they tacitly accepted the inevitability of Pakistan by proposing the partition of the Punjab and Bengal themselves.

Attlee and Cripps, however, seemed unable to read the writing on the wall: events in India were now moving so fast that it was difficult for them to keep up. Mountbatten's instructions, set out in a letter on 18 March, were 'to obtain a unitary government for British India and the Indian States, if possible within the British Commonwealth, through the medium of a Constituent Assembly, set up and run in accordance with the Cabinet Mission's plan'. The major parties could not be compelled to accept it, of course, but Mountbatten was given until 1 October to try to persuade them. If by that time there was no prospect of agreement, he was to report back to the British government, with his proposals for how to hand over power on the due date. This was 'flexible to within one month; but you should aim at 1st June 1948, as the effective date for the transfer of power'.[23]

'Plan Balkan'

Ismay, Miéville and an advance party of Mountbatten's staff left London's Northolt aerodrome on the morning of 19 March 1947, aboard the York aircraft MWI0I, which had been allotted to the king during the war. The viceroy-designate left next day in his trusty MWI02, with Edwina, their daughter Pamela, Ronnie Brockman and Peter Howes. They arrived in Delhi three days later, only two hours after the advance party, largely because Ismay had insisted on regular stops at civilized hours in Malta, Fayid in Egypt, and Karachi. Mountbatten, of course, was in too much of a hurry to bother with such niceties.

Both parties were met at Palam airport by Auchinleck, who 'more than astonished' Ismay by appearing in a beret. 'Have you gone mad, Claude?' Ismay blurted out. 'Where is your topee?' Ismay had been brought up, he says, 'in the belief that anyone who failed to wear a pith helmet while the Indian sun was still in the sky was a lunatic'. Auchinleck replied that 'on the contrary, we had all been mad for a hundred years or more to wear such an uncomfortable and unnecessary form of head-gear'.[1] Auchinleck's beret may have seemed a small thing, but it was somehow symbolic of the radical changes that the British needed to make in their thinking on India. To his credit, Ismay was quick to adapt to the new climate, and to appreciate the enormous developments since he had last been there, not least the scale of communal bitterness, which came as a great shock.

Auchinleck had changed his beret for a regular service cap when he returned to the airport to greet Mountbatten. Nehru and Liaquat Ali Khan joined him in the reception committee; Nehru in a white Gandhi cap and long *sherwani* coat, Liaquat in a grey Persian lamb Jinnah cap above a European lightweight suit, both thereby making their positions clear from the outset. The Mountbattens were driven through the wide, dusty avenues of New Delhi in an open landau, escorted by the governor-general's bodyguard of cavalry in full dress, to the Viceroy's House where Lord and Lady Wavell were waiting on the red-carpeted steps to greet them. Mountbatten always liked to claim that this was a unique break with tradition and that no incoming viceroy had ever met his predecessor on Indian soil. This was romantic nonsense, of course – Wavell himself had spent more time with Linlithgow in 1943 than he now did with Mountbatten. In any case, however, the two men were closeted together from 4.30 p.m. till 7.00, discussing the Indian political situation. The main problem, they agreed, was that the Indian politicians did not seem to appreciate just how little time there was to arrange the whole transfer of power before June 1948. They questioned whether the Cabinet mission plan allowed for Punjab and Bengal to be partitioned.

Mountbatten said he thought there had to be some strong authority to which power could be handed over, and that any solution must be based on the Indian army.[2] He then explained his plans to make 'a political gesture' by reducing the sentences of the 15 INA men who were still in gaol. He also proposed to write that very day to Gandhi and Jinnah, inviting them to come and see him – 'One more viceroy, I suppose,' Wavell noted sadly, 'who hopes to reconcile these intractable personalities.' He spoke, too, of his hope of 'getting India to accept some form of Dominion status', something that would have been welcomed 30 years earlier but which seemed deader than the dodo in 1947, when Nehru had already declared his aim to be 'a sovereign and independent republic'.[3]

Queenie Wavell and Edwina, meanwhile, discussed more practical matters – the problems of running the Viceroy's House. The task facing the new vicereine was formidable. The place was enormous, with 340 rooms and one and a half miles of corridors. So, too, was the staff – there were some 7,000 on the viceregal estate – although they seemed to have done nothing in the house since the start of the war. Once, Lutyens's masterpiece had epitomized the splendour of the Raj at its height, but after seven years of neglect it had begun to look down at heel. Behind the grand doors of many of the once magnificent reception rooms, with their handles in the shape of a lion couchant wearing the imperial crown, lay dust and cobwebs and fading grandeur. Like much of official India, everything was in need of a good spring clean and a fresh coat of paint.

After seeing the Wavells off at the airport at 8.15 a.m. on Sunday 23 March, the Mountbattens prepared for the swearing-in ceremony next day. This was held in the Durbar Hall, a vast, domed, circular room in which two oversized gilded thrones upholstered in crimson velvet, stood side by side before a 30-foot high canopy, also in deep crimson velvet, from which strategically-placed lights illuminated the thrones. The room was packed with the great and the good. On either side of the thrones sat the new Indian leaders, including both Nehru and Liaquat but not Gandhi or Jinnah – Gandhi was tramping the dusty tracks of Bihar, trying to bestow peace upon that troubled province, while Jinnah was in Bombay, recuperating from his latest bout of illness.

Also missing were two of the most prominent Indian princes, the Nawab of Bhopal and the Maharaja of Bikaner, whose seats were whisked away at the last minute to avoid the embarrassment of empty chairs.[4] These were Mountbatten's oldest personal friends in India, and their absence was an indication of the depth of the split in the ranks of the princes over support for the constituent assembly and all that it meant for their future: Bhopal and Bikaner were on opposite sides, and refused to sit together at the ceremony, even if it implied a discourtesy to the new viceroy.

The ceremony began with a deafening fanfare of trumpets, as a procession of ADC's led the Mountbattens to their thrones on the marble dais. Looking as slim and handsome as any film star in his white naval uniform, Mountbatten glittered with medals and orders. He wore the dark blue sash of a knight of the Garter, no fewer than three grand crosses, the KCB and the DSO, plus his campaign medals and the golden aiguillette of an ADC to the king-emperor. Around his neck, he wore the 'Viceroy's Heirloom', an enormous diamond passed to him the night before by Wavell. Beside him, Edwina looked positively unostentatious in a dress of ivory brocade on which she wore her own war medals and other decorations, plus her new order of the Crown of India.

The whole ceremony took about 15 minutes. The lord chief justice of India, Sir Patrick Spens, administered the oath, then Mountbatten made a four-minute speech, drafted for him by George Abell. He reiterated the British determination to leave India by June 1948, stressed the urgency of finding a solution to the constitutional problems, and promised to give the Indian leaders all the help he could in doing so. He appealed to everyone to do their best to avoid exacerbating the communal bitterness, and begged for 'the greatest goodwill of the greatest possible number' in his difficult task.[5] It was the closest he could get to the king's speech from the throne, and it was another break with tradition – no other viceroy had ever had the nerve, or felt the need, to say anything at the swearing-in ceremony. And there was yet another new feature: for the first time, the scene was filmed and photographed for posterity, for the eyes and ears of the world, and it was to them that Mountbatten was speaking. Unfortunately, the effect was marred by the abominable acoustics – hardly anyone could hear a word he said.[6]

That same afternoon, the new viceroy began the business of getting to know the Indian leaders and charming them into trusting him. Over the next six weeks, he was to hold 133 personal interviews, each following much the same pattern. He aimed to disarm his visitors by talking to them alone in his study, sitting informally in comfortable armchairs with no secretary taking notes, a practice he continued throughout his time in India. Immediately after each meeting ended, he would call in a secretary and dictate a résumé of what had been said – he claimed to have a 'photographic memory' giving him perfect recall, but inevitably what he dictated was his own version of what had taken place. The overwhelming impression given by his accounts of meetings, and equally by his reports back to London, is of the incessant use of the pronoun 'I'.

The first meeting was with Nehru, whom Mountbatten already knew and liked: he could identify with the old-Harrovian Brahman's easy manners, patrician self-confidence and socialist ideals. Nehru, according to Mountbatten, was 'in expansive mood', and their talk lasted three hours, covering all that had happened since the Cabinet mission. Once Nehru had been put at his ease, Mountbatten asked him what he thought of Jinnah, encouraging him to denigrate his opponent. Nehru obliged with a vitriolic piece of character assassination. Jinnah, he said, was a man to whom success had come very late in life, at over 60: before that, he had not been a major figure in Indian politics – an assertion that ignored the fact that as early as the First World War Jinnah had been one of the great white hopes of both Congress and the League. He was, Nehru said dismissively, a successful lawyer but not a very good one. He had succeeded politically only by taking up a permanently negative attitude, because he knew that Pakistan could never stand up to constructive criticism.[7]

The talk ranged over most of the other issues of the day before the time came for Nehru to leave. In parting, Mountbatten told him: 'Mr Nehru, I want you to regard me not as the last viceroy winding up the British Raj, but as the first to lead the way to the new India.' Nehru turned and smiled. 'Now I know what they mean,' he said, 'when they speak of your charm being so dangerous.' Mountbatten recounted Nehru's riposte rather proudly next morning to the inner circle of his staff at the first of their regular daily meetings: each day he would describe to them in dramatic detail all that had happened the day before, and float ideas for future action and discussion.

When asked what was the biggest single problem facing India at that time, Nehru had said it was the economy, and blamed the League for sabotaging any economic planning from the centre. Since Mountbatten's next appointment was with Liaquat, he was able to get the other side of the story at once. He spent two hours with him, but although Liaquat was also an aristocrat and an Oxford graduate, he did not have the same quicksilver brain and open personality as Nehru, and there was no immediate rapport. Liaquat at that time was in the middle of a crisis over his first budget as finance minister. It was an honest and carefully thought-out attempt to tackle India's immense economic problems: while giving money back to the lower levels of society by abolishing the Salt Tax and raising the minimum exemption levels for income tax, Liaquat had created a furore by imposing new taxes on the rich. The most important of these were a graduated tax on capital gains, new measures to combat tax evasion, and a 25 per cent tax on business profits over 100,000 rupees, to replace the now defunct wartime excess profits tax.

Liaquat's proposals had been approved unanimously by the Indian Cabinet, as the Executive Council was now generally known. They had also been received with great enthusiasm by the Central Legislative Assembly as 'India's first national budget' and 'the poor man's budget'. Unfortunately, they were greeted with howls of protest by Indian big businessmen – who happened to be mostly Hindu and who were also Congress's financial backers. Suddenly, the right-wing Congress ministers, led by Patel and Rajagopalachari, began furiously attacking Liaquat and his budget, not as anti-Congress, but as anti-Hindu. It was a sharp lesson for Mountbatten on how deeply communal divisions were affecting every aspect of Indian life. Eventually, Liaquat was forced to compromise, and reduce the profits tax to 16.6 per cent, if only because the League could not afford to offend its wealthy supporters either – some things at least were common to both sides.

By the end of March, Mountbatten had held individual interviews with every member of the Indian Cabinet. He had also established a pattern of entertaining which was designed to bring him into contact with a much wider range of Indian opinion. He started on 28 March 1947 with a garden party for delegates to the Asian Relations Conference which had been held in Delhi during the week, plus all the members of the Central Legislative Assembly and senior officials; some 700 guests in all. From then on, he held two garden parties and several lunch and dinner parties every week, allowing literally thousands of Indians to see the splendours of the Viceroy's House for themselves.

It was all brilliant public relations, calculated to create the maximum amount of goodwill among the maximum number of middle- or upper-class Indians – especially when coupled with Mountbatten's stock response to admiring comments: 'It's all yours – we are only trustees. We have come to make it over to you.' No former viceroy had ever wooed the Indian people so assiduously. But then, Mountbatten's viceroyalty was unique: he had been sent not to rule India, but to give it back to the Indians.

Nevertheless, Mountbatten had still not met the two men who counted most for his mission: Gandhi was still on walk-about in Bihar, while Jinnah was trying to regain his strength in Bombay. Gandhi arrived first, at 3.00 p.m. on Monday, 31 March, providing an historic photo session for 'every accredited cameraman in the sub-continent' whom Campbell-Johnson had assembled in the Mughal gardens outside the viceroy's study.[8] As usual, Gandhi performed 'with great good humour', putting himself out to be co-operative. But it was at the very end that Max Desfor, the brilliant Associated Press photographer, caught the image that was to last, when Gandhi, turning to re-enter the study, put his hand on Edwina's shoulder to steady himself. It was a gesture of trust and friendship – carefully calculated, of course, for Gandhi was acutely aware of the symbolic importance of his every move – and it spoke volumes to the rest of India, and the world.

The talks lasted two and a half hours, and were little more than a getting-to-know-you session. Edwina was present for the first 75 minutes. When Gandhi was invited to vet the press communiqué at the end, he shrewdly said he would be happy to leave the wording to the viceroy. Obviously, if it was not to his liking, he could later repudiate it, but meanwhile he opted for a gesture of trust.

There were more talks next day, again lasting two and a quarter hours and again with Gandhi in his role as loquacious old buffer. Only 15 minutes were devoted to business, when Gandhi presented his solution to the whole communal problem in government. He suggested that Mountbatten should dismiss the existing Cabinet and call on Jinnah to form a new one, with total freedom to appoint whomever he chose – they might be all Muslims, all non-Muslims, or whatever. Congress would guarantee full co-operation, so long as all the measures the new government put forward were 'in the interests of the Indian people as a whole' – and the sole judge of this would be Mountbatten 'in his personal capacity'. Jinnah, for his part, should undertake to do everything possible to preserve peace, and the Muslim National Guards and all other private armies should be abolished. Within those limits, Jinnah would be free to do whatever he liked, including planning for Pakistan and even putting those plans into operation, as long as he did not use force. The sting came at the end: if Jinnah refused, the same offer should be made to Congress.[9]

This startling suggestion was nothing new, of course – Gandhi had made it at least twice before, the last time to the Cabinet mission. One of the older hands on Mountbatten's staff later dismissed it as 'an old kite flown without disguise',[10] but Mountbatten was hearing it for the first time and he was both astonished and intrigued. He asked Gandhi what he thought Jinnah's reaction would be. 'Jinnah will say, "Ah, it is the wily Gandhi again"' the Mahatma replied. 'And won't he be right?' Mountbatten asked with a smile. 'No,' said Gandhi, 'I am being absolutely sincere.' He went on to say that the British must face the consequences of their historic policy of divide and rule, which 'had created a situation in which the only alternatives were a continuation of British rule to keep law and order or an Indian blood-bath. The blood-bath must be faced and accepted.'[11]

For the first time, Mountbatten had been brought face to face with Gandhi's ruthless idealism. This was putting principle above practicality with a vengeance. Nevertheless, he told Gandhi he found his suggestion of inviting Jinnah to govern 'attractive', and promised to consider it sympathetically if Congress agreed to it. He was probably just being polite, but if so his politeness backfired on him, for Gandhi took his interest as an invitation to draw up a detailed plan, and pursued it relentlessly for several days, during which he met Ismay twice to discuss detailed drafting. It was not until Nehru and the Congress Working Committee told him bluntly on 11 April that his plan was unacceptable that he reluctantly gave up – and even then he told Mountbatten that if he believed in the plan he could go ahead without him.

The following day, however, Gandhi returned to the attack from a different angle, but one which, as H.V. Hodson put it, 'perhaps revealed his mind more frankly'.[12] Now, he suggested that the viceroy should strengthen the existing interim government, make it govern properly over the next 14 months, then simply hand power over to it. This, as Mountbatten and Ismay spotted at once, would mean handing over power to Congress, to the disadvantage of the League, which would cause strife and possibly civil war. But Gandhi had an answer to that up his sleeve: he and Jinnah were just about to sign a joint appeal for a truce between Hindus and Muslims, which Mountbatten had been urging on them for several days. The document included a call for all sides to avoid any spoken or written incitement to violence and disorder, or any provocation of communal hatred. Once Jinnah had signed that, Gandhi argued, he could not use force for political purposes. 'I was speechless to find,' Mountbatten recorded, 'that he proposed . . . to take advantage of this to impose a Congress Government over the Muslims. Here again, I find it hard to believe that I correctly understood Mr Gandhi.'[13] The truth was that he was just beginning to understand him, and was finding what he understood hard to swallow.

Mountbatten still considered Gandhi to be 'a figure of the first importance', and that it was imperative not to alienate him. He quickly realized, however, that this was not a practical politician with whom he could reach pragmatic agreements: Gandhi's role was increasingly that of a figurehead or an oracle. In fact, he had already been sidelined by the Congress high command, most notably Nehru and Patel. They had not even told him, never mind consulted him, about the Working Committee's resolutions calling for the partition of the Punjab and Bengal. And they had certainly not involved him in their decision to remove the problem of the Muslim League by accepting the principle of Pakistan.

Gandhi told the journalist, Durga Das, that: 'His followers had let him down badly. Now that power was within their grasp, they seemed to have no further use for him.' He even fondly recalled the memory of Subhas Chandra Bose, who had once been such a thorn in his flesh. At least, he said, Bose had shown in his organization of the INA how Hindus and Muslims could work together in a great cause. Echoing what he had said to both Wavell and Mountbatten, he was adamant that 'he would rather have a blood-bath in a united India after the British quit than agree to partition on a communal basis and give rise to two armed camps, perpetually in conflict'.[14]

Later, when Das spoke to Patel, the Sardar dismissed Gandhi's views almost contemptuously, blaming him for what had happened. After all, he argued, it was he who had invoked the bogey of self-determination for the Muslims and, by holding talks with him in 1944, had made 'a hero of Jinnah in Muslim eyes'. To Das, such comments confirmed Gandhi's earlier complaint that Patel and Rajendra Prasad had ceased to be his yes-men. Patel clearly believed that Gandhi trusted only 'Jawaharlal to bring about Hindu-Muslim unity' – and he resented it. He described Nehru as 'the only nationalist Muslim today' – a phrase he had recently coined and which he used at every possible opportunity. Nehru, he declared, had always leaned on someone: first it was Gandhi, now it was Mountbatten. As for the other Congress leaders, Patel thought them confused and wrong-headed. Azad, he said, was concerned only about the Muslims. Ominously, Patel wanted to save India from the chaos that would ensue from what he saw as 'Anglo-Muslim moves' to weaken central authority. He was counting on 'Hindus and Sikhs and patriotic Civil Servants and Princes to support him'.[15]

While Gandhi was busily preparing his plan, Mountbatten had been forging ahead on several other fronts. On I April, he tackled one of the most sensitive outstanding issues, the vexed question of the INA prisoners. He called a meeting that afternoon with Nehru, Liaquat, Baldev Singh and Auchinleck, in the hope of sorting something out. Auchinleck – 'more difficult to deal with than I can remember at any time since October 1943' as Mountbatten noted – was threatening to resign if the men's sentences were commuted. They had been found guilty, he reminded everyone, not of political offences against the British but of acts of brutality and even murder against their fellow Indian soldiers. If discipline was to be maintained in the army, they must serve their full terms.

Since there were both Hindus and Muslims among the INA men, Liaquat and Nehru found themselves on the same side for once. They both appreciated the problem, but neither could afford to be seen as siding with the British against men whom many Indians regarded as patriots and freedom fighters. It was a tense and difficult three-hour meeting, but eventually Auchinleck was prevailed upon to accept – and even to write out in his own hand – a formula in which the Federal Court would consider and advise upon each individual case, thus removing all responsibility from both politicians and the army and placing it in the hands of the judiciary. It was a great relief to everyone, not least Nehru, who had been worried lest Auchinleck, whom he liked and respected greatly, be replaced by Field Marshal Slim, who was said to be significantly pro-Muslim. Far more seriously for everyone, if the C-in-C had resigned, most of the senior officers in the armed forces would have followed him.

Nehru shepherded the formula through the Legislative Assembly next day, successfully fighting off a resolution calling for the immediate release of the prisoners. For Mountbatten, this was encouraging proof of Nehru's steadfastness. But he was quick to claim the credit for himself. Cock-a-hoop at his first success at mediation, he wrote to his daughter Patricia of his 'unbelievable triumph' – and put the agreed formula into action before anyone could change their mind.

Jinnah first met Mountbatten shortly before noon on Saturday 5 April. It was an altogether more formal occasion than the viceroy's first meeting with Gandhi at the beginning of the week, and there were fewer photographers present – largely due to Jinnah's notorious reserve and his refusal to go out of his way to woo the foreign press. During the photo session, he was placed between the two Mountbattens, but still made a quip about 'A rose between two thorns'. Mountbatten saw this as a piece of pre-prepared gallantry gone wrong, with Edwina, whom Jinnah expected to stand between himself and her husband, as the rose. But with Jinnah, one can never be sure. Movie film of the occasion shows Jinnah smiling and chatting easily, but Mountbatten was obviously put out that the Quaid-i-Azam seemed impervious to his famous charm, and he found the meeting itself hard work. 'My God, he was cold,' he told Campbell-Johnson afterwards. 'It took most of the interview to unfreeze him.'

Following his usual custom, Mountbatten refused to discuss serious business at their first meeting, saying he needed to get to know Jinnah personally. Jinnah was a little put out by this, but was eventually persuaded into telling the story of the League and his own part in reviving it. He also succumbed to Mountbatten's technique of encouraging his visitors to talk freely about their opponents, so that he could show sympathy for their views and seem like a friend. Jinnah was not, of course, as indiscreet or as outspoken as Nehru, who was a born gossip, but he did supply a sharp analysis of the divisions within Congress that made it impossible for any of its leaders to speak for Congress as a whole. This applied especially to Gandhi who represented nobody, had enormous responsibility but no authority, and whose word was therefore worthless. Jinnah contrasted this with the League, where there was only one man to deal with – himself. If the League refused to ratify any decision he made, he said, he would resign and that would be the end of the League.[16]

Mountbatten invited Jinnah and his sister to dinner the following evening. Edwina tried her own brand of Mountbatten charm, but was equally unsuccessful in 'unfreezing' Fatima Jinnah, who proved to be as austere as her brother. 'Fascinating evening,' Edwina wrote in her diary that night. 'Two very clever and queer people. I rather liked them but found them both fanatical on their Pakistan and quite impracticable [sic].'[17] The Jinnahs must have enjoyed the dinner, however, for they stayed until well after midnight, by which time, according to Mountbatten, 'the ice was really broken'. Jinnah spent some time describing the horrors of the Muslim massacres in Bihar and elsewhere, and said a quick decision was needed. He insisted there was only one way of preventing India from perishing altogether, and that was 'a surgical operation'. Mountbatten said he had not yet made up his mind, but reminded him that 'an anaesthetic was needed before an operation'.[18]

From 5 to 10 April, Mountbatten met Jinnah every day, but failed utterly to make him shift his position. Jinnah simply refused point blank to accept the Cabinet mission plan, or to enter the constituent assembly. He dismissed Mountbatten's warning that Britain might not accept Pakistan into the Commonwealth by informing him that legally Britain did not have that choice – Pakistan would automatically be a member, and Britain would find it difficult if not impossible to expel her.

When Mountbatten made the point that all the arguments in favour of the partition of India applied equally to the Punjab and Bengal, and would have to be applied to them, so that half of each would go to India, Jinnah professed himself most upset at the idea of being fobbed off with 'a moth-eaten Pakistan'. But his distress was purely tactical. He was, as always, way ahead of Mountbatten: a whole year earlier, the League Planning Committee had considered the implications of 'a smaller but sovereign Pakistan State' and concluded that it would still be viable without the non-Muslim districts of east Punjab and west Bengal. By the end of the final three-hour session on 10 April, Mountbatten, baffled and frustrated, was forced to admit defeat. Jinnah, he said, was a 'psychopathic case', and 'impossible to argue with'.[19]

That night, Mountbatten saw Liaquat, whom he found easier to deal with than Jinnah, and tried to make him see the light. He should have known it was hopeless, for Liaquat had told him a week earlier: 'If Your Excellency was prepared to let the Muslim League have only the Sind Desert, I would still prefer to accept that and have a separate Muslim State in those conditions than to continue in bondage to the Congress with apparently more generous conditions.'[20] Now, Mountbatten told Liaquat the way his mind was working.

I started off with Pakistan and complete partition of the Punjab and Bengal and Assam. I told him that I had no doubt that the Indian leaders and their peoples were in such an hysterical condition that they would all gladly agree to my arranging their suicide in this way. He nodded his head and said 'I am afraid everybody will agree to such a plan; we are all in such a state.' I told him that the worst service I could do to India, if I were her enemy or completely indifferent to her fate, would be to take advantage of this extraordinary mental condition to force the completest partition possible upon them, before going off in June 1948 and leaving the whole country in the most hopeless chaos.[21]

What Mountbatten still did not seem to realize was that 'the completest partition possible' was exactly what all the Muslim leaders, not just Jinnah, wanted.

It had been clear to Jinnah and Liaquat since 8 April that Pakistan was in the bag, and that it would come sooner rather than later. All that remained to be settled were the details. Perhaps the most urgent and important of them all was the question of the Indian armed forces, for it was essential to any state's independence that it should have its own army, navy and air force. There could be no doubt that dividing the Indian armed forces would be an incredibly difficult piece of surgery, and that planning needed to start immediately. Liaquat wrote to the viceroy on 8 April suggesting that the forces should be reorganized so that they could be more easily divided when partition came. The British reaction at all levels was one of horror. Ismay advised Mountbatten that the Cabinet mission plan envisaged one national army, and that there could be no division until the government in London abandoned the plan. Mountbatten agreed. There would be no splitting of the Indian army before the withdrawal of the British, he said, for two reasons: 'The mechanics won't permit it, and I won't.'[22] In the event, neither proved to be true.

Auchinleck, who had devoted his life to the Indian army, was opposed to any suggestion that this magnificent machine, built up over two centuries, should be dismantled. Although Liaquat had asked only that a plan should be prepared, the C-in-C first said it was impossible to divide the army into two self-contained forces, then that it would take several years and could only be done in stages. He refused to allow the proposition to be discussed, even in Cabinet or the Defence Council, for fear of leaks and the effect they would have on the morale of the men. Baldev Singh, as defence minister, agreed, warning of the dangers as he saw them:

> Respect for law and order is rapidly waning. In certain parts, large sections of the population have lost confidence in the ability of the police to protect life and property. The only relieving feature in this dark picture is that the integrity of the Armed Forces is still unsullied ... It would indeed be an irreparable disaster if a Force such as this was exposed to risks that would not only weaken but ultimately destroy its worth.[23]

In fact, a plan already existed for reorganizing the army on communal lines — it had been prepared for Wavell, as part of his evacuation scheme. It showed that such a division was perfectly feasible, but would take at least a year, during which time the units affected would be out of action. This meant, of course, that they would not be available for peace-keeping or security duties, an alarming prospect with the eruption of communal violence in the Punjab and the

NWFP, not to mention Bihar, Calcutta, Bombay, the UP, and even Delhi. Jenkins reported that if partition was imposed on the Punjab by force rather than by agreement between the main parties, he would need at least four divisions of troops to keep order.

For the whole of April, Mountbatten and his team struggled to find ways of making the Cabinet mission plan work. At first, Mountbatten toyed with the idea of granting dominion status immediately, either to an Indian union, or to three dominions – India, Pakistan and the Indian States – linked by a common centre and with himself as a 'constitutional viceroy'. But he quickly dropped this idea when Ismay and Miéville pointed out that as soon as he did so, he would cease to have any personal power or any control over the armed forces.

On 8 April, Nehru told Mountbatten that he thought all provinces, including partitioned ones, 'should have the right to decide whether to join a Hindustan Group, a Pakistan Group, or possibly to remain completely independent'. This was a radical change for Congress, but it still depended on there being a strong centre responsible for common subjects such as defence. Mountbatten seized on Nehru's suggestion as one way of keeping some sort of union, and asked Ismay to begin drawing up a new plan based on it – though he omitted to mention Nehru's insistence on a strong centre. For the next few days, Ismay beavered away at producing the 'bare bones' of what everyone referred to as 'Plan Balkan', to distinguish it from 'Plan Union'. On 11 April, Mountbatten told him to send it to V.P. Menon, asking Menon to put flesh on the bones.

Menon did not like what he was presented with. It was very different from the plan he and Patel had agreed, and he believed the absence of a strong central government was an invitation to anarchy. But when his objections were dismissed he set to and did as he was asked, like the good civil servant he was. Plan Balkan did not mention Pakistan as such, but allowed for power to be demitted to the provinces or sub-provinces, which would be free to join together in groups; the states could join the groups if they wished; the interim government would remain until June 1948; Muslim and non-Muslim members of the assemblies in the Punjab and Bengal would vote separately on partition of their provinces, which would take place if both sections voted for it; the predominantly Muslim district of Sylhet in Assam could choose to join the Muslim part of Bengal; and there would be fresh elections in the NWFP to enable its people to decide for themselves where they wanted to go. The idea was to allow the Indian people to make their own decisions on partition, so that Britain could not be blamed if things went wrong.

Menon's fleshed-out draft was ready on 14 April, and was presented next day to a conference of all the provincial governors in the Viceroy's House. The governors gave it their general approval, though Jenkins thought the communities in the Punjab, especially the central part, were so closely interwoven that any attempt to divide them would be disastrous for everybody. Sir Frederick Burrows, the governor of Bengal, was ill and unable to attend, but his secretary, J.F. Tyson, spoke for him. He was against the partition of the province, maintaining that east Bengal, cut off from Calcutta on which it depended for the processing, marketing and exportation of its jute, which was virtually its only product, would become a vast rural slum. He said many Bengali Muslims were against partition – a statement that was borne out soon afterwards when Suhrawardy began pressing for Bangladesh, an undivided and independent Bengal with its own dominion status alongside India and Pakistan. The prospect was welcomed by Jinnah but denounced by Nehru and Patel, who feared that an independent Bangladesh, with a Muslim premier, would inevitably line up with Pakistan rather than India.

The discussions he had had with the various governors, especially those whose provinces were worst affected by communal strife, were enough to convince Mountbatten that speed was essential. As soon as the conference was over, he wrote to Pethick-Lawrence, telling him that a decision had to be made very soon, 'if we are to avert a civil war and the risk of a complete breakdown of the administration'. He said he expected to have a plan prepared within the next 10 days, and would send Ismay home with it by the end of the month for approval by the Cabinet. He planned to present the plan to a conference of all the Indian leaders at Simla on 15 May.[24]

While Plan Balkan was being prepared, with a new draft every day, Mountbatten was pursuing Britain's need to keep India in the Commonwealth. He started on Baldev Singh after he had spoken to Nehru on 8 April, pointing out that if India left, no British officers would be able to stay on in the Indian army – a line that had probably been suggested to him by Major 'Billy' Short, Cripps's expert on the Punjab and the Sikhs. During the visit to London with Wavell the previous December, Baldev Singh had told Short he was anxious to keep the British connection with the army going for as long as possible, maybe for ever, with British officers remaining in their posts, or acting as advisers. Now, he told Mountbatten that he had already proposed that India should remain in the Commonwealth for the sake of defence, even if it meant postponing the declaration of an independent sovereign republic for 10 years. Mountbatten hinted that the British government was not keen on keeping India, and asked Baldev to persuade the other minority representatives in the government – Matthai for the Indian Christians, Jagjivan Ram for the Scheduled Castes, and C.H. Bhabha for the Parsis – to join him in pressing Congress to stay in the Commonwealth.

Baldev, according to Mountbatten, was 'quite thrilled at the prospect of playing an important part',[25] and went to work with a will. He returned a week later, reporting good progress: Bhabha was enthusiastic, and even Nehru had said he was 'very interested', though he wanted 'at least another month or six weeks to think it over'.[26] But Baldev was painting an over-optimistic picture. Nehru may have expressed interest, but he had also told him that he was not bothered about the defence issue: if all the British officers left, he said, it would encourage the Indians to be more self-reliant. In any case, leaving the Commonwealth would release India from the dangers posed by association with British power politics: India standing alone would be under no threat from any major foreign power. If the British officers were to leave, he said, 'I shall accept that without losing a night's sleep.'[27]

Baldev was not the only one trying to persuade Nehru of the benefits of remaining in the Commonwealth: Rajagopalachari, backed by senior Indian officers, held that full Indianization of the army must be spread over a five-year period. But Nehru was not to be moved from his dream by such pragmatic concerns. 'Under no conceivable circumstances is India going to remain in the Commonwealth, whatever the consequences,' he wrote to Baldev on 14 April. 'Any attempt to remain in the Commonwealth will sweep away those who propose it and might bring about major trouble in India.'[28] Mountbatten urged Baldev to go on lobbying, suggesting that he could use as a 'very strong lever' on Congress the fact that Jinnah was not merely willing but insistent that Pakistan should be a member. It was something he was using himself at every opportunity, along with the tactical untruth that the British government did not want to keep India in the Commonwealth, and needed to be persuaded to do so.

Mountbatten used those same arguments on Krishna Menon, Nehru's close friend and regular channel to Cripps. He had returned to India and was staying in Delhi, Mountbatten noted, 'specially in the hope of being of use to me ... to help to give me the background of what was going on in Congress circles, and to help me to put over any points that I found too delicate to handle directly myself.'[29] Mountbatten told him that if Congress insisted on staying out of the Commonwealth, India would be left with 'a rotten army', while Britain and the other members would be relieved at not having the worry and expense of defending India from Russia.

When Mountbatten pressed Krishna to get Congress to make the first move, Krishna suggested that there was another way: 'If the British were voluntarily to give us now Dominion Status, well ahead of June 1948, we should be so grateful that not a voice would be heard in June 1948 suggesting any change, except possibly in the word dominion if that had been actually used up to that date.' Mountbatten told him that if the Muslims had been prepared to stay in a Union of India, he 'would certainly recommend Dominion Status next month', but he could not give it to the interim government, where they were in a permanent minority. Krishna then came up with the idea of giving immediate dominion status to both India and Pakistan, with the states free to join either. Mountbatten leapt at the idea, provided he could be joint governor-general with full powers over defence, 'since I would have to co-ordinate the use of the single army for both Indian dominions'.[30] He sent Krishna away to think about it, and to work on Nehru.

Next day, Mountbatten told his staff that following his meeting with Krishna Menon he had 'the germ of a new plan' in his mind. He discussed it with them over the following few days, and asked his joint private secretary, John Christie, whom Ismay had brought into the team working on Plan Balkan, to prepare a document setting out the details, seeing it not as an alternative to Plan Balkan, but as a corollary to it. In fact, much of the work had already been done, because, as Ismay pointed out, Mountbatten's 'new plan' was based on 'what we generally refer to as "the V.P. Menon Plan"', which Mountbatten had seen in London.[31]

By 22 April, Mountbatten was able to report that the Muslim League, the Scheduled Castes, and some princely states, together representing about half the population of India, were asking to remain in the Commonwealth. The campaign was going well. When he met Krishna Menon again that day, he noted, 'we properly let our hair down together and discussed every aspect of the plan now being worked on'. In particular, Mountbatten hammered home the benefits that Pakistan would gain by remaining in the Commonwealth. Although he personally would not support keeping Pakistan in if India opted out, there was little he or even Britain could do about it. It would be up to all the other members of the Commonwealth to decide whether or not to expel Pakistan, which was unlikely. Pakistan would then be able to call on British officers for all services, send its own officers for training at British establishments and staff colleges, and receive secret military hardware and information. As a result, Pakistan's armed forces would soon be 'immensely superior to those of Hindustan', and she would also have a large Commonwealth naval base at Karachi.[32]

Mountbatten recorded that Krishna 'absolutely shuddered' at the prospect presented to him. The viceroy followed this up by stressing that none of it need happen, and outlined the latest state of the plan for two dominions, with himself as joint governor-general. Menon, according to Mountbatten, was 'rather smitten with this idea', but said Congress, and Nehru and Patel in particular, were committed to leaving the empire. Then, with machiavellian guile, he lamented that Nehru had been 'overworking to the point of breakdown', and suggested Mountbatten might take him away for two or three days' holiday, to somewhere restful where they could get to know each other. 'For,' he said, 'between you, you can solve all the problems of India.'[33]

Throughout April, the smell of blood hung over much of northern India. Bombay,

Benares and Calcutta were placed under dusk-to-dawn curfew, though the violence in each was mercifully sporadic. The worst disturbances were in the NWFP and its neighbour, the Punjab, where by mid-April the death toll after a month of havoc had reached 3,500. Jenkins complained of the 'extreme complacency' of the League leaders, 'who say in effect that "boys will be boys". Every British official in the ICS and IP [Indian Police] in the Punjab, myself included, would be very glad to leave it tomorrow,' he continued. 'We now feel that we are dealing with people who are out to destroy themselves.'[34]

In the NWFP, Congress Muslims and League Muslims were at each other's throats. The Khan brothers, Abdul Ghaffar Khan and the prime minister Dr Khan Sahib, were clinging to power against increasing agitation, and had thrown 5,000 of their opponents into prison. Their relationship with the governor, Sir Olaf Caroe, had also reached rock-bottom. Clamouring for his removal, they accused Caroe of being biased in favour of the League, and even of having conspired to have Nehru murdered during his visit the previous October. Mountbatten discussed the situation with Caroe during the governors' conference, and two days later called Dr Khan Sahib to Delhi for a meeting with himself, the governor and Nehru. It was agreed that there would not be a new election – which would almost certainly vote the League into power – but there might be a plebiscite for the people to decide whether to join India or Pakistan. Meanwhile, in keeping with the Jinnah-Gandhi appeal for peace, all political prisoners not convicted for violence would be released, and the ban on public meetings lifted. Mountbatten reported to London that Sir Olaf was straightforward, impartial and statesmanlike, but was 'suffering badly from nerves' – he was clearing the ground for Sir Olaf's removal.

The grand gesture of releasing the prisoners was spoiled when most of them refused to leave the gaols unless an election was called or the Congress ministry resigned. There was a new wave of unrest, with trains being attacked and the frontier tribes rising in open rebellion. With the position seeming critical, Mountbatten decided to visit the NWFP for himself. It was his first visit to a province since his arrival, and it proved to be a dramatic one.

Mountbatten flew into Peshawar on the morning of Monday 28 April, with Edwina and their daughter Pamela in the party. A vast crowd of between 50,000 and 100,000 Pathans, all supporting the League, had converged on the state capital from all over the frontier. Unfortunately, they had gathered in the largest open space available – which happened to be the airfield, so before the Mountbattens' York could land, the governor had to get them to move. They settled in Cunningham Park, between the fort and the railway embankment, only a few hundred yards from Government House. The previous night, some of them had actually invaded the governor's garden, and a shot had been fired through a window – frontier tribesmen all carried long rifles everywhere.

The tribesmen were still making a great deal of noise when the Mountbattens arrived, and were preparing to march on the house to present their grievances to the viceroy. If things got out of hand and they decided to attack *en masse*, there would be absolutely nothing the police could do to stop them. The only solution, though a risky one, was for the viceroy to go to them. Mountbatten agreed, and Edwina insisted on accompanying him. Hand-in-hand, they climbed the railway embankment and looked down on the great crowd thronging the park and stretching away into the distance. 'There was much gesticulation,' wrote Alan Campbell-Johnson, who was with Mountbatten, 'and the waving of innumerable but illegal green flags with the white crescent of Pakistan, accompanied by a steady chant of "*Pakistan Zindabad*".'[35] Caroe picks up the tale:

> The Viceroy, not resplendent in stars and orders, but a fine figure as always, wearing a green bush-shirt of Burma provenance – there were not wanting those who noted that this was the right colour for a *Haji* [one who has made the pilgrimage to Mecca] – brought his hand to the salute and stood facing the crowd. The moment was dramatic, the gesture superb. The atmosphere changed. Cries of *Pakistan Zindabad* died away, and I heard more than one voice of admiration.[36]

Mountbatten was not able to speak to the crowd, but he and Edwina stood for half an hour, waving and smiling. The situation had been defused, and the tribesmen later dispersed peacefully. Mountbatten went back to Government House and held meetings with local leaders from both sides – the League members demanded to be taken from gaol under armed escort, but were refused the gesture, since they were now voluntary prisoners. He told both sides they would have to trust him to see that they got fair play during the transfer of power. Next day, the viceregal party travelled to the Khyber to talk to tribal leaders, who told him they would rather come to terms with Afghanistan than be ruled by a Hindu raj.

That afternoon, the party flew the short hop to Rawalpindi in the Punjab, where Jenkins met them and escorted them on a tour of the nearby small town of Kahuta. This had recently been the scene of fierce rioting, during which Muslims had destroyed the homes and businesses of local Sikh traders. The devastation, 'as thorough as any produced by fire-bomb raids during the war' according to Campbell-Johnson,[37] brought home to Mountbatten something of the scale of the problem. After talking to more local leaders, he returned to Delhi, while Edwina stayed on in the Punjab to tour other riot-torn areas and try to organize some sort of relief operation, drawing on her wartime experience as superintendant-in-chief of the nursing division of the St. John Ambulance Brigade.

The visit to the NWFP had helped to take the edge off the violence there, at least for a while, though agitation and disturbances continued. But its most important effect was on Mountbatten and his close entourage. Campbell-Johnson spoke for his chief when he wrote: 'The whole visit has brought home to us the need for achieving wider agreement on India's future as quickly as possible. If we do not, there will be a complete disintegration of what remains of law and order both in the Frontier and the Punjab, not to speak of the other northern provinces. It is certainly a great dispensation that south and central India should be remaining so calm.'[38]

Back in Delhi, Mountbatten found that the seeds he had been planting so assiduously for Commonwealth membership were showing signs of germination. On I May, V.P. Menon confirmed to Miéville that Patel might accept an early grant of dominion status 'for the time being'. Miéville also reported that Nehru had invited Sir Walter Monckton, the eminent British lawyer then in India as legal adviser to the Nizam of Hyderabad, to dine with him on 3 May, to discuss 'some form of continued allegiance to the Crown'.[39] It all looked very promising.

While Mountbatten was away, the final version of Plan Balkan had been typed. Ismay was suffering with 'Delhi belly', so it was left to Miéville to show it to Jinnah and Nehru on 30 April. Jinnah, as always, refused to commit himself without further thought, but repeated his demands that the constitutional assembly be dismissed and power transferred at once to the existing provinces. That evening, however, he issued a press statement attacking the proposal to partition the Punjab and Bengal as an attempt to unnerve the Muslims by emphasizing that they were going to get 'a truncated or mutilated, moth-eaten Pakistan'. He demanded the full six provinces of NWFP, the Punjab, Bengal, Assam, Sind and Baluchistan.[40]

When Nehru read Plan Balkan, he raised only comparatively minor points – much of it, after all, followed his own suggestions. His biggest criticism was over the provision for fresh elections in the NWFP. Mountbatten was relieved to hear this, and was even more pleased when he received a letter from Nehru written the next day, telling him that the Congress Working Committee had accepted the principle of partition by self-determination.[41]

Ismay and Abell left for London on 2 May, taking the plan to the Cabinet. They also took the draft of the alternative plan, based on V.P. Menon's paper, with instructions that it was not to be shown to the India Committee unless they rejected the first plan. Mountbatten asked for Cabinet approval by IO May, so that he could present it to all the party leaders at Simla one week later.

'Thirteen Months Means Mischief to India'

Mountbatten had lived up to his reputation for speed – when Ismay and Abell left for London he had been in Delhi for two days short of six weeks, and in that time he believed he had found the answer to the problems that had stumped his predecessors for years. If all continued to go as planned, and both the government at home and the Indian leaders accepted his solution, he would have achieved his goal in less than two months. But, as always, charging ahead at full speed meant that some things got left behind in the rush – most notably a proper understanding of the complexities of the situation. Ismay had written to his wife while still preparing Plan Balkan: 'We have made almost innumerable alternative drafts ... but it is impossible to get Dickie to go through them methodically. He's a grand chap in a thousand ways, but clarity of thought and writing is not his strong suit.'[1] John Christie, while working on redrafting the V.P. Menon plan, commented that the atmosphere in which he was working was 'more Alice in Wonderlandish than one could believe'.[2]

In London, Ismay was faced with a new secretary of state for India. It had become clear that Pethick-Lawrence was now too old and too exhausted to complete the final lap, and on 26 April, Attlee brought on a younger substitute – the 40-year-old 5th Earl of Listowel, who had been under-secretary at the India Office from 1944 until the end of the war, and since then postmaster-general and deputy leader of the House of Lords. A Fabian Society socialist who had been interested in India for many years, Listowel was a long-time supporter of Congress. The change, however, made little if any difference to Ismay and Mountbatten, since Attlee and Cripps made all the policy decisions, anyway. Typically, Mountbatten later claimed that it was he who had suggested 'Billy' Listowel for the position.

Ismay was summoned to a meeting of the India Committee immediately he arrived in London, to present and explain the new plan. 'I emphasised that it was a case of "Hobson's Choice",' he wrote in his memoirs. 'No one in India thought it was perfect. Yet nearly everyone agreed that it was the only solution which had any chance of being accepted by all political parties, and of ensuring a fairly equitable deal for all minorities. It was not a gamble. There was no other way.'[3] Faced with such a definite statement, Attlee and his colleagues, though perturbed at the prospect of partition, felt they had no option but to approve the proposals. They felt, however, that some of the wording could be improved, and called in a Parliamentary draftsman to make the necessary revisions. The new version would be ready by the end of the week.

Ismay believed it would all be plain sailing from then on, and that he could afford to relax for a few days before returning to India. Back in Delhi, however, all was not so calm. The cracks in Mountbatten's hastily constructed edifice had started to appear even while his envoy was in the air *en route* for England. Jinnah's hostile reaction to the plan was swiftly followed by protests from the Congress Working Committee over what it saw as the appeasement of those who were employing 'brutal and terroristic methods' in the NWFP. Nehru had told the committee what was in the plan, in confidence, so that he could report their views to Mountbatten and thus 'avoid any misunderstanding at a later stage'. But someone on the committee leaked the information to the *Hindustan Times*, the paper owned by G.D. Birla and edited by Gandhi's son, Devadas. In a lead story it accused Mountbatten of dishonesty and 'not playing fair' and attacked the proposals to remove the Congress government in the NWFP and hold fresh elections there. A couple of days later a Congress report demanded the removal of Caroe.

Mountbatten tried to get round Congress by suggesting a referendum in the NWFP instead – which upset Jinnah. Jinnah demanded a public assurance that elections would follow the referendum – which was unacceptable to Nehru and Congress. And so the squabbling started all over again. Gandhi poured fuel on the fire once more by denouncing the idea of partition, repeating his call for power to be given at once to either a League or Congress government, and asking 'Was Pakistan to be seized by terrorism?' He followed this with what Christie described as the start of a 'sly Quit India campaign' by telling a Reuters correspondent: 'It would be a good thing if the British were to go today – 13 months means mischief to India.'[4]

Mountbatten was feeling the strain of 16 or 17 hours' work every day for six weeks, and even his apparently boundless energy was beginning to flag. He decided to follow his doctor's advice and take a short break, to prepare himself for the vital negotiations that were due to start in mid-May. He decided after the weekly Cabinet meeting on 6 May to go to Simla, where he hoped to spend three or four days of relative peace and quiet. There would be some business to be done, of course, for he had followed Krishna Menon's suggestion and invited Nehru along, but the main idea was for them both to relax and enjoy the cool mountain air. Mountbatten would travel light and take the minimum staff – though this turned out to be no fewer than 180 officers and servants. With Ismay and Abell in London, and Christie and a few others left to hold the fort in Delhi, Miéville and V.P. Menon accompanied him to Simla.

The inclusion of Menon in the party proved to be the turning-point in the whole saga. Menon was one of the most truly remarkable men in India. As reforms commissioner and constitutional adviser to the viceroy he was the highest-ranking Indian in government service, and yet he was not a member of the ICS, had no university degree or qualification, and had not even matriculated. Born in Malabar in 1889, the eldest of 12 children of a Jain farming family, he had left home at the age of 15 to earn his own living and send money home to the family after the death of his father. He taught himself to type, proved he was clever and good at figures, but his lack of a school certificate always counted against him. However, in 1929, after a succession of jobs – labouring in the railway workshops, contract overseer in the Kolar goldmines, clerk in a tobacco firm in Bangalore, and so on – he managed to talk his way into a clerkship in the Home Department of the government of India. After that, his rise was meteoric. In 1931 he attended the round-table conference; by 1940 he had made himself an expert on Indian constitutional affairs; and by 1943, after being passed over once because he was an Indian, he was appointed reforms commissioner by a reluctant Linlithgow, when H.V. Hodson resigned. Linlithgow had kept him firmly in his place, but Wavell had appreciated his talents and his open, forthright character, and had made him one of his closest advisers.

Until he went to Simla on 6 May 1947, Menon had been kept out of Mountbatten's inner circle, partly because he was an Indian, and partly because of the close relationship he had developed with Patel since their first meeting in 1946. Even now in Simla he and his wife did not stay in Viceregal Lodge but were given a room at the Cecil Hotel. Because of this distancing, Menon had not had a chance to discuss his own plan with Mountbatten in any detail – and as a result, the viceroy had never seriously considered it, or really understood it. Had he done either, he might have saved himself and everyone else a great deal of trouble.

Now, with the viceroy virtually to himself, Menon expatiated on his objections to Plan Balkan, with its implication that the provinces should initially become independent successor states, free to choose individually whether or not to come into a united India. He did not believe that Congress would ever accept this. He then explained the thinking behind his own plan, for power to be handed over as quickly as possible to two central governments, each with dominion status and a governor-general, and each with its own constituent assembly, freed from communal pressures. The 1935 India Act, suitably amended, would continue as an interim constitution for both until they had framed their own new constitutions – though in point of fact, the 1935 Act applied only to the provinces, having never come into effect for the central government, which still operated under Montagu's 1919 legislation. As dominions, both states would be members of the Commonwealth as a matter of course. Mountbatten liked what he heard, and asked Menon to discuss his plan with Nehru when he arrived. He did not mention, however, that Nehru had seen and approved Plan Balkan, and he forbade Menon from talking to him about it – presumably, he was afraid that V.P. would convince Nehru that it couldn't work.

When Nehru did arrive with Krishna Menon on 8 May, he brought good news and bad news. The good news was that an emergency session of the Congress Working Party had agreed to accept dominion status. The bad news was that they wanted it to apply to a single interim government for all India, with one constituent assembly drawing up a new constitution. Nehru estimated that it would take about three months to work out the principles of a constitution. Only after that would those provinces or parts of provinces that rejected it be free to opt out – until then the Muslims would have to remain in the central government, and accept their share of responsibility, which he thought would help to make them 'face realities'. He wanted power to be handed over as early as June 1947, with full independence, under the new constitution, following as planned a year later.[5]

Although this was at odds with the plan that Ismay had already presented to the Cabinet in London, Mountbatten felt that it was 'essential to meet Pandit Nehru's views as far as possible'. He cabled London, hoping that any statement on the plan would emphasize the 'Union of India', and refer not to Pakistan but to 'provinces which were contracting out of the Union'. He followed this later in the day by another cable, asking Ismay to distribute V.P. Menon's plan to the India Committee, and to tell the ministers that Nehru and Patel both now wanted 'a form of early Dominion Status (but under a more suitable name)'.[6] Next day, however, he changed his mind, and sent another cable telling Ismay to hold back the Menon plan after all. He planned to spend the weekend of 10–11 May working out the details of the original plan with Nehru, and thought there was 'a sporting chance' of the main Union of India remaining in the Commonwealth indefinitely. Jubilantly, he told Ismay: 'This is the greatest opportunity ever offered to the Empire and we must not let administrative or other difficulties stand in the way.'

The next two days in Simla passed in an endless round of meetings, with and without the staff. Nehru talked at length with V.P. Menon about his plan, which he found very interesting, and argued with him and Mountbatten about dominion status and the big question of whether partition should come before or after the transfer of power. But it was all highly civilized, and there was time for peaceful strolls in the grounds of Viceregal Lodge, and for the Mountbattens and

Nehru to take a relaxed afternoon tea with the Campbell-Johnson family, who were staying in a house called 'The Retreat', tucked away in a fold in the hills at the end of a mule track. After playing with their children, Nehru demonstrated his agility by walking backwards up the steep hill in the orchard, saying it made breathing easier in high altitudes, and rested the calf muscles.[7]

The personal friendship between Nehru and Mountbatten deepened quickly. So, too, did the friendship between Nehru and Edwina. Both were unashamedly promiscuous – Nehru was not the lonely widower so often depicted, but had lived for some years with Padmaja Naidu, Sarojini's daughter, who observed sadly that 'Jawahar is not one woman's man.'[8] He had numerous affairs, one of which, with a young woman called Sharanda Mata, resulted in a child. It is doubtful whether Nehru and Edwina consummated their friendship at Simla, but they certainly did so later, when it ripened into a full-scale love affair. This raised eyebrows in Delhi for a number of reasons, not least the danger of Edwina's influencing her husband in favour of Congress and against the League – surprisingly, no one ever thought the affair might have turned the cuckolded husband against Nehru and Congress. Nor did it.

The approved version of the official plan was cabled from London on Saturday, 10 May, and Mountbatten joyfully announced to the press that he would officially present it to Nehru, Jinnah, Patel, Liaquat and Baldev Singh at a conference in Delhi on the morning of 17 May. With his usual eagerness, he even cabled London a digest of the speech he intended to make to the Indian leaders. But as the day wore on, he began to have doubts. The amendments made to the plan in London seemed at first sight to be minor improvements, but on closer inspection they could be seen as fundamental changes. The whole plan was now very different not only from the Cabinet mission plan but even more so from Menon's plan, which Mountbatten knew Patel and Nehru supported. Beset by an uncharacteristic uncertainty, he told his staff that afternoon that he had a 'distinct hunch' that he ought to take advantage of his new-found friendship with Nehru to ask his personal opinion of the new draft. The staff disapproved, since it had been agreed that all five leaders would see the draft at the same time. But Mountbatten was still uneasy, and decided to follow his hunch.[9]

Before bed that night, Mountbatten invited Nehru into his study for a glass of port, took the revised plan from his safe, and gave it to him to read, 'on the understanding that he was going to advise me merely as a friend of the likely reception it would have on May 17'.[10] Nehru took it to his bedroom. At midnight, he called Krishna Menon to his room. 'He was almost beside himself,' Krishna wrote, 'and said that this plan was very different from what he had accepted and was quite unacceptable.'[11] He spent the next four hours raging over the document and preparing his response.

What Nehru most objected to in the revised plan was that it encouraged the Balkanization of the country by allowing individual provinces such as Bengal and the NWFP to break away as independent sovereign states, rather than forming groups as envisaged in the Cabinet mission plan. Attlee had struck at the very roots of Congress doctrine by removing from the plan any recognition that the provinces now in the constituent assembly represented the Union of India, the successor state to British India, from which those forming Pakistan would be seceding. As for the princes, the revised plan was a direct invitation to them to remain independent kingdoms, presumably as allies or clients of Britain.

Clearly, there had been a serious misunderstanding over the draft plan which Nehru had seen, all too briefly, on 30 April. In Mountbatten's frantic haste to get agreement in principle before the plan was rushed to London, neither Nehru nor anyone else had been given time to reflect on the deeper implications, nor had Nehru seen the changes that had been made on the following two days, including the inflammatory matter of voting procedures in Bengal. The additional revisions that had been made in London had aggravated the problem, with the result that on the morning of Sunday, 11 May, Mountbatten found disaster staring up at him from his breakfast table in the shape of a letter, written during the night, which he described as 'Nehru's bombshell'. In it, Nehru denounced the revised plan, which he said had produced 'a devastating effect' on him:

> The relatively simple proposals that we had previously discussed now appeared, in the garb that HMG had provided for them, in an entirely new context which gave them an ominous meaning. The whole approach was completely different from what ours had been and *the picture of India that emerged frightened me*. In fact, much of what we had done so far was undermined and the Cabinet Mission's scheme and subsequent developments were set aside, and an entirely new picture presented — *a picture of fragmentation and conflict and disorder, and, unhappily also, of a worsening of relations between India and Britain*. Instead of producing any sense of certainty, security and stability, they would encourage disruptive tendencies everywhere and chaos and weakness.

Nehru concluded by saying that he was writing a note on the proposals, but in the mean time, his letter was 'some indication of how upset I have been by these proposals which, I am convinced, will be resented and bitterly disliked all over the country'.[12]

V.P. Menon's warnings had been all too right, and the first thing Mountbatten did was to send for him. Menon, as it happened, was having coffee with Nehru at that moment, listening to his diatribe against the plan and trying in vain to persuade him that all was not lost and that they could find a new approach. But, as Menon wrote, 'He was too agitated to listen to me.' He found

Mountbatten agitated, too, severely rattled by the prospect of what would have happened if he had gone ahead with the planned conference of leaders on 17 March without having shown the plan to Nehru. Typically, Mountbatten was most exercised about the threat to his own reputation. As he told Campbell-Johnson later in the day, if he had not followed his hunch and shown the plan to Nehru – against the advice of most of his staff, he was at pains to emphasize – 'Dickie Mountbatten would have been finished and could have packed his bag. We would have looked complete fools with the Government at home, having led them up the garden to believe that Nehru would accept the Plan.'[13]

The problem now was how best to retrieve the situation. Menon suggested that 'the most promising line of action was to proceed on the basis of my plan'.[14] He had good reason to believe that Congress would accept it since it gave them an early transfer of power and, unlike the plan Nehru had just rejected so emphatically, would retain the essential unity of India, while allowing Pakistan to secede. As for Jinnah, even Mountbatten had gained the impression that he was reconciled to the idea of a truncated Pakistan.

Menon's quiet assurance – backed, of course, by his close contacts with Patel – calmed Mountbatten's panic. There was a way out: an alternative plan was already in place and needed only to be activated. The viceroy told Menon to invite Nehru to a meeting with himself and his staff at once. The meeting started with Nehru restating his objections, which he had listed in a 2,500 word document. Then Menon and Mountbatten together went to work to convince him of the merits of Menon's plan for twin dominions. At the end, Mountbatten asked him if Congress would accept a new draft plan based on what he had just heard. But having been once bitten, Nehru was not prepared to commit himself. 'I cannot say,' he replied. 'I would have to see the new draft first.'

By this time, Mountbatten was running at full throttle again. Nehru was leaving for Delhi that evening, he told Menon, and it was vital that he should see the new draft before he went. Could Menon have one ready for him to read before the evening train departed? Menon nodded, though it was already 2.00 p.m. He walked quickly back to his hotel room and poured himself a stiff whisky – the first time he had ever drunk whisky before 6.00 p.m. Then he set to work. Four hours later, with Miéville leaning over him impatiently, he wrote the last word. Miéville grabbed the pages and rushed them back to Viceregal Lodge. Menon took four aspirins and went to bed.[15]

While Menon had been writing, Mountbatten had kept himself busy. He sent a stream of cables to Ismay in London, telling him to hold everything, that the draft plan was cancelled, that he was to stand by for a revised plan, and that Mountbatten had good reason to believe that both sides would accept dominion status if power could be transferred earlier than June 1948. It is small wonder that Ismay confessed himself 'bewildered, out of touch with the situation in India, and useless as an envoy'.[16] Campbell-Johnson, meanwhile, was summoned to Viceregal Lodge from a tea-party he was holding for a party of pressmen, and told to find a face-saving way of saying that the leaders' conference announced with so much triumphalism only the day before was now cancelled. After more cables to London to obtain clearance, he settled for a pointless white lie, which nobody believed: 'Owing to the imminence of the Parliamentary recess in London, it has been found necessary to postpone H.E. the Viceroy's meeting with the Indian leaders announced to begin on Saturday 17th May, until Monday 2nd June.'[17]

At 9.00 p.m. that evening Menon was due for dinner at Viceregal Lodge. Nehru had already left, and there seemed to be no one who could tell him what had happened. Menon later told the British journalist, Leonard Mosley, that when Mountbatten and Edwina made their formal entrance, he was at one end of the receiving line and his wife was at the other. He watched as the viceroy and vicereine greeted Mrs Menon warmly, then had to wait five minutes as they worked their way down the line. Eventually 'Lady Mountbatten came up to him, [and] gave him an affectionate peck on the cheek while she whispered in his ear: 'He accepted it, V.P.'[18] Mountbatten, who according to Menon 'had completely regained his buoyant spirits and good cheer', told him that Nehru had said the approach contained in his paper 'was on proper lines and that it would not be unacceptable to the Congress'. Later that night, Menon phoned Patel in Delhi to bring him up to date on the developments of the day. Patel was delighted, and assured him there would be no difficulty with Congress.[19]

The viceregal party returned to Delhi on Wednesday, 14 May. Their week in Simla could hardly be described as a holiday, but at least it had been a change, and a break from the relentless heat of the capital, which was now soaring above 115°F in the shade every day. There was heat of a different kind, too – awaiting Mountbatten was a 'courteous but firm' summons to return to London for consultation.

Attlee and the Cabinet were understandably confused by the sudden changes of tack over the last few days, and wanted explanations. Ismay was unable to give them, and had suggested either that he should return to Delhi for two or three days for a new briefing, that Miéville should be sent to replace him, or that Mountbatten himself should come home. Attlee had another option: that a ministerial mission should fly out to Delhi with full powers to settle everything on the spot. Realizing that the minister involved would be either Attlee himself or more probably Cripps, and knowing what Mountbatten's reaction to that would be, Ismay urged him to come back at once. The matter was settled when Attlee decided he would recall the viceroy.

Mountbatten's first impulse was to refuse. If the government refused to accept his recommendations he would resign. Edwina and V.P. Menon soon talked him out of that, however, and he cabled Ismay to send his York aircraft back for him. He then called in Campbell-Johnson and told him to prepare a press statement making it clear he was returning to London 'of his own volition, and not simply by urgent summons' – the Mountbatten face had to be saved at all costs.

The next 48 hours were spent in a frenzied effort to get guarantees from both Congress and the League that there would be no more bombshells. Mountbatten asked Menon to draw up a draft heads of agreement, which he would give to all the Indian leaders for their approval before leaving for London. The completed document listed eight sections, including, briefly: acceptance of the procedure for ascertaining the wishes of the people on whether or not there should be partition; transfer of power on a dominion status basis to one or two central governments responsible to their constituent assemblies; transfer of power on the basis of the 1935 Act, suitably modified; reappointment of the present governor-general as common governor-general of both dominions; and in the event of partition, a commission to be appointed to demarcate boundaries, and the armed forces to be divided according to territorial recruitment rather than on a simple communal basis, since many Muslims in the forces came from areas that would not be included in Pakistan. There were to be special arrangements for separating mixed units.

Menon took the draft heads of agreement to Nehru, Patel and Baldev Singh. Miéville took it to Jinnah and Liaquat. None of them raised any objections, and when Mountbatten met each of them they agreed to the terms – though Jinnah refused to put that in writing. Nehru did write, saying that Congress approved the scheme generally, on condition that the other parties accepted it as a final settlement and made no further claims. He said Congress saw it as a continuation of the Cabinet mission plan, adjusted to fit the existing situation, and that if the League failed to accept it, they would insist on full implementation of the original plan. Baldev Singh, as a Sikh, was reluctant to accept, but after Menon had warned him that there would be a blood-bath in the Punjab if it were not divided, Singh said that he would not stand out if Congress accepted. And so, amazingly, Mountbatten and Menon had obtained agreement from all sides in only two days.

Now things were really moving, all Mountbatten's jitters were forgotten. He left Palam airport for London at 8.30 a.m. on Sunday, 18 May, accompanied by Edwina, Vernon Erskine Crum and V.P. Menon, who was now firmly established as a trusted member of the viceroy's entourage. Mountbatten was determined to make this one of the fastest-ever flights to London, with special long-range fuel tanks fitted to the MW102, and double crews to keep it flying. They would touch down only twice, for refuelling at Karachi and Fayid, in Egypt, and were expected to land at Northolt at 10.30 next morning, after barely 24 hours in the air.

At Northolt on the morning of Monday, 19 May, the party was met by an anxious Ismay, who took Mountbatten straight from the airport to meet Attlee. Explaining the new plan – 'Plan Partition' as everyone now labelled it – he reported that 'It had become clear that the Muslim League would resort to arms if Pakistan in some form were not conceded.' That afternoon, they attended a meeting of the India Committee, where Mountbatten ran through all that had happened since his arrival in India. He told the ministers that the turning-point had come when 'certain Congress leaders' had offered to accept partition and dominion status in return for an early transfer of power, well before June 1948. They had also assured him, he said, that although they must be free to secede from the Commonwealth, they would not wish to do so once dominion status had been accepted. With this in mind, Congress had agreed to accept a common governor-general for both dominions, and wanted him to stay on in that position and to act as arbitrator between the two. Jinnah, of course, had made no response to that suggestion yet.

Mountbatten had been nervous about the reception both he and his new plan might get from the committee. But his fears proved to be groundless. 'We could hardly do less than agree without a murmur', Listowel said later, 'to a scheme that had the blessing of the Viceroy and the two communities.'[20] In any case, it was soon obvious that the ministers had no desire to delay anything: they wanted to get India off their hands as quickly as they decently could. Mountbatten stressed that everything now depended on speed. Congress had only agreed to the new plan on condition that power be handed over virtually immediately – Nehru had even talked about June, though this was clearly impossible. Patel was speaking of a more realistic two months. Any delay might give them, and even more so Jinnah and the League, time to change their minds. It must be done by early autumn at the latest. The committee agreed.

Herbert Morrison, Attlee's deputy prime minister and lord privy seal, ever the practical administrator, pointed out the problems of getting the necessary legislation through Parliament before the summer recess. Could it be done? The question was referred to the lord chancellor, Lord Jowitt, who reported that it was just about possible for an amending Bill to the 1935 Act to be prepared within six or seven weeks from deciding exactly what was required, but that there would be no hope whatever of getting it through Parliament without the full co-operation of the opposition parties. If Churchill chose to make trouble, there would be no hope.

Attlee said the Tory leaders had promised to co-operate, if they could be sure that both the main Indian parties accepted the new plan, but Mountbatten would have to convince them that he had got it right this time. Next day, Mountbatten met Churchill, Eden, Sir John Anderson and Lord Salisbury, and put his case to them. The morning after, Churchill telephoned him to say they had agreed in principle, but asked him to come round to his house to discuss the details.

When Mountbatten arrived at the Churchill residence at 28 Hyde Park Gate, he found the great man still in bed, sitting up with a quilted dressing-gown draped across his shoulders. It was nothing unusual for Churchill to conduct interviews in this way, and the two men got down to business at once. Churchill wanted reassurance that both India and Pakistan would become members of the Commonwealth, which he believed would bring the whole of Britain behind the plan, and would certainly ensure the support of the Conservative Party. Mountbatten told him Nehru had definitely committed himself, provided power was transferred during 1947, but that Jinnah was holding back.

'By God,' Churchill exclaimed, 'he is the one man who cannot do without British help!' He then offered Mountbatten advice on how to handle Jinnah: 'Threaten. Take away all British officers ... Make it clear to them how impossible it would be to run Pakistan without British help.' Mountbatten politely agreed to try to 'follow some such policy', and persuaded the old man to give him a personal message for the Muslim leader. Churchill obliged: 'This is a matter of life and death for Pakistan, if you do not accept this offer with both hands.'[21]

Jinnah, however, was still trying to squeeze the final drops of advantage from the situation. That same day he gave a statement to the Reuters correspondent in Delhi reiterating his demand for his big Pakistan, with the Punjab and Bengal undivided, and causing consternation by adding a new demand: for an 800-mile corridor linking east and west Pakistan, a corridor that would cut India in two. It was a fairly clumsy attempt to stay in the game by creating a new bargaining counter which could be offered as a quid pro quo for concessions in the disputed provinces. There was little chance of its being taken seriously, but his options were now so limited that anything was worth a try. It did, however, succeed in concentrating the minds of the Congress leaders. Nehru declared the whole idea absurd and some Congressmen wondered if Jinnah really wanted any settlement at all. The prospect that he might be prepared to drag things out at such a delicate moment was alarming to Congress. But if nothing else, Jinnah's latest ploy had finally removed any lingering doubts Nehru might have had over partition. Let Jinnah have Pakistan, he declared: 'By cutting off the head we will get rid of the headache.'[22]

While the Indian press was full of Jinnah's strident demands and Nehru's contemptuous rebuttals for the rest of the week, Gandhi was doing his bit to keep the political pot bubbling. At his daily prayer meetings he was loudly demanding a united India, and was calling on the British to impose the Cabinet mission plan, by force if need be — despite the fact that he had been largely responsible for persuading Congress to reject it a year before. Alarmed by this, Sir John Colville, Bombay's governor who was acting viceroy in Mountbatten's absence, saw Gandhi and managed to extract a promise from him that although he was unhappy with Plan Partition, he would not push his opposition to the point of actually sabotaging it.

Colville was even more alarmed by disturbing reports from Burrows in Bengal: communal tensions in Calcutta were now so great that violence seemed imminent. *The Times* correspondent, Eric Britter, told Campbell-Johnson that Muslims and Hindus had already taken up battle posts in the city: 'Houses and whole streets have become prepared positions, providing strong points and fields of fire.'[23]

Bengal, and the British government's policy on Suhrawardy's demand for an independent state, was the only outstanding item left for Mountbatten to discuss with the India Committee by 28 May. Nehru solved the problem the day before, however, by announcing that Congress could only agree to Bengal remaining undivided if it stayed in the Union. This unequivocal statement not only removed the possibility of a third dominion, it also destroyed Jinnah's arguments against the partition of Bengal, and hence the Punjab, too. He had won the battle for Pakistan, but he would have to be satisfied with his moth-eaten version.

By the end of the week, Saturday, 31 May, Mountbatten and his party were back in Delhi, after another journey at what Ismay described as 'breakneck speed'. 'A long flight with Mountbatten', he recalled in his memoirs, 'was an experience which I was careful not to repeat. The idea of a reasonable degree of comfort never entered his head. Speed was all that mattered.'[24] They arrived in the early hours, and plunged back into work immediately, knowing there was only the weekend between them and the fateful conference called for 2 June. Mountbatten's adrenalin level was still running on high. Campbell-Johnson noted admiringly that his physical and mental strength were astounding: 'He seems in no way tired by his journey or the protracted high-level discussions in London; on the contrary, he is more resilient than ever, and pours out directives to his staff.'[25]

At 10.00 a.m. on the Monday morning, the Indian leaders were driven into the north court of the Viceroy's House in their large American cars: Nehru, Patel and Kripalani representing Congress; Jinnah, Liaquat and Abdur Rab Nishtar the Muslim League; Baldev Singh the Sikhs. Jinnah, as always, kept everyone waiting, making his entrance a carefully-calculated 10 minutes late. Then they were all shown into the viceroy's study, which had been magically transformed since their last visit: Mountbatten had had the oppressive dark wooden panelling painted a refreshing shade of pale green, to match the study he had discovered in Simla. The new feeling of light and air was somehow symbolic of the new hope surrounding the men who gathered in the room that morning. But for the moment, as Mountbatten reported: 'The atmosphere was tense, and I got the feeling that the less the leaders talked, the less the chance of friction and perhaps the ultimate breakdown of the meeting.'

Mountbatten and the seven leaders sat round a small circular table, with Ismay, Miéville and Erskine Crum sitting immediately behind the viceroy. Mountbatten began by giving a closely reasoned analysis of the situation and of recent developments. Then, after confirming that the Cabinet mission plan was dead, he presented the leaders with copies of the new plan, drawing their attention first to the new paragraph 20 of the British government's statement. Headed 'Immediate Transfer of Power', it read:

> The major political parties have repeatedly emphasised their desire that there should be the earliest possible transfer of power in India. With this desire His Majesty's Government are in full sympathy, and they are willing to anticipate the date of June 1948, for the handing over of power by the setting up of an independent Indian Government or Governments at an even earlier date.
>
> Accordingly, as the most expeditious and indeed only practicable way of meeting this desire, His Majesty's Government propose to introduce legislation during the current season for the transfer of power on a Dominion Status basis to one or two successor authorities according to the decisions taken as a result of this announcement. This will be without prejudice to the right of the Indian Constituent Assemblies to decide in due course whether or not the part of India in respect of which they have authority will remain within the British Commonwealth.[26]

The meeting lasted about two hours, with Mountbatten doing most of the talking as he took the leaders through the statement, paragraph by paragraph. After the first few tense minutes the atmosphere became distinctly hopeful, especially after Mountbatten had described how the British government and opposition were both being most helpful. He admitted that the Sikhs had so far not got a satisfactory settlement, but at least they would be represented on the commission to demarcate the boundaries in the partitioned Punjab, and could make their own demands then. As for defence, Britain was ready to assist the defence forces of both dominions and supply British officers to assist in administration. But he warned that there would be problems if either dominion allowed foreign countries to establish bases on their territories.

There followed an involved but good-humoured semantic argument about the difference between agreement with and acceptance of the plan. Although none of the leaders agreed with it in its entirety, they accepted the need to make the plan work. 'Mountbatten', Campbell-Johnson recorded, 'cordially agreed, and, from that moment knew that the essential battle was won.' He asked for the reactions of the Congress and League Working Committees, and of the Sikhs, by midnight. Kripalani and Baldev Singh promised to let him have a letter that evening. Jinnah said he would not be able to have anything in writing by then, but agreed to come and see the viceroy at 11.00 p.m. and give him a verbal report.

To round off the meeting, Mountbatten said he would broadcast to the nation the following evening, and persuaded Nehru, Jinnah and Baldev to follow him with their own speeches. He promised to let them see his script next morning – at which Patel, who had been silent for most of the two hours, pointed out with a mischievous grin that it was the general rule for all scripts to be submitted for approval to the honourable member for information: in other words, himself. Jinnah retorted that he would say what came from his heart: in other words, whatever he liked.[27]

Gandhi, who never came together with the other leaders since he could not speak officially for anyone but himself, was due at 12.30. Aware that the League might claim that this was giving Congress preferential treatment, Mountbatten kept Jinnah back after the others had left, to talk briefly in private, and 'to impress on him that there could not be any question of a "No" from the League'. But Jinnah made no comment – Mountbatten would have to wait until 11.00 p.m. for his reaction.

Mountbatten was not alone in not looking forward to his interview with Gandhi. Nehru and Patel, he understood, were also apprehensive of what Gandhi's unpredictable inner voice might prompt him to do or say. 'He may be a saint,' Mountbatten wrote, 'but he seems also to be a disciple of Trotsky.' To his delight, however, Gandhi entered the room with his finger to his lips, indicating that it was his day of silence. Mountbatten spent 45 minutes trying to break down his resistance to the new plan. Gandhi smiled and scribbled a few, mostly friendly notes on the backs of used envelopes and scraps of paper with his blunt pencil stub. One note repeated the call for the removal of Sir Olaf Caroe from the NWFP. Another said: 'Have I said one word against you during my speeches? If you admit that I have not, your warning is superfluous. There are one or two things I must talk about, but not today.' It seemed clear that Gandhi would keep his promise to Colville not to sabotage the plan.[28]

The only remaining hurdle now was Jinnah. Fortunately, Mountbatten had no time to brood before he returned that evening, for there was a huge garden party in the grounds of the Viceroy's House for holders of the Burma Star, timed to coincide and exchange messages with the London rally in the Royal Albert Hall. Following that, he entertained the commanders-in-chief of the army, navy and air force and army commanders to dinner, when he let them into the secret of the new plan. All of them reluctantly agreed that partition was the only solution.

The generals and admirals and air marshals were still enjoying their port and cigars when Mountbatten and Ismay left the party to meet Jinnah. The League leader, according to Ismay, 'was in one of his difficult moods'.[29] He spent half an hour protesting against the 'scandalous' partition of the provinces, and demanding a proper referendum in Bengal 'in justice to the Scheduled Castes'. Mountbatten refused to consider any amendment to the plan unless it was agreed to by all parties, and asked Jinnah straight out whether his Working Committee was going to accept it. Jinnah remained amiably non-committal. He would, he said, do all in his power to persuade the All-India Council of the League to agree to the plan, and he was hopeful that they would. He had called an urgent meeting of the Council for next Monday. Mountbatten warned him that if the League did not accept the plan, Congress would reject it. If they did, there would be chaos and he would lose his Pakistan, probably for good. 'What must be, must be,' replied Jinnah.

Mountbatten told his staff meeting next morning that he had then responded:

> Mr Jinnah! I do not intend to let you wreck all the work that has gone into this settlement. Since you will not accept for the Muslim League, I will speak for them myself. I will take the risk of saying that I am satisfied with the assurances you have given me, and if your Council fails to ratify the agreement, you can place the blame on me. I have only one condition, and that is that when I say at the meeting in the morning, 'Mr Jinnah has given me assurances which I have accepted and which satisfy me,' you will in no circumstances contradict that, and that when I look towards you, you will nod your head in acquiescence.

Jinnah said nothing, but nodded his head. Mountbatten pressed on. Would he be justified, he asked, in advising Attlee to go ahead and make his announcement in London tomorrow? This time, Jinnah did speak – one word: 'Yes.'

Shortly after Jinnah had gone, the promised letter from Kripalani on behalf of Congress arrived. Although a long letter containing various cavils and reservations, it was a firm acceptance. But it had been extracted from a fiery Working Committee meeting with great difficulty. The younger left-wing members had hurled accusations of betrayal at Nehru and Patel, while Azad sat chain-smoking in bitter silence and Abdul Ghaffar Khan had confined himself to a few curt words of disappointment. The ghost of Gandhi's disapproval had cast a giant shadow over the entire meeting. Baldev's letter did not reach the Viceroy's House until early next morning. That, too, contained reservations, in this case about instructions to the proposed boundary commission, but it accepted the plan.[30]

The following day, Tuesday, 3 June, was devoted to removing, as far as possible, any remaining obstacles that lay in the path of the agreement. Mountbatten sent Menon to talk to Patel about the points raised in the Congress letter of acceptance, and invited Nehru to come and see him at 9.30, immediately before the next meeting with all the leaders.

The Congress letter contained two contentious points, which needed to be disposed of at once. It asked that the NWFP be allowed a third choice in its referendum on whether to join India or Pakistan – the option of independence as a separate state. And it complained that the final sentence of the all-important paragraph 20 of the British government's statement allowed Pakistan to stay in the Commonwealth even if India left. Mountbatten dealt firmly with both points. How could Congress ask for the NWFP to be given the option of independence, he asked, when they had insisted on denying the same option to Bengal? As far as Commonwealth membership was concerned, the British government did not run it: all the states in it were free and equal partners, and the only way Nehru could have Pakistan removed was by appealing to all members at a Commonwealth conference. He had no intention, he told Nehru, of raising such a controversial matter now, which would only infuriate Jinnah. And with that, they went into the meeting.

Mountbatten was still nervous of letting the leaders speak, so he spoke for them. He said they had all raised objections to various points in the plan, but since he knew from experience that none of the suggestions would be acceptable to the other parties he did not intend to raise them. He would simply ask them all to signify their consent, which they did, Jinnah nodding as agreed. None of them objected when he said, with enormous relief, that he would now announce the plan officially. But when he appealed to them all for restraint, asking them to bury the past so that they could build a fine future, Liaquat could not resist saying he was speaking to the wrong people: it was Gandhi who needed to exercise restraint, instead of using his prayer meetings to incite people to rebel against their leaders. Instantly, all the old rancour was back, as the two sides began hurling abuse across the table.

Mountbatten stepped in hurriedly to quieten them. Reaching for a thick document behind him, with a dramatic gesture he raised it high above his head and slammed it down on the table with a bang. It was a master plan prepared at great speed by John Christie, entitled 'The Administrative Consequences of Partition', dealing with all that would have to be done to provide for continuity of the administration in the two new dominions – the division of staff organizations and records, services and institutions, assets and liabilities of the government of India; future economic relations; domicile, diplomatic relations, and so on. At 34

458 The Proudest Day

closely-typed foolscap pages it was a masterpiece of compression, but it presented a daunting prospect, enough to bring the Indian leaders down to earth with a bump. 'The severe shock that this gave to everyone present,' wrote Mountbatten, 'would have been amusing if it was not rather tragic.'[31]

The climax of the day was the broadcast that evening of the four speeches on All-India Radio. Mountbatten spoke first, in a slow and deliberate voice that was in great contrast to his normal quick-fire speech. He said he had always believed in a unified India, but that it had proved impossible to achieve. The boundaries between Muslim and non-Muslim areas would be established by a Boundary Commission, on which all the various parties would be represented. He wished India well and hoped that their decisions would be wisely guided and carried out in the peaceful and friendly spirit of the Gandhi-Jinnah appeal.

Nehru said that he, too, had hoped for a united India, but that it was not to be. In the event, he believed the new proposals represented the only way forward. He abhorred the violence that was tearing the country apart, and praised the viceroy for his efforts on behalf of India. 'We are little men,' he said, 'serving great causes, but because the cause is great some of that greatness falls upon us also.' Jinnah, too, praised the viceroy and appealed for peace and order. As for the plan, 'It is for us to consider whether ... [it] should be accepted by us as a compromise or a settlement. On this point,' he added rather ominously, 'I do not wish to prejudge.' Nehru ended his speech with '*Jai Hind!*'; Jinnah with '*Pakistan Zindabad!*' – which he pronounced in such clipped tones that many listeners thought he had said 'Pakistan's in the bag!' Baldev Singh spoke last. He called on Indian defence forces, so many of whom were Sikhs, to remain loyal and uphold their high standards of discipline in what would inevitably prove to be the testing time ahead. He contradicted Jinnah on one point – he referred to the plan not as a compromise, but as a settlement.

Meanwhile, in the House of Commons in London, Attlee announced what had come to be known as the 3 June Plan. It was cautiously welcomed by Churchill on behalf of the opposition.

It was left to a newsman in the press conference held in the Viceroy's House next morning to extract the final and perhaps most important piece of information. 'For how long,' he asked, 'would "His Excellency" remain "His Excellency" and thereafter as governor-general?' In other words, when would the transfer of power actually occur? 'That is a most embarrassing question,' Mountbatten replied. 'I think the transfer could be about the 15th of August.'[32]

'A Treaty of Peace Without a War'

Mountbatten's announcement of 15 August as the date for the handing over of power was greeted with delight by most of the people of India, but with consternation by officials in both London and Delhi. To them, the idea that the Raj could be wound up in a mere 72 days was unthinkable. Listowel prepared a draft cable to Mountbatten, querying the date. Before sending it, however, he submitted it to Attlee, whose principal private secretary, Leslie Rowan, noted his own comment on it: 'If we had trouble in Parliament it might not be feasible to fix appointed day as 15 August.' Attlee, as terse as ever, simply wrote across it: 'Accept Viceroy's proposal.'[1]

Throughout the rest of his life, Mountbatten gave a variety of explanations for choosing 15 August. In later years, he liked to romanticize his decision as yet another flash of inspiration, another Mountbatten hunch. He told Larry Collins and Dominique Lapierre in a recorded interview: 'The date I chose came out of the blue . . . I was determined to show that I was master of the whole event. When they asked: had we set a date, I knew it had to be soon. I hadn't worked it out exactly then – I thought it had to be about August or September and I then went to the 15th of August. Why? Because it was the second anniversary of Japan's surrender.'[2] It was also, as he told others, the anniversary of his own appointment as supreme commander, so his choice seems perfectly in character.

In fact there is evidence that the date had been carefully thought out in advance. Mountbatten had written to Listowel the day before the press conference, saying that he wanted to wind up the Raj on 15 August. And he said elsewhere that he had agreed the date with the Indian leaders at the beginning of June. There is no written record of this, but it is interesting that it happens to coincide almost exactly with Patel's demand for independence in two months – that, after all, had been the deal. 'The August transfer of power,' Mountbatten wrote in his Final Report, 'was inherent in the Partition solution.' Bearing in mind that the necessary legislation could not be drafted until decisions had been taken on the partition of the Punjab and Bengal, 15 August was, to within a day or two, the earliest possible date after the new Act would became law. It was also, in Mountbatten's opinion, about the latest possible date that the interim government could be kept functioning.

The collapse of the interim government was a serious possibility, with fresh squabbles breaking out across the Cabinet table virtually every day. Most of the time, only Mountbatten's genius for genial and unflappable chairmanship saved the situation. At the very first meeting after the announcement, for example, he suggested that no new high-level appointments should be made until the two new administrations had been set up. Everyone agreed. Then Nehru said he wanted to pick a few ambassadors straight away but since they would be representing India, this was no business of Pakistan. Liaquat immediately protested — there were certain countries, he said, to which Pakistan would not wish to see an ambassador appointed, such as the Soviet Union. This was a mischievous barb, since everyone knew that Nehru intended to appoint his own sister, Mrs Lakshmi Pandit, to the Moscow post. Nehru snapped angrily that such interference was intolerable. Liaquat snapped back. Nehru threatened to resign. There was instant pandemonium, with everyone shouting at once. Mountbatten managed to restore order, then admonished the ministers: 'Gentlemen, what hopes have we of getting a peaceable partition if the first discussion leads to such a disgraceful scene as this?' As they sat glaring at each other with sullen resentment, he addressed them like naughty schoolboys: 'I am not going on with the next item until I see a row of smiling faces in front of me.' Everyone laughed, the tension was broken, and the meeting continued. But there had to be a limit on how long such tactics would work, especially in dealing with more serious matters.[3]

For all his careful thought, there was one aspect of the date which Mountbatten had not considered: its astral significance. Barely a week before independence, the astrologers suddenly gave it a universal thumbs-down, pronouncing that 15 August was a most inauspicious day for such a momentous event. For anyone, even the viceroy, to go against the astrologers was the surest way of alienating vast numbers of the population, but having named a day, Mountbatten felt his pride was at stake. Fortunately, the 14th was regarded as highly suitable, and it did not take great ingenuity to suggest that midnight on that day would be acceptable to everyone.

Only one man in India carried more weight than the astrologers, and that man was Gandhi. The most relentless questioner at the morning press conference on 4 June had been Devadas Gandhi, and it seemed likely that he had been influenced by his father. On his return to the Viceroy's House, Mountbatten learned that Gandhi senior was planning to speak against the plan at his prayer meeting that evening. He called him to the house an hour before the prayer meeting was due to begin, and set about convincing him that the new plan should really be called 'the Gandhi Plan', since everything in it had been suggested by him. Eventually, Gandhi was persuaded. As he left, he turned and said to Mountbatten with grudging admiration: 'You and your magic tricks!'

At his prayer meeting, Gandhi gave the plan his blessing. 'The British government,' he said, 'is not responsible for partition. The viceroy has no hand in it. In fact, he is as opposed to division as Congress itself, but if both of us – Hindus and Muslims – cannot agree on anything else, then the viceroy is left with no choice.' This plan, he said, was the only basis on which agreement could be reached, and so it must be implemented.[4] When the AICC met in Delhi on 14 June to ratify the Working Committee's decision, Gandhi clinched its acceptance by giving it his support. The resolution was passed by 157 votes to 29, with 32 abstentions: the main opposition coming from nationalist Muslims, and Hindus living in the provinces that would become Pakistan.

Meanwhile, the various Sikh organizations met in Lahore and approved the plan in principle, including the division of the Punjab. But they had ominously declared that no partition of the province would be acceptable to them unless it preserved 'the solidarity and integrity of the Sikh community'.[5] The Hindu Mahasabha, unsurprisingly, was totally opposed to the plan, and even called for an All-India 'Anti-Pakistan Day', swearing there would never be peace while India was divided, but this had little effect.

The Muslim League's All-India Council had met, in the ballroom of Delhi's Imperial Hotel, on 9 June; a meeting that was considerably more stormy than any of the others. Militant Muslims from all over India, but especially from the Punjab and Calcutta, angrily branded the plan as a 'betrayal' and 'a tragedy for Pakistan' – they wanted a single Pakistan stretching unbroken from Karachi to Chittagong. Jinnah's old enemies, the Khaksars from Lahore, besieged the hotel and burst through the doors from the garden, swinging their sharpened spades and screaming 'Get Jinnah!' They charged through the hotel lounges and were halfway up the staircase to the first-floor ballroom before League National Guards managed to halt them. Finally, police with lathis and tear gas brought them under control, arresting 50 would-be assassins while hotel guests 'ran helter-skelter' from the lounge, their eyes streaming.[6] Jinnah continued unperturbed through the disturbances, and the Council agreed 'to accept the fundamental principles of the Plan as a compromise, and to leave it to him, with full authority, to work out all the details of the Plan in an equitable and just manner'.[7]

Jinnah was playing his usual game of 'you show me yours', refusing to commit himself until Congress had done so in case he should somehow find himself outmanoeuvred. The League resolution, carefully framed to avoid an outright acceptance of the plan as a final settlement, raised howls of protest from Nehru and Patel, but no matter how much Mountbatten pleaded and reasoned, Jinnah and Liaquat refused to budge. Finally, the viceroy overcame the problem by extracting an oral promise from Jinnah and then writing to Kripalani as president of Congress, saying Jinnah had assured him he would sign a joint document accepting the plan as a final settlement if Congress did likewise.

During the rest of June, the disputed provinces voted on their futures. Everything went exactly as forecast, and by the end of the month they had all voted by substantial majorities for partition and Pakistan. The NWFP referendum was not held until 6–17 July, by which time Caroe had been persuaded to take 'sick leave' and had been replaced by Lieutenant-General Sir Rob Lockhart, in deference to the continuing Congress demands for Caroe's removal. Abdul Ghaffar Khan's Congress supporters and Red Shirts abstained. To everyone's relief the referendum passed off peacefully, as did the voting in most other places. Even in Calcutta there was only sporadic violence, though rioters there did sometimes use sten guns. The exception, inevitably, was the Punjab, where the Legislative Assembly had to be protected by armed guards while its members were making their fateful decisions.

The latest trouble had started in the predominantly Hindu Gurgaon district of the Punjab, only 50 miles north of Delhi, where local Hindus began making their own preparations for partition by trying to wipe out the Muslims of the local Meo community. Muslims in nearby communities retaliated, and soon there was fighting along a 50-mile front, with whole villages put to the torch. Troops on security duty were increased from a battalion to a brigade, and gradually brought the situation under some sort of control. By then, however, trouble was flaring up again in Lahore and Amritsar; not full-scale riots this time, but stabbings, beatings and arson, which were all difficult to control by normal police or military methods. 'Having discovered how easy it is to burn down an Indian city,' Campbell-Johnson commented in his diary, 'the incendiaries are particularly dangerous. Throwing fireballs through windows and skylights and making full use of roof-tops and narrow city lanes, they are almost impossible to catch in the act.'[8]

On 23 June, Jinnah appealed to Mountbatten to be absolutely ruthless in putting down the disorder: 'I don't care whether you shoot Muslims or not, it has got to be stopped.' Nehru wanted the viceroy to pull out the police, who were mainly Muslim and no longer impartial, and declare martial law in the cities, but Jenkins, on the advice of his military commanders, thought that troops were helpless against 'cloak and dagger' tactics. Their failure would actually make things worse, since they, too, would then be accused of bias. When Mountbatten announced this to the Indian Cabinet, both sides attacked him furiously. 'Nehru,' he reported, 'as usual, completely lost control of himself and demanded the sacking of every official, from the Governor downwards, that same day. I had to reprimand him publicly for this irresponsible suggestion.'[9]

Although the referendums in the NWFP and the Sylhet district of Assam were still to come, voting in the provincial assemblies was completed on 26 June, when the Sind Assembly decided by 33 votes to 20 to join Pakistan. On 27 June, Mountbatten announced this to his staff meeting, concluding: 'Thus we can now look upon the creation of Pakistan on the 15th August as legally decided upon.'[10] It was time to put the machinery of partition into motion, as outlined in Christie's document.

The Cabinet's Partition Committee was disbanded and replaced by the Partition Council, consisting of Mountbatten as chairman, Patel and Prasad for Congress, with Rajagopalachari as alternate member, and Jinnah and Liaquat for the League, with Abdur Rab Nishtar as their alternate member. Any disputes that could not be settled by agreement in the Partition Council were to be referred to an Arbitral Tribunal of three men with high judicial experience, but finding a mutually acceptable chairman proved difficult. Listowel suggested Sir Cyril Radcliffe, a distinguished English lawyer – and yet another fellow of All Souls. The Congress leaders objected to anyone from outside India, and proposed their old solution to such matters, the Federal Court, which Jinnah refused. Eventually, they all agreed on the resigning Chief Justice of India, Sir Patrick Spens, though in the end his services were never called upon.

The Partition Council was to work through a Steering Committee of two officials; Chaudry Muhammad Ali, financial adviser to the Military Finance Department, representing Pakistan, and Hiralal Muljibhai Patel, the Cabinet secretary, for India. Fortunately for everyone, Muhammad Ali and H.M. Patel were civil servants of the highest order, as intelligent and skilful as any in the distinguished history of the ICS. They had also known each other for many years.

While the politicians bickered and postured, Muhammad Ali and H.M. Patel got on with the job in hand quietly and efficiently. They set up 10 expert committees whose responsibilities reflected the mind-numbingly dull but essential minutiae of government: organization, records and personnel; assets and liabilities; central revenues; contracts; currency and exchange; budget and accounts; economic relations (controls and trade); domicile; foreign relations; and finally, the Armed Forces Reconstitution Committee. The committee was so named because Auchinleck, in a despairing protest against the dismemberment of his beloved Indian army, refused to allow the word 'partition' to be used. Assisting these expert committees, in typical bureaucratic style, was a burgeoning network of departmental committees – 20 for organization, records and personnel, 21 for assets and liabilities, and so on. Membership of all committees was carefully balanced, with equal numbers of Muslims and non-Muslims on each, augmented on the armed forces committees by a number of British officers.[11]

And so, in both Delhi and London, the preparations for independence and partition got under way, at a rate that was fast enough to satisfy even Mountbatten's relentless craving for speed. To make doubly sure everyone got the message, he had special calendars printed, with tear-off sheets for each day giving the date and, in bold black letters several inches high, proclaiming 'XX DAYS LEFT TO PREPARE FOR TRANSFER OF POWER', for all the world like a National Service soldier's demob chart.

Somehow, the viceroy still found time to pursue his obsession with extending his genealogical tree. And in an unrelated bit of heraldry, he also managed to design new flags for both dominions, adding a Union Flag, one ninth in area, to the upper canton of the Congress and League flags. He sent the result to Nehru and Jinnah, but both found ways of politely rejecting his offer. Jinnah pointed out that it would be repugnant to Muslims to have a Christian cross alongside the Islamic crescent. Nehru escaped by saying that Congress extremists were already accusing the leadership of pandering to the British and he did not think it would be wise to push them further. He sent Mountbatten the new design already approved by Congress, which exchanged the spinning wheel at the centre of the Congress tricolour with the wheel of the ancient Sarnath Asoka, symbol of the third century BC emperor who had brought most of India and Afghanistan under one rule.

The business of the flags – which was to be repeated shortly afterwards when he produced his own designs for the personal standards of the governors-general – was a small dent in Mountbatten's pride, but there was a much bigger one on the way. It was V.P. Menon who drew his attention to the provision in the draft Bill relating to the role of the governor-general. 'The India Office,' he pointed out, 'appear to be assuming that His Excellency would be asked by both parties to become Governor-General of the two new Dominions. It appears that the India Office were expecting both Mr Jinnah and Pandit Nehru to write letters asking the Viceroy to accept this post, and that it would be possible to quote these letters in Parliament.'

The trouble was, although Nehru had already asked Mountbatten to continue as governor-general of India, Jinnah had remained conspicuously silent. He had originally suggested that there might be a 'super governor-general' above the governors-general of the two dominions, as an impartial arbitrator. This was obviously impractical, but the same result could be achieved by having Mountbatten as a common governor-general. Mountbatten raised the matter again with Jinnah just before he flew to London with the Menon plan, but got nothing from him but a promise that he would think about it and let Mountbatten know his decision.

Since Jinnah now neither liked nor wholly trusted the viceroy – 'flash and second-rate' he had called him – it is hardly surprising that he refused to be stampeded into any quick decision on such an important matter. It is more surprising that Mountbatten, having spent nearly two months negotiating with him, had so little understanding of Jinnah's character. Jinnah could, with difficulty, sometimes be persuaded; he could not, however, be bounced into anything. Yet Mountbatten persisted. When he returned from London he raised the subject again. At one point he even considered asking Sir Walter Monckton to prepare a legal case for submission to Jinnah, but was sensibly dissuaded by Ismay.

On 20 June, Mountbatten sent Miéville to enlist the support of Liaquat, who agreed to approach the Quaid-i-Azam. Three days later, when he had still not heard anything, Mountbatten returned to Jinnah personally, but still failed to get an answer. He even sent for his old friend the Nawab of Bhopal, the leading Muslim prince, and asked him to use his influence. Bhopal flew to Delhi in his private plane specially to see Jinnah, but was no more successful than Liaquat had been in eliciting a response. Finally, on 1 July, Jinnah gave Mountbatten his answer. He told him that initially he wished to have British governors in all the provinces of Pakistan except Sind, and had already appointed three British officers as chiefs of the armed services. The only way this could be made acceptable to his people, he said, was if he became governor-general himself. He said he had been most reluctant, but had been advised to do this by three or four intimate friends and colleagues. Liaquat would be prime minister.

Mountbatten was furious. He noted that he did not know who the friends could be, since both Liaquat and Bhopal had said they favoured his own appointment. 'I therefore had difficulty,' he wrote caustically, 'in not reaching the conclusion that the only adviser to whom Mr Jinnah listened was Mr Jinnah.'[12] The Congress and League leaders were at that moment sitting in separate rooms at the Viceroy's House, working on the draft of the independence Bill. Chaudry Muhammad Ali recalls that he was sitting with Jinnah and Liaquat when Mountbatten burst in. 'He belaboured the Quaid-i-Azam with arguments and bluster,' Muhammad Ali recalled.

> He maintained that the proposal for a common Governor-General was inspired by the highest motives and was in the best interests of Pakistan. Without him as common Governor-General, Pakistan would put itself at the gravest disadvantage. It was with the greatest difficulty that he was securing for Pakistan what was due to her and, unless it was known that he would continue in this position even after partition, his power to help Pakistan would rapidly diminish. The responsibility for the immeasurable loss to

Pakistan would rest on the shoulders of Jinnah. He threatened to make all this public and let the world judge.[13]

Jinnah, Muhammad Ali wrote, 'bore this onslaught with great dignity and patience'. He emphasized that his decision had not been made on personal grounds, but on his estimate of what was best for his people.

Mountbatten continued to bluster, pointing out that as constitutional governor-general, Jinnah's powers would be severely restricted: he would only be able to act on advice. Jinnah's retort was withering: 'In my position, it is I who will give the advice, and others who will act on it.'[14] Aware of Mountbatten's hurt, he assured him that his one wish was for him to stay on as governor-general of India, or as a super governor-general, but Mountbatten was not assuaged. His own version of the end of the interview reveals his pique: 'I asked him "Do you realise what this will cost you?" He said sadly, "It may cost me several crores [tens of millions] of rupees in assets," to which I replied somewhat acidly, "It may well cost you the whole of your assets and the future of Pakistan." I then got up and left the room.'[15] 'From this stage on,' Muhammad Ali noted, 'there was a noticeable change in Mountbatten's attitude toward the problems of partition and toward Pakistan. Mountbatten had barely tolerated Jinnah in the past; now there was active hostility.'[16]

Only one person in the Viceroy's House had read the runes correctly. 'What I thought might happen funnily enough,' Edwina wrote to her elder daughter Patricia back in England, 'and which neither Daddy nor any of his staff EVER contemplated has occurred, and Mr Jinnah himself wants to be Governor-General of Pakistan.'[17] Edwina could afford to treat the matter lightly; her husband could not. He saw Jinnah's rejection as a betrayal, a deliberate and vicious besmirching of the Mountbatten myth, and he was acutely aware that it would be seen in London as a loss of face. He, too, wrote to Patricia:

Your poor old Daddy has finally and irretrievably 'boobed' and I've now landed myself in a position from which I cannot conceivably extricate myself with honour. Either I shall be accused of taking sides ... or I let down the Congress leaders ... Mummy feels I should preserve my dignity and go on 15 August. The others feel I cannot let down Nehru and must stay. In both cases I'm in the wrong. In fact I've at last made a mess of things through over-confidence and over-tiredness. I'm just whacked and worn out and would really like to go. I'm so depressed, darling, because until this stupid mishandling of the Jinnah situation I'd done so well. It has certainly taken me down a few pegs.[18]

Realizing the dangers created by Mountbatten's wounded *amour propre*, his staff held an emergency meeting at 9.30 next morning in Ismay's bungalow, 'to devise a formula whereby His Excellency the Viceroy could remain Governor-General of both Dominions and at the same time satisfy Mr Jinnah's vanity'! As some of them feared, His Excellency was throwing a giant tantrum and threatening to resign. They managed to dissuade him for the moment, but he remained unsettled and for several crucial days the question remained at the top of his personal agenda. He even sent Ismay and Campbell-Johnson back to London to canvass opinion on what he should do. Campbell-Johnson was to talk to his contacts in the press and elsewhere, Ismay to the government, the opposition, and not least, the king himself. All, naturally, thought Mountbatten should stay on as governor-general of India, and could not see what he was worrying about. Personal messages from King George, Attlee and Churchill did the trick, and on 9 July he told his staff he had made up his mind to stay.

Ismay did not return to India until 22 July 1947, having been away for 17 days during the most hectic period. He had, however, been in London during the passage of the Indian Independence Bill through Parliament, which was the official reason given for his trip. The drafting of the Bill had only been able to begin in earnest once the Indian provinces had decided on partition. To have it ready and on the statute book in time for power to be transferred on 15 August was a prodigious achievement. No comparable piece of legislation had ever been completed so quickly. The 1935 India Act had taken six years overall: the 1947 Act was completed in less than six weeks.

In Delhi, V.P. Menon was responsible for overseeing the Bill's progress and clearing it with the Indian leaders, aided by a lawyer sent out from London, and Sir George Spence, a former law secretary who was just about to retire and return to England. Spence was in poor health, but volunteered to stay on and work under Menon – who had once been a clerk in his department. It was a gesture of love for the country he had both served and helped to rule that was typical of so many Britons then.

The Bill was introduced to the House of Commons on 4 July by Attlee, received its second reading six days later, and its third on 14 July. There were no amendments, no dissenting voices – Anthony Eden had been given the task of keeping Churchill out of the way, for fear that the old lion might be unable to resist letting out a few roars and upsetting everything. The following day it was passed through the House of Lords, with several fine speeches cheering it on its way. Halifax, himself a former viceroy, was lavish in his praise for both Attlee and Mountbatten. But it was Lord Samuel who found the most memorable phrase to mark the occasion: 'It may be said of the British Raj,' he declaimed, 'as Shakespeare said of the Thane of Cawdor, "Nothing in his life became him like the leaving of it." This Bill is a moral to all future generations; it is a Treaty of

Peace without a war.' Fine words indeed − but had Samuel been a theatrical, he would have known better than to tempt fate by quoting from Macbeth, a sure way to bring ill fortune.

While Ismay was away, all had been proceeding apace. The partition committees had been told to submit their completed reports within one month of starting work, a desperately short period of time even though the work of partition was given absolute priority over everything else. They all met the target, thanks largely to their professionalism and an amazing absence of friction. The same could not be said for the politicians. Inevitably, many administrative decisions were also highly political, and there were frequent clashes of interest. A typical example was the question of printing presses. There was only one official press in Karachi, where the new Pakistan government would initially be based, and that could not cope with the needs of the provincial government of Sind, let alone Pakistan's. The government of India had six presses in Delhi, and Liaquat asked for one of them to be moved to Karachi, to be used for printing government documents, banknotes, and so on. It was a reasonable enough request, and Mountbatten had no hesitation in putting it before the Partition Council. Sardar Patel refused point blank. 'No one asked Pakistan to secede,' he declared. 'We do not mind their taking their property with them, but we have no intention of allowing them to injure the work of the government of India merely because they have not enough resources of their own.' He was finally persuaded to make one press available, but only on condition that it remained in Delhi and that the Pakistanis would stop using it the moment a new press arrived in Karachi from London.[19]

The affair of the printing press highlighted the biggest problem being faced by Pakistan. India, which had finally been recognized by the British government as the successor state on 17 June after further pressure from Mountbatten, would simply take over a going concern with everything in place. Pakistan, on the other hand, would be starting from scratch, without an established administration, without armed forces, without records, without equipment or military stores.

All these handicaps were exacerbated by Mountbatten's mad rush to complete the hand-over in 72 days, which the Muslims understandably regarded as a deliberate attempt to sabotage their new country even before it was born. As early as 9 May, during his stay in Simla with Nehru, Mountbatten had admitted the problem. 'What are we doing?' he had asked then. 'Administratively it is the difference between putting up a permanent building, a nissen hut or a tent. As far as Pakistan is concerned, we are putting up a tent.'[20] It was Nehru and Patel, to say nothing of Gandhi, who had consistently demanded a fast conclusion, and Mountbatten had given way to them, adding to the suspicion of favouritism. Of all the charges levelled against him, that, with all its tragic consequences, was the one that would still remain 50 years later.

Karachi, the capital of Sind, had been chosen as the first capital of Pakistan for various reasons. For a start, the new capital would have to be in West Pakistan, since East Bengal would still be in the throes of partition and establishing its own provincial capital at Dacca. In West Pakistan, Sind was the only province with a Muslim League government. As a fairly new province itself, Sind had a recently-built, modern assembly building, which could be used for the Central Assembly. The Sind government offered the governor's house as the official residence of the new governor-general – it was hardly the same as Lutyens's and Baker's monumental complex in New Delhi, but it would have to do. Added to that, Karachi had a mild climate, an international airport and a fine harbour. It also happened to be the birthplace of the Quaid-i-Azam, though he had never shown much attachment to it on that score.

But Karachi, although a modern town, was not a large town. It had a population of only about 350,000 and the sudden arrival of 25,000 people strained its resources and its accommodation to the limit. The mayor, Dr Hakim M. Ahsan, made over most of his municipal offices to supplement the provincial government offices that were taken over, but still there were nowhere near enough. Part of the secretariat could be accommodated in the assembly building, the rest took over the army's Napier Barracks. Elsewhere, temporary wooden buildings were erected, and private offices requisitioned. Living accommodation was equally short. Even ministers could find no houses and were put up as guests in the homes of provincial ministers and officials. Other newcomers had to make do with a tented reception camp. 'By 15 August,' wrote Chaudry Muhammad Ali, who was in overall charge of the arrangements, 'somehow or other, shelter had been found for the thousands of families that poured into Karachi, and office accommodation for every ministry and department had been found or hastily constructed.'[21]

Dr Ahsan recalls:

When people started working there were no desks, there were no chairs, they started by squatting on the floor. To tell you the truth, we didn't even have money enough to disburse their salaries. I had some 75,000 lakhs at that time in my reserve funds, the Sind government had some reserve funds, so we volunteered that, and so the first few months were tided over. And suddenly, we received money, our share, from the division of assets. A trickle came down to us, and so we started to manage things.

Until then, even the simplest things were in short supply: with no pins or paper-clips, for example, officials and secretaries resorted to using thorns to fasten their papers together. But all were borne along on a wave of euphoria and what Dr Ahsan describes as missionary zeal.[22]

Before anything could be divided between India and Pakistan, everything had to be counted. The assets of provinces which were not going to be partitioned naturally remained their property. But in the Punjab, Bengal and Assam as well as in central government offices in Delhi and elsewhere, clerks checked inventories and counted every table, chair, typewriter and paper-clip. It is intriguing to see the resources some of the departments of the mighty Raj had at their disposal. The Department of Food and Agriculture, for example, boasted '425 clerks' tables, 85 large tables, 85 officers' chairs, 850 ordinary chairs, 50 hat pegs, 6 hat pegs with mirror, 130 bookshelves, 4 iron safes, 20 table lamps, 170 typewriters, 120 fans, 120 clocks, 110 bicycles, 600 inkstands, 3 staff cars, 2 sets of sofas and 40 chamber pots.' It is extraordinary that, with no more equipment than that, the British had attempted to keep 400 million Indians fed, and oversee their agriculture.

There was, of course, more than furniture and equipment to be sorted out and counted. There were also people. The vast majority of government servants in British India had always been in the provinces, especially since the 1919 and 1935 Acts had increased provincial autonomy, but there were some 3,000 civil servants and Indian Police officers forming what were known as the Secretary of State's Services. These had to decide for themselves where they were going, and generally it was a simple if reluctant choice.

There were other services, however, which were much more complicated. Not least of these were the railways. Rolling stock and equipment were relatively simple to divide, but what about the employees? There were about 925,000 people working for the Indian railways at the time of partition. About 73,000 of those working in the Pakistan portions of the North-Western Railway and the Bengal-Assam Railway opted for India, while around 83,500 employees in the other companies working in India opted for Pakistan. This meant that arrangements had to be made for the transfer of 156,500 employees without, if possible, disrupting vital rail services.[23] There was no way this could possibly be done by 15 August. The result was rail chaos over the critical period, which contributed to the catastrophe that was to engulf the Punjab.

When it came to dividing up the non-human assets, there were some items that could be shared equally on a 50–50 basis. In Lahore, for example, when the superintendent of police, Patrick Rich, divided the police equipment between Muslim and Hindu and Sikh representatives, it was strictly half and half – one set of leggings for the Hindus and Sikhs, one for the Muslims, and so on through rifles, lathis and so on. But this even-handedness broke down when it came to sharing the instruments of the police band. It began well enough – a flute for Pakistan, a flute for India, a drum for Pakistan, a drum for India, and so on.

At the end, however, a single trombone remained, and to Rich's astonishment the two representatives came to blows over an instrument neither of them could play.

More serious, at the central level, was the dispute over money – always the most contentious part of any divorce, after the children. In essence, it was a question of how the cash balances, the sterling balances and the public debt were to be divided up. On the credit side, there was money in state banks, gold in the vaults of the Bank of India, and so on, as well as various properties belonging to the Raj. Cash balances amounted to about Rs 4 billion (£300 million). The Pakistan representatives asked for 25 per cent of this, based on population, resources and requirements. The Indians offered 5 per cent, Rs 200 million, arguing that the large cash balances were due to anti-inflationary measures, and that the working balance was really only Rs 500 million, a tortuous piece of logic which the Muslims found impossible to fathom. On the debit side, however, the Indians proposed that Pakistan should be responsible for 20 per cent of India's huge uncovered debt, and assume joint responsibility for the equally large public debt to securities holders.

The two sides were soon deadlocked, and in fact did not reach final agreement until late November, when H.M. Patel and Muhammad Ali shut themselves in a bedroom in Vallabhbhai Patel's house, after he and various other ministers agreed to give them a free hand. They swore not to come out until the matter was settled – which after all the months of wrangling they achieved in only 45 minutes. The final agreement which the two friends reached was that Pakistan would take 17.5 per cent of the cash and sterling balances and in return would cover the same proportion of India's national debt. They also agreed to divide up the remaining movable assets of the Raj on a ratio of 1.4.

The question of finances revealed other problems facing Pakistan, one of the most serious of which was a shortage of experienced banking staff. Banking in India had always been very much the preserve of non-Muslims, largely because usury, the lending of money for profit, is forbidden under Islamic law. Partly for this reason, it was agreed that the Reserve Bank of India would continue to manage Pakistan's financial affairs until 1 October 1948. The existing Indian currency would remain in use in both countries until the end of March 1948, which was the earliest Pakistan could expect to start introducing its own coins and banknotes. From that time, Indian notes would remain in use, but were overprinted with the words 'Government of Pakistan'. In fact, the system was to break down in December 1947, when the Indian government instructed the Reserve Bank to withhold Pakistan's agreed share of the cash balances, provoking a new crisis between the two dominions. The date for Pakistan's taking control of her own financial affairs was advanced by three months. The State Bank of Pakistan was established on 1 July 1948, with a capital of Rs 30 million, only half of which came from the government, with the remainder subscribed by the public.

On the everyday commercial banking front, most Hindu-owned and managed banks in the provinces that were to join Pakistan transferred their headquarters and funds to India. Only one Muslim-owned bank, the Habib Bank, moved in the opposite direction. As the disturbances in the Punjab increased, the Hindu banks panicked, closing 418 branches in West Pakistan, and leaving only 69 in the entire country after partition.

Dividing the armed services was one of the most difficult and delicate tasks of all. It was not made any easier by the stubborn reluctance of Auchinleck, who still believed it should never be done at all, and in any case would take from three to five years to complete. He was not the only sceptic: Ismay, who was also deeply attached to the Indian army, where, he said, no communal differences had ever disturbed the *esprit de corps* of mixed regiments, was grief-stricken at the thought that 'these magnificent units were to be mutilated'.

Ismay had done his utmost to persuade Jinnah not to insist on splitting the army, reminding him that in the early days of their nationhood both the new governments would have special need of an army on which they could depend. Ismay wrote in his memoirs:

> I asked him to remember that an army was not merely a collection of men with rifles and bayonets and guns and tanks: it was a living entity ... Why not divide the Army on numerical lines in the first instance, India getting two-thirds and Pakistan one third? Later on, when things were more settled, it might be found more expedient to transfer the Hindu element in the Pakistan Army to India, and vice versa.[24]

As a military man, Ismay should have known he was fighting a hopeless rearguard action. Jinnah was very polite, but dismissive. 'Lord Ismay,' he said, 'we are very grateful to you for coming out to India to try and help us, but you know nothing about Hindus and you know nothing about Muslims.'[25]

On Monday, 23 June, Field Marshal Montgomery, chief of the Imperial General Staff, arrived in Delhi to discuss the situation with the viceroy and Auchinleck. Mountbatten eagerly seized on his visit as an opportunity to impress. The viceregal servants normally wore Mountbatten's personal insignia embroidered on their livery: 'M of B' (Mountbatten of Burma), set within the Order of the Garter. In the sort of *noblesse oblige* gesture he loved to make, Mountbatten arranged that the monogram should be changed to read 'M of A' for Montgomery of Alamein, who was also a member of the Order of the Garter. Montgomery was delighted. Ismay found the whole business 'a scream'. 'Both concentrated on their "ego" and on their own personal achievements — so discussion became a bit confused,' he wrote to his wife next day.[26]

One of Montgomery's reasons for visiting India was to persuade Auchinleck to accept the inevitability of the dismemberment of the Indian army. At the same time, he discussed the possibility of replacing Auchinleck with Field Marshal Slim. Nehru, who by now was suspecting Auchinleck of being pro-Muslim, was reported to be agreeable, but Mountbatten was not – this was no time to be changing horses. And so Auchinleck stayed, and supervised the operation with his usual thorough professionalism, though in the end it broke his heart.

The Joint Defence Committee, which was to monitor the business of dividing up the armed forces and their various assets, was set up on 30 June. Of all the committees it needed perhaps the greatest combination of sensitivity and firmness, and finding the right men was crucial to its success. It was V.P. Menon who suggested Sir Chandulal Trivedi, then governor of Orissa and soon to become the first governor of East Punjab, one of the most difficult of all the new appointments in India. Trivedi had been secretary of the War Department until 1946, and probably knew more about military administration than anyone in the country. More to the point, though a Hindu and on good terms with the Congress high command, he was also a lifelong friend of Liaquat. He was thus in the unique position of enjoying the confidence of Hindus, Muslims and the armed forces. Choosing Trivedi was an inspired idea, since none of the other members trusted each other an inch, and the politicians were scarcely talking to each other. It was largely thanks to him that the committee was able to complete its task successfully and even amicably.

In terms of personnel, the division of the Indian army seemed basically very simple. The original plan to divide on territorial citizenship rather than religious lines, but allowing those whose home community was in a minority to transfer if they chose, had been dropped by the Partition Council. Now, soldiers were to be separated along religious lines and relocated in either India or Pakistan by 15 August. The army sub-committee set up to oversee this had, in its ignorance, assumed that all Muslims would choose to go to Pakistan, and all non-Muslims to India. When some did not, confusion reigned. There were Muslims from India who had no intention of going to Pakistan and wished to continue serving in the new Indian army. Similarly, there were non-Muslims who looked upon provinces that were to be in Pakistan as home. In theory, all a soldier had to do was fill in a questionnaire, and the authorities would arrange everything for him. But some soldiers havered and wavered and changed their minds at the last minute, or even after the last minute. Some had their minds changed for them.

Captain (later Lieutenant-General) L.S. Menèzes, commanded a rifle company at Thal in Kurram in the NWFP. He was a Christian and his men were Muslim. They wished to return to India, and were duly replaced on the Frontier by two companies of Dogras, who had chosen Pakistan. *En route* to their base,

Menèzes's company was forcibly taken off the train at Lahore, because the Pakistani authorities were suspicious of a company of Muslims returning to India.[27]

This monstrous game of musical chairs was further complicated by the fact that, by 15 August, there were well over 400,000 Indian soldiers in the sub-continent, and more were returning every day from Japan, Iraq, Africa and elsewhere. The country was awash with soldiery, many of whom had no idea where they were supposed to be going, or had not yet made up their minds. Menèzes believes that this proved to a blessing in disguise. He argues that the presence of hundreds of thousands of experienced, well-trained men on the move prevented the coming intercommunal massacres from being much worse than they were.

Compared to the army, dividing up the navy and the air force was simple. For one thing, there were fewer assets to worry about, and far fewer personnel. No major problems were anticipated. Nevertheless, as with the division of any property anywhere, what Jonas Chuzzlewit called 'the rule of bargains' applied: 'Do other men, for they would do you.'

The air force presented few complications, and was divided quickly and fairly. The navy was slightly more involved. The naval sub-committee consisted of two Muslim and two Hindu naval officers: Captains Soman and Shankar representing India, and Captain H.M.S. Choudhri and Commander I.K. Mumtaz Pakistan. There was no problem over shore bases and training establishments, which had to go to the country where they were located – those in Bombay, for instance to India, those in Karachi to Pakistan. The ships included six sloops, four River Class frigates, 16 Bathurst/Bangor mine-sweepers, and various trawlers, motor mine-sweepers, motor launches and harbour craft. According to Shankar, everything began amicably, with India and Pakistan sharing the frigates evenly and the smaller vessels on a proportional basis – India receiving 12 mine-sweepers to Pakistan's four, and so on. The only difficulty arose over the sloops. The flagship, HMIS *Narbada*, was the largest of these, and the Pakistanis wanted her. It had already been agreed that the fairest division was for India to have four because of her longer coastline, and Pakistan two. Shankar proposed that India should keep the two oldest, *Sutlej* and *Jumna*, and the two newest, *Kistna* and *Cauvery*, leaving Pakistan *Narbada* and *Godavari*, the two ships in between. Soman, the other Indian negotiator, was uneasy about this – why should they give up the largest sloop?, he argued. But he was persuaded into agreeing to the division by his colleague.[28]

Unfortunately, the *Times of India* got hold of the story and accused the Indian team of betraying the nation by handing over its flagship to Pakistan. The two captains were hauled before a committee of senior Congress leaders, including Vallabhbhai Patel, Baldev Singh, and three others. Patel was intimidating in the extreme, accusing the two men of betraying their trust and being 'traitors of the worst kind'. They could see themselves appearing before a court martial, if not a firing-squad. Shankar, however, pointed out that neither Patel nor the journalist who had written the piece were sailors. They knew nothing about ships in general, and the *Narbada* in particular, whereas he did. 'I have just completed a term on that ship,' he said, 'and I know for sure [she] will not be seaworthy for at least two years, maybe more ... In my considered view, India is better off letting Pakistan have it, if they are so keen on it.'[29]

And so by common sense, experience, and a fair bit of shrewd horse-trading, the division of the spoils in the armed services was achieved. It would all take a little time to complete, and there were several bitter battles ahead over military stores and the ordnance factories, all of which stayed firmly in India, but it was agreed that by 15 August both countries would have sufficient forces of their own to be able to defend their borders and keep the peace internally. These forces would be under their own local operational command, with commanders-in-chief answerable directly to the new governments, and would provide the basis for the future national armies, navies and air forces.

A limited number of British officers on short-term contracts would be retained by both the Indian and Pakistani armed forces. However, the remaining British forces were to begin withdrawing from the sub-continent by 15 August. The last British troops were to leave by 28 February 1948. To begin with, the commanders-in-chief of both armies, navies and air forces were to be British – General Sir Rob Lockhart as C-in-C of the Indian army and General Sir Frank Messervy of the Pakistani army. Auchinleck was to serve in the new post of supreme commander, maintaining overall administrative, but not operational, control and answerable to a Joint Defence Committee which would include the governors-general of both new dominions and their defence ministers. The plan was that this arrangement should continue until 1 April 1948, by which date the 'reconstitution' of the armed forces was to be complete. In the event, however, it lasted only until 26 September 1947, when Auchinleck was forced to offer his resignation after Patel accused him of pro-Pakistan bias – at the same time that Liaquat was complaining that he was under the thumb of the Indian government. The Supreme Headquarters was closed down at the end of November, with Auchinleck retiring and refusing Attlee's offer of a peerage.

The last British unit, the Somerset Light Infantry, left Bombay on the last day of February 1948, slow-marching through the great arch of the Gateway of India past an honour guard of Sikh and Gurkha troops. As they were ferried out to the waiting troopship, the sound of singing wafted across the water to speed them on their way. It was a spontaneous rendering from the immense Indian crowd gathered on shore, of that old Scottish anthem of farewell, *Auld Lang Syne*: 'Should auld acquaintance be forgot, and never brought to mind ...'

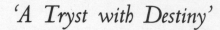

'A Tryst with Destiny'

Besides the division of the Punjab, the other major problem overshadowing the transfer of power was the question of the princes. They had, after all, wrecked the central government provision of the 1935 Act by refusing to enter a federation, and now they threatened the successful conclusion of the transfer of power. Nobody had told Mountbatten that the princes might be difficult: 'I had been given no inkling,' he wrote later, 'that this was going to be as hard to solve as British India, if not harder.'[1] As a result, he had not bothered to give it much thought until the decision for partition suddenly brought the princely states into focus. 'When the date was fixed for August 15,' recalled Sir Conrad Corfield, who as political adviser was responsible for the states, 'it became more important than ever that he should appreciate the difficult position of the Indian States. It proved impossible, however, to distract his attention from British Indian problems.'[2]

Two-fifths of the land area of the sub-continent, and 100 million of its 400 million inhabitants, were ruled by the princes – Maharajas, Nawabs, Rajas and so on. These were medieval monarchs, complete autocrats, with all internal power concentrated in their own hands or those of their families and favourites. They looked upon their states' revenues as their own personal piggy-banks, squandering their wealth on women, horses, Rolls Royces, planes, gambling – all the playthings of the super-rich. Not surprisingly, their states suffered, tending to be more backward than the rest of India. In matters of law and order or civil liberties, or health, in economic and educational terms, the princely states remained firmly trapped in the Middle Ages.

In all, there were 562 princely states in India, ranging in size from Hyderabad and Kashmir, each of which was almost as big as mainland Britain, to mere dots on the map. The rulers of this crazy patchwork of political dependencies all owed allegiance to the British crown. To British India, the viceroy was the governor-general; to the princes, he was the crown representative. It had suited Britain to leave the states as they were in 1858 – it would have stretched the nation's resources beyond their limits to have added another two-fifths to the land area it directly administered. The states were not directly ruled by Britain, but were looked after by her for defence, foreign policy and communications, in return for which they each acknowledged British 'paramountcy' through individual treaties. Their citizens were not British subjects, like the other Indians, but 'British protected persons'.

It had been Linlithgow's policy as viceroy not to do anything that might 'alarm or dishearten' the princes, who he believed were 'the only solid and dependable element in India, on which the British could rely'. Others saw things differently. Ever since his membership of the Simon Commission, Attlee had regarded the princes as the major stumbling block on the road to Indian independence. The problem was what to do with them and how to do it. It is not surprising that the Cabinet mission plan attempted to clarify the issue by simply washing its hands of the whole matter: 'It is quite clear that with the attainment of independence by British India, whether inside or outside the British Common-wealth, the relationship which has hitherto existed between the Rulers of the States and the British Crown will no longer be possible. Paramountcy can neither be retained by the British Crown nor transferred to the new Governments.' In other words, after independence the princes would have to fend for themselves and make their own deals with the new governments of India or Pakistan, whichever was appropriate. 'The precise form which their co-operation will take,' the plan continued, 'must be a matter for negotiation during the building up of the constitutional structure, and it by no means follows that it will be identical for all the States.'[3]

The vast majority of the states were in the territory that would become India: only 14 of the 562 were in or adjacent to Pakistan. But here again there were complications. Some princes were of a different religion from the majority of their subjects – Hindu princes ruled Muslims and vice versa – and what made things worse was that this applied to some of the biggest states. In Hyderabad, the Nizam was a Muslim while 86 per cent of his people were Hindus – 14.62 million out of 17 million – and the land-locked state was entirely surrounded by India. In Jammu and Kashmir, the situation was reversed: there the ruler was a Hindu, while 77 per cent of his population were Muslim, a proportion rising to 96 per cent in the valley of Kashmir itself, and the state was largely, though not completely, bordered by Pakistan.

Most of the princes saw themselves as Indian Englishmen, men of two worlds, as much at home at Lords or Henley as they were in India. They had been educated in England, many of their friends were English, and they looked to the British for support and encouragement against what they saw as an attempt by native politicians to strip them of their power and wealth. In this, the Muslim

Nawab of Bhopal – a friend of Jinnah and a man of great influence – was typical. When he learned that his old friend Louis Mountbatten, whom he had known since the 1920s, was to be the new viceroy, he believed the princes now had nothing to fear. Mountbatten, he told other friends, would never let them down. He was to be disappointed.

Bhopal had recently been elected chancellor of the Chamber of Princes, and rather improbably hoped to transform what was little more than a gentlemen's debating club, of which the viceroy of the day was the president, into a vital third force in Indian politics. He wanted the princes to have the same kind of political clout as the Muslim League or Congress. But as he well knew, the only circumstance in which this might happen was if the future independent British India opted to become a loose federation of states, with power at the periphery, as envisaged in the 1935 Act. With the League and Congress permanently at each other's throats, he believed the princes would hold the balance of power. In theory at least, Jinnah was not averse to such a structure; Gandhi and Congress, however, were. They demanded a strong central government – which meant government by them, the Hindu majority.

The coming of the constituent assembly brought discord among the princes. Bhopal believed that those who agreed to take part in drafting the new constitution had weakened the position of the princes as a whole, and had made themselves the unwitting tool of Congress. He was also exercised about the time limit the British had set on their departure, even before Mountbatten brought it forward. June 1948, he thought, would be impossible to meet and 'if enforced must lead to bloodshed and chaos'.[4]

The other main faction, led by the Sikh Maharaja of Bikaner, argued that the states could not afford to be left out of the constitution-making process. They could not adopt a wait-and-see policy but must co-operate fully with the work of the constituent assembly. He pointed out the danger of any of the states failing to carry their own people with them: 'nothing must be done which could impair their loyalty and support'.[5] He believed that the interests of the people could only be served by establishing a union or federation with real political power at the centre – the very reverse, in fact, of what the Nawab of Bhopal advocated. This fundamental disagreement was the reason why Bhopal and Bikaner had refused to sit together at Mountbatten's inauguration ceremony.

It was Mountbatten's announcement of independence on 15 August that finally sabotaged any ideas the princes may have had of holding the balance of power. Bhopal immediately resigned his chancellorship of the Chamber of Princes, on the grounds that as soon as paramountcy was withdrawn all Indian states, his own included, would automatically become independent: each state, he said, would have to forge its own political relationship with India or Pakistan. A week later, Travancore, one of the most southerly of the states, declared it would opt for independence. Hyderabad followed suit. Congress feared that others would join them, fragmenting India and bringing the chaos that everyone dreaded. This could cause untold damage to India's fragile infrastructure: under the British, the states and provinces had been welded together into an administrative whole, enabling railways, postal and telegraph services to cross boundaries without any problems. Food and agriculture policy, too, was conducted on a national basis, as was the control of narcotics, arms and ammunition, the extradition of criminals and the surrender of fugitives.

At a meeting of party leaders called by Mountbatten on 13 June to discuss the problem of the states, Jinnah and Nehru clashed over the question of the states' independence. Jinnah agreed with Bhopal's reading of the situation – indeed, he had probably advised him on it. Nehru, however, approached the situation as an emotional politician rather than a punctilious constitutional lawyer. Only those states that could demonstrate their sovereignty, he maintained, could be considered truly independent, and the test of sovereignty was twofold: first, the capacity to conduct a foreign policy, second the capacity to wage war. By those criteria, very few could claim even partial sovereignty. It followed, he argued, that in order to prevent the spread of anarchy within the sub-continent, the existing British political and administrative machinery for the states must be preserved, until it could be taken over *in toto* by the new government. Any state opposing this policy would be considered to have committed an unfriendly act towards that government, and would have to bear the consequences.

The British government had no intention of allowing itself to be stuck with the problem of the princes once it had handed power to the Indians – for Attlee, this would destroy the whole object of the exercise. He made it quite clear that once paramountcy ceased, so did Britain's responsibility. As soon as the Independence Act was passed, Mountbatten dissolved the interim government, with enormous relief, and set up two parallel interim governments for India and Pakistan. The old Political Department, under Sir Conrad Corfield, which had looked after the states and provided them with residents, advisers and support, was wrapped up and its duties handed on to the new governments' States Department. This in itself instantly made things easier, for Corfield had long identified far too closely with his 'clients', the princes, and had been working diligently to sabotage the efforts of Mountbatten and the party leaders to persuade them to accede quickly to one or other of the new dominions. Corfield believed that the longer the princes held out, the stronger their bargaining position would be: indeed, it would be best for them if they could hold out until after partition, when they could, he believed, name their own terms.

Corfield's chances of success in continuing his obstructive tactics plummeted when the new Indian states minister was appointed – it was the iron man of Congress, Vallabhbhai Patel. And they hit zero when Patel began by persuading V.P. Menon, whose task as reforms commissioner was finished now that the Act had received the royal assent, to become secretary of his new department. Menon had been on the verge of retirement, but Patel informed him that his country needed him. As Menon himself recorded, Patel told him 'people like myself should not think in terms of retirement ... I should consider it my bounden duty to work for the consolidation of freedom.'⁶ Menon and Patel, already a well-practised double act, were to make a formidable team. Corfield retired, with bad grace, but not before Mountbatten had given him one last order: to organize a conference of princes at which the viceroy would apply pressure on them to accede gracefully. Corfield made sure, however, that he left for home two days before the conference, which started on Friday 25 July.

The conference was Mountbatten's first and only official meeting with the princes. The red carpet at the Council House was rolled out for the occasion, and the new chancellor of the Chamber of Princes, the massive, six-foot-four-inch Sikh Maharaja of Patiala, stood at the door to welcome the viceroy, dwarfing Menon, who stood beside him. All previous viceroys, even Wavell, had dressed in formal grey morning suit for such occasions, but Mountbatten dazzled in his white admiral's uniform with his full array of orders and decorations, looking every inch a prince himself. Previously, too, viceroys had always sat in solitary splendour on a dais, but this time there were two chairs, one for Mountbatten and one for the dour figure of Patel. The Maharwal of Dungapur, for one, correctly interpreted this as meaning that pressure was being brought to bear on the princes, not only by the viceroy but also by the future government of India. The message was 'do as we want, or else'. As if to drive the message home, the princes were told that the session, which would normally last anything up to two or three days, was being reduced — to about two hours.

Mountbatten needed to persuade the rulers to hand over their states and accede to India or Pakistan. Patel urged him to get them to sign individual instruments of accession. If they refused to co-operate, India would almost certainly take over their states after the transfer of power, by force of arms if necessary. It was a tricky situation, but, inevitably, it was V.P. Menon who came up with a practical, face-saving solution. He proposed that the rulers should be persuaded to hand over just three functions of their states to central government: defence, external relations, and communications — the same functions which had always been exercised by the British government. Few if any of the states were equipped to conduct their own defence, and external affairs was by definition tied to defence. Communications, which included postal services, telegraph, and broadcasting as well as railways and road links, were the life-line of the new nation and could not reasonably be left to the whims of individual rulers.

Mountbatten thought his task would be easier if he could offer the rulers something in return, such as retaining their perks — titles, palaces, privy purses, their right to British decorations, and so on. Patel was blunt: Mountbatten could offer them whatever he liked, so long as Patel got his 'full basket of apples'. In other words, all the rulers must sign their instruments of accession and abandon their claims to independence, before the transfer of power.

At the conference on 25 July 1947 Mountbatten explained to the princes that accession would cost them nothing – they would incur no financial liability at all – nor would signing the so-called standstill agreement. This was one of those convenient constitutional documents which preserved the political status quo until, in legal parlance, such time as 'new arrangements in this behalf' could be made. He assured them that states that were 'viable', even small states which grouped together into 'viable units', would have a future – they would have nothing to fear from the Dominion of India.

The Nawab of Bhopal was a notable absentee from the conference. He said the princes had been invited 'like oysters to attend the tea-party with the Walrus and the Carpenter'.[7] Presumably, he saw Mountbatten in the role of the Walrus ('"I weep for you," the Walrus said,/"I deeply sympathise."/With sobs and tears he sorted out/Those of the largest size.'), while the gruff, monosyllabic Patel was ideal casting for the Carpenter. As if to substantiate Bhopal's theory, there actually was a party three days later, when Mountbatten gave a reception for over 50 rulers and 100 states representatives. Campbell-Johnson recorded:

> Those of Their Highnesses who had not already signified their intention of signing the Instrument of Accession were duly shepherded by the ADC's one by one for a friendly talk with Mountbatten. He in his turn passed them on in full view of the company to VP, who conducted them across the room to see Patel. There were Maharajas three deep in a semi-circle watching this process. One veteran prince was heard to remark, 'Who's HE getting to work on now?' Craning forward to see, he added with relish, 'There's no need for him to work on me. I'm signing to morrow!'[8]

It was not until Thursday of the following week, at a meeting of the full negotiating committee held in Bikaner House, that the drafts of the Instruments of Accession and the standstill agreement were approved. But by 14 August, Patel's basket was almost filled with 'apples'. Only three were missing. One was the relatively small state of Junagadh, but the others were the two largest – Hyderabad and Kashmir.

Mountbatten addressed the constituent assembly on the morning of 13 August:

> It is a great triumph for the realism and sense of responsibility of the rulers and the governments of the States as well as for the Government of India

that it was possible to produce an Instrument of Accession which was equally acceptable to both sides; and one, moreover, so simple and so straightforward that within less than three weeks practically all the States concerned had signed the Instrument of Accession and a unified Standstill Agreement. There is thus established a unified political structure.

V.P. Menon's reaction was more honest – he just thanked God they had managed to bring it off, and so avert the threatened fragmentation of India. He wrote: 'We had obtained a breathing space during which we could evolve a permanent relationship between the Government of India and the States.' If anyone's contribution to the final stages of India's independence deserves to be celebrated, it is surely Menon's.

The Punjab and Bengal had voted for partition – but who was to draw the lines? After the obligatory wrangles, with Jinnah playing for time by suggesting calling in the United Nations, which could have delayed things for months if not years, it was decided to set up two boundary commissions, each with an independent chairman and four High Court judges, two nominated by Congress and two by the League. Finding the judges was simple, but agreeing on two chairmen was impossible. In the end, Sir Cyril Radcliffe, Listowel's rejected nominee for the Arbitral Tribunal, was accepted as a compromise candidate, and at Jinnah's suggestion he was appointed chairman of both commissions, with a casting vote. Congress and the League both agreed to accept his awards, and to enforce them.

Sir Cyril was one of Britain's most distinguished lawyers, who had served as director-general of the Ministry of Information during the war, when Mountbatten had got to know him. Son of a wealthy sportsman, educated like Attlee at Haileybury, he had won a first at Oxford and became a fellow of All Souls. One of his main qualifications for the job in the eyes of the Indian politicians, however, was that he had never been to India, had no connections with it, and was therefore deemed not to be prejudiced in favour of either community.

Radcliffe would be responsible for the separation of 88 million people, most of whom wished to be at each other's throats, and for dividing 175,000 square miles of territory between them as equally as possible. Yet his only briefing was a 30-minute session with the permanent under-secretary in the India Office, poring over a large-scale map of India. It was an impossible task, but Sir Cyril seems to have had no doubt that he was up to it. What he did have justifiable doubts about was the time in which he was expected to accomplish the partition. He expected to be given several months at the very least, but when he arrived in Delhi on 8 July, he was shattered to find that he had just five weeks.

The terms of reference for the commissions were simple: they were 'to demarcate the boundaries on the basis of ascertaining the contiguous majority areas of Muslims and non-Muslims, and in doing so to take into account also other factors'. What constituted these 'other factors' was never defined, but clearly they gave Radcliffe considerable room for manœuvre, which he was going to need if he was to satisfy everyone. Obviously, they included such features as natural boundaries, communications, watercourses and irrigation systems. But there was a host of other, less tangible considerations to be taken into account, too, and the Partition Council deliberately refrained from attempting to list or define them – they knew that once they started, they would never finish.

After briefly visiting Lahore and Calcutta to meet the members of the two commissions, Radcliffe settled into the Controller's House on the edge of the viceregal estate, avoiding contact with the viceroy as far as possible, to minimize any suspicions of influence and impropriety. Since he could not sit with both commissions, he sat with neither, studying the reports and records of their proceedings and all the material submitted to them by counsel representing Congress, the League, Sikh members of the Punjab Legislative Assembly, and other interested parties, which were flown to him in Delhi each day. He soon realized, however, that there was an added complication to his task – the distinguished Indian judges on the commissions were hopelessly partisan and could hardly bear to speak to each other, let alone work together harmoniously. One of them at least had good reason for an anger he could hardly contain: the wife and two children of the Sikh judge in Lahore had been murdered by Muslims in Rawalpindi a few weeks earlier. It was clear that Radcliffe would have to make all the decisions himself – and that his role would not be that of a surgeon with a sharp scalpel but that of a butcher wielding a blunt and bloody axe.

In both Bengal and the Punjab, any dividing line was bound to run through densely populated areas, cutting through road and rail communications, irrigation schemes, electric power systems and even individual landholdings – a hastily-drawn boundary might well separate a peasant from his fields, a factory from its warehouse yards. The Bengal commission was also responsible for the Sylhet district and other Muslim majority areas in Assam, and for the hill tracts around Chittagong, which were inhabited by Buddhist hill tribes. But the big question was who should get Calcutta. Without Calcutta, Muslim East Bengal would almost certainly decline into the rural slum already foretold. But could Calcutta itself survive without its hinterland and the river systems which flowed through Muslim-inhabited countryside? In the city, Muslims were only a quarter of the population, therefore it seemed proper for it to go to India – but a large proportion of the population were Scheduled Castes, who supported the League against Congress. There could be no easy answers.

The Punjab commission faced equally insoluble puzzles, with both sides laying claim to Lahore. Although there was in fact a slight Muslim majority in the city, the Hindus and Sikhs were so convinced it would be theirs that they refused to consider preparing any alternative capital for East Punjab. They felt any sign of moving from Lahore might prejudice their claim to the city. The situation in the Punjab was, of course, complicated by the presence of the Sikhs, whose heartland was at the very centre of the area where the line would have to be drawn. Whatever happened, some of their most holy shrines and historic sites would be given to the hated Muslims. What was more, much of their richest land was in West Punjab: they had been largely responsible for building and financing much of the British-designed canal system which had turned arid semi-deserts into the fertile breadbasket of India. Radcliffe was made aware of this, but he was also aware that while the Sikhs owned 40 per cent of the land in those areas, much of that land was worked by Muslim peasantry, who outnumbered them by four to one.

Through July and into August, Radcliffe toiled away in his bungalow, suffering terribly in the oppressive heat and humidity – the monsoon was unusually late that year. 'The heat is so appalling,' he told Leonard Mosley some years later, 'that at noon it looks like the blackest night and feels like the mouth of hell. After a few days of it, I seriously began to wonder whether I would come out of it alive. I have thought ever since that the greatest achievement which I made as Chairman of the Boundary Commission was a physical one, in surviving.'[9] Despite the hardships and the incredible workload, Radcliffe would accept no payment – he regarded the service he was performing as nothing more than his patriotic duty, to be carried out without fear or favour.

While Radcliffe was toiling away in his bungalow in Delhi, the Sikhs were planning to take matters into their own hands. There had been warnings of what was to come as early as March, when the chief secretary of the Punjab reported to Delhi that they were planning to set up their own state by force: 'Their plans embrace the whole community in the Punjab and it is said they also involve the Sikh States. The Sikhs are being regimented, they are being armed, if they are not armed already and they are being inflamed by propaganda both oral and written.'[10] Race memories of the atrocities committed against the Sikhs by Aurangzeb were still very much alive, fuelling fears of future persecution under renewed Muslim rule. After the 3 June plan had been announced, the main Sikh organization, the Shiromani Akali Dal, had distributed a circular saying that 'Pakistan means total death to the Sikh Panth [community] and the Sikhs are determined on a free sovereign state with the [rivers] Chenab and the Jamna as its borders, and it calls on all Sikhs to fight for their ideal under the flag of the Dal.'[11]

The Sikhs were organized on semi-military lines into *jathas* or armed bands, most of whom were ex-soldiers. It was the religious duty of every Sikh to carry a sword, the *kirpan*: in normal times this was often no more than a miniature token, but in times of crisis it became the real thing, full-sized, razor sharp, and ready for business. Now, the swords were augmented by pistols, rifles, sub-machine guns and even mortars. The *jathas* were trained and co-ordinated, able to link up with each other to form larger forces, and to join with the RSSS. The menace was unmistakable, and was regularly reported to Delhi by Jenkins and his staff.

Ismay, too, was worried about the Sikhs, much as he sympathized with 'this warrior sect, which had provided many thousands of splendid recruits for the Indian Army', and felt it 'had every cause to feel aggrieved'. Before he left for London on 5 July, he and Miéville had two or three talks with Giani Kartar Singh and his fellow leader, Master Tara Singh — his honorific title, incidentally, came from his having been a third-grade schoolteacher. 'They arrived,' Ismay recorded, 'carrying villainous-looking curved swords and many volumes of Hansard, from which they quoted interminably. They refused to budge an inch from their preconceived ideas, and occasionally used threatening language. We told them that if they resorted to violence, either before or after Partition, they would be very roughly handled; but we did not feel that our warnings had the slightest effect.'[12]

Knowing he was not getting through to Mountbatten, Jenkins asked if Ismay would meet him on 10 July, to discuss 'the serious situation'. Ismay, of course, was in London by then, but George Abell drove up to Simla to talk to the worried Punjab governor. Next day, he reported the conversation to Mountbatten, telling him Jenkins had stressed that there was no doubt the Sikhs were in a very dangerous mood, and that the tensions between Muslims and Hindus were building in the Punjab as a whole, but particularly in Lahore and Amritsar. 'The Muslims and Hindus,' Jenkins had told him, 'are in touch about everything except law and order ... Your Excellency should talk to Nehru and Patel and pray them to get the Congress and the Sikhs to drop their claim to stay in Lahore and hold up all the partitioning proceedings until the Boundary Commission reports.'[13]

To underline the seriousness of his message, Jenkins also wrote to Mountbatten direct, telling him the Sikhs were intent on causing trouble if the boundary commission's decisions were not to their liking, 'or if the new Governments of Pakistan and India are set up before the decision is given'. He reported on a meeting he had had with Giani Kartar Singh, who had said 'there would have to be an exchange of population on a large scale. Were the British ready to enforce this? He doubted if they were, and if no regard was paid to Sikh solidarity a fight was inevitable.'

Jenkins, who had always been opposed to partition in general and the partition of the Punjab in particular, told the Giani the Sikhs had only themselves to blame, since they had insisted on it. The Giani countered by saying they had never intended it to be based on population alone, and that they were just as entitled to their own land as the Hindus and Muslims. They must have their holy shrine at Nankana Sahib and at least one canal system, and there must be arrangements to bring 'at least three-quarters of the Sikh population from West to East Punjab'. In the exchange, property must be taken into account as well as population, since Sikhs were, on the whole, better off than the Muslims. If they did not get what they wanted, he warned again, 'they would be obliged to fight ... on revolutionary lines by murdering officials, cutting railway lines, destroying canal headworks and so on'.

When Jenkins told him this would be very foolish, the Giani retorted that Jenkins would feel the same if Britain were invaded. As for trust between the communities, the Giani said: 'The Muslims were now putting out some conciliatory propaganda about their attitude towards the Sikhs in their midst, but their intention was that of a sportsman who is careful not to disturb the birds he means to shoot. He believed the Muslims would try to make the Sikhs of West Punjab feel secure and then set about them in earnest.'[14]

Three days later, having had no response from Mountbatten, Jenkins wrote to him again, saying that 'The communal feeling is now unbelievably bad' and that the Sikhs 'threaten a violent rising immediately'. He begged him at all costs to announce Radcliffe's findings before 15 August, 'to stop panic and the mad hurrying to and fro of populations' between the two new dominions. He asked for a military force to be positioned along the likely line of the new border at once to preserve peace. 'I believe,' he ended, 'that if the representatives of the future Dominions can make it clear now that there is no question of a chaotic changeover, that they mean business, and that they are sending an imposing organisation here to protect the people, with appropriate publicity, it will do much to steady the Punjab.'[15]

With Liaquat and Jinnah also drawing Mountbatten's attention to the dangerous situation in the Punjab, and demanding the arrest of the Sikh leaders, the viceroy at last began to take serious notice. He called a staff meeting on 15 July to discuss it, but it was five days later before he visited Lahore to see the situation for himself, and to talk to Jenkins and members of the Punjab Partition Committee. The Committee tried to make out that 'things were going very well', but Jenkins soon put the record straight, telling Mountbatten that in fact they were going 'very slowly indeed'. 'Hatred and suspicion are entirely undisguised,' he said, adding that meetings of the Committee 'resemble a peace conference with a new war in sight'. The Committee members, however, followed the governor's earlier example by urging Mountbatten to announce the boundary award before 15 August.

On 27 July, Mountbatten received yet more disturbing intelligence from the Punjab:

Information from a reliable source has been received that if Nankana Sahib, about twelve miles north of Lahore, is not included in the Boundary Award to East Punjab, the Sikhs intend to start trouble on big scale. It is reported that the Sikhs intend to act on or about 7 August, and during the ten days before this, large meetings will be held to work up agitation. It is already known that the Sikhs have collected large quantities of arms. It is also reported that the Muslims are fully aware of the preparations and are, in fact, making counter-preparations. Both sides have attempted to subvert troops in the area and several of these attempts are said to have been not wholly unsuccessful. Promises of assistance from some troops have been received.[16]

V.P. Menon came up with another of his brilliant suggestions at the viceroy's staff meeting. Why not approach Jinnah and persuade him to declare Nankana Sahib 'a sort of Vatican'? Jinnah would have nothing to lose, and it could well help to calm the Sikhs. The suggestion was noted, and forgotten.

From Lahore itself, Jenkins made another bold suggestion. He urged Mountbatten to approach all the political leaders and ask them not to wait for the boundary commission but to make certain concessions which would ease the tension. Despite all the Hindu and Sikh dreams, it was pretty certain that Lahore must go to Pakistan. If Nehru and Patel were to concede it now, it would create the maximum of goodwill. As a quid pro quo, Jinnah could be asked to recognize that the Sikhs did have a case for a share in the canal colonies in the west. The Montgomery district, although populated by nearly a million Sikhs and only a quarter of a million Muslims, was geographically in West Punjab, and the boundary commission could not alter that. But the two parties themselves could do something about it, by negotiation 'out of court'. He asked Mountbatten to bring them together at once. This suggestion was not followed up either, and another possible opportunity for peace was lost.

Mountbatten's visit to Lahore, however, had finally persuaded him that something had to be done to contain if not forestall trouble in the Punjab. After consulting Auchinleck, he proposed to the Partition Council that a Punjab Boundary Force should be set up and put in place at once. The new force would be commanded by Major-General 'Pete' Rees, who was then in command of the 4th Indian Division, a famous and battle-hardened formation that had fought its way through Eritrea, the Western Desert including El Alamein, and Italy, including Monte Cassino. This division would form the nucleus of the force, which was to be 50,000 strong, with a high proportion of British officers, but no British units. It would be composed mainly of mixed units that had not yet been partitioned, and would be in place in the 12 disputed districts by 1 August. Rees would have two advisers, Brigadier Digambhar Singh for India, and Colonel Ayub Khan for Pakistan. After 15 August Rees would remain in operational control of the forces of both new states in the area.

A week after ordering the setting up of the Punjab Boundary Force, Mountbatten paid a visit to Calcutta, where Suhrawardy took the opportunity of making a last plea to be allowed to form an independent Bengal. It was futile, of course, but he would not have been Shaheed Suhrawardy if he had not tried. The city was relatively peaceful, but uneasy, and Mountbatten asked Lieutenant-General Sir Francis Tuker, the GOC, if he, too, would like a special boundary force. Tuker thanked him, but declined. He was already organized, and could handle the situation with the existing troops under his command, even though they were far fewer than 50,000. And so he did.

The Punjab Boundary Force was said to be the largest military force ever assembled for the express purpose of maintaining civil peace – but it was still too little, too late. In all, it provided no more than one soldier per square mile. The killing squads had little difficulty in avoiding contact with the troops – though there were times when they chose to fight them, especially when several gangs linked up to outnumber them. Jenkins had earlier said he would need at least four divisions to keep the peace during an enforced partition – and given the numbers of people who were already starting to criss-cross the vast, dusty spaces of the area, even that size of a force would have been hard pressed to prevent catastrophe.

By the time the Boundary Force was in position, the casualty figures in the Punjab since the beginning of March were conservatively estimated at 4,632 killed and 2,573 seriously injured. The difficulties the force faced were illustrated by the fact that 3,588, or over 77 per cent, of the killings took place not in the cities, but in rural areas. In the cities nearly twice as many victims were wounded rather than killed – it was obviously harder to finish off the job in close packed urban surroundings. Despite the militancy of the Sikhs, Jenkins estimated that at that time the dead included three times more non-Muslims than Muslims.[17]

As 15 August approached, the killings mounted on both sides, with retaliation provoking retaliation. In Amritsar, Master Tara Singh was holding court in the Golden Temple like an Old Testament prophet, preaching doom and breathing fire into his people as he exhorted their warriors 'to rise and destroy the Mughal invader'. A massacre of Muslims in the city followed, after the newly-appointed superintendent of police, a Hindu, had ordered all Muslim policemen to be disarmed. The governor quickly removed the superintendent and reversed his order, but by then the damage had been done. The Muslims in Lahore went on a rampage of revenge, unhindered by the mainly Muslim police force, many of whom joined the rioters.

In the cities and near the dividing line, most people clung hopefully to their homes, but further back in what would soon be enemy territory, hundreds of thousands began packing up their belongings and starting the long trek to what they imagined would be safety. Their winding caravans provided the marauding bands, whose mounted outriders were scouting the countryside, with easy targets. But the attacks were still sporadic, and the number of casualties, though serious, was still not astronomical.

On 5 August came another worrying intelligence report, this time brought by Superintendent Gerald Savage, head of the CID in the Punjab, who was sent by Jenkins to deliver it to the viceroy in person. He arrived during a meeting of the Partition Council, and Mountbatten had to be called out to see him. When he had heard what Savage had to say, Mountbatten adjourned the Council but kept back Jinnah, Liaquat and Patel to hear it for themselves. Savage told them that Sikhs arrested during demonstrations had made statements alleging that Master Tara Singh and other leaders were involved in bomb-making and in plots to destroy canal headworks, blow up the special trains which had started carrying Pakistani officials from Delhi to Karachi on 1 August, and to assassinate Jinnah by throwing a bomb into the open Rolls Royce car he would be using for his state drive to the new Assembly for the declaration of independence.

Jinnah and Liaquat immediately demanded the arrest of Tara Singh and the other Sikh leaders. Patel demurred, saying it would only provoke trouble. Mountbatten thought they should be arrested, but that he would take the advice of the men on the spot. Jenkins had already discussed the question with the two governors-designate of East and West Punjab, Sir Chandulal Trivedi and Sir Francis Mudie, and all had agreed that arresting Tara Singh and the others would be disastrous in the current climate. To the fury of Jinnah and Liaquat, Mountbatten bowed to the governors' decision – he could hardly be accused of indifference to Jinnah's safety, however, since he would be riding in the open car alongside him.

Three days later, Mountbatten may well have had qualms about leaving Tara Singh and his accomplices free, when the special train making its daily run to Karachi was blown up by a bomb on the line. Fortunately, a number of linked bombs failed to detonate at the same time, but three coaches were smashed and three more derailed, killing one woman and her four-year-old son and wounding a dozen other passengers. Waiting gangs of Sikhs swooped on the wrecked train, but were driven off by the military escort.

Approaching the end of his mammoth task, Radcliffe informed the viceroy that he expected to have completed his award for the Punjab on 9 August. Meanwhile, Jenkins had been pressing with increasing urgency to be given some advance warning of where the line was to be drawn, so that he could deploy troops in areas where there was the most likelihood of violence over the decisions. Like all the political leaders, the Punjab governor believed that every day, almost every hour, that the awards could be advanced would help to reduce bloodshed. As the final draft was being prepared, Christopher Beaumont, Radcliffe's secretary, told George Abell where the line had been drawn, so that he could make a sketch map and send it to Jenkins.

Abell's map, with a covering letter, arrived in Lahore on 8 August. Jenkins noted that one of the most contentious areas, the Muslim majority *tehsils* or sub-districts of Ferozepur and Zira had been given to Pakistan. The two *tehsils* had a combined population of over half a million, and formed a salient east of the Sutlej river. This salient had two significant features: it contained the headwaters of the canal which irrigated the princely state of Bikaner, which was acceding to India; and it also housed an important army arms depot, which would give the Pakistan army virtually its only source of weapons and the major part of its military stores and equipment.

On 11 August, Jenkins received an urgent telegram from Abell. It read, simply: 'Eliminate salient'. In other words, the whole of the Ferozepur district, complete with its canal headwaters, its military stores and its Muslim population, was now to go to India. What had happened during those three days was that Nehru and Patel had been informed of the contents of the highly secret document, possibly through Mountbatten, who had seen the draft on 9 August (though he later somewhat unconvincingly denied having seen it), but more likely through a leak by Radcliffe's Indian assistant secretary, V.D. Ayer. They had asked Mountbatten to have this part of the award changed. There is no written proof that Mountbatten did in fact pressure Radcliffe to change his award, but in recent years strong circumstantial evidence has emerged that he did so, despite his many denials. It was typical of the bias he was already displaying towards India and against Pakistan, a bias that was to become increasingly marked over the remainder of his time in India. His close relationship with Nehru, and his antipathy towards Jinnah, undoubtedly affected his judgement at a time when he should have been strictly impartial.

The content of the awards was not the only thing that concerned Mountbatten at that time. He had from the start been urging Radcliffe to speed up his report. But when it was reported at his staff meeting on 9 August 'that Sir Cyril Radcliffe would be ready that evening to announce the Award of the Punjab Boundary Commission' he abruptly changed his tune. Was it desirable, he asked the meeting, to publish it straight away? 'Without question,' he said, 'the earlier it was published, the more the British would have to bear the responsibility for the disturbances which would undoubtedly result.'

At last, Mountbatten had got the message – after no fewer than 23 warnings from Jenkins alone – that there was going to be mayhem, and that his helter-skelter timetable meant there would be no time to make anything like adequate preparations to deal with it, let alone prevent it. But he could at least try to cover his own tracks, and protect his own reputation. He 'emphasised the necessity for maintaining secrecy, not only on the terms of the Award, but also of the fact that it would be ready that day'.[18] Making the excuse that 'the printers were on holiday, and we were leaving for Karachi', he put the awards in his safe, where they were to remain like a ticking bomb until after the independence celebrations – *nothing* was going to spoil his party, no matter what the possible cost in human suffering.

The Jinnahs left Delhi for Karachi in the viceroy's Dakota aircraft on the morning of 7 August. Jinnah had sold his New Delhi house for a handsome profit to a Marwari merchant, but could not bring himself to part with his Malabar Hill mansion in his beloved Bombay – there was always the chance that he might be able to return to it in his declining years. Instead, he leased it to a European consulate. In Karachi, he had bought Flagstaff House to use as his private residence, but he was never to live in it. Instead, he moved into Government House, the former residence of the governor of Sind, with its pleasant, park-like grounds.

On Monday, 11 August 1947, he attended the first meeting of Pakistan's constituent assembly, where he was unanimously elected president. Liaquat presented the national flag of the Federation of Pakistan to the assembly, telling the members 'This flag stands for freedom, liberty and equality to all those who owe allegiance to it. This flag will protect the legitimate rights of every citizen, will protect and defend the integrity of the State, and will not be used for the exploitation of other nations, but will be an emblem of peace.' Jinnah, in his presidential address, described for the first time his vision of the new nation. If anyone had any fears that it would be a strictly Islamic nation, or anything other than a secular state, they were soon disabused. It might have been the old 'ambassador of Hindu-Muslim unity' of 1915 speaking:

> You are free; you are free to go to your temples, you are free to go to your mosques or to any other place of worship in this State of Pakistan ... You may belong to any religious caste or creed – that has nothing to do with the business of the State ... We are starting the State with no discrimination, no distinction between one community and another, between caste and creed ... We should keep that in front of us as our ideal, and you will find that in the course of time Hindus would cease to be Hindus and Muslims would cease to be Muslims, not in the religious sense, because that is the personal faith of each individual, but in the political sense – as citizens of the nation ... My guiding principle will be justice and complete impartiality, and I am sure that with your co-operation, I can look forward to Pakistan becoming one of the greatest nations of the world.[19]

Two days later, on 13 August, the Mountbattens flew in. They were met at Karachi airport by the governor-designate of Sind and driven straight to Government House, where the Jinnahs were waiting to greet them. The house had been 'decked up to look like a Hollywood film set'. A state banquet had been arranged for the evening. It had originally been proposed as a luncheon, but had had to be hastily rearranged when it was remembered that it was Ramadan, the holy month when Muslims are required to fast between sunrise and sunset – apparently Jinnah, never the most devout follower of Islam, had forgotten.

Next morning, with the reported assassination threat very much in mind, Mountbatten accompanied Jinnah in the open car to and from the constituent assembly. It was the kind of challenge Mountbatten could never resist. 'It occurred to me,' he boasted to Stanley Wolpert in an interview in 1978, 'that the best way for me to protect him would be to insist on our riding in the same carriage, you see. I knew that no one in that crowd would want to risk shooting me!' The journey passed without incident. There were no bombs, just wildly cheering crowds. 'But such was Jinnah's vanity, you know,' Mountbatten told Wolpert, 'that no sooner did we get inside the gates of Government House than he tapped my knee and said, "Thank God I was able to bring you back alive!"'[20]

That afternoon, the Mountbattens flew back to Delhi, leaving Jinnah to enjoy his moment of glory next day alone at centre stage. As they crossed the Punjab, they could see the smoke rising from numerous large fires – where Hindus and Muslims were marking independence by murdering each other and torching each other's property. Delhi was packed to overflowing, with peasants from the surrounding countryside, with refugees from the Punjab who had been pouring into the city and camping in its parks for days, and with all manner of humanity. Triumphal arches decorated the streets, there was an air of festivity everywhere. In the evening, members of the constituent assembly gathered to wait for midnight. As the clocks struck twelve, the new independent dominion was ushered in with blasts from conch shells, and then India's first prime minister, Jawaharlal Nehru, stepped on to the rostrum to make a speech that would take its place in the history books of the future. It was a noble piece of oratory, as flowery and as charged with emotion as only Nehru could have made it:

> Long years ago we made a tryst with destiny, and now time comes when we shall redeem our pledge, not wholly or in full measure, but very substantially. At the stroke of the midnight hour, when the world sleeps, India will awake to life and freedom. A moment comes, which comes but rarely in history, when we step out from the old to the new, when an age ends and when the soul of a nation long suppressed finds utterance. It is fitting that at this solemn moment we take the pledge of dedication to the service of India and her people and to the still larger cause of humanity.

Next day, at 8.30 a.m., Mountbatten was sworn in as governor-general of the dominion of India, by an Indian chief justice and before an audience of former freedom fighters. He almost failed to make it back to Government House, as the Viceroy's House had now become — the crowds outside the Council Chamber were so dense that even the 400-strong bodyguard could not force a passage for him to his carriage. But Nehru climbed on to the roof, and waved back the throng, and they obeyed him as they would have obeyed no one else that day.

The rest of the day was one vast party, culminating at six in the evening with the main event, the raising by Nehru of the flag of the new country at India Gate. Military bands — including the band of the INA — were in place, an elaborate ceremony had been arranged and rehearsed, but the crowds were again so enormous that the carriages of Nehru and Mountbatten were quite unable to get through. The planned parade and speeches had to be abandoned. Nehru gave the signal for the flag to be raised and the guns to boom out their salute. As the flag broke out at the top of the pole, a beautiful rainbow appeared in the sky behind it, its colours seeming to echo the saffron, white and green of the flag. It was a fitting piece of magic, a fitting welcome to the new, and a farewell to the old.

After 122 eventful years, Macaulay's proudest day had finally arrived.

Epilogue

After the party came the reckoning. Radcliffe left India on Independence Day; so, too, did Jenkins, Abell and the remaining members of the ICS. None of them felt like joining in the celebrations. Neither did Gandhi, who had decided to take himself to Calcutta as a 'one-man boundary force', hoping that by his very presence he could prevent any fresh outbreak of killings there. Ismay was absent, too, laid low by a severe bout of dysentery. 'This dispensation was painful,' he wrote, 'but not altogether unwelcome. I was convinced that the right thing had been done, but I was in no mood for unrestrained rejoicing ... I had deep forebodings about the immediate future ... Many of my Indian friends were likely to lose their lives, and many more were certain to lose their homes.'[1]

At 5.00 p.m. next day, Saturday, 16 August, the newly-elevated Earl Mountbatten of Burma handed copies of Radcliffe's awards to the Indian and Pakistani leaders — Liaquat and Muhammad Ali had flown to Delhi from Karachi that morning for an emergency meeting of the Joint Defence Council. They were all given two hours to take the documents away and study them, before returning to Government House for another meeting.

Both sides were incensed by what they read. As expected, Calcutta had gone to India, and Lahore to Pakistan — in both cases there was sadness, but no shock. The Indians were angry to find that the Chittagong Hill Tracts had gone to Pakistan, while the Pakistanis were furious to discover that not only Ferozepur but also an important part of the Muslim-majority district of Gurdaspur, in the northern Punjab, had gone to India.

Gurdaspur was not a rich district by any standard, but it had great strategic and symbolic significance, since it provided India's only road into Kashmir. Like the legendary Shangri-La, the valley of Kashmir is protected on all other sides by mountains, with few passes. All Kashmir's other road and rail communications with the rest of the sub-continent ran through West Pakistan. So did the great rivers Indus, Jhelum and Chenab, the lifeblood of West Pakistan, which flowed down from Kashmir into the dusty plains, carrying Kashmiri timber exports with them. With the maharaja, Hari Singh, still dithering over accession to either dominion, Gurdaspur had become the key to Kashmir's future. Without it,

Kashmir would have no viable land connection with India, and would be obliged to accede to Pakistan.

The Indian leaders, of course, were well aware of the strategic importance of Kashmir, despite its significant Muslim majority. If Kashmir became part of India, then West Pakistan would be virtually surrounded, and India would also control the great rivers on which Pakistan's economic survival depended. This might well hasten the collapse of Pakistan, which most Indian leaders thought was inevitable within a few months anyway, and lead to the reunification of the sub-continent under a Congress government.

For Nehru, there was also an emotional involvement: Kashmir was the home of his Brahman ancestors, and its political leader, Sheikh Muhammad Abdullah, was a close personal friend. While Radcliffe was working on his awards, Nehru worried about the fate of Kashmir and of Sheikh Abdullah and his followers, who supported Congress: how would they fare in Pakistan? Congress must be able to defend its own, which meant being able to get troops into the valley if necessary. He badgered Mountbatten mercilessly about the boundary line, so much so that Mountbatten described him as 'pathological' on the subject.[2]

On 9 August, the day after Abell's sketch map had reached Jenkins in Lahore, Jinnah and Liaquat told Muhammad Ali, who was making a flying visit to Karachi from Delhi, that they had heard disturbing reports about the likely border between East and West Punjab, particularly in the Gurdaspur district. They gave him a message for Ismay, which he delivered as soon as he returned to Delhi later that day, driving straight from the airport to the Viceroy's House. When Muhammad Ali arrived, however, Ismay was closeted with Radcliffe. He had to kick his heels for an hour before he could tell Ismay of Jinnah's fears that the award in Gurdaspur would be political rather than judicial: 'if the boundary actually turned out to be what these reports foreshadowed, this would have a most serious impact on the relations between Pakistan and the United Kingdom, whose good faith and honour were involved in this question'.[3]

The reports turned out to be correct. Clearly, Nehru had prevailed. When he finally saw the awards on 16 August, Liaquat immediately accused Radcliffe of bending to pressure from Mountbatten and Nehru. Once again, there is no documentary proof of this, only strong circumstantial evidence. But at the time, there was nothing to be done. Both sides had given their word, as had Baldev Singh for the Sikhs, that they would accept whatever Radcliffe decided, and they stood by their promises. Baldev complained bitterly of the wrongs done to the Sikhs by having many of their sacred places left in Pakistan, but he was silenced by Muhammad Ali, who pointed to the many Muslim-majority areas that had been assigned to India. Nehru and Patel said nothing. Next day, Jinnah broadcast his reactions to his new nation:

The division of India is now finally and irrevocably effected. No doubt we feel that the carving out of this great independent Muslim State has suffered injustices. We have been squeezed in as much as it was possible, and the latest blow that we have received was the Award of the Boundary Commission. It is an unjust, incomprehensible and even perverse award ... and it may not be a judicial but a political award, but we have agreed to abide by it and it is binding upon us. As honourable people we must abide by it.[4]

By the time Mountbatten unlocked his safe on 16 August, it had been just one week since Radcliffe had finished drafting his award for the Punjab. But a week is a very long time for communities riven by uncertainty and fear. During that week confidence in government, in the police and in the army had finally collapsed. Policemen were themselves Hindus, Muslims and Sikhs, and were affected like everyone else by the fear of being caught in the wrong place at the wrong time. They had seen their own people butchered, raped and dispossessed. For them, the safety of their families came before their duty as policemen. Given time, the police force, like the army, could have been reorganized and prepared, under impartial British officers. Given time, local and national governments could have made arrangements for an orderly transfer or exchange of populations. Given time, and firm government, it is even possible that some of the worst fears could have been allayed. But time was precisely what no one was given, so panic set in, and catastrophe became inevitable and unstoppable.

With no announcement of the awards, many towns and villages in the Punjab had greeted independence nervously with the flags of both India and Pakistan flying defiantly in competition with each other. There were reports that Sikhs in Amritsar had celebrated on the morning of 15 August by rounding up a group of about 30 Muslim women and girls, stripping them naked and forcing them to parade in a circle before a jeering crowd. They had then picked out the most attractive and repeatedly raped them, chopping down the rest with their *kirpans*. When news of the outrage reached Lahore, Muslims there took their revenge by attacking the chief *gurdwara*, the Sikh temple, where scores of Sikhs had taken refuge. They burned it to the ground with the Sikhs trapped inside, while Muslim police stood by, doing nothing to stop them. But this was only the beginning of the holocaust.

The emergency meeting of the Joint Defence Council on 16 August agreed to strengthen the Punjab Boundary Force as quickly as possible. Nehru and Liaquat visited Lahore, Ambala, Jullundur and Amritsar together, to see for themselves what was going on and to appeal for peace. They tried to remind everyone that both India and Pakistan had pledged to protect the minorities after partition, and that there was no need for anyone to move home. But they were shouting against a hurricane. Each new outrage, each new murder or massacre, brought a thirst for revenge and a desperate need to flee from the terror. As the scale of the disaster mounted, Tara Singh and other Sikh leaders toured the province in military vehicles, appealing for an end to the violence, but their followers had tasted blood, and it was too late for Tara Singh to stop what he had begun.

When the boundary commission awards were finally made public on 17 August, they did nothing to bring peace but only increased the general frenzy not to be trapped on the wrong side of the line. The flow of refugees soon became a raging torrent. In the sub-continent as a whole, some 14 million people left their homes and set out by every means possible – by air, train, and road, in cars and lorries, in buses and bullock carts, but most of all on foot – to seek refuge with their own kind. Ten million of them were in the central Punjab. In an area measuring about 200 miles by 150 miles, roughly the size of Scotland, with some 17,000 towns and villages, 5 million Muslims were trekking from east to west, and 5 million Hindus and Sikhs trekking in the opposite direction. Many of them never made it to their destinations.

The long, winding columns of frightened souls trudging through the landscape carrying as many of their worldly possessions as they could manage, to say nothing of their old and their young, were easy targets. Some of the columns stretched for miles – the longest was some 50 miles long (some say 74 miles), with 800,000 refugees heading towards India from West Punjab and it is said to have taken eight days to pass any given spot. Sometimes, when columns heading in different directions passed on the road, they fell upon each other with whatever weapons they had to hand, before moving on, leaving a trail of dead and dying behind them.

The massacres and slaughters have become the most abiding memory of that time. Sadly, in northern India and much of Pakistan, people talk of the horrors of partition rather than the joys of independence. There have been hundreds, possibly thousands, of books and memoirs written by those who lived through it. Perhaps the most succinct writings are a number of pieces by the Urdu poet, Saadat Hasan Manto, such as one entitled 'Compassion':

> Please don't kill
> my young daughter
> before my eyes . . .
>
> All right, let's do as he says . . .
> Strip her
> and drag her away[5]

One of the most powerful and recurring images is of the trains. They left Delhi and Lahore and other stations packed with refugees as only Indian trains can be packed; with people clinging to the sides and roof like a vast swarm of bees. As often as not, the trains arrived at their destinations filled with nothing but bloated, butchered corpses, stinking and silent apart from the buzzing of flies. Some coaches were scrawled with chalked graffiti: 'A Present from India', 'A Present from Pakistan'. Both sides stopped trains in the countryside, or fell upon them in sidings while the drivers watered their engines, systematically sorting out the travellers from the other side and hacking them to pieces, while studiously avoiding any harm to Britons and other Europeans heading for home. Manto again captured the essence, in another short piece, this time entitled 'Hospitality Delayed':

Rioters brought the running train to a halt.

People belonging to the other community were pulled out and slaughtered with swords and bullets.

The rest of the passengers were treated to halwa, fruits and milk.

The chief assassin made a farewell speech before the train pulled out of the station: 'Ladies and gentlemen, my apologies. News of this train's arrival was delayed. That is why we have not been able to entertain you lavishly – the way we wanted to.'[6]

Not even the trains carrying Indian troops back from Pakistan were safe, presenting an especially tempting target for Pathan tribesmen. General Menèzes recalls that his own battalion was twice attacked whilst travelling home by train, having 26 soldiers killed and 72 wounded, including seven officers.[7]

The Punjab Boundary Force did its best, but could do little to prevent the killings. The one obvious way in which the exodus could have been monitored and protected, in which the armed gangs on both sides could have been spotted and wiped out, was with aircraft: there were eight squadrons of modern Tempest fighter-bombers from the old RIAF, seven of which had been given to India and one to Pakistan. Between them they could easily have covered likely trouble spots in the open country, and protected trains and railway lines. But for some reason both sides refused to use them, or to declare martial law. The Boundary Force was confined to acting 'in assistance to the civil authorities' and forbidden from mounting any offensive operations. As the then Brigadier Ayub Khan explained: 'The force could only rush to a place that was being attacked, and by the time the troops arrived it was looted, burnt and the Muslim inhabitants massacred. In the end, all that this force could do was to try and keep the roads clear for the refugees. This was done by patrolling the main thoroughfares and the railway lines.'[8]

By the end of August, communal distrust had reached such levels that both sides were accusing the Boundary Force of bias, of failing to protect *their* people, and it was wound up amid general recriminations. Most of its British officers, who had been sickened both by the hopelessness of their task and the gruesome horrors they had been forced to witness, were relieved. Mountbatten decided he could retire to Simla for 10 days' much-needed rest. Meanwhile, the killings continued.

It is impossible to give an accurate figure for those who perished. Most were massacred by the other side, but many were struck down by cholera, dysentery and all those other diseases that afflict undernourished refugees everywhere, or died from starvation, or sheer exhaustion. The official British estimates at the time were between 200,000 and a quarter of a million – but it was in the British government's interest to minimize the extent of the slaughter for which they bore the ultimate responsibility. At the other extreme, there were those with other political axes to grind who claimed two million had perished. Over the years, a consensus has been reached that the true figure was around one million. It is a truly terrible indictment.

Looking back after 50 years, the horror of those days is not diminished by the passage of time. But it is worth remembering that the real trouble was confined to that one part of the Punjab, though it did eventually spill over into neighbouring areas, including Delhi and part of the UP. For the first two weeks after partition, the rest of India remained quiet, with little trouble. The south, as usual, stayed that way. Bengal began quietly, then threatened to erupt as news of what was happening in the Punjab arrived. Serious trouble, however, was prevented by one man, who somehow managed to work a miracle that had been beyond General Rees and his 50,000 men in the Punjab. That man, of course, was Gandhi.

Gandhi had chosen to go and live in Hydari House, an old Muslim residence, open on all sides, in Beliaghata, an area of Calcutta which had been torn by earlier riots. To highlight his pleas for communal unity, he invited Suhrawardy – the man most Hindus blamed for inciting the Calcutta killings the year before – to stay there with him. Suhrawardy, who with partition was about to lose his position as chief minister of Bengal, agreed readily, and together the two men set an example which most of Calcutta, and indeed most of Bengal, followed. Independence Day itself was marked in Calcutta by unbelievable scenes of fraternization, with Hindus and Muslims embracing each other and dancing together in the streets. Gandhi's public prayer meetings on the *maidan* attracted crowds estimated at half a million. That year, the great Muslim festival of Id el Kebir fell on 18 August, while the spirit of friendship and reconciliation was still at its height. When Gandhi greeted the crowd in Urdu with '*Id Mubarak*', 'Happy Id', they went wild with delight.

By 31 August, however, the tensions had returned and the first communal killings began. At 10.00 p.m. that night, as Gandhi lay sleeping naked between his two great-nieces, Hydari House was besieged by a gang of young Hindu fanatics from the RSSS. Stones were thrown, Muslims in the street nearby were attacked, Gandhi himself was in danger. The police arrived before he was harmed, and managed to restore order. Severely shaken, Gandhi told his followers, 'The miracle of Calcutta has proved to be a nine-days wonder.' Next day, as the flames of communal hatred threatened to consume the city again, he prayed for guidance. The answer he received was a familiar one: a fast unto death, to be broken only when all sides repudiated their violence.

It would not be a long fast: Gandhi was now nearly 78 years old, and in failing health. Even after one day, his condition was giving his doctors cause for alarm. The riots continued, and so did he – but suddenly the message seemed to get through, and by the second day the calls for peace were becoming louder than the noises of riot, as an anxious crowd began to build in the street outside the house. By the end of the third day, peace had returned and the *goondas* responsible for much of the killing had come to bow before the frail old man and surrender their weapons, literally by the truckload. Rajagopalachari, now governor of Bengal, sent a handwritten message telling Gandhi complete calm had been restored.

At 9.15 p.m. on 4 September, after just 73 hours, Gandhi broke his fast with a few sips of orange juice. The miracle had been worked once again, and this time it lasted. There was no more trouble in Calcutta, and very little elsewhere in either part of Bengal. The province that had always been the epicentre of violent rebellion had become India's exemplar of peace. Gandhi celebrated his success by announcing that he would leave next day for the Punjab.

At almost exactly the same time as Gandhi was breaking his fast in Calcutta, Mountbatten was receiving a telephone call in Simla. It was from V.P. Menon in Delhi, telling him he must abandon his holiday and return. The troubles in the Punjab had spread to Delhi and were threatening to engulf the city. There were wild rumours that the Muslims, hundreds of thousands of whom were seeking sanctuary in the vast refugee camps in parks and open spaces, were plotting to seize the city and restore the Muslim hegemony of the Mughal emperors. The rumours were fuelling murder and mayhem by Hindus and by the embittered Sikhs who were flooding in from the Punjab. Under these pressures the administration was breaking down. If the government were to lose control of its own capital, then the whole new state might collapse in anarchy and chaos.

Nehru and Patel were at their wits' end. They had had years of experience of agitation and prison, but virtually none of the administration of a huge and complex country. And certainly, they did not have the knowledge or the experience to deal with what Ismay described as 'a cataclysm of this kind'. It was

V.P.'s idea to ask Mountbatten to come back and take charge of the emergency. Patel agreed at once. So did Mountbatten, and he and Edwina returned next day.

Mountbatten liked to claim that Nehru and Patel had offered him executive power to run India, and that he had replied 'My God, I've just got through giving you the country and here you two are asking me to take it back!' In fact, they asked him to set up and chair an emergency committee, on which they would serve. This was something entirely within Mountbatten's training and experience, and he swung into action with all his usual dynamism. He formed a committee of 15 members, consisting of Cabinet ministers and representatives of all the appropriate military and civil services, and set up a military style operational headquarters in Ismay's office, complete with map room, covering the whole area of the Punjab. Alongside this, V.P. and H.M. Patel, who was then Cabinet secretary, set up a similar emergency committee to deal exclusively with the situation in Delhi.

Mountbatten was in his element, and at his most effective. 'He was captain of a destroyer flotilla, chief of combined operations, supreme commander, and governor-general, all rolled into one,' wrote Ismay. 'The Emergency Committee was in practically permanent session; and questions which would have taken days, or even weeks, to settle by the normal procedure were decided in a matter of minutes.'[9] For once, Mountbatten faced a situation where speed really was vital, and he revelled in it. Edwina, meanwhile, plunged into relief work in the refugee camps, where the misery was compounded by the arrival of the monsoon, turning the dust of the camps into a morass of mud. Both Mountbattens rendered great service to the new dominion over this terrible period.

Gradually, over a period of weeks, things were brought under control, both in the city and in the Punjab. By the end of the year, the killings and the mass migrations were coming to an end, and some sort of order was restored. But the scars would be slow to heal. Much of the bitterness and hatred of those traumatic days still remain in both India and Pakistan. And the arguments still rage over whether Mountbatten's madcap rush to grant independence was the main cause of so much suffering. It is easy to be wise 50 years after the event, but on balance the answer must surely be yes. Too many dangerous loose ends were left undone, too many complex problems left unresolved or botched for the sake of speed. In the final analysis, when all the excuses about the threat of civil war and total breakdown of public order are stripped away, we are left with the conclusion that those million lives and several million homes were sacrificed to fulfil a deal between Mountbatten and Vallabhbhai Patel to keep India in the Commonwealth in return for the transfer of power in two months. And we are left with another question: was it worth it?

Among the loose ends left dangling after independence were the three states that had avoided acceding to either dominion: Hyderabad, Kashmir and Junagadh. Junagadh, the smallest of the three with an area of 3,337 square miles and a population of about 700,000, was the most easily dealt with. A maritime state on the Kathiawar Peninsula, it was more or less equidistant by sea from Karachi and Bombay, and by land was about 150 miles south of the Pakistan border. It was also surrounded by smaller Indian states. The nawab, Sir Mahabthakhan Rasulkhanji, was a Muslim though 80 per cent of his subjects were Hindu. After partition, he declared his intention of acceding to Pakistan, which he was legally entitled to do, in spite of the geopolitical chaos it would cause.

Jinnah was happy to accept the state, which could of course connect with Pakistan by sea. The government of India, however, retaliated by imposing an economic blockade of Junagadh, and surrounding it with troops, supplemented by troops from the neighbouring Hindu states, which had acceded to India. A provisional government of Junagadh was formed in Bombay, with Gandhi's nephew Shamdaldas as president. At the end of October, the nawab fled to Karachi, and a week later a Hindu people's liberation army, 20,000 strong and armed and equipped with armoured cars and other modern weaponry by India, marched in and seized the state. Some months later, a referendum produced a vote for accession to India.

Hyderabad was a very different matter. The state lay in the very centre of India, covered an area of 82,000 square miles, had a population of 16 million and annual revenues of Rs 260 million. It had its own currency, issued its own postage stamps, had its own army and even its own airline, Deccan Airways. Its ruling dynasty had been founded in the early eighteenth century by Nizamul Mulk, one of Aurangzeb's most successful generals, whose descendant, His Exalted Highness the Nizam Sir Mir Osman Ali Khan, was one of the richest men in the world. He was also one of the most tight-fisted — the local joke was that he didn't know the word 'spend' was in the dictionary — shuffling around his palace in old carpet slippers and threadbare pyjamas.

The nizam had declared his intention of reverting on 15 August to his status as an independent sovereign of an independent state. He had hoped to acquire separate dominion status for Hyderabad, and was horrified to discover that this was impossible under the Indian Independence Act. Various attempts were made, largely by Sir Conrad Corfield, to win Hyderabad time to come to terms with India. Eventually, Nehru and Patel accepted a one-year moratorium, with the state's future to be decided in August 1948. When the time was up and the nizam still refused to accede, Patel sent in two divisions of the Indian army, in what he described as a 'police action', code-named 'Operation Polo'. After four days' fighting, Hyderabad became part of India.

Kashmir was more complicated, and more dangerous. At 84,471 square miles it was the biggest of all the princely states. It had boundaries with Tibet,

China and Afghanistan, and was separated from the Soviet Union only by a small strip of Afghan territory. But although its area was bigger than that of Hyderabad, its population was only about 4 million, the vast majority of whom were Muslims. They celebrated 15 August as Pakistan Day, but the Dogra Hindu maharaja, Hari Singh, continued to procrastinate. As V.P. Menon put it, he was 'in a Micawberish state of mind, hoping for the best while doing nothing'. He played with various political options without following through on any of them. One was to declare Jammu and Kashmir an independent state under his own rule, another was to achieve some sort of *rapprochement* with Jinnah, or with India. In the face of some local unrest, he decided to remove his most dangerous political adversary from the scene and arrested Sheikh Abdullah, who was immediately seen as a prisoner of conscience.

Still trying to buy time, Hari Singh signed a standstill agreement with Pakistan. Patel, however, showed no inclination of signing one on behalf of India – indeed, he took a leaf out of the maharaja's book and did nothing. His policy, as with all the states, was no standstill agreement without accession. And in any case, he was not particularly keen to have Kashmir and all the problems it would bring: he had earlier said that if the maharaja chose to accede to Pakistan, it 'would not be taken amiss by India'.

Unfortunately, Patel's prudence was overtaken by events. On 21 October, some 5,000 Pathan tribesmen from the NWFP invaded Kashmir in lorries and buses. Incensed by crude attempts by the Hindus of Jammu to alter the communal balance in their part of the state, they had declared a jihad in defence of their co-religionists. It was passed off as a spontaneous action, and not an invasion by Pakistan. Others saw the tribesmen as Pakistan's Afghan mercenaries. By the time news reached Delhi three days later, the Pathans had been joined by most of the Muslim soldiers of the maharaja's army, and were well on their way to the Kashmiri capital, Srinagar. Kashmir's only airfield was at Srinagar, and if they could take that before the winter snows closed off the road through Gurdaspur, there would be no way Indian troops could get in for several months. Auchinleck wanted to send in British troops immediately, to protect the 200 or so British residents of Kashmir, but Mountbatten overruled him, refusing to allow British troops to become involved in Kashmir, just as he had refused to allow them to be used in the Punjab. The Defence Committee sent V.P. Menon by plane to Srinagar, to assess the situation and report back.

The maharaja was in a high state of panic, begging to be allowed to accede to India, and calling for military aid. Menon advised him to flee at once to his other palace in Jammu, then himself flew back to Delhi. Mountbatten by this time was advocating immediate military action to defend Srinagar and the Kashmir valley from the tribesmen, but this could only be done if Kashmir was part of India. If the maharaja wanted to accede, then the Indian government should agree. A plebiscite could be held later, after the raiders had been driven out, giving the Kashmiri people the choice of staying with India, joining Pakistan, or becoming independent. The committee agreed. Menon was dispatched to Jammu, with the instrument of accession. The maharaja signed. At first light next morning, the first aircraft carrying Indian troops took off, and by nightfall 329 men of the 1st Battalion the Sikh Regiment had secured Srinagar airport. By the end of the month two more battalions and their support units had secured Srinagar itself and the surrounding area.

Kashmir was now firmly part of the Union of India, but was to remain a running sore, poisoning relations between India and Pakistan for at least the next half century, keeping them perpetually on the brink of war and actually tipping them over the brink in 1965, when General Ayub Khan, by then the president of Pakistan, sent Muslim infiltrators into Kashmir to provoke a rising. The Indian government retaliated by invading West Punjab, pushing its tanks to within gunshot range of Lahore before calling a halt and withdrawing. Since then, Kashmiri guerrillas and Indian police have been keeping the conflict alive, conducting a secret war – a continuing cycle of outrage and reprisal, terror and repression, that seems more reminiscent of Ireland or Algeria than India, a seemingly permanent reminder of the consequences of the mindless haste of 1947. The plebiscite promised 50 years ago is still to be held.

Gandhi never reached the Punjab. He got no further than Delhi, where he stayed in G.D. Birla's luxurious Birla House – his usual abode in the sweepers' quarter was swamped by refugees. He held daily prayer meetings, received deputations, toured the city visiting many of the refugee camps, growing increasingly pessimistic. His feeling of helplessness was profound. On 12 January 1948, he announced another fast unto death, saying he did not wish to live unless there was total peace between India and Pakistan. He was soon in genuine danger of his life: his kidneys stopped working on the third day, and there was acid in his urine. But many Hindus regarded Gandhi's fasts as weakness in the face of Muslim demands. Hindu extremists stood at the gates of Birla House shouting 'Let Gandhi die!' This enraged Nehru, but does not seem to have surprised the object of their anger. Just over three weeks before, Gandhi had written in a letter: 'I know that today I irritate everyone. How can I believe that I am right and all others are wrong?'

Gandhi had done more than irritate people, however. He had driven four members of the Hindu RSSS to plot his assassination. They were Madanlal Pahwa, a 20-year-old refugee from the Punjab; Vishnu Karkare, 37-year-old head of the Poona branch of the RSSS; Narayam Apte, 34, chairman of the RSSS newspaper, the *Hindu Rashtia* (*Hindu Nation*); and Nathuram Godse, 37, editor of the *Rashtia*. On 14 January, Pahwa set off a bomb while the Mahatma was circulating among the crowds in the grounds of Birla House. A second assassin,

Digambe Badge, was to start shooting at Gandhi from a window in the servants' quarters. Although the bomb went off, the attempt was a failure. Pahwa was caught by the police, but Badge got away. Gandhi treated the whole thing as little more than a tiresome inconvenience – as did the police, who increased the guard of four men to 16 but otherwise did little to improve security. This was later to become a scandal, reflecting badly on the minister responsible – Patel.

Gandhi continued with his fast, holding court on his death bed as various notables, including the Mountbattens, came to see him. Every hour, on the hour, All-India Radio broadcast bulletins on the state of his health. Clement Attlee, caught up in the drama, sent a message to Jinnah suggesting he make some gesture of reconciliation in order to save Gandhi's life. Jinnah did not respond. It was left to Maulana Azad to negotiate Gandhi's return to life. If total peace was not possible, he asked, what would Gandhi settle for? As so often in the past, the answer turned out to be far less grandiose than the initial demand, and altogether more practical. Gandhi said he was prepared to give up his fast if Hindus would promise to permit the feast day of a local Muslim saint to be celebrated without interference; if 117 mosques were restored to the Muslims; if Muslims were allowed to move freely about the country, and even return from Pakistan if they wished, without threats or intimidation; and if there was no economic boycott of Muslim businesses. Finally, the Indian government must repay the £40 million it had been refusing to hand over to Pakistan as its share of government assets. The government agreed, and Gandhi ended his fast.

On 30 January, Gandhi was late for his prayer meeting – Patel had visited him after a particularly violent row with Nehru at that day's cabinet meeting. At 4.30 p.m. Gandhi left the house and headed for the prayer ground in the large garden to the left of the house, supporting himself as usual with one hand on the shoulders of each of his 'walking sticks' as he called his two young great-nieces, Abha and Manu. As he climbed the steps to the raised wooden platform on which he sat during the service, Nathuram Godse thrust his way towards him through the crowd. Manu tried to stop him, but he pushed her aside so violently that she fell. He drew a Biretta pistol from his jacket pocket and shot Gandhi twice through the abdomen. Gandhi fell. As he was lying on the ground Godse fired a third shot, which lodged in his lung. Gandhi's last words were '*Hey Ram!*' 'Oh God!' The Mahatma was dead, killed by a Hindu who believed he had betrayed his own people, his own religion, his own country.

Jinnah did not survive his old adversary by very long. He was now 72; he had won the longest and most difficult case of his distinguished career, representing the cause of Indian Muslims before the court of history with skill, panache and iron determination. More to the point, he had won for them what he believed they needed. He had defeated the tiresome little Hindu 'god-man' and seen him gunned down by people Jinnah would have described as his fellow fanatics, men who worshipped cows. Surely now, like any successful professional man, he had earned the right to sit in the garden of his house in Mount Pleasant Road on Malabar Hill in Bombay, a welcome glass of Scotch in one hand and one of the Craven-A cigarettes which were undoubtedly killing him in the other, and talk shop with fellow lawyers, or taste the frivolous pleasures of Bombay society. But it was not to be. By now, he was a mere shadow of the man who had, single-handedly, brought Pakistan into being. When a Parsi friend from Bombay, Jamshed Petit, visited him in Karachi, he found him asleep in a chair in the garden of the modest Government House. Jinnah awoke, and whispered, 'I am so tired, Jamshed, so tired.' He looked like a skeleton.

In June, accompanied by Fatima, he flew to Quetta to ease his lungs by breathing the cool mountain air of Baluchistan. His coughing stopped, and he was able to sleep and eat well for the first time in months. Indeed, Fatima recorded that 'For the first time in years, he seemed relaxed.'[10] On 1 July, he was due to speak at the opening ceremony of the State Bank of Pakistan in Karachi. Fatima tried to persuade him not to go, but he insisted. The trip totally exhausted him, and on 6 July his doctors advised him to return to the mountains, this time to Ziarat, which was several thousand feet higher than Quetta. But his condition got worse. Lieutenant-Colonel Ilahi Bakhsh of the Pakistan Medical Service flew from his home in Lahore to examine him. He diagnosed lung cancer. Other doctors confirmed his diagnosis. Mirza Abol Hassan Ispahani, head of the Calcutta financial empire, flew in from the USA to offer the services of an American consultant if Dr Bakhsh thought fit. Dr Bakhsh did not: everything that could be done was being done.

The doctors moved Jinnah back down the mountains to Quetta. By then his weight was down to less than 80 pounds and he was diagnosed with pneumonia as well as tuberculosis and cancer of the lung. He needed oxygen to help him breathe. On 11 September he was flown back to Karachi. His stretcher was placed in a military ambulance at the airport, which then set off for the city, but after a few miles the ambulance broke down. Fatima later recalled: 'There was no breeze, and the humid heat was oppressive. To add to his discomfort, scores of flies buzzed around his face, and he did not have the strength to brush them away.' It took over an hour for a replacement ambulance to arrive. They finally reached Government House at 6.10 p.m. Jinnah slept for two hours, then opened his eyes. The last word he spoke was his sister's name. He died at 10.20 p.m.

The following day, Pakistan's Quaid-i-Azam was buried in Karachi, a few hundred yards from the place where he was born. It was just seven and a half months after Gandhi's body had been cremated at Raj Ghat in Delhi, on the bank of the river Jumna. Gandhi's ashes were consigned to the waters at Triveni, the confluence of the rivers Ganges, Jumna and the underground Saraswati at

Allahabad, where nearly four years earlier the ashes of his wife, Kasturbai, had been scattered to begin their journey to the ocean. Today, Jinnah lies in a magnificent pink marble mausoleum, still a potent icon for the citizens of the country he created.

What of the remaining major players in the independence drama? Vallabhbhai Patel, the eldest at 73, became home minister and deputy prime minister under Nehru, but the differences between them increased. In March 1948, he suffered a major heart attack, brought on, it is said, by accusations surrounding the police failure to round up Gandhi's would-be assassins before the murder. He recovered, however, and resumed his posts in time to direct the 'police action' against Hyderabad, before dying of a second heart attack on 15 December 1950.

Liaquat Ali Khan was a sick man, suffering from stomach ulcers, but remained prime minister of Pakistan while the chief minister of East Pakistan, Khwaja Nazimuddin, became Pakistan's second governor-general. On 16 October 1951, Liaquat was gunned down at Rawalpindi. The assassin, an Afghan, was himself immediately shot. No one was ever charged with Liaquat's murder. Liaquat had been described by Jinnah as 'mediocre' but he was one of the few men the Quaid completely trusted. He was always a decent, honest and honourable man – after his death, it was discovered that he was virtually penniless, having always rejected bribes, lived on his salary and, as long as other refugees were still suffering financial hardship, refused to claim the compensation due to him for his lost family lands back in the UP.

Nehru died from a stroke on 27 May 1964, at his home in Delhi, aged 74. He had been prime minister for nearly 17 years, had become a world statesman, a figure of international importance and the undisputed leader of the non-aligned nations. 'When Nehru left the scene,' wrote S.S. Gill in his recent book *The Dynasty*, 'idealism and greatness walked out of Indian politics.' That may or may not be true, but he had left India a great legacy, the legacy of a stable democracy, a secular republic with no state religion and full protection under the constitution for all minorities. He was largely responsible for defeating the efforts of Hindu nationalists to eject the 30 million Muslims who chose to remain in India after partition – with the ironic result that there are now more Muslims in India than in Pakistan. In the years since his death, he has been followed by 10 prime ministers, each of whom has assumed and relinquished office peacefully and constitutionally with the exception of his own family: his daughter, Indira, was gunned down by her Sikh bodyguards in 1984; her son, Rajiv, succeeded her, but having been voted out of power in the general election of November 1989, was himself assassinated 18 months later while campaigning for re-election.

Mountbatten left India in May 1948, handing over to the first Indian governor-general, Chakravarti Rajagopalachari. He was back in the navy in June, as planned, and resumed his interrupted career with conspicuous success, starting with command of the 1st Cruiser Squadron. In due course, he achieved his lifetime's ambition by filling his father's old post as first sea lord, and then went one better by becoming supremo over all three armed services as chief of the defence staff, retiring as an admiral of the fleet. He was assassinated on 27 August 1979, not by anyone connected with India or Pakistan but by IRA terrorists at Mullaghmore harbour in County Sligo, Ireland, where he holidayed each year with his family in Classiebawn Castle, a neo-gothic pile inherited by Edwina from her father's family, the Ashleys. At about 11.30 a.m. that morning, Mountbatten climbed down the harbour steps and boarded his 29-foot fishing boat, *Shadow V.* The boat had just cleared the harbour wall when it was torn apart by a massive 50-pound bomb, killing Mountbatten and three of his passengers, including his 14-year-old grandson Nicholas Knatchbull, and seriously injuring three others.

Having spent the previous few years planning his state funeral in great detail – an interest that had replaced the family tree as his principal hobby – he was buried with all the pomp and circumstance he had wished for. In New Delhi, every shop and office closed, and a week's state mourning was declared. For a while, India remembered the joys of independence, and forgot the sorrows of partition.

There is, the authors of this book have been gratified and astonished to discover, a vast residue of goodwill and even affection in India and Pakistan not only for the British but even for the relatively unlamented British Raj. Gandhi once told a viceroy to leave India to anarchy or to God. Largely because they could not do otherwise, the British did just that – and it has almost worked.

Source Notes

Abbreviations used in notes:

CWMG	Collected Works of Mahatma Gandhi
IAR	Indian Annual Register
INC	Indian National Congress Records, New Delhi
IOL	India Office Library, London
IOR	India Office Records, London
NAI	National Archives of India, New Delhi
NML	Nehru Memorial Library, New Delhi
PRO	Public Record Office, London
SWJN	Selected Works of Jawaharlal Nehru

Prologue

1 Fisher, pp. 33–4
2 PRO: CAB 27/91. Vol. VI, Statement of Government of Punjab
3 PRO: CAB 27/92
4 PRO: CAB 27/93
5 Sir Verney Lovett, KCSI, in the *Yorkshire Post*, 28 May 1920
6 Briggs, quoted in Colvin, pp. 174, 177

Chapter I

1 IOL: Revised constitution of the East India Company, 1783
2 Spear, p. 67; Wolpert, *A New History of India*, p. 174
3 Quoted in Mason, p. 8
4 *The Travels of Peter Mundy*, quoted in Mason, p. 15
5 Kushwant Singh, *A History of the Sikhs*, pp. 82–4
6 Macaulay, Speech to the House of Commons on 10 July 1833 on the Government of India Bill. *Works*, Vol VIII, p. 125
7 Ibid., p. 126
8 Quoted in Lapping, p. 20
9 Muir, p. 82

10 Quoted in Mason, p. 49
11 Ibid., p. 50
12 Ibid., p. 57
13 Wolpert, *History*, pp. 194–5
14 Spear, p. 100

Chapter 2

1   Griffiths, p. 96
2   Mason, p. 84
3   Griffiths, p. 179
4   Quoted in Edwardes, *The Myth of the Mahatma*, p. 124
5   Moorhouse, p. 86
6   *Life and Letters of Rammohan Roy*, quoted in Chandra, p. 82
7   Moorhouse, p. 87
8   Brailsford, p. 165
9   Ibid.
10 *Life and Letters of Rammohan Roy*
11 Lapping, p. 26
12 Ibid., p. 140
13 Ibid., p. 142
14 Macaulay, *Works*, Vol. VIII p. 122
15 Ismay, p. 3
16 Macaulay, *Works*, pp. 137–9
17 Macaulay, Minute on Indian Education
18 Mason, p. 145
19 Mason, p. 145; Moorhouse, p. 104
20 Wolpert, p. 222

Chapter 3

1   Chandra, pp. 41–2
2   Griffiths, p. 179
3   Lunt, pp. 24–5
4   Macaulay, *Works*, VIII, p. 120
5   Muir, pp. 352–78
6   Ibid., p. 160
7   Chandra, p. 36
8   Ibid., p. 35
9   IOL (725): Sir John Kaye's Mutiny Papers, 35
10 Hibbert, p. 74
11 Kaye, Vol. 3, p. 646

Chapter 4

1 St. Aubyn, p. 307
2 Philips, pp. 10–11
3 Ibid.
4 Nehru, *Discovery*, p. 257
5 W.W. Hunter, *The Indian Mussulmans*, London, 1870, quoted in Akbar, *Nehru* pp. 32–3
6 Quoted in Beg, p. 76
7 Akbar, *Nehru*, p. 32
8 Chandra, p. 113
9 Dutt, *Economic History of India Under Early British Rule*, London, 1956, pp. xi, 420, quoted in Chandra, p. 97
10 Quoted in Chandra, p. 97
11 Quoted in Wolpert, p. 252; Edwardes, *The Myth of the Mahatma*, p. 140
12 Edwardes, *The Myth of the Mahatma*, p. 140
13 Quoted in Edwardes, *The Myth of the Mahatma*, p. 141
14 The *Bengalee*, 2 April 1883, quoted in Chandra, pp. 106–7

Chapter 5

1 Tinker, p. 44
2 Ibid.; Masani, p. 70
3 Quoted in Edwardes, *The Sahibs and the Lotus*, p. 215
4 Mason, p. 250; Moorhouse, p. 198
5 Quoted in Akbar, *Nehru*, p. 45
6 Lapping, p. 29
7 Chandra, pp. 67–8
8 Ibid., p. 70
9 Ibid., p. 68
10 IOL: Dufferin Papers, Vol. 47, Reel No. 528.
11 Ibid., Vol. 18, Reel No. 517
12 Ibid., Vol. 54, Reel No. 534
13 INC, I, p. 3, quoted in Chandra, p. 77
14 Beg, pp. 206–7
15 Chaudry Muhammad Ali, p. 7
16 Quoted in Akbar, *Nehru*, p. 16
17 Ibid.
18 *Writings and Speeches of Sir Syed Ahmed Khan*, edited by Shan Mohammad, Meerut, 1972, quoted in Chandra, p. 87
19 *The Pioneer*, Allahabad, 14 January 1888
20 INC, I, 19, p. 25
21 Allana, p. 1
22 *The Pioneer*, op. cit.
23 Sayeed, pp. 4, 22; Chandra, pp. 43, 410; Edwardes, *Myth of the Mahatma*, p. 146

24 Quoted in Edwardes, *Myth of the Mahatma*, p. 148
25 Ibid., p. 151

Chapter 6

1   Morris, p. 115
2   Quoted in Mason, p. 262
3   Quoted in Morris, p. 113
4   Quoted in Moorhouse, *India Britannica* p. 202
5   Ibid.
6   Ronaldshay, p. 321
7   Proceedings of the House of Lords, 30 June 1908, cols. 510–13
8   Chandra, p. 125
9   Morris, p. 97
10 *Manchester Guardian*, 23 and 27 October 1905
11 *The Times*, 6 November 1906
12 Chandra, p. 127
13 G.D. Birla, *In the Shadow of the Mahatma*, quoted in Ross, p. 25
14 Morris, p. 98
15 Bence-Jones, p. 199
16 Allana, pp. 7–10
17 Ibid.
18 Mary Minto, pp. 47–8
19 Pirzada, *Foundations of Pakistan*, p. 6
20 Aga Khan, pp. 122–3
21 Fatima Jinnah, *My Brother*, unpublished manuscript preserved in National Archives of Pakistan, Islamabad, F/143. Quoted in Wolpert, *Jinnah of Pakistan*, p. 7
22 Wrench, p. 132
23 Fatima Jinnah, *My Brother*, quoted in Wolpert, *Jinnah*
24 Ibid.
25 Ibid.
26 Beg, p. 180; Syed Sharifuddin Pirzada, *Some Aspects of Quaid-i-Azam's Life*, National Commission on Historical and Cultural Research, Islamabad, 1978, quoted in Wolpert, *Jinnah*, p. 14
27 Allana, p. 27
28 Wolpert, *Jinnah*, p. 18
29 INC, I, 19, p. 68
30 INC, I, p. 796
31 INC, II, pp. 853–4

Chapter 7

1   Wolpert, *History*, p. 283
2   Wolpert, *Tilak and Gokhale*, p. 187

3 Sumit Sarkar, *The Swadeshi Movement in Bengal, 1903–8*, New Delhi, 1973, p. 65, quoted in Chandra, p. 128

4 Chandra, p. 129

5 Wolpert, *History*, p. 280

6 Chandra, p. 140

7 Ibid., p. 139

8 *Kesari*, XXVIII, 19, 12 May 1908, p. 4

9 Wolpert, *History*, p. 283

10 Mason, p. 281

11 Curzon to Balfour, 31 March 1901, British Library, BL Add Mss 49732, quoted in Judd, p. 239

12 Judd, p. 237

13 Beg, pp. 241–2

14 Lapping, p. 35

15 Akbar, *Nehru*, p. 70

16 Morley, *Recollections*, Vol. II, p. 172

17 Morley, *Indian Speeches*, p. 91

18 Moorhouse, p. 217

19 Pirzada, *Foundations* p. 258

20 Naidu, p. 11

21 *Al-Hilal*, quoted in Sayeed, p. 43

22 Abdul Waheed Khan, p. 22–3

23 Sayeed, pp. 43–4

24 Bence-Jones, p. 218

Chapter 8

1 Fisher, p. 4

2 Benians, Butler and Carrington, p. 642

3 Wolpert, *Tilak and Gokhale*, pp. 264–5

4 Kushwant Singh, *History of the Sikhs* Vol. 2, p. 176

5 Chandra, p. 152

6 Kushwant Singh, op. cit., p. 179; Chandra, p. 152

7 Kushwant Singh, op. cit., p. 179; Chandra, p. 152

8 Mason, p. 284

9 O' Dwyer, p. 200

10 Chandra, p. 162

11 Chandra, p. 163

12 Ibid.

13 Edwardes, Report to the Secretary of the Government of India, Home Department, 19 January 1916, quoted in Beg, p. 287

14 Mohammad Noman, *Muslim India*, Allahabad Law Journal Press, 1942, p. 134, quoted in Sayeed, p. 39

15 Pirzada, *Foundations*, pp. 353–4

16 Ibid., p. 361
17 *The Leader*, 8 February 1931
18 Akbar, p. 59
19 Ibid., p. 60
20 Wolpert, *History*, p. 294; Chaudry Muhammad Ali, p. 15; Munawwar, p. 93; Sayeed, p. 41; Akbar, p. 99

Chapter 9

1 Bence-Jones, p. 223
2 Ibid.
3 Montagu, p. 157
4 Ibid., pp. 8–10
5 Ibid.
6 Ibid, pp. 194
7 Chelmsford Papers, quoted in Draper, p. 33
8 Bence-Jones, p. 224
9 Fisher, p. 6
10 Montagu, pp. 363
11 Mason, p. 275
12 Fisher, p. 188
13 Montagu, pp. 8–10
14 Saiyid, pp. 238–9
15 M.K. Gandhi to G. Arundel, 4 July 1919, reported in *Bombay Chronicle*, 12 August 1919

Chapter 10

1 M.K. Gandhi, *An Autobiography*, p. ix
2 Brown, pp. 24–5
3 M.K. Gandhi, *Autobiography*, p. 182
4 Chandra, p. 175
5 M.K. Gandhi, *Autobiography*, p. 132
6 Smuts to Sir Benjamin Robertson, 21 August 1914, quoted in W.K. Hancock, *Smuts, The Sanguine Years 1870–1919*, CUP, Cambridge, 1962, p. 345
7 Kumar and Puri, p. 40
8 M.K. Gandhi, *Collected Works*, XIII, p. 9
9 Ibid., pp. 332–4
10 Kumar and Puri, p. 47
11 Chandra, p. 179
12 W.H. Lewis to W.B. Heycock, 29 April 1917, NAI, Appendix D to Proceeding no. 323 of Home Political files, A, July 1917; Brown, p. 111
13 Montagu, p. 58
14 M.K. Gandhi, in *Indian Review*, April 1918, quoted in Fisher, p. 50

15 M.K. Gandhi, CWMG, Vol. XIV, p. 262
16 Ibid., pp. 339–40
17 Ibid., pp. 377–8

Chapter 11

1 CWMG, Vol. XV, pp. 101–2
2 H.F. Owen, 'Organizing for Rowlatt Satyagraha', in Kumar, p. 81; Brown, p. 130
3 Kumar and Puri, p. 53
4 PRO: Report of Hunter Committee, CAB 27/91
5 PRO: CAB 27/91
6 Kumar, p. 281; Draper, p. 48
7 PRO: CAB 27/91
8 M.K. Gandhi, *Autobiography*, p. 291
9 Colvin, pp. 116–18
10 Colvin, pp. 116–18
11 Horniman, p. 176
12 PRO: CAB 27/93: *Report, Proceedings and Memoranda of Cabinet Committee on Indian Disorders (1920)*
13 INC 1:63
14 IOL: MSS Eur E 264, Chelmsford papers
15 Tendulkar, Vol. I, p. 263
16 Sir Chimnanlal Setalvad, quoted in Swinson, pp. 95–6
17 PRO: CAB 27/91
18 Ibid.
19 Central Statistical Office, London
20 Nehru, *Autobiography*, pp. 43–4

Chapter 12

1 Nehru, *A Bunch of Old Letters*, p. 12
2 Nehru, *Autobiography*, p. 51
3 Ibid., p. 52
4 *The Times*, 22 March 1920
5 Sayeed, pp. 50–1
6 CWMG, Vol. XIV, p. 504
7 Brown, p. 154
8 Ambedkar, *Pakistan or the Partition of India*, p. 141
9 IAR 1921, Vol. III, pp. 106–8
10 Sir Dinshaw Wacha to G.A. Natesan, 6 October 1920, NML, G.A. Natesan papers, quoted in Brown, p. 155
11 Saiyid, pp. 264–5
12 Wolpert, *Jinnah*, pp. 71–2
13 Moorhouse, p. 239

14 Nehru, *Autobiography*, p. 69
15 Quoted in Akbar, *Nehru*, p. 141
16 Prabhudas Gandhi, *Recalling Memories of 1921*, quoted in Chandra, pp. 187–8
17 Lord Willingdon to Montagu, 11 February 1922, IOL: Mss EUR.F.93(4), Willingdon Papers.
18 NAI: Home Political 342–54 and KW, A, February 1920
19 *Imperial Legislative Assembly Debates*, Vol. I, 1921, pt. II, p. 1520
20 IAR 1922, Vol. I, pp. 172–4
21 Ambedkar, *Pakistan or the Partition of India*, p. 149
22 IAR 1922, Vol. I, pp. 187–8
23 Ambedkar, *Pakistan or the Partition of India*, p. 150
24 *Young Indian*, 24 November 1921, CWMG, Vol. XXI, pp. 466–7
25 Tendulkar, *Mahatma*, ii, 95, quoted in Kumar, p. 311
26 CWMG, Vol. XXII, p. 178
27 IOL: MSS Eur E 316, Reading Collection, Reading to Montagu, private telegram, 24 December 1921
28 IOR: H. Poll, 461/1921
29 *Young India*, 16 February 1922, CWMG, Vol. XXII, pp. 415–16

Chapter 13

1 Wolpert, *Jinnah*, pp. 80–1
2 Pirzada, *Foundations*, Vol. I, pp. 576–7
3 Moraes, p. 66
4 Mihir Bose, p. 48
5 Amery to Baldwin, 10 April 1927. Amery Papers, quoted in Louis, p. 27
6 Morris, p. 291
7 IOL: MSS Eur E 316, Reading Collection, Letter to Lord Reading, 4 December 1924
8 IOL: MSS Eur C 152, Halifax Collection (Irwin Papers), Birkenhead to Irwin, 3 September 1926
9 Harris, p. 76
10 IOL: MSS Eur C 152, Halifax Collection (Irwin Papers), Birkenhead to Irwin, 16 June 1927
11 Simon to Birkenhead, 16 May 1927. Simon Papers 61–4, Bodleian Library, Oxford
12 Quoted in *The Times*, London, 28 November 1927
13 Pirzada, *Foundations*, Vol. II, p. 114
14 Ibid., p. 127
15 Chagla, p. 94
16 IOL: MSS Eur C 152, Halifax Collection (Irwin Papers), Birkenhead to Irwin, 5 January 1928
17 Birkenhead to Irwin, 19 January 1928. Birkenhead, p. 255

Chapter 14

1 CWMG, Vol. XXXVI, p. 15
2 Chandra, pp. 261–2
3 Attlee, draft autobiography, cited in Burridge, p. 269
4 Das, p. 131
5 Ibid.
6 Nehru to Gandhi, 23 February 1928. CWMG, Vol. XXXVI, p. 58
7 IOL: MSS EUR C 152/29, Halifax Collection (Irwin Papers), Irwin to Birkenhead, 15 March 1928
8 Birkenhead, p. 519
9 *All Parties Conference 1928*. Report of the Committee appointed by the Conference to determine the principles of the Constitution for India. Allahabad, General Secretary, All-India Congress Committee, 1928
10 Qureshi, p. 55
11 IOL: Simon MSS, Eur F77/3/76, Simon to Irwin, 18 September 1928.
12 Neville Chamberlain Diary, 30 March 1928
13 Chandra, p. 249
14 Nehru, *A Bunch of Old Letters*, p. 68
15 Cited in Nanda, *Mahatma Gandhi*, p. 272
16 Saiyid, pp. 428–9
17 Ibid., pp. 432–5
18 Kanji Dwarkadas, *Ruttie Jinnah*, self-published, Bombay, 1963, p. 58, quoted in Wolpert, *Jinnah*, p. 97
19 Chagla, p. 121
20 Qureshi, pp. 321–4; Sayeed, pp. 72–3
21 Saiyid, pp. 450–1
22 Birkenhead, pp. 522–3
23 Nehru, *Autobiography*, pp. 194–5
24 S.C. Bose, *The Indian Struggle*, pp. 169–70
25 Nehru, *Autobiography*, p. 187
26 Chandra, p. 249
27 National Archives of Pakistan, F 15/5, MacDonald to Jinnah, 14 August 1929
28 Nehru, *Autobiography*, p. 196; Wolpert, *Jinnah*, p. 110
29 Nehru, *Autobiography*, p. 197
30 Brailsford, p. 21
31 National Archives of Pakistan, F/15, 54–9
32 Nehru, *Autobiography*, p. 201
33 Ibid.
34 Ibid., pp. 612–13

Chapter 15

1 Nehru, *Autobiography*, pp. 209–10
2 CWMG, Vol. XLII, p. 389

3 CWMG, Vol. XLIII, pp. 3–7

4 Ibid., p. 7

5 Nehru, *Autobiography*, p. 212

6 Webb Miller, *I Found No Peace*, New York, Simon and Schuster, 1936, quoted in Sengupta

7 Chandra, p. 275

8 Nehru, *Autobiography*, p. 214

9 Gandhi to Irwin, CWMG, Vol. XLIII, pp. 411–16

10 Chandra, pp. 252–3

11 Dutton, p. 97

12 Letter dated 15 August 1930. Nehru, *Autobiography*, Appendix B, pp. 613–14

13 Gilbert, p. 30

14 *The Times*, 13 November 1930, p. 14

15 Pirzada, *Foundations*, Vol. II, p. 159

16 K.K. Aziz, (ed.) *Complete Works of Rahmat Ali*, Islamabad, National Commission on Historical and Cultural Research, 1978, Vol. I, p. 4, quoted in Wolpert, *Jinnah*, p. 131

17 National Archives of Pakistan, F/15, 92, Simon to Dube, 26 February 1931

18 Menon, *The Transfer of Power in India*, p. 46

19 Nehru, *Autobiography*, p. 247

20 Gilbert, p. 34

21 Muggeridge, p. 43

22 Bence-Jones, p. 272

23 Muggeridge, p. 18

24 Ross, p. 67

25 Ibid.

26 Edwardes, p. 219

27 Mercer, p. 407

28 Ross, p. 68

29 Ibid., p. 69

30 Das, p. 152

31 Ibid., pp. 154–5

Chapter 16

1 Menon, *Transfer*, p. 48

2 Nehru, *Autobiography*, p. 323

3 Low, p. 173

4 Ibid., p. 122

5 IOR: TP5, Willingdon to Hoare, 29 May 1932; *The Civil Disobedience Movement 1930–34*, New Delhi, Govt. of India, 1936

6 Chandra, p. 291

7 Ibid.

8 IOR: H Poll 31/95/32, Viceroy to SoS, 1 November 1932

9 Ibid.
10 IOR: H Poll 4/2/33, Haig's note, 18 March 1933
11 IOR: H Poll 117/33, Haig's note, 9 July 1933
12 IOR: TP7, Willingdon to Hoare, 9 April 1934; TP12, Tel, 19 April 1934
13 CWMG, Vol. LIX, pp. 3–12
14 NML: Ansari Papers, Pant to Ansari, 25 November 1934
15 NML: Satyamurti Papers, Gandhi to Satyamurti, 14 November 1934
16 IOR: TP8, Willingdon to Hoare, 11, 19 November 1934
17 IOR: TP8, Willingdon to Hoare, 3 December 1934
18 Jinnah to Abdul Matin Choudhury, 30 March 1933, Allana, pp. 91–2
19 Pirzada, *Foundations*, Vol. II, p. 233
20 Judd, p. 270
21 IOR: MSS Eur D 609, Zetland Collection (Lawrence Papers), Linlithgow to Zetland, 21 December 1939
22 Menon, *Transfer*, p. 51
23 John Glendevon, *The Viceroy at Bay: Lord Linlithgow in India, 1936–43* London, 1971, p. 52, quoted in Chandra, p. 319
24 Ross, p. 98
25 Ibid., p. 99
26 Nehru, *Letters*, pp. 182–91
27 Ibid. pp. 191–2
28 Ibid., p. 200

Chapter 17

1 Morris, p. 479
2 Ibid.
3 Quoted in Butler, pp. 276–7
4 Sarvapalli Gopal, *Jawaharlal Nehru*, Vol. I, London, 1975, p. 255; quoted in Louis, p. 126
5 Ibid. Vol. 58, p. 11
6 Akbar, *Nehru*, p. 258
7 Ibid.
8 Sayeed, p. 176
9 *Annual Report of the All-India Muslim League for the Years 1932 and 1933*, Delhi, n.d., quoted in Sayeed, pp. 176–7
10 Pirzada, *Foundations*, Vol. II, p. 258
11 *Return showing the Results of Elections in India, 1937*, Cmd 5589, HMSO, November 1937
12 Ibid.
13 Ibid.
14 IAR 1937, Vol. I, pp. 177–8
15 M.N. Roy, quoted in Akbar, p. 283
16 Nehru, *Letters*, p. 225
17 IAR 1937, Vol. I, pp. 264–70

18 Rajmohan Gandhi, pp. 11–14
19 Quoted in Rajmohan Gandhi, p. 16
20 Nehru at Ambala, January 1937. SWJN, Vol. VIII, p. 119
21 *The Statesman*, Calcutta, 7 January 1937
22 SWJN, Vol. VIII, p. 121
23 Khan, pp. 73–4
24 Dwarkadas, pp. 466–7
25 Gandhi to Jinnah, 22 May 1937, CWMG, Vol. LXV, p. 231
26 Nehru, letter to Prasad, 21 July 1937, from *Rajendra Prasad's Correspondence*, Vol. I, quoted in Rajmohan Gandhi, pp. 19–20
27 Ibid., p. 22
28 Jamil-ud-Din Ahmad, *Glimpses of Quaid-i-Azam*, p. 11
29 Pirzada, *Foundations*, Vol. II, pp. 265–73
30 *Resolutions of the All-India Muslim League from October 1937 to December 1938*, Delhi, All-India Muslim League, 1944, pp. 78–82
31 IAR 1939, Vol. I, p. 374

Chapter 18

1   Nehru, *The Discovery of India*, p. 313
2   Ibid., p. 314
3   Mason, p. 303
4   Ibid., p. 316; Anita Inder Singh, p. 36; Moore, pp. 22–3
5   Hodson, p. 70
6   Mason, p. 303
7   Nehru to Gandhi, 28 April 1938. Nehru, *Letters*, pp. 276–7
8   Rajmohan Gandhi, *The Rajaj Story 1937–72*, p. 7, quoted in Chandra, p. 327
9   Akbar, *Nehru*, p. 309
10 Nehru, *Letters*, pp. 256–7
11 Nehru, *Autobiography*, p. 604; Tariq Ali, p. 61
12 Nehru, *Letters*, pp. 276–7
13 Nehru, *Autobiography*, p. 604
14 Ibid., p. 605
15 Harris, p. 152
16 Nehru, *Autobiography*, p. 607
17 Ibid.
18 Ross, p. 132
19 Khaliquzzaman, pp. 206–7
20 Zetland, pp. 248–9
21 Khaliquzzaman, p. 207
22 Zetland, p. 249
23 Nehru, *Discovery*, p. 364
24 Ibid., p. 363
25 Glendevon, p. 136

26 Ibid., p. 137
27 Ibid., p. 135
28 IOL: MSS Eur D 609, Zetland Collection, Vol. 18, Linlithgow to Zetland, 5 September 1939
29 Menon, p. 60
30 SWJN, Vol. IX, p. 292
31 Nehru, *Discovery*, pp. 366–7
32 Menon, pp. 66–7; Hodson, p. 78
33 Chandra, pp. 449
34 Jamil-ud-Din Ahmad, *Some Recent Speeches and Writings of Mr Jinnah*, Vol. I, pp. 112–20
35 Ibid., pp. 110–11
36 Nehru, *Letters*, p. 403
37 Cripps's diaries, quoted in Estorick, pp. 198–9
38 Ibid., p. 199
39 Ibid., pp. 200–1
40 *Bombay Chronicle*, 19 December 1939 – cutting preserved in CAB 127/60, PRO
41 Cripps's diaries, quoted in Estorick, p. 205
42 Ibid., p. 206; Cooke, p. 256
43 10 January 1940. CWMG, Vol. LXXI, Appendix II, pp. 433–5

Chapter 19

1 IAR 1940, Vol. I, p. 218; Azad, p. 30
2 Pirzada, *Foundations*, Vol. II, pp. 327–30
3 Ibid., pp. 335–7
4 Ibid., p. 340
5 IOL: MSS Eur F 125, Linlithgow Collection, Vol. 19, Linlithgow to Zetland, 8 April 1940, Telegram
6 Linlithgow to Jinnah, 19 April 1940. Pirzada, *Quaid-i-Azam Jinnah's Correspondence*, p. 201
7 Zetland, p. 296
8 Amery, *My Political Life*, Vol. II, p. 211
9 Amery to Simon, 20 March 1897, Simon Papers 47, quoted in Louis, pp. 43–4
10 Amery, *Diaries*, Vol. II, p. 617
11 Amery MS Diary, quoted in Louis, p. 127
12 IOR: L/PO/6/105d, Amery to Churchill, 14 July 1940
13 Linlithgow Papers, IOL: MSS Eur F125/9, Amery to Linlithgow, 'Private', 30 May 1940
14 Amery, *Diaries*, Vol. II, p. 641, quoted in Louis, p. 130
15 Glendevon, p. 182
16 26 May 1940, CWMG, Vol. LXXII, pp. 100–1
17 *Harijan*, 6 July 1940. CWMG, Vol. LXXII, pp. 229–31
18 IAR 1940, Vol. II, pp. 193–4
19 David Dilks, *The Diaries of Sir Alexander Cadogan*, p. 316
20 Churchill to Amery, 'Secret', 17 July 1940. Amery Papers, quoted in Louis, p. 131

21 SWJN, Vol. I, p. 266
22 IAR 1940, Vol. II, p. 201
23 *India and the War: Statement issued with the authority of His Majesty's Government by the Governor-General on August 8, 1940* Cmnd 6219
24 Jamil-ud-Din Ahmad, *Speeches*, Vol. I, pp. 386–7
25 Das, p. 198
26 Menon, *Transfer*, p. 82
27 Mihir Bose, p. 143
28 *Forward Bloc*, 15 June 1940, quoted in Hauner, p. 238
29 Mihir Bose, p. 161
30 Amery, *Diaries*, II, p. 661, quoted in Louis, p. 142
31 IOR: HC 371, 5s, 22 April 1941, cols. 53–7
32 IAR 1941, Vol. I, p. 327. Italics in the original.
33 Pirzada, *Foundations*, Vol. II, pp. 360–1
34 Ibid., p. 371
35 Menon, *Transfer*, pp. 109–10

Chapter 20

1 Hodson, p. 91
2 Churchill to Attlee, (T), 7 January 1942, TP, Vol. I, p. 14
3 Ibid., p. 49.
4 Quoted in Reginald Coupland, *The Cripps Mission*, London 1942, p. 20
5 Fergusson, pp. 71–2
6 Hauner, p. 428
7 Attlee to Amery, 2 February 1942, TP, Vol. I, p. 60
8 Hodson, p. 91
9 TP, Vol. I, pp. 282–3
10 Amery MS Diary, 26 February 1942, quoted in Louis, p. 157
11 PRO: CAB 127/70; Parliamentary Papers, India (Lord Privy Seal's Mission), pp. 4–5
12 Churchill to Linlithgow, 10 March 1942, TP Vol. I, pp. 394–5
13 PRO: CAB 127/70
14 Quoted in Moore, *Churchill, Cripps and India*, p. 82
15 Mass Observation file report No 1166, quoted in Addison, p. 200
16 Malcolm MacDonald, *Titans and Others*, Collins, 1972, pp. 109–10, quoted in Addison, p. 205
17 Jamil-ud-Din Ahmad, *Speeches*, pp. 401–2; CAB 127/70
18 Hodson, p. 98
19 PRO: CAB 127/70
20 Gandhi interview with Louis Fisher, quoted in Estorick, p. 305
21 Coupland, p. 26
22 Nehru, *Discovery*, p. 389
23 PRO: CAB 127/72

24 PRO: CAB 127/70
25 Ibid.
26 SWJN, Vol. I, p. 280, quoting from General Molesworth's *Curfew on Olympus*
27 PRO: CAB 127/70
28 Ibid.
29 US National Archives, 123 Johnson, Louis, 1/2
30 Hodson, p. 99
31 PRO: CAB 127/70
32 Ibid.
33 Ibid.
34 Hodson, p. 103
35 Telegram dated 11 April 1942, received 3.00 a.m. 12 April 1942, marked 'no distribution'. Churchill Papers, 20/73 quoted in Gilbert, *Road to Victory*, p. 88

Chapter 21

1 Rahman, p. 91
2 Chaudhuri, p. 694
3 Ibid.
4 *Harijan*, 26 April 1942
5 *Harijan*, 10 May 1942
6 'Secret and Personal' telegram, 14 June 1942, Churchill Papers, 20/76
7 Prime Minister's personal minute to the Secretary of State for India, M250/2, 14 June 1942, Churchill Papers, 20/67
8 PRO: CAB 127/80
9 Statement issued to the foreign press, 31 July 1942, quoted in Jamil-ud-Din Ahmad, *Speeches*, Vol. I, pp434–9
10 CWMG, Vol. LXXVI, pp. 384–96
11 Linlithgow to Churchill, 31 August 1942, TP, Vol. II, p. 853
12 Linlithgow to Amery, 5 September 1942, TP, Vol II, p. 908
13 Amery to Linlithgow, 17 November 1942, TP, Vol III, p. 570
14 Mira Behn, p. 249
15 Gandhi to Linlithgow, 29 January 1943, CWMG, Vol. LXXVII, pp. 55–6
16 Nanda, *Gandhi*, p. 236
17 Linlithgow to Amery, 2 February 1943, TP, Vol. III, p. 570
18 Amery to Linlithgow, 8 February 1943, ibid., p. 617
19 Ibid., pp. 631–2
20 Gandhi to Sir Richard Tottenham, 8 February 1943, CWMG, Vol. LXXVII, p. 61
21 'Strictly Secret Note' on the proceedings at Delhi, 24–6 April 1943, TP, Vol. III, pp. 918–20
22 Ibid., p. 922
23 Linlithgow to Amery, 10 June 1943, TP, Vol. IV, p. 36
24 Amery to Linlithgow, 28 June 1943, TP, Vol. IV, p. 36
25 Linlithgow to Amery, 4 October 1943, ibid., p. 349

26 Das, p. 208
27 Cited in Lewin, p. 208
28 Wavell, p. I
29 Ibid.
30 Cited Lewin, p. 219
31 Amery to Linlithgow, 8 June 1843, TP, Vol. III, p. 1048
32 Amery, MS Diary, 9 June 1943, quoted in Louis, p. 169
33 Wavell, p. 8
34 Wavell, appendix I, pp. 467–70
35 Wavell, pp. 20–3
36 Ibid.
37 Ibid.
38 Ibid.
39 Ibid., p. 33
40 Amery, *Diaries*, II, p. 988

Chapter 22

1 Mihir Bose, p. 208
2 Ibid., p. 211
3 Peter Heehs, article: 'India's Divided Loyalties?', in *History Today*, July 1995, p. 19
4 Ibid.
5 Mihir Bose, pp. 210–11
6 Cited in Mihir Bose, p. 220
7 Hamid, p. 16
8 Kiani, p. 126
9 Hamid, p. 16
10 Mira Behn, pp. 254–5
11 Mira Behn to Amrit Kaur, 10 July 1944, NML, Amrit Kaur Papers, file No M8
12 Menon, *Transfer*, p. 154
13 Ibid., p. 156
14 Wavell to Amery, 5 May 1944, TP, Vol. IV, p. 952
15 Amery memorandum, 5 May 1944, TP, Vol. IV, pp. 953–3
16 Amery to Wavell, 11 May 1944, Ibid., pp. 965
17 IAR 1944, Vol. II, pp. 129–30
18 Gandhi to Jinnah, 17 July 1944 Jamil-ud-Din Ahmad, *Speeches*, Vol. II, p. 148
19 Jinnah to Gandhi, 24 July 1944, ibid.
20 Ibid., pp. 135–47
21 IAR 1944, Vol. VII, p. 193
22 TP, Vol. IV, p. 1058
23 CWMG, Vol. LXXVIII, p. 101
24 Jamil-ud-Din Ahmad, *Speeches*, Vol. II, pp. 179–84
25 CWMG, Vol. LXXVIII, p. 122
26 Jamil-ud-Din Ahmad, *Speeches*, Vol. II, p. 223

27 TP, Vol. V, pp. 56–7

28 TP, Vol. V, pp. 68–9 and 140

29 V.P. Menon to Evan Jenkins, 27 January 1945, TP, Vol. V, p. 476

30 Minute by Churchill, 16 January 1945, ibid., p. 404

31 Menon, *Transfer*, p. 178

32 Ibid.

33 Amery, *Diaries*, II, p. 1039

34 PRO: CAB 127/77

35 TP, Vol. V, p. 1076

36 Wavell, p. 152

37 TP, Vol. V, pp. 1077–80

38 Wavell, p. 142

39 Wavell to Amery, 15 June 1945, TP, Vol. V, pp. 1126–7

40 Wavell, pp. 145–7

41 Ibid.

42 Wavell to Amery, 25 June 1945, TP, Vol. V, p. 1155–6

43 Wavell, p. 153

44 Amery to Wavell, 10 July 1945, TP, Vol. V, p. 1224

45 Wavell, p. 154; and Wavell to Amery, TP, Vol. V, pp. 1224–5

46 Wavell, p. 155 (italics in original); and Wavell to Amery, 14 July 1945, TP, Vol. V, pp. 1247–8

47 Amery to Wavell, 10 July 1945, TP, Vol. V, p. 1224

48 PRO: CAB 65/33, Cabinet meetings 31 May and 8 June 1945

49 Amery, *Diaries*, II, p. 1045

50 Wavell, pp. 152–3

Chapter 23

1 Lady Felicity Harewood (Felicity Attlee), *Clem, Father and Politician*, The Third Attlee Memorial Lecture, 20 February 1985, quoted in Hennessy, p. 86

2 Menon, *Transfer*, p. 216

3 Wavell to Pethick-Lawrence, 19 August 1945, TP, Vol. VI, p. 39

4 Wavell, p. 165

5 Harris, p. 366

6 Wavell, p. 169–70

7 TP, Vol. VI, pp. 282–3

8 Patel to Birla, 20 September 1945, G.M. Nandurkar (ed.), *Sardar's Letters – Mostly Unknown*, Ahmedabad, 1977–8, Vol. I, p. 174, quoted in Moore, pp. 75–6

9 Mihir Bose, p. 247

10 Hodson, p. 250; Menon, *Transfer*, p. 225

11 Hodson, p. 251

12 TP, Vol. VI, p. 387

13 Ibid. pp. 305–6, 360

14 Ibid., p. 507

15 Governor Casey to Wavell, 2 January 1946, Ibid., p. 725
16 Casey to Wavell, 2 December 1945, Ibid., p. 589
17 Cunningham, governor of NWFP, to Wavell, 27 November 1945, Ibid., p. 546
18 Ibid., p. 512
19 Auchinleck to Wavell, 24 and 26 November 1945, Ibid., pp. 533 and 545
20 Hamid, p. 20
21 Ibid., p. 19
22 Hamid, Appendix I, pp. 303–6
23 Ibid.
24 Sarkar, p. 422
25 Wavell to Pethick-Lawrence, 22 February 1946, TP, Vol. VI, p. 1048
26 Ibid., pp. 1117–18
27 Ibid., pp. 1082–3
28 Jamil-ud-Din Ahmad, *Speeches*, Vol. II, p. 363

Chapter 24

1 Menon, *Transfer*, p. 226
2 Maurice Zinkin, Government of India Finance Department, sent to India Office by Cripps 16 January 1946, TP Vol. VI, pp. 801–5
3 Ibid., p. 1173
4 Ibid., p. 1125
5 Note by Wyatt, 28 March 1946, TP, Vol. VII, pp. 22–4
6 Nehru to Dorothy Norman, 1963, quoted in Akbar, p. 370
7 Sonia Gandhi, *Two Alone, Two Together*, p. 528
8 TP, Vol. VII, pp. 59–60
9 Cameron, p. 93
10 Wavell, p. 236
11 TP, Vol. VII, pp. 117–18
12 Ibid., pp. 111–13
13 Pirzada, *Foundations*, pp. 522–3
14 Ibid., pp. 514–15
15 Ibid., pp. 516–20; Wolpert, *Jinnah*, p. 262
16 Pirzada, *Foundations*, pp. 523–4
17 TP, Vol. VII, p. 179
18 Ibid., pp. 220–1
19 Ibid., p. 263
20 Azad, pp. 150–2
21 *Alexander Diaries*, entry for 16 April 1946, quoted in Anita Inder Singh, p. 158
22 Wajid Ali, Lahore, personal interview with authors
23 TP, Vol, VII, p. 342
24 Ibid., p. 345
25 Cameron, p. 96
26 Wavell, p. 260

27 TP, Vol. VII, p. 591
28 *Harijan*, 17 May 1946, quoted in TP, Vol. VII, p. 615
29 Wavell to the king, 8 July 1946. TP, Vol. VII, pp. 1092–3
30 Ibid., pp. 636–7
31 Wavell, pp. 276–7
32 TP, Vol. VII, p. 638
33 Ibid.
34 Ibid., p. 1037

Chapter 25

 1 SWJN, Vol. XV, pp. 236–8
 2 Ibid., pp. 242–3
 3 Jamil-ud-Din Ahmad, *Speeches*, Vol. II, pp. 407–21; Pirzada, *Foundations*, pp. 546–9
 4 Pirzada, *Foundations*, Vol. II, pp. 557–8
 5 Ashraf, p. 291
 6 Pirzada, *Foundations*, p. 560
 7 Ashraf, p. 373
 8 Wavell, pp. 239 and 407
 9 TP, Vol. VIII, p. 239
10 Tuker, p. 158
11 Ibid., pp. 599–600
12 Wavell, p. 335
13 Quoted in Moorhouse, *Calcutta*, p. 220
14 Wavell, p. 340
15 TP, Vol. VIII, pp. 312–13
16 Wavell, p. 341; TP, Vol. VIII, p. 313
17 TP, Vol. VIII, p. 328
18 TP, Vol. IX, p. 24
19 Jamil-ud-Din Ahmad, *Speeches*, Vol. II, p. 444
20 TP, Vol. VIII, p. 323
21 Ibid., p. 350
22 Ibid., p. 332
23 Jamil-ud-Din Ahmad, *Speeches*, Vol. II, p. 425
24 TP, Vol. VIII, pp. 532, 648
25 Khawaja Ahmad Abbas, *Who Killed India?* quoted in Mumtaz Hasan, *India Partitioned: The Other Face of Freedom*, Vol. 2, Roli Books, 1995
26 Menon, *Transfer*, p. 306; Wolpert, *Jinnah*, p. 289; TP, Vol. VIII, DOC 275, n. 3
27 Attlee, p. 209
28 TP, Vol. VIII, p. 570
29 IOR: HP 5/55/46, pp. 32–3, Governor of Bengal to viceroy (T291)
30 Brown, p. 376
31 Akbar, p. 384

32 TP, Vol. VIII, pp. 732–3
33 Sonia Gandhi, p. 540
34 Wavell, p. 410
35 Mosley, p. 52

Chapter 26

1 Attlee, *Autobiography*, I/I3, quoted in Moore, p. 205
2 General Sir Philip Christison, 'Life and Times', p. 106, Imperial War Museum
3 Quoted in Lambton, p. 215
4 Quoted in Ziegler, p. 53
5 Mountbatten's Diary, 30 June 1937, quoted in Ziegler, p. 98
6 A.P. Cole to Mountbatten, 19 September 1940, Broadlands Archive A115, quoted in Ziegler, p. 132
7 Ziegler, pp. 138–9
8 Hoey, p. 182
9 Sir David Fraser, quoted in Roberts, p. 72
10 Keegan, p. 220
11 Ziegler, p. 701
12 Collins and Lapierre, *Mountbatten and the Partition of India*, pp. 10–11
13 Broadlands Archive, D92, 8 January 1947, quoted in Ziegler, p. 356
14 Hough, p. 244
15 TP, Vol. IX, pp. 397–400
16 TP, Vol. IX, p. 451
17 Ismay, p. 410
18 'Indian Policy', Cmd 7047: TP, Vol. IX, p. 774
19 IOR: Viceroy's Personal Report No. 17, 16 August 1947, Appendix IV
20 Ibid.
21 Jenkins to Pethick-Lawrence, 25 February 1947, TP, Vol. IX, p. 815
22 Wavell to Pethick-Lawrence, 25 February 1947, TP, Vol. IX, p. 819
23 TP, Vol. IX, pp. 972–4

Chapter 27

1 Ismay, p. 416
2 TP, Vol. IX, pp. 1011–12
3 Wavell, p. 432
4 Campbell-Johnson, p. 43
5 Menon, p. 350; TP, Vol. X, p. 9
6 Campbell-Johnson, p. 42
7 Campbell-Johnson, p. 44
8 Campbell-Johnson, p. 51
9 IOR: Annexe 1 to Viceroy's Personal Report No. 2, 9 April 1947

10 Campbell-Johnson, p. 55
11 Ibid., p. 52
12 Hodson, p. 223
13 IOR: Viceroy's Personal Report No. 2, 9 April 1947
14 Das, p. 239
15 Ibid., p. 240
16 Hodson, p. 220; TP, Vol. X, pp. 137–9
17 Morgan, p. 394
18 TP, Vol. X, pp. 138–9
19 Ibid., p. 190
20 Ibid., p. 102
21 Ibid., pp. 331–2
22 Campbell-Johnson, p. 58
23 Hodson, p. 259; Hamid, p. 332
24 Viceroy's Personal Report No. 3, 17 April 1947, TP, Vol. X, pp. 296–303
25 Mountbatten Archives, IOL file 191
26 S. Gopal, *Jawaharlal Nehru*, p. 353
27 Ibid.
28 Ibid.
29 TP, Vol. X, p. 310
30 TP, Vol. X, pp. 312–13
31 Ismay to Mountbatten, 25 April 1947, TP Vol X, p. 437
32 Ibid., pp. 371–4
33 Ibid.
34 Note by Jenkins, 16 April 1947, ibid., pp. 282–3
35 Campbell-Johnson, p. 74
36 Caroe, unpublished memoir, quoted in Ziegler, pp. 376–7
37 Campbell-Johnson, p. 79
38 Ibid., p. 80
39 Viceroy's staff meeting, 1 May 1947, TP Vol. X, p. 524
40 TP, Vol. X, DOC 276, Annex 1, p. 543
41 Ibid., pp. 517–19

Chapter 28

1 Ismay to Lady Ismay, 23 April 1947, Ismay Papers, III 8/5A, quoted in Ziegler, p. 378 and Moore, p. 275
2 Christie's diary, 24 April 1947, IOL, MSS Eur. 718/2
3 Ismay p. 420
4 *Hindustan Times*, 6 May 1947
5 TP, Vol. X, pp. 673–5
6 Ibid., p. 699
7 Campbell-Johnson, p. 88

8 Gill, p. 372

9 Viceroy's Personal Report No. 7, 15 May 1947; TP, Vol. XI, p. 836

10 Ibid.

11 Record of conversation between Mountbatten and Krishna Menon, Mountbatten Tour diaries, 24 June 1970, quoted in Ziegler, p. 379

12 TP, Vol. X, p. 756

13 Campbell-Johnson, p. 89

14 Menon, *Transfer*, p. 362

15 Menon, interview with Leonard Mosley; Mosley, p. 125

16 Ismay, p. 421

17 Campbell-Johnson, pp. 89–90

18 Mosley, pp. 125–6

19 Menon, *Transfer*, p. 365

20 Harris, p. 383

21 TP, Vol. X, pp. 944–6

22 Campbell-Johnson, p. 98

23 Ibid., pp. 96–7

24 Ismay, p. 422

25 Campbell-Johnson, p. 97

26 Campbell-Johnson, Appendix, p. 367

27 Ibid., pp. 99–101: Viceroy's Personal Report No 8, 5 June 1947, TP Vol XI, pp. 158–65

28 Ibid.

29 Ismay, p. 424

30 Campbell-Johnson, pp. 102–3; Viceroy's Personal Report No. 38, TP, Vol. XI, pp. 161–2

31 Ibid., p. 163

32 Mountbatten, *Time Only to Look Forward*, p. 43, quoted in Ziegler, p. 387

Chapter 29

1 Harris, pp. 383–4

2 Collins and Lapierre, *Mountbatten*, p. 72

3 Viceroy's Personal Report No. 9, 12 June 1947, TP, Vol. XI, p. 303

4 Pyarelal, Vol. II, p. 217

5 Menon, *Transfer*, p. 384

6 Campbell-Johnson, pp. 115–16; *Morning Herald* and *Morning News*, quoted in Pirzada, *Foundations*, Vol. II, pp. 566–7

7 Ibid., p. 568

8 Campbell-Johnson, p. 126

9 Viceroy's Personal Report No. 10, 27 June 1947, TP, Vol. XI, p. 680

10 Viceroy's Personal Report No. 10, TP, Vol. XI, p. 139

11 Chaudry Muhammad Ali, p. 168

12 Report on the Last Viceroyalty
13 Chaudry Muhammad Ali, p. 177
14 Report on the Last Viceroyalty
15 Viceroy's Personal Report No. 11, 4 July 1947, TP, Vol. XI, pp. 899–900
16 Chaudry Muhammad Ali, p. 178
17 Morgan, p. 408
18 Lady Mountbatten Papers, 5 July 1947, quoted in Ziegler, pp. 398–9
19 Hodson, p. 326; Chaudry Muhammad Ali, pp. 170–1
20 Campbell-Johnson, p. 87
21 Chaudry Muhammad Ali, p. 199
22 Dr Hakim Ahsan, personal interview
23 Chaudry Muhammad Ali, pp. 178–80
24 Ismay, pp. 427–8
25 Hodson, p. 263
26 Ismay to Lady Ismay, 24 June 1947, Ismay Papers, quoted in Ziegler, p. 391
27 Menézes, pp. 428–30
28 Rear Admiral Satyindra Singh, 'A Division of the Spoils', in *Maritime International*, December 1996; and personal interview with authors
29 Ibid.

Chapter 30

1 Report on the Last Viceroyalty
2 Mosley, p. 160
3 TP, Vol. VII, p. 523
4 Campbell-Johnson, p. 44
5 Menon, *States*, pp. 74–5
6 Ibid., p. 93
7 Allen, pp. 239–40
8 Campbell-Johnson, p. 144
9 Mosley, p. 197
10 Notes on the Sikh Plan, Lahore, West Punjab Government, 1948
11 Ibid.
12 Ismay, pp. 430–1
13 TP, Vol. XII, pp. 117–21
14 Ibid., pp. 71–4
15 Ibid., pp. 131–7
16 Ibid., p. 369
17 IOR: Viceroy's Personal Report No. 17, 16 August 1947, Appendix IV, Memorandum by the Governor of the Punjab, 4 August 1947
18 Viceroy's Staff Meeting minutes, 9 August 1947, TP, Vol. XII, pp. 611–12
19 Jinnah, *Speeches as Governor-General*, pp. 7–9
20 Wolpert, *Jinnah*, p. 342

Epilogue

1 Ismay, p. 431
2 Akbar, *Kashmir*, p. 99
3 Chaudry Muhammad Ali, p. 218
4 Jinnah, *Speeches*, pp. 32–3
5 Bhalla, p?
6 Ibid.
7 Menézes, p. 430
8 Lapping, p. 95
9 Ismay, p. 436
10 Fatima Jinnah, *My Brother*, quoted in Wolpert, *Jinnah*, pp. 369–70

Bibliography

We have consulted the following books, in whole or in part, during the research and writing of *The Proudest Day*. All books are published in London unless otherwise indicated.

Addison, Paul, *The Road to 1945*, Pimlico, 1994
Aga Khan, H.H., *The Memoirs of Aga Khan*, New York, Simon & Schuster, 1954
Ahmad, Ausaf, *Indian Muslims*, New Delhi, Khama, 1993
Ahmad, Aziz, *Studies in Islamic Culture in the Indian Environment*, Oxford, Clarendon Press, 1964
Ahmad, Jamil-ud-Din, *Some Aspects of Pakistan*, Lahore, Ashraf, 1943
—— (ed.) *Some Recent Speeches and Writings of Mr Jinnah*, 12 Vols., Lahore, Ashraf, 1952
—— *Glimpses of Quaid-i-Azam*, Karachi, Educational Press, 1960
Ahmad, N., *Muslim Separatism in British India: A Retrospective Study*, Lahore, Ferozsons, 1991
Ahmed, Akbar S., *Resistance and Control in Pakistan*, Routledge, 1991
—— *Postmodernism and Islam*, Routledge, 1993
Ahmed, Syed Jaffar, *Federalism in Pakistan: A Constitutional Study*, Karachi, Pakistan Study Centre, University of Karachi, 1990
Akbar, M.J., *Nehru: The Making of India*, Viking, 1988
—— *Kashmir: Behind the Vale*, New Delhi, Viking (India), 1991
Ali, Chaudry Muhammad, *The Emergence of Pakistan*, Lahore, Research Society of Pakistan, University of the Punjab, 1973
Ali, Tariq, *The Nehrus and the Gandhis: An Indian Dynasty*, Picador, 1985
Allana, G. (ed.), *Pakistan Movement: Historic Documents*, Karachi, Department of International Relations, University of Karachi, 1967
Allen, Charles and Dwivedi, Sharada, *Lives of the Indian Princes*, Century, 1984
Ambedkar, B.R., *Thoughts on Pakistan*, Bombay, Thacker, 1941
—— *What Congress and Gandhi Have Done to the Untouchables*, Bombay, Thacker, 1945
—— *Pakistan or the Partition of India*, Bombay, Thacker, 1946
Amery, L.S., *My Political Life*, 3 Vols., Hutchinson, 1953–5
Ansari, Iqbal A., *Diaries The Muslim Situation in India*, New Delhi, Sterling, 1989
Anwar, Muhammad, *Jinnah Quaid-i-Azam*, Karachi, National Publishing House, 1970
Ashraf, Mohammad (ed.), *Cabinet Mission and After*, Lahore, Ashraf, 1946
Attlee, Lord, *A Prime Minister Remembers*, Heinemann, 1961

Azad, Maulana Abul Kalam, *India Wins Freedom: The Complete Version*, New Delhi, Orient Longman, 1993

Aziz, K.K., *The Making of Pakistan*, Lahore, Islamic Book Service, 1986

Aziz, Qutubuddin, *The Murder of a State*, Karachi, Islamic Media Corporation, 1993

Bahadur, Om Lata, *The Book of Hindu Festivals and Ceremonies*, ND

Barnes, John and Nicholson, David (eds.), *The Leo Amery Diaries*, 2 Vols., Hutchinson, 1980, 1988

Beg, Aziz, *Jinnah and His Times*, Islamabad, Babur & Amer, 1986

Behn, Mira (Madelaine Slade), *The Spirit's Pilgrimage*, Longman, 1960

Bence-Jones, Mark, *The Viceroys of India*, Constable, 1982

Benians, E.A., Butler, J., and Carrington, C.E. (eds.), *The Cambridge History of the British Empire*, Vol. 3, 1870–1919, Cambridge University Press, 1959

Bhalla, Alok (ed.), *Stories About the Partition of India*, 3 Vols., Delhi, Indus, 1994

Birkenhead, The Earl of, *Frederick Edwin, Earl of Birkenhead: The Last Phase*, Thornton Butterworth, 1935

Bolitho, Hector, *Jinnah: Creator of Pakistan*, John Murray, 1954

Bose, Mihir, *The Lost Hero*, Quartet Books, 1982

Bose, Subhas Chandra, *The Indian Struggle, 1920–42*, Calcutta, Netaji Research Bureau, Asia Publishing House, 1969

Brailsford, H.N., *Subject India*, New York, John Day, 1943

Brown, Emily C., *Har Dayal: Hindu Revolutionary and Rationalist*, Tucson, University of Arizona Press, 1975

Brown, Judith M., *Gandhi: Prisoner of Hope*, New Haven and London, Yale University Press, 1989

Burridge, Trevor, *Clement Attlee: A Political Biography*, Jonathan Cape, 1985

Cameron, James, *An Indian Summer*, Macmillan, 1972

Campbell–Johnson, Alan, *Mission with Mountbatten*, Robert Hale, 1952

Chagla, M.C., *Roses in December: An Autobiography*, Bombay, Bharatiya Vidya Bhaven, 1974

Chandra, Bipan, *et al.*, *India's Struggle for Independence*, New Delhi, Penguin, 1989

Chaudhuri, Nirad C., *The Autobiography of an Unknown Indian*, New York, Macmillan, 1951

—— *Thy Hand, Great Anarch!*, New York, Addison-Wesley, 1987

Churchill, Winston S., *The Second World War. Vol. 1: The Gathering Storm*, Penguin, 1985

Collins, Larry & Lapierre, Dominique, *Freedom at Midnight*, Collins, 1975

—— *Mountbatten and the Partition of India*, New Delhi, Vikas, 1994

Colvin, Ian, *The Life of General Dyer*, Blackwood, 1929

Connell, John, *Auchinleck: A Critical Biography*, Cassell, 1959

Cooke, Colin, *The Life of Richard Stafford Cripps*, Hodder & Stoughton, 1957

Copley, Antony, *Gandhi*, Oxford, Blackwell, 1987

Coupland, Sir Reginald, *The Cripps Mission*, Oxford University Press, 1942

Das, Durga, *India from Curzon to Nehru and After*, Collins, 1969

Dharmavira, *Lala Har Dayal and Revolutionary Movements of his Time*, New Delhi, Indian Book Company, 1970

Dilks, David, *Curzon in India*, 2 Vols., Hart-Davies, 1969–70

—— (ed.) *The Diaries of Sir Alexander Cadogan, 1938–1945*, Cassell, 1971

Draper, Alfred, *Amritsar: The Massacre That Ended the Raj*, Cassell, 1981

Dulta, David, *Simon: A Political Biography*, Aurum Press, 1992

Duncan, Emma, *Breaking the Curfew: A Political Journey Through Pakistan*, Arrow, 1990

Duncan, Ronald (ed.), *Selected Writings of Mahatma Gandhi*, Faber & Faber, 1951

Dutton, David, *Simon: A Political Biography*, Aurum Press, 1992

Dwarkadas, Kanji, *India's Fight for Freedom, 1913–1937*, Bombay, Popular Prakashan, 1966

Edwardes, Michael, *The Myth of the Mahatma: Gandhi, the British and the Raj*, Constable, 1986

—— *The Sahibs and the Lotus: The British in India*, Constable, 1988

Estorick, Eric, *Stafford Cripps*, Heinemann, 1949

Fein, Helen, *Imperial Crime and Punishment: The Massacre at Jallianwala Bagh and British Judgement*, Hawaii, University of Honolulu Press, 1977

Fergusson, Major Bernard, *Wavell: Portrait of a Soldier*, Collins, 1961

Fischer, Louis, *The Life of Mahatma Gandhi*, Granada, 1982

Fisher, Fred B., *India's Silent Revolution*, New York, Macmillan, 1919

Franks, Norman, *31 Squadron: First in Indian Skies*, RAF Collection, 1987

Gandhi, M.K., *Young India, 1919–1922*, 3 Vols., Madras, S. Ganesan, 1922, 1923, 1924

—— *An Autobiography, or The Story of My Experiments with Truth*, Ahmedabad, Navagivan, 1927; Cape, 1966

—— *Non-Violence in Peace and War*, Ahmedabad, Navagivan, 1942

—— *The Collected Works of Mahatma Gandhi*, New Delhi, Government of India, 1958–84

Gandhi, Rajmohan, *India Wins Freedom Errors*, New Delhi, Radiant, 1989

Gandhi, Sonia (ed.), *Two Alone, Two Together: Letters between Indira Gandhi and Jawaharlal Nehru, 1940–1964*, Hodder & Stoughton, 1992

Gill, S.S. *The Dynasty*, Delhi, HarperCollins, 1996

Gilbert, Martin, *Winston Churchill: The Wilderness Years*, Macmillan, 1981

Glendevon, John, *The Viceroy at Bay: Lord Linlithgow in India, 1936–1940*, Collins, 1971

Goodrich, Leland M. (ed.), *Documents on American Foreign Relations, Vol IV*, Boston, World Peace Foundation, 1942

Gopal, Ram, *A Political History of Indian Muslims*, New Delhi, Criterion, 1989

—— *Hindu Culture During and After Muslim Rule*, New Delhi, MD Publications, 1994

Gopal, S., *Jawaharlal Nehru*, Vol. I (1899–1947), New Delhi, OUP, 1976

—(ed.) *Selected Works of Jawaharlal Nehru*, 14 Vols., New Delhi, Orient Longman, 1972–81

Griffiths, P.J., *The British in India*, Robert Hale, 1946

Gupta, Brijen Kishore, *Sirajuddaullah and the East India Company 1756–1757*, Leiden, E.J. Brill, 1962

Halifax, Earl Of, *Fullness of Days*, Collins, 1957

Hamid, Major-General Shahid, *Disastrous Twilight: A Personal Record of the Partition of India*, Leo Cooper in association with Secker & Warburg, 1986

—— *Early Years of Pakistan*, Lahore, Ferozsons, 1993

Hardy, Peter, *The Muslim of British India*, Cambridge University Press, 1972

Harris, Kenneth, *Attlee*, Weidenfeld & Nicolson, 1982

Hasan, Mushirul, *India Partitioned: The Other Face of Freedom*, 2 Vols., Delhi, Lotus Collection, Rolli Books, 1995

Hassan, Mushira, *India's Partition: Process, Strategy, Mobilization*, Delhi, Oxford University Press, 1993

Hauner, Milan, *India in Axis Strategy*, Munich, Kleth-Cotta, 1981

Heehs, Peter, *India's Freedom Struggle*, Oxford University Press, 1988

Hennessy, Peter, *Never Again: Britain 1945–1951*, Jonathan Cape, 1992

Hibbert, Christopher, *The Great Mutiny, India 1857*, Allen Lane, 1978

Hodson, H.V., *The Great Divide: Britain – India – Pakistan*, Hutchinson, 1969

Hoey, Brian, *Mountbatten: the Private Story*, Sidgwick & Jackson, 1994

Horniman, B.G., *Amritsar and Our Duty to India*, T. Fisher Unwin, 1920

Hough, Richard, *Mountbatten: Hero of our Time*, Weidenfeld and Nicolson, 1980

—— *Edwina, Countess Mountbatten of Burma*, Weidenfeld and Nicolson, 1983

Indian National Congress, *Report of the Commissioners Appointed by the Punjab Sub-Committee*, New Delhi, Deep Publications, 1920

Ismay, General the Lord, *Memoirs*, Heinemann, 1960

Ispahani, M.A.H., *Quaid-i-Azam Jinnah As I Knew Him*, Karachi, Forward Publications, 1966

Jalal, Ayesha, *The Sole Spokesman: Jinnah, the Muslim League and the Demand for Pakistan*, Lahore, Sang-e-Meel Publications, 1992

Jinnah, Quaid-i-Azam Muhammad Ali, *Speeches as Governor-General*, Karachi, Pakistan Publications, 1963

—— *Speeches*, Lahore, Sang-e-Meel Publications, 1989

Jones, Thomas, *Whitehall Diary*, Oxford University Press, 1969

Kabir, Humayun, *Muslim Politics 1906–47 and Other Essays*, Calcutta, Firma K.L. Mukhopadhyay, 1969

Kaye, John William, *A History of the Sepoy War in India, 1857–58*, W.H. Allen, 1880

Khaliquzzaman, Choudry, *Pathway to Pakistan*, Lahore, Longman, 1961

Khan, Abdul Waheed, *India Wins Freedom: The Other Side*, Karachi, Pakistan Educational Publishers, 1961

Kiana, Major-General Mahommad Zaman, *India's Freedom Struggle and the Great INA*, New Delhi, Reliance, 1994

Kumar, Chandra and Puri, Mohinder, *Mahatma Gandhi: His Life and Influence*, Heinemann, 1982

Kumar, Ravinder, *The Making of a Nation: Essays in Indian History and Politics*, New Delhi, Manohar, 1989

—— (ed.) *Essays on Gandhian Politics: The Rowlatt Satyagraha of 1919*, Oxford University Press, 1971

Lambton, Anthony, *The Mountbattens: The Battenbergs and Young Mountbatten*, Constable, 1989

Lapping, Brian, *End of Empire*, Granada, 1985

Lewin, Ronald, *The Chief*, Hutchinson, 1980

Louis, William Roger, *In the Name of God, Go!: Leo Amery and the British Empire in the Age of Churchill*, New York, W.W. Norton, 1992

Low, D.A. (ed.), *Congress and the Raj: Facets of the Indian Struggle 1917–47*, Heinemann, 1977

Lunt, James (ed.), *From Sepoy to Subedar: Being the Life and Adventures of Subedar Sita Ram Pande, Related by Himself*, Routledge & Kegan Paul, 1970

Macaulay, Thomas Babington, *Complete Works*, (8 Vols.), Longmans, Green, 1866

Mansergh, N. and Lumby, E.W.R. (eds.), *Constitutional Relations Between Britain and India: The Transfer of Power*, (12 Vols.), Her Majesty's Stationery Office, 1970–83

Masani, R.P., *Britain in India*, Oxford University Press, 1960

Mason, Philip, *The Men Who Ruled India*, Jonathan Cape, 1985

Mehta, Ved, *Mahatma Gandhi and His Apostles*, New Haven and London, Yale, 1993

Mellor, Andrew, *India Since Partition*, Turnstile Press, 1951

Menèzes, Lieutenant-General (Ret'd) S.L., *The Indian Army*, Delhi, Viking, 1993

Menon, V.P., *The Story of the Integration of the Indian States*, Longmans, Green, 1956

—— *The Transfer of Power in India*, Longmans, Green, 1957

Mercer, Derrik (ed.), *Chronicle of the 20th Century*, Longman, 1988

Minto, Mary, Countess of, *India, Minto and Morley, 1905–10*, Macmillan, 1934

Montagu, Edwin, *Indian Diary*, Heinemann, 1930

Mookerjee, Girija K., *Subhas Chandra Bose*, New Delhi, Publications Division, Ministry of Information and Broadcasting, Government of India, 1975

Moore, R.J., *The Crisis of Indian Unity*, Oxford University Press, 1974

—— *Churchill, Cripps and India, 1939–45*, Oxford University Press, 1979

—— *Escape from Empire: The Attlee Government and the Indian Problem*, Oxford University Press, 1983

Moorhouse, Geoffrey, *Calcutta: The City Revealed*, Penguin, 1974

—— *India Britannica*, Harvill, 1983

Moraes, Frank, *Witness to an Era*, Weidenfeld & Nicolson, 1973

Morgan Janet, *Edwina Mountbatten*, HarperCollins, 1991

Morley, John, Viscount, *Indian Speeches*, Macmillan, 1910

—— *Recollections*, Macmillan, 1918

Morris, James, *Farewell the Trumpets: An Imperial Retreat*, Faber & Faber, 1978

Muggeridge, Malcolm, *Chronicles of Wasted Time, Vol. 2: The Infernal Grove*, Fontana, 1975

Muir, Ramsay, *The Making of British India, 1766–1858*, Manchester, Manchester University Press, 1923

Mujeeb, M., *The Indian Muslims*, George Allen & Unwin, 1967

Munawwar, Muhammad, *Dimensions of Pakistan Movement*, Rawalpindi, Pap-Board Printers, 1989

Muni, S.D. and Amuradha, *Regional Co-operation in South Asia*, New Delhi, National Publishers, 1984

Naidu, Sarojini (ed.), *Mohammad Ali Jinnah: His Speeches and Writings, 1912–1917*, Madras, Ganesh, 1918

Nanda, B.R., *Mahatma Gandhi*, Delhi, Oxford University Press, 1958

—— *The Nehrus*, Delhi, Oxford University Press, 1962

—— *Gokhale: The Indian Moderates and the British Raj*, Princeton University, 1977

Nehru, Jawaharlal *The Discovery of India*, Meridian Books, 1946

—— *An Autobiography*, Bodley Head, 1958

—— *A Bunch of Old Letters*, Bombay, Asia Publishing House, 1958

Noon, Firoz Khan, *From Memory*, Lahore, Ferozsons, 1966

O'Dwyer, Sir Michael, *India as I Knew It 1885–1925*, Constable, 1925

Patel, I.J., *Sardar Vallabhbhai Patel*, Publications Division, Ministry of Information and Broadcasting, Government of India, 1985

Philips, C.H. (ed.), *The Evolution of India and Pakistan, 1858 to 1947: Select Documents*, Oxford University Press, 1962

Philips, C.H. and Wainwright, M.D. (eds.), *The Partition of India: Policies and Perspectives*, George Allen & Unwin, 1970

Pirzada, S.S. (ed.), *Foundations of Pakistan: All-India Muslim League Documents*, Karachi, National Publishing House, 1969

—— *Quaid-i-Azam Jinnah's Correspondence*, Karachi, East and West Publishing Company, 1977

Poolman, Kenneth, *The Kelly*, William Kimber, 1954

Prasad, Rajendra, *India Divided*, Bombay, Hind Katabs, 1947

Pyarelal, *Mahatma Gandhi: The Last Phase*, 2 Vols., Ahmedabad, Navagivan, 1956–8

Qureshi, Ishtiaq Husain, *The Struggle for Pakistan*, University of Karachi, 1965

Rai, Lajpat, *Young India: An Interpretation and a History of the Nationalist Movement From Within*, Home Rule for India League, 1916

Rai, Satya M., *Partition of the Punjab*, Asia Publishing House, 1965

Raman, T.A., *What Does Gandhi Want?*, Oxford University Press, 1943

Roberts, Andrew, *Eminent Churchillians*, Weidenfeld & Nicolson, 1994

Ronaldshay, Lord, *The Life of Lord Curzon*, Vol. II, Ernest Benn, 1930

Ross, Alan, *The Emissary: G.D. Birla, Gandhi and Independence*, Collins Harvill, 1986

Royle, Trevor, *The Last Days of the Raj*, Michael Joseph, 1989

Sadullah, Mian Muhammad *et al*, (eds.), *The Partition of the Punjab*, 4 Vols., Lahore, National Documentation Centre, 1983

St. Aubyn, Giles, *Queen Victoria: a Portrait*, Sinclair-Stevenson, 1991

Sarkar, Sumit, *Modern India 1885–1947*, Macmillan, 1989

Saiyid, M.H., *Mohammad Ali Jinnah*, Lahore, S.M. Ashraf, 1945

Sayeed, Khalid Bin, *Pakistan: the Formative Phase, 1857–1948*, Karachi, Oxford University Press, 1968

Seervai, H.M., *Partition of India: Legend and Reality*, Rawalpindi, Services Book Club, 1989

Sengupta, Padmini, *Sarojini Naidu*, Bombay, Asia Publishing House, 1966

Shirer, William L., *Gandhi: A Memoir*, New York, Simon and Schuster, 1979

Singh, Anita Inder, *The Origins of the Partition of India 1936–1947*, New Delhi, Oxford University Press, 1987

Singh, Kushwant, *Train to Pakistan*, New Delhi, Time Books International, 1989

—— *A History of the Sikhs*, 2 Vols., New Delhi, Oxford University Press, 1991

Singh, Patwant, *Of Dreams and Demons: An Indian Memoir*, Duckworth, 1994

Singh, Rear Admiral (Ret) Satyindra, *Under Two Ensigns: The Indian Navy 1945–1950*, Bombay, Lancer International, 1996

Sitarmayya, B. Pattabhi, *The History of the Indian National Congress*, Bombay, Padma Publications, 1946

Spear, Percival, *A History of India*, Penguin, 1990

Storry, Richard, *A History of Modern Japan*, Penguin, 1960

Swinson, Arthur, *Six Minutes to Sunset*, Peter Davies, 1964

Tahmankar, D.V., *Sardar Patel*, George Allen & Unwin, 1970

—— *Lokamanya Tilak*, John Murray, 1956

Tendulkar, D.G., *Mahatma*, New Delhi, Publications Division, Government of India, 1960

Tinker, Hugh, *The Foundations of Local Self-Government in India, Pakistan, and Burma*, Athlone Press, 1954

Tuker, Francis, *While Memory Serves*, Cassell, 1956

Tully, Mark & Masani, Zareer, *From Raj to Rajiv: 40 Years of Indian Independence*, BBC Books, 1988

Tyler, Froom, *Cripps: A Portrait and a Prospect*, Harrap, 1942

Warner, Philip, *Auchinleck: The Lonely Soldier*, Sphere, 1982

Wavell, Field Marshal Earl, *Wavell: The Viceroy's Journal*, Oxford University Press, 1973

Wedderburn, Sir William, *Allan Octavian Hume*, T. Fisher Unwin, 1913

Wilkinson-Latham, Christopher, *The Indian Mutiny* (Men-at-Arms Series 67), Osprey Military, 1977

Wolpert, Stanley, *Tilak and Gokhale*, New York, Oxford University Press, 1961

—— *Jinnah of Pakistan*, New Delhi, Oxford University Press, 1985

—— *Zulfi Bhutto of Pakistan*, New Delhi, Oxford University Press, 1989

—— *A New History of India*, New York, Oxford University Press, 1993

Wrench, Sir John Evelyn, *The Immortal Years, 1937–1944*, Hutchinson, 1945

Zaidi Z.H. (ed.) *M.A. Jinnah – Ispahani Correspondence, 1936–1948*, Karachi, Forward Publishing Trust, 1976

Zetland, Lord, *Essayez: the Memoirs of Lawrence, 2nd Marquess of Zetland*, John Murray, 1956

Ziegler, Philip, *Mountbatten: The Official Biography*, Collins, 1985

India (Lord Privy Seal's Mission), Comd 6350, HMSO, 1942

Proceedings of the Indian Round Table Conference (Cmd 3778) 12 November 1930–19 January 1931, HMSO, 1931

Report of the Committee to Investigate the Recent Disturbances in Bombay, Delhi and the Punjab (The Hunter Committee), HMSO, 1920

Report of the Indian Statutory Commission, Cmd 3569, May 1930, HMSO, 1930

Report, Proceedings and Memoranda of Cabinet Committee in Indian Disorders (1920), HMSO, 1920

The Indian Annual Register, for the years 1919–47, Calcutta, The Annual Register Office

Kesari, Vol. XXVIII, No. 19, 12 May 1908

Maritime International, Bombay, Vol. II, No 12, December 1996

The Oracle, Calcutta, Netaji Research Bureau, Vol. XV, April 1993, No. 2; Vol. XVI, January 1994, No. I

Index

Abbas, Khwaja Ahmad 400
Abdullah, Sheikh Muhammad 495, 503
Abell, George 398, 401, 408, 419, 426,
    441–2, 485, 490, 494: London 444;
    map 490, 495
Addiscombe military academy 30
Aden 84, 115, 368
Administrative Consequences of Partition 457–8
Afghanistan 12, 22, 29, 41–2, 49, 66, 86,
    120, 183, 191: invasions 20, 66, 169;
    Lohanas tribe 94; wars 66–7, 69–70
Aga Khan 91, 93–4, 99, 218: Poona palace
    329, 332
Age of Consent Act (1891) 80
Agra 12–13, 15, 29, 53, 123
Agriculture, Department of 85
ahimsa doctrine 143, 153, 160
Ahmed, Sir Sultan 307
Ahmedabad, Gujarat 70, 89, 155, 158–60,
    176: All-India Central Committee 228;
    Congress 194–5; disturbances 400;
    mayor 199; revolts 329–30; *satyagraha*
    movement 166
Ahmednagar Fort gaol 329, 333, 346–7, 352,
    355
Akbar (son of Hamayun) 12, 56
Akyab port 331, 335
Al-Hilal newspaper 111
Alam, Shah (Mughal emperor) 21, 29
Alamgir 'World Conqueror' 15, *see also*
    Aurangzeb
Alexander, A.V. 373–4, 382, 387–8, 390,
    401–2
Alexander, Horace 375, 384
Ali, Asaf 251, 317, 364, 403
Ali, Chaudhry Muhammad 463, 465, 465–6,

494–5
Ali, Choudhry Rahmat, *Now or Never* 234, 276
Ali, Muhammad 111, 120, 183, 188–9, 191,
    199, 202–3
Ali, Rashid 367
Ali, Shaukat 120, 183, 185, 188–9, 191,
    202–3, 274
Ali, Wajid 48–9, 53, 382
Aligarh 29, 77–8, 92–3, 111; Muslim
    University 189, 271
Alipore Central Gaol 202, 251–2
Allahabad (North-West Provinces) 21, 53,
    75, 124, 126, 128; Brahmans 124; fort
    55; Gandhi, Mahatma Mohandas
    179–80, 235; High Court 123; Khilafat
    Committee 184; Muslim League 129,
    263, 294; riots 368; Working
    Committee 327
All-India; 'Anti–Pakistan Day' 461; Cabinet
    323; Depressed Classes 290, 379;
    Executive Council 316; federation 233,
    249, 256, 284, 295; Khilafat Conference
    191; National Convention 217–18;
    Radio 319, 354, 458, 505; States'
    Peoples' Conference, Ludhiana 281;
    Students' Conference 328; Trade Union
    Congress 182, 221, 317, 328; union
    379, 383
All-Indian Village Industries 262
All-Parties Conferences 212–15, 218
Almora gaol 258
Ambala 496
Ambedkar, Dr Bhimrao Ramji 185, 243–4,
    248, 252, 265, 288, 290–1, 337–8,
    377, 379. *See also* Independent Labour
    Party; untouchables

Amery, Leo 204, 296–8, 300, 302, 305–8:
Bengal famine relief 340; Churchill,
Winston 327, 353–4; Gandhi, Mahatma
Mohandas 331–2; *History of the War in
South Africa* 297; House of Commons
206, 300–1, 354; India Committee
311–13, 320, 323, 351–2, 357–8;
Linlithgow, Lord 331, 333;
Rajagopalachari's formula 349; viceroy
selection 333, 335–6; Wavell, General
Sir Archibald 335–6, 347, 354
Amrita Bazar Patrika 67, 157
Amritsar (Sikhs' holy city) 2–5, 8, 16, 164–5,
167; Brigadier–General Reginald Dyer
192; Gandhi, Mahatma Mohandas 177;
Gobind Garh fort 169; Golden Temple
1, 5–7, 16; *hartal* 164; Indian National
Congress 180; Khan, Liaquat Ali 496–7;
massacre 127, 173–8, 224, 228–9, 296;
Nehru, Jawaharlal 496–7; Sikhs 379,
407, 496; unrest 168–9, 171–2, 421,
462
Anand Bhavan 125–6, 129, 280
Anandamath (The Abbey of Bliss) 79–80, 91
Andaman Islands 343–4
Anderson, Sir John 336: Government of India
Act (1935) 452; India Committee 313
Anderson, Sergeant William 7
Anglo-Afghan war 180
Anglo-American unity 308
Anglo-Indians 69, 72, 74, 84–5, 104, 106,
108–10, 137, 164–5, 176–7, 190, 317,
337–8: law codification (1860) 39–40,
61; newspapers 70, 85
Ansari, Dr M.A. 188, 212–13, 217, 236, 251
Anti-Compromise Conference 303
Apte, Narayam 504–5
Arab lands 119
Arakan 36, 334–5
Arbitral Tribunal 463
Armed Forces Reconstitution Committee
463–4
Arnold, Sir Edwin, *The Light of Asia* 145
Arya Samaj (Society of Noble Men) 65, 89,
102–3, 192
Ashley, Edwina (later Mountbatten) 193,
412, 508
Asian Relations Conference 428
Asquith, Herbert 132–3, 135, 175, 203, 411

Assam 36, 87, 92, 234, 269, 289, 344, 433:
Cabinet Mission plan 390; Congress
370; Fifth–column 311; Pakistan 441;
partition 435, 470; premier 273, 307
provincial legislature 108; Sylhet district
463, 483
Astor, Lady 281
Atlantic Charter 308
Attlee, Clement 207, 211–12, 255, 310–12,
316, 353: All-party Parliamentary
delegation 372–3; Auchinleck, General
Sir Claude 475; British general election
359; British withdrawal plans 402, 423;
broadcast 262; Cabinet Mission 379,
398; Gandhi, Mahatma Mohandas 505;
House of Commons 250, 418, 420–1,
458, 467; India Committee of the
Cabinet 313, 360–1, 385, 418; Interim
Government 399; Labour Party leader
260; Listowel, Earl of 442;
Mountbatten, Lord 409–10, 416–19,
449, 451, 467; Nehru, Jawaharlal 281,
406–7; Plan Balkan 447; prime minister
359; princes 477, 479; round-table
conferences 242, 249–50; San Francisco
conference 353; Simon Commission
409, 477; 3 June Plan 458–9; Wavell,
General Sir Archibald 398, 402, 408
Auchinleck, General Sir Claude 311, 363–4,
366–7, 369–70, 401: Armed Forces
Reconstitution Committee 463–4;
Indian army 473; Kashmir 503;
Mountbatten, Lord 415, 424, 431, 434,
487, 503; peerage offer 475; supreme
commander 475
August Offer 300–1
Aurangzeb (great–grandson of Akbar) 14–16,
43, 78, 484
Australia 73, 115, 214, 412
Ayer, V.D. 490
Azad Hind Fauj 342, *see also* Indian National
Army (INA)
Azad, Abul Kalam 111–12, 119–20, 183,
188, 191, 230
Azad, Maulana 265, 271–2, 282, 301,
309–10, 505: Ahmednagar Fort gaol
329; Attlee, Clement 359; Cabinet
Mission 377, 380–1, 383–4, 389–91;
three–tier scheme 379–81, 386; Calcutta

killings 396; Congress president 293,
327, 390; Congress Working Committee
316–19; East Bengal riots 404; gaol
308–9; India Committee draft
declaration 319–21, 325; *India Wins
Freedom* 269; Muslim Conference 295;
Parliamentary Committee 268; Roosevelt
mediation plan 327; Simla Conference
355–7; Simla talks 383–4; Wavell,
General Sir Archibald 321, 396;
Working Committee 377, 380, 383

Babur 'The Tiger' 12, 17
Badge, Digambe 505
Bahadur, Tegh 16
Bahrain 119, 368
Baisakhi Day 1–4, 6, 9, 16
Baker, Sir Herbert 112–13
Baker, Colonel R.J. 153
Bakhsh, Lieutenant-Colonel Ilahi 506
Baldwin, Stanley 203–4, 237, 257, 260, 281,
298
Balfour, Arthur 91
Balkans 111
Baluchistan 12, 41–2, 169, 345, 441, 506
Bande Mataram (Mother India) 91, 102, 349
Banerjea, Surendranath 65–6, 82, 104, 110,
134, 187: *Bengalee* 68, 88; Imperial
Legistation Council 108, 127; Indian
Association 70–1; Indian Civil Service
exams 63–4; *Swadeshi movement* 89;
Vernacular Press Act 67–8
Bang-i-Islam 234
Bangladesh 87, 436
Bania caste 201
Bank of India 471
Bardoli, Gujarat 193, 195
Basu, Rash Behari 116–17, 326, 341–2
Batliwala, S.S. 279
Battenberg, Prince Louis of 410–11, *see also*
Mountbatten, Lord
Beaumont, Christopher 490
Behn, Mira 237, 241, 329, 346, *see also*
Slade, Madeleine
Belgaum, Muslim League 200
Benares (holy city) 88–9, 248:
Congress 126; curfew 438–9;
Gandhi, Mahatma Mohandas
181; Hindu University of India

120; INA trials protest 365;
Indian National Congress 126,
181
Bengal 12, 16, 21–2, 25, 34, 52, 68,
325, 377: army 24; Cabinet
Mission plan 390, 425, 447;
commerce 47; commission
483; East 87–8, 92, 110, 334,
405, 436, 483–4; riots 103,
403–5; education 31, 41;
famine 339–40; Fort William
14, 19; government 202, 398;
governors 188, 338, 365, 379,
436, 500; Haq, Fazlul 332–3,
332–4; *hartal* 164; Hindus 110;
independence 488; Indian Army 58;
Indian Association 66, 70–1; Japanese
raids 326; Lahore resolution 350; League
government 402; Legislative Council 22,
63, 130; lieutenant–governor 70, 105;
Muslim League 307, 332–3, 370, 378,
382, 394; Muslims 130, 289, 295, 436;
Nawab of 20, 22; New Party 105;
Pakistan 234, 441, 452; partition of
86–9, 100, 109, 111, 126, 433, 435,
441,453, 460, 470, 482–3; Permanent
Settlement system 266; premier 273,
307, 332; presidency 86–8, *see also* Bihar,
Orissa and Chota Nagpur; Provincial
Congress 283; Provincial elections 266;
Provincial legislature 108; rebellions 45;
reunification 88, 109; terrorism 91–2,
106, 201, 229, 245; West 87, 90;
zamindars 59
Bengalee 207
Bentham, Jeremy 32–3, 80
Bentinck, Lord William 34–7, 39–41
Berlin 2, 208
Besant, Annie 120–1, 125, 137, 162, 185–6,
209; Home Rule League 121, 129, 134,
163
Best, Captain Thomas 13
Bevin, Ernest 360, 418
Bhaba, C.H., interim government 403, 436–7
Bhagavad Gita 145
Bharmal, Raja of Amber 12
Bhave, Acharya Vinoba 302
Bhopal, Nawab of 426, 465, 478–9, 481
Bhowali hills 258

Bihar 14, 21–2, 52, 86–7: Congress 269, 370, 404–5; Fifth-column 311; Gandhi, Mahatma Mohandas 425, 428; *hartal* 164; lieutenant-governor 157; massacres 432–3; and Orissa province 109, 206, 249; prisoners 278, 377; riots 229–30, 329–30, 404, 434–5

Bikaner 490; Maharaja of 426, 478

Bilgrami, S.H. 102

Birkenhead, Lord 204–6, 209–10, 212–13, 215, 223, 233

Birla, G.D. 90, 261, 264, 290–1, 337–8, 362, 370, 443: Delhi house 504; Gandhi, Mahatma Mohandas 155, 241, 257, 302

Birmingham cruiser 414

Blaker, George 374

Blavatsky, Madame 72, 120, 144

Board of Control, London 23, 27, 35

Boer War 147

Bombay 13–15, 21–3, 29, 38, 47, 52, 70, 101, 176, 400–1: Wardha Working Party decision 328; All-Parties Conference 213–15; Bandra Convent School 99; Brahman institution 74; British withdrawal plans 401–2; Congress 121, 193, 262, 269, 370; Corporation 199; curfew 438–9; Defence of India Act arrests 328–9; Gandhi, Mahatma Mohandas 145, 147, 155, 159, 193, 245; Goculdas Tejpal Sanscrit College 74; government 279; governors 42, 73, 82, 122, 296; *hartal* 164; High Court 99, 105, 121; Home Rule Leagues 121, 134, 186; industries 330; Interim Government 400; killings 400; Muslim League 271, 391–2; Muslims 108, 121–2; Nariman, K.F. 269; Parsi community 129; Presidency 74–5, 155, 163; provincial legislature 108, 265; Regulation XXV (1827) 230; revolts 329–30; RIN mutiny 368–9; riots 194, 220, 369–70, 421; Simon Commission 211; *swadeshi* movement 89; University 65

Bombay Chronicle 163, 173, 207, 291

Bonaparte, Napoleon 27, 41

Bonnerjee, Womesh C. 71, 73–4, 77

Bose, Kudiram (bomber) 105, 110

Bose, Nandalal 263

Bose, Sarat 283, 365, 395–6, 403

Bose, Subhas Chandra 187–8, 201–2, 214, 221, 223, 257, 287: Afghanistan 304; aircrash 363; arrest 304; Asia, south–east 341–5; Bengal 343; Bengal Provincial Congress 283; broadcasts 326, 341, 345, 363; Burma 342; Congress Party 251–2, 275, 280, 282–3, 287; Congress Socialist Party 272; Forward Bloc 283, 303, 307, 365, 370; Germany 305, 312, 341; Government of India Act (1935) 257; INA trials 363; Independence for India League 217, 342; Indian Legion 341; Indian National Army (INA) 342–5, 430; Mandalay prison 255–7; Netaji 342, 345, 362–3; Provisional Government of Azad Hind (Free India) 343; Rani of Jhansi Regiment 343; Singapore 341–3; Swarajists Party 199; Tojo, General Hideki 341, 343, 363; Tokyo 341

Bostock, Captain 169

Bosworth Smith, Mr 172

Botha, General Louis 151

Bottomley, Horatio, *John Bull* 411

Boundary Commission 458, 482–7, 490, 494–7

Brahmans 31, 38, 46, 184, 201, 263; Allahabad 124; Benares 89; scholars 28–30

Brahmo Samaj (Sacred Society) 32–3, 65

Briggs, Captain F.C. 'Tommy' 4–6, 169

Bright, John 98

British: Communist Party 208; Commonwealth of Nations 233, 237, 372, 477; French mandates 183; Labour Party 103–4, 208; Labour Party annual conference (1925) 206; Liberal Party 58, 69, 91, 97, 126, 203; Parliamentary delegations 368, 372–3, *see also* Cabinet Mission; Raj 58, 73, 78, 83, 87, 105, 113, 116–7, 150, 166, 169, 174, 185, 196, 221, 228, 330; Raj assets 471; withdrawal plans 401–2, 408–9, 417–18, 422–3, 425

Britter, Eric 453

Broadway, Mr Justice 175

Brockman, Captain Ronald RN 420, 424

Brockway, Fenner 213

Brodrick, Sir John 86, 88

Brooke, Field Marshal Sir Alan 340, 416

Brooks, F.T. 125

Brydon, Surgeon William 42

Buddhism 140

Burke, Edmund 23, 98

Burma 36, 74, 92, 255, 308, 311, 314,
  409–10, 415: Bose, Subhas Chandra
  342; East India Company 75; Gandhi,
  Mahatma Mohandas 155, 222;
  government 202; Independence Army
  310; lieutenant–governor 190–1; Simon
  Commission 215; World War II 325,
  331, 335, 344, 353. *See also* Rangoon

Burnham, Lord 207

Burrows, Sir Frederick 379, 395–6, 436, 453

Butler, Sir Harcourt 92, 113, 180

Butler, R.A. 257, 260, 283, 336, 358

Byron, Lord 347

Cabinet Mission 374–93, 397–9, 406–7,
  423: Azad, Maulana, three–tier scheme
  376–7, 379–80, 383, 386–90, 392,
  397–8, 406, 425, 429, 434–5, 446–7,
  454. *See also* Simla talks

Cabinet Partition Committee 463

Cadogan, Sir Alexander 300

Cadogan, Edward 207

Calcutta (Bengal) 14, 19–20, 22–3, 29, 37–8,
  47–8, 52–3, 87–8: *Amrita Bazar Patrika*
  67; bhadralok 59, 63, 65, 85; Black
  Hole of 19, 30, 53; Board of Revenue
  102; bomb incidents 105, 202;
  Boundary Commission award 494;
  Colleges 31, 41, 188; Congress 216–17;
  courts 60, 68, 70; Dum Dum, RAF
  mutiny 368; *durbar* 110; East India
  Company 75; Fort William College
  30–1, 39; Gandhi, Mahatma Mohandas
  155, 217–18, 494, 499–500;
  Government House 30, 84, 108; *hartal*
  164, 194; Hooghly river 343, 396;
  Imperial Legislative Council 82, 127;
  Independence Day 499; Indian National
  Congress 75, 100–1, 135, 147, 184–5;
  Indian Mirror 70; Jinnah, Mohammad Ali
  209, 274; killings 394–8, 403–4, 499;
  Mountbatten, Lord 488; Muslim League
  274, 303; Nehru, Jawaharlal 362;

partition 379, 436, 483; Presidency Gaol
  303; Prince of Wales 194; proposed air
  raid 344; refugees 312; riots 104, 106,
  193, 205, 365, 367, 369–70, 421, 462;
  seat of government 109–10, 113; Simon
  Commission 211; *Statesman* 239; stock
  exchange 396; Union Bank 33;
  University 64, 71, 85–6, 99; Viceroy's
  House 193; violence 434–5; Wavell,
  General Sir Archibald 338–9;
  Willingdon Hospital 388, 401

Calcutta Statesman 343, 396–7

Calicut port and city 25

Caliph 111–12, 119, 271

Caliphate 182, 199

Cambridge 127–8, 234

Cameron, James 376, 384

Campbell-Bannerman, Sir Henry 91–2, 126

Campbell-Johnson, Alan 420, 428, 432,
  440–1, 446, 448–50, 453, 455, 462,
  467: princes 481

Canada 73, 115, 214; Ghadr Party 116:
  governor-general 92, 239; *Komagata Maru*
  affair 130

Candy, Major-General 347

Canning, Charlotte 56

Canning, Lord 48–9, 52–3, 55, 57, 70

Canning, Paul 13

Cape Comorin 17, 29

Carberry, Captain D. H. M. 4, 6, 171

Carnatic 25, 27; Nawab of 17–18

Caroe, Sir Olaf 422, 439–40, 443, 455, 462

Casey, Richard G. 365

Cassel, Sir Ernest 412

Catherine, Queen 13

Cawnpore (Kanpur) 53, 60

Central Legislative Assembly 25, 198, 199,
  218, 222, 224, 232, 235, 248–9, 269,
  307–8, 346: Chamber 277; Delhi 285;
  elections 364, 370, 388; Khan, Liaquat
  Ali 428

Central Provinces: British withdrawal plans
  401–2; Congress government 269, 370;
  premier 279

Ceylon 325–6, 415, 418

Chagla, M. C. 209, 215, 217–18

Chaki, Prafulla (bomber) 105, 110

Chamber of Princes 285–6, 317, 337–8, 409,
  477–8, 480

Chamberlain, Austen 133, 204

Chamberlain, Joseph 147

Chamberlain, Neville 204–5, 215, 281, 296

Champaran, Bihar 156–7, 159–60

Charles II, King 13

Charter Act: (1813) 31, 33, 35, 37; (1853 renewal) 63

Chatterjee, Bankim Chandra: *Anandamath (The Abbey of Bliss)* 79–80, 91; novels 105

Chattopadhyaya, Virendranath (Chatto) 208

Chaudhuri, Nirad C. 326

Chauri Chaura, United Provinces 195, 197

Chelmsford, Lord, viceroy (1916–) 132–3, 135–40, 157, 160, 163, 170, 173–5, 184, 190–1

Chelmsford, Margaret 133

Chenab river 484

Chhatari, Nawab of 265, 307

Chiang Kai-shek 287, 311

Child, Sir Josiah 11

China 287, 290, 312, 327

Chitpavan Brahman families 80–1

Chittagong (eastern Bengal) 11, 89, 231, 245, 331, 343, 461, 483: Hill Tracts 494

Chota Nagpur 86–7

Choudhri, Captain H. M. S. 474

Christie, John 438, 441–4, 457: *Administrative Consequences of Partition* 457–8

Chundrigar, I. I., interim government 403

Church of England in India 35

Churchill, Lord Randolph 73, 204

Churchill, Winston 176, 204, 297–300, 299, 302, 366: Atlantic Charter 308; August Offer 300–1; Bengal famine relief 340; British general election 339; constitution of India 136, 223, 233, 237, 255, 352; Desai-Liaquat pact 352; eastern front 415; Executive Council 331–2, 308–9; Gandhi, Mahatma Mohandas 149, 241, 327, 338, 347; Government of India Act (1935) amending Bill 451–2; India Committee 312–13, 315, 320–1, 323–5, 358, 360; Mansion House speech 314; Mountbatten, Lord 414–15, 452, 467; National Government 297; Roosevelt, President 307–8, 310, 314; 3 June Plan 458; viceroy selection 333, 335–6; War Cabinet 309; Wavell, General Sir Archibald 335–6, 338–40,

353–4, 361

Civil & Military Gazette 118

Civil Liberties Union 291

Civil Service Commission 64

Clemenceau, Georges 182

Clive, Robert, of Plassey 18–22, 24, 226

Cockin, Major C.W. 366

Collins, Larry 459

Columbia University, New York 243

Colville, Sir John 453, 455

Colvin, Sir Aukland 73

Comintern 208–9

Commerce and Industry, Department of 85

Committee of the Cabinet, plan 390

Commonweal 120

Communist Party 278

Comrade newspaper 111

Congress, Indian National, 71, 73–8, 128, 221, 246, 251, 277: Ahmedabad, Gujarat 194–5; Amritsar 180; Assam 370; Benares 126, 181; Bengal 88–9, 266; Bihar 370; Bombay 100, 121, 193, 262, 370; Cabinet Mission plan 383, 390, 406; Calcutta 75, 100–1, 135, 147, 184–5, 365; Central Committee (AICC) 187, 192, 228, 252, 267–9, 283; Bombay, Wardha Working Party decision 328; Independence Day 461; Central Legislative Assembly, Delhi 285; Central Provinces 370; Commonwealth membership 437–8; constitution 255, 352; council reforms 152–3; Extremists 82, 101–2, 104; Faizpur, Maharashtra village 263; Gandhi, Mahatma Mohandas 156, Gaya 198; Government of India Acts, (1919) 253 and (1935) 255–7, 267–8; governments 269; Hindu Mahasabha 276; INA relief funds 364; interim government 403; Jinnah, Mohammad Ali 94, 152–3; Khan, Liaquat Ali's budget 428; Khilafat leaders 191; Lahore 224–5; leaders 82, 191, 202, 221, 233, 279, 352, 430, *see also* Nehru, Jawaharlal and Patel, Vallabhbhai; Lucknow 156; Madras 77, 207, 253, 370; ministries 279; minorities 243–4; Moderates 82, 101–2, 104, 120, 126, 134, 154; Muslim League 93, 129–30, 276, 306–7, 327;

Muslims 273, 389, 403; Nagpur 188; National Volunteers 194; Nationalists 251, 253–4, 266; newspapers, India Committee draft declaration 325; North-West Frontier Provinces (NWFP) 370; Orissa 370; political prisoners 278, 377; provincial election 259, 370–1; Ramgarh 293, 301; Simla Conference 355–8; Socialist leaders 279; Socialist Party 251, 257, 272; Surat (1907) 104; Tripuri 282; United Provinces 283, 370; Volunteers 404

Congress-Khilafat Swaraj Party 198–200, 203, 251–2

Congress-League alliance 122, 135, 137, 272, 352

Congress Working Committee 232–3, 236–7, 246, 258, 276, 282–3, 286, 293, 307: Ahmednagar Fort gaol 329, 333, 346–7, 352, 355; Allahabad 327; Azad, Maulana 316–19; Cabinet Mission 388; Defence 321; dominion status 445; India Committee draft declaration 316–20; Madras 327; Nehru, Jawaharlal 267, 293, 317; Plan Balkan 443; Second World War 299–300, 302; Transfer of Power 456–7; Wardha 287, 289, 327–8; World War II 115, 120

Constituent Assembly 388, 390, 399, 401–2, 406–8, 407, 423, 478: London meeting 406–7; Objectives Resolution 407

Corfield, Sir Conrad 476, 479–80, 502

Cornwall (British cruiser) 325

Cornwallis, Lord 24–5, 29, 37, 59

Cotton, Sir Henry 75, 100

Council of State 136–7, 357

Coupland, Professor Sir Reginald 305, 315–16, 318

Craddock, Sir Reginald 191

Cranbourne, Lord 336

Crete, battle for 414

Crew, Lord 109

Crimea war 49

Criminal: Intelligence Division 230; Penal Code 109

Cripps, Sir Stafford 265–7, 281, 290–2, 297, 313–24, 371–3, 442: Azad, Abul Kalam 230; British withdrawal plans 401–2,

418, 423; Cabinet Mission 377, 379, 382, 387–8, 390, 392; Congress and Gandhi, Mahatma Mohandas 375; constitutional questions 352; Gandhi, Mahatma Mohandas 317–19, 376–7, 383, 391, 398; health problems 388, 399, 401; House of Commons speech 391; India Committee 360–1; India Committee proposals 313–26, 338, 347; Jinnah, Mohammad Ali 291, 318, 375–6; Linlithgow, Lord 315–16; Menon, Krishna 398, 437; Mountbatten, Lord 416–17, 449; Nehru, Jawaharlal 281, 265–7, 290, 292, 313, 316, 319–23, 375, 383; plan (1942) 360–2, 372, 374–5; Roosevelt mediation plan 327; Simla talks 384–5

Croft, Sir Frederick Leigh 95–6

Croft, Sir William 374

Cunningham, Sir George 365

Cunningham, Admiral Sir John 415, 417

Curtis, Lionel 305

Curzon, Lord George (viceroy 1898–) 30, 82–9, 104, 107, 109, 132, 136, 197, 203–4

Curzon–Wyllie, Lieutenant–Colonel Sir William 106

Dacca 34, 88–9: Muhammadan Educational Conference 93; Nawab of 266

Dalhousie, Marquess of 47–9, 70, 333

Dane, Sir Louis 296

Das, C.R. 185, 187–9, 194–5, 199–200, 202

Das, Durga 212, 238, 242–3, 302–3, 334, 430–1

Das, Jatindranth 222

Dass, Durgas 6–8

Davar, Justice D.D. 105

Dawn Muslim daily 333, 355

Day of Deliverance 289–90, 292

Day, Ernest 201

Dayal, Lala Har 116

Deccan 15: Airways 502; towns 80

Defence of India Act (1915) 120, 138, 330: Bombay arrests 328–9

Defence of India Rules 404

defence system 402

Dehra Dun 335

Delhi 11, 29, 37, 43, 52–4, 132, 155, 176,

498, 504: All-India Central Committee (AICC) 192, 461; All-Parties Conference 212; Azad, Maulana Muslim Conference 295; Central Legislative Assembly 285, 293, 302–3; *durbar* 83, 109–10, 112; emergency committee 501; Gandhi, Mahatma Mohandas 165; *hartal* 164, 166; House of Tamerlane 17; Hunter Committee of Inquiry 175–7, 182; Kashmir gate 53; Khilafat conference 183; King of 441; King's Way (now Raj Path) 112; Mughal emperor 16, 20; Muslim League 333, 377–8; police force 123; Raisina Hill 112; Red Fort 29, 364; revolts 329–30, 500–1; seat of government 109–10, 112; Simon Commission 211; Sultan of 12; Sultanate 17; Viceregal palace 237; violence 434–5, 500–1
Derby, Lord 55–6
Desai, Bhulabhai 223, 251, 352, 364, 366
Desai, Mahadev 188, 241, 290, 329, 345–6
Desai-Khan, Liaquat Ali pact 352
Desfor, Max 428
Dev, S. D. 259
Devonshire (British cruiser) 325
Devonshire, Duke of 336
Dharamsi, A. N. 75
Dharasana, Gujarat 229
Dharmsala 168
dharna doctrine 142–3
Dieppe raid 415
Direct Action Day 393–5
Disraeli, Benjamin 66, 69
Dominion. Constitution for India 223, 290–1, 318, 181, *see also* India, dominion status; Prime Ministers 233
Dorman Smith, Sir Reginald 384, 410
Douglas Graham and Company 95–7
Doulatram, Jairamdas 232
Doveton, Captain 172
Dow, Sir Hugh 404
Dublin 127, 169
Dufferin, Lord 72–4
Dundas, Henry (later Lord Melville) 23, 27
Dungapur, Maharwal of 480
Dupleix, Joseph Francois 17–19, 21
Durban 145–7
Durga 91, 105: Puja, Bengali festival 90

Dutch East India Company 10
Dutch East Indies 364
Dutt, Batukeswar 222
Dutt, Romesh Chandra 63–4, 92: *Economic History of India* 63–4
Dwarkadas brothers 223
Dwarkadas, Jamnadas 163, 249–50
Dyer, Brigadier–General Reginald Edward Harry 3–9, 19, 169–72, 175–8, 180, 182: Amritsar 192

East India College, Hertford Castle 30
East India Company 10, 12, 17, 23, 30, 32, 34, 38, 54–5, 75, 123, 226: Parliamentary committee report and charter (1833) 37
Eden, Anthony 316, 335: Government of India Act (1935) 452; India Office 260
Edge, Sir John 123
Edward VII, king-emperor 83–4, 107, 109, 206
Edward VIII, king-emperor 413
Edwardes, Commissioner S. M. 122
Egypt 3, 115, 281, 312, 418
Elgin, Lord 149
Elizabeth I, Queen 10
Ellenborough, Governor-General Lord 35, 43
Elphinstone, Mountstuart 28–9, 42
Emergency Committee 501
Emergency Whipping Act 330
Emerson, Ralph Waldo 150
The Englishman 70
Erskine, Lord 279
Erskine-Crum, Lieutenant-Colonel Vernon 420, 450, 454
Etawah, revolt (1857) 71

Fabian Society 120
Faizpur, Maharashtra village, 263
Fatehpur Sikri 85
Fatwa, Royal Canadian Air Force officers 329
Federal Court: Arbitral Tribunal 463; Cabinet mission statement 393, 407
Federal Government 351
Fergusson, Major Bernard 312
First World War 2, 114–20, 152–3, 160–2, 218, 285: pilots 4
Fisher, Fred B. 1–2, 114, 136
Flanders 114–15

Foreign Cloth Boycott Committee 222
Fort St. David 14
Fort William, Calcutta 14, 19, 30–1, 39,
    394–5
Forward Bloc 283, 303, 307, 365, 370
Fox, Charles James 23
Fox, George Lane 207, 211
France 4, 22, 160
Francis, Philip 22–3
Freedom at Midnight 416
freedom movements, Young Italy and Young
    Ireland 121
'Freedom Pact' 129
French: East India Company (Compagnie des
    Indes Orientales) 17; Nawab 18–19
Fujiwara, Major Iwaichi (later Colonel) 342,
    345

Gainsford, Superintendent D. 294
Gandhi, Devadas (son of Mahatma
    Mohandas) 241, 443, 460–1
Gandhi, Karamchand (father of Mahatma
    Mohandas) 142, 145
Gandhi, Kasturbai (wife of Mahatma
    Mohandas) 143–5, 147–8, 151, 153,
    155, 160, 166, 229, 323, 329, 331,
    345–6, 507
Gandhi, Mahatma Mohandas 82, 94,
    142–64, 173, 228, 345–9: Aga Khan's
    Poona palace 329, 332, 345–6; *ahimsa*
    182; Ahmedabad 166; All-India Central
    Committee 267–8; All-Indian Village
    Industries 262; All-Parties Conferences
    212–14; Allahabad 179–80, 235;
    Amery, Leo 306; Amritsar 177; Anti-
    Compromise Conference 303; anti-war
    speeches 302; arrested 165–8, 196, 230;
    ashram 160, 267, 283, 317, 332;
    assassination plot 504–5; Attlee,
    Clement 399; Azad, Cabinet Mission
    plan 380; Benares 181; Bihar 425, 427;
    Bombay 155, 193, 235, 245; Bose,
    Subhas Chandra 201; Brahmo Samaj 33;
    bramacharya 148, 405–6; British
    withdrawal 326–7; Burma 155, 222;
    Cabinet Mission plan 376–7, 380,
    387–9, 397–8, 429; Calcutta 151,
    217–18, 494, 499–500; campaign
    against the Raj 182–96; Casey, Richard

G. 365; Churchill, Winston 327, 338,
    347; civil disobedience campaign 222,
    226–44, 246–7, 249–52, 262, 289,
    301–3, 332; Congress 184, 199–200,
    252–3, 258–9, 263, 270, 282, 293,327;
    leadership resignation 310; Congress
    Working Comittee 269, 286, 319;
    constitution 289, 352; cremation 506–7;
    Cripps, Sir Stafford 317–19, 375–6,
    391, 398; Desai-Liaquat pact 352;
    dominion status 223; east Bengal 405;
    England 144–5, 152–3, 286; fasts 248,
    250–1, 282–3, 331–2, 348, 500,
    504–5; gaol 246, 248, 250; Gujarat
    227–9; Gurjar Sabha (Gujarat Society)
    154; health problems 346–7, 349; *Hind
    swaraj* (Indian Home Rule) 150, 154,
    184–6; Hindu-Muslim accord 271;
    Independence Day 460–1; India 145,
    147, 153–61; India Conciliation Group
    359; Interim Government 400; Irwin,
    Lord 224, 226–7, 230, 236; Jinnah,
    Mohammad Ali 333, 349–50; Kaiser-i-
    Hind gold medal 154, 184; Karachi 238;
    Khilafat Committee 184; Linlithgow,
    Lord 261, 285, 288–9, 328–9, 331;
    MacDonald, Ramsay 248; Madras
    Presidency 222; Moderates 186–7;
    Mountbatten, Lord 49–30, 425,
    428–30, 455, 505; Nehru, Jawaharlal
    216, 221, 327, 383–4, 504; new
    Congress 187, 190; new Government of
    India Act (1935) 257; Noakhali riots
    404; non-co-operation movement 194;
    Pakistan 349; Pethick–Lawrence,
    Frederick 376, 391, 398; Plan Balkan
    443; Poona, Lady Thackersey 347;
    princes 478; programme of boycott and
    non–co-operation 198; Punjab
    499–500; Quit India campaign 328,
    346, 399; Rajagopalachari, Chakravarti
    348–51; Reading, Lord 191; RIN
    munity 369; round-table conference
    241–4; Sabarmati Ashram members 251;
    satyagraha 157, 262; Second World War
    299; Simla Conference 355–6; Simla
    talks 384–5; Simon Commission 211;
    South Africa 85, 109, 145–52, 155,
    297; *swaraj* 188, 192; Transfer of Power

455; two–nation theory 350, 452; untouchables *Harijans* 247–9; Wardha *ashram* 267, 302, 317; Wavell, General Sir Archibald 346–8, 355, 365, 376,397–9, 430; Willingdon, Lord 245–7, 258; Yeravda Central Gaol 230, 232, 237; *Young India* 121

Gandhi, Manilal (son of Mahatma Molandas) 229

Gandhi Plan 461

Gandhi, Shamdaldas (nephew of Mahatma Mohandas) 502

Gandhi-Irwin Pact 237–8, 245–6

Ganges (holy river) 53, 123, 236

Garhmukteswar, massacre 405

Gaya, Congress 198

Gazette of India 284–5

General Service Enlistment Act (1856) 48–9

George III, King 339

George V, king-emperor 109–10, 112, 115, 166, 174, 233, 242, 260, 411, 413

George VI, King 409–10, 413, 415–17, 467

Germany 183, 240

Ghadr movement 119

Ghadr Party 116–17

Ghadr (Rebellion) newspaper 116

Ghadrites 118

Gharjakh 171

Ghose, Dr Rash Behari 104

Ghosh, Sudhir 384, 398

Gill, S.S., *The Dynasty* 507

Gladstone, William Ewart 69, 97

Glasgow cruiser 369

Gloucester, Duke of 412

Goculdas Tejpal Sanscrit College 74

Godse, Nathuram 504–5

Goebbels, Joseph 305

Gokhale, Mahatma Gopal Krishna 81–2, 100, 151–5: Congress 101, 104, 120; Congress President 88–9, 92; death 129, 155; Gandhi, Mohatma Mohandas 147, 153–4; Imperial Legislative Council 127; Morley reform proposals 102, 107–8; Servants of India Society (SIS) 81–2, 107, 154–5, 159,186; South Africa 151

Golden Temple, Amritsar 1, 5–7, 16

Gosh, brothers, Sisir Kumar and Motilal 67

Government of India Acts: (1858) 55; (1919) 199, 205, 253, 445; (1935) 254–8, 260–1, 267–8, 276, 284, 288–9, 294,

311, 336, 352, 444–5, 452, 467, 476, 478

Grancy, Baron von 411

Grand Trunk Road 37

Granth (Sikh holy book) 117

great revolt (1857) 103, 123, 330, 369

Great War *see* First World War

Grigg, Sir James 313, 358

Gujarat 12, 16, 94, 142, 156, 229: Home Rule 134

Gujarati 95, 144, 163

Gujranwala 170–1

Gupta, Behari Lal 63

Gupta, K. G. 102

Gurdaspur (northern Punjab) 494–5, 503

Gurjar Sabha (Gujarat Society) 154, 158–9

Gurkhas 29, 58, 169

Gwalior, Maharaja of 115

Haig, Sir Harry 247–53, 277, 332

Haileybury 207; East India College 30, 37, 39, 63

Hali, Altaf Husain, *Musaddas (The Ebb and Flow of Islam)* 79

Halifax, Lord 205, 261, 296–7, 336, *see also* Irwin, Lord; Wood, Edward

Hallett, Sir Maurice 308

Hamayun (son of Babur) 12

Hance, Sir J.B. 339–40

Hankey, Sir Maurice 419

Haq, Fazlul 264, 266, 273, 295, 307, 332–34

Hardie, James Keir 104

Hardinge, Diamond 113

Hardinge, Lord (viceroy) 112–14, 116, 132, 151–2, 326

Harijan 290, 302, 325

Harrington, Henry 60

Harris, Kenneth 361

Harrison, Agatha 375, 384

Hartal 68, 88, 163–4, 193

Hartshorn, Vernon 207, 211–12

Hasan, Abid 341–2

Hastings, Marquis of (viceroy) 29, 419

Hastings, Warren 21–5, 28, 33

Hatch, G.W. (District Magistrate) 121

Hawkins, Captain William 12–13

Hermes carrier 326

Heron, Mr (superintendent of police) 170

Herring, Miss Bertha 296

Hesse-Darmstadt, Prince Alexander of 411
Hesse, Princess Victoria of 411
Hesse and the Rhine, Grand Dukes of 411
Hewart, Lord, Lord Chief Justice 205
hijrat (religious emigration) to Afghanistan 183
Hindu Mahasabha 192, 202, 207, 209,
    212–13, 241, 255, 265–6, 276, 288,
    291, 301, 307, 317, 328, 349, 404, 461
Hindu Rashtia (Hindu Nation) newspaper 504
Hindu-Muslim: negotiations 249, 379, 430;
    rioting 245; unity 129–30, 180, 182,
    184, 199, 219, 271
Hinduism 65, 77, 88, 140, 243, 248
Hindus 46, 60, 75–6, 78–9, 105, 126,
    129–30, 192, 248–9: banks 472;
    divisions 142; federal authority 351;
    festivals 80–1; Leaders' Conference 248;
    money–lenders 118–19; newspapers
    295; provinces, British withdrawal plans
    401; Raj 273, 275; scriptural writings
    150; University of India 120; votes 108
Hindustan 27, 379, 385: armed forces 438;
    Group 435; Republican Army 201;
    Socialist Republican Army 201, 216,
    222; Workers of the West Pacific Coast
    116
Hindustan Times 443
Hitler, Adolf 205, 280–1, 283, 296, 299,
    305–7, 343, 363
HMIS: *Hindustan* 369; *Narbada* 369, 474–5;
    Talwar 368–9
HMS: *Dufferin* 138; *Kelly* 413–14
Ho Chi Minh 208
Hoare, Sir Samuel 240, 242, 249, 252–3,
    257–8, 260: Government of India Act
    (1935) 336; House of Commons 246;
    possible viceroy 336
Hodson, H.V. 305, 315, 322, 430, 444
Hodson, Lieutenant William 52–4
Holwell, J. Z. 19
Home Rule Leagues 121, 130, 134, 156,
    162–3, 186: Besant, Annie 121, 129,
    134, 163; Bombay 186
Home Rule movement 120, 133
Hong Kong 116–17, 367
Hooghly river, Calcutta 343, 396
Hope, Lord *see* Linlithgow, Lord
Hopkins, Harry 324
Horniman, B. G. 163, 170, 173, 175

House of Commons 97, 133, 176–7, 242,
    281, 296: Amery, Leo 300–1, 306, 354;
    Attlee, Clement 250, 418, 420–1, 458,
    467; Chamberlain, Neville 281;
    Churchill, Winston 299; Cripps, Sir
    Stafford 391; Hoare, Sir Samuel 246;
    MacDonald, Ramsay 242; Montague,
    Edwin 133
House of Lords 176, 182, 223, 296, 391
Howes, Lieutenant–Commander Peter 420,
    424
Hume, Allan Octavian 71–3, 75–6
Hunter Committee of Inquiry 175–7, 182
Hunter, Lord 175–6
Hunter, Sir William 60
Huq, Mazhar-ul 122
Huxley, Thomas Henry 150
Hyderabad (princely state) 19, 22–3, 28, 118,
    476, 479, 481, 502: Nizam of 16, 18,
    27–8, 102, 441, 477, 502

Ibbetson, Sir Denzil 103
ICS *see* Indian Civil Service (ICS)
Id el Kebir (holiday) 349, 400, 499
Ilbert Bill 69–70, 85, 88
Ilbert, Sir Courtney 69
Imam, Hossain 357
Imperial Conference (1926) 214
Imperial Legislative Council 59–61, 67, 74,
    78, 81–2, 107–8, 126–7, 130, 136,
    138–9
Imperial War Conference (1917) 132
Imphal 343–5
INA prisoners 431–2
Independence: Act (1947) 460, 467–8,
    479–80, 502; bill 465; governor-general
    role 464; Menon, V.P. 464, 467; Day
    459–61, 476, 478, 494; Gandhi,
    Mohatma Mohandas's declaration
    225–6; Nehru, Jawaharlal 493; for India
    League 217, 342
Independent Labour Party 265, 290
India: administration 402; ambassadors 460;
    Association, Bengal 66, 70–1; Cabinet
    (Executive Council) 428–9; central and
    southern, *hartal* 164; Christians 137, 207,
    403; Committee of the Cabinet 312–19,
    358, 361, 418; Committee of the
    Cabinet defence clause 315, 318;

Committee of the Cabinet draft declaration 314–24, 325; Commonwealth membership 436, 438, 441, 452, 454, 501; Communist Party 182, 328; Conciliation Group 359; Constituent Assemblies 454; constitution 247, 249–50, 257, 261, 268, 290–1, 193–4, 300–1, 305, 349, 352, 360, 374, 377, 426; Constitution White Paper 249–50, 254; constitution-making body 361, 385; constitutional settlement 360; Council 108–9, 153, 354–6; Councils Act (1861) 61, 96–7, 102, 107; currency 471; debts 471; defence 327, 373–4, 379, 458; Defence Minister 318–19, 321–2, 475; division with Pakistan 470–5, 496–7; Dominion status 223, 232–3, 290, 318, 422, 425, 436–7, 445, 451, 454; Education Despatch (1854) 204–5; elections 360; European business community 317; Executive 374; federal government 377; full independence 255, 314, 501–2; future government 480; government 12, 134, 176; Governor-General 223, 256–7, 464–6, 475, 493; Home Department 191, 247, 330; interim government 350, 391, 393–4, 397–403, 405–6, 408, 430, 445, 460, 479; law 145; leaders 426, 433, 495; Mountbatten, Lord 426, 449–50, 453–5, 457; League 398; Legislative Assembly 207; Liberals 317; Medical Service 153, 168, 339; Mountbatten, Lord Louis, governor-general 464–6, 493; navy 474–5; new government 477, 485; Provincial Committee 215; railways 470; self-government 351, 354; strikes 368; War Department 342; World War II 309, 322, 325–7, 330–1

Indian air force 474

Indian Army 58–9, 119, 286, 304, 334, 436, 472–3

Indian Civil Service (ICS) 61–4, 66, 69, 92, 110, 128, 188, 223, 257, 277, 353, 444, 463, 494; examinations 198; Punjab 439

Indian Expeditionary Force 114–15

Indian Independence League 326, 341–2

Indian Mirror, Calcutta newspaper 70

Indian National Army (INA) 342–5; demonstrations 370; Gandhi, Mahatma Mohandas and Azad brigades 345; trials 362–8, 364, 372, 425, 431

Indian National Congress *see* Congress

Indian Ocean 325

Indian Opinion newspaper 148, 150, 152, 173

Indian Penal Code 138

Indian Police Act (1861) 61, 103

Indian Republican Army 231

Indian Social Reformer 137

Indo-China 364

Indonesia, Indian troops 368

Insein prison 202

Instrument of Accession 481–2, 504

International Labour Organization 208

Invergordon 240

Iqbal, Dr Muhammad 234, 263–4, 276, 294

Iran 75, 120

Iraq 183, 306

Ireland 73, 105, 203: Easter Rising (1916) 2, 129; Free State 214; Home Rule 97, 115, 120; Republican Army (IRA) 2, 508; Sinn Fein 2, 127

Ironside, General 281

Irving, Miles 2–5, 7, 165, 167–8, 170

Irwin, Lord: viceroy 204–7, 210, 212–13, 215, 220–3, 232, 236; Gandhi, Mahatma Mohandas 226–7, 230, 235–6; train bomb 224. *See also* Halifax, Lord

Isaacs, Rufus *see* Reading, Marquess of

Ismailis 94

Ismay, Lord Hastings 'Pug' 38–9, 441, 448, 450–1, 453–4, 456, 494–5, 500–1: Cabinet mission plan 448–9, 454, 456; Gandhi, Mahatma Mohandas 430; governor-general 465, 467–8; India Committee 442–3; Indian army 472; London 444; Mountbatten, Lord 419–20, 424, 434–5, 450–2; Plan Balkan 438, 441–3, 449; Sikhs 485

Isna Ashari sect 99

Ispahani, Mirza Abol Hassain 264, 303–4, 506

Jafar, Mir 19–20

Jahan, Shah 15
Jahangir 'World Seizer' 13, 16, *see also* Salim
Jains 74, 140, 142–3, 151
Jalandhari, Hafiz 263
Jallianwala Bagh 5–9, 170, 173, 175, 192,
    209; massacre 127, 173–8, 176–8, 224,
    228–9, 296
Jambusar, Nehrus 228
Jamiat Ulama-i-Hind 218
Jamiat-ul-Ulama 272
Jammu 43–4: instrument of accession 504;
    and Kashmir 477, 503. *See also* Singh,
    Gulab
Jamna (holy river) 123, 484
Jamshedpur 90, 330
Japan 310–2: Arakan attack 334; First Air
    Group 310; food rioting 2; *Komagata
    Maru* ship 116–17; naval forces 35, 326;
    propaganda broadcasts 326; surrender
    360, 362–3; war against 330, 354
Jayakar, All-Parties Conferences 212–15
Jayakar, M. R. 232, 236
Jenkins, Sir Evan: Punjab governor 421,
    435–6, 439–40, 485–90, 494–5;
    Wavell, General Sir Archibald 337–8,
    353, 360, 398
Jenkins, Sir John 109
Jerusalem, Grand Mufti 306
Jhansi, Rani of 57
Jinnah, Dina (daughter of Jinnah) 139–40,
    235
Jinnah, Fatima 96–9, 235, 273–4, 432, 506
Jinnah, Mohammad Ali (Mamad) 152, 238,
    377–8: All-India Council meeting 461;
    All-Parties Conferences 195, 212–15;
    All-Parties Muslim Conference 218;
    Baluchistan 506; Bengal partition 100–1;
    Bombay 99, 101, 209, 254, 506;
    Boundary Commission awards 494–6;
    Cabinet Mission 377, 379–83, 388–9,
    391–2, 406, 433; Cabinet Mission
    Working Committee 383; Calcutta 209,
    274; Central Assembly 199, 253; Central
    Parliamentary Board 264; Committee
    199–200, *see also* Muddiman Reforms
    Inquiry Committee; Congress 100, 107;
    Congress-League Pact 137; Constituent
    Assembly 406; constitution 289, 352;
    Cripps, Sir Stafford 291, 318, 376;

Darjeeling 129; Day of Deliverance
    289–90, 292; Desai-Liaquat pact
    352–3; Dominion status 223–4;
    Douglas Graham and Company 95–7;
    Executive Council 108–9; Gandhi,
    Mahatma Mohandas 154, 186–7, 294,
    333, 349–50, 505; Government of India
    Act (1935) 255, 276, 294; governor-
    general of Pakistan 464–7; Gujarat
    Society 154; health problems 306,
    348–9, 385, 402, 425–6, 428, 506;
    Hindus and Muslims truce 430; Home
    Rule Leagues 134; Imperial Legislative
    Council 108, 127; INA trials 364; India
    Committee draft declaration 317, 323;
    India elections 360; Indian Army 472;
    Indian Cabinet 429; Interim Government
    393–4, 397–8, 400, 402; Junagadh state
    502; Karachi 94–6, 491; Lahore 293–5;
    legal career 98–9, 105–6, 121–2;
    Linlithgow, Lord 285–6, 288, 349;
    London 152–3, 213, 215, 235, 242–3,
    253–4, 406–7; Lucknow Pact 130–2;
    Menon plan 450; Morley, Lord John 97;
    Mountbatten, Lord Louis 425, 427,
    432–3, 451, 453–6, 462, 464–5, 486;
    Muslim League 111, 180, 182, 184–5,
    199–200, 209, 211, 215, 217–18, 234,
    263–5, 270–1, 301, 306, 333, 360–1,
    392–3; Mussulmans 382; Naoroji,
    Dadabhai 97, 99–100; National Defence
    Council (NDC) 307; New Delhi 254;
    NWFP 443; Pakistan 332, 349, 362,
    370–1, 373, 376–8, 422, 434, 441,448,
    452; Pakistan Day 316; Partition
    Council 463–4; Plan Balkan 436, 441,
    443, 445–6; princes 478; provincial
    elections 270; Punjab 370; Quaid-i-
    Azam 283, 332, 375, 392, 432, 465,
    506; Quit India campaign 328, 332;
    Rajagopalachari's formula 348–9;
    resolution 218–20; RIN mutiny 369;
    round-table conference 233; Rowlatt Act
    138–9; *sherwani* 273; Shiite Isna Asharis
    99; Sikhs 487; Simla Conference 355–8;
    Simla talks 384–5; Simon Commission
    213; Transfer of Power 454–7; Viceroy
    House proposed meeting 337–8;
    Wavell, General Sir Archibald 393,

356–7, 381, 391, 401; Wyatt, Major
  Woodrow 375, 388–9
Jinnah, Ruttie 129, 187, 213, 218, 239, 253
Jodhpur 15
Johannesburg 146–7, 149–51: Tolstoy Farm
  150–1, 156
Johnson, Colonel Frank 167, 172
Johnson, Colonel Louis 322–3, 338
Joint Defence: Committee 473, 475; Council
  494, 496
Joint Parliamentary Commission 255
Jones, Tom 204, 281
Jowitt, Lord 451
Jubbulpore, Central Provinces, riots 368
Judaic heritage 77
Jullundur 3–4, 169, 496
Junagadh state 481, 502: Nawab of 502

Kabaw valley 345
Kabul 16, 42, 311
Kakindada port 325
Kali (goddess) 14, 36, 90–1, 105
Kalighat *see* Calcutta
Kalinin, Soviet president 209
Karachi 94–5, 97, 438, 461: Gandhi,
  Mahatma Mohandas 238; Jinnah,
  Mohammad Ali 491–2, 506;
  Mountbatten, Lord 492; RIN mutiny
  369; riots 369–70, 400; Sind Muslim
  League 276
Karkare, Vishnu 431
Kashmir (princely state) 43–4, 476–7, 481,
  494–5, 502–4: Brahmans 123–4;
  Cabinet Mission 380–2; Maharaja of
  503–4; standstill agreement 503; Union
  of India 504. *See also* Jammu
Kassim, Karim 95
Kathiawar peninsula, Gujarat 94, 142–3, 502
Kaul, Kamala *see* Nehru, Kamala
Kaul, Pandit Jawaharmul (father of Kamala)
  128
Kaur, Rajkumari (Princess) Amrit 346, 375
Kayastha sub–caste 201
Keble, John 205
Kemal, Mustafa (Turkish president) 199
Kennedy, Mr (Calcutta bomb victim) 105
Kesari (The Lion) newspaper 80–1, 90, 101,
  105
Keynes, John Maynard 127

khadi 189–90
Khajuraho, temples 85
Khaksars 293–4, 461
Khaliquzzaman, Choudry 211, 271–2,
  283–4, 378
Khan, Abdul Gaffar 231, 245, 266, 293, 370,
  384, 405, 439,456, 462
Khan, General Ayub 487, 498, 504
Khan, Ghazanfar Ali 403
Khan, Ghengis 12
Khan, Nawab Ismail 271–2, 384
Khan, Khan Abdul Qayyum 378
Khan, Khizar Hyat 357, 370–1, 420–1
Khan, Liaquat Ali 253–4, 264, 290–1, 352,
  357, 431: Ambala 496; ambassadors
  460; Amritsar 496–7; assassination 507;
  Boundary Commission 495; Central
  Legislative Assembly 428;
  Congress–League coalition 352; Cripps,
  Sir Stafford 290–1; Desai, Bhulabhai
  pact 352; INA prisoners 431; Indian
  Cabinet 428; interim government 402–3,
  406; Jinnah, Mohammad Ali 253–4,
  264; Jullundur 496; Lahore 496;
  London Constituent Assembly meeting
  406–7; Menon plan 450; Mountbatten,
  Lord Louis 424–5, 427–8, 433, 453–4,
  457, 465, 486; Pakistan 434; Partition
  Council 463–4; Plan Balkan 445–6;
  provincial elections 370; Simla
  conference 357, 384
Khan, Nizam Sir Mir Osman Ali 502
Khan, Sir Mohammed Zafrullah 337–8
Khan, Nawab Salimullah 93
Khan, Sir Shafaat Ahmad 397, 403
Khan, Lieutenant–Colonel Shah Nawaz
  344–5
Khan, Sir Sikander Hayat 266, 273, 286, 291,
  293–5, 307,318, 332
Khan, Sir Syed Ahmed 75–80, 92, 100, 108,
  112, 124, 131: *Essay on the Causes of the
  Indian Revolt* 76; *The Loyal Muhammadans of
  India* 76; Muslim Univtersity 189
Khan, Zafar Ali 111
Kheda, Patidars 159–60
Kher, B. G. 269, 271
Khilafat 4, 182–5, 188, 190–2, 195, 199,
  201, 203, 274
Khoja sub–sect 77, 94–6, 99

Khudai Khidmatgars (Servants of God) 231
Khyber Pass 11, 41
Kiani, Colonel Mohammad (later
     Major–General) 345
Kidwai, Rafi Ahmed 272
Kingsford, Douglas 105
Kipling, Alice 118
Kipling, John Lockwood 118
Kipling, Rudyard 118, 260, 292: *Kim* 37;
     Mesopotamia 133
Kisan sabhas (peasant associations) 181–2, 188,
     328
Kitchener, Lord 86, 92, 109, 132, 136
Kitchlew, Dr Saifuddin 127, 167–8, 174,
     176–7, 189
Knatchbull, Nicholas 508
Kohima 344–5
Komagata Maru, Japanese ship 116–17
Kripalani, Acharya 423
Kripalani, J.B. 188, 259, 453–6, 462
Krishak Proja Party 266
Kyber Pass 175–6, 183, 440

Lahore (capital of Punjab) 3, 11, 17, 43, 68,
     103, 118, 164–5, 291: Boundary
     Commission award 494, 498; Congress
     224–5; garrison 170–1; *hartal* 166;
     Hunter Committee of Inquiry 175;
     Jinnah, Mohammad Ali 293–4; Khan,
     Liaquat Ali 496; Mountbatten, Lord
     487; Muslim League 209, 284, 293–5,
     348, 421; Nehru, Jawaharlal 496;
     Pakistan 494; partition of India 483–4,
     487; Pearl Mosque 85; People's
     Committee 167; resolution 350; Sikhs
     379, 461, 483, 485–7, 496; unrest
     293–4, 462
Lake, Lord 29
Lamington, Lord 296
Lampson, Sir Miles 335
Lansbury, George 208
Lapierre, Dominique 459
Laval, Pierre 260
Law, Andrew Bonar 203
Lawrence, Sir Henry 45–6, 53
League against Imperialism 208
Leese, Sir Oliver 415
Legislative Assembly 136–7
Lester, Muriel 241

Lewis, W. H. 157–8
Liberal Charter 37, *see also* Charter Act (1813)
Liberal Party, *see* British Liberal Party
Linlithgow, Doreen 261, 334
Linlithgow, Lord (viceroy) 239–40, 278,
     283–86, 307–8, 335, 366: Amery, Leo
     298, 300, 331, 333; August Offer
     300–1; Chamber of Princes 285–6, 477;
     Cripps, Sir Stafford 292, 315–16;
     Executive Council 307–8; Gandhi,
     Mahatma Mohandas 261, 285, 288–9,
     298–9, 302, 328–9, 332, 339;
     Government of India Act (1935) 255–7,
     261, 268–9, 311; India Committee
     proposals 314–16, 318, 321, 354;
     Jinnah, Mohammad Ali 285–6, 288,
     295–6, 349; Menon, V. P. 444; Nehru,
     Jawaharlal 261, 281, 288, 298; Patel,
     Vallabhbhai 261, 298; round-table
     conference 249; successor 336; Wavell,
     General Sir Archibald 339; Zetland
     295–6
Listowel, Lord 'Billy' 360, 442, 451, 459,
     463
Lloyd George, David 135–6, 139, 182–4,
     203, 220
Lockhart, General Sir Rob 462, 475
Loganadhan, Lieutenant-Colonel 344
Lothian, Lord 257–8, 268, 278, 281
Loyalty hospital ship 115
Lucknow (capital of Oudh) 53, 75, 156, 211,
     215–16, 236: Muslim League
     conference 273–4; Pact 130, 132,
     136–7, 156, 209
Ludhiana Conference 281
Lumley, Sir Roger 336
Lutyens, Sir Edwin 112, 425
Lutyens, Emily 112
Lyttelton, Oliver 336
Lytton, Lord 66–7, 69–70, 112, 338

MacArthur, General Douglas 310
Macaulay , Lord Thomas Babington 16,
     39–41, 47, 69, 493; codification of
     Anglo–Indian law (1860) 39–40, 61;
     House of Commons speeches 37–8, 41;
     The Lays of Ancient Rome 40; Minute on
     Indian Education 40–1
MacBride, Richard 116–17

MacDonald, Malcolm (son of Ramsay) 316
MacDonald, Ramsay 260: Communal Award
247–8, 251, 254, 263; Gandhi,
Mahatma Mohandas 230, 248; Jinnah,
Mohammed Ali 213, 222; Labour
government 204–7, 220; National
government 240; round-table conference
233, 235, 241–4
Mackinlay, Brigadier J. P. C. 395
Maclagen, Sir Edward 175
MacPherson, John Molesworth 99
Madras 14, 17–18, 21–3, 38, 52, 188: British
withdrawal plans 401–2; Congress 77,
207, 253, 269, 327, 370; Gandhi,
Mahatma Mohandas 155; government
279; governors of 35, 82, 190, 239,
253, 279; Home Rule League 121;
Justice Party 265; Muslim League 306;
provincial legislature 108; Simon
Commission 211; Vellore 35–6
Mahabharata 145
Maharashtra 15–6, 65, 81, 106, 181, 211,
267
Mahavira 142
Mahmood-ul-Hasan, Maulana 120
Mahmud, Dr Syed 232, 269
Maisky, Ivan 281
Malabar coast 25, 192
Malaviya, Madan Mohan 134, 185, 187, 192,
195, 202, 209, 216, 241, 248, 251,
253–4: All-Parties Conferences 212–15
Malaya 310–1, 375–6, 418
Malcolm, John 28–30
Mamdot, Nawab Khan of 378, 421
Mandal, Jogendra Nath 402–3
Mandalay 85, 353: palace 85; prison 106,
115, 120, 202, 255–6
Manipur 343–4
Manto, Saadat Hasan 497–8
Marathas 13–14, 16, 18, 20, 22–3, 28–9, 42,
48, 54, 60, 65, 71: Peshwa of 53, *see also*
Sahib, Nana; states 58
Marseilles 241
Martineau, Captian E. M. 50–1
Mason, Philip 118, 136–7, 277–9, 342
Mata, Sharanda 446
Matthai, John, interim government 403, 436
Mazumdar, Ambika Charan 129
Mazzini, Giuseppe 66

Mazzotta, Orlando (Bose, Subhas Chandra)
305
Meares, Sir Grimwood 123
Mecca 13, 120
Meerut, United Provinces 43, 51–2, 76, 222,
423
Mehta, Dr Dinshaw 345
Mehta, Sir Pherozeshah 74–5, 82, 99–101,
104, 120, 186
Menèzes, General L. S. 473–4, 498
Menon, Krishna 398, 437–8, 443–6
Menon, Mrs 449
Menon, V.P. 372: Delhi riots 500–1; Desai-
Liaquat pact 352–3; Independence bill
464, 467; Instrument of Accession 482;
Jammu 504; Joint Defence Committee
473; Kashmir 503; Mountbatten, Lord
449–51, 500–1; Patel, Vallabhbhai 444;
Plan Balkan 435–6, 444–5; Plan for
twin dominions 119–50, 422–3, 438,
441–8 448; princes 480–1; reforms
commissioner 480; Simla conference
357; Wavell, General Sir Archibald 360,
383, 444
Mesopotamia (today's Iraq) 115, 119, 133,
175
Messervy, General Sir Frank 475
Middle East 111, 139, 418
Miéville, Sir Eric 419–20, 424, 441, 448–50:
Mountbatten, Lord 444, 454, 465;
Sikhs 485
Milford Haven, Marquessate of 411
Mill, John Stuart 80, 97–8
Millar, James 238
Miller, Webb 229
Milner, Sir Alfred (later Lord) 297
Minto, Lady 93
Minto, Lord (viceroy) 91–2, 102–4, 106–10,
360
Modh Banias 142, 144, 261
Moghuls 11–15, 24
Mohammed, Dost 42
Molesworth, General G. N. 321
Monckton, Sir Walter 441, 465
Monghyr, RAF crews 329
Montagu, Edwin 107, 133–40, 173–6, 194,
197, 223, 239: Gandhi, Mahatma
Mohandas 158; 'Report on Indian
Constitutional Reform' 13, 445

Montagu-Chelmsford Reforms 136, 138, 162, 176, 180, 190, 205
Monteath, Sir David 399
Montgomery, Field Marshal 472–3
Moplahs (Muslim group) 192
Moraes, Frank 201
Morley, Lord 89, 92, 97, 102–4, 106–9, 115, 133, 149, 359–60: *On Compromise* 97
Morley-Minto reforms 126, 129, *see also* Indian Councils Act (1861)
Morning Post 177
Morris, William 262
Morrison, Herbert 451
Moscow 209, 304
Mosley, Leonard 449, 484
Mosley, Oswald 240
Mountbatten, Edwina 375–6, 412–13, 416–17, 424–6, 432, 449–51, 508: Jinnah 466; Nehru, Jawaharlal 375–6, 446; North-West Frontier Provinces (NWFP) visit 439–41; relief work 501
Mountbatten, Lord (viceroy) 193, 336, 375, 409–41; assassination 508; Attlee, Clement 409–10, 416–19, 449, 451; Auchinleck, General Sir Claude 415, 424, 431, 434, 487, 503; Bhopal, Nawab of 465, 478; Boundary Commission 490, 494, 496; British withdrawal plans 426; Burma 415–16; Cabinet Mission plan 434–5; Calcutta 488; Captain of HMS *Kelly* 413–14; Chamber of Princes 480; Churchill, Winston 414–15, 452; Combined Operations 414–16, 419; constituent assembly 481–2; Cripps, Sir Stafford 416–17; dominion status 445–6; Earl of Burma 494; emergency committee 501; Final Report 460; Gandhi, Mahatma Mohandas 49–30, 425, 428–30, 460–1, 505; governor-general 493–7; INA trials 364–5, 425; inauguration ceremony 478; Indian Cabinet 428; Indian Cabinet Committee 451, 453; Indian leaders 426, 449–50, 453–5, 457, 479; Jinnah, Mohammad Ali 425, 427, 432–3, 462, 464–5, 490; Karachi 492; Kashmir 495, 503–4; Khan, Liaquat Ali 424–5, 427, 433; Lahore 487; marriage 412;

Montgomery, Field Marshal 472–3; mother 419; naval career 410–17, 419, 507–8; Nehru, Jawaharlal 375, 424–5, 427, 435, 438, 443–4, 446,448, 464, 490; North-West Frontier Provinces (NWFP) 439–41; NWFP referendum 443; Partition Council 463–4; Patel, Vallabhbhai 438, 441, 453–4, 459, 501; Plan Balkan 442, 445–8; Plan Partition 451; princes 476, 480–1; Punjab 489; Sikhs 485–6; Simla 443–4, 449, 499–500; Singh, Baldev 431; swearing–in ceremony 45–6; Transfer of Power announcement 454–60; Wavell, General Sir Archibald 415, 424–6
Mountbatten, Pamela 424, 432, 439–41
Mountbatten, Patricia 466
Mudaliar, Sir A. Ramaswami 337–8
Muddiman, Sir Alexander 199
Mudie, Sir Francis 398, 489
Muggeridge, Malcolm 239–40
Mughals 11–12, 16, 20, 24–5, 28, 30, 54, 76, 107, 113, 123: armies 46; capital *see* Delhi; Court of St James's 32–3; culture 12, 14; dynasty 60
Muhammadans 92–3, 154: Anglo-Oriental College, Aligarh 77; Educational Conference 93
Muirhead, Colonel 283
Mukherjea, P. M. 107
Mulk, Nizamul 502
Mumtaz, Commander I. K. 474
Munro, General Sir Charles 135
Munro, Major Hector 20
Murshidabad 19–20
Musaddas (The Ebb and Flow of Islam), Altaf Husain Hali 79
Muslim League 93, 102, 110–11, 115, 120, 128–30, 132, 154, 139, 187, 202, 263, 266, 276, 283, 332–3, 352–3, 374: All-India Council 391–2, 456, 461; Allahabad 129, 263, 294; annual expenditure 263; Bankipur 110–11; Bengal 307, 370; Bombay 121–2; Cabinet Mission plan 392, 406–7; Calcutta 274, 303; Commonwealth membership 438; Congress 135, 276, 307, 379; constituent assembly 418; constitution and policy 110–11, 271;

Delhi 333, 377–8; INA trials 364;
interim government 401–3, 406; Jinnah,
Mohammad Ali 111, 180, 182, 184–5,
199–200, 209, 211, 215, 217–18, 234,
253–4, 263–5, 270–1, 291, 301,392–3;
Lahore 209, 284, 293–5, 348, 421;
Lucknow Conference 273–4; Madras
306; Muslim parties 273; National
Guards 404, 421, 429, 461; Pakistan
380–1, 451, *see also* Pakistan; Permanent
Settlement system 266; Planning
Committee 433; Rajagopalachari's
formula 348–50; resolution 295, 348–9;
Second World War 300; Sind 370;
Subjects Committee 295; Working
Committee 283, 288, 301, 348–9, 383,
392–3

Muslims 46, 60, 76–9, 88–9, 110, 111, 126,
129–30, 137, 139–40, 142–3, 191,
192, 200, 209, 210, 242–3, 249, 256,
263, 270, 274, 323, 377, 382, 505; 60,
89, 110, 191, 200, 209, 274, 294, 382:
invaders 11; laws 15; Muhurram 80;
newspapers 111, 120; parties 264, 273;
provinces, British withdrawal plans 401,
422; separatism 234; states 295;
University, Aligarh 189, 271; votes 108,
348, 382. *See also* Pakistan

Mussolini, Benito 260, 280, 283, 299
Mutaguchi, General Renya 344
Muzzafarpur 105
Mysore 23: Maharaja of 27–8

Nagpur 48, 89, 186–8
Naidu, Padmaja (daughter of Sarojini) 446
Naidu, Sarojini 209, 223, 228–9, 232, 237,
241, 329, 376
Naini prison 232, 235, 246
Nair, C. Sankaran 187
Naiyar, Sushila 329
Nankana Sahib shrine 485–7
Naoroji, Dadabhai 64, 74–5, 77, 82, 97,
99–101
Napier, General Sir Charles 42
Nariman, K. F. 267, 269
Natal 145–6, 148–9
Nath, Brij Gopi 6
National: Agriculturist Party 265, 271;
Coalition government 260; Defence

Council (NDC) 307; Government 297;
Negro Congress 281; Planning
Committee 281–2; Week 228–9
National Liberal Federation 186, 207, 255
Nava Jivan, Gujarati journal 173
Nawanagar, Jam Saheb of 337–8
Nawaz, Begum Shah 307
Nawaz, Mumtaz 'Tazi' Shah 375
Nayar, Pyarelal 241
Nazimuddin, Khwaja 402, 507
Nazism 258, 275, 287, 299, 305, 327
Nehru family 195–6, 221–2, 224, 228
Nehru, Indira (daughter of Jawaharlal) 129,
208, 258, 280–1, 405, 507
Nehru, Jawaharlal 125–9, 189: Ahmednagar
Fort gaol 329; Alipore gaol 251–2; All-
India States' Peoples' Conference 281;
All-Parties Conferences 212–15;
Allahabad 199, 251; Almora gaol 258;
ambassadors 460; Amritsar 496–7; anti-
war speech 302; arrests 230, 302; Attlee,
Clement 406–7; Bengal 251, 266; Berlin
208; Bihar riots 405; Boundary
Commission 490, 495; British election
campaiagn 362; Brussels 208; Cabinet
Mission 377, 397; Calcutta 362; Ceylon
238; Chiang Kai-shek 287; civil
disobedience campaign 238;
Commonwealth membership 436–7;
Congress President 258–9, 282, 384,
390–1; Congress Working Committee
267, 293, 317, 320, 430; Constituent
Assembly, Objectives Resolution 407;
constitution 283, 289, 445; Constructive
Programme 262; Cripps, Sir Stafford
265–7, 290, 292, 313, 316, 319–23,
375, 383; death 507; Delhi riots 500–1;
Dominion Constitution for India 233;
Egypt 281; election results 277; Europe
280–1, 283; Executive Council 400;
Faizpur Congress 263; father's death
236; Gandhi, Mahatma Mohandas
179–81, 216, 221, 327, 383–4,430,
504; Gandhi-Irwin talks 237; Ganga
Dhar 123; Government of India Act
(1935) 255, 257; Hyderabad 502;
Independence Day 493; Independence
for India League 217; Indian National
Army (INA) 364; Interim Government

393–4, 397, 399–400, 401, 403;
Japanese war 327; Kashmir 495; Lahore
496; Lahore Congress 224–5; Legislative
Assembly 431; Linlithgow, Lord 261,
281, 288, 298; London 258, 281,
398–9; Malaya 375–6; Menon, V.P.,
plan 450; Moscow 209; mother 251,
280; Mountbatten, Edwina 375–6, 446;
Mountbatten, Lord 45, 375, 424–5,
427, 435, 438, 443–4, 446, 448,
453–4, 464; Naini prison 232, 235,
246, 252; National Planning Committee
281–2; North-West Frontier Provinces
(NWFP) 405; Pakistan 423; Plan
Balkan 436, 441, 445–9; Plan Partition
451; prime minister (1947) 181;
princely states 479; provincial elections
370; Punjab 492; Report 214, 217–18,
242; RIN mutiny 369; Salt Tax 226;
Second World War 287; Simla talks
384; Simon Commission 207–8;
Singapore 375, 377; transfer of power
452, 454–7; United India 458; United
Provinces 245; Unity Board 272;
Viceroy House proposed meeting
337–8; Wavell, General Sir Archibald
321, 375, 391, 397–8; World War II
300–2
Nehru, Kamala (wife of Jawaharlal) 128–9,
180, 189, 208,229, 236, 258
Nehru , Krishna (daughter of Motilal) 125,
189, 229
Nehru, Lakshmi (daughter of Motilal) 123
Nehru, Motilal 122–31, 180, 187, 189,
198–200, 208–9, 228: All-Parties
Conferences 212–15; Amristar trials
175, 177; Calcutta Congress 216–18;
death 235–6; dominion status 223–4,
290; Home Rule League 185; Imperial
Legislative Council 108, 127; Khilafat
Committee 184; Naini prison 232;
Nationalist coalition 199; Rowlatt Act
140; swadeshi home 228, 246; Swarajists
200, 203; United Provinces 126–7, 194
Nehru, Nand Lal 125
Nehru, Rajiv 507
Nehru, Sarup Kumari 125
Nehry, Bansi Dhar 124
New Delhi 112: Bose, Subhas Chandra 202;

dominion status 223; Mountbatten,
Lord burial 508; Plan for co–operation
304; Tariff Board 198; Viceroy's House
112, 240, 337, 374, 412, 424–5, 428,
455. See also Delhi
New India newspaper 120
New Party 102–5
New Zealand 115, 412
newspaper censorship 246
Nguyen Ai Quoc see Ho Chi Minh
Nicholson, Brigadier John 54
Nicobar Islands 344
Nightingale, Florence 71
Nishtar, Abdur Rab 384, 403, 453–4, 463–4
Noakhali and Tippera districts, east Bengal
403–5, 421
Non-Party Conference 351
Noon, Sir Firoz Khan 378, 392
Norris, Justice 68
north Africa 111, 306, 327, 331
North, Lord 21
North-West Frontier Provinces (NWFP)
231, 244, 329: Afghanistan 175–6, 183;
Cabinet Mission plan 390, 447;
Congress 245, 266, 269, 370; elections
435, 439; Gaffar Khan's Red Shirts 245;
governor 365–6; Great Mutiny 52;
Hume, Allan Octavian 72; Muslim
voters 273, 382, 422; Nehru, Jawaharlal
405, 214–15; Pakistan 378, 441; Punjab
86, 118; referendum 443, 457, 462–3;
riots 245, 422, 434–5, 439–40; World
War II 119. See also United Provinces
(UP)
North-West Indian Muslim State 234, 284,
286
Norway 296
NWFP see North–West Frontier Provinces
(NWFP)

Obaidullah, Sub-inspector 5
O'Brien, Colonel A. J. 171
Ochterlony, Sir David 394–5
O'Connell, Daniel 73
O'Dwyer, Sir Michael 117–19, 135, 164–70,
173–6, 296
Ollivant, Sir Charles 99
Operation Rutter 415
Orissa 12, 14, 21, 86–7, 249, 473: British

withdrawal plans 401–2; Congress 269, 370; Fifth-column 311
Ottoman empire 111, 139, 162, 182
Oudh, kingdom of 16, 22, 28–9, 48, 52–3, 58–9: Nawab-Vizier of 22
Owen, David 316
Oxford Movement 205

Pacific 331: War Council 337–8
Page-Drake, Mrs. F. E. 96
Pahwa, Madanlal 504–5
Pakistan 234–5, 295, 306, 332–3, 338, 348–51, 356–8, 361, 370, 373–89, 391–2, 423, 427, 429, 433–6, 443, 445,447–8, 461: ambassadors 460; Amery, Leo 313; British governors 465; Commonwealth membership 437–8, 452, 454, 457; constituent assembly 491–2; creation of 463, 497; Day 316, 503; defence minister 475; division with India 470–5; dominion status 436, 454; Federation of 491; finance 471; Gandhi, Mahatma Mohandas 349; government 12, 231, 505; Governor–General 464–7, 475; Group 435; interim government 479; Jinnah, Mohammad Ali 295, 332, 349, 362, 370–1, 373, 376, 464–7; Medical Service 506; Muslim League 451; new government 477, 485; Punjab 332; Resolution 295; Sind 441, 463; six provinces 441; Wavell, General Sir Archibald 337–8; West 494–5. *See also* Assam; Bengal; North–West Frontier Province; Punjab; Sind
Pal, Bipin Chandra 102–3, 106, 127, 185, 187
Palestine 183, 283, 306, 312, 418
Pan-Islamic movement 112, 234–5
Pande, Mangal 50
Paneli village, Gondal 94, 96
Pant, Govind Ballabh 216, 253, 272, 277, 279, 355
Paris 241, 303: Peace Conference 139
Parliamentary Committee 268, 271
Parsis 74, 106, 142, 154, 207, 288, 403
Partition Council 463–4, 473, 483, 489: army sub-committee 473; naval sub-committee 474–5; Steering Committee 463, 487

Patel, Hiralal Muljibhai 501: Partition Council, Steering Committee 463
Patel, Vallabhbhai: Ahmedabad 159, 166, 199; Ahmednagar Fort gaol 329; Bengal government 398; Bombay 269, 271; Boundary Commission 490, 495; Cabinet Mission 377, 389, 422, 435; Calcutta riots 365; civil disobedience campaign 238; Congress 221, 259, 282, 301, 383–4, 391; constitution 267; Delhi riots 500–1; Executive Council 400; Gandhi, Mahatma Mohandas 159–60, 188, 198, 383, 431, 505, 507; Hyderabad 502; India Committee draft declaration 319; Indian states minister 479–80; interim government 402–3, 406; Jinnah, Mohammad Ali 448; Kashmir 503; Khan, Liaquat Ali budget 428; law courts boycott 189; Linlithgow, Lord 261; London Constituent Assembly meeting 406–7; Menon, V. P. 444, 450; Mountbatten, Lord 438, 441, 453–4, 459, 501; Parliamentary Committee 268; Partition of India 422–3, 481; Partition Council 463–4, 474–5; Plan Balkan 436, 445–6, 449; Plan Partition 451; princes, conference of 480–1; provincial elections 370; RIN mutiny 369; round-table conference 232; Simla talks 384–5; Transfer of Power 454–7, 459; Wavell, General Sir Archibald, plan 362; World War II 345
Patel, Vithalbhai 199, 224
Pathans 50, 118–9, 122, 149, 498, 503: Afghan frontiers 86; mercenaries 29
Patiala, Maharaja 48, 480
Patna (capital of Bihar Province) 52, 404–5
Pearl Harbor 309–10, 326
Peel, Lord 198, 215, 233
Persia 41, 94
Peshawar, North–West Frontier Provinces (NWFP) 3, 11, 37, 231, 238, 304, 439–41
Peshwa 15–16, 23, 65
Pethick-Lawrence, Frederick 359–60, 442: British withdrawal plans 401–2; Cabinet Mission 372–4, 376, 379, 381–2, 387–8, 390, 406,423; interim government 391, 393, 398–9; Simla

talks 384–5
Petit, Sir Dinshaw 129
Petit, Jamshed 506
Petit, Jehangir 154
Phadke, Vasudeo Balwant 71
Phillips, William 338
Pillay, Chidambaram 106
Pitt, William the Younger 23
Plan Balkan 435–6, 438, 441–7, 449
Plan Partition 451, 453
Plassey, battle of 19, 30, 178
Pollitt, Harry 208
Pondicherry 17–18
Poona 13–15, 65, 71, 80–1, 154–5, 250–2,
      347: Gandhi, Mahatma Mohandas 197,
      250; Home Rule League 121;
      Maharashtra Provincial Congress
      Committee 267; revolts 329–30;
      Sarvajanik Sabha (PSS) 65–6, 81; Simon
      Commission 211; *swadeshi* movement 89
Poonja, Jinnahbhai 94–8
Poonja, Manbai (sister of Jinnahbhai) 95, 99
Poonja, Mithibai 94, 96, 98
Porbandar, Gujarat 142–3
Portugal 2, 10, 13
post–war Commission 351
Pound, Admiral Sir Dudley 415
Prarthana Samaj (Prayer Society) 65
Prasad, Rajendra 188, 198–9, 254, 258–9,
      269, 283, 289, 431: constituent
      assembly 407; interim government 403;
      Parliamentary Committee 268; Partition
      Council 463–4
Pratt, Mr (commissioner) 166
press censorship 329
Pretoria 145–6, 152
Prince of Wales, battleship 310
princely states 255–6, 476–80, *see also*
      Chamber of Princes
princes 476–8: conference of 480–1;
      Instrument of Accession 481–2;
      standstill agreement 481
Privy Council 235, 243
proscribed organizations 246
Providence, dispensation of 82
provinces, decisions 435
Provincial: Autonomy 257; elections 265–7,
      277, 314, 370, 372, 374; legislative
      councils 136, 259, 265

PSS, Poona Sarvajanik Sabha (All People's
      Association) 65–6, 81
Public Works Department 85
Punjab (land of the five rivers) 1–2, 5, 16, 29,
      42–6, 289, 370–1, 377: Boundary
      Commission 496–7; Boundary Force
      487–8, 490, 496, 498–9; Cabinet
      mission plan 425; commission 483–4;
      Council 357; Curzon, Lord 86; East
      486–7; Gandhi, Mahatma Mohandas
      165, 499–500; government 167, 173–4,
      176, 182; governors 317, 421, 485, 489;
      great revolt 52; *hartal* 164; Imperial
      Legislative Council 130; independence
      492; Indian Army 58, 286; Ismailis 94;
      Jinnah, Mohammad Ali 370; Lahore
      resolution 350; Legislative Assembly
      462, 483; lieutenant–governors 103,
      117–19, 164, 296; martial law 170,
      172, 174, 192; Mountbatten, Lord 489;
      Muslims 357, 378, 382, 420; Nehru,
      Jawaharlal 492; Pakistan 441, 452, 484;
      Partition Committee 486; partitioning
      433, 435, 441, 453–4, 460, 470, 476,
      482–3, 485, 489–90; premier 273, 307;
      provincial elections 266; riots 103,
      118–19, 230, 370, 420, 439, 462,
      488–9, 500–1; Sikhs 116, 137, 315,
      317, 379, 484; *swadeshi* movement 89;
      violence 434–5, 470, 472; West 504
Punjabee newspaper 103
Pyarelal 329

Quaid-i-Azam 283, *see also* Jinnah,
      Mohammad Ali
Quaroni, Pietro 304
Quit India campaign 328, 332, 338, 346,
      365, 368, 443
Qur'an 77–8, 91, 111, 150, 192

Radcliffe, Sir Cyril 463, 482–4, 486,
      489–90, 494–6
Rahimtoola, Sir Ibrahim 253
Rai, Gobind (son of Aurangzeb) 16
Rai, Lala Lajpat 89, 102–4, 106, 182, 187,
      194, 202, 216, 222: All-Parties
      Conferences 212–15
Raj, Hans 175
Rajagopalachari, Chakravarti, Bengal governor

188, 500: Congress 259, 327;
constitution 267, 318–19, 321; formula
348–50; Gandhi, Mahatma Mohandas
198, 348–51; governor-general 507;
Indian Army 437; interim government
403; Japanese war 327; law courts
boycott 189; Nehru, Jawaharlal 279;
Partition Council 463–4; Tamil
Congress 252; World War II 200–2,
310–11, 327
Rajkot 94, 142–3, 147, 154, 282–3
Rajputs (Hindu warrior race) 11–12, 15, 29,
43, 46, 58, 94
Ram, Jagjivan 143, 379, 403, 436
Ram Naumi festival 1, 3, 165, 167
Ramachandra, Baba 181
Ramgarh, Congress 293, 301
Ranade, Justice 71, 81–2: Poona All People's
Association 65–6, 81
Rance, Brigadier Sir Hubert 410
Rand, Mr, (Poona plague officer) 80–1
Rande, Mahadev Govind 65
Rangoon (capital of Burma) 54, 84, 314, 343
Rani of Jhansi Regiment 343
Rani, Swarup (wife of Motilal Nehru) 125,
229
Rasul, Abdul 89
Rasulkhanji, Sir Mahabthakhan 502
Rawalpindi, Punjab 103, 440, 507
Rawlinson, Lord 191
Reading, Lord, viceroy 191, 193–7,
199–200, 213, 221, 338
Reay, Lord 73
Red Dragon 13
Rees, Major General 'Pete' 487, 499
Regulating Act (1773) 21
Regulation III (1818) 73, 202
Rehill, Superintendent J. F. 4–5, 7
Ribbentrop, Joachim von 304–5
Rich, Patrick 470–1
Richards, Professor Robert 372
Ripon, Lord, Viceroy 69–70, 72, 85
Risley, H. H. 88
Roberts, Field Marshal Lord 85
Robeson, Eslanda 281
Robeson, Paul 281
Roe, Sir Thomas 13
Rolland, Romain 208
Rommel, Erwin 306–7

Roosevelt, President 307–8, 310, 322–4, 415
round-table conferences 233, 235, 237–44,
249
Rousseau, Jean–Jacques 80
Rowan, Leslie 459
Rowlatt Act (1919) 138, 139–40, 162–163,
165, 188, 285, 470
Roy, Dr B.C. 347
Roy, Raja Rammohan 31–5, 67, 77
Royal Air Force (RAF) 171, 329–30;
Canadian Air Force 329; Garhwal
Regiment 238; Indian Air Force (RIAF)
368, 498; Indian Navy, mutiny 369;
Navy, Trincomalee base 326; Public
Services Commission 213; Society for
Asian Affairs 296
RSSS (Rashtriya Swayamsevak Sangh,
'National Personal Service Society') 404,
421, 485, 500, 504
Ruskin, John 144, 150: *Unto This Last* 147–8,
150
Russia 66, 88, 105, 201, 250–2, 331, 385:
Revolutions; (1905), Black Sea fleet
mutiny 369; (1917) 2, 119, 209
Russo-Japanese War 90, 125
Rutherford, Sir Thomas 339

Saadullah, Sir Muhammad 273, 307
Sabarmati Ashram 227, 230, 241–2, 251
Sabarmati river 155, 158
Saha, Gopinath 201
Sahib, Imam 229
Sahib, Dr Khan 245, 356, 370, 422, 439
Sahib, Nana 19, 53, 57
Sahib, Nawab 76
Saklatvala, Shapurji 206
Salim (son of Akbar, known as Jahangir) 12
Salisbury, Lord 97, 452: Government of India
Act (1935) 452
Salt Tax 226, 230, 238, 247, 377, 427
Samaj, Arya 264
Samarkand 11–1, 14
San Francisco 116, 353
San, U Aung 310, 410
Sanskrit 31, 63
Santiniketan, West Bengal 154–5
Sapru, Sir Tej Bahadur 187, 191, 196, 207,
224, 232, 236, 306, 10, 351: INA trials
364

Sarabhai, Ambalal 155, 158, 160
Sarabhai, Anasuya 158, 160, 166
Saraswati festival 128–9, 202
Sarwar, Ghulam 404
Sastri, Srinivasa 236, 349
Satyagraha: Ashram 155, 180; Association
    149; Sabha 163–4, 179
satyagrahis 148–9, 151–5, 158–60, 163–4,
    166, 173–4, 179, 188–90, 193, 195–6,
    222, 228–9, 302
Satyamurti, S 251, 253
Satyapal, Dr 167–8, 170, 174, 176–7, 216
Saunders, police officer 216
Savage, Superintendent Gerald 489
Savarkar, V. D. (leader of Hindu Mahasabha)
    317, 349, 337–8
Saw, U 308, 310
Sayani, R. N. 75
Scheduled Castes 328, 379, 407, 483:
    Commonwealth membership 438;
    Federation 207
Scoones, General Sir Geoffrey Scoones 366
Scott, Ian 407
Scott, Sir Robert 412
Scott, Superintendent 216
Second World War 24, 115, 284–7, 289,
    298–303, 306–9, 325–7, 337
Sen, Surya 231
Servants of India Society (SIS) 81–2, 107,
    154–5, 159, 186
Seth, Jagat 19–20
Shafi, Sir Muhammad 209, 375
Shah, Akbar II (Mughal emperor) 75
Shah, Bahadur 54; Behadur II 41, 52, 60
Shajehanabad (Delhi foundation stone site)
    112
Shankar, Captain 474–5
Shankarlal, Lala 304
Shaw, George Bernard 127, 242
Sheridan, Richard Brinsley 23
Sherwani, Tasadduq 245–6
Sherwood, Miss Marcia 3, 168, 172
Sheth, Dada Abdullah 146–147
Shiromani Akali Dal (Sikh organization) 404,
    484
Shivaji (father of Maratha nation) 15, 48,
    80–1
festival 80–1
Shore, John 25

Short, Major J. McL. 'Billie' 374–5, 436
Siddiqi, Abdur Rahman 283, 303
Sikhs 15, 17, 43, 337–8, 386–7, 484–7, 489:
    Akali Dal Party 421; Akali Sena 421;
    All-Parties Conference 213; Amritsar
    379, 407, 496; Boundary Commission
    495, 497; Indian Army 58; interim
    government 403; Khalsa High School
    and Boarding House 171; organizations
    404, 461, 484; Pakistan 323, 328, 379,
    386–7, 453–4; World War II 323
Simla (summer capital) 72, 91, 169, 288:
    Conference, Wavell, General Sir
    Archibald 354–8, 360; meetings 445–6;
    Mountbatten, Lord 443–4, 449,
    499–500; Muslims 92–3; talks 384–5;
    Viceregal Lodge 444–46, 448–9
Simon, Sir John (later Lord) 175, 205–7,
    211, 215, 221–2, 297: Commission
    206–13, 211, 215–16, 220, 254, 409;
    Commission report 222, 232, 242; India
    Committee 313, 358
Sinclair, Sir Archibald 336
Sind 16, 29, 41–2, 183, 244, 249, 289, 394:
    Madressa-tul-Islam school 94; Muslim
    League 276, 370, 382; Pakistan 441,
    463, 465
Singapore 119, 311–2, 367, 373, 375, 377
Singh, Ajit 103
Singh, Baldev 406–7, 434, 436–7, 453–7,
    495: Executive Council 400; interim
    government 403; Menon plan 450;
    Partition Council 463–4, 474–5; Plan
    Balkan 445–6
Singh, Bhagat 222, 238
Singh, Brigadier Digambhar 487
Singh, Giani Kartar 485–6
Singh, Gianni Pritam 342
Singh, Gulab 43
Singh, Maharaja Hari 494–5, 503
Singh, Captain Mohan 342–3
Singh, Ranjit 42–4
Singh, Sardar Arjan 7–8
Singh, Master Tara 297, 379, 421, 485,
    488–9
Singh, Udam 296
Sinha, Sir Satyendra P. (later Lord Sinha) 107,
    122, 127, 206
Sinha, Sri Krishna 269

Siraj-ud-daula 19–20
Sirhind, Muslim governor 16
Sitaramayya, Pattabhi 282
Slade, Madeleine 237, *see also* Behn, Mira
Sleeman, Captain William 36
Slim, Field Marshal William 344, 415, 431, 473
Smith, F. E. 204, *see also* Birkenhead, Lord
Smith, Lieutenant-Colonel Henry 167–8
Smuts, General Jan Christian 149, 151–2, 297
Socialist League 265
Society for the Promotion of National Feeling, Bengal 65
Soman, Captain 474
South Africa 57, 73, 85, 109, 150, 214: Indian Christians and Tamils 149; Indians 147; Newcastle 151–2; Phoenix Farm 148, 151, 154, 156; Supreme Court judge 151; Union Buildings, Pretoria 112; Zulu Rebellion (1906) 148
Soviet Union 290, 306, 460, *see also* Russia
Spain 2, 280
Spens, Sir Patrick 426, 463
Srinagar (capital of Kashmir) 503–4
Srirampur, east Bengal 405
SS: *Arabia* 153; *Clyde* 144
Stalin, Marshal 363
Stalingrad 341
Standstill agreements 481–2, 503
Stanley, Oliver 336
Stansgate, Lord (former William Wedgwood Benn) 360
Stephen, Ian 343
Sterling Area 308
Stevenson, Adlai 275
Stilwell, General 'Vinegar Joe' 335
Strathcona, Lord 207
Sudharak newspaper 81
Suez Canal 3, 94, 142, 307, 373
Suhrawardy, Hussain Shaheed 264, 378, 394–5, 404, 436, 453, 488, 499
Sun Yat-sen, Madame 208
Surat (Gujarati seaport) 12–13, 16–17: Congress (1907) 104; magistrate 230
Sutlej river 29, 43
swadeshi movement 89–90, 103, 115, 150, 190
swaraj 185–7, 192–3, 199

Swaraj Sabha (Home Rule League) 186
Swarajist Party *see* Congress-Khilafat Swaraj Party
Swinton, Captain 112
Switzerland 208, 258, 418
Sykes, Sir Percy 296

Tagore, Debendranath 33
Tagore, Dwarkanath 33
Tagore, Sir Rabindranath 33, 154–5, 173–4, 248
Tagore, Satyendranath 63
Taj Mahal 15, 85
taluqdar system 181
Talwar, Bhagat Ram 304
Tanjore 17
Tashkent 201
Tata Iron and Steel Works 115, 330
Tata, Jamshed N. 90, 337–8, 398
Tegart, Charles 201–2
Tenasserim province 36
Terauchi, Field Marshal Count 343–4
Thakur, S. B. 63
Theosophical Society 120, 140, 144–5
Thoreau, Henry David, *On the Duty of Civil Disobedience* 150: 3 June Plan 458, 484, *see also* Transfer of Power
thugi 105
Tibet 86
Tilak, Bal Gangadhar 184: Congress 104, 120, 122, 129–30, 282; *dharma* 106; Extremism 102; Hindu nationalism 80–2; Home Rule League 121, 134, 162; *Kesari* 80–1, 90, 101, 105; *Swadeshi* movement 89, 103; World War I 115
The Times 67, 176, 268, 297, 453
Times of India 474
Tipu, Sultan of Mysore 25, 27
Tirur, Toplahs 192
Tiwana, Khizar Hyat Khan 332
Tobruk, Libya 316
Tojo, General Hideki 326, 341, 343, 363
Tolstoy, Count Leo 144, 150, 262
Topi, Tantia 57
Transfer of Power 454–60, *see also* British withdrawal plans
Transvaal 148–9, 152
Travancore state 478–9
Treaty of Sèvres 197

Trevelyan, Sir Charles 34
Tribune 265
Trichinopoly fortress 18
Tripuri, Congress 282
Trivedi, Sir Chandulal 473, 489
Tsushima, straits of 90, 125
Tuker, Lieutenant–General Sir Francis 395, 488
Turkey 111, 119–20, 182–4, 197
Turku-Afghan dynasties 11
Turnbull, Frank 315, 374, 381, 399
two-nation theory 350
Tyabji, Justice Badruddin 77, 99–100
Tyson, J.F. 436

Union of India 437, 445, 447, 504
Unionist Party 266, 273
United Indian Patriotic Association 75
United Muslim Party 266
United Nations 353, 482
United Provinces (UP) 92, 155: Congress 283, 370; Congress government 269; council 189; Emergency Powers Ordinance 246; governor 180; *hartal* 164; Muslim League 271–2, 274; Muslim parties 264; Nehru, Motilal 126–7; prisoners 278, 377; provincial government 272; provincial legislature 108; revolts 329–30, 405; riots 229–30, 245, 421, 434–5. *See also* North–West Provinces
United States 312
Unity Board 272
Untouchability Abolition Week 248
untouchables 243–4, 247–9, 252, 288, 379, 386–7

Vampire destroyer 326
Vancouver, Sikhs 116–17
VCOs, viceroy commissioned officers 367
Vedic India 262, 264–5
Vernacular Press Act (1878) 67–9
Viceregal Lodge 93, 356–7, 385
Victoria, Queen 41, 58: Empress of India (1877–1990I) 66, 411; Loyal Opposition 74; proclamation (1858) 55–7, 63, 70, 146
Vincent, Sir William 190–1
Vivekananda, Swami 188

Vizagapatam port 325

Wacha, Sir Dinshaw E. 186
Wadya, H.A. 104–5
Wales, Prince of (later Edward VII) 193–4, 412
Waqt, Lahore Urdu newspaper 6
Wardha 282, 291–2: *ashram* 259, 291–2; Congress Working Committee 287, 289, 327–8
Watson, Admiral 19
Wavell, General Sir Archibald (viceroy) 311, 314–15, 335–40, 346, 363–4, 372: Amery, Leo 335–6, 347; Attlee, Clement 398, 402, 408; Azad, Maulana 321, 396; Bengal famine 339–40; Bihar riots 405; British withdrawal plans 401–2, 408–9, 417–18, 434; broadcast 354–5; Cabinet meetings 338–9, 371; Cabinet Mission 376, 378, 383, 385, 387–90; Calcutta killings 395–8; Chamber of Princes 480; Churchill, Winston 335–6, 338–40, 353–4, 361; Desai–Liaquat pact 352–3; earldom 420; Eden, Anthony 335; Executive Council 351, 353–5, 362, 371, 374; Gandhi, Mahatma Mohandas 346–8, 355, 365, 376, 430; INA trials 363–4, 366; independence within the Commonwealth 352; India Committee 361, 418; India defence 327; India elections 360–1; Interim Government of India 397–8, 400, 406–7; Jinnah, Mohammad Ali 356–7, 381, 391, 393, 401; Linlithgow, Lord 339; Menon, V.P. 444; Mountbatten, Lord 424–6; Nehru, Jawaharlal 375, 391, 393, 397; parliamentary delegation 374; Rajagopalachari's formula 351; replacement 416, 418, 420; RIN mutinies 369–70; Simla conference 354–8, 360, 384; Simon Commission 409
Wavell, Lady Queenie 336, 356–7, 424–5
Webb, Beatrice 127, 232
Webb, Sidney 127
Wedderburn, Sir William 75
Wedgewood Benn, William (later Lord Stansgate) 220–1, 223

Wellesley, Arthur (later Duke of Wellington) 28–9

Wellesley, Lord 25, 27–30, 35, 47–8

Wilkinson, Ellen 360

Willingdon, Lady 240

Willingdon, Lord (viceroy) 122, 237, 239–40, 245–7, 249, 252–3, 258, 261, 419-420

Wilson, Geoffrey 290

Wilson, President of US 218

Wolpert, Stanley 492

Wood, Sir Charles 61, 204–5

Wood, Edward *see* Halifax, Lord; Irwin, Lord

World War II 331

WRINS (Womens Royal Indian Naval Service) 368

Wyatt, Major Woodrow 374–5, 388–9

Yamashita, General 311

Yeravda: Central Gaol 230, 232, 237; Pact 248

Yokohama 117

Young India, national bi–weekly 121, 173

Younghusband, Major Francis 86

Ypres, Battle of 114

Zaheer, Syed Ali 403

Zamindar newspaper 111

Zentralstelle Freie Indien (the Free India Centre) 305

Zetland, Marquess of: India Office 297; viceroy 260, 281, 283–4, 286, 289, 295–6

Ziegler, Philip 416